Murauer · The Belief of an Unwilling to believe

Paul Klee, Hauptweg und Nebenwege (Main Way and Byways), 1929

Michael Murauer

The Belief of an
Unwilling to believe

Philosophical Life Orientation Today

Michael Murauer, born 1955 in Munich, Studies in Philosophy and Medicine in Regensburg and Munich. Many years of work as a doctor (internist and general practitioner). Lives and works in Deggendorf/Lower Bavaria.
Other books: »Gott & die chinesische Teekanne oder Diogenes wusch seinen Kohl. Eine Reise in die Bilderwelt der Philosophen«, Edition BoD 2006. Kommentarband, 2008, second expanded edition 2012, third revised edition 2022 (online only)
English editions (currently online only): God and the China Teapot or Diogenes washing his cabbage. A journey into the philosophers' world of metaphors, 2022
Commentary Volume 2022   www.murauer.info

In this book general terms are used alternately in feminine, masculine or neutral forms. It is conceivable and it seems desirable to me that this could become normal use of language in the long run.
Gender-neutral or gender-inclusive language is not that much of a problem in English (because of the decline of grammatical gender it has gone through), as it is, for instance, in German, where nouns generally expose their gender. I generally sympathise with the efforts to develop new language habits in order to end the centuries of discrimination, be it against women, people with sexual minority orientations, ethnical or social groups that still appear even in the way we talk. But this should not make language uglier, less clear, or more awkward, or impair its flow more than by eliciting brief (and desired) moments of increased attention. Inconsistencies should be seen with serenity and tolerance. I recommend Navid Kermani's nuanced essay on this topic: Mann, Frau, völlig egal (Man, woman, whatever), Die Zeit, 3 January 2022, p. 46. What I have no sympathy for is the retroactive correction of historical texts. This is a distortion of history which makes it impossible for the readers to make their own historical judgements. But explanations helping the readers in doing this may be an option, especially in children's literature.

German editions: first edition 1985, second revised and expanded edition 2011, third revised and expanded edition 2025, English edition 2025
Text and Data mining is prohibited (§44b UrhG)
©2025 Michael Murauer
Herstellung und Verlag (published by): BoD – Books on Demand GmbH, Überseering 33, 22297 Hamburg, bod@bod.de
Druck (printed by): Libri Plureos GmbH, Friedensallee 273, 22763 Hamburg
ISBN 978-3-8192-3864-2

Alpha

Reasonable belief, believing reason

"Never does a man come to reason by reason."[1]

Montesquieu

"Nothing sillier than to believe that someone who is able to think accurately should not be able to feel and that thinking would not be passionate."[2]

Günther Anders

"Let me point out at the outset that belief and faith, though by their nature they include a non-rational element, need not be either irrational or anti-rational, unscientific or anti-scientific. They can perfectly well be coherent with reason and with scientifically established fact, and any belief-system which is going to be of value in the world of today must be thus coherent with reason and science, because rationality and scientific knowledge are an important part of that world. And this implies further that it must not be dogmatic: to be coherent with science it must surrender the completeness of its certitudes, and with that its own unchange-ability."[3]

Julian Huxley

"But how to come to an understanding on something that does not meet the criteria of scientific objectivity? This question assumes that there is nothing between objective method and personal confession. But this is wrong for even if evidence of truth and cogent proof are not possible, there is at least the possibility of prudent deliberation and reasonable discussion with results that may never be certain and unshakeable but nevertheless probable, plausible and acceptable."[4]

Franz Josef Wetz

"In the beginning and in the end is the conviction. The struggle for integrity lies in between."[5]

Ronald Dworkin

Contents

Introduction

The future belongs to philosophy, not to religions or secular ideologies

"We have learned nothing from historic experience if we have not learned that man lives by more than his applied intelligence alone."[1]

Lewis Mumford

Today religion is socially acceptable again, even among intellectuals. Criticism of religion in the Enlightenment tradition is denounced as outdated. After criticising religion, philosophy has criticised itself. From logical empiricism and the philosophy of Wittgenstein to analytic philosophy of language it tried to ban philosophy of life from its sphere. This movement reached its peak from the sixties to the eighties of the 20th century. After that the short-lived period of postmodernism chose all kinds of feuilletonistic frills as philosophical topics. No wonder that thereafter the interests in question of ethics, morals and philosophy of life has increased again.

But lo and behold: society has got philosophy's self-criticism down the wrong throat. Philosophy is widely considered as a museum-like or ivory tower enterprise that leads to more or less arbitrary results, not convincingly committing anybody to anything. This kind of philosophy is allowed to participate to some extent in the market of life and business counsellors and coaches. But when it comes to serious problems of personal life and society it does not suggest itself to seek advice from philosophy and philosophers. Many people still prefer to turn to a priest, a bishop, possibly his boss in Rome, or the friendly, seemingly unmissionary Dalai Lama, or whoever the respective religious denomination recommends.

Meanwhile, philosophers write lots of intelligent articles and books in which they weigh up values on the basis of rational consideration and try to provide decision-making aids for important personal and social problems. And how many people are interested? Not too many. No wonder, as philosophers have dismantled themselves beforehand.

The term "existential deficit" of philosophy was originally coined to

13

reproach philosophy for its lack of engagement with existential questions. (Rahner[2]) In the meantime, it rather describes the lack of social receptiveness and social effects of philosophical thought and philosophical results in contemporary society. Philosophy presents itself far to humbly to be perceived adequately in a noisy and multimedia excited society.

This book stands in the tradition of Enlightenment thought. This is the basis for the concepts and demands on the task of philosophy in our time that will be discussed in the following.

There is no acceptable alternative to a rational debate on the issues of philosophy of life and morals. Absolute truth will not be found by such a debate, but reasoned value-based choices. This procedure is far preferable to choices based on untenable religious and ideological pretensions of truth or even dogmas.

Philosophers should definitely claim far more social participation and attention. They are the right people to shape future discussions on adequate life orientation and guidance and not the theologians, clergymen, gurus and ideologues with their dogmatic doctrines of faith which have long ago shown to be untenable by the standards of critical reason.

Only a life orientation guided by philosophical thinking is adequate for modern human beings. The indifferentist humbleness which often characterises the appearance of today's philosophy in social debate is therefore completely misplaced. It means to draw a wrong consequence from the justified relativisation of absolute claims to truth and certainty.

It must be made clear again that scientific and especially philosophical thinking is in sharp contrast to religious life orientation and religious world views, that it leads – if it is keeping up with modern times –inevitably to a naturalistic world view and a naturalistic concept of humans, and that it is definitely willing and able to provide support and orientation concerning the crucial questions of life based on rational weighing of values and moral choices resulting therefrom. It also is a commitment for philosophers to stand up against political procedures which still impose on all members of society values and moral choices that are convincing only from a religious position (concerning, for example, bioethical issues). (1)

Lessons in philosophy and critical evaluation of philosophies of life must become a compulsory subject at school. Religious instruction, however, should be a private matter of religious denominations. Each bigger university should be ambitious to have minimum one philosopher or philosophically interested and renowned scholar in its ranks whose public presence and impact is a match for religious leaders, at least those of regional importance.

A secular philosopher may well have personal respect and personal sympathy for people with a religious life orientation and may feel closer to some of them than to unthinking areligious people. But this should not lead to covering up the fundamental differences in the way of thinking and their consequences for the shaping and guidance of life. Religions and ideologies are relics from former stages of human history of ideas – albeit regrettably still very much alive. Up-to-date philosophy is applied critical reason. It is not willing to accept assumptions without good reasons and is therefore inevitably opposed to religions and ideologies. Where these have been and are confronted with a process of enlightenment, present themselves in a moderate way, and respect the attitude of ideological tolerance, peaceful coexistence is possible. But even then, the fundamental conflict should not be disguised or talked to death. Putting it from the psychological point of view contributes to clarification: Religious people think that the areligious lack an important dimension of life. Areligious people think that the world view of the religious is illusionary to a considerable extent. By tolerance and affection, it is possible to build all kind of personal bridges across this rift, but the rift will stay.

Criticism of religion remains to be a way to secure an adequate position for philosophy in social debate. This way has been taken again with strong commitment in our time as well. (2) Often enough this is not really intellectually thrilling anymore, but it is absolutely necessary in the interest of our future. On the one hand, we need a sober and self-critical atheism that accepts religion as a cultural and social phenomenon. Without emotional ties to religion, it is able to acknowledge the positive aspects of this phenomenon and to cooperate with religious people and with representatives of religious denominations on certain social tasks without reservation. On the other hand, we still need a somewhat aggressive atheism, at times ironical to the point of sarcasm, that is mocking religious thinking without crossing the border of malice and bad taste. It has to make perfectly clear how astonishing, and even downright consternating, it is that in the twenty-first century the old religious ideas are still believed in and regarded as an adequate life orientation to such an extent. The provocative question »How can one still believe such things today?« may not always make appear the questioner likeable. But it is no fusty, epistemologically outdated, loudmouthed nineteen century atheism. This question may have an emotional enlightening effect that goes beyond dry rational argument.

Particularly with regard to radical but also already conservative traditionally interpreted Islam, the necessary, wise politics of prudent de-escalation must not be confused with a misguided appeasement policy that accepts an erosion of human and civil rights by rotten compromises and may therefore be used by other religions as well to stabilise or re-expand their claim to social and political power. (3) A religion which – despite many reasonable individual voices – has so far proved incapable to regard the contempt for life expressing itself in suicide attacks committed in its name en masse on an international level as its very own continuous moral and educational problem deserves a high degree of distrust for this reason alone, not to mention other problems with current mainstream Islam, like its poor record concerning the rights of women, homosexuals, apostates, or critics of religion. Being shocked by Islamic terrorism we should not lose sight of the fact that this is only the most extreme phenomenon of a widespread intolerance in the Islamic world that is also embedded in many ways in its legal and political systems. Historical assignments of guilt must not be accepted as an excuse for this. The debate and the struggle with an Islam that is dominated by an intolerant interpretation will continue for decades to come and must be conducted at all levels, from the education system to, unfortunately, military force.

However, we must not view religions too pessimistically. As human-made systems of interpretation and attribution of meaning they are open to reinterpretation by humans. All major religions contain sufficient starting points for a relatively humane reinterpretation under the influence of Enlightenment thinking, as has already been achieved to a considerable extent for Christianity, at least in modern pluralistic societies.

The scope of rational criticism of religion is limited. Therefore, it is important to find ways to satisfy the psychosocial needs underlying religions in a better way than they do. Hence the maxim expressed by the physicist Frank Wilczek: »So to me the important challenge is not to debunk religion, but to address its issues in better ways«. (4) An adequate, comprehensive approach combines the »destructive« and the constructive elements of enlightenment – shifting the emphasis according to times and personalities.

This book constantly balances on the ridge between systematic philosophical treatise and personal confession and, furthermore, it integrates the cultural world of its author in a broad concept of philosophy. (5) It hopes to approach truth by viewing together partial truths and avoiding half-truths. (6) While determined to keep up with the edge of modern thinking and striving for a maximum of coherence, it is fortunately not bound by the constraints of scientific rituals. I consider it unusual and necessary insofar as it attempts to sum up the contemporary state of philosophical criticism of weltanschauung taking into account the world view developed by modern science while simultaneously offering life orientation and guidance – the author exposing himself with his personal framework of philosophical life orientation. It is about a synthesis of the world-view and world-view relevant findings of modern science. And it is about really drawing consequences from this by translating this synthesis into concrete personal life orientation. This objective also justifies the wide range of subjects, which may seem presumptuous at first glance. As modern knowledge is no longer even remotely comprehensible for a single person it is nevertheless important that time and again some people overcome their fears of incompetence and attempt an overview under the aspect of life orientation.

I insist that nobody has to offer more than a weltanschauung which in last consequence can »only« be founded and justified subjectively (although many people still cling to opposite illusions). But at the same time, I insist that such a philosophy of life does not necessarily have to do anything with arbitrary decisions and may well be a serious contribution to philosophy, especially if it attempts to limit subjectivity to a minimum which is inevitable for a sufficient life orientation. That still leaves a lot of room for argument over what is really inevitable, leading finally to questions such as: Should this subjectivity be extended to a faith in (perhaps even the Christian) god or another religious offer? It will become clear beyond doubt that my concept of a minimum is different and that it actually means »minimum«.

To prevent misunderstandings definitely and to counter the somewhat to personal title of this book - which is nevertheless inevitable – let me state once more: What I advocate is anything but a subjectivist philosophy. I reject claims to objectivity wherever they are not sufficiently well-founded, and I accept subjectivity where it is inevitable. However, I am completely convinced that there are correct answers to scientific questions and especially to the questions that are decisive for our world view. There is truth, but no final certainty. And if we have to modify or even revise knowledge, that we believed to be correct, from a later point of view, then even in these cases there is a best possible knowledge at a certain point in history. It is the knowledge we arrive at by means of a rationality that strives for the greatest possible impartiality.

One should look at this book as a house that is again and again in need of all kinds of alterations and additions, getting not only more rooms but, above all, more and bigger windows and doors. These can be opened easily. You can look outside, stick your head out, or step out in order to perceive and follow ever new paths of philosophical debate and search for orientation.

I wrote this book first and foremost to clarify things for myself, to keep hold of acquired knowledge, and develop it further, and to have a better thought-out guideline for practical life. Even where it cannot come up to the wide range of its pretensions it still makes private and individual sense. And perhaps it can contribute some interesting pieces to the puzzle that represents the spirit of our age.

It cannot be denied that unwillingness-to-believe in philosophy of life (though it may be given different names) is a reality and a significant tendency in our social and historical situation, albeit only in a qualified minority. To emphasise this reality one more time is just a sideline for me. My main concern is to clarify in which form the necessary life-determining belief is possible under the premise of unwillingness-to-believe.

This book wants to help sceptics and so-called unbelievers to gain clarity and consistency. It wants to help them to define their unbelief concerning traditional systems of belief more precisely, namely as »unwillingness to believe«. It wants to contribute to the overcoming of an insufficiently thought-out and therefore often half-hearted unbelief, which is still too much stuck in agnosticism, an attitude widespread in modern affluent societies. It wants to show once again that it is possible to consciously shape one's life, to gain sufficient confidence in life, and to realise moral attitudes and values without a belief in god or a substitute religion that elevates theses of social or natural philosophy to dogma. This book fights for unwillingness to believe and the courage to set subjective, individual, and conventional norms and goals on the basis of a minimum of belief. It is an attempt to find a philosophical modus vivendi for those unwilling to believe. It is an attempt to overcome the existential deficit of philosophy without falling behind the criticism of ideologies it has provided. Philosophy's obligation to practice is to be fulfilled in a manner appropriate to the intellectual situation of modern time.

This book is equally opposed to the underestimation (in positivism, for example) of the theoretical difficulties involved in breaking with the traditional doctrines of faith, and to the overestimation of the practical difficulties (a position religious people are inclined to – and especially religious doubters).

Thus, it invites non-religious people to become aware of the belief they have already tacitly embraced and to make conscious decisions of belief after thorough consideration, that is to justify convictions by choices. For the undecided, it wants to encourage them to create a basis for their life orientation through a minimum of conscious decisions of belief – far from the traditional metaphysical offers. Finally, it also addresses those who have not only lost a faith but also the conviction that life is worth to be lived and to be shaped consciously. Perhaps it can help one or another among them to find the courage for a new beginning.

I want to make a contribution to the fight against all dogmatic world views. History bears impressive witness to their harmful consequences right up to the present day. However, apart from their many evils, they have undeniably also produced great cultural and social achievements. And at times they have even shown an at least partial and temporary ability for tolerance. We must be aware of their criminal history and their cultural history and not fixate on just one of the two. And if we conclude after all that a certain weltanschauung has predominantly negative consequences, this is not an argument against its truth in the first place, but only one against its adherents (just as, conversely, desirable consequences, contrary to the rhetoric of tolerance from Lessing's "Nathan the Wise", do not constitute an argument for its truth). This sort of balancing argumentation has a certain heuristic value in prompting us to devote equal attention to the criminal and oppressive and the cultural and charitable history of dogmatic ideologies. And from a practical point of view this sort of balancing argumentation is still a weapon of enlightenment that should not be underestimated (although it can also be turned against itself).

But the decisive problem, the significant demarcation, lies elsewhere today. In former times dogmatic world views were a reasonable looking proposal for orientation in the world. For most people, apart from a few extraordinary minds, they were almost inevitable. People simply knew too little. Meanwhile, however, this type of weltanschauung falls far short of what is possible for human beings. All kinds of dogmatic ideology – religious or secular - are outdated and implausible.

As the "belief" presented in this book is founded on a world view that tries to take into account the scientific state of the art as far as possible (which includes a permanent revisability in the light of new knowledge), and as it does not include any dogmatic assertions about the world, but only guidelines for personal actions, it has little in common with the kind of belief demanded by religions and secular ideologies. So why is the word »belief« still in the title?

The convictions of an unwilling to believe are founded on pre-rational – not: irrational – choices too. These convictions do not require to sacrifice reason on the altar of religion or ideology or to condemn it to silence in essential questions of life. However, as they are not convictions of minor significance either, but life determining, philosophical convictions, it is nevertheless adequate to speak of the "belief" of an unwilling to believe. But it is not justified to equate these convictions with dogma just because they have the orientation function that is filled by dogmas in religions and ideologies.

In this book quite a few battles are fought once again that have been won by enlightenment long ago - but they have been won only in the field of intellectual debate. Amongst the leading scholars of our time only a few remain who - be it for social, psychological, spiritual or moral reasons - still put trust in religion or secular ersatz religion for explaining our world or providing orientation for our philosophy of life or morals. But the fact that a small percentage of humankind has internalised the results of enlightenment does not suffice to determine either the predominant life orientation or the development of society or the course of history. Therefore, the old battles will have to be fought again and again in ever new variations and constellations for an unpredictable time. If all would just depend on the intellectual avant-garde, this book could bear a more neutral (though perhaps also less interesting) title, such as: "Scientific World View and Philosophical Belief". As it is, however, I still prefer to define myself to a considerable extent by unbelief in traditional systems of belief respectively of faith, and this will probably still be necessary for a long time to come for anyone who does not want to pursue intellectual debate on weltanschauung and philosophy in a very restrained and withdrawn manner.

In secular philosophy of life there is a considerable naming confusion. To get the differences clear, it is helpful to think out for oneself that different designations refer to different philosophical problems. »Agnosticism« stands for a principled last reservation of doubt meant to keep a little bit of distance to all our assumed knowledge. "Atheism" stands for the confrontation, forced upon us by cultural and intellectual history, with all the untenable doctrines assuming one or several gods to explain the world and ascribe meaning to it. »Naturalism« stands for an adequate, reality-based and revisable explanation of the world. »Secular Humanism« stands for a moral orientation and creation of meaning which can be defended with good reasons and makes no recourse to metaphysical fictions and speculations.

Even if used in a meaning which seems adequate to me, each of these terms represents only a part of what I consider important for orientation in the world and in personal life. Hence "the belief of an unwilling to believe" which brings it all together.

It would be desirable to characterise this fundamental philosophical attitude by a shorter, catchier, and nevertheless differentiated term with positive connotation, which therefore might have a good prospect of wider dissemination, but this is difficult. No doubt Richard Dawkins und Daniel Dennett are »bright« themselves, but their idea that atheistic naturalists and humanists could organise themselves better and reach better reputation in society using this label has not been very successful so far. The term has some charm, but among other problems (like a certain touch of arrogance) it has the disadvantage that it does not translate easily into other languages.

This book also wants to tie in deliberately with the classical and modern »art of living« tradition of philosophy. This may always be threatened by triviality. Nevertheless, I do not share Kersting's view that contemporary philosophy could only regain a state of directness in moral counselling at the price of self-denial and intellectual regression. The fact that too many philosophers regard personal convictions and statements on the art of living, morals and the meaning of life as a private matter and no longer as a part of their philosophical work contributes significantly to the regrettably low importance contemporary society attaches to philosophy. It is a mistake to send everything in philosophy that sounds like »contemporary Seneca« into an ideologically disarmed exile of psychological counselling. (7)

"Although philosophy as counselling corresponds to the everyday notion of philosophy, it is not integrated in the academic philosophical studies as a rule. This is very regrettable. As a consequence, the common needs for orientation and for recipes for a life that is as fearless and happy as possible are only met by the teachings of some guru, saviour or religion, all of which have in common that they fulfil their task only at the price of a sacrifice of the intellect."[3]

Joachim Buhl

"And still, I profess loyalty to enlightenment, specifically to the *classical* enlightenment - as a *philosophia perennis* that contains all of its own cor-rectives, so that it is an idle game dialectically to dissect it."[4]

Jean Améry

1. Choices

Strongholds in a sea of chance

"We are in fact the sum total of our choices ..."[1]

Woody Allen

The choices described in the following make some fundamental statements on how to shape one's life. To make choices means to decide consciously. Choices do not create convictions, they only clarify, justify and stabilise them. At first choices are always "afterwards", but once made a basis of life orientation they are also "before".

One can also choose to make convictions, such as those justified by choices in the following, the basis for the shaping of one's life without making choices, as a belief »without justification« and thus simply speak of fundamental attitudes concerning philosophy and philosophy of life. One can simply state the existence of certain convictions without feeling the desire to justify them, for instance by choices. One can be unwilling to believe without making choices as a philosophical justification. The desire for a philosophical justification of life determining convictions and the gain in coherence that can be achieved thereby could be no more than a (transitory) peculiarity of Western intellectual history.

However, the justification of convictions by choices corresponds to my feeling (which in this case is in accordance with a general human feeling most people share) that I am able to change or stabilise personal convictions by conscious subjective decisions. It appears sensible to me, to distinguish and stabilise some decisions as choices - choices that are of particular importance for the shaping of life and that have been made after intensive reflection. This is also to make clear that these decisions are not arbitrary or easily changeable and that they can be just as convincing as, for other people, statements on philosophy and philosophy of life with a (never redeemable) pretension of objectivity. Furthermore, I consider the justification of convictions by choices to be a good prevention of unwarranted pretensions of objectivity. By simply stating convictions you can easily forget to make sure that you have good reasons for them. And you can easily forget that you too are »just« believing. You can fall into the illusion of being beliefless and confuse a belief without justification with belieflessness.

To build on choices as a foundation of last resort of our weighing up does not mean that we underestimate the role of the uncontrollable in human life. (For a discussion of fortune see also 2.3.) Of course, the quote from Woody Allen's movie is only half the truth. In fact, we are the sum total of our choices plus chance. And strictly speaking, even our possibilities to make choices depend on chance. Our choices are part, consequence and cause in an incalculable, not even remotely comprehensible, not predetermined, and thus not predictable web of chance that makes us what we are (and that is, of course, subject to the laws of nature).

Is there still any point, then, in talking about decisions and choices? Well, life means to make decisions. And this is valid both in a descriptive and a normative sense. First, we describe an essential characteristic of central nervous systems and especially the human brain thereby: they are complex decision-making systems that have acquired considerable degrees of freedom in the course of evolutionary development, as too rigid decision-making mechanisms are not advantageous in a continuously changing world, at least not for organisms of higher complexity. Second, we do not have any sound alternative to set norms for ourselves and our societies. By elaborating and communicating our thinking, by taking, making clear, justifying, and defending our point of view we find our place in life and make our contribution to the web of chance which forms our world – a contribution according to our possibilities, more or less momentous, more or less novel, and more or less valuable.

If life determining choices (considerably influenced by chance themselves) appear to be no more than an inescapable personal necessity for some humans from a deterministic point of view (which is irrefutable to a certain degree), they nonetheless make a big difference to the thinking and acting of the person who makes them.

It is possible (and it should be done) to acquire and to practise philosophical and moral attitudes much the same way we can acquire and practise skills in playing a musical instrument or in exercising a particular kind of sport. This book wants to show that there are good reasons for choosing choices, and specific choices, as a basis of such an acquisition and practice and for preferring them to other – be it more indifferentist or more objectivist – ways of a philosophical life orientation. (For a more elaborate discussion of the problems of justification and the compatibility of choices and determinism see 2.1.)

"We human beings are always more our accidents than our choice. Note that I do not say that we human beings are only our accidents; I only say that we are not only our choice, and that we human beings are always more our accidents than our choice."[2]

Odo Marquard

1.1. The Fundamental Choice to Consciously Shape One's Life

The usual is not enough

"Acting and acting consciously are two different things."[1]

Epictetus

If you discover the attitude of unwillingness to believe in yourself, it follows that you must decide yourself whether to consciously shape your life (whereas most traditional systems of belief save their followers this decision) and to do so by making choices and act according to them or whether to be no more than an observer and executing body of impulses arising in yourself, subject to any fluctuation. The possibility of letting oneself drift through life without principles and of making one's decisions only according to the momentary mood and situation in the world must first be excluded. If unwillingness to believe is presupposed, this can only be justified by choices. It makes sense, then, to begin with a fundamental choice to consciously shape one's life. On this basis, further convictions, which can be used to guide the shaping of one's life in detail, can then be justified by choices. (1)

The fundamental choice to consciously shape one's life does not in itself necessarily lead beyond the mere statement of convictions, a drifting through life without principles, or Pyrrhonean scepticism. A person who is disappointed by philosophy or who interprets the determinism of modern neuroscience in a passive way can consciously and explicitly set, by making such a choice, the mere stating of convictions or the drifting without principles, that is, decisions only according to the momentary mood and situation in the world, as the principle of the shaping of her or his life. These options may be called conscious shaping of life insofar as life is not simply lead without fundamental choices even if the conscious shaping of life is thus reduced to only one general principle and you remain completely dependent on the circumstances, being no more than observer and executive organ of impulses arising in yourself, just as those people who try to live completely without principles.

The specific dilemma of Pyrrhonean scepticism is illustrated by the nice story Bertrand Russell tells of Pyrrho: "He maintained that we never know enough to be sure that one course of action is wiser than another. In his youth, when he was taking his constitutional one afternoon, he saw his teacher in philosophy (from whom he had imbibed his principles) with his head stuck in a ditch, unable to get out. After contemplating him for some time, he walked on, maintaining that there was no sufficient ground for thinking he would do any good by pulling the old man out. Others, less sceptical, effected a rescue, and blamed Pyrrho for his heartlessness. But his teacher, true to his principles, praised him for this consistency."[2]

Since Pyrrho did not have a sufficient reason either to leave the old man stuck in the ditch, this must have happened out of a momentary mood, or Pyrrho chose walking on as the more passive option, assuming that this would fit better with his sceptical attitude. This, however, would express a new principle of decision that goes beyond scepticism, for it does not at all follow from the indecisiveness created by scepticism that one always decides in favour of the more passive option.

Pyrrhonean sceptics differ from those who confine themselves to merely stating their convictions and from those who explicitly decide according to the momentary mood and situation in the world, by the desperate (and futile) attempt to get along with reason alone, trying to avoid decisions which in the last resort must have an irrational (or better: pre-rational) justification. As far as they indulge in passivity, you see them fighting against the impulses of common sense time and again and also against even the simplest customs without justifying or being able to justify why they are doing this.

This is why Sextus Empiricus already argues that sceptics can, without giving up their scepticism, make the inevitable decisions on how to shape their life according to "unphilosophical experience", that is, they can orientate themselves to the customs of the society into which they were born and to the moral concepts they were taught through their upbringing. The truth of moral rules being undecidable, no objection can be raised against sticking to the ideas you are accustomed to since youth.[3]

The first objection to this argument is that it does hardly seem satisfactory to base moral decisions on socially given moral concepts in a certain historical situation without thinking twice. Sceptics may possibly acknowledge this with a shrug of the shoulders, albeit hopefully a regretful one. They should also make clear to themselves, however, that an orientation towards the usual is not a necessary consequence of scepticism. Basically, it is just a variant of striving for the greatest possible passivity which also includes a decision going beyond scepticism.

A fundamental choice to merely state one's convictions, a fundamental choice to let oneself drift without principles and to decide only according to the momentary mood and situation in the world, or a fundamental choice for Pyrrhonean scepticism do not correspond to my idea of a good shaping of life. Therefore, they are excluded by the following fundamental choices and the choices based on them.

To set a guideline for one's life does not have to mean that spontaneous action is made impossible or only more difficult. It is precisely those who want to let themselves drift or only get by with the principle of doubt who can be hindered in the spontaneity of their actions by the resulting uncertainty.

"Have you been able to think out and manage your own life? You have done the greatest task of all."[4]

Michel de Montaigne

1.2. The Fundamental Choice of Unwillingness to believe

Criteria of a rational belief

> "I never gave up reason,
> Not even for the most enticing promise."[1]

Theodor Storm

After the attitude of unwillingness to believe, which was initially noted as a mere fact, has necessitated a fundamental choice to consciously shape one's life, it in turn requires justification. Again, only another fundamental choice offers itself for this. This will be discussed below. But prior to that I want to explain what unwillingness to believe means to me.

First, unwillingness to believe means to doubt all concepts of the world again and again. "It is of course possible that all or any of our beliefs may be mistaken, and therefore all ought to be held with at least some slight element of doubt." (Russell[2]) In other words: We should emphasise the hypothetical character of all knowledge. (Vollmer[3]) This is also beautifully expressed by an old Spanish saying: *De las cosas mas seguras la mas segura es dudar.* "Of the most certain things doubt is the most certain." (1)

Second, unwillingness to believe means to never assume something just because you cannot disprove it – or, put positively – only to assume that for which you have good reasons. Good reasons are those that are based on logic, observation and simplicity. Good reasons are those that result from a critical examination according to these criteria. Otherwise, one must not shy away from admitting one's own ignorance. This requires not only an overcoming of human vanity but above all a mastery of the human desire for handy and certain explanations of the entire world (including that which remains inexplicable on sober reflection) and for an objective, absolutely valid morality. In the complete absence of good reasons, however, it is not enough to nobly suspend our judgement; rather, we should explicitly reject the assertions in question.

The demand for good reasons includes the conviction that different sources of knowledge are not equally valid, that the different paths that have been and are proposed as leading to knowledge do not actually achieve this with the same degree of probability, and that it cannot be claimed with the same right that the results allegedly gained by using them are comprehensible. Therefore, one should not accept certain ways as a sufficient justification of knowledge. The definition of unwillingness to believe has to include the paths to knowledge that are considered insufficient in this sense. For those unwilling to believe these are the following:

1. the path of revelatory experiences, of religious or spiritual experiences, if claiming to be more than mental experiences of individuals and groups and demanding to be accepted as a criterion of reality and truth,
2. the path of mere authority, that is to say, the gaining of knowledge by accepting the assertions of others and deriving from them without ensuring that these assertions have been confirmed by repeated systematic verification and are, at least principally, accessible to one's own examination (2),
3. the path of esotericism, that is to say, the explanation of facts, the prediction of future events and the influencing of the world by alleged mysterious special psychic abilities or allegedly recognised special laws that are only valid occasionally and cannot be systematically reproduced.

That does not mean that assertions based on revelatory experiences, authority or esoteric procedures must be wrong in every case. It only means that such a justification of assertions is not considered convincing.

Belief founded on revelatory experience or esotericism is more than a mere variant of belief in authority. It differs from this by its subjectively impressing character of illumination (if honestly felt and not only displayed for the pursuit of material interests or power).

In addition to the willingness to revise one's own thinking and the demand for good reasons, there is a third essential component of unwillingness to believe. This is restraint in making personal decisions of belief that cannot be justified further (which, on the other hand, are the only remaining possibility, as a last resort, for those unwilling to believe – as for anybody else - to justify their thinking and their way of life). Restraint means that one wants to summarise one's conception of a good life by as few choices of belief as possible and therefore subjects the necessity of every choice of belief to critical scrutiny. (3)

This is not to propagate or suggest a total supremacy of reason at the expense of feeling. Although unwillingness to believe means wanting to use one's mind in questions of philosophy and weltanschauung without taboos, even the belief of an unwilling to believe cannot be justified by reason alone. The life orientation proposed here does not want to have anything in common with a shallow rationalism which, due to a lack of life experience, believes in the complete controllability of human life by reason or believes at least that this would be desirable. (4) If those unwilling to believe abstain almost completely from religious feelings, such as, for instance, the hope of redemption, this does not mean that they would be less able of intense feelings than religious people, be it in questions of their philosophy of life or their personal relationships, or that they must lack emotionally accentuated qualities such as enthusiasm or a sense of adventure. There is a good reason why the mottos of this book already reject such misunderstandings.

Unwillingness to believe stands in clear contrast not only to religious faith, but also to credulity in general (although the contrast to credulity is not so much a philosophical problem). (See also 3.1.7.)

Unwillingness to believe also stands in clear contrast to any ideological promises of redemption, be it religious or secular myths of salvation. We humans can improve our lot if we behave morally on the basis of reasonable weighing, but we will never be able to eliminate injustice, suffering, and (premature) death completely. Secular promises of salvation that demand present sacrifices of humanity in the interest of a future paradise on earth deserve the utmost distrust too. The history of the twentieth century has shown in a depressing manner, at the cost of the lives of millions of people, that they can lead to catastrophic consequences at least equal to those of religious promises of salvation.

Unwillingness to believe does not mean to flirt with doubt or the inadequacy of one's own knowledge and to quickly retreat to the admission of one's own ignorance. Such an admission by no means always indicates intellectual superiority; it can also indicate a lack of effort to gain knowledge, idle indifference, or an unfair immunisation strategy with regard to one's own position (by retracting one's statements as soon as they are attacked).

The value of the described unwillingness to believe cannot be proved. It is itself a value. As the Storm quotation says it: Do not let psychologically comfortable offers hinder you to face the truth. Moreover, one can argue for unwillingness to believe by resorting to other values, that is by presupposing a certain morality on the part of the interlocutor.

If somebody strives for knowledge (which is not exactly the same as the determination, already expressed in unwillingness to believe itself, to avoid illusions as far as possible), one can point out that reliance on the paths to knowledge considered unreliable by the unwilling to believe has obviously led to errors quite often if a later consideration in the light of logic, observation and simplicity is used as a criterion for this.

However, such errors (or – as far as the old religions and myths are concerned – more justly: explanatory models of the world that belong to former times and are outdated) can often be denied by a subtle interpretation of the original statements. With a little hermeneutic skill one can present authoritative interpretations of the world as »symbolic« and thus »timeless«.

Let us consider a Christian example – in accordance with the cultural background of the author. Using historical and textual criticism the two biblical stories of creation, which, taken literally, have always been contradictory because of the different sequence of creation, can be interpreted as follows: The priestly source with its six or seven day work story can be read as the symbolisation of an order of the world created and guaranteed by god, whereas the approximately five hundred years older Jahwist source in which the creation of man precedes that of the rest of the world can be read as a foundation of human morality and a setting of norms in an obligatory reference to god. (5) The fact that historically inhomogeneous texts have been compiled in the Bible, which, if regarded as realistic descriptions of events, already must have appeared contradictory to attentive readers in the past, allows the interpretation that this has been done with the intention to explain the world in an allegoric manner and to create meaning and morality therewith. Looked at that way it appears inadequate to see a contradiction between the biblical stories of creation and scientific concepts of the origin of the world, life, and humankind. But even if we do not attach much importance to the fact that such an allegoric interpretation contrasts sharply with the overwhelming majority's understanding of the bible throughout history, the crucial problem remains: such an allegoric interpretation does not provide any good reasons for including the idea of god in an explanation of the world. The timeless appeal of an authoritative interpretation of the world is no argument for its adequacy and no reason to accept it. The long-lasting importance of certain myths and interpretations of the world does not change the fact that they have been created by human beings. On the contrary, this is abundantly clear by the results of religious studies, as those referred to above concerning the bible.

But the aforementioned interpretations of the biblical texts make at least comprehensible what Ratzinger has in mind, when he tells us – in a phrasing which is skilful and presumptuous at once – that the belief in creation "moves on the ontological level", "marvels at the miracle of being itself," answering the question why things exist at all instead of others or nothing and what this means. The theory of evolution, on the other hand, he wants to be classified as situated on a phenomenological level, just explaining why the actually occurring forms in the world are the way they are in detail.[4] After domesticating evolutionary theory like that, Pope John Paul II was then able to accept it in 1996 in a message to the Pontifical Academy of Sciences, though defending a last stronghold: "If the origin of the human body comes through living matter which existed previously, the spiritual soul is created directly by God."[5]

But is it not much more plausible, then, to confine oneself to the "phenomenological" level for the explanation of the soul as well, that is to say, to an evolutionary, biological and biographical level? Why should we cherish a mere speculative respectively spiritual intuition of truth as a basis of an "ontology" of the soul? Or more generally: Why should we look for a way to justify meaning and morals that is obviously quite pleasing to human wishful thinking?

In the field of morals the apologists of traditional religious world orientation extract from the contradictory, unrealistic, rigorous and often sectarian demands that can be found in the scriptures of the great "book religions", a selection which, despite its questionable aspects, impresses by a certain grandness (such as the Christian charity or principle of loving one's neighbour and one's enemy) or that appears as useful or relevant for the respective present. The rest is (fundamentalist currents left apart) either ignored deliberately or dismissed as insignificant in order to preserve revelation and authority as sources of ideological certainty, emotional security, moral orientation, and a means to spell out the contents of spiritual experiences. I consider this subjectivist and decisionist procedure, which can always produce the results that suit the respective zeitgeist, to be dishonest. I am convinced that none of the religions rooted in times long past, Christianity included, can provide us with more than starting points for thought, and in any case no acceptable overall moral orientation. I consider religious morality to be equally time-dependent and outdated in many points as religious explanations of the world. (6)

But those who disagree, can weigh and play off the great importance of knowledge for our orientation in life allegedly to be obtained by revelation and authority against the errors (perhaps even considered as insignificant or unreal) to which we have succumbed or still may succumb if we accept these paths as trustworthy paths to knowledge. This pattern of argumentation has long been explicitly put forward or realised in their thinking and life in different variations by eminent philosophers time and again, for example by Pascal in his "wager"[6] or by William James in "The Will to Believe"[7]. And even in our time a man like C. F. v. Weizsäcker has attributed such great importance to religion that an excellent overview of the modern scientific world view has not prevented him from holding on to Christianity, or at least to a religious life orientation. And Weizsäcker is indisputably both a scientist and a Christian: in contrast to simpler minds, he does not allow religion to interfere in areas that are accessible to scientific knowledge, but only allows it to have a say beyond the "scope of science". (7)

This leads us to a better understanding of unwillingness to believe. In areas where the scientific way of thinking is overwhelmingly successful, there is no need to choose it (although unscientific and anti-scientific episodes of the zeitgeist may pose considerable practical problems and educating people to think scientifically is an important task). Those who rely on revelation, authority and esotericism in areas accessible to scientific investigation, may occasionally have s stroke of luck but will not be right in the long run: they are not religious but credulous, uncritical, blinded, indoctrinated, uneducated, or simply stupid. The argument of convergence, which has been illustrated by C. F. v. Weizsäcker very convincingly, makes the situation perfectly clear: "That physics is science, but dialectical materialism is not, became quite obvious, for instance, in 1955 at the First Geneva Conference on the Peaceful Uses of Atomic Energy. Many Western and Soviet physicists met there for the first time, and much information kept secret until then was made public. It was an expected and yet astonishing experience that the numerical values of certain atomic constants, which had been measured under top secret conditions in different countries under opposite political systems and creeds, proved to be identical to the last decimal when compared. Nothing similar happened with regard to the two sides' theories of state and society. The

Soviet and the Western scientist are united by a bond that no political disagreement can break: by a common truth."[8]

In fact, nobody rejects scientific thinking and the technology based on it in general. There is always only a selective rejection of science, a refusal of scientific thinking for certain areas. Let us listen once more to C. F. v. Weizsäcker: "The European Christian and the European sceptic live out their common unreflective belief in technology whenever they flick the switch entering a room and expect the light to come on. The romantic writer, who has written a book against the world view of science, calls his publisher by telephone because he is late in proof-reading; and even by this small act he bows to the God he rejects in his conscious thought."[9]

For all its practical importance, criticism of credulity or of selective rejection of science does not point to the very core of unwillingness to believe. The example of C. F. v. Weizsäcker shows that this criticism is close to the heart of some religious people as well. (8) Unwillingness to believe goes further: It means to reject religious speculation even where science cannot give an answer, for instance in cosmology beyond the fundamental physical laws of our universe (or possible universes) and in morality as far as the justification of all principles going beyond morality as reciprocity is concerned. In cosmology those unwilling to believe have no alternative to agnosticism beyond such a threshold (which nevertheless is equivalent to atheism for all practical purposes and also should be named as such). And in morality – despite all the horrors and disappointments of human history – they can only trust in the norm-setting power of the individual human being and of human society (and that is the only way to permanently overcome a scientism whose lack of moral standards can indeed lead to disaster).

Unwillingness to believe is on the one hand a psychological fact and on the other hand a central value decision - a value decision for a philosophy of life in which striving for truth and a view of the world without illusions have a high placement in the ranking of values. The honour of human beings (and here it has still a place, this term that one hears only with suspicion today) lies in the morality set by themselves and it lies in not lying to oneself, in trying to understand the world as good as possible, in viewing it as adequately as possible. This is the pathos of Theodor Storm, of Camus (though he overdid it with his heroic humanism of revolt against meaninglessness) and many others, including me, despite all efforts at unpathetic formulations. Bertrand Russell expressed this attitude both succinctly and amusingly when he was asked what he would say to God if, contrary to all his expectations, he found himself before his throne after his death: "Sir, why did you not give me better evidence?"[10]

Where good reasons are lacking, one does not decide according to speculation or spiritual experiences (what a variety of ideas does our brain produce without an equivalent in the outside world), but one suspends judgement and solves the practical problems that require a decision without assumptions offending reason (which does not mean: without feeling and morality). Spirituality and moral religiosity are no support the unwilling to believe can, wants to, or must accept.

Finally, there is another way of arguing for unwillingness to believe: If somebody believes in the value of tolerance, one can possibly convince her or him by pointing out that people who have gained or think they have gained knowledge by using one of the paths rejected by unwillingness to believe are often quite intolerant in this respect because they are all too convinced of the objectivity of their "knowledge". (9) But since this is not always the case, unwillingness to believe does not follow necessarily even if we presuppose the moral attitude of tolerance.

Unwillingness to believe cannot be deduced. Unwillingness to believe needs to be justified by a fundamental choice. (10 –12)

> "… the question of differentiating between knowledge and belief is of minor philosophical interest, in comparison with the more general question how our acceptance of different sorts of propositions is to be justified. What is important is to elicit the criteria of rational belief, rather than to determine the point at which it deserves a different name."[11]
>
> Alfred J. Ayer

> "How often has our view of the world been clouded by mind-bewitching myths and ideologies."[12]
>
> Franz M. Wuketits

1.3. The Fundamental Choice to Live

Those who want to live also speak themselves

"'One has to live', it is said, and 'one wants to live' is the fact in front of us. But not everyone has to be 'one'."[1]

Jean Améry

"Deciding whether life is or is not worth living, that is to answer the fundamental question of philosophy."[2]

Albert Camus

Even if one presupposes the fundamental choice to shape one's life consciously, those unwilling to believe have to make a choice about whether to live their life and about whether to regard it worth living.

I share Jean Améry's opinion that we should not call the people who come to a negative judgement here and then also plan and act accordingly "self-murderers". This term for suicides (still very common in German) contains a Christian-religious prejudice and is also semantic nonsense. (1) When Améry proposes a general replacement by the term »voluntary death« or »free death«, however, this contains an almost equally questionable, undifferentiated idealisation of suicide. The adequate summarising terms, which allow an open-minded consideration of the individual case, are »taking one's life« or »suicide« (although in German this word of Latin origin has the disadvantage to be regarded as a mere translation of »self-murder« making it more difficult to notice the questionable character of the original German term).

Taking one's own life does not have to contradict the fundamental choice to consciously shape one's life. If it is not a rash action but the consequence of a balance, it is definitely a possibility to shape one's life consciously. "Whoever must die is in the condition of answering a destiny and his rejoinder consists of fear or braveness. But potential suicides or suicides speak themselves." (Améry[3])

The irrevocability of the decision for suicide is not a suitable criterion for considering it as incompatible with unwillingness to believe. Many decisions about the shaping of our life are necessarily irrevocable since the concrete

38

situation in which they are possible does not occur again and their consequences can no longer be corrected.

Invoking the generally observable self-preservation instinct of the majority of all living beings, including most humans, only describes the facts and does not give us a norm, just as in other cases biological propensities or preferences of a majority cannot justify norms (although this is assumed often enough and may even be quite reasonable in many cases from a social and pragmatic point of view).

Life is actually the »default« (and thus more passive) situation given to us by nature, and most humans will only consider suicide if they get into an unbearable situation of personal or social suffering. However, the boundaries are drawn very differently. People kill themselves for a wide variety of reasons, not only for "generally understandable" or "clearly pathological" ones. Even a physically and mentally healthy person can come to the conclusion that the joys of life do not outweigh the hardship, suffering and adversity it brings. It is a fact that we humans can, at least from late childhood on, revoke our willingness to live and reject and end life.

There is a wide spectrum of motives for suicide. It ranges from fanatical and altruistic self-sacrifice to political demonstration and agitation and to the most diverse, in part perfectly understandable sufferings and burdens inherent in the personal circumstances of life. It also includes those cases, admittedly extremely rare, and in so far practically unimportant, but nevertheless philosophically interesting, where a person kills herself when feeling at the peak of happiness because she does not want to live with less and does not want to experience decline and decay. "Better pass boldly into that other world, in the full glory of some passion, than fade and wither dismally with age." (Joyce[4]) One can also feel like that without believing in another world. And although only few of us take their own life due to such a feeling, it is not at all uncommon to see a potentially suicidal behaviour by taking unnecessary high, avoidable, life-threatening risks, as for instance in rashly heroism, extreme sports, or various kinds of dangerous thrill-seeking experiences by adolescents or also bored wealthy older people.

That the position of a happy suicidal person is in itself reasonable and consistent, if taken consciously and after thorough consideration, can hardly be disputed. Equally reasonable, however, is the opposite position: what we can still learn and know, what we mean and can still mean to other people, now and during the years to come, the joys we can experience in the further course of life (also: why should it be only the peak that counts?). So this is a value decision, a philosophical decision of fundamental importance. And whatever we decide, whatever reasons we give: all of them are »natural«, given by nature, inherent in the human nature (which includes the possibility of deliberate self-destruction).

That other people »throw away« their lives may appear grotesque to those who, for example due to an incurable disease, have to die involuntarily before reaching an average lifespan or at least much sooner than they hoped. Furthermore, such a behaviour is also an affront to those who fight to preserve human life (although it does not call the meaning of their work into question, for most of the people concerned thank them for their efforts). Nevertheless: To be willing to live is not a matter of course for human beings.

It is possible to perceive suicide as a genuine philosophical temptation in a time of radical questionability. "If all answers dissolve again and again, a peculiar paralysis threatens to spread over existence." (Weischedel[5])

The fundamental choice of unwillingness to believe and the fundamental choice to consciously shape one's life speak neither for nor against suicide. Therefore, this alternative – be it a concrete temptation or an extreme possibility recognised by philosophising – must first be excluded. This can only be justified by a fundamental choice to live.

The questionability – or clearer: the lack of a meaning going beyond biological existence – is confronted with the human ability to spontaneously enjoy life and to make conscious decisions. Humans can give their life a foundation through choices, they can set moral attitudes, values and thus meaning. This does not mean to indulge in an inflationary decisionism. Those unwilling to believe want to confine themselves to a minimum of belief decisions necessary for a sufficient life orientation.

The decision to live cannot be deduced. Ultimately, the decision between life and suicide cannot be made on rational grounds. But those unwilling to believe can nevertheless influence this decision in favour of life. They can make the fundamental choice to live more attractive for themselves and others by seeking and pointing out perspectives for life and contrasting them with suicide as an escape from life – an escape which in all probability leads to the dissolution of personality. But, admittedly, such a prospect may also promise a desirable state of tranquillity, or, at any rate, the settlement of their problems to some people.

However, it is often the case that if one (re)commits oneself to life, bonds to life develop in the form of interest in the world, relationships with other people and responsibility for other people. From the responsibility for other people follows that in certain individual cases even for secular humanism suicide can be a morally wrong decision, a flight from responsibility.

However, it will not always be possible to point out good reasons and positive perspectives for living on that outweigh the concrete reasons for fleeing. Just think of advanced stages of incurable diseases. The weighing of values which leads to a person's wish to end her life is not always wrong and we must not always try to exert our influence in order to avoid suicide. (2) Actually, the conjecture that a person who attempts suicide might be mentally disturbed is always justified without detailed knowledge of the circumstances of the individual case. This is supported by the relatively low repetition rate of 10 to 20 percent after attempted suicides. But: "Those who leap have not necessarily fallen into delusion, they are not even 'disturbed' or 'deranged' in all circumstances." (Améry[6])

We do not know how we ourselves will think and act in certain "borderline situations". Nor do we know whether we will perhaps belong to the unfortunate ones who are subject to a long-lasting and so gradual decline that they are deprived of the possibility of self-determination. More than an unreserved, unconditional affirmation of life, Seneca's statement seems to me worthy of a philosopher, in which he formulates a middle way between the extremes of a happy suicide on the one hand and an unconditional obligation to endure life to the bitter end on the other (as we encounter in Christian resignation to God's will): "It is this, that I shall not abandon old age, if old age preserves me intact for myself, and intact as regards the better part of myself; but if old age begins to shatter my mind, and to pull its various faculties to pieces, if it leaves me, not life, but only the breath of life, I shall rush out of a house that is crumbling and tottering. I shall not avoid illness by seeking death, as long as the illness is curable and does not impede my soul. I shall not lay violent hands upon myself just because I am in pain; for death under such circumstances is defeat. But if I find out that the pain must always be endured, I shall depart, not because of the pain but because it will be a hindrance to me as regards all my reasons for living. He who dies just because he is in pain is a weakling, a coward; but he who lives merely to brave out this pain, is a fool."[7]

"Somebody who leaves life without compelling reason in full possession of his mental powers, without misery or illness, has not understood that the meaning of life is life itself."[8]

Bernulf Kanitscheider

"Believe that life is worth living and your belief will help create the fact."[9]

William James

1.4. The Fundamental Choice of Moral Attitudes and Values

At the cradle of weigh up thinking

"Reason and education, though we are willing to put our trust in them, can hardly be powerful enough to lead us to action, unless besides we exercise and form our soul by experience to the way we want it to go."[1]

Michel de Montaigne

Montaigne's sentence succinctly emphasises the limited utility of moral principles. And yet such principles are necessary as a guideline.

By the preceding choices, we have gained, bit by bit, a necessary measure of orientation against the uncertainty following from unwillingness to believe on a rational level. However, we are still lacking essential elements to distinguish our conscious shaping of life from that of the Pyrrhonean sceptic or of a person who explicitly decides according to the momentary mood and situation in the world. The previous choices only provide very broad guidelines for our actions (by excluding, for instance, religious faith or suicide as a result of a philosophical rejection of life). The question "What should I do?" calls for more detailed guiding principles. Therefore, a fundamental choice to adopt moral attitudes and values is made here. This is the systematic, connecting basis on which moral attitudes and values can be justified by choices in particular.

The fundamental choice to adopt moral attitudes and values is not rendered superfluous by the fundamental choice to consciously shape one's life. The choice to shape one's life consciously could be the only fundamental choice we make, except one more fundamental choice, namely the choice to make all further moral decisions according to the momentary mood and situation. The fundamental choice of moral attitudes and values, on the other hand, involves seeking reasonable grounds as a foundation of the moral attitudes and values for which we then decide. And it involves seeking, wherever

43

possible, reasonable grounds and making rational weighings on the basis of previously accepted moral attitudes and values prior to particular moral decisions. Rationality plays an important role in clarifying the premises of our moral decisions, but it cannot replace these decisions.

The fundamental choice of moral attitudes and values is in clear contrast to the pretension made by some people that they may decide according to arbitrary, free-floating moral intuitions by appealing to moods and feelings. Such intuitions may be diametrically opposed to a rational consideration of values, for instance, a weighing of interests between different people concerned. Those who decide consciously in favour of certain moral attitudes and values thereby also assume the obligation to face the discussion about the reasons for their moral decisions concerning concrete problems and to provide good reasons for their decisions or to admit the questionability or inconsequence of certain weighings and decisions. The latter alternative must not be used lightly as an excuse and has to be limited to as few particular cases and problems as possible if somebody wants to be taken seriously in a moral sense.

The choices on the basis of the fundamental choice of moral attitudes and values, that are discussed below, do not necessarily follow from the fundamental choices already made, even if they are partly suggested by them (such as the attitude of tolerance). Those who share the preceding choices can now nevertheless decide quite differently in any particular case. To an even greater extent than hitherto from now on "only" a personal example is given for the shaping of the belief of an unwilling to believe.

I do not agree with Weischedel when he says: "First and foremost it must be stated that a sceptical ethics, if it is to be philosophical, needs a principle from which its recommendations can be derived; without such a principle it could only lead to a more or less accidental compilation of ethical directives."[2] What a concrete person decides for after thorough deliberation is no accidental compilation. That morality needs *one* principle, from which all particular moral attitudes and values can be derived, does not become an intellectual necessity just because it is a tradition, a habit of thought and a desire of some philosophers. I cannot see any principle from which a sufficiently differentiated morality could be convincingly derived. (More on this in section 3.3.) In any case, the morality of a sceptic described in Weischedel's "Sceptical Ethics" does not necessarily follow from his fundamental choice of scepticism but requires a wide variety of further choices. Nor does the morality described here necessarily follow from the fundamental choice of unwillingness to believe (and not even from all my fundamental choices together). Best of all, essential parts of morality and law can be derived from an interest in self-preservation and survival most people share – or, in general, from the undeniable elementary interests of a majority of humans (briefly: existence, subsistence, development) and from interculturally traceable, evolutionary developed moral behavioural dispositions. But if such facts are to be acknowledged as a basis for norms this too requires decisions.

Different moral attitudes and values can come into conflict with each other. In great part moral thinking means to weigh moral attitudes and values against each other. Therefore, the description of moral attitudes and values is often very fuzzy. A precise description of moral attitudes and values in general sentences is not possible, they remain more or less vague. Agreement on the meaning of the terms used, which remains problematic principally despite all efforts at definitional clarity and yet is a prerequisite for meaningful communication, can only be assumed here to a reduced extent.

What one understands exactly by particular moral attitudes and values depends on one's personality and mindset as a whole and ultimately only manifests itself in the statements and actions in concrete situations. And even then, a false impression can be created due to a personal lack of strength in realising moral attitudes and values although the person concerned is definitely serious about them. "The philosopher is a human being subject to human passions and weaknesses, he needs to be granted leniency." (d'Holbach[3])

Nevertheless, even with a limited number of moral statements one can achieve two things: set oneself a guideline for one's life and give others an impression of one's moral attitudes and values. And this impression, which one conveys to others, is an important contribution to philosophical debate, and even more so if it is supported by one's own conduct of life.

Seneca's remark (certainly also made on his own behalf) "Philosophers do not carry into effect all that they teach. No; but they effect much good by their teaching, by the noble thoughts which they conceive in their minds..."[4] describes very accurately that philosophers are masters of theory, not necessarily of practice, or that they are at least often forced to make considerable concessions and lower their ideals when they clash with practice. However, it is not always "Unfortunately, philosophers do not carry into effect all that they teach«. Sometimes we may well find: »Fortunately, philosophers do not carry into effect all that they teach."

"Be a philosopher; but, amidst all your philosophy, be still a man."[5]

David Hume

1.4.1. The Choice to Strive for Knowledge

A risky decision with a threefold possibility of gain

"It goes without saying, however, that there would be no truth at all if the question of how to live with it were to be the criterion for truth."[1]

Theodor Lessing

The fundamental choice of unwillingness to believe does not yet include an explicit decision as to whether one wants to regard knowledge as worth striving for and the striving for it an essential goal of one's life. The principles of doubt and of the demand for good reasons, which belong to unwillingness to believe, suggest this, but principally they also allow to regret the spread of doubt as well as laziness or indifference beyond destructive contributions concerning knowledge. Therefore, a separate choice to strive for knowledge is necessary.

Knowledge is not only scientific knowledge. If one takes the choice to strive for knowledge seriously, however, it is an obvious consequence that one also strives for an overview of scientific knowledge that allows to assess one's own position in the world as appropriately as possible for a human being at a certain moment in history. C. F. v. Weizsäcker has summed up the significance of science in a nutshell: "The gain that science brings us is threefold. It is a gain in knowledge, a gain in the possibilities of action, and a gain for the development of a conscious human personality. It is, to use three foreign words, a theoretical, a practical, and a moral gain."[2]

However, the striving for knowledge may come into conflict with shared humanity. In pursuit of knowledge one can forget to communicate with others, the help others and to respect others. There is, for example, the scientist who neglects his family and exaggerates the degree of ruthlessness that is often an inevitable side effect and prerequisite of great achievements. Or, as a blatant example for of an excessive pursuit of knowledge: foreseeably harmful scientific experiments on humans without consent. (1)

The choice to strive for knowledge must also be tempered by the choices to enjoy life and to strive for personal development. Nietzsche's criticism elucidates this aptly, in spite of the arrogant-elitist tendency: "Now, this paradox, the scientific man, has in recent years got into a frantic hurry in Germany, as though science were a factory and every minute's slacking incurred punishment. Nowadays he works as hard as the fourth estate, the slaves; his study is no longer an occupation but a necessity, he looks neither to right nor left and goes through all the business of life, and its more questionable aspects, with the half consciousness or the repellent need for entertainment characteristic of the exhausted worker."[3] (2)

Striving for knowledge has its dark side, it is anything but a harmless undertaking. Knowledge often means disillusionment. This disillusionment may have a destructive or at least very disturbing effect on some people's lives. Knowledge and science bestow power. This power can be abused. The pursuit of knowledge has brought humankind to a point where it can destroy the earth to the point of making it uninhabitable. The pursuit of knowledge alone will not prevent humans from doing so. The consequences of one of the most valuable and appealing goals humans can set themselves could cost them their existence if it is not accompanied by an adequate progress in cultural development.

1.4.2. The Choice of Shared Humanity

Neither holy nor unconcerned

Shared humanity means not only that we feel connected to other human beings in the human condition and that we respect them, but also that we want to help them if they are in need of help and we can help. Shared humanity begins in our immediate surroundings by taking the interests, wishes and fears of others seriously – without losing ourselves. Only if we try to live shared humanity in our personal contacts and vicinity will the otherwise all to presumptuous moral grandiloquence of general and universalising pronouncements about it be alleviated and the inevitable discrepancy between aspiration and reality become bearable.

What a person understands in detail by shared humanity depends on her or his other moral attitudes and values. The essential goals of shared humanity are to protect human beings from attacks on their life and physical integrity, from physical and mental illness, economic hardship, social disadvantage and political oppression, to free them of these scourges or at least to alleviate their consequences and to stand up for their freedom to live according to their own ideas as long as they do not harm others. Shared humanity means being aware that prosperity and opportunities for personal development are to a large extent dependent on fortunate circumstances and chance as an indispensable basis for personal achievement, and that people in need often do not lack the will to shape their lives, but have simply had bad luck.

Even if all this still remains vague and noncommittal enough and should be seen in the light of the limited possibilities of every individual human being and not be misunderstood as a moral dream of omnipotence or a fantasy of universal happiness, it is, on the other hand, not a banal formulation of goals.

An explicit choice is required to justify shared humanity as an essential goal of one's life. As can be seen from the state of the world, shared humanity is not even an essential goal besides others for many people, or at any rate they do not realise it - or else their moral attitudes and values are so different from mine that I am no longer willing to call shared humanity what they mean by that. This applies, for example, to all those religious and ideological fanatics in whose morality tolerance does not stand next to shared humanity, to all those who believe (and often even call this »true« shared humanity) that people must be forced to their happiness – if necessary with violence and terror – and that everyone must live as they see fit by virtue of their higher insight.

Shared humanity can be a motive for the pursuit of knowledge, as one wants to know in order to be able to help others.

The choice of shared humanity is also closely related to the choice to enjoy life. That an obligation to make sacrifices can arise from shared humanity does not need to be explained further. The problem lies in the extent of sacrifice that should follow from shared humanity. This must be discussed again and again while taking a realistic look at the state of the world (as, for instance, Singer[1] does). However, helping others can also increase one's own joy of life. "People for whom we are a source of strength give us our support in life." (Ebner-Eschenbach[2]) In searching an appropriate balance it seems desirable to me to avoid an altruistic doggedness that sees the meaning of one's life only in the help for others, only in the service for a good cause. Using the help for others as an escape from meaninglessness can lead us to a point where we would no longer see meaning in a world without drudgery, evil, and disaster. I want to enjoy life and help others not only for the sake of a moral obligation but also so that they can enjoy life (again). I respect the honestly meant exclusive orientation of an
48

individual life towards the service to others, but I do not accept it as exemplary. (See also note 3.6.3. (1))

Altruistic self-sacrifice oscillates between being a necessary, arousing, extraordinary example and a fanaticism going back to a pathological structure of personality and a need to compensate for psychological maldevelopments. Through their personality and their actions "moral saints" point out intolerable and unacceptable grievances and injustices that call for remedy. Some of them may suffer from an exaggerated need for recognition or a guilt complex. But they have the merit of breaking through the defence mechanisms again and again with which we not only rightly protect ourselves against excessive demands but often make ourselves all to comfortable: This and that is too far away or none of our business or we as individuals could not do anything about it anyway.

Ascetic altruism (apart from the fact that it can concretely save the lives of some people) has an important moral function in society as a motivating attitude of a small minority. Its moral basis, however, are those people who, in their place and in their immediate surroundings, inconspicuously try to realise moral attitudes and values in everyday life, people, for whom altruism plays an essential but not an utterly dominant role. On the one hand, it is regrettable that altruistic motives do not play a more important role in the value system of many people; on the other hand, it is fortunate that the value system of most people does not only know altruistic motives, otherwise our joy in life would be greatly diminished and our culture considerably impoverished.

Montaigne already saw the appropriate balance very well when he wrote: "He who lives not at all unto others, hardly lives unto himself." And then a few lines later: "Just as anyone who should forget to live a good and saintly life, and think he was quit of his duty by guiding and training others to do so, would be a fool; even so he who abandons healthy and gay living of his own to serve others thereby, takes, to my taste, a bad and unnatural course."[3] Camus continues these thoughts in his own way: "One must stand up for those who suffer. But if you stop loving anything else, what do you stand up for?"[4]

Expediency must also be included in the moral evaluation and speaks against altruistic one-sidedness and doggedness: *medicus sine hilaritate sanare nequit* - without cheerfulness the doctor cannot heal. Thus, what Appiah formulates as a modern weighing up ethics has long been present in the philosophical tradition: "But life is complicated and we face many, often conflicting, demands; the needs of other people aren't the only thing that matters. So there will be difficult trade-offs between different values."[5]

Just as each individual must find an appropriate way between indifference and ascetic altruism according to his or her inclinations, talents and possibilities, the same goes for modern affluent societies as a whole. An exaggerated feeling of guilt, not uncommon today, that our societies are basically living at the expense of the rest of the world, is not a good basis for searching this appropriate middle way. Viewed impartially, only the modern affluent societies manage to provide most of their citizens with a satisfactory level of economic security, medical care, and cultural stimulation. And they do this not mainly by exploiting others, but as a result of a long philosophical, cultural, social and economic development. To break the structures of misery in the economically underdeveloped countries of the world, we do not only need fairer economic relations, but these countries also have to get rid of disorganisation, corruption, and religious prejudice. Economic fairness and political pressure from the affluent countries can help, but to a considerable extent the poor countries will have to achieve this themselves in a long and painful historical process, even if we reach a much fairer international economic order than we have today. (1)

Therefore, for me shared humanity does not mean considering equal opportunities for all humans as a goal achievable within a foreseeable timespan and demanding an equal distribution of the available resources among all. If one wanted to do this, one would have to accept, in view of the population explosion in the economically underdeveloped countries, the end of any cultural and civilisational development that also allows for luxury, i.e. the end of our individualistic way of life. (See also the comments on the topic of »equality« under 3.8.2. and 3.9.)

However, the people in the developing countries have an immediate moral claim to a degree of solidarity that seriously combats the structures of misery they are confronted with. In the interest of the poor (and also of our own descendants) shared humanity undoubtedly demands that we should at least succeed in refraining from thoughtless, stupid, and reckless ways of wasting resources in which often only a perverted idea of freedom is expressed and that are co-determined essentially by short-term and short-sighted economic interests and can be avoided without serious disadvantages. Moreover, we also pragmatically serve our own security interests when we fight against poverty and exploitation.

For a long time to come, we will have to accept an unfair degree of inequality for the sake of other values. But we should not accept this fact with resigned indifference. At least in the long term – which means here beyond the next fifty years – simply combating misery is not enough. Richard Rorty is right when he adopts the slogan "No future without dreams!", and argues, with exemplary unpretentious passion, for a social and democratic reformism which is as sober as it is tenacious and which - even if this can only be a utopia - adheres to the goal "that sooner or later all human children should get the same opportunities in life".[6]

To make progress on this path, it is certainly advisable for most of us to heed Wolfgang Kersting's admonition: "The same applies to morality: dwell in the land and you shall be fed."[7] As Kersting shortly after mentions the human interest in existence, in subsistence and in development as the »material support« of a sober universalism, it quickly becomes apparent that for him »sober universalism« by no means refers to a minimal concept. At the same time, it is his intention to denounce the hollow and unrealistic words of a rhetoric of human rights based on a supposed »law of nature« or other highly questionable philosophical concepts of justification.

From a moral point of view, every single human life, that is in some way worth living for the respective individual, has an equal value, but from a political point this is far from being the case. We must fight to bring the moral and political perspectives closer together, even if we will hardly ever be able to bridge the gap between the two perspectives completely.

(2)

1.4.3. The Choice to Enjoy Life

A plea for a paradox

> "Who hasn't experienced how thin the barrier is, nature has put up between gaiety and sadness?"[1]

> Julien Offray de La Mettrie

> "We should spread joy, but cut down sadness as much as we can."[2]

> Michel de Montaigne

For me, the choice to enjoy life means to indulge in what I can perceive as beautiful and valuable in this world, to take pleasure in the diversity of the world, in nature and in the creative achievements of human beings, in truth and the striving for truth; it means to take pleasure with and in other people, in oneself, in what one succeeds in, in what one likes, in what one would not have it any other way, and finally also in what one could imagine to be much worse. True to Lichtenberg's remarks: "'Many are less fortunate than you' may not be a roof to live under, but it will serve to retire beneath in the event of a shower." "One complains so much of every pain, and rejoices so seldom when one feels none." "To make us truly feel a fortune appearing indifferent to us, we must always think that it be lost, and we got it back this moment. But some experience in all kinds of suffering is required to perform these attempts successfully."[3]

The choice to enjoy life also means for me to want to bring joy to others and enrich the life of my fellow human beings – and to find enrichment therein myself. This effect or even egoistic motive observable in altruistic programs and actions does not devaluate them, but rather gives them an additional, albeit secondary value. Why should we be ashamed of our own joy arising from the choice of shared humanity? However, the knowledge of the benefit we ourselves derive from bringing joy to others or helping them can guard us against complacency.

A choice to enjoy life may seem paradoxical. Isn't joy something emotional and spontaneous? Either one rejoices in life or one does not. But this is thinking too simplistic. Of course, external conditions determine one's ability to rejoice to a considerable degree. It is not a sound philosophical advice to sugar coat a miserable situation. But one's own personal readiness to rejoice, the readiness to let things you can rejoice in touch you, is an essential prerequisite for being able to experience joy (just as the effort to ignore more or less insignificant nuisances or at least not to get affected by them for a longer period of time). To be aware of the positive aspects of life and one's personal life situation is an essential part of psychological and philosophical art of living. To a certain – not insignificant – degree, we ourselves are responsible for whether we enjoy life. That is why a choice to enjoy life makes sense.

Moods in which everything seems boring and worthless are one of the facets of a free, open, and sensitive human life. They can also be a prerequisite for extraordinary productivity and must not be anxiously suppressed right at the outset by an overly rigid order of thoughts and the course of life. On the other hand, one should not get lost in such moods either. These two aspects are well expressed in the following quotations: "Ah, that's what one has to pay for the Promethean fire! It isn't enough to suffer, you have to love the melancholy and respect your doubts and questionings: they represent the surfeit, the luxury of life, and mostly appear on the summits of happiness, where there are no coarse desires; people who are in need and sorrow are not bothered by them; thousands and thousands of people go through life without knowing anything about this fog of doubts and the anguish of questionings … But to those who have met them at the right moment, they are not an affliction, but welcome guests." (Gontscharov[4]) "Life is too short to be interested in everything, but it is good to be interested in as many things as are necessary to fill our days. We are all prone to the malady of the introvert, who, with the manifold spectacle of the world spread out before him, turns away and gazes only upon the emptiness within. But let us not imagine that there is anything grand about the introvert's unhappiness". (Russell[5])

For me, it also follows from the choice to enjoy life that one strives for a basic mood of serenity – not a desperate cheerfulness when external problems stand in the way, but neither black sternness nor grumpiness as the normal state.

> "Whether young or old, you have to acquire cheerfulness and energy anew every day."[6]
>
> Otto Flake

1.4.4. The Choice to Strive for Personal Development

Between the possible and the impossible

> "Our life is like a journey on which, as we advance, the landscape takes a different view from that which it presented at first, and changes again, as we come nearer."[1]
>
> Arthur Schopenhauer

> "In the interplay of the possible and the impossible we expand our possibilities. That we create it, this tension in which we grow, that, I think, is what

53

matters; that we orientate ourselves towards a goal which however, when we approach, recedes once more."[2]

Ingeborg Bachmann

The choice to strive for personal development leads beyond knowing, helping, and rejoicing. It means wanting to work on oneself in order to live up to one's own standards and thus be content with one's life in hindsight, not with every single action of course – that would only be possible with arrogance and self-deception - but with the balance. I want to do all in my power to be able to write someday what Bertrand Russell wrote in old age: »This has been my life. I have found it worth living, and would gladly live it again if the chance were offered me.«[3]

Insights, principles, and advices on wisdom and art of living, which seem essential to me, are the subject of this section. Where it cannot be said better the literary and philosophical tradition is plundered.

– It is about viewing the world realistically, not only in a cosmological and biological but also in a moral sense. If this were an easy exercise to follow, there would be no need for Goethe's admonition: "After all, to look at the world adequately (…) you should not judge it as to good or to bad; love and hate are very closely related, and both make our vision cloudy."[4]

– It is about reviewing and improving again and again one's own processes of thinking, acquisition of information, planning, decision-making as well as action strategies and it is about avoiding inadequate simplification, short-sightedness, loss of reality, activism or actionism or else resignation.

– It is about a middle way between spreading oneself too thin between too many interests and tasks and accepting one-sidedness to easily; it is about coping decently with the tension arising from the limitations of one's own possibilities and the lack of inclination to accept them. "Just as our physical path on the earth is always only a line and never a surface, so in our lives, whenever we wish to grasp and possess a thing, we have to leave countless others behind to our right and to our left, renouncing them. If we cannot decide, and instead, like children at a fair, reach for everything that tempts us in passing, then this is a mistaken endeavour to transform the line of our path into a surface: we zigzag about, wander like a will-o'-the-wisp, and attain nothing. He who would be everything cannot be anything." (Schopenhauer[5])

– It is about recognising one's personal limits, about adapting responsibilities and obligations to one's own capability.

– It is about reviewing, preserving and developing further the goals for one's own life, since these goals are not discovered and regarded as an externally determined, objective truth, but are felt and found as a personal desire and commitment.

– It is about the realisation of these goals in life, about making one's choices more than mere declarations, it is about practising and living moral attitudes and values and about consequently pursuing the goals and obligations resulting from them. "It is more important for you to keep the resolutions you have already made than to go on and make noble ones. You must persevere, must develop new strength by continuous study, until that which is only a good inclination becomes a good settled purpose. … There is no reason why you should put confidence in yourself too quickly and readily. Examine yourself; scrutinise and observe yourself in diverse ways; but mark, before all else, whether it is in philosophy or merely in life itself that you have made progress." (Seneca[6]) "But understanding is not the same as doing. Quickness of understanding is a mental faculty, but right doing requires the practice of a lifetime." (Goethe[7])

– It is about making progress in dealing with other people, about progress in communication and human leadership. (1)

– It is about advancing in the realisation of what one considers valuable, which means also to bring oneself in a position that allows to advocate for it more effectively – power as a means, not an end in itself (it goes without saying that it depends very much on the personality of the individual and the respective social situation to what extent and in what manner such »political« demands on oneself can be realised). (2)

– It is about accepting responsibility, in personal relationships and in certain social roles and positions, and at the same time it is about not doing so with too much willingness to compromise, but to maintain autonomy and distance and a productive readiness for change.

– It is about learning from failures as well; they can make us more experienced and mature and make us appreciate success all the more; moreover, one can realise moral attitudes and values even in futile efforts.

"Lack of success does not signify lack of meaning." (Frankl[8])

- It is about not letting get yourself down by the personal burdens and wounds inflicted on you by life (sometimes with your own active assistance), it is about keeping your head up or at least trying to rise it above personal and social problems, constraints and prejudice again and again, that is, to strive for a standpoint "au-dessus de la mêlée". (3) To keep distance from the present situation and to look ahead, as good and as long it is possible, is advice already given by Shakespeare: "Come what come may, time and the hour runs through the roughest day."[9]

- It is about accepting imperfection, failure, and suffering as an inevitable part of life. In this Schopenhauer's dictum may be of some help: "A good supply of resignation is of the first importance in providing for the journey of life."[10]

- It is about finding the right middle way between sympathetic understanding for the emotional needs of fellow human beings and an appropriate distance from emotional aberrations.

- It is about the right balance between being close to everyday life and stepping back from its seemingly self-evident necessities and keeping some distance in thinking and acting. (4) I see philosophy as an essential prerequisite as well as an essential element in the realisation of a meaningful life. "One should be a human being and not 'withdraw' from life but take part in all that it entails. Thus, one should marry and have children (in the 'Mastersingers' there is a definition which wants that one can speak of mastery only when the ability to sing a beautiful song still proves itself in the midst of child baptism, business, strife and quarrel) ... ." (Thomas Mann[11]) "True, our first duty in life is to perform our practical tasks, to meet the demands of the day. But if we desire to lead a philosophical life, we shall not content ourselves with practical tasks; we shall look upon the mere work in whose aims we immerse ourselves as in itself a road to self-forgetfulness, omission and guilt. And to lead a philosophical life means also to take seriously our experience of men, of happiness and hurt, of success and failure, of the obscure and the confused. It means not to forget but to possess ourselves inwardly of our experience, not to let ourselves be distracted but to think problems through, not to take things for granted but to elucidate them. There are two paths of philosophical life: the path of solitary meditation in all its ramifications and the path of communication with men, of mutual understanding through acting, speaking, and keeping silence together." (Jaspers[12])

- It is about the right degree of resolute personal commitment without becoming completely absorbed and getting lost in the hustle and bustle of the world. Montaigne: "It is for little souls, buried under the weight of business, to be unable to detach themselves cleanly from it or to leave it and pick it up again."[13] (5)

- It is, on the one hand, about accepting and cultivating habits that determine life and make it easier and thus make it possible for us to cope with everyday life and concentrate on certain aims and pursue them rather consistently and efficiently and, on the other hand, about keeping an open mind and the readiness for change and for breaking habits.

- It is about achieving contentment and overcoming the notorious discontent human beings tend to – sometimes even when and just when external reasons for discontent seem limited. This tendency is expressed succinctly in the sentence "There, where you are not, is happiness". (6) A somewhat different fruitful perspective on this is opened up by the sentence: "Wherever you go, you take yourself with you." The challenge is to find a way between contenting oneself to easily and insatiable discontent, between the "carpe diem!" and an orientation to the future. One has to become and stay aware of the fact that our orientation in life should take into account, evaluate and cherish the past, the present, and the future. This may sound obvious and even banal and nevertheless it is difficult enough to put it into practice a whole life long. The temptation to emphasise just one aspect proves to be overpowering time and again. "The habit of looking to the future and thinking that the whole meaning of the present lies in what it will bring forth is a pernicious one." (Russell[14]) "Don't spoil what you have by desiring what you don't have; but remember that what you now have was once among the things only hoped for." (Epicurus[15]) "… taking each day as if it were the last and yet living it faithfully and responsibly as if there were yet to be a great future." (Dietrich Bonhoeffer[16]) "Hear the voice of the past. Don't lose yourself arrogantly to the fleeting present … Reverence for the past and responsibility to the future provide the right attitude in life." (Klaus Bonhoeffer[17]) (7)

Here, in the realm of maxims for the conduct of life, I also see the place for the »existentialist« call for concentration on the moment, for appreciation of the moment, for a direct, undisguised and wondering perception of the world that transcends everyday life. But this call does not form a good basis for entire philosophies and it is certainly good for nothing if used as an antirational attitude claiming to provide a privileged path to knowledge.

– Finally, it is about the right way to deal with inevitable limitations, with losses of possibilities, abilities and persons: »When he was young, he told her, each phase of his life, each self he tried on, had seemed reassuringly temporary. Its imperfections didn't matter, because he could easily replace one moment by the next, one Saladin by another. Now, however, change had begun to feel painful; the arteries of the possible had begun to harden.« (Rushdie[18]) "…Wisdom. Is that to be seasoned or is it the ability to integrate adversities? I would like to understand wisdom in this second sense, as the ability to integrate the adverse and to have thereby gained more distance from positive things and from oneself. … we have to integrate adversities throughout our whole life and not just in old age, but more so in old age. … If we accept our own inabilities, we remain alive in relation to them." (Tugendhat[19])

> "No two of us have identical difficulties, nor should we be expected to work out identical solutions. Each, from his peculiar angle of observation, takes in a particular sphere of fact and trouble, which each must deal with in a unique manner. One of us must soften himself, another must harden himself; one must yield a point, another must stand firm – in order the better to defend the position assigned to him."[20]
>
> Owen Flanagan

> "Who does not take himself seriously is soon lost … ."[21]
>
> Thomas Mann

(8)

1.4.5. The Choice of Tolerance

A mental head guard

> "… the step from absolute morality to bloody massacre is short; ideology's claim to absolute authority takes it quickly and as a matter of course."[1]
>
> Karl Schlechta

> "When they saw they would never be able to set a catholic head on his shoulders they at least struck off the protestant one."[2]
>
> Georg Christoph Lichtenberg

> "Since each, incapable of ruling
> His inner self, would gladly rule his neighbour's will
> In the manner that his proud mind dictates to him …"[3]
>
> Johann Wolfgang von Goethe

In the case of tolerance it becomes particularly clear that the content of moral attitudes and values depends on the personality and the views of a person as a whole and can only be formulated vaguely in isolation.

First of all, tolerance means letting people live the way they want to, even if you do not approve of their way of life, as long as other people are not significantly harmed.

The vagueness of this formulation lies in the concept of significant harm to others. Just offending religious or ideological feelings and rules of conduct through deviant behaviour and actual or supposed dangers for the peace of mind or the salvation of the soul of religious adherents or for the »right« ideological orientation of other people associated with the »bad example« do certainly not constitute significant harm in the sense of the concept of tolerance advocated here. Unfortunately, committed religionists and ideologues often have a different concept of tolerance (in which only their own freedom of religion and belief is adequately represented) even if they do not, like fundamentalists or fanatics, reject tolerance altogether. Those who are psychologically too dependent on the certainty of their own truth can hardly tolerate the provocation of divergent thinking.

The choice of tolerance does not follow, however, from unwillingness to believe or from scepticism or atheism. There may be intolerant people who are unwilling to believe or sceptics and there have already been and there are more than enough intolerant atheists who in their ideological stubbornness did and do in no way rank behind religious fanatics and have been responsible for the killing of millions of people. Atheism can be compatible with totalitarian secular doctrines of salvation and totalitarian regimes and does not necessarily go hand in hand with secular humanism. On the other hand, there are fortunately many tolerant religious people who live humanist values.

The choice of tolerance cannot be derived from the choice of shared humanity either; its independence has to be emphasised. Without tolerance shared humanity may be interpreted in such a way that one feels obliged to impose one's own ideas about the right life on others.

Tolerance moves between the poles of a symmetric attitude in which the people involved concede true equality to their different attitudes and ways of life and an asymmetric attitude of mere toleration as often shown by majorities towards minorities.

The closer you are to the person whose actions are at stake, the less tolerance will have to do with non-interference. Clear statements and determined efforts to influence may also be a moral duty. Tolerance is not tantamount to indifference.

The choice of tolerance is, in contrast to the choices discussed earlier, more orientated towards toleration than towards action. But it contains a call to action insofar as it entails the obligation to stand up for the enforcement and the maintenance of tolerance in society and to prevent people who are driven to intolerance by their aversions from determining decisively the course of events.

Tolerance needs a clear relationship with other cultural-conventional values: it must find its limits where the human and civil rights guaranteed in liberal democracies are in danger.

"Toleration requires a concept of the intolerable."[4]

Kwame Anthony Appiah

"There is no such thing as a 'culturally authentic' suppression, or a 'culturally authentic' murder. There is only suppression and murder, and both should be treated as such, with determination if necessary."[5]

Paul Feyerabend

1.4.6. Further Choices of Moral Attitudes and Values

Even more prospect of conflict

The fundamental choices and the choices made so far are of fundamental significance for the shaping of my life. But there are further moral attitudes and values which I consider essential and which I want to take into account in the conduct of my life. Some of them may seem to suggest themselves given the choices already made. But it must not be overlooked that they cannot be derived conclusively from them and that the acceptance of any further moral attitude and any further moral value can only be justified by a choice as well.

Of course, it is possible to proceed differently and to define, for example, shared humanity in such a way that truthfulness, openness, gratitude etc. are also included in the definition. But nothing is gained by this. The choices one has to make then refer to whether one should include a certain moral attitude in the definition of another moral attitude which one has chosen. The number and the character of choices remain the same in this approach, but one runs the risk of overlooking this. Furthermore, there are difficulties with overly complex terms if we want to express conflicts and weighings between different moral attitudes and values. If, for instance, truthfulness is seen as a constituent of shared humanity, how should we describe the conflict between truthfulness and shared humanity that can arise when doctors have to decide on the extent of information they should give to an incurably ill patient? However, there are certainly several, essentially equivalent possibilities of formulating certain moral attitudes and values in the form of choices.

The further moral attitudes and values that I have chosen (that is, I have chosen to accept them as valuable and to try to realise them) shall only be enumerated here in a possibly incomplete list with just a few brief remarks. For the most part, they shall be just mentioned as a stimulus for reflection because a more detailed description would mean treading to well-trodden paths. (1) It seems to me that that it makes less sense and is less necessary today to write another detailed moral treatise and to try the patience of one's fellow human beings with its presentation in euphonious speech than to stimulate reflection, to recall moral attitudes and values and to exemplify one's morals through one's own life, that is by trying to apply and demonstrate one's morals in concrete situations. "The world would be in better shape if people would take the same pains in the practice of the simplest moral laws as they exert in intellectualising over the most subtle moral questions." (Ebner-Eschenbach[1]) And already 250 years earlier Pascal says: "All good maxims are in the world. We only need to apply them."[2] This concerns everyone in equal measure in the first place; it is not a specific task of philosophers. But they have the additional task of examining moral weighing in detail and of undermining rash prima vista arguments. And above all, they also have the task to demonstrate the justifiability of morals – beyond mere social utility - in an age when traditional justifications have lost their credibility due to their overblown pretensions.

Moral attitudes:

Truthfulness (2), openness, frankness, rationality, objectivity, readiness to depart (3), modesty, magnanimity, benevolence, mercy, serenity, patience, compassion, justice, fidelity (4), gratitude, moderation, responsibility, reasonableness (5)

Values:

Life (6), justice (7), equality (8), freedom, health, peace, material security, diversity, individuality, friendship, love, beauty, (9)

When setting up a morality for oneself, one should, in my opinion, especially avoid a narrowness which is a characteristic of many attempts to shape morality and is briefly and precisely described by Richard Robinson: "There is a tendency to set up as one's great goods either personal goods or political goods but not both."[3] (In accordance with this tendency many philosophers are then also predominantly interested only in problems from one or the other of these realms.)

I see an essential moral obligation and achievement in striving for unprejudiced and differentiated moral weighing. Excellent examples for this gives, for instance, Peter Singer in his book "Practical Ethics"[4] (even if I do not agree with his results in some essential points, as will be discussed in later sections). When subjected to this kind of scrutiny some of the things we take as a matter of course in our everyday life suddenly look rather bad, while, on the other hand, one or the other politically produced compromise turns out to be astonishingly wise. Weighing values at this level requires a clear and persistent mind, paired with moral courage. Moral weighing without prejudice is associated with the risk of being treated with considerable hostility and only being recognised by a minority, and of course there is still the risk of making mistakes.

Part of my morals are - beyond the choices already described – my statements on concrete moral questions. This is an important point, because, first of all, the meaning of concepts like "justice" is by no means the same for all people, it is probably not even so much the same for two of us that we would, even with access to the same level of information, always agree in our judgements of just and unjust throughout our lives. Apart from this, people do not agree on the ranking they assign to certain moral attitudes and values within their morals.

The result of weighing values can therefore by no means be derived directly from the presupposed moral attitudes and values but is ultimately the consequence of decisions of conscience, which can only be justified philosophically by separate choices to be made in each case. These decisions of conscience do not become justified but understandable (which is nowhere near predictable) by the different intelligence, character structure and life experience of each individual.

Only the decisions and the moral weighing in specific cases make a morality really concrete and often characterise it much better than its general principles; at least they are indispensable to complete the characterisation. There is more subjectivity in morality than just making choices of certain moral attitudes and values. In the unavoidable recourse to conscience as an instance for concrete decision-making and to choices to be made in the respective situation, subjectivity proves to be inescapable even in a way that can no longer be described systematically.

> "The problem of values is in the first place the problem of conflicts of values, and this problem cannot be solved by means of rational cognition. The answer to these questions is a judgment of value, (ultimately) determined by emotional factors, and, therefore, subjective in character – valid only for the judging subject, and therefore relative only."[5]
>
> Hans Kelsen

Ultimately, we are forced to make personal moral decisions, of which, moreover, the premises remain fraught with uncertainty and the consequences of which can never be fully foreseen. This is not, however, to advocate a rash invocation of conscience, an inconsiderate individualisation and subjectivisation of moral decisions without thorough consideration and discussion of the interests involved and the consequences to be expected, and finally a weighing of moral attitudes and values relevant to the problem at hand. From an ethics that does not know any absolute values, we arrive at a morality of weighing in which appropriate decisions in conflicts of values are prepared with the help of reason.

From this follows a concept of moral guilt that differs significantly from that which the proponents of absolute value systems have anchored in our consciousness. Günther Patzig has impressively explained this (especially with regard to Albert Schweitzer): "A particularly critical and questionable aspect of Schweitzer's conception – and this objection is directed against all philosophers and theologians who allege an inevitable entanglement of man in moral guilt – is the following: Schweitzer believes that every human being must incur moral guilt because, forced to make decisions, we cannot conform to ›the will to live‹ of all living beings: we are obliged to respect values and interests; in many situations we cannot take into account all the values and interests involved; therefore we incur moral guilt in these situations by any possible action. However, it is a very dangerous – and moreover psycho-hygienic very questionable - inflation of the concept of guilt, when it is alleged that doctors who kill bacteria in order to save a person's life are thereby necessarily entangled in moral guilt, namely towards the bacteria whose right to life and will to live they must violate. Moral guilt, I insist, can only incur those who in a conflict situation do not adequately take into account the most important competing interests in an appropriate manner although such a course of action would have been open to them. Whoever, in such cases of a preference decision under compulsion to act, which in extreme cases must be called tragic, chooses the best of the available alternative courses of action or one of several equally justified alternative courses of action, is free of moral guilt. But he should nevertheless regret that human life constantly involves us in situations in which we cannot equally consider all the interests and values at stake."[6]

How much sense makes philosophical weighing after all? Can we act in any other way than that determined by personal dispositions and historical circumstances? Let us anticipate a little bit the next section on the meaning of choices. Neither the subjective mental and philosophical phenomenon of moral guilt nor that of free will disappear because of a naturalistic-neurobiologically founded determinism. Philosophical thinking and philosophical maxims are part of the incalculable web of factors influencing how we act. The world is changed by philosophical thinking just as by other emotional and social occurrences, scientific findings of a different kind, technical achievements or natural events. And philosophical thinking, too, does not always lead to positive consequences for people. Nevertheless, I am convinced that we have better prospects of living good and rightly if we strive to think philosophically and to let ourselves be guided by philosophically justifiable and justified maxims.

To know, to help, to enjoy life, to develop personally and to realise other essential moral attitudes and values: this is the short version of the fundamental life goals to which I always strive to find my way back, especially when the adversities of everyday life threaten to bury them. This is a worthwhile and sustainable proposal for a life orientation even if everyone will set their priorities differently.

2. The Meaning of Choices

Beating the drum for a philosophical last resort

"The practical question is not whether to reject persuasion, but which persuasion to reject."[1]

Charles L. Stevenson

"An interesting parallel between skepticism and determinism exists here. Just as skepticism denies the possibility of *knowledge*, so determinism denies the possibility of *freedom*. Yet both knowledge and freedom to act on it are required for reasonable choice. Such choice would be denied to someone genuinely convinced – to the very core of his being – of both skepticism and determinism. He would be cast about like a dry leaf in the wind."[2]

Sissela Bok

2.1. Choices and Justification

The "game of justification": coherence instead of grand gesture

> "'First ground', 'last foundation' are un-human words (how in this superhorizon ›first‹ and ›last‹ merge!)."[1]
>
> Wolfgang Stegmüller

> "'Fundamental decisions' may be intelligent or unintelligent – they are not always, or merely, arbitrary."[2]
>
> Sidney Hook

Ultimately, I see no other possibility for those unwilling to believe to justify their life orientation than to do this through conscious subjective decisions, that is, by making choices.

When it comes to the problem of how one should behave, or ultimately: how one wants to behave, one cannot evade the decision by weighing up probabilities. Probability considerations are only possible if the question is what the world is like. Even then, probability considerations always presuppose decisions about our behaviour. Probability considerations can in turn serve as justification for further decisions about our behaviour, but they cannot replace these decisions.

The questions "How should human beings behave?" and "How should I behave?" can, however, also be understood as questions about the nature of the world if they ask about norms for human behaviour that have been established or exist independently of humans or at least independently of the individual human being. Accordingly, one can then make probability considerations, for example, as to whether and which commandments a god may have set humans for their behaviour; or one may assess which rules of behaviour can be found in a certain legal system.

But with this, the question of how one should behave, in the meaning: according to which principles one wants to orient one's behaviour, cannot be answered without decisions either. Even if we want to grant a certain degree

69

of probability to the existence of a god or several gods and their commandments (or to the existence of other absolute rules of behaviour for human
beings), prior decisions about our behaviour (at least with regard to
knowledge) are unavoidable – just as before all other probability considerations about the nature of the world. If the question is whether one should
accept the rules of a legal system, one must at least tacitly make a judgement
about its bindingness and validity. These decisions cannot be replaced by
probability considerations.

If one then assumes the existence of one or several gods and of commandments set by them, human beings have still to make the decision whether they
want to accept the (presumably) divinely set rules of conduct. They could also
consider another morality to be better. In the same decision-requiring situation
we find ourselves in relation to any morality that has arisen through biological
and cultural evolution. Thus, even if one assumes the existence of absolute or
natural norms for human behaviour, the ultimate decision on how to behave
cannot be based on probability considerations.

One can object to the call to justify convictions by choices saying that, conversely, choices are justified by convictions as a rule. In fact, the cause of our
convictions is not to be found in choices. How and why we come to our convictions, what causes, what explanations there are for them, is not primarily a
philosophical but a historical, sociological, psychological and neurobiological
question. (1) In contrast, our convictions are the cause of our choices.

In order to understand why it makes sense, nevertheless, to speak of a justification of philosophical convictions through choices, it is necessary to distinguish between different meanings of the term "justification", namely "factual justification" and "normative or philosophical justification". In everyday
usage, "justification" generally means to give a factual reason for a certain
attitude or conduct, that is, justification is actually used in the sense of "explanation", "motive" or "good reason". The common use of the term "justification" in science also differs very slightly from this. Known or assumed
facts, recognised laws or theories are used as "explanation" or "good reason",
or the accordance of a newly formulated law with observations is emphasised.
Thus, justification is derived from facts that are considered to be established.
This is what I call "factual justification". It always presupposes a "normative
or philosophical foundation" that justifies a certain method of gaining
knowledge and hence its results.

"Philosophical justification" or "normative justification", on the other hand, means to give a normative ground for a certain conviction (for example, the conviction to accept or reject certain methods of gaining knowledge). Such a ground cannot be found by a mere selection from what is. It is about a vindication of convictions, a "justification" for which no further justification can be offered. In this sense convictions can be justified through choices. That and why one should indeed use the term »justification« in this way (even if many modern philosophers do not like it) will be discussed in depth in this section.

For those unwilling to believe, not just the only philosophically tenable justification for their own views is to be found in choices. They cannot see any other »last« foundation for other philosophies of life either than subjective decisions of belief, whether they are made consciously or unconsciously. Therefore, it is completely inappropriate to object that a philosophy of life based explicitly on choices it is not binding enough, since the choices depend entirely on the individual and could be changed at any time. Every weltanschauung is based on conscious or unconscious decisions of belief of an individual, there is no more binding justification.

Those who believe in a god and his commandments or in a certain necessary course of history, to which one has to adapt, need decisions of belief to shape their lives just as much as those who are unwilling to believe. The weltanschauung of these believers is equally based on subjectivity because they have to decide to believe in their specific belief, they have to decide to accept the experiences of faith, which make their faith seem objectively correct, as a path to knowledge, they have to assume that these experiences of faith convey a correct description of the world and the right guideline for action beyond the subjective experience (or at least reveal an authority that is able to accomplish this).

The argument that a belief is indubitably certain and self-evident without such decisions of belief loses its persuasive power the moment there are people (obviously mentally healthy in everyday matters) for whom this does not apply. In other words: I do not know of any belief that is indubitably certain and self-evident nor can I imagine that there could ever be such a belief. Alleged self-evidence of philosophical statements amounts to a quasi-religious revelatory belief and thus falls – like religious faith in revelation in the narrower sense – under the paths to knowledge rejected by the fundamental choice of unwillingness to believe.

Lange described the situation very pointedly as early as 1866: "There is no rational religion without dogmas, which are incapable of proof."[3] With a similar tenor Popper speaks of an »irrational faith in reason«: "We may choose some form of irrationalism, even some radical or comprehensive form. But we are also free to choose a critical form of rationalism, one which frankly admits its origin in an irrational decision (and which, to that extent, admits a certain priority of irrationalism)."[4]

Lange and Popper, however, go too far with this. We should rather speak of a pre-rational than of an irrational foundation of the belief in reason. It is by no means the same whether one merely recognises that an ultimate justification of convictions by reason is impossible, or whether one is prepared to make much more far-reaching concessions at the expense of reason. How misleading it is to speak of an irrational faith in reason is demonstrated by the following statement by the theologian Feil: "Under Popper's presupposition, (Christian) faith can only be rejected from another faith position, but not by invoking rationality only of one's own and irrationality of the faith position."[5] What is lost here is that the pre-rational decision for the restriction to reason and the pre-rational decision for a pantheistic, deistic or, under certain circumstances, even a theistic belief in God are only on the same level insofar as the latter do not *have to* produce irrational consequences either (although they often do). But they definitely differ with regard to the more or less great »parsimony« or "redundancy" – or plainly: simplicity - of their explanation of the world. And, above all, they differ in their demand for good reasons. While a pantheistic and deistic faith believe themselves to be already justified by the fact that they cannot be refuted, the unwilling to believe demands good reasons why one should decide in favour of such a faith. And the decision for revelation and authority, which underlies the Christian version of theistic faith, definitely requires clear violations of reason, a »sacrifice of the intellect« (for instance, in concepts such as an omnipotent and omnibenevolent god benevolent or the immaculate conception, to name just two particularly obvious examples). To speak of an "irrational faith in reason" is inadequate. It can easily lead to an undifferentiated exaggeration of philosophical relativism.

The terminology of choices, to which some readers may take exception (especially if it is misunderstood as if a philosophy of life were to be created out of nothing by choices at the philosopher's desk), is an adequate expression of my personal attitude to life. It makes sense in order to draw attention to the fact that one's life can ultimately only be built on subjective decisions, and to document that these decisions are made consciously. To say it again: Choices differ from other conscious decisions within momentaneously unquestioned systems of thought in that their subjectivity becomes directly apparent.

However, the terminology of choices does not only serve the accuracy of thinking. It also makes sense in order to stabilise convictions and give them inner, subjective necessity - and thus, at first indirectly, social effectiveness. After having examined the coherence of one's moral intuitions through thorough consideration, one is able to codify them by choices on a private level – at least provisionally. Admittedly on a social level some new aspects come into play, but here as well, there is no other and better way of setting norms in principle. Here the convictions of the individuals lead to a conventional setting of norms by the community. (See also 3.3. und 3.7.1.)

When choices are avoided, it will be difficult for an admittedly subjective philosophy of life, as a belief without justification, to counter convincingly all the doctrines of faith with a claim to objectivity. Choices, in other words, also gain a rhetorical function, rhetoric understood here in the sense of a skilful - not an insidious, inadmissibly simplifying or truth-indifferent - influencing in the direction of the desired value system. This rhetorical function serves both to convince oneself and to be persuasive in society.

For the unwilling to believe there is no realistic hope that more absolute knowledge might ever be attained.

Some philosophers, professional or not, persistently contradict me (in a mixture of anger and pity) and say: "Values cannot be justified." I am always pleased to hear that the lesson "values cannot be justified", which should mean nothing else than "no 'ought' can be derived from an 'is'", has been learned quite well by philosophers in the meantime – even if it has taken a good two hundred years since Hume to spread this insight to some extent and there is still some argument about it.

Formulated in today's terms, Hume's insight is: Descriptive und prescriptive statements differ, but they are both a part of the "is" and from this fact nothing can be directly gained for the selection among prescriptive statements. In the consequence of naturalism and determinism the "ought" belongs to the "is", values are simply a part of reality. Thus, although the difference between "is" and "ought" is flattened, we are left nevertheless with the problem of choosing between values. Even though this choice is also a part of the "is", we can at least discuss this part of the "is", the choice of values and the weighing up between them, and influence it through various activities and social structures and arrangements. Our discussions can lead us to decisions for which good reasons can be given. The conditions under which the complex decision-making apparatus at our disposal, our brain, operates are constantly changing. Our decisions and choices, and the communication about them, are part of this change. The selection and ranking of values and thus biographical and historical developments are, among other things, influenced by philosophical explication and deliberation. In a long-term perspective, their influence is greater than it may appear in day-to day-business. (2) (See also 3.3.)

Some now believe to discover an "is" in the choices from which an "ought" is derived. This is a misunderstanding. Choices are not a justification in this traditional and no longer tenable sense. Values are not derived from choices but are by them merely accepted in a conscious decision, and thus reinforced and stabilised (without claiming a more than subjective or conventional bindingness for them). Choices are a procedure of conscious acceptance and affirmation of values towards me and others (and of course a method of reflection, but more on this in 2.2.). And although this has nothing to do with the common use of "justification" in connection with values (which in fact amounts to the is-ought fallacy), it remains meaningful to use the term »justification« for it since this procedure is proposed instead of the justification of values by deriving an ought from an (alleged or arbitrarily-intentionally selected) is.

Instead, one can also advocate a conception of rationality which "takes into account the unjustifiability of knowledge and decision by giving up the idea of justification together with the striving for certitude or certainty" to say it as proposed by Hans Albert.[6] He wants to build on "criticism" or critical examination instead of "justification". Such attempts to declare the concept of "justification" as outdated for a modern philosophical conception, proved and prove very popular in contemporary philosophy – and especially among its serious representatives. This kind of terminological refusal is quite understandable as a reaction to the concept of justification (or foundation) of classical rationalism and to the Münchhausen trilemma[7] described by Albert. However, it remains conceptually unclear and turns out to be inadequate, especially with regard to philosophy's obligation to praxis and its task in the social, intellectual and ideological debate.

To speak of an "idea", a "postulate" or a "principle" of criticism remains conceptually unclear for the following reason: On the one hand, it is made quite clear what is meant by criticism, namely more or less what follows for me from the choice of unwillingness to believe. What is not so clear, however, is what is hidden behind the concept of an "idea", "postulate" or "principle".

Admittedly, Albert makes it clear that a moral decision is meant, he speaks of the "moral content" of criticist philosophy and of a decision not "for an abstract principle with no existential significance, but for a way of life".[8] But why then not call a spade a spade and speak of a »choice of criticism or critical examination« and thus refrain from subliminally conveying a claim to objectivity of which one is aware enough that it is not tenable at this point. The fact that the consequent application and the procedural rules of "criticism" are also in need of justification and that such a way of thinking is also based on subjective decisions does not, as can be seen, become any clearer if one avoids the concept of justification or foundation (even if this is indisputably burdened with a heavy objectivist mortgage). It is meritorious and necessary to analyse the different uses of this concept. But the attempt to eliminate it altogether evokes bad memories of the dismissed positivist-analytical procedure of banning certain concepts considered suspicious from philosophy.

There is another reason why it is inappropriate to avoid the concept of justification: The principle of critical examination alone does not provide us with a sufficient minimum of life orientation. Thus only a small part of the philosophical life orientation described in the first main section of this book can be derived from it in a fairly straightforward manner. For life, a conscious shaping of life and particular moral attitudes and values the most diverse pros and cons can be presented (which depend very much on the personal situation), but a critical examination of these arguments cannot ultimately replace the respective life-determining philosophical and moral decisions. These decisions are not taken away from us, as is largely the case in scientific questions, by applying consequently the once accepted principle of critical examination. Accordingly, the philosophy of the critical rationalists remains rather impersonal and has difficulties to gain the necessary emotional significance for a personal life orientation and an adequate social appeal and attraction. As the name of this philosophical direction already suggests, the ideas of critique and rationality – necessary and meritorious as they are – have too much the upper hand in it. Constructive efforts for a philosophical life orientation going beyond this, which ultimately must always include emotional decisions too, are neglected or relegated to a sphere of weltanschauung or philosophy of life not regarded as part of serious philosophy.

On closer consideration the "principle of critical examination" turns out to be another variant of the incorrect view, also advocated by Weischedel in his "fundamental choice of scepticism", that philosophical life orientation can and must be derived from one fundamental principle. The fact that the proposed fundamental principle appears important and congenial to us should not lead us to agree with such a simplifying view.

Using the concept of "justification" or not, one can firmly and sufficiently defend oneself against the denunciation that subjective decisions (choices) for a minimum of philosophical life orientation, made after careful consideration, are arbitrary decisions. Albert himself gives an impressive example of what this can sound like in the passage quoted again in context below, and at the same time expresses how resolutely he stands up for very specific subjective decisions and the philosophical thinking justified by them: "Thus it is possible to overcome positivist resignation in questions of moral philosophy without lapsing into the existentialist cult of commitment, which replaces rational discussions of such problems with irrational decisions. Criticist philosophy, which presents us with this opportunity, has a moral content itself. Whoever adopts it does not decide for an abstract principle without existential significance, but for a way of life. One of the immediate ethical consequences of criticist philosophy is the conclusion that unshakable faith, impervious to rational argument, valued so highly by many religions, is not a virtue, but a vice."[9] Despite the fact that I myself see good arguments for retaining the concept of justification, I also want to emphasise in the face of this convincing plea for a critical philosophy that its proponents should not divide themselves all too much in a discussion about the concept of justification. Although this discussion is interesting and not unimportant, it often only reveals mainly terminological differences while at the same time there is a great deal of agreement on the objectives of philosophy. (See also the apt statement by A. J. Ayer quoted at the end of section 1.2., 1.2.[10]) If Albert explicitly opposes a thinking of justification that wants to create certainty by recourse to dogmas (which was also the conception of classical rationalism)[10], one can only agree with him. Such a use of "justification" does no longer make sense today, it is simply outdated. Those who advocate it today may still gain political influence, if they manage to find enough supporters, but they are no longer to be taken seriously in philosophical debate.

Because this is a crucial point, once again in other words: I do not want to contest that, when it comes to problems of justification, it is possible to continue the regress of justification infinitely and thus to ask also for the justification of choices. But I suggest to terminate the regress of justification by choices because this kind of termination does not contain any (dogmatic) propositions about the world, no logical contradictions and thus no avoidable impositions on reason, and admits honestly without any ifs and buts that the regress of justification is terminated (namely with the justification »choice«). The termination of the regress of justification by choices is in no way intended to immunise the content of these choices against criticism. In every other, at some point unavoidable termination of the regress of justification there are also subjective decisions, but this is often not recognised or one does not want to admit and or acknowledge it.

The philosophical position of the unwilling to believe is not at all adequately represented by the terms "subjectivism" or "decisionism" since these are conventionally equated to a large extent with "arbitrariness".

If by "arbitrary" ("at will") is meant that a philosophical concept is ultimately founded on subjective decisions, on our will, then this applies to all philosophies and philosophies of life. This is rightly expressed by Ernst Topitsch when he says: "There are fundamental values between which only a choice beyond scientific argumentation is possible."[11] However, a person who wants to limit the unavoidable subjective decisions to an inescapable, consciously conceived minimum, namely the unwilling to believe, thus at the same time also tries to realise the highest possible degree of objectivity. (3)

If, on the other hand, "arbitrary" is supposed to mean "not thoroughly considered", "rashly accepted without careful consideration of the consequences", then this merely divides the exponents of different philosophies of life into different intellectual (which is not the same as moral) quality classes. This, however, does not change anything as to the inevitability of fundamental philosophical decisions.

If, finally, "arbitrary" is supposed to mean "situational ad-hoc-decisions without – or almost without – recognisable principles", then this does hardly apply to anybody participating in philosophical discussions, except – to a certain extent – the rare specimens of Pyrrhonean sceptics.

So, the notion of arbitrariness has only a very limited discriminatory power in philosophical debate, and especially in its first meaning mentioned above, in which it is used by »objectivists«, it is completely pointless.

I do not want to finish this section without emphasising very firmly that there are clear limits to the content of choices. Thus, I am absolutely convinced that deciding against modern science means to pay a high price, namely, to forgo the best possible approximation to truth. And this also applies to those people (not so few) who only think scientifically in their own field of expertise and leave room to all kinds of speculations and snap judgements in other fields also accessible to scientific thinking.

What science and individual scientists are interested in, undoubtedly depends to a considerable extent on the respective social and historical situation, but what counts in the end is intersubjectively verifiable truth (even if it is never absolutely certain).

If, driven by necessity, choices are described here as the only ultimately tenable philosophical justification, this does not express any anti-rational tendency. The principle of the unwilling to believe is: Make only the inevitable minimum of choices and do so after carefully weighing the pros and cons. Certain fundamental choices and choices can be argued for rationally. Nevertheless, choices are in the end an emotional termination of the regress problem of philosophical justification. Choices serve the clear recognition and critical evaluation of preferential tendencies and they serve to stabilise and accept attitudes consciously. They are not a metaphysical deus ex machina of a disguised idealistic philosophy, but they are cultural and, on another level of explanation, also neurophysiological facts, that are determined by a complex interplay of multiple causes. Choices are in no way contradictory to a deterministic psychology, neurobiology and neurophilosophy. Reinhard Merkel states the facts clearly: "When certain processes take place in the brain, a mental state is created, for instance, the decision to act in a certain way. But the reverse is not true: when somebody makes a decision, certain neuronal processes in his brain are created."[2]

Metaphorically, the philosophy of choices presented here can be seen as a play that takes place on a stage created by the phenomenon of free will. This phenomenon of free will emerges when we construct our self, and it enables us to use the associative and integrative capacities of our brain to explicate and deliberate alternatives for decision and action, and then also to absorb social influences and create social effects through communication and argumentation. (4) This play can also be given the title "elbow room". (See the final passage of 3.2.) It is not a meaningless play and – here the metaphor has its limits– it is more than a play because it decides how we shape our lives.

If we deal with the question of free will with a neurophysiological plausible theory of natural autonomy which includes the concept of identification as a central element, we can say: "Identification is the process through which a person makes her volitions *her own*." (Walter[13]) Choices, then, bring such an identification - in other words: the formation of authenticity — to our mind

78

and they are an ultimately emotional mechanism that terminates the regress problem of such a concept of identification (though rational considerations also play an essential role in bringing about choices). There are concrete, if not yet sufficiently clear and unambiguous concepts concerning the brain processes leading to identification and authenticity. Philosophically and morally fundamental choices of philosophy of life and morality are thus an ability of our brain that we can make use of philosophically. And we can (and should) use this ability in such a way that we come to a philosophical life orientation without dispensable speculative, metaphysical assumptions.

Human beings preparing their decisions by rational weighing will always remain an idealisation. The task of philosophy is to come a little closer to this idea.

What choices mean philosophically can also be very well expressed in Peter Bieri's diction[14]: Let us practise the craft of freedom by appropriating our will. This happens by articulating, understanding and evaluating it. When we work on ourselves in this way, we give our will a profile that was not there before.

> "We cannot do without an element of risk, of sovereign decision and highly personal choice, which always includes the possibility of failure. But how much calmer we could be if we knew that every decision of sufficient weight springs from a rational weighing of the various possible points of view, that it was preceded by an unbiased apprehension of the facts, undistorted by prejudice, and that every morally relevant decision is incorporated into a life experience which may later suggest a revision of that decision!"[15]
>
> Günther Patzig

> "Deliberation presupposes a gradient of certainties and priorities of rules and valuations, which makes it possible in the first place to establish systematic connections between separate convictions and thus make the uncertain more certain. That is what the game of justifying is about and not the futile digging for a hidden foundation on which all our moral and extra-moral convictions are allegedly based."[16]
>
> Julian Nida-Rümelin

2.2. Choices and Morality

On sandy soil

"The causes which have led to the development of morality in mankind, which have guided or impelled us all the way from the savage to the civilised state, will not cease to operate because a number of ecclesiastical hypotheses turn out to be baseless."[1]

Thomas Henry Huxley (1)

"… for the question 'What shall I do?' is one that we cannot for long evade; the problems of conduct, though sometimes less diverting than crossword puzzles, have to be solved in a way that crossword puzzles do not. We cannot wait to see the solution in the next issue, because on the solution of the problems depends what happens in the next issue."[2]

R. M. Hare

Despite certain constants in the moral judgement of human beings and societies (for example, with regard to certain types of homicide), there is no objective standard of comparison for judging human beings in terms of their moral qualities in a universally valid way. Each individual and each society can only come to a judgement based on their own morality, even if they are strongly influenced by cultural traditions. The valuation as »good« or »bad« ultimately refers to the comparison with one's own morality. Nevertheless, there is much to discuss on a rational level. Sections 3.3., 3.6., and 3.7. will show with many examples that this position does not have to result in a decisionistic subjectivism in ethics.

It depends only to a very limited extent on the way of its justification whether a morality is good or bad, and it depends only to a very limited extent on the way someone justifies her or his morals whether she or he is a good or bad person. A good or a bad morality is possible both with a justification by choices and with a seemingly more objective justification. A morality explicitly justified by choices will have to struggle with human weakness and baseness just as much as any other. (2)

Among the adherents of the most diverse philosophies of life there are both good and bad persons (in all conceivable gradations). This makes it impossible to judge the truth of the great world religions and a philosophy of life in general according to the moral qualities of their adherents as suggested (cunningly for a distant future) by the judge in the Ring Parable in Lessing's "Nathan the Wise". But there is no good reason for such a procedure anyway (except as a rhetorical figure and a pragmatic crutch for tolerance). Why should a belief whose adherents appear to be decent people to an above-average degree not nevertheless contain false propositions and even a completely false conception of the world? Or, conversely: Why should a correct explanation of the world not go hand in hand with bad morals?

It is also undeniable that there are personal crisis situations in which a religious morality, for example, by strictly prohibiting suicide, can provide a better support and prevent a catastrophe more effectively than a secular, humanist morality and a counselling and psychotherapy based on it – which in turn can offer more help in other conflict situations. As a fellow human being, a friend or a therapist one can use a person's philosophical orientation to cope with a crisis. However, the suitability or unsuitability of a certain morality for overcoming a certain crisis is neither a criterion for the »truth« of this morality nor for its moral value (which depends on an overall evaluation).

As for the resilience of a morality in difficult times, it is limited by the strength and the courage that the individual can muster. I do not believe that the admittedly subjective character of a morality impairs the strength and the courage to stand up for that morality, at least not in those who cannot recognise a superiority of another morality in terms of its philosophical justifiability.

Due to the prevalence of religious views a large number of testimonies of faith from dark times have been handed down. These I want to contrast here with a testimony of standing firm of an unwilling to believe: "I entered the prisons and concentration camps as an agnostic and, on April 15, 1945, freed by the British in Bergen-Belsen, I left the inferno as an agnostic. At no time could I discover within me the possibility of belief, not even when I lay bound in confinement, knowing that my file was stamped 'Troop Demoralization', and for that reason constantly expecting to be hauled off for execution." "Only in exceptional cases did the magnificent example of comrades make a

Christian or Marxist *engagé* of the sceptic intellectual. Mostly he turned away and said to himself: an admirable and redeeming illusion, but an illusion, nonetheless. At times he also rebelled ferociously against his believing comrades' exclusive claim to the truth. To speak of God's boundless mercy appeared outrageous to him ... ."(Améry[3])

But if the belief in the superiority of one's own morality with regard to its philosophical justification – the illusion of objectivity which usually characterises a morality justified by religious faith – would actually make this morality more resilient, then those unwilling to believe could only state this without being able to indulge in such an illusion for that reason. And, if truthfulness is valuable to them, this could only in extreme situations be a reason to contribute to the maintenance of such an illusion in society. Moreover, although the resilience of a morality in crisis situations will be seen as positive, provided one shares its contents or can at least respect them, it seems hardly convincing, on the other hand, to use this resilience as a criterion for the value of a morality or a way of justifying morality. The fanatics' blinded insistence, in extreme cases at the price of their own life, can also be called resilience.

The same applies to the question of the durability or changeability of a morality and philosophy of life. It is not so important whether a morality and a philosophy of life justified by a religious faith or by choices are more durable. One can also hold on to bad principles in a durable – or: stubborn – way, just as good things can fall victim to change. The morals of people who call themselves Christians, for example, also change in practice according to the changed historical, social and personal situation – and sometimes quite considerably. Moreover, not every religious believer remains believer throughout his or her life. Religious believers can become unbelievers or unwilling to believe and vice versa. Human beings sometimes change their decisions and choices, whatever they may be. Whether a weltanschauung admits that it is based on subjectivity or not, does not principally but at most statistically make a difference in terms of its resilience and durability.

However, if one presupposes an admittedly subjective basis for one's own morality, one must be particularly aware that one is responsible both for the observance of one's own morality and for its contents and the preservation of these contents. Our conduct of life, our thoughts and actions are not only influenced by our morals and those of other people around us, but in turn have an effect on them themselves. "Good as well as evil becomes dear to us through long intercourse", says Seneca.[4] And Marcus Aurelius writes in his meditations: "Such as are thy habitual thoughts, such also will be the character of thy mind; for the soul is dyed by the thoughts." "How can our principles become dead, unless the impressions [thoughts] which correspond to them are extinguished? But it is in thy power continuously to fan these thoughts into a flame." "Look within. Within is the fountain of good, and it will ever bubble up, if thou wilt ever dig."[5] Not only disposition, upbringing, social environment, but also self-education, one's own thoughts and actions (and, very importantly, the experience gained from the consequences) influence a person's morality. This aspect is of particular importance if we recognise our subjective value judgements as the ultimate basis of morality.

Here, things are generally easier here for those who justify their morality by a belief shared with a religious community. As a rule, there are then representatives of this religious community who remind them again and again of the respective morality and swear them to its content and its objectivist foundation. A reminder of and a reflection on certain moral demands are institutionalised in various ways within the community. In contrast, those unwilling to believe are to a much greater extent alone with the responsibility for their morality, even though certain moral attitudes and values will with some probability be brought to them again and again from the respective cultural tradition. Those who are unwilling to believe (but by no means only they) can, if they do not remain vigilant, overlook or neglect moral attitudes and values that could actually mean something to them, and likewise they can lose their morals or parts of them unawares. Even if they are reminded of them later, it is questionable whether they will gain inner necessity for them once more.

Admittedly, one could say: What do I care about the morals once lost or given up if they are not absolute or objective? But – regardless of the way it is justified – one must consider the morality one has in a certain moment, if one is serious about it and if is to be alive at all, to be so valuable that one cannot wish for its loss. Furthermore, convictions can return and then you will have to answer to your conscience. The feeling of guilt is not dependent on a religious justification of morality (a statement that represents a psychological truism, but is by no means banal in the social and philosophical debate in view of what religious dignitaries and correspondingly influenced politicians say). One can also feel guilty if one violates self-imposed morals, and especially if one violates the morals according to which one was brought up, even they were not justified religiously. (But: One can also feel guilty for no reason, feelings of guilt are not always justified: they are a psychological phenomenon, not a philosophical-moral criterion for truth or appropriateness.)

In any case, it is clear from all this that it is particularly important for those unwilling to believe, for persons who explicitly justify their morals subjectively, to think carefully about what moral attitudes and values they should strive for, and to keep in mind certain aspects which they believe they have neglected so far or may be in danger of disregarding or forgetting in the future. There are various ways of doing this: regular reflection, reading, notes in a diary, for some people also the structured summary of one's own views, as attempted in this book (which, because of its less detailed, more general character, can only supplement but not replace other possibilities), and – not to be forgotten –-the discussion of value questions with other people. We come back here to a part of what the choice to strive for personal development contains.

It should be emphasised once again that the changeability of morality does not only entail risks but also chances, because it offers the possibility of personal development and an adaptation to a changed and changing environment. However, anyone who believes in an objective morality that is equally valid for all people at all times in each of its sentences will hardly be able to make friends with such a statement.

At the end of this section, it is time once again to firmly address
– the misunderstanding that choices are meant as an attempt to create a morality quasi out of »nothing«,
– the misjudgement that a morality which is justified by choices, and whose ultimately subjective justification is thus admitted, is unsuitable as a basis for the morality of a community.

Joseph Ratzinger rightly points out that a decisionism that disregards our intellectual and cultural tradition, be it existentialist or of whatever provenance, leads to nothing good: "Every morality needs a we with its prerational and superrational experiences, in which not only mastery of the moment speaks, but wisdom of generations flows together."[6] Well, the morality that those unwilling to believe set for themselves by their choices, does by no means have to disregard our cultural tradition (it is even hardly able to do this). Where we distance ourselves from the »wisdom of generations«, we should do so with good reasons – which, however, does not mean that we do not have to make decisions.

Ratzinger continues: "In other words, the experiences that have condensed in the communal forms of life of the various peoples and religious communities are valuable as orientation marks for human action. However, we must immediately add: They are not in themselves a sufficient source of morality." With these statements we can also agree. However, those unwilling to believe cannot see a sufficient source of morals in the appeal to god, to divine revelation and authority, either, because the tempting objectivity that seems to be attained in this way remains only an illusion for them. And the "communal ways of life of the various peoples and religious communities" also contain some highly inhuman moral and penal rules.

For those unwilling to believe even their choices are no source of morality to be lightly regarded as "sufficient" and yet they must ultimately content themselves with that. In concrete moral weighing, the individual character, the individual conscience, and the personal life experiences come into play additionally. The result of such weighings cannot be derived directly from previously made choices (but it cannot be derived directly from a specific religious faith either).

The morality of a community can and will only ever emerge from the discussion and conflict between individual members with different moral views, regardless of how they justify their morality for themselves. We have no good reason to grant a privileged position to those who claim an objective justification of morality and an absolute morality for themselves. The absence of such claims would not change the fact that a morality of the community comes into being, only that one could hope for a more tolerant dispute and for a quicker and less painful adaptation to changed circumstances. Here, I want to refer once again to Schlechta's apt remark which precedes section 1.4.5. as a motto: It is a short step from absolute morality to concentration camps, massacre and mass murder. This is a lesson taught by the great historical catastrophes up to the immediate present.

(3)

"In some respects, we are obviously forced to build on sand, and contrary to a widely held view, we can definitely do so. However, one should not aim to high with the building one erects on such ground."[7]

Rainer Hegselmann

2.3. Choices and the Meaning of Life

Transience is no excuse

"I don't know whether this world has a meaning that transcends it. But I know that I do not know that meaning and that it is impossible for me just now to know it. What can a meaning outside my condition mean to me? I can understand only in human terms."[1]

Albert Camus

Changing the Wheel

I sit by the roadside
The driver changes the wheel.
I do not like the place I have come from.
I do not like the place I am going to.
Why with impatience do I
Watch him changing the wheel?[2]

Bertolt Brecht

"Wherever you go, you take yourself with you."[3]

N. N.

"In fact, the frantic pace of life can be readily understood if we take it as an attempt at self-numbing: Man is fleeing from an inner dreariness and emptiness, and in this flight, he plunges straight into a bustle."[4]

Viktor E. Frankl (1)

"He who has a *why* to live for can bear almost any *how*."[5]

Friedrich Nietzsche

"If man is to retain his sanity, the world *must* make sense for him ..."[6]

Dennis Gabor

She who has made the fundamental choice of unwillingness to believe and therefore cannot do without the use of reason when dealing with the question of the meaning of life, will first consider what scientific knowledge tells us about the situation of humans in the world. (2)

Human individuals live their life as one among billions of fellow human beings. They themselves and humankind as a whole are the product of a cosmic development which, once set in motion, required no further influence to produce humankind, among other things. Humankind lives on a planet among billions and billions within a galaxy of one hundred billion stars and a diameter of one hundred thousand light years, which in turn is only one among more than one hundred billion others in a universe with an (expansion) age of almost fourteen billion light years.

It is possible that this universe even is only one among many. There could be an eternal oscillation of expansion and contraction in which we are »only« the product of one of these cycles. And: Even small deviations of fundamental physical constants lead to other universes that do not allow the emergence of life due to their temporal and thermal conditions and their elemental composition. Thus, it is quite plausible to assume that our universe is not the only one that exists, has existed or will exist, but that it is extraordinary (which does not necessarily mean unique) in that it has produced its own observers. The universe could be a multiverse or megaverse consisting of many »pocket universes« (one of them ours) which have different physical constants and thus quite different properties. (3) However, this is only one example from the wide range of cosmological models for which serious mathematical and physical arguments can be put forward. (4) Still and for the time being the following applies: "At these outermost frontiers of explanation mathematical analysis and metaphysical speculation mingle for the moment." (Kanitscheider[7])

But let us return to our universe in the "narrower" sense. If we presuppose the above-mentioned dimensions, which meanwhile have been made very plausible, and if we assume that only every billionth star has a planet that offers suitable conditions for higher forms of life, we still come up with ten thousand billion such planets. Nevertheless, we are not really able to estimate the probability (or improbability) of the occurrence of such environmental conditions and the emergence of life under suitable environmental conditions. Due to the multiplication of a multitude of necessary factors, the improbability of suitable environmental conditions for intelligent life must be considered very high. This is countered by the presumably large number of possible planets. Our historical experiences with geocentric and anthropocentric explanatory models and claims to singularity give reason to assume that we are once again on the wrong track if we make the assumption that life, or at least intelligent life, exists in the cosmos only on earth and that intelligent life exists only in form of us humans. However, this argument, drawing on analogy to other historical "wounds" to human narcissism we had to accept in the course of the history of ideas, is only a hint, the significance of which we have to assess on the basis of scientific facts.

Such an argument from the history of science can also lead us astray. Astrophysics shows us what an amazing chain of improbable coincidences was necessary to create the planet earth with its favourable conditions for the development of intelligent life. (5) In addition, the history of evolution shows us at how many points the evolutionary process could have taken a different direction – depending on accidental changes of the environmental conditions, a direction which would not have led to the emergence of living beings endowed with higher intelligence and self-awareness. It is therefore possible that the emergence of intelligent life did not happen more than once, even take into account the unimaginably large number of planets in the universe.

If the probability for the emergence of intelligent living beings in the universe is low, it becomes extremely improbable that this should have happened again within the cosmic "vicinity" of light-year distances up to about a human lifespan which could allow a more than »archaeological« communication. Even if we assume that intelligent beings, which have developed under different environmental conditions in different evolutionary processes, would in principle be able to communicate with each other, it remains very questionable, due to the cosmic dimensions of space and time, whether they will ever learn anything about each other - whether we will ever learn anything about other intelligent beings - let alone be able to establish any contact or even a contact of any actuality. Besides of having arisen at all, other civilisations in the universe would also have to be sufficiently close and simultaneous to ours for communication to come about. Our civilisation has the technical means to communicate over astronomically relevant distances only since the first half of the 20th century. And we do not know how long it will still survive. On the other hand, already the closest spiral galaxy similar to our Milky Way, Andromeda, is 2.5 million light years away, far longer than Homo sapiens has existed. Blumenberg has described the situation succinctly: "Contrary to its title, relativistic physics set the absolute limit, against which all technical finesse becomes powerless and in view of which even our Milky Way already far exceeds the order of magnitude that would allow communicative 'simultaneity'. ... It is the insurmountable wall constituted by the speed of light that finally denies man an existence of cosmical importance."[8]

In view of the cosmic dimensions, the belief in a god who cares about the fate of humankind or even of the individual human being and who is even supposed to intervene in a directing way, appears to me as a childlike human hubris. It only deserves a more detailed discussion in a later section because the willingness of many people to believe and the entire history of human culture and human thinking forces this upon us.

Some want to derive the continuation of the species and its further participation in the evolutionary process as a »meaning« from the situation described (the evolutionary process is then usually perceived one-sidedly as directed towards the development of ever more complex biological and then also cultural structures). Let us listen to Julian Huxley, for example: "There is thus a new categorical imperative that has taken form and voice from the facts of post-Darwinian science and human studies – that man's destiny, his duty and privilege in one, is to continue in his own person the advance of the cosmic process of evolution."[9] When scientists, as Huxley undoubtedly does here, want to give not only an interpretation and extrapolation of the development so far but also a goal, this cannot be derived from the facts any more than any other way of giving life a meaning but requires a value judgement. I consider this way of giving life a meaning, which sees the meaning of an individual's life - not unlike the Marxist – in the integration in a historical development, to be insufficient. Only very little concrete meaning for the individual life can be derived from it and, if one were to confine oneself to this, the individual would largely be treated as a means (not to mention the vagueness of such a goal: hardly anything is thus said about the direction we would like the evolutionary process to proceed).

Moreover, while growing complexity is an essential characteristic of the cosmic (although here probably not in the long run) and especially of the biological evolutionary process, it is wrong, on the other hand, to see this process as a continuous progress towards more differentiation and complexity. (6) Again and again new successful variations of relatively »primitive« organisms emerge (dangerous new viruses are a particularly impressive example for us humans). And it is by no means the most differentiated and complex organisms that are the most stable in evolutionary terms (horseshoe crab species, for example, have existed nearly unchanged for about 450 million years and thus far outshine Homo sapiens in this respect). In general, only some living beings follow a path towards ever greater complexity. The criterion of success in biological evolution is successful occupation of ecological niches, reproductive success. Differentiation and complexity are only means to this end and a conditionally occurring consequence of the evolutionary process. What counts is expediency – and differentiation and complexity only count insofar as they are expedient in a certain environment. The statement that the evolutionary process has brought forth life in ever more complex forms is only true in a historical and summarising sense: with increasing duration of biological evolution more and more and among them ever more complex living beings have appeared (and for the most part also died out again). This is a consequence of the evolutionary mechanisms working according to the laws of nature, a fact of the evolutionary history of life on our earth, but not a goal inherent in the evolutionary process.

Thus, a value judgement to accept "a duty to continue the advance of the cosmic process of evolution", does not yet provide a useful guideline if one does not select certain lines of development from this process as worthy of support by further value judgements. This shows even more clearly that thinking in terms of evolutionary progress is an unsuitable detour to establish moral standards for human beings. It is sensible to judge the value we assign to certain organisms produced by evolution (as far as we have to make such a decision at all) according to their properties and capabilities and not their historical position in the evolutionary process. And if we speak of evolutionary progress in a historical and cultural context, this is always an analogy into which we (must) put our moral values.

The abilities to which most of us attach the highest value emerged only late in the evolutionary process: self-consciousness (or, emphasising individuality: self-awareness), empathy and compassion, the development of a complex culture with art and science and a level of knowledge that finally also allows us an adequate assessment of our position in the cosmos. The fact that evolution took a long time to produce these abilities does not mean, however, that they are therefore so valuable, and it also does not mean that in an advanced phase of evolution living beings or features of living beings do not arise which are decidedly negative from our human point of view. The fact that the characteristics to which we attach the greatest moral value are characteristics of very complex living beings does not mean that complexity or simplicity alone provide a reasonable moral standard of value. It is also not at all certain that the most complex living beings created by the evolutionary process on our earth, we humans, will not ultimately be responsible for the disappearance of all higher life on this earth, and it is even quite probable that we will at least be responsible for the extinction of a considerable part of the evolutionarily created living beings. (And not even in the field of cultural evolution complexity is necessarily a positive feature: there are also highly complex criminal organisations or forms of organisation whose complexity brings ineffectiveness.)

The world view brought forth by science explains, on the basis of certain regularities ("laws") which are tested again and again on the world accessible to us, why what exists became possible and how it develops. It does not speak for evolution being directed towards the development of humans. (7) It does not speak for a meaning of individual human life or of the existence of humankind that goes beyond this existence. Of course, it cannot provide proof against this either (which, however, is not a justification for believing in all kinds of speculations).

It is a consequence of the fundamental choice of unwillingness to believe to renounce knowledge about an objective meaning of the individual life, of the existence of humankind and the world, as far as »objective« would imply that this meaning is determined beyond one's own consciousness and beyond socio-cultural agreements and conventions. Moreover, unwillingness to believe makes it impossible to cherish at least a life-determining hope that such a meaning might exist. (By the way: An objective meaning, if it could be recognised, would first have to be accepted by individual human beings or humankind.) The universe is meaningless in the sense that it is empty of meaning ("das Universum ist sinnlos im Sinne von sinnleer"[10]), to follow a conceptual differentiation by Joachim

Kahl, because in it there is no manifestation of a planning intention, no »absolute« meaning. This is not a dry quibble, for an adequate description of man's (humankind's) position then goes like this: "Now does he at least realise that, like a gipsy, he lives on the boundary of an alien world. A world that is deaf to his music, just as indifferent to his hopes as it is to his suffering or his crimes." (Monod[11])

But the universe is not meaningless in the sense of absurd; first, because it has a recognisable order based on the laws of nature, and second, because it enables us humans to create meaning. And then we may even rightly say that it is no longer empty of meaning. On the other hand, we can speak of meaninglessness in a different, not a factual but a moral sense, based on mistaken human decisions, if individual and social meaning is not created or this is done in a chaotic or destructive manner.

Those unwilling to believe can only give meaning to their life themselves. Personally, I do not want to give my life a meaning that consists in just one or a few concrete goals (although I have, of course, all kinds of goals that are of greater or lesser importance to me). Rather, a life appears meaningful to me in which I try to realise all my choices for the shaping of my life and thus my moral attitudes and values (while weighing them against one another). (8)

To build on choices does not mean neglecting the role of destiny in life and developing a hubris of calculability. "Destiny" is indeed a term that should arouse suspicion, or perhaps better: critical attention, a term to think about carefully, as the German word "bedenklich" (questionable) (9) expresses aptly, because "destiny" is often associated with the idea of predestination or providence, of a puppeteer of some kind in the background. Such an idea is so speculative and implausible that it should play no role in questions of life orientation. If, however, "destiny" means the uninfluenceable personal genealogy and place of birth, the – at least to a considerable extent – always undeserved, and, moreover, at any time endangered present as well as the incalculable future, that is the chances and dangers of the given, the accidental, of all that which is exempt to our command, then this concept rightly claims an essential place in our consciousness. (10)

The loss of the "objective" meaning seemingly guaranteed by the traditional philosophies of life and of the emotional security associated therewith obviously still weakens the ability of many people to experience their lives as meaningful. I hope that this is only a symptom of a transitional period and that it will become natural for many more people than today to follow their own sense of meaning and to create their own meaning, regardless of whether there is an objective meaning of their lives and actions, or even in the awareness that there is most probably no such meaning.

As a symptom of such a transitional period, in which people still suffer emotionally from the loss of the seemingly objective offers of meaning (that is, they feel a lack of stability, grief or at least regret therefore), I also see heroic humanism, the pathetic philosophy of revolt, as Camus devised it. His philosophy of defiance (despite and precisely because life is probably meaningless and the course of events in the world is cruel and unjust, one must adopt a morality and thus meaning for oneself and fight against the current state of the world) is still deeply rooted in Christianity (here it is said: despite and precisely because it appears to be absurd and all indications speak against it, one must believe in a benevolent and omnipotent God, according to whose will and plan the events in the world take place: credo quia absurdum). Both use paradox as a philosophical »justification« although it is nothing more than a rhetorical device.

In contrast, an autonomous shaping of life is undertaken with the choices of an unwilling to believe, beyond the shock of the loss of religious commitment or of an idealistic philosophy. The fact that there is no meaning of individual human lives that goes beyond the meaning human beings create themselves (insofar as one does not want to accept as meaning the mere participation of this life in an evolutionary process that has no predetermined goal), or, in any case, the inability of humans to recognise such an objective meaning if it would exist, have become so familiar that a revolt against these facts appears completely inadequate. Rather, well-considered conscious decisions, choices, are the way of conduct that suggests itself now and that also enables us to create the necessary meaning.

Existentialism pursues an insufficiently reflected cult of decision which can justly be called decisionism. In contrast to that, I see decisions simply as the unavoidable end of philosophical regresses of justification (one can only avoid to make oneself aware of such decisions and to admit them to oneself). And I plead for limiting these decisions to a minimum necessary for life orientation.

"The great lamentation about loss of meaning has its origin merely in exaggerated expectations of meaning."
"One must refrain – especially at the present time – from the nonsense of binding the affirmation of life to an absolute proof of meaning."[12]

Odo Marquard

"Human beings have to understand themselves as autonomous, ultimate, but at the same time – since they cannot dogmatically prescribe their own giving of meaning to others – relative instance of giving meaning."[13]

Hubertus Mynarek

"No one knows whether our life has a ›meaning‹, let alone what it is. But everyone can make it meaningful without thus becoming a defrauder or a fool."[14]

Karlheinz Deschner

"There is no more purpose or meaning in the world than you put into it."[15]

Hans Reichenbach

"There can be no guarantee that our finite life on this earth is meaningful. At any rate, such a life can only be meaningful insofar as we ourselves give it meaning by setting us tasks whose fulfilment we can regard as valuable and by devoting ourselves to activities that are either satisfying in themselves or contribute to the fulfilment of such tasks. The fact that all happiness on earth is temporary is not in itself a reason to regard this happiness as worthless, and the transience of all states, even of those we value most highly, does not in any way make their positive valuation illusory."[16]

Hans Albert

"Mentioning personalities of influence on intellectual history should not lead us to assume that the concept of meaning is in any way tied to the fulfilment of a high cultural task or to the legacy of a historically significant work. Those who are not given the opportunity to perform a socially accepted or even highly valued function can as well find fulfilment and meaning in the sphere of activity accessible to them. In the normal case, the simple everyday existence characterised by the monotonous rhythm of work, it is only necessary that one or more goals in life are consciously conceived and that the person concerned works with commitment and perseverance to achieve them."[17]

"In the long run, all life, all intelligence and all mind will perish in the tide of transience."[18] (11)

Bernulf Kanitscheider

"One always feels how the question of meaning is fed by the tacitly presupposed and never doubted conviction that the self of the questioner is so precious that it has to leave some traces of meaning in the world. This is what I call metaphysical arrogance."[19]

Jacques Wirion

"Everything is temporary. That don't excuse nothin'."[20]

Dialogue from the movie »Moonstruck«

3. What Does Unwillingness to Believe Lead to?

In search for good reasons and the reasons of the good

"Philosophy has to be concrete and practical,
without forgetting its origin for a minute."[1]

Karl Jaspers

What is probable if one has made the choice of unwillingness to believe and applies logic and observation on this foundation? What consequences are to be drawn from the views thus gained if one chooses the moral attitudes and values recommended in part 1?

3.1. Knowledge

Scepticism and Naturalism

Unwillingness to believe means that one must also fundamentally question the human ability to gain knowledge. On the other hand, this ability is so undeniably successful, as can be seen in the extension of human scope of action, that any exaggerated doubt about the human capability to gain knowledge appears to be unworldly and a mere intellectual eccentricity.

Even, for instance, radical constructivists have to acknowledge that we are able to acquire knowledge that allows us to achieve objectives. Therefore C. F. v. Weizsäcker says: "In answer to the question as to reasons for the historical success of science, I know no other answer except its truth. … If one can manipulate an instrument on the surface of Mars about 250 million miles away, can this be explained in any other way than through knowledge of the laws of motion of and of wave theory?"[1]

But let us first deal with some of the many objections to human ability to gain knowledge.

That our ability to gain knowledge depends on the condition of our sense organs is only the most trivial objection, but it already justifies a certain distrust of individual testimony. Nevertheless, a concept of normality (even if it is only a statistical one) concerning the capabilities of human sense organs helps quite good to overcome this objection. If normally functioning sense organs would frequently give us an unreliable or even completely wrong picture of the world, they would not have evolved, and humans would not exist. Furthermore, we are able to check the coherence of our sensory impressions with the information we obtain through objectified, largely subject-independent measuring procedures (albeit, in applying them, we always need our sense organs in some way).

Human ability to gain knowledge, human perception, and the interpretation and evaluation of this perception are, however, not only influenced by the condition of the sense organs but to a considerable degree also by the inner state, by the respective intrinsic activity of the brain. In short: Our brain influences our perception just as much as our perception influences our brain. The intrinsic activity of our brain and our perception (and consequently also our memory) depend on generally and individually predetermined biological structures, on our respective cultural tradition, on our entire life history, on our beliefs and our state of knowledge, on our respective emotional state, our motives and intentions, on mental and physical illness or health (with all the difficulties of demarcation in the transitional area). (1) Thus, Kant's scepticism is aggravated, in that human ability to gain knowledge is relativised not only in general, but also in the individual, in a way that, beyond obvious individual limitations, in principle affects everyone. The critique of pure reason is extended beyond the general and becomes definitely and unequivocally the critique of your and my reason.

There is nothing fundamentally new about this, either. Francis Bacon, who was sometimes reduced to a mere founding father of empiricism and inductionism (and who was underestimated by me too long enough due to insufficient knowledge and his time-conditioned bows to traditional religion), already described a great part of this in his teaching about the idols of the mind as early as at the beginning of the 17th century: "… all the perceptions both of the senses and the mind bear reference to man and not to the universe… ." "…for everybody (in addition to the errors common to the race of man) has his own individual den or cavern, which intercepts and corrupts the light of nature, either from his own peculiar and singular disposition, or from his education and intercourse with others, or from his reading, and the authority acquired by those whom he reverences and admires …; so that the spirit of man (according to its several dispositions), is variable, confused, and as it were actuated by chance … ."[2] (2)

Nevertheless, it is plausible and probable that – as suggested by evolutionary epistemology – our organs of cognition have been shaped by evolution to fit the world we encounter and that we thus only occasionally succumb to sensory illusions and serious errors of interpretation. Obviously, we belong to a structured world that we can explain, at least in part. If we found ourselves in a complete chaos, any striving for knowledge going beyond the mere assessment of such a situation would be pointless and unsuccessful (apart from the fact that our very existence would then be inconceivable). And, as to the influences of psychological or mental constitution on our cognitive ability: existentially endangering variants of interpretations did at least not prevent humankind from having made it this far.

Evolutionary epistemology is able to relativise a subjectivist reservation about human ability for knowledge, but it does not make this reservation irrelevant or superfluous. It presupposes the acceptance of a scientific way of thinking and thus contains a rest of subjectivity itself. And if, on the level of a hypothetical realism, we see humans as (at least dimensionally) insignificant observers of the universe, they are at the same time the epistemological centre of the (their) universe, and none of us can be completely certain how »objective« her or his conception of the world is.

On the one hand, it must be avoided that philosophical objections against the human ability to gain knowledge are misused to open the door to gratuitous subjectivism and to discredit the scientific process of gaining knowledge beyond a healthy mistrust. On the other hand, it is inappropriate to dismiss them lightly as hair-splitting and to side once and for all with an all to resolute and unconcerned objectivism and realism (as it corresponds to our »natural« feeling). Rather, we must bear a certain epistemological uncertainty; anything else is basically a surrender of human intellect to the need of the human psyche for certainty and decision-making.

From the mere fact that people argue and argue rationally, it does not follow that they are obliged to use rational argumentation. The idea that whoever enters the ground of argumentative, rational discourse has thereby necessarily accepted it, is also based on an inadequately idealising conception of human beings. A certain factual way of acting does not automatically imply consequence in behaviour; at best such a consequence arises from conscious philosophical and moral decisions, insofar as the strength of a certain human being is sufficient for this in the first place. Arguments from convergence and efficiency (such as those of C. F. v. Weizsäcker quoted here and at the end of section 1.2.) are of a pragmatic nature and justify rationality without further ado "only" insofar as they are simply irrefutable if one does not want to expose oneself to ridicule in the long run. (In this way, even ideological bulwarks such as the Catholic Church eventually come to recognise scientific findings that can hardly be doubted any longer.)

Anyone who discusses and strives for results thereby, that is to say, who does not argue arbitrarily but rationally and, as a rule, finally decides with reasons for one of the alternatives, does still not necessarily express the conviction that humans have the ability to gain knowledge – in principle she or he could also leave this question undecided or even deny it – but they are at least willing to live as if human beings are able to gain knowledge. Although a different stance – a radical epistemological scepticism – cannot be finally refuted, I do not see any good reasons for it. And it is part of unwillingness to believe to demand such good reasons and not to regard the mere conceivability of a position as a sufficient reason for accepting it.

3.1.1. Logic

The indispensable but not necessarily accepted formal sciences

Logical rules and consistent logic systems are a kind of knowledge, regardless of whether or not used to describe the world. The term »logic« is used here to represent all formal sciences (as for example also mathematics, formal linguistics, modern extensions of logic like fuzzy logic etcetera).

The acceptance of logic includes a logical notion of truth as a necessity of thought without which logic cannot be formulated consistently. Such a logical notion of truth is not to be confused with an epistemological notion of truth where truth means a representation of reality as adequate as possible and it must by no means be confused with an objectivist epistemological notion of truth according to which propositions about the world acquired in a certain way are considered to represent truth beyond any doubt. If the logical and the »real« notion of truth are confused, it is possible to talk past each other for a long while. Concerning "real" truth we are confronted with the uncertainty as to how far we are able to recognise it and as to when we have recognised it and to what extent. On the other hand, formal sciences are "ontologically neutral" (Vollmer[1]) beyond their own existence.

The perfection, the seemingly unarguable certainty of some fundamental findings of the formal sciences, especially of mathematical axioms and theorems, which urges us to assume that they should be valid for every possible species of intelligent beings capable of abstraction and even in other universes, if these should exist, has indubitably something platonic to it. That such knowledge is possible remains to be surprising and fascinating. (1)

A formulation according to logical rules is a precondition for meaningful propositions about interrelations of facts, that is hypotheses, and for any systematic description of the world. If it makes sense to use a certain logical and terminological system (be it formalised or verbal) for describing certain partial aspects of the world, depends on whether it allows to interrelate observations in a way that creates an increase in information, that is to say, in a way that opens up possibilities for a more satisfying explanation of events and for better predictions of events to be expected under certain conditions.

The use of the wording "more satisfying" points out that a subjective factor is at play here and that a further criterion which allows to decide on the acceptance of propositions is needed. (See 3.1.3.) Logic as a criterion of selection for propositions is far from trivial. Just consider the logical contradictions that are often inherent to religious belief systems. These contradictions cannot be eliminated by interpreting these belief systems as if they would not intend to contribute directly to the description of the world but just convey a myth or poetic truth about the relation between god and the world or even humans and god which is supposed to help us to cope with our life. One of these contradictions is the first and final nail in the coffin of at least Christian religion: The problem of theodicy can only be "solved" if one abandons logic or accepts intolerable intellectual twists and turns.

3.1.2. Observation

Revolution or sleight of hand?

> "Faith has hitherto been unable to move any real mountains …, but it is
> able to place mountains where there were none before."[1]

Friedrich Nietzsche

Observation (and this includes self-observation) is a main way to knowledge. Hypotheses have to be confirmed by observations if they shall be considered as knowledge.

The question of testability, of falsifiability, or verifiability of hypotheses and theories (these gradual processes are deliberately used in the same breath here, see also 3.1.5) constitutes an important criterion of critique representing the necessary scepticism about theories which are too vaguely formulated and too open to interpretation. But doubt about the falsifiability or verifiability of theoretical statements should not serve to nip speculative thinking in the bud as it plays an important role for the advance of human knowledge. Often enough theoretical considerations, which appear very speculative first of all, prove to be falsifiable or verifiable only in the light of further scientific development. Examples abound especially in physics and cosmology.

The importance of observation should not be overestimated. Albert has put this very aptly: "Observation, measurement, and experiment are without doubt important elements of the scientific process, but not as a means of providing a firm basis for the inductive acquisition and founding of theories, as sources of guaranteed truth. Rather, they are means for criticising and thus running a check on theoretical conceptions."[2] On the one hand, observations are the stimulus for a theory in many cases first of all. On the other hand, what we observe is influenced to a considerable degree by previous knowledge, by theories we assume, and by particular knowledge interests. (1) We see more easily what we already know, assume, believe, or want to believe. (This was already emphasised in different variations by, for example, Goethe, Einstein and Heisenberg.)

It is of great importance under which conditions observations shall be considered to be reliable and hypotheses to be sufficiently corroborated. Although the position about this does not change the answer to the question "Which ways to knowledge am I prepared to accept?" in principle, it determines our individual concept of plausibility in everyday life and our concept of science and, thus, it is crucial for our decisions on particular theoretical and practical issues and provides a critical clarification as to what observation means to us.

Those unwilling to believe will apply their general principle of doubt to observations as well, and they will mistrust them all the more as they are just isolated observations and the more difficult they are to reproduce. To overrate isolated observations is amongst the most frequent intellectual sins. We humans tend to ascribe an all to privileged persuasive power to our personal observations. If we have an economic interest in particular results, or if our observations are emotionally influenced to a considerable degree, as with issues of health and disease or even life and death of individual human beings, there is an increasing risk that we judge the significance of isolated observations all to uncritically and that we infer all to far-reaching, unjustified conclusions from them, and are led astray by a tendency to assume causality even

104

when there is only association and parallelism. (2) (About causality see also note 3.4. (9))

Observations are inevitably selective. In every situation we can only be aware of a small fraction of what would be accessible to our senses. But selectivity is not only – as unconscious selectivity - an inevitable characteristic of our cognitive situation and a necessity for survival, it is also - and here not only as unconscious but also as conscious and intentional selectivity – a prerequisite for hypotheses, theories, and a meaningful interpretation and valuation of the world, in short: a prerequisite to make knowledge and progress of knowledge possible. On the one hand, the awareness that our perception is selective justifies a critical attitude towards our ability of knowledge. On the other hand, it is completely inadequate to derive exaggerated reservations of subjectivity from this. Selectivity does not have to be tantamount to wrongness or inappropriateness.

The following statement seems appropriate to me as a general guideline for assessing the value of observations (and theories as well): Observations are all the more dubious as they call into question everything else we know. "There have been times in the history of science when the whole of orthodox science has been rightly thrown over because of a single awkward fact. It would be arrogant to assert that such overthrows will never happen again. But we naturally, and rightly, demand a higher standard of authentication before accepting a fact that would turn a major and successful scientific edifice upside down, than before accepting a fact which, even if surprising, is readily accommodated by existing science. … If I saw a man levitating himself, before rejecting the whole of physics I would suspect that I was the victim of a hallucination or a conjuring trick. There is a continuum, from theories that probably are not true but easily could be, to theories that could only be true at the cost of overthrowing large edifices of successful orthodox science." (Dawkins[3]). Considering a logical system, we expect inner consistency. Analogously external consistency is an essential criterion for assessing observations.

3.1.3. Simplicity

The double-edged razor

> "So, the principle of parsimony calls for minimum explanations: Which the-
> oretical concepts and assumptions are the minimum necessary to explain the

observed phenomenon completely and consistently? This does not guarantee the unambiguity of an explanation, but it reduces the arbitrariness of interpretations considerably."[1]

Gerhard Vollmer

Our explanation of the world should be as simple as possible, that is to say, as simple as logic and observation allow (and if it is like that, and only then, it is satisfying). Or the other way round: »It is unjustified to explain something in a more complex way which could be explained using less or more parsimonious assumptions." This is "Occam's razor" (1) or Mach's principle of economy of thought (and it has been stated similarly by many other philosophers). It is all but self-evident und does not at all follow directly from the epistemological criteria "logic" and "observation".

The discussion of simplicity becomes much clearer if we make a fundamental distinction: On the one hand, simplicity is a heuristic concept with aesthetic, philosophical, sometimes even religious appeal. (Such a motivation played an important role for Copernicus and Newton, for instance.) This heuristic concept may lead to truth but as well may lead us astray. Beauty is no criterion of truth. On the other hand, simplicity - mostly called parsimony when this meaning is intended - is a fundamental, morally important philosophical principle characterising a person's approach to knowledge. Then, simplicity means not to accept assumptions without good reasons (and - more so - not to accept assumptions contrary to reasonable judgement). Good reasons make us assign a smaller or greater probability to assumptions, but they do not provide absolute certainty. If we keep in mind this distinction, much confusion about simplicity can be avoided.

The criterion of simplicity or parsimony shall be discussed here considering the intervention of god at certain points of cosmogony and evolution postulated by some theologians. Such an intervention is claimed, for instance, at the origin of our specific universe or of human mind with its (in the world we know up to now) unique capacities for abstraction or complex symbol-based communication (and thus for reflection on the world and ourselves). Those who feel committed to the criterion of parsimony will look for an explanation within the framework of natural processes as observed otherwise as well whereas a divine intervention will appear to them as "greater expenditure". In general terms: Continuity is a substantial postulate of economy of thought.

The ongoing argument on the theory of evolution, as outlined in its essentials by Darwin and elaborated and confirmed in many aspects since, shows us that there may be a long-lasting resistance against simpler scientific solutions and that this resistance may not founded on logical flaws of the new scientific concept or conflicting observations but on an emotionally and ideologically motivated refusal to accept facts which appear disagreeable.

Referring to logic and observation alone does evidently not provide a sufficiently hard criterion to reject arbitrary suppositions going beyond theories that can be justified convincingly by logic and observation. We need the principle of economy of thought as an additional criterion – and it is, often tacitly, assumed in science as a rule. This has nothing to do with inadequate and inconsiderate oversimplification (though it may carry this risk).

"A good example of the significance of the law of parsimony is provided by a controversy that Galileo had regarding the mountains he discovered on the moon. A certain Ludovico delle Colombe attempted to refute him by maintaining that the apparent valleys on the moon were really filled with an invisible crystalline substance. Galileo replied sarcastically by saying that this suggestion was so excellent that he would apply it further and that, accordingly, it seemed probable that the mountains on the moon were, because this same invisible substance was piled on top of them, ten times higher than he had estimated! Galileo's mocking answer was particularly devastating because it showed that Ludovico had disregarded the principle of parsimony and that once this was done, the door is opened to a thousand and one absurd hypotheses and wild vagaries."[2]

Corliss Lamont

Logic, observation and simplicity are principles of knowledge accepted unavoidably to a large extent by everybody in dealing with the world, and this is also valid for religious believers and even for religious fanatics. But to really take these principles seriously, as required by the demand for good reasons which is part of the fundamental choice of unwillingness to believe, means to adhere to them and to accept the evidence gained thereby even if they conflict with personal wishes and emotional desires. Therefore, in this book the principle of economy of thought shall be applied consequently to the fundamental questions of philosophy of life as well. Which philosophical assumptions constitute the minimum that is necessary for a sufficient and fully adequate orientation in life?

Certainly "simpler" must not mean »easily understandable on the first attempt« or "better explicable to a child". Rather it means "more compelling", »more convincing for the one who knows the relevant facts to be explained«, "in better correspondence with established facts, also in the sense of a better predictive value", "producing a better explicatory value and a better coherence of a world view", "more consistent in the framework of a successful comprehensive explanatory system" (thus, "simpler", contrary to the first impression, comprises more conservatism than readiness for revolution). These expositions can reduce the vagueness of the principle of simplicity to some degree.

The principle of simplicity may lead astray if the theoretical basis and the possibilities of observation are still insufficient for a more adequate word view. C. F. v. Weizsäcker illustrates impressively why the Ptolemaic geocentric system must have appeared simpler and more convincing to the ancient Greeks than the heliocentric concepts already devised then.[3] To many contemporaries of Galilei a geocentric cosmology will still have appeared as the simpler solution. To the one who has to explain no more than the everyday world classical Newtonian physics may still appear as the simpler solution compared to relativistic physics. Therefore it is important to insist on the formulation "more convincing for the one who knows the relevant facts."

Scientists often and with a high degree of consensus agree on what they want to accept as a "simpler" solution whenever convincing observations are available. There is, nevertheless, a subjective, democratic, conventional element even here, though, other than in democratic elections, not every vote counts the same regardless of the level of information of the person concerned. The criterion of simplicity comprises a certain vagueness as other criteria of scientificity do as well, for instance the already mentioned postulate of falsifiability or verifiability. In specific circumstances there may be an intense debate on which point of view meets the criterion of simplicity better, for example, if there are conflicting observations regarding a certain hypothesis or if a hypothesis appears to be non-confirmable by observation at the time given or even in the long run. Discussion also gets difficult if the foundations of the scientific world view generally accepted up to now or the personal philosophy of life of scientists are called into question or if some concrete interests are linked to the preservation of a certain scientific view. Then, Kanitscheider's statement applies: "Furthermore, it has turned out as notoriously difficult to reach agreement on the character of simplicity of hypo-theses."[4] (2)

The criterion of parsimony cannot be made redundant by other criteria for the evaluation of theories, for instance consistency or testability. Not fully developed or unnecessary complicated and clumsy theories may also be consistent and testable. Furthermore, the criterion of simplicity represents the claim for good reasons for theories that are consistent but not or not yet testable. If we take the explanation of the fine tuning of the universe as an example, the assumption of a (deistic) god and the multiverse theory are both consistent and not testable for the moment and possibly even in the long run. Nevertheless, the multiverse theory is definitely simpler because it stays within the usual framework of physical theory building whereas the assumption of the existence of a god is supported by nothing and constitutes a mere ad hoc solution to explain the fine tuning of the universe just evading the explicatory problem by presenting a deus-ex-machina »solution« and shifting the problem of explanation one level up. Now, we have to explain how a god who is able to guarantee the fine tuning of the universe could have come into existence from nothing and we have to answer the question which other reasons we have to suppose such a god's existence except of our desire and wish to explain the fine tuning of the universe.

But the principle of simplicity has a double face as well, Occam's razor is two-edged. The ingenious speculation, proved to be right later on, may fall prey to it. And it may cause – rightly or wrongly – that any effort to solve certain questions is abandoned or that certain questions are not even posed anymore. Einstein already warns us against the dangers carried by the principle of simplicity and his sentence basically comprises all that matters in this context, anything else is just decoration, circumlocution, clarification: "Everything should be made as simple as possible but not simpler."[5] I am convinced, nevertheless, that overemphasis of the principle of simplicity has hindered the progress of human knowledge far less than the willingness to accept emotionally comfortable but objectively unjustifiable additional assumptions and speculations. (3)

3.1.4. Realism

A strong hypothesis

> "There is no bridge that leads beyond our thoughts to the objects of them."[1]
>
> G. Chr. Lichtenberg

> "Achilles: That's quite a bit to swallow. I never imagined there could be a world above mine before – and now you're hinting that there could even be one above that. It's like walking up a familiar staircase, and just keeping on going further up after you've reached the top - or what you'd always taken to be the top!
> Crab: Or waking up from what you took to be real life and finding out it too was just a dream. That could happen over and over again, no telling when it would stop."[2]
>
> Douglas R. Hofstadter

> "Already in the first beginnings of western epistemology, during the time of the pre-Socratics, some thinkers understood that the idea of knowledge as a more or less truthful reflection of an actually independent ontological reality leads into an inextricable paradox. As such a reality is only accessible by experiencing it, the experiencing subject can never assess to which degree the experience is altered, distorted or generated by the specifics of its activity of experience."[3]
>
> Ernst von Glasersfeld

Even if we do not doubt the reality of the world spontaneously, we must, nevertheless, confront the assumption that the only thing we can be certain about is the existence of our mind. Could it be that only our consciousness exists, and all the rest be no more than a subjective imagination, or that my personal imagination is just a very unrealistic reflection of some real world I have no direct access to? Life as a dream or a voyage through more or less thick fog.

If life were no more than a dream, it would suggest itself to consider birth and death as no more than subjective ideas as well and to assume that the individual consciousness still exists in another world.

Against the idea that life might be a dream one may object that we usually have a seamless feeling of reality while what occurs to us in our dreams is mostly locally and temporally discontinuous and ignores the laws of physics in various ways. Popper[4] and Vollmer[5] give an overview of further arguments. Convincing arguments for realism are provided especially by the already mentioned evolutionary epistemology as it demonstrates the adaptation of our organs of knowledge (not just our sense organs) to the segment of the world relevant most directly to our survival.[6] That we can extend our segment of knowledge by mental and technical means from the subatomic to the cosmic scale, contrary to the limitations of all other beings we know to their immediate area of life, appears to me as one more strong argument for realism. Admittedly, to be able to accept this reasoning a considerable degree of realism is already presupposed.

Thus, several well-founded deliberations may make it probable or very probable that our life is not just a dream, but they do not provide ultimate certainty. Various objections can be raised, like the one that the dream »life« and dreams within life cannot be compared. Against every proof of reality one may object that we only dream what we feel as reality. Even by death reality or irreality of life cannot be proved. If we could carry on a philosophical discussion with the deceased, the same objections that can be raised against our feeling of reality could be raised against a feeling of reality they might have in relation to their level of consciousness and an analogous argumentation could be applied to any level of "reality" coming into sight.

Unquestionably it would be of greatest significance if life were only a dream within a wider existence of consciousness. We would not necessarily have to live such a life in a different way than a real life, but one could not deny a temptation to experiment with life. One could try if one could reach another level of consciousness by putting oneself in extreme situations or by even sacrificing one's life (similar to awakening before impact when experiencing a fall during a dream). Furthermore, there would be much less reason to orientate one's life to moral attitudes and values. What does it matter how you behave in a dream as it is not about real events (unless there would be an authority drawing sanctioning consequences for real life from your dream behaviour)? Finally, life as a dream would bring with it a completely different and much narrower meaning of "knowledge" restricted to grasping a dream reality, that is to say, knowledge would be no more than knowledge about intrapsychic events.

Perhaps these considerations may become more comprehensible by the following illustration. If we put it a little bit pointed and provocative, for religions focused on afterlife life is not much more than some kind of dream or at least just a part (and mostly the less important) of our existence though this part wins some significance as we may influence our position in the »true« other-worldly world by our behaviour during this transient state. A considerable part of Kamikaze operations by fanatics may be understood as a consequence of such ideas though – to be just – these ideas may lead to impressive examples of altruism as well.

Descartes has sharply put the problem of doubt about the reality of the world (a doubt extending on human capability for knowledge as a whole): "For how do we know that the thoughts that come to us in dreams are any falser than the others, seeing that they are often no less vivid and clear? However much the best minds choose to investigate this matter, I do not believe that they will be able to furnish any argument which is sufficient to remove this doubt, unless they presuppose the existence of God."[7] Descartes found his way out in believing in a benevolent god who would not mislead human beings when something appears certain to them beyond doubt. Conversely, he believed to find a rational basis for the faith in god by the idea that human beings to whom something appears certain beyond doubt could not err because the existence of such a god appeared certain beyond doubt to him. It is evident that his »rational« justification contains a vicious circle, and that Descartes cannot avoid a decision of belief: Either he believes in a benevolent god first of all who does not mislead a human being to whom something appears certain beyond doubt, or he believes first of all that a human being to whom something appears certain beyond doubt does not err and infers the existence of such a benevolent god from that.

The unwilling to believe cannot take either of these decisions. And neither of them is required at all as the decisive weakness of all anti-realistic reflections is not that realism cannot be proved but that there are no good reasons for an anti-realistic position. Therefore, just as concerning human capability for knowledge, a fundamental choice about realism appears no longer necessary to me. That things which appear real after thorough examination exist independently of our own consciousness as a rule and are not just a dream reality and that it is possible – despite all subjectivist reservations - to adequately perceive and interpret at least partial aspects of a world which exists independently of humankind and individual human beings and which is principally equal for all beings capable of knowledge seems no more or just as doubtful to me as any other scientifically well founded concept.

With good reason Vollmer proposes a hypothetical realism which we should consider as a hypothesis to test and which draws a distinction between psychological certainty and epistemological uncertainty.[8] At the very least such a hypothetical realism is what follows as a consequence from the epistemological principle of simplicity. Admittedly, realism would be a severe, unjustified and not easily identifiable simplification if the world were not real – whereas in the case of single erroneous findings about the world we will someday be confronted with conflicting observations showing us that our assumptions have been wrong (even the invisible crystalline matter on the moon would have become apparent to us meanwhile). And yet there are no more good reasons for an anti-realistic position than for any other highly speculative proposition about the world, there are no more good reasons for it than could have been brought forward in favour of such an invisible crystalline matter on the moon during the time of Galilei. Bertrand Russell puts it straight: "There is no logical impossibility in the supposition that the whole of life is a dream, in which we ourselves create all the objects that come before us. But although this is not logically impossible, there is no reason whatever to suppose that it is true; and it is, in fact, a less simple hypothesis, viewed as a means of accounting for the facts of our own life, than the common-sense hypothesis that there really are objects independent of us, whose action on us causes our sensations."[9] (The ensuing reflections on the hunger of Russell's cat are, as the little book on "The Problems of Philosophy" as a whole, a worthwhile reading experience for everybody interested in philosophy, likewise enjoyable and instructive.)

It is possible, admittedly, to formulate an epistemological agnosticism sophisticated enough to cope with all everyday necessities. Thus the constructivist Ernst von Glasersfeld says: "... to claim that human knowledge should reflect an ontological world independent from man may appear indispensable, but it is not indispensable; a knowledge enabling us to reach goals set by ourselves in the world of our experience suffices completely to justify science, philosophy, and art." And: "... such a knowledge ... gives us the possibility, nevertheless, to distinguish between subjective figments and the objective world of experience of the community."[10] But if we are able to know this much, what difference remains between constructivism and a critical and hypothetical realism? A practically irrelevant, highly questionable reservation. It is no surprise to find the proponents of constructivism mainly amongst psychologists, psychotherapists, educationalists and related academic disciplines for which differences in subjective individual interpretations and valuations of human beings play an important role. To scientists working in the traditional natural sciences, however, constructivism is far less attractive because they are much more impressed by the convergence or even identity of scientific results across individual, moral, philosophical, social and political barriers (let me point again here to the account by C. F. v. Weizsäcker quoted at the end of section 1.2.). They experience the success of hypotheses and theories directly. For them this is a strong argument for realism and an even stronger perhaps is that hypotheses and theories fail time and again. (Vollmer[11])

Our striving for knowledge produces a complex web of interactions: We invent concepts of order in ever new varieties and thereby discover an order independent of us in ever better ways. (1) We cover the world by our structures of knowledge with such a success – and sometimes our failure to do so becomes evident sooner or later as well – that this justifies the assumption that we are able to understand a real world adequately to a considerable degree. (2)

> "Reality is that which, when you stop believing in it, doesn't go away."[12]
>
> Philip K. Dick

3.1.5. Science

Engine of progress, stumbling when it comes to the critique of religion and ideology and to morality

> "Scientific thinking does not differ in its nature from the normal activity of thought, which all of us, believers and unbelievers, employ in looking after our affairs in ordinary life. It has only developed certain features: it takes an interest in things even if they have no immediate, tangible use; it is concerned carefully to avoid individual factors and affective influences; it examines more strictly the trustworthiness of the sense-perceptions on which it bases its conclusions; it provides itself with new perceptions which cannot be obtained by everyday means and it isolates the determinants of these new experiences in experiments which are deliberately varied."[1]
>
> Sigmund Freud

"Science by itself cannot advocate courses of human action, but it can certainly illuminate the possible consequences of alternative courses of action."[2]

Carl Sagan

As an unwilling to believe one can only accept a systematic quest for knowledge as scientific if it refrains from the ways to knowledge rejected by the fundamental choice of unwillingness to believe and demands good reasons guided by logic, observation and simplicity as criteria of knowledge.

Thus theology, for example, is no scientific discipline for those unwilling to believe as far as it is based on revelation and authority, that is to say, as far as it claims to be able to attain knowledge about a hereafter, god or divine commandments for human beings. It is more than doubtful that such a »scientific« discipline has any real subject outside its own tradition at all: this is even highly implausible. To stick to scientific rituals may serve well for social positioning as an academic discipline, but it does not bring real scientificity. In contrast, the unwilling to believe will concede their place among scientific disciplines to the study of religion or ecclesiastical history as a matter of course.

It is unjustified to denounce those unwilling to believe as positivists when they take such a position. In contrast to a positivist the unwilling to believe is well aware of the fact that science cannot assess what science is. There is no final objective concept of science and each of its definitions comprises subjective prerational decisions and – on a societal level – conventions and settings.

Science can establish rules for itself and can strive to have them generally accepted. Thereby it can create a more or less reliable basis for scientific communication and can define the necessary societal criteria of demarcation. Though indubitable practical success may decide in its favour in many cases, it cannot completely evade subjectivity and conventionality as far as a certain scientific methodology and an exclusive definition of science is at stake.

The knowledge that there is some residue of subjectivity in her or his definition of science should not hinder the unwilling to believe in the effort for a broad acceptance of a strict concept of science which comprises as little belief as necessary and to advocate it as an adequate basis for government policy. This means in concrete terms, for example, to stand up against carrying on theology and other pseudoscience like homeopathy at public universities, or at least against governmentally institutionalising and financing it any longer. (1)

Within the scope of what is accepted as science by the unwilling to believe further decisions are necessary concerning the ways of application of logic and observation that should be accepted or judged as more or less reliable in case of dispute and concerning the degree of trust to be put in certain methods of a discipline. (See the deliberation on the criteria of knowledge in sections 3.1.1. to 3.1.3.)

Popper has pointed out the requirement of falsifiability as decisive criterion for ascribing scientificity to hypotheses and theories. This is a useful thought-provoking concept especially when dealing with too vague and arbitrarily adaptable theories. It is understandable that Popper ascribed special importance to the requirement of falsifiability considering psychoanalytic tenets that could hardly be tied down to unambiguous predictions, appeared to be able to offer an "explanation" for everything after the fact and tended to immunise by referring to alleged psychological defence mechanisms in their opponents.

But the importance of the falsifiability criterion must not be overrated. Even if accepted, we are left with the problem to come to terms regarding criteria of falsifiability and falsification. As Kuhn[3], who has complemented Popper's ideal presentation of science by valuable enquiries on the actual historical proceedings of science, has stated correctly, falsification and verification are a gradual process – at least in scientific practice – and we may argue over criteria of verification as well as over criteria of falsification. In scientific practice attempts of verification often precede attempts of falsification. Verification often is the immediate goal and falsification results from attempts of verification or as a reaction thereupon.

Admittedly, there is some asymmetry between verification und falsification. Just a few facts contradicting a hypothesis or theory may unsettle it so severely that a multitude of facts supporting it cannot compensate for that. On the other hand, we are highly suspicious of facts contradicting hypotheses and theories that already seem verified very well. Such hypotheses and theories are not jettisoned easily. For good reason we cast doubt on the contradicting facts first of all or look for an explanation conforming with the tried and tested theory or a modification or extension meeting the new facts. This is nicely expressed in a remark ascribed to Lakatos: "If you see one bright red swan, you are not likely to give up a theory that says that all swans are white; you will instead go looking for the person who painted it." (2) That we can go wrong as well when sticking to the tried and tested theory is shown by the fact that at least black swans exist.

Even if a theory is still scarcely verified, we will not dismiss it easily for some contradicting observations as long as it has a high explanatory power and produces fertile hypotheses – and the more so if there is a lack of a better alternative.

Hence the asymmetry between verification und falsification is of lesser importance than one might think at first glance. (3)

Whatever we give priority to in the discussion of verification and falsification: in the long run and at least from today's point of view we have less trouble with non-falsifiable theories than with the lack of willingness to apply the strict traditional criteria for falsification or verification of modern science consequently, including the discussions on philosophy and philosophy of life, and to abandon falsified theories. Again, we find ourselves confronted more and more with unscientific and anti-scientific thinking, partly even making claims to constitute a concept of scientificity of equal rank by invoking an unavoidable rest of subjectivity that can be found at the basis of every concept of science and thus constructing a subjective arbitrariness of any concept of science whatsoever. Such pseudoscience is advertised as »conceptual pluralism in science« and its magic formula is "internal consensus". (4)

Thus, all sorts of old and new abstruse theories enjoy an undreamt-of standing. Even for experts with a scientific education it is by no means a matter of course that they abandon falsified theories. Taking homeopathy as an example, we realise that a lack of falsifiability is not at all the problem. Homeopathy is falsifiable and it is falsified. Modern physics and biochemistry do not yield any evidence at all that the theory underlying homeopathy could be true (on the contrary they would have to be changed completely just for its sake). If a medical theory alleges unknown physical forces for which no indications have been found elsewhere after two hundred years, no scientifically valid proof of efficacy surpassing placebo effect has been produced during this long timespan, and all alleged effects can easily be explained by suggestion and suggestibility, then this theory is falsified. Nevertheless, its attractiveness is unbroken, and we still see – at least in Germany – a considerable financial support for and social recognition of this theory. (See also note 3.1.2 (2))

If one considers the historical development of science and pseudoscience and the ever new varieties in the course of time in which the latter appears and partly receives a lot of attention, though in most cases quite fleetingly, there is some plausibility to Gordin's proposition that pseudoscience is a permanent and inevitable concomitant of science. In some cases, fruitful ideas can even come from it. For the rest, all of us, and scientists in particular, can counteract its influence by certain wise behaviours (communication, explanation of the scientific way of working including its procedures of recruitment, control and sanctioning in case of misconduct).[4]

Let us have a look at another example we find in the philosophical debate: Considered as a hypothesis (and only then it has a comprehensible content) the statement that there is a god both all-benevolent and all-powerful is falsifiable and clearly falsified by the state of the world. But that does not prevent even distinguished scientists from still accepting and supporting a religion which counts this statement amongst its fundamental convictions.

Unfortunately, there a falsified theories and hypotheses that have such a high speculative appeal and satisfy human desires and wishes to such a high degree that they develop a tenacious life of their own beyond the death of their original protagonists and beyond all falsification.

This kind of pseudo-scientificity cannot be combatted just by discussing what epistemological justification means or what it should mean. It is possible, no doubt, to define and accept a concept of science that allows revelation, authority, and esoteric procedures as criteria of knowledge, a concept that gives up or only inconstantly pursues the requirement that theories have to be logically consistent and ascribes more importance to subjectively convincing individual observations than to intersubjectively verifiable procedures of observation that strive to eliminate subjective factors as far as possible. Against that we can only resort to a historical argument in the end: it is not this kind of »science« that has provided humankind with the amount of knowledge and power it has at its command today. But if somebody believes that knowledge and truth are subordinate values and that we humans already have too much knowledge and power and consequently holds the opinion that it would be preferable to still have children regularly die from appendicitis or pneumonia if we would on the other hand have no nuclear weapons either, then what to discuss about? Here the only question left is who can win through.

For discussing the scientificity and the scientific value of theories it is important to realise that the term "theory" is used with two very different meanings. (A clarification I owe to Collins.[5])

118

On the one hand, what is meant by "theory" is speculations and conjectures about causes and facts. We constantly set up this kind of theories in our private life, for instance, concerning the intentions and motives of behaviour of other people, but they also appear in science, namely as hypotheses, and are a significant factor in scientific progress. The concept of multiverses, the conjecture that there might be several or multiple universes with different natural constants, is an example of such a scientific "theory".

On the other hand, what is meant by "theory" are fundamental principles of sciences or social and artistic fields of activity. These fundamental principles are suggested by a wealth of facts, they are "proved", or they have been developed and tested in a long cultural tradition. Examples from the realm of the natural sciences that fall into this second category are the theory of relativity or the theory of evolution. Concerning this kind of theories, the statement that "it is just a theory" is no longer justified because these are scientific or social concepts tried and tested again and again. These concepts are no mere speculations and conjectures. To the contrary, they are the current state of a scientific explanation of the world or the social formation of conventions – which does not mean that we will not be prompted or forced to modify them by future changes of our knowledge.

Admittedly, the transition between the first and the second way to use the term "theory" may be gradual in the sciences, depending on the respective state of knowledge.

At this point let us make a small digression considering the issue of »science and religion«. One can, at least with some practice, interpret religious texts like the Bible allegorically in a way that they do no longer contradict scientific knowledge. On the one hand, this allows many renowned scientists to stay religious, and on the other hand, it allows many religious people to accept scientific results to a greater degree than forced by everyday necessities. Thus, science and religion are not unconditionally incompatible. But they come into conflict, at the latest, whenever a religious fundamentalism demands that religious texts should be taken literally and replace a scientific explanation of the world.

Furthermore, the following question definitely arises: Why, after all, should we undertake ever new allegorical interpretations of religious texts as soon as they come into conflict with the results of science? Or to put it in another way: It seems much more sensible to look upon religious texts as documents of historical interest demonstrating how bygone times attempted to explain the world and orientate in it. These texts are sometimes impressive and instructive in a timeless manner, sometimes they are dismaying, and in many ways, they are no longer adequate for today. There is a big problem with the allegorical interpretation of religious texts and religious tradition (especially for Christianity see also 1.2.): The way of the world does not show any effect of a god's hand. There are no hints that the course of the universe would be influenced by moral criteria (except of those brought into the world by humans). Everything can be explained much more easily if we consider it as a consequence of morally indifferent laws of nature.

Nowadays it is popular to state that there is no fundamental contradiction between modern scientific thinking and religion and that they simply deal with different spheres of knowledge and life. As long as both would just be willing to accept this they would not have to come into conflict. Well, this view is hardly more than a modish prejudice and the adequate comment on it is given by quoting the famous evolutionary biologist Ernst Mayr: "Frankly I've never been able to understand it because you would need two completely different compartments in your brain, one that deals with religion and the other with everything else."[6] That some people are able to reconcile scientific thinking and religion for themselves does not change the fact that scientific thinking – if not only learned as an armamentarium for a specific purpose – brings with it a strong critical impulse concerning metaphysics and religion. This cannot be waved aside as a historic phenomenon. The euphoria that meant to get religion over and done with, characteristic of the belief in science during the decades of transition from the 19th to the 20th century, was followed by an exaggerated swing of the pendulum to the other side, namely a considerable timidity of scientific thinking concerning its consequences for philosophy and philosophy of life. As a matter of course that could and cannot be the last word either.

Religion is the wrong answer to the question that science alone cannot give us moral orientation. The moral orientation we humans (and thus also scientists and science) need has to be found (which means elaborated and set) in a better and less questionable manner.

As far as the modish tendency is concerned to disparage science and scientists morally or to be especially suspicious of them, the confrontation with negative sequels of the scientific and technological progress does not explain this completely. It is also a consequence of exaggerated and illusionary moral expectations and demands (furthered by some scientists' proneness to self-glorification). It is possible to have a mere instrumental relationship to science, that is to say, to consider it as a tool like a hammer or a machine-gun or, in one's personal plans, as a means to earn a living and make a career. And therefore, it is possible to be both an excellent scientist and a bigoted, philosophically backward, morally irresponsible or fanatic person. It is disappointing that scientific and technological progress does not automatically lead to an enlightened philosophy of life and a tolerant, democratic, and just society but we had and have to accept the fact.

Time and again scientists and engineers become collaborators and underlings of fanatic ideologies, totalitarian regimes and scheming power politicians. Scientists too may misjudge their duties and the appropriate conduct in certain historic situations. Scientists too may be seduced, bribed, put under pressure, urged, blackmailed.

In private life as well one should not necessarily expect scientists to be a shining example. A particular allure of scientific work, in basic research especially, lies in pushing the boundaries of knowledge to ever new spheres, formerly out of reach. That is sort of working on the frontline of something »eternal«, as a small cog in a great project of humankind which is always changing but perpetual at the same time. Compared to this, the usual everyday worries, the ordinary biographical events, the course of personal relationships, rise and fall in politics, economy and culture may all appear as a tedious and relatively unimportant repetition of pretty much the same. But those who think like that, neglect, like other people with obsessive ideas, the obligation to their fellow human beings and to the respective contemporary society, that is, they actually fail to be humane. On the other hand, scientific progress – contrary to more dubious obsessive ideas – deserves a high degree of commitment, and scientific work may ease or compensate personal problems.

As soon as at the end of the 19th century T.H. Huxley already warned against an overestimation of scientists: "So far as my experience goes, men (!) of science are neither better nor worse than the rest of the world. Occupation with the endlessly great parts of the universe does not necessarily involve greatness of character, nor does microscopic study of the infinitely little always produce humility."[7]

If scientists are no better and no worse than other groups of people in society, there is no reason to discredit science and scientists as a whole. Nor is there any reason to place trust in them beyond measure.

Finally, we should not forget that we realise the world not only by systematic scientific effort. It is not science alone that is telling us what is. And it is not science that tells us what ought to be. (But science can tell us a lot about the extent to which particular ought statements correspond to the interests of sentient beings, individual human beings and a majority of human beings and which prospects of success these statements may have.)

At this point I want to comment briefly on the Verstehen-Erklären controversy and thus the concept of "understanding" that played a considerable role especially in German 20th century philosophy and was and is used particularly to delimit natural and human sciences. This concept can be productive if it draws our attention to the specifics applying to our striving for knowledge concerning human needs, human behaviour, personal relationships, social structures, historic situations and processes, intellectual and artistic expressions and products. It emphasises that apart from general explanations an individual consideration and judgement is of considerable importance concerning these matters. But it is misleading to confront »understanding« as a specific method of human sciences to a notion of explanation allegedly reserved for problems dealt with in the natural sciences.

Is "understanding" really so much different from "explaining"? As far as "understanding" is meant as a comparison with one's own feelings, as emotional and cognitive empathy and convergence it has no doubt considerable importance for human emotional life and enjoyment of life, but it is only indirectly - as a source of interest and motivation - connected to the scientific process of gaining knowledge. But if "understanding" means to acquire a language or terminology, to gain knowledge on natural, historic, biographic, or personal factors in order to come to well-founded judgements concerning these matters, then I am not able to see a fundamental difference to the approach used in the natural sciences. In this way we come just as well to an interpretation and evaluation according to the principles of logic, observation, and simplicity. It does not contradict this view that, compared to a clearly structured experiment in natural science, the observational situation is considerably more difficult if we want, for instance, draw conclusions from the behaviour of a person to her feelings, from the work of an artist to what she or he intends to express, or if we want to filter truth from historic sources.

But natural science as well does not only consist of experiments but has to deal with a lot of complex problems presenting a difficult observational situation with a multitude of different factors influencing the picture. And natural sciences as well do not only strive to establish general laws, they are not (in the sense of Popper's differentiation) mere "theoretical" sciences, but not seldom they are also "historical" sciences that deal with the explanation of one-time events. (See Vollmer[8]) Think of problems of cosmology, Earth's history, palaeontology, history of evolution, or just an individual medical history. Popper rightly defends the unity of scientific method[9] (though some of his statements in this context may be controversial). Undeniably, different scientific disciplines have their specifics. But a fundamental methodological difference, as alleged often enough, between natural and human sciences can only be postulated after constructing an inductionistic travesty of the method of natural science. It must be conceded that many natural scientists have furthered this travesty by inadequate and oversimplified concepts concerning their own epistemological presuppositions and their own method (for instance by taking their subspecialty as a generally applicable model).

The concept of "understanding" represents an extended approach on how to gain knowledge but it is no new or even privileged way to knowledge. It is imprecise, prone to misunderstandings and vulnerable to misuse. (5) But »understanding« thought also reminds us of the methodologically and morally valuable attitude to get ourselves involved with some object thoroughly, to learn about it in-depth, before allowing distancing and criticism. (See also 3.1.9., p. 135/136). On the other hand, understanding thought has a tendency not only to postpone distance and criticism but to disregard them altogether and, finally, to deny the existence and recognisability of truth at all and to give up the striving for the highest possible degree of objectivity. Then, everything is accepted in an attitude of understanding, a specific value and legitimation as knowledge is ascribed to whatever has some systematics, tradition or social importance without casting an unbiased critical eye on the foundations of such "knowledge". Thus, even theology is considered as a serious scientific discipline and the critical potential towards untenable speculative theories and pseudoscientific and quasi-religious (political) ideologies suffers. This is another facet of the general observation that successful work as a scientist and unprejudiced, critical thinking are not necessarily associated.

> "The fact that an authority may be qualified in one field does not necessarily mean that he or she will exercise critical intelligence in others; and in some domains the scientist may be as credulous as the ordinary person."[10]
>
> Paul Kurtz

3.1.6. Knowledge – Interpretation – Judgement

The pitfalls of putting it all together

Observations do not lead to knowledge directly. They have to be interpreted, that is to say, they have to be put into a theoretical framework and into the context of our world view as a whole using logical conclusions and taking into account other observations and the principle of parsimony. In a next step we attach value to what we judge to be knowledge, that means, we assess the scientific value and the personal significance for ourselves, position ourselves to it, and decide on the consequences we draw.

This may be illustrated by two examples from natural science: A multitude of biological observations can best be explained by the theory of evolution; the cosmic microwave background radiation can best be explained by assuming an expanding cosmos producing a redshift. That are the widely accepted and the most plausible interpretations. But the consequences we draw from these phenomena and the respective interpretations regarding the significance we ascribe to individual human beings and humankind as a whole, and especially the question whether we see them as part of an argument against religious cosmogonies and a religious interpretation of the world in general, is a question of judgement.

Most of us make interpretations and judgements - at least during long periods of our lives – that allow us to integrate ourselves sufficiently into the environment we live in. But in unfavourable cases our interpretations and judgements may lead to severe suffering or personal disaster (for instance, in persons running amok, in crisis induced suicide, or in outlaws and martyrs for philosophical, religious or political reasons). Given enough power one of us can drag millions of fellow human beings into the abyss. And these problems are not limited to occasional misinterpretations and misjudgements of the world, as, for example, in the case of persons wrongly convicted and sentenced to death based on false evidence or in the case of deadly love dramas caused by alleged or real infidelity. It may also happen that the view of the world goes through a selective narrowing in a long process and the undue importance ascribed to correctly observed partial aspects creates a progressive vicious circle leading to wrong judgements with possibly deleterious consequences. (See also the literary example from note 3.1. (1). At the polar opposite our personal judgement of the world may lead to astonishing equanimity or unselfishness in desperate situations.

In interpreting the world, we presuppose just a few philosophical decisions concerning knowledge. We measure our success - as long as we proceed rationally – according to the predictive power and the durability of our assessments. As a rule, we check our interpretation of the world continuously comparing it to other people's. That are the ways we try to attain objectivity and certainty. We come closest to objectivity where our emotional involvement is relatively low, namely in problems of natural science and technology. In this field we reach a relatively high degree of consensus concerning the interpretation of observations and information, though already much less concerning our judgement about them.

In historical, political, and social questions, and in the assessment of persons in our immediate surroundings, of ourselves, and our personal relationships even our interpretations of the world become more and more wavering and questionable. The influence which our personality with all our biography exerts on our interpretation of observations becomes more important. But even here objectivity does make sense as a criterion and appears relatively unproblematic as long as only as few as possible philosophical decisions concerning knowledge are presupposed and the striving for objectivity is understood in a broad analogy to the mathematical concept of infinity which allows to reach a lot though we always just think in approximation.

Contrary to this, the judgement of knowledge is determined subjectively to a much higher degree. Our judgement of the world is influenced by our further moral attitudes, values, and decisions, and ultimately by our entire psychological and social situation.

3.1.7. Credulity

Innocuous horoscopic simplicity?

> "What philosopher has not at one time or another cut the queerest figure imaginable, between the affirmations of a reasonable and firmly convinced eyewitness, and the inner resistance of insurmountable doubt?"[1]

> Immanuel Kant

When discussing the fundamental choice of unwillingness to believe it was stated that not only religious faith but also credulity in the most general sense stand in marked contrast to unwillingness to believe. Here, some more attention shall be given to this human weakness.

First of all, credulity is an intellectual and personal deficiency (surely acquired to a considerable degree) comparable to the deficiency of a mathematician who miscalculates, for lack of intelligence, for wishful thinking, or for sloppiness though he or she accepts the principles of mathematics. Commonly credulous people accept logic, observation, and simplicity as a basis of their assessments quite as other people do. They just do not realise or do not want to realise when they do not or at least do not sufficiently comply to this standard. Credulity becomes attractive because it provides a relief from the complexity of the world and creates an ordering structure in a (though all too) simple way. It allows to reject or at least alleviate the disillusionment caused by modern science and opens the door for emotionally comfortable wishful thinking and solace. Often credulity is an uncontrolled, uncritical straying of the capability to look for structure and to interpret signs which, on the other hand, is so important for human ability of knowledge.

Credulity can be found among people with very different philosophies of life. It is by no means confined to adherents of the traditional religions. On the contrary, many of them think absolutely critical and realistic concerning problems of everyday life whereas the adherents of allegedly rationally justifiable systems of belief, "unbelievers" of very different shades, and even some of those who seem to have reflected intensively on their philosophy of life, sometimes show considerable credulity, not only by accepting a just seemingly completely rational justification for their belief but also by an astounding degree of superstition. Even people who have a seemingly rational philosophy of life often cannot overcome the deeply ingrained human propensity to interpret the world irrationally or at least to recklessly assume causal relationships between observations. You can have a lot of factual and specialised knowledge and think very uncritical, nonetheless. "... somebody can be afraid of Friday and the number 13 and yet create excellent drugs." (Neurath[2]) The life of many people is shaped much less by consequent thinking than by traditional patterns and habits of thought. (See also note 1.2. (2))

Credulity can be an outlet for unreflective and unfulfilled wishes to be an important and chosen person. Therefore, some people turn to astrology, for instance. This variety of credulity – like some others posing in a pseudoscientific outfit – was already aptly criticised by Schopenhauer: "Astrology furnishes a magnificent proof of this miserable subjective tendency in men, which leads them to see everything only as bearing upon themselves, and to think of nothing that it is not straightway made into a personal matter. The aim of astrology is to bring the motions of the celestial bodies into relation with the wretched *Ego* and to establish a connection between a comet in the sky and squabbles and rascalities on earth."[3] In our days the disposition to interpret the world by relying on esoteric practices is still quite widespread, and we can find the same kind of concise analysis too: "Enlightened contemporaries who would shrug shoulders and smile when accidentally coming across what the prophet Isaiah says (brilliantly translated by Luther): 'Fear not, for I have redeemed you, I have called you by name, you are mine' – these very same contemporaries read their horoscopes every day. They do not care whether the assertions of astrology and the horoscope industry have been dismissed as desolate superstition a hundred times. No matter if it's true. These horoscope believers do not want to be an anonymous grain of sand in the tempest of time. They want to be called by their name and want to be approached about their birthday and their sign of the zodiac. That's what they long for. What they are advised to – restraint in matters of love, caution in monetary matters– is of minor importance. The main thing is to have a destiny."[4]

Astrology exemplifies frequent characteristic of credulous pseudoscience: people believe to follow a privileged way of knowledge that allegedly leads to insights otherwise not attainable at all or that pretends to enable them to reach insights otherwise only attainable by sophisticated scientific procedures in a much easier individual and empiric-intuitive way - if there only is a strong enough aptitude and an appropriate initiation. The complexity of the world to which everybody is exposed today continuously, and which cannot be evaded seriously, is answered by illusionary simplification.

There is no convincing evidence that would justify the various esoteric claims to knowledge. And regarding these special psychic capabilities some people claim to have – be it clairvoyance or other alleged parapsychological skills like telepathy or telekinesis – there is, furthermore, one very convincing argument against their existence (already presented by Stanislaw Lem[5]): if these capabilities would exist, they should have had a considerable evolutionary advantage and, therefore, should have spread accordingly.

Credulity in its innumerable varieties may be quite amusing; but it may also cause great harm if (wrong) decisions are made based on avoidably erroneous presuppositions. This may still be relatively innocuous if »just« a wrong decision concerning human resources based on graphology or a wrong allocation of resources in scientific funding is at stake. But it may also take a more or less heavy toll on human lives, for instance as a consequence of wrong decisions made by political leaders advised by astrology or by parents withdrawing their sick children from promising (though sometimes burdensome), evidence-based, scientific treatments and trusting in so-called alternative medical procedures instead. This brings us back to the emotional comfort credulity may offer. For these parents, for instance, credulity also has the advantage to spare them the confrontation with the question whether it is their own feelings or the health and well-being of the child what matters to them first of all.

This book wants to make a contribution against credulity, among other things. But we should not harbour illusions about the prospects of success of this struggle as it is directed against one of the oldest and most persistent weaknesses of humanity. Nevertheless, this battle has to be fought over and over again. Though the concrete external uncertainties for the individual have diminished in many aspects, at least in most of the modern western societies, there is intellectual and philosophical insecurity and an increased geographical, social, and biographic mobility against which many people evidently want to set simple models of explanations as a comforting counterbalance. If individual situations of crisis or misery like disease or poverty are added, people fall prey to credulity even more easily.

Credulity is a complex phenomenon that can only be understood by a differentiated approach of explanation. My intention here was to discuss just some of the relevant aspects. (1) Especially the rule for the critical analysis of observations described at the end of section 3.1.2. in the impressing wording of Dawkins appears to me as a good safeguard against credulity. And – read properly – in this attack against undue credulity, in this call for suspicion against the all to unusual, there is as well an invitation to appreciate the capabilities of the human mind constituting its positive antipole: curiosity, impartiality, openness to the new.

"In our more or less irreligious age everything is possible. There is such an immense bullshit amongst the intelligentsia no longer supervised by the church that one wonders what for we had the Enlightenment after all. Just have a look at the movie listings; you can cash in on every witches sabbath, on every satanic nonsense, on whatever you want, and in the therapeutic scene too. Just everything."[6]

Gerd B. Achenbach

"It might seem that the serious matters of life have precious little to do with the validity of horoscopes, the probability of reincarnation, or the existence of Bigfoot, but I maintain that susceptibility to bad arguments in one domain opens the door to being manipulated in another domain. A critical mind is critical on all fronts simultaneously, and it is vital to train people to be critical at an early stage."[7]

Douglas R. Hofstadter

3.1.8. Intuition, Imagination, Fiction, Speculation, Meditation, Mystical Experience, Communication

Convoluted paths

"You can only feel sorrow for a philosopher who confines himself to dry truths and for whom the treasures of imagination and feeling are lost."[1]

Voltaire

"Let us speak specifically of rational understanding, particularly in the sciences. It is customary to present science as a system of more or less logical inferences from either axioms or experiences. That is the image of science as a fortress and the way it is defended against criticism once it has been discovered. But it is not being discovered that way. It is a well-known phenomenon in mathematics that one ›sees‹ a theorem prior to its proof, an intended structure prior to the formulated sentence and seemingly incoherent segments of a proof prior to the completed proof."[2]

C. F. v. Weizsäcker

Logic and observation do not lead to knowledge of their own accord. Neither logical systems nor hypotheses which can be confirmed by observation come into being without intuition and imagination. The conditions under which intuition and imagination become effective cannot be predicted reliably and even less in a generally valid manner because they are highly dependent on human individuality and the specific situation and task. Varying from case to case, intuition and imagination may be furthered by distraction and idleness as well as by hard work and everyday bustle, but lacking opportunities for education and an all to overwhelming pressure to secure subsistence are certainly bad prerequisites. Intuition and imagination are no ways to knowledge in a strict sense, but just a prerequisite, or, to stay with the metaphor, a means of transportation on this way. Intuition may be very successful in finding shortcuts on the way to knowledge (which may even be relevant to survival), but, on the other hand, it is vulnerable to errors to a considerable degree. (1)

What has been grasped or guessed intuitively or has been created by imagination, has to be formulated clearly and confirmed by logic and observation if it is to have an impact beyond the moment and shall be accepted as knowledge. Fictive ideas and stories train our power of imagination and improve our ability to conceive and achieve something new. It is to speculation, to speculative thinking, that we owe substantial stimuli for the progress of knowledge time and again - but stimuli only. Then, good reasons have still to be procured, and the wilder speculation diverges from established science the less probable it is that this can be done. On the one hand, a considerable degree of tolerance and interest for speculative approaches is substantial for the progress of knowledge, on the other hand, it deserves little tolerance if pretensions to truth are glibly raised on a basis of no more than mere speculation.

Meditation and communication with others, (self-)contemplation and conversation may be the sources of surprising insights which cannot be reached or at least can only be reached much slower by strictly controlled straight thinking.

As to meditation and mystical experience: This is a book in the rational tradition of western philosophy. It concedes that eastern wisdom – and western mystical tradition – contribute interesting ideas and rewarding methods to our approach to knowledge, but it does not accept the idea that meditative philosophy may lead to completely different contents, to a knowledge not requiring and not accessible to validation by logic and observation. The report of meditative experiences that can be given in words may appear inadequate as holds true for other psychological and emotional events – like the experience of love – as well. But: Contemplation is always an experience of the self. Logic and observation provide no good reason to suppose that the suspension of the border between the individual and the world, as it can be experienced in meditation, would be more than an intrapsychic process. Meditative experiences are liminal experiences (and as such they are also an interesting research topic in neurobiology). Metaphysical they are only in so far as this may be said about all psychological experiences (and such a way of talking is highly questionable for all the misunderstandings that can be related to it).

Meditation and mystical experience are no royal road to knowledge. They may lead us to knowledge or to errors about the world or just about ourselves. Meditative experiences, too, have to undergo an examination by logic and observation. Their interesting psychological and psychotherapeutic effects must be separated from their philosophical content. The connection between meditation and religion is just a historic fact. Meditation can, should and will continue to be practised and bring personal and social benefit on the basis of a secular, naturalistic philosophy of life as well.

Beyond meditation in a strict sense the ability of spiritual experience is an interesting property and peculiarity of the human brain. But I do not see any good reason for interpreting spirituality and religiosity as crossing boundaries in such a way as is often ascribed to them. They are products of the human brain allegedly pointing to a reality outside this brain without presenting any better argument for that than the often impressing subjective experience of epiphany connected to them.

Communication and the signs and media used for it lend an intersubjective existence to intellectual achievements and allow them an existence surpassing the individual human brain (and its capacity), in spite of some losses occurring in the process of transmission. However, these signs and media are not more than dead physical objects if there is no brain to decode them and realise there meaning.

Communication, as stimulating as it can be and as important it is for the progress of knowledge and for a pleasant living together, may degenerate to mere activism and its value depends on the contents that are brought in.

Apart from their usefulness (and their dangers) all these »convoluted paths« to knowledge can bring a lot of joy and enrich our lives.

3.1.9. Knowledge and Language Style
Which sort of language does the job?

For the purposes of this section I understand »language« in a broad sense including, for instance, symbolic languages, as those of mathematics.

The exposition of facts of different areas of knowledge and different domains of science, or, to put it even more generally, the presentation of different cultural achievements requires different languages suited or suited best for the specific case. Here I want to make some remarks on the language of philosophy without going into a more detailed discussion of problems of philosophy of language as, for instance, the mutual dependence of language and knowledge. (1)

It is a fact that the languages which have been used and are used today by different philosophers to express and present their thought differ a lot. Let us have a look on some landmarks within the spectrum of philosophical languages – regardless of the historic sequence: At one end of the spectrum we find silence or the utmost reduction of verbal utterances and a more or less direct presentation of the advocated philosophy by the behaviour and the way of life a philosopher – as with Diogenes, for example. Then you have philosophers, like the logical positivists, advocating that philosophy is a critique of language first of all and that symbolic languages are a tidier way to deal with philosophical problems. At the other end of the spectrum there are those using a highly abstract conceptuality, like Hegel. Some philosophers develop a decidedly distinct language, be in it in an often unwieldy and dry way, as in Kant's case, or in a more or less existentially appealing or artistic form, as in Nietzsche's expressive or in Heidegger's neologistic way of speaking. Over those who think they have to use a philosophical technical jargon without a convincing necessity just to demonstrate their status as a philosopher I throw the cloak of silence here. Regretfully even philosophers who have to say something are not immune against this plague. Finally, there are philosophers, like Bertrand Russell, who try to express themselves in ordinary, generally used, everyday language wherever possible or, at least, try to explicate and define the concepts they need therewith, as good and as simple as they are able to do.

This outline is heavily simplified, of course, for the reason alone that the very same philosopher may chose different languages depending on the problems he or she is working on (Bertrand Russell serving as an example for that again). Needless to say, that specific fields of philosophical work need specialised terminology and that there are problems that require symbolic languages in addition to ordinary language. And symbolic language may also, last not least, help to analyse ordinary language and matters distorted or blurred by it. My simplifying outline draws its justification from the fact that by far not all special philosophical languages and »private« conceptual systems are well-founded and indispensably necessary for the matter dealt with.

From the order of the enumeration presented above one may already guess that I have a special sympathy for philosophers using ordinary language. This sort of philosophical language is mine as well – at least as something to aim at. I strive for a way of expression that is as simple, generally intelligible, and as close to everyday language as possible because such a philosophical language has an enlightenment impetus and is linked to a philosophical tradition furthering critical reason (though one should not argue from form to content too easily, especially in philosophy). We should not distrust ordinary language in an exaggerated manner and instead try to use it as clearly as possible. It may appear paradoxical at first glance, but to formulate a philosophy in an as generally intelligible language as possible means to set oneself the most difficult task. The substantive quality of philosophical deliberations has to be the greater the more it abstains from making itself interesting by a difficult, obfuscated, idiosyncratic, or artistic-inventive language.

Though a specific terminology is necessary to a certain degree for any philosophy and science, I have a reluctance against philosophies you have to immerse in to understand them and even have to literally live in to preserve an understanding of their conceptual system in the length of time and whose concepts are only meaningful and applicable within the respective system. To me such a philosophy is a constricting imposition.

But we should avoid in principle the frequent mistake to claim exclusiveness for just one style of philosophical language (and especially the one chosen by ourselves) and to restrict our cognitive interest just because of an antipathy against the language chosen by certain philosophers and schools of philosophy. It is not only that different fields of philosophical work require different languages as a consequence of the problems they are dealing with. The variety of philosophical languages and language styles also makes philosophy more appealing. One may find the language of a philosopher as interesting as the style of a painter – and like or dislike it as much.

And it is always worthwhile asking these questions: Which motive drives a philosopher to choose a certain language? What does justify her or his choice and what is achieved by it?

Kant, for instance, though his language rises to a considerable power and originality time and again, has delivered, in my opinion, unpleasant examples of an unnecessary inaccessible and tiring language of little aesthetic appeal, thus being a bad model for German philosophy, emulated far too often. But Kant had strong excuses – contrary to later philosophers with the same deficiency: In his day the German language still had no big philosophical tradition, and he could feel entitled to expand its philosophical conceptual possibilities and to provide it some reputation as a language of philosophy first of all. Furthermore, the wealth of contents he dealt with was more important to him than an elegant language style. Kant himself was not always satisfied with his language and when finishing his "Critique of Pure Reason" he uttered that he had refrained from further stylistic revision to get it ready in substance. Finally, the critical potential of his teachings and deliberations was so big that he would have had to give up his social integration if he would have declared all that in the language of the people. (2)

Another example is Heidegger. He has developed a very idiosyncratic, archaising-neologistic language often based in etymology respectively starting out from the dissection of literally meaning. And with what he tells us in this language he is permanently oscillating between triviality and a partly inventive presentation of elementary insights just as he oscillates in his life between the ridiculous and even repulsive and the impressive. Concepts like, for instance, that of "Jemeinigkeit" ("mineness") as an explication of the ultimate loneliness of the individual and its inability to act by proxy at death's door have a certain appeal, no doubt, and capture fundamental conditions of life quite well (though it appears improper and vain at the same time to exploit common key events of the human condition, such as the ultimate loneliness of human beings in the face of death, for terminological inventiveness. And, after all , there a very different types and degrees of such loneliness in practical life.) Heidegger demonstrates very well that it is possible to make oneself conspicuous and attract attention for a longer timespan by using an individualised, characteristic, philosophical language. In his case the language he has chosen is not so much artistic and all the more determined by an absolute striving for inventiveness, and he boosted that by his quaint way of life with quirks like his Heimattümelei ("homelandliness"), wearing traditional costumes and misusing the honest German term "Bodenständigkeit" ("down-to-earthness") to promote his kind of backward provincialism and obstinate nationalism. Admittedly, by looking at the word radically from the subject's point of view, by undertaking an analysis of the lifeworld, Heidegger has shown a certain inventiveness, though this is less distinct to us today after there have been so many other philosophers of existence and existentialist philosophers. Nevertheless, I very much doubt that Heidegger would be recalled and discussed today to an only remotely comparable extent if he had said what he had to say in a generally comprehensible ordinary language as clear as possible. The spectrum of his philosophical interest was simply to narrow. I am convinced that he basically knew this too and that he deliberately wanted to make himself interesting and style himself as a great philosopher by the choice respectively the creation of his language. (He was able to write plainly and generally understandable as well if he wanted to, see, for instance, large parts of his small booklet "What is Philosophy?"[1]) It is often claimed that Heidegger has opened such a fundamentally new philosophical perspective that he consequently needed a new language. I do not agree. This opinion overrates the inventiveness of his contents. There is a general propensity to consider Heidegger's undeniable importance as a part of the cultural history of the 20th century (though mainly in France and Germany) as a measure of his philosophical inventiveness. Howsoever, we can learn one or the other thing here and there from his writings and we may like him or not as we may like or not, say, the paintings of an artist like Chagall (though we get, in Heidegger's case, unavoidably into a discussion on the connection between intellectual achievements and moral attitude). (3)

One may (and should) cultivate an aversion against (self-)alleged »profundity«; such an aversion has done a lot of good in philosophy. I share Arthur Schnitzler's thrust when he says: "Profundity has never thrown light on anything. Clear thinking looks deeper into the world."[2] (And he has carried out this in his works.) But Schnitzler is not completely right: We should be prepared to find knowledge in what is presented with profundity too and should not close shutters too quickly. An idiosyncratic, not easily accessible turn of phrase sometimes actually opens new perspectives. Before we blame a philosopher for her or his language, we should try to understand what motivated them to choose just this language. And even we still do not like their language and think that they should have expressed themselves simpler, clearer, and more generally understandable, this should not hinder us to learn from them. To a certain degree we have to keep apart the phrasing and the content of a philosophy just as the life and the work of a philosopher.

From the hermeneutically oriented philosophers and theologians we can learn a thorough approach in analysing and interpreting texts. Prior to them Nietzsche has already formulated this approach in an unsurpassed manner (though I rarely wanted to follow his recipe fully): "Love as an artifice. – He who really wants to get to *know* something new (be it a person, an event, a book) does well to entertain it with all possible love and to avert his eyes quickly from everything in it he finds inimical, repellent, false, indeed to banish it from mind: so that for example, he allows the author of the book the longest start and then, like one watching a race, desires with beating heart that he may reach his goal. For with this procedure one penetrates to the heart of the new thing, to the point that actually moves it: and precisely this is what is meant by getting to know it. If one has got this far, reason can afterwards make its reservations; that over-estimation, that temporary suspension of the critical pendulum, was only an artifice for luring forth the soul of a thing."[3]

An independent, individual way of thinking, talking and living holds a certain fascination by its peculiarity alone, even if its contents are wrong or at least questionable to a considerable degree. We are reinforced in such a fascination if we have a special connection to the respective way of life due to similar experiences or if it realises or seems to realise some of our dreams, that is to say, if it has a certain substitute function. But we should never succumb to fascination for such motives, and especially to the fascination of mere consequence, all too much and more than briefly without critically considering the substance. Phenomena, like for instance the fame and the appreciation won by the eloquent Ernst Jünger in spite of his glorification of war, show that fascination for an impressive figure may hinder a critical examination of his or her questionable way of thinking.

Concerning "private" philosophical languages and the languages of philosophical schools it has to be stated, anyhow, that in the long run none of these has been able to spread beyond a narrow circle of followers and gain acceptance within the "scientific community", within a community of experts, in a way comparable to other scientific terminologies, say that of mathematics, physics or evolutionary biology, to mention just three of many possible examples. Still more than in other disciplines the concepts of philosophers with an idiosyncratic turn of phrase have to be looked upon as rungs of a ladder which may well bring us to a higher level of knowledge but then turn out to be very questionable and insufficient. That is because they describe individual concepts of thought rather than reality or, at least, they describe reality to a lesser degree or less directly than other scientific terminologies. Philosophers can contribute specific concepts to the history of ideas but hardly comprehensive terminologies. And even concepts which prevail, like

136

»naturalistic fallacy«, are often subject to a change of meaning from one philosopher to the other or one time to the other and become more ambiguous by their widespread use. (Concerning this example see also note 3.3. (3))

Good philosophy, at least as far it deals with existentially significant issues, can reach us more directly and unfold a more lasting persuasive power if it stays as close as possible to ordinary language. This is not tantamount to the use of an uncritical everyday language. (And one can be trivial or interesting in both an idiosyncratic and an ordinary language.) "This academic style does not suffice. Another style is necessary. It has not to be extravagant. To the contrary, one has 'just' to take a step back to ordinary language. In ordinary language you talk *to* somebody and about things concerning this somebody and in a tone this somebody understands. And those who do not reach this normality will never have to say anything however much they may have to 'say'."[4] Although the use of ordinary language as such does not guarantee that we achieve the way of communication described as desirable here by Günther Anders, it enhances our chances to do so.

A clear language should and must not come along with utter conviction. Clarity does not exclude the awareness of complexity.

Last but not least we should not forget that the pleasure one may take in philosophical deliberations depends to a considerable degree on their phrasing and style. For my part, I have more pleasure with those philosophers who keep a good sense of (self-)mockeryand humour and do not take themselves too seriously.

> "How sad are totalising systems of thought, how ponderous are concepts, when they cannot make light of themselves. A little humor is the antidote; Montaigne and Hume have it; Kant and Hegel do not."[5]
>
> André Comte-Sponville

3.2. Freedom of the Will and Determinism

Overrated Alternatives

"One way to gain some perspective on the free-will question is to replace it by what I believe is an equivalent question, but one which involves less loaded terms. Instead of asking, 'Does system X have free will?' we ask, 'Does system X make choices?'"[1]

Douglas R. Hofstadter

"It is a simple fact that human beings all along adjust what they do and what they refrain from according to norms, commandments and prohibitions, whether institutionalised or not."[2]

Walter Schulz

"But in the higher range of the biological sector certain configurations of the world-stuff have definite mental attributes. Regarded objectively, these configurations are the special arrangements of nervous tissue we call brains; physiologically they are organs for co-ordinating and directing action on the basis of sense-data and memory; but subjectively, certain of their activities are apprehended as mental or psychological – perception, thought, emotion, and will."[3]

Julian Huxley

"Man can do what he wills, but he is not able to will what he wills."[4]

Arthur Schopenhauer

2Whatever the intellectual position one wants to claim for the mental hare of volition and decision to maintain its freedom, and by which conceptual finesse one wants to do this, the neurophysiological hedgehog is always already there. Because without it nothing mental is conceivable at all, neither a will nor any other process of consciousness. Therefore, it appears unavoidable to come to terms with just that in giving a justification for freedom."[5]

Reinhard Merkel

Weischedel thought that he would have to make a fundamental choice of freedom within a framework of a morality founded on choices.6 But you are free or not; you cannot make a choice of freedom if you are not free. What remains to be considered is a choice of a belief in freedom (that is what Weischedel too probably meant) or a choice of a provisional belief in freedom. One may argue that to believe in freedom, or to live as if humans were free, is a prerequisite

– for being able to speak seriously of "choices",
– that the formulation of moral principles as guidelines for decisions makes sense,
– to justify a responsibility of human beings for their acts and a punishment for certain acts.

With special regard to these arguments I want to discuss here if the alternative between free will and necessity has clear philosophical and practical consequences. If this would be the case, and no decision for one of the two alternatives could be attained based on the choices made up to now, a choice concerning freedom might become necessary.

The psychological and social reality of human will, of the human ability to make decisions and choices, of the phenomenon of conscience, and the feelings of responsibility, guilt, regret and remorse coming along with it, cannot be doubted even if one denotes human willing and acting as »necessary« in a naturalistic-deterministic sense. But then one would say: "Even if somebody believes to be able to make free decisions, these decisions are necessarily made the way they are made." Would it be more adequate, therefore, to address the fundamental choices and the choices described in this book as fundamental convictions and convictions? But this would not eliminate the subjective experience that these attitudes can be justified and changed by choices, nor would it eliminate the fact that both, convictions and choices, are sometimes actually abandoned and replaced by others due to changes of experience and thought.

And the sometimes nagging doubts about the rightness of one's own acting, possibly leading to the opinion that past actions have been wrong, do not disappear because of determinism either. Doubt or remorse cannot be removed by the conviction that our acting is determined by necessity. They are also necessary (in a twofold sense of "neurophysiologically caused, irrefutable" and "morally and socially needed").

So is it the essential characteristic of a belief in the necessity of human will-ing to state unalterable fixations of behaviour and attitudes and insurmounta-ble conflicts between human beings? But "necessary" must always mean as well: "depending on determining factors of influence". Among these factors of influence are, for instance, other people's attempts to persuade and con-vince. These attempts may perhaps "necessarily" be successful, but, on the other hand, it is impossible to predict reliably the kind of influence inducing »necessarily« a human being to a certain behaviour. Consequently, attempts to persuade and convince make equal sense against the backdrop of a belief in necessity and of a belief in free will. And as attempts to persuade and con-vince still make sense in the light of a belief in the necessity of human willing and the acting following therefrom, the same is valid for all other ways of trying to influence human behaviour (making sense not always being tanta-mount to »desirable«): norms, commandments, prohibitions, rewards, punish-ments, moral appeals, inducing compassion and shame, self-criticism and self-discipline, attention, encouragement, contempt or humiliation.

Statements on the freedom or necessity of the will do not have as simple consequences, by far, as it appears at first glance. To concede a high degree of free will to human beings does not necessarily mean that we ascribe a high degree of moral responsibility to them. Some varieties of existentialism as-sume a very high degree of human freedom of the will and at the same time, they conclude from the lack of objective morals that human beings have to be exonerated from all conventional moral claims.

The belief in the necessity of human willing and acting may, if free of moral rigorism, lead to understanding and compassion – and even to an exaggerated leniency at the expense of other people. On the other hand, it is compatible without contradiction with social Darwinist ideas and with the conviction that a great number of people, whose behaviour one rates as intolerable or whose capabilities one considers as insufficient, are incorrigible and that society should be protected from them with utmost severity at all costs, respectively that one can confidently feel justified to allocate them to the less privileged classes. The assumption that people must necessarily act the way they act does not have to be a source of tolerance and social balance. No logical or moral necessity follows from this assumption for treating people less harshly or more humanely whose acts one disapproves or whose efforts one considers as insufficient. One can also draw the opposite conclusion from this assumption without logical contradiction. Thus, death penalty can be defended or attacked

140

from an indeterministic as well as from a deterministic position. Areligious and deterministic ideological zealots often have the same special preference for it as religious indeterminists.

All this shows that it is less important than generally assumed where human willing and acting is located between the opposite poles of free will and necessity. Wherever the position on this continuum may be – the existence and the justification of philosophic ethics and individual morals comes from the undeniable fact that human beings make decisions and that their decisions are influenced and that they are motivated or demotivated not only by information but also by rules of behaviour, by positive and negative incentives, by emotional impulses and by the example of other people.

Neither for the shaping of our individual life, nor for the shaping of our social life we need to make a fundamental choice of freedom. Following a thinking in the causal and deterministic tradition of natural science does not change the fact that we approve certain ways of behaviour and reject others, that we think that a certain conduct should be encouraged or at least tolerated, and that we disapprove or even want to suppress another.

Even if the concepts of "moral responsibility" and "guilt" are no longer understood in their original sense, dependent on a metaphysical concept of free will, they nevertheless remain psychological and social realities and indispensable cultural products, without which neither individual nor social life can be adequately ordered and influenced in a morally positive sense. (On the question of what a sensible concept of guilt in criminal law, independent of an illusionary concept of free will, might look like see 3.7.6.).

It cannot be denied that the concepts of free choice, moral responsibility, and guilt can be misused. They may be used to foster irreconcilability and social barriers or to discipline human individuals by creating guilt complexes or to bend them to an ideology's ideas. Feelings of guilt are powerful social factors of influence and regulation which can be exploited by ideologies to secure their regimen. In such a situation critical reason can clarify and destabilise the underlying dogma.

Having reduced their significance to an adequate measure we can now calmly apply ourselves to realistic considerations on freedom of the will and necessity. That we are not all too free in our willing and acting is commonplace today. Beyond all mechanistic conceptions of the human brain it is evident that our behaviour is determined to a considerable degree by our genetic dispositions (1), our socialisation, and a wealth of biographic and historic accidents. (2) These complex, confusing, and often more or less hidden influences in an ever changing environment together with the complexity of the human brain itself lead to a high variability and unpredictability of human behaviour (even without bringing into play "real" random effects respectively probabilities of quantum physics, hardly of any importance in this context). The complexity of influences and of their processing allows human beings to permanently produce something new, initially existing in a human mind only, be it in the field of concepts, technics, society, politics, art, and – regrettably – also criminal and terroristic activities.

To test alternatives – even in comparison to currently successful ways of behaviour – seems to be an evolutionary developed strategy of more complex brains (already detectable in mice[7]) that serves not only to find the most successful pattern of behaviour but also to prepare possibly more efficient options for the eventuality of a changing situation. "Freedom" appears to be an evolutionary achievement arising and becoming more distinct with the growing complexity of central nervous systems. Yet again too sharp a demarcation between humans and animals fades away. Admittedly, only humans have the capability for deliberation on an explicitly conceptual level and for presenting good reasons. But leaving aside mainly positive specifically human aspects, we must also accept that only human beings have a variability in their behaviour that may lead them to choose suicide, on the one hand, or to commit monstrous mass murder, on the other hand. (3)

The "elbowroom" of human willing is a function of the human brain and no supernatural gift beyond the laws of physics. Today the statement that human thinking and human mind is bound to neurophysiological processes is no longer a provocative proposition of a materialistic and deterministic philosophy of life but a matter of course, nearly generally accepted in (at least natural) science. Already decades ago Julian Huxley has formulated pointedly and suggestively how things stand in principle: "The only possible conclusions from the facts of evolution are that mental and psychological events are also material events, but experienced from inside instead of studied from the outside; that the mental properties of life – knowing, feeling, willing – on the whole make for biological success, since they have been intensified during evolution."[8] (4)

Though such a perspective cannot be the only way to look at our feelings and our will, it definitely has its merits: Feelings and will are no divine gifts but products of our brain which we owe to the fact that, taking stock of evolution, they have contributed to the success of the human species up to now. And this holds true as well for phenomena following from our capability to feel, will and acquire knowledge: morals, culture and civilisation.

Psychological events are electrochemical and chemical processes in and between complex neuronal structures, these structures also disposing of highly specialised media of storage or being able to develop or activate such media in response to certain stimuli. Studying these processes will always encounter limits. It will never be possible to completely describe the processes in an individual human brain at some point x. "... for after a certain point, in its individual creations at least, the mind lies beyond scientific research. Scientific research recognises this limit without indulging in mystical exercises or illusions. The reason for the limit is straightforward: The forms of embodiment that lead to consciousness are unique in each individual, unique to his or her body and individual history." (Edelman[9]) (5)

As soon as an existence of mind and freedom of the will independent of human brains as a material substrate is posited, that is to say, as soon as a dualistic concept with a metaphysical idea of free will is proposed, I will be found unequivocally on the side of the "materialists" und "determinists". As a vehicle of metaphysical speculations mind and freedom of the will belong to a bygone period of human intellectual history, at least if we orient ourselves by the frontline of the best possible knowledge and not by social reality.

In a way, however, mind and freedom of the will may rightly be called "metaphysical", in so far as – though they are products of the human brain and their identity with certain processes in this brain cannot seriously be denied – they cannot be described sufficiently by any description, ever so detailed it may be, of the physical and chemical processes taking place therein. We need psychological, sociocultural, and philosophical concepts to deal adequately with the phenomenon "mind".

An increasing understanding of the mind in neurological, neurophysiological and neurochemical terms is fundamental in a certain sense and will open up new possibilities of intervention to us. But such an understanding becomes possible only because our mind (emerging in our brain) provides us with concepts that tell us and let us think what we want to explain and have to explain.

A neurobiological explanation of the mind is neither sufficient nor exhaustive. It will influence the philosophical, psychological, emotional, cultural, and social concepts we use in our examination of the phenomenon "mind", but it will not replace them (and should not even strive to do so). Concepts of the humanities are also appropriate to examine mental and emotional phenomena from "outside". These are complementary levels of knowledge. "Ideas influence one another, they provide stimulation for the emergence of new ideas, they supersede or transform other ideas. All that materialism could offer for the treatment of these phenomena is a metaphorical reference to the notion of contagion. The comparison is superficial and does not explain anything. Diseases are communicated from body to body through the migration of germs and viruses. Nobody knows anything about the migration of a factor that would transmit thoughts from man to man." (Mises[10])

The better we understand our situation in the world and the functioning of our brain the more concepts like "freedom of the will" and "necessity" are reduced to starting points for our thinking (and we still need them as such, though we owe a lot of confusion and many false conclusions to them). Human willing and acting is neither free in a metaphysical sense (what should be the substrate for that?) nor is it necessary in a plain mechanistic sense. It is complexly influenced and (at least potentially) flexible; it is predictable only with considerable uncertainty and only within limits amenable to purposeful influence.

The traditionally sharp line between freedom of the will and determinism becomes blurred and turns out to be of such little moment that it is verging on insignificance, and this not only as far as practical, moral and social consequences are concerned. One can very consequently and fruitfully adopt a position that formulates and states a compatibility of free will and determinism in a certain sense. Daniel Dennett describes this as the »elbow room« we owe to our biological and cultural evolution. "What we want when we want free will is the power to decide our courses of action, and to decide them wisely, in the light of our expectations and desires. We want to be in control of ourselves, and not under the control of others. We want to be agents, capable of initiating, and taking responsibility for, projects and deeds. All this is ours, I have tried to show, as a natural product of our biological endowment, extended and enhanced by our initiation into society. ... Yes, we can imagine a rational *and deterministic* being who is not deluded when it views its future as open and 'up to' it. Yes, we can imagine a responsible, free agent of whom it is true that whenever it has acted in the past, it could not have acted otherwise … There are real threats to human freedom, but they are not metaphysical. There is political bondage, coercion, the manipulation inducible by the dissemination of misinformation, and the 'forced move' desperation of hunger and poverty."[11] (6)

"Elbow room" is a metaphor for the capability of humans to make decisions after deliberate consideration, taking into account moral norms, visions for the future, wishes and plans and shaping and changing their present and future thereby. Thus, the drama we perform on the stage set by the psychological phenomenon of free will gets its title. (See also the final passage of section 2.1.) Such metaphors are justified because they describe a concrete and exclusive ability which we find only in the most complex decision-making apparatus produced by nature we know: the human brain. This capability means, on the one hand, that our future is open to a certain degree and, on the other hand, it does not change the fact that the decisions we make are biographically and situationally inevitable if looked upon in hindsight. This capability of explication, deliberation, and decision making will continue to have and should have a determining influence on the way we deal with each other and the rest of the world.

That said, we should be aware of the risk to misunderstand determinism: To simpler minds it may appear as if the fact that we are not free in a metaphysical sense could be a reason or excuse for discouragement, passivity or fatalism though it is neither an argument nor a justification for such a conduct or attitude.

3.3. Ethics and Morals

Older and younger than religion

"… moral concepts, principles, and practices have developed by some process of biological and social evolution. Their origin and persistence are due somehow to the fact that they enable human beings, whose natural situation includes a mixture of competitive and co-operative forces, and a need for co-operation, to survive and flourish better, by limiting the competition and facilitate the co-operation." – "… morality has a genuine causal source of its own. It is basically a matter of feelings and attitudes, partly instinctive, developed by biological evolution, and partly acquired, developed by socio-historical evolution and passed on from generation to generation less by deliberate education than by the automatic transmission of cultural traits. Since it has such a source, quite independent of religion, it is certain to survive when religion decays."[1]

John Leslie Mackie

"It is impossible to infer a reign of absolute values from empirically perceived values. One cannot speculate behind whatever may appear acceptable or preferable to us. To presume an unalterable, absolute reign of values behind what the people of a certain community perceive as acceptable and justified is a completely unprovable hypothesis, and moreover an impracticable one: what, after all, should serve us as a standard for errors by which we might recognise the perspective distortion of just our view of the world?"[2]

Reinhold Zippelius

"… morality, this law allegedly given by nature, that is so indefinitely variable and arbitrary, given different weight in each country and assessed in a new way by each expert, be it a priest or a legislator, and permanently modified by the whole world."[3]

Guy de Maupassant

146

I think that a conceptual distinction between ethics and morals facilitates the discussion.

By ethics I will understand all reflections concerning the justifiability and justification of moral attitudes and values, their emergence and origin, the way they are conveyed, and their linguistic and logical structure. Understood in this way ethics is a scientific discipline. Philosophical ethics may even adopt the (erroneous) position that a philosophically founded morality is impossible. (1)

By morals I will understand the moral attitudes and values themselves, the justification presented for them by the individual, and the statements derived therefrom. They can be discussed rationally, but ultimately they require personal decisions.

Ethics and morals together are subject and task of moral philosophy. (One may prefer to call ethics "metaethics" and divide morals into "normative ethics" and "applied ethics" which may sound more "scientific" but does not make things clearer in my opinion.)

For various reasons it was regrettably not possible up to now to sufficiently establish such a conceptual distinction: The call for it is still not widespread enough, and it has to prevail against a long tradition of vague usage of these terms. With »morals« some people think of questionable social conventions first of all. And a considerable part of humankind deliberately wants to justify ethics and morals in an absolute, ideological (religious) manner, and in this case distinctions that bring with them a certain tendency of relativisation are just disturbing. Finally, a lot of people do not want to give up the hope that science might provide us with a morality and a foundation for it. One wants to look upon and present moral attitudes and values as a result of science and this can (seemingly) be done more successfully if you call the morals you stand up for "ethics".

According to the proposed conceptual distinction the choices described in part 1 are an example of a personal morality and sections 2.1. and 2.2. are a contribution to ethics which shall be somewhat expanded here, especially by criticising ethical conceptions that believed or still believe to be able to found morality on anything else than subjective decisions on an individual level and conventions on a social level.

First, let us consider the "is" of the "ought". What becomes probable if one applies logic and observation as an unwilling to believe? Morality is a result of special human capabilities. The human scope of decisions and actions is considerably greater in comparison with animals in many respects. Humans show a variability in their individual and group behaviour exceeding considerably what we can observe in other species. They dispose of conceptual thinking, language, and an evaluation of consequences reaching beyond the actual situational context. All that allows a highly differentiated cultural development. (2) Even if a human being consciously strives to just follow impulses and instincts and is seemingly able to evade morals by doing so, he or she inevitably expresses a moral conviction thereby, because they could orientate their behaviour according to other principles.

Morality is influenced substantially by personal predisposition and external circumstances of life. Against this background education and self-education shape and preserve our morals. The availability and presence of moral content within the consciousness of an individual depends on the number, the frequency, and the circumstances of the respective processes of impression and reminder, as with other content of memory and learning as well, though such a dependence may not be valid to the same degree for moral principles after they have passed a process of identification.

Moral attitudes and values develop and change in the course of a lifetime. "As the preferences of every human individual undergo changes, experience of values does not even provide individual insight with an invariable system of value conceptions." (Zippelius[4]) Moral attitudes and values change also in the course of cultural development and different cultural spheres influence each other.

These facts do not exclude that a certain morality could be set independently of humans, that is to say "objectively", but they indicate to the contrary. As an unwilling to believe one cannot see any convincing arguments for the existence of an order and a ranking of moral attitudes and values that would exist not only in human brains and societies but would be set by a higher authority, be it a god, nature or - like in Marxism – "the laws of history". All attempts to define a highest good or a ranking of moral attitudes and values amongst all that what human beings have regarded as valuable hitherto in a way based on more than subjective conviction have failed – even if a specific conviction of this kind may appear especially impressing when supported by a locally prevailing tradition or even by elementary norms found near-universally in human societies.

The moral attitudes and values we observe are very different and in part

148

highly contradictory. From their mere existence follows no decision on their rightness. The "ought" is a part of the "is", but no "ought" can be derived from the "is". No prescription follows from the description, no choice amongst the norms from describing them. This a statement of little originality since Hume (3) and (though less clear) also Kant[5] which, nevertheless, cannot be repeated often enough in our time as well.

We can hope that understanding our evolutionary heritage contributes to a reasonable, humane morality. "During the years to come an evolutionary ethics will probably be based analogously on the discoveries of sociobiology which takes into account the genetic foundations of our social behaviour and strives to formulate norms and values in a way that makes them compatible with our evolutionary heritage, rationally comprehensible, intersubjectively enforceable, and suitable to secure a humane life for humans at least in the medium term." (Vollmer[6]) But we should nevertheless keep in mind clearly that no moral standards can be derived from biological evolution (though it has created the possibility and the necessity for such standards first of all by developing the human brain). An "evolutionary ethics" can just clarify preconditions relevant for the setting of our norms. It allows us to take a look at our origin, our past, and our moral status quo and gives us interesting hints as to which morals might have prospects to become generally accepted and to which degree. Taking into account the knowledge of evolutionary biology may thus influence the process of setting norms. But this knowledge does not provide us criteria of selection as to which norms we should accept. It cannot take setting norms of our shoulders, be it in the realm of concrete personal morals or regarding a specific cultural development or social norms. Neither natural sciences nor social sciences can make the decisions for a certain morality for us.

"Verifiable is only what is, not what ought to be", says Ayer[7]. Therewith the still popular method to derive values from nature – and especially the nature of humans – is criticised once and for all in a few words. Moral behaviour is a product of nature as well, and in so far nature is not morally indifferent. But there is no moral criterion in nature to judge the behaviour it creates, nature's only criterion is reproductive success. "The 'true good' and the 'true evil' did not come into the world but with human beings. As a result of their considerable degrees of freedom they can set moral norms, observe or neglect them, and they have to take the responsibility following from that." "Ethics does not need an authorisation by evolutionary biology nor is this possible at all."

149

(Vogel[8, 9]) (4) (5)

Ethics and morals – and the complete cultural development they are a part of – are a consequence of biological evolution just as egoism, parochialism, and brutality. What is natural for human beings is the range of decision making and actions available to them, from murder to self-sacrifice, for instance. Howsoever human beings behave: if a certain behaviour is possible, it is automatically "natural" as well (even if it may be a very rare variant, and perhaps only as a rare variant compatible with human existence). The person running amok, the fanatic suicide assassin (in this case the German term "self-murderer" is adequate for once) or the mass murderer practising cannibalism, they are as "natural" as the women or men sacrificing their lives to save others. Without any additional criteria of demarcation classifying behaviour as "natural" is nothing more than a description of reality, of the status quo, of the individually or statistically observable ways of behaviour.

We should not idealise to much that human beings are capable of far-reaching altruism. This altruism is linked very closely to the extended human range of perception, action and influence, and often enough it is »just« reciprocal altruism, morality in terms of usefulness. If we want to assess altruistic behaviour adequately, it is always worthwhile to look at it from the aspect of self-interest as well. The more we feel threatened and burdened by tides of refugees, for instance, the more many of us become reluctant to welcome refugees and the more willing we are to invest in measures to prevent their arrival or to repel them, on the one hand, and to take action against the misery in their countries of origin, on the other hand.

If altruistic ways of behaviour have selfish aspects too just we should not belittle them just because of that. To many of us the misery of others produces psychological discomfort, and we want to see it relieved. Frequently our behaviour is determined or co-determined to a considerable degree by emotional motives which – even if we consider it as a form of selfishness to strive for the fulfilment of emotional wants and needs –have little to do with what can be understood as the self-interest of a rational egoist. Thus, we can aim primarily at relieving the misery of others and receive the improvement of our own well-being caused thereby just as a side-effect.

On closer consideration our behaviour is often determined by a mixture of altruistic and selfish motives. Shaftesbury already took into account very well this kind of influences which are often enough neglected by philosophers: "You have heard it, my friend, as a common saying, that interest governs the world. But, I believe, whoever looks narrowly into the affairs of it will find that passion, humour, caprice, zeal, faction, and a thousand other springs, which are counter to self-interest, have as considerable a part in the movement of this machine."[10]

The sentence "No 'ought' can be derived form an 'is'!" is sometimes underestimated. Its real significance lies not only in the fact that it is illicit to derive an ought from an is but also in this being nearly impossible or at least completely unattractive to most people without introducing further criteria of selection. In committing the is-ought fallacy de facto never all of nature or all of the culture created on this basis is taken as a norm because any discriminatory power would be lost thereby and the procedure would become absurd. Then it would mean no more than accepting the status quo as the moral ideal and to elevate it to a norm (what would include, alike, discussions in moral philosophy, moral heroes, Nazi extermination camps or human capability for mass murder). Is and ought would be identical, not only in a descriptive but also in a prescriptive or normative sense. Therefore, the normative is always obtained by some kind of selection from the spectrum of the natural. Instead of recommending us this selection as a proposal for a norm which we should accept by an individual and cultural effort, it is then presented to us as the "true" and "one and only" nature, or as the nature privileged as such by divine commandments.

To identify the is-ought fallacy the name of the game for critical thinking is: "Look for the normative sentence hidden in the 'justifying' factual statements!"

"Back to nature!" is as inappropriate as a watchword as "Leave nature behind!" Neither are human beings evil as natural beings nor good as cultural beings and the reversal is equally wrong. Which dispositions and varieties of behaviour can be acted out to which degree depends largely on the respective cultural and historic situation. Murderers and rapists are amongst us in every society (and their impulses are in us too), as well as moral heroes and saints and in between we, the majority, showing less extreme moral qualities and a sufficient control of socially negative impulses, in different gradations. And one has to be jolly glad if one lives in a social structure that keeps negative extremes within bounds and represses them (though the capability to create such cultural structures is also part of the spectrum of our evolutionary developed behavioural dispositions).

Reason alone does not provide us with morals, nor can we justify morals or reach a consensus on certain morals by reason alone. But reason may help us to see and formulate moral problems clearly, to recognise the consequences and options for acting following from the positions we take, to develop positions as consistent as possible based upon that, and, finally, to make adequate decisions. It may help us to assess and to overcome differences in moral judgement caused by different levels of information that people with identical or rather similar morals may have (a point of great practical importance!). And it may help us to recognise differences resulting from the application of identical or similar moral attitudes and values on different historic and social situations.

Reason enables us to gain clarity about human natural dispositions affecting moral behaviour. If a morality ignores evolutionary shaped ways of reaction and behaviour, it will lead to hypocrisy the more likely the more it does so. But this does not mean that it would always be desirable to allow for or to consent to "natural" moral dispositions of a majority, nor does it mean that a morality complying with such dispositions would necessarily be accepted, as historic and cultural facts play an important role in that too.

If we find, for example, that men, by their genetic heritage, have a lower inclination to sexual fidelity than women (statistically speaking, as we should always do in such statements), then this does mean that a morality accommodating for that is easier to observe for men, but it does not mean that we would have to or ought to accept such a morality. Such a finding by reason does not change the fact that a man and a woman have to determine individually the conditions under which they can and want to live together and that these conditions will not be the same for different people.

By evolutionary theory we have acquired a fascinating extension of our knowledge about or own nature and a better understanding of our behaviour. Sociobiology, evolutionary psychology, and developmental psychology enable us to better describe the biological part of causes for our moral status quo. But we should beware of believing that its cultural and historic causes could be inferred more or less necessarily therefrom and would already be described thereby too. Culture and history could have taken a completely different course on the same biological basis if other configurations of events would have occurred by chance – and they have taken quite a different course under different overall conditions in human societies showing just a slight genetic divergence. The distinctive intercultural variation of moral systems is rightly considered as an important distinguishing mark to even our closest animal relatives. (6)

If we are able to explain our morality better, the individual and social process of setting norms is not rendered unnecessary or meaningless thereby. It is one thing to explain morals and another thing to judge it and to make one's choice for a certain morality.

Now it is time to proceed from the is of the ought (whose analysis philosophy shares with a variety of other scientific disciplines) to the specific task of moral philosophy: How to make a choice amongst the various ought-offers and ought-claims?

To find and to justify a morality that would be indubitable for every reasonable human being is a driving force for the formulation of fundamental moral rules attempted again and again. These fundamental rules are often described as a part of ethics, but they belong to morals - at least if their acceptance is concretely recommended. They are presented in different varieties as procedural rules whose application promises the answer to moral questions without a need to bring in values and moral attitudes going beyond the respective fundamental moral rule.

Confucius: "What you do not want done to yourself, do not do to others."[11]

Kant: "So act as if the maxim of your action were to become through your will a universal law."[12]

And – in the Anglo-Saxon utilitarian tradition – R. Robinson: "Any kind of thing is bad if it, or the pursuit of it, increases the misery of living things upon the whole. – No kind of act may be forbidden unless its discontinuance would lessen misery upon the whole. – Anything is good if the pursuit of it pleases somebody and does not increase misery."[13]

A serious morality without some principle of universalisation is hard to imagine. It does not follow from this, however, that such a principle of universalisation, or a concrete formulation thereof as in one of the procedural rules mentioned above, would be self-evident. To the contrary, they have to be accepted by decisions which are anything but obvious. It is imaginable, for instance, that a thief rejects Kant's imperative deliberately, relying – very realistically – on the assumption that the maxim of his acting will not be generally adopted. We consider this behaviour as morally wrong, as a rule, but that does not necessarily mean that it is unreasonable. "In other words, an imperative demanding that I be guided only by norms which I might wish to be universal has itself no logical or psychological foundation; I can reject it without falling

153

into contradiction, and I may admit it as a supreme guideline only by virtue of an arbitrary decision unless it appears within the context of religious worship." (Kolakowski[14]) However, it has to be stated (as already discussed earlier, see 2.1. and 2.2) that thoroughly considered decisions of conscience are not "arbitrary" and that decisions for a religious moral codex are certainly not less "arbitrary" than those for a morality that is justified otherwise. There is not only no logical or psychological basis for applying rules of the kind of the categorical imperative but not even a convincing moral justification. Absolutising single moral values like it was done by Kant in his essay "On a Supposed Right to Lie from Altruistic Motives"[15] turns into unreason. To avoid this one may try to save rules of universalisation by including exceptions or saving clauses (you have to tell the truth except if you would harm yourself or someone else severely by doing so). But Kant consequently rejected such exceptions from »true principles« in his essay (because they "would nullify their universality"). He felt very well that exceptions carry a kind of vagueness which transforms these principles into nothing more than heuristic instruments of moral considerations. And that is indeed the status they deserve, but then they no longer fulfil Kant's lofty ambitions of justification.

Applying rules of universalisation without exception is not adequate to the complex reality we find ourselves confronted with. Those who want to follow rules of universalisation without compromise will not only be compelled to morally erroneous decisions in some cases, but be predestined to become victims, and their behaviour often has to be considered rather as stupidity and rigidity than as moral heroism.

Take the Golden Rule as an example. We will have to neglect it, time and again, in order to defend fundamental values of our society. Criminals and terrorists cannot be treated the way we would like to be treated ourselves (though we are obliged to deal with them according to the rule of law and human rights). And for much smaller moral problems too the following is valid: if you want to live and survive without sacrificing yourself as a "saint" (which may be seen as a highly dubious ideal), you will have to renounce now and then to applying the categorical imperative on the basis of your own moral attitudes and values (let alone an absolute moral duty) in a strict sense, even if you accept it as an important moral criterion in principle. In a weighing up morality it is justified to look upon principles of universalisation just as heuristic criteria. This is an imperative of an "ability to cope with life" following from a realistic assumption of the level of moral behaviour we can expect from other people.

Let me clarify this by an example which is rather harmless but close to everyday life: If a state imposes an unfair system of taxes and social security charges that burdens disproportionately already relatively modest incomes that have been acquired by personally done, socially useful work under hard conditions, and at the same time disproportionately low wages are paid for this work, then it may be morally justified that, for example, a nurse disadvantaged by such circumstances makes use of modest possibilities of tax evasion if able to do so, while, on the other hand, the tax evasion of a highly paid sports star or manager lacks moral justification and hardly deserves any understanding.

What has a universalisation rule, let us take Kant's imperative as a concrete example here, to say about the behaviour of our nurse? The principle that everybody bends the rules of law as he or she feels appropriate can certainly not be a general principle of morality or legislation. Nevertheless, it is morally justifiable that even the citizens of a democratic society defend themselves against excessive demands and overtaxing of the state, and that they do this in a completely private manner too, without necessarily engaging in political resistance and taking the considerable burden associated therewith. In a weighing up morality such a behaviour finds its place, but it cannot be formulated as a general principle of legislation. Of course, for reasons of legal certainty, the legal system of the state cannot tolerate the morally justifiable limited breach of law of even relatively economically disadvantaged ordinary people (though the wrong path of disloyalty to law is not really taken in a substantial sense thereby). But the range of punishment for such offences, from relatively mild financial penalties to non-suspended prison sentences depending on the amount of money involved, already reflects the (reasonably) strongly differentiated moral judgement depending on the circumstances.

That a general legislation can also deal quite well practically with such a behaviour of the citizens is shown by the fact that it does indeed live with such incidents without taking serious efforts to prosecute such offences more than by chance and sporadically (to do otherwise would not make any sense by just considering the cost-benefit ratio and the more so because it would promote disaffection with the state). One may even state it as a principle that the more narrowly and out of touch with reality a society regulates and restricts freedom the more it will have to accept tacitly that a consequent enforcement of its norms is impossible. All sorts of examples may be found in every society (for our own take, amongst others, unreported employment in household work and home care). In extreme cases it may be true what Heinz Bethge, former president of the Leopoldina in Halle, stated concerning his steadfast struggle for a science that could be taken seriously in the so-called German Democratic Republic: "In our country the state lived on the deviation from the rules." (quoted from memory)

Let us consider another existentially more important example: A human being fighting for survival in a desolate situation of misery within a severely unjust class society lacking social security mechanisms cannot be morally bound to an unconditional prohibition of theft. Nevertheless, the morally justified softening of the prohibition of theft in such a situation is not suitable as a maxim for general legislation.

Examples like this show that it depends on the respective social circumstances to which degree people behave and can behave morally and are able to consider rules of universalisation in their behaviour.

Universalisation rules have a limited scope regarding the behaviour they demand and justify. Often enough it is not easy at all to decide whether we should follow a certain universalisation rule and, if so, which and why and how far. As far as moral philosophy formulates ideals by universalisation rules it should denote them as such – or as aids for weighing up – and it should not maintain that a violation of such ideals and a well-considered modification of rules which may follow from a weighing of different moral attitudes and values in a concrete life situation would necessarily be immoral. There are responsible moral decisions which are guided by maxims that would not be suitable, or would be suitable as such only by a considerable amount of subtlety, as principles of a general legislation – decisions of which we know this and of which we also know that they will never become an (explicit) principle of a general legislation even if that would be basically possible. (7)

Consequences from universalisation rules can be drawn on very different levels of abstraction and generalisation. And it is not at all clear in advance that more general consequences lead to more adequate moral weighing. Let us follow up on the examples from the social sector mentioned above. A universal rule on a low level of abstraction could be: "A person who has no other possibility to secure home care for close relatives does not behave morally wrong if he or she violates social security or tax law in need" (which could principally be converted in a legal text too: "… is not guilty of an offence if …"). Is such a universal rule morally less adequate than a rule that obliges to

156

respect law without exception on a higher level of generalisation in the interest of legal certainty or does it not even represent a more adequate moral weighing?

And also in decisions concerning not only individual welfare universalisation rules like Kant's imperative have their limits. Thus, the maxim that one should proceed against societal developments considered as undesirable and threatening, such as armament, environmental damage, or "moral decay" (for not to forget another side of the political spectrum) by acts of coercion – even if only in the form of coercive 'non-violent' action – cannot be made a principle of general legislation, as this could impair social life to the point of impossibility. And nevertheless, such acts may be morally justified or even morally required in specific cases. People differ considerably in their moral judgement on concrete cases and general moral rules contribute little to resolve these differences (which does not mean that we cannot and should not discuss rationally under which circumstances such acts may be justified).

General fundamental moral rules do not justify moral decisions sufficiently without further presuppositions. Even after one has made the choice to accept such a rule one still has to set other values as these rules lead to different results depending on the presupposed morals. (See also Topitsch[16]) There may be quite different opinions on what one does not want to be done to oneself and what one should not do to others therefore, or on what one wants as a maxim for a general law, and on what increases or lessens the misery of living things, and, furthermore, on the priority of different interests of different living things in case of conflict. These differences are due to conceptions of moral value that go beyond general moral rules and that fill these rules with moral content first of all.

Let me illustrate this by an example from the history of Christianity: the inquisitor who condemns the heretic to be burned at the stake for a double reason, namely, to use the »bad« example to set a warning one against it and to save the soul of the heretic, may well feel himself in accordance with the rule of Confucius. He may argue that, as for him the salvation of one's soul is the ultimate goal (of much greater importance than the sustainment of earthly life), he himself would want to be burned at the stake if he were a heretic (in principle at least, as long the concrete situation is not to be expected). Furthermore, the maxim of his will, namely, to save the souls of as many human beings as possible, appears suitable to him to be valid as a principle of general legislation. For him, burning heretics at the stake does not increase the misery

157

of living things upon the whole, it does not even appear as a misfortune for the heretic himself as the inquisitor supposes that death is not the end of his or her life. On the contrary, he believes that by prohibition and punishment of heresy misery is lessened upon the whole. Burning heretics at the stake may also please himself and others while not appearing to increase misery.

Convinced National Socialists could have accepted Kant's categorical imperative too, by just doing relatively little mental acrobatics and invoking alleged special rights of the strongest or a superior race and the irrefutable necessity to eliminate a Jewish world conspiracy. Admittedly, it would have been much more difficult for them, or would have been possible only by practising outrageous hair-splitting, to see themselves in accordance with the rules of Confucius or R. Robinson.

What follows from these examples? Even if accepted by a moral decision, universalist procedural rules face the problem of lack or deficiency of moral content and, consequently, of limited practical utility and possible deformability.

We are confronted with the sometimes completely different conclusions that are drawn from general moral rules according to the presupposed philosophy of life and morality. George Bernhard Shaw has expressed this very pointedly and elegantly in his comment on Confucius' Golden Rule: "Do not do unto others as you would have that they should do unto you. Their tastes may not be the same."[17] This hyperbole reaches further than it might appear at the first moment: A distinct majority of people will be able to agree largely on the consequences that should be drawn from a golden rule (be it formulated negatively or positively) to satisfy basic human needs and respect basic rights – and that does already mean a lot. Nevertheless, Shaw has formulated a corrective that deserves due regard alongside Confucius' rule. Shaw's dictum does not only point to the diversity and relativity of moral conceptions but also to the obligation to respect them as long as there are no grave reasons against it, in other words, it points to the obligation to respect the autonomy of others (and especially of minorities).

Hans Kelsen justly draws our attention to the fact that the Golden Rule does not give the answer to the question of the right moral and legal order but already presupposes such an order. "Somebody might not mind at all that others tell lies to him, since he – rightly or wrongly – thinks himself to be clever enough to find out the truth and thus to protect himself against the liar. Then, according to the golden rule, he is allowed to lie."[18] One may object that it would be very exhausting and not very promising in the long run to find out the truth in a completely mendacious society and that it would surely be no fun to live in it. But that does not alter the fact that all sorts of extreme and socially harmful wishes and moral ideas are principally compatible with the Golden Rule.

Let us have a look on another social conflict, now fortunately belonging to the past more and more, to illustrate the vagueness and interpretability of universalisation rules. The Golden Rule will hardly prompt smokers to spare non-smokers their harmful and annoying smoke in restaurants as they themselves do not object getting shrouded by it (as demonstrated by the insufficient effect of all efforts for voluntary smoking bans). Even if interpreted as a general principle not to harm or bother others without good reason, the Golden Rule would still allow smokers to see their pleasure as a sufficiently good reason to do so.

Universalisation rules are a subjectively and intersubjectively valuable heuristic principle of morals, but they are insufficient to create an intersubjectively justifiable morality. And they are certainly no way to reach the illusionary goal of an objective morality.

What matters more? Space for people living in the way of modern civilisation or the protection of the way of life and the culture of indigenous people and the habitat of animals? The life of animals or the culinary pleasures of humans? The preservation of life for as many human beings as possible or cultural and aesthetic needs and wishes? To keep alive five ordinary people or one closely related person or an eminent sportsperson, scientist or politician? No rule of universalisation spares us the moral decisions that must be made here. (8)

Now I want to make some comments on discourse ethical concepts, a variant of moral procedural rules that has gained some importance in the present. These concepts strive to establish rules of communication for the process of knowledge and the sciences and for setting and justifying moral and social norms, and they claim that we could find rationally justified, objective (or may be better: privileged) intersubjective guidelines for our acting by following these rules. If not emphasising that the decision for discourse and for accepting the results obtained by a certain kind of discourse and the consequences thereof ultimately have a subjective or at least conventional character, despite all the rationality (hopefully) invested in the discourse (and admitting this runs contrary to the discourse ethicists' hope for objectivity), these concepts commit a variant of the is-ought-fallacy by deriving an obligation for discourse respectively a certain kind of discourse and for the acceptance of the results gained thereby from the mere existence of discourse respectively a certain kind of discourse. Why should we regard certain discourses and their results as morally binding just because they meet the requirements of a fair discourse? To do this we have to accept, first of all, values like autonomy and equal rights of persons and the discourse itself as an instance bringing about morals, and we have to accept all this by moral decisions, and thus, we find ourselves in the same situation as with other moral procedural rules.

Apart from the problem of justification we face here again, it is hardly feasible to define sufficiently the circumstances and precautions telling us if and when an ideal and fair discourse takes place or has taken place which could become the source of our individual and social morals. Could it be denied (to choose examples from a democratic society deliberately) that the McCarthyism of the 1950s or the sometimes rigid system of pressure of "political correctness" concerning groups and individuals facing social marginalisation and discrimination or some kind of disadvantage (as well as the following countermovements) are forms of discourse or the result of certain discourses? It has been clear to Seneca already (see his remark quoted in 3.7.1., p. 302) that democracy too is capable of moral errors and crimes (even if it should be able to achieve "a discourse free of coercion"). And, on the other hand, one cannot seriously maintain that morally significant discourses take place only in democratic societies.

But even we take for granted a rational and fair discourse, an "ideal speech situation", we will have to make decisions finally, moral decisions and decisions for and between values in our private lives and norm setting decisions for our societies, and the latter will not get beyond a conventional foundation, and it will by no means be possible to found them on a "postconventional" authority. I point to my discussion of Peter Singer's positions to clarify this (see especially different chapters of section 3.6.) by which, I believe, one can realise quite well that even a rational discourse of moral questions leaves us with very different alternatives to decide between. Such decisions require a hierarchy of values and moral attitudes and a weighing between them. They cannot appeal to rational arguments alone. As reasonable a morality gained by discourse may appear – it always presupposes ideals like those of a good life and of justice. The catchword "postconventional morality" (Apel[19]) promises too much. For the justification of morals, we still have to rely on subjective convictions, decisions and choices in the personal sphere and on convention in the social sphere – and this holds true even if a rational discussion of moral questions free of ideological and religious prejudice should have become the norm someday.

Though their merits for the justification of morals remain limited, the concern of discourse ethical concepts, namely, to call for and to further a thorough, rational, pluralistic and democratic discussion of moral questions is estimable and worthy of support.

As far as Habermas is concerned, growing doubts as to the normative power of the principle of discourse shine through in later publications, and it appears as another, very formal, just newly formulated kind of a universalisation rule on the model of Kant's imperative. "For the justification of moral norms, the discourse principle takes the form of a universalisation principle."[20] Therewith discourse ethics is subject to the same limitations already discussed for other universalisation rules. Discourse ethics can only free itself form the charge of formalism, respectively of being indifferent or void of content, by alleging that a discourse undistorted by authority would be able to determine something like a »enlightened interest of human beings« and to bring about its acceptance.

This is where the interest-based concepts in moral philosophy start from. Why should we read all those circuitous, convoluted books on discourse (9) if such an enlightened interest can be determined by moral philosophy in a reasonable discussion and thus can provide us with a foundation for our value system? The dependency on questionable and possibly erroneous majority opinions is supposed to be eliminated by an intersubjective rationality of enlightened interest.

Let us take a short look on two worthwhile examples of interest ethics: Hoerster's "interest-founded ethics"[21] as a German, continental European, more value oriented concept and Singer's "equal consideration of interests"[22] as an Anglo-Saxon more preference utilitarian oriented concept.

Hoerster puts the enlightened interest of human beings on this planet centre stage, if not the interest of everybody then at least that of the overwhelming majority, an interest that we can supposedly determine in a rationally plausible way and then make an intersubjective basis of morality. The fact that there are deviant interests of a small number of fellow human-beings does not devalue this concept, even if these deviant interests, together with the manipulation of a great number of other people concerning the consideration of their own well understood interest, has led to historic disasters time and again and will, alas, lead to such disasters in the future too. Hoerster's concept comes from the philosophy of law originally and is therefore discussed in more detail in the related chapter 3.7.1.. At this point I want to give only one hint about the limitations of this concept: If we do not want to introduce a far-reaching (and therefore inevitably controversial) idea of a good life under the notion of "enlightened interest", we can only make plausible thereby some elementary moral demands, like a general prohibition of killing and theft, or a general obligation to help those in need, and even then we do not get a sufficient basis for argumentation against all kind of exceptions claimed by different cultures and regimes.

Singer's preference utilitarian concept postulates that the interests of all people and – in a further step – all living beings capable of suffering or experiencing enjoyment have to be considered equally to the extent they are existing. This is appealing because it conveys the impression that the only thing we have to do, is to assess interests empirically without any need to judge and select them as, for example, "enlightened". Equal consideration of equal interests, for example, the interest in life and in a life as free from suffering and as fulfilled as possible, has a lot of explosive potential that can be used to question and extend our moral views, as exemplarily done by Singer in his "Practical Ethics". The problem is, however, that we have to and want to consider a large variety of different interests. Therefore, we cannot avoid a ranking of interests. And even if we have accepted such a ranking in principle, we have to address problems of weighing. What takes priority, the survival interest of as many human beings as possible or of small populations of animals threatened with extinction? Is it morally required that higher-ranking interests, like the survival interest of human beings, should completely oust the pursuit of other interests, like the desire for beauty or cultural enjoyment? Is the elimination of interests of lower priority really conducive to the pursuit of interests of higher priority – especially in a long-term perspective?

In spite of their limitations, the concepts of interest ethics elucidate one more time the important role reason plays in moral questions, and how inadequate it is to regard the terms "good" and "evil" or "morally right" and "morally wrong" as nothing more than an expression of our approval or disapproval, our liking or disliking. Yes, moral judgements are »only« a consequence of what we have set as our morality, but they are more than an expression of emotions. This is true, in any case, if these judgements are based on thorough moral weighing.

Partly people hold on with great obstinacy to attitudes and ways of reaction that are long since nowhere near adequate to the altered situation they find themselves in. These may be notions of honour or possession, the rules of a tribal society, or traditional religious patterns of thought. Nevertheless, we can call people's prejudices into question. We should feel encouraged to do so by the surprisingly quick, though relative success produced thereby at least in the part of the world influenced by the Enlightenment. Well, the authority of religion has been undermined here for centuries already. But then, in the last fifty to a hundred years things got going rather dynamically, despite the setbacks of National Socialism, Stalinist communism, Maoism, their totalitarian aftermath and the renewed threat by politically instrumentalised religion, as represented especially by Islamic fundamentalism.

The right questions once asked (Why should women have an inferior status and inferior rights than men? What justifies discrimination of homosexuality and other minority sexual or gender orientations? and so forth ...), positions that are ill-considered, or can only be justified in an authoritarian manner, fall behind sooner or later. Regarding problems like euthanasia or our treatment of animals the change is underway though comparably broad aha experiences are yet to come. The persistent questioning, the ever newly revived Socratic midwifery, which does not have to confine itself to Socratic doubt, will eventually bring forth the change.

Fundamental and procedural rules of morality do not provide us with a ranking of interests, values, and moral attitudes and do not spare us the weighing between them. Tacitly these rules build upon morals taken for granted in advance. Without an "infusion" of values and moral attitudes they remain half-empty and do not cope sufficiently with the complexity of our real life. Such rules are valuable, nevertheless. They can help us to review the contents, the consistency, and the adequacy of a morality and can thus contribute to moral change and progress. They can help us in finding decisions on the basis of a certain morality. They can make much clearer what the consequences of certain ways of acting and certain decisions are. They have, in other words, an important auxiliary function in preparing moral weighing. In this sense they are "generators of morals".

But even after a rational weighing of interests we cannot do without controversial value decisions under certain circumstances, and we cannot spare ourselves those moral dilemmas and conflicts where only casting lots appears

adequate. To accept this does not mean to make a case for a subjectivist decisionism.

> "A man who sincerely makes a factual judgement may be said to be express-
> ing his belief about a factual issue, but that does not support a subjectivist
> view of factual judgements. The subjectivist interpretation comes in when
> one says that one who makes a moral judgement expresses his attitude, and
> *that is all there is to be said about it.*"[23]
>
> Bernard Williams

> "I do not believe that a god has handed us over moral laws on stone tablets.
> Instead we have to rely on ourselves and on reason to develop a position as
> consistent as possible."[24]
>
> Peter Singer

3.4. God and Religion

Inevitable antiques?

> "I take this opportunity to remark that the word »atheism« contains a surreptitious presupposition insofar as it presumes theism as self-evident."[1]

> Arthur Schopenhauer

> "Instead of asking whether God, reincarnation, immortality, or other paranormal phenomena exist, we should ask *why* there is such a strong propensity to believe in them."[2]

> Paul Kurtz

Belief in god or gods and religion astound as lastingly successful phenomena of human culture with an almost worldwide appearance and importance, regretfully still not belonging to bygone times. On the one hand, these phenomena call for explanation, and on the other hand, they have to be examined concerning their possible truth and psychosocial value – and be it as nothing more than fictions in the sense of a philosophy of "as if". (Vaihinger[3])

Meanwhile it is quite hard to keep track of the diversity of explanations offered for the phenomena god and religion. There are genetic, evolutionary biological, psychological, psychiatric, sociological, economic, political, and comparative historical approaches of explanation. Eventually also brain research strives to contribute to the explanation of religion by gaining information about the representation of religious experiences and ideas in the brain. Here I just want to give a short account of all these approaches, not intended to be exhaustive but enabling the reader to proceed further in any of these directions on his own.

Since E. O. Wilson proposed an evolutionary explanation of religion in his book "On Human Nature"[4] the attention of many scientists has been drawn to its evolutionary benefit. This is pointedly expressed by Daniel Dennett: "To an evolutionist, rituals stand out like peacocks in a sunlit glade."[5] (1)

Attempts to explain religion genetically are closely related to evolutionary biologically ones because a genetic anchoring and the spread of a genetic predisposition to religion is not conceivable on a broader level without an evolutionary advantage of such a predisposition. Any details concerning a genetic anchoring of religiosity and spirituality are first of all proximate (directly explaining the predisposition to religiosity), not ultimate (explaining the evolutionary advantage) causes of religiosity and spirituality. In his book "The God Gene"[6] Hamer gives a good overview (despite the simplifying, eye-catching title) of scientific findings concerning a genetic predisposition to spirituality (respectively an emotional religiosity which can be seen as a basis for an "intrinsic" religiosity, which will be discussed here later, in contrast to a predominantly social or "extrinsic" religiosity). Findings range from twin research to the impact of neurochemical processes and their genetically determined variations on spirituality to the interaction between population genetics and religious regulations of mate selection. Hamer´s findings are certainly only a simplifying start for explaining the genetic part in the causation of spirituality. (For critical remarks see Vaas[7] and Wikipedia article on God gene) Regrettably Hamer does not have the critical distance to religion brought about by an epistemological position for which the postulate of good reasons as a presupposition to accept concepts and statements about the world is of central significance in the realm of philosophy of life as well and so he declares that the act of believing "is one of the greatest gifts of being human."(See the last page of the book cited above; but it should not be withhold that he strictly advocates a tolerant conception of religion.)

If an evolutionary approach actually wants to contribute something significant to the explanation of religion, it must make plausible that there is a specific evolutionary advantage of religiosity and religion. All explanatory attempts of this kind have to confront the question whether religion really is evolutionary adaptive in a direct manner, or if it is just exaptive, that is to say, first of all a by-product of other evolutionary advantageous traits, or if it is even nothing more than such a by-product.

Religious ideas could be adaptive because they may confer an advantage for the struggle against disease via placebo effect. They could be a psychological reward and "provide human beings with an innate sense of optimism" (Hamer, p. 12), contributing to a better coping with stress and the inevitable sufferings and burdens of life. Other theories have some attractiveness too: Religion might go back to magical fertility rites and mother cults by which archaic women's alliances tried to enhance their reproductive success and which have been transformed by a patriarchal takeover of power later. (Sommer[8]) Developing religiosity might have been of crucial importance for the survival of human groups in critical periods of human history as during population bottlenecks 80000 to 60000 years ago when human population possibly dropped to around 2000 fertile individuals, thus coming closer to extinction as ever since. (Rossano[9])

Already in the early phase of evolutionary reflection on religion E. O. Wilson[4] proposed that the readiness to be indoctrinated could be a neurologically based learning rule that evolved through the selection of clans competing one against the other. Later concepts of group selection have been elaborated further especially by his namesake D. S. Wilson.[10] Nevertheless it remains highly controversial whether selection at group level really is a significant evolutionary factor. We do not necessarily need biological group selectionist hypotheses to explain, for instance, xenophobia and religious fanatism. If advantages of religion play a significant role for the evolutionary development of cooperativity is doubtful to the present day. On a historic scale religion is old but on an evolutionary scale it is young (which is a very weighty argument that religion is just to be regarded as a by-product of evolutionarily traits useful for other reasons, and is only later influencing the historical success - or also failure - of certain groups of people as a cultural and power-political factor, no longer causing any major evolutionary changes).

There are other more exaptive attempts of explanation: Religious people could be more attractive as spouses and life partners if they were as well more sensitive, more musical, more eloquent, and more interested in ornaments and aesthetics (just think about the affinity for the ritual of church weddings persisting especially in women even in relatively secular societies like ours). Various evolutionary advantageous capabilities show up in religious conceptions: cooperativity with mutual exchange and promotion of social cohesion, sanctioning of cooperative and uncooperative behaviour (and especially coping with the problem of free riders), conceptualisation, creating theories about the world and the intentions of other acting beings in this world, empathy, and finally also the capability of romantic, irrational love, with the potential to stabilise human bonds. Nothing of all that is necessarily bound to religion, but religiosity could thus be a by-product of other evolutionary advantageous capabilities. When discussing such approaches of explanation, we should not overlook, however, that just by making religions possible evolutionary developed capabilities make no big contribution to explain why religions and certain specific religions have actually emerged. (2) Many of these capabilities make possible science and art too. But that is not very revealing for their historic origin either.

Among all the evolutionary advantageous capabilities that may have played a role for the development of religion as exaptive factors let us finally have a somewhat closer look on the human capability of intentional thinking. To ascribe intentions to natural phenomena and especially moving objects is no doubt an evolutionary strategy essential for survival in many cases, for example, when fleeing from predators. But this intentional thinking roves around. We know from child psychology that children think animistically and dualistically as well as finalistically and teleologically, that is to say, they ascribe a soul to many objects and regard it as independent from the body or object and, furthermore, they tend to allege a meaning and purpose to everything. Adults too have more or less difficulties to break away from such ideas, as we can see from the widespread belief in life after death or from the difficulties with overcoming the propensity to search for a meaning in diseases. (3)

Belief in authority, to be considered as evolutionary advantageous at least for children as a rule, contributes only to a limited extent to explain the formation of religions, but it is a good candidate for explaining the successful passing on and persistence of religious ideas. (See note 1.2. (2))

Evolutionary approaches to explain religion open up a lot of interesting aspects but we should not overestimate them. Historical and social psychological explanations, addressing later developments, make an indispensable contribution to explaining the formation and the success of religions. It is certainly an important stabilising factor for religion that individuals can derive psychological and social benefits from it. Allport investigates this aspect of an instrumentalisation of religion by his concept of "extrinsic religiosity".[11] He already presents a multitude of interesting reflections and empirical findings concerning the analysis of the religious status quo of a (his) society. But he is biased in favour of religion; and by developing the distinction between "extrinsic" and "intrinsic" religiosity, based on an earlier concept of "mature" und "immature" religiosity, he has also impeded a realistic investigation of the psychosocial benefit of religions, despite the considerable amount of work initiated by him.

In contrast, William James, the founder of modern psychology of religion, envisages predominantly the individually stabilising psychological effect of religion, see his book "The Varieties of Religious Experience"[12], still well worth reading. Among other things he initiated the studies in religious conversion, a scientific field still active until today. (4)

Psychological explanations of religion date back the farthest in the history of philosophy. From today´s perspective already their older versions point to possibly evolutionary advantageous or at least psychosocially useful mechanisms (which transcend the limits of reality in a religious context and, nevertheless, unfold a considerable real effect even as fictions).

By projecting their own characteristics onto their gods, humans try to gain explanatory power, to formulate ideals, and to reach better control of the world. The thought that human conceptions of gods often appear all-too-human can already be found in ancient times. In the 6th century BC Xenophanes remarked that "if oxen and horses or lions had hands, and could paint with their hands, and produce works of art as men do, horses would paint the forms of the gods like horses, and oxen like oxen, and make their bodies in the image of their several kinds", and that "the Ethiopians make their gods black and snub-nosed", and "the Thracians say theirs have blue eyes and red hair".[13] "God created man in his own image, says the Bible; the philosophers do the exact opposite, they create God in theirs", Lichtenberg[14] then remarks. And even shorter Schiller: "Mankind portrays himself in his gods."[15] Montesquieu too pursues the thought, drawing on an earlier formulation of Spinoza: "It has been very well said, that if triangles were to make themselves gods, they would give them three sides."[16] But it would make sense as well to say: "If triangles were to make themselves gods, they would imagine them as circles", namely if it would be an unattainable ideal of triangles to be round. What appears in human conceptions of gods are their own properties, the systems of power and rule they are used to in their specific historic situation (5) and their unaccomplished and unattainable ideals. All this does not come as a big surprise, actually, as human beings can only speculate with human concepts. The all-too-human character of the conceptions of gods does not refute them, but neither does it inspire confidence that these speculations might have to do anything with describing a reality.

Feuerbach then goes so far as to see a divinisation of man in the human conceptions of god from which a sufficient orientation for moral and social progress could be derived if only supernaturalism were eliminated. One would only have to bring back into the world the properties projected on god. "If human nature is the *highest nature* to man, then practically also the *highest* and *first law* must be *the love of man to man. Homo homini Deus est:* – "[17] If we consider historic conceptions of god, especially the Jewish-Christian one as presented in the Old Testament, it is really remarkable how even Feuerbach still clings to an idealised New Testament Christian conception of god with this thought.

Not only the human desire for interpretation and meaning but also our need for causality, indubitably of evolutionary benefit, roves around and goes astray in religious contexts. Lichtenberg's résumé of this discussion is still second to none: "It is truly astonishing that we have erected our belief in God upon vague ideas of causation. We know nothing of Him, and can know nothing, for to conclude that the world must have a creator is never anything but anthropomorphism." And elsewhere: "This means to think to where there are no thoughts anymore."[18]

On the basis of a neurobiological conception of altered states of consciousness Lewis-Williams begins his analysis of religious experience in stone age cultures and he does not see a fundamental difference to experiences of ecstasy and transcendence in the religions accepted today. He leaves no doubt that spiritual states of consciousness do not allow statements about a reality beyond our consciousness. "What is in our heads is in our heads, not located beyond us."[19]

"Neurotheology" (Newberg[20]) uses modern imaging techniques to analyse the processes in our brains correlated with different types of religious experience. Left aside the problems in reproducing the alleged connections of neural structures with intense religious experiences, there is another problem here: Though he cannot escape the conclusion that these experiences are culturally suggestible to a high degree and subject to indoctrination, Newberg does not look on religious experience with sufficient distance because he is biased by a constructivist theory of knowledge and truth. (6)

Something like a psychiatric approach to explain religion can already be heard in what Hume writes in 1757 in his "Natural History of Religion": "Examine the religious principles, which have, in fact, prevailed in the world. You will scarcely be persuaded, that they are any thing but sick men's dreams: Or perhaps will regard them more as the playsome whimsies of monkeys in human shape, than the serious, positive, dogmatical asseverations of a being, who dignifies himself with the name of rational."[21] 170 years later Freud asks in "The Future of an Illusion", to what it is that religious ideas and doctrines "owe their efficacy, independent as it is of recognition by reason" and being not "precipitates of experience or end-results of thinking", and the core of his answer is: they owe it to wishful thinking, to conscious and unconscious, originally infantile wishes, which often remain, completely or partly, unfulfilled in our life, especially the wishes for protection and protection through love (by a mighty father), the fulfilment of the demands of retributive or restorative justice, for an afterlife, and for a meaningful and moral order of the world.[22] Later Metzinger condenses the comforting psychosocial effects of religious belief systems, by which they can decrease subjective suffering, in the nice dictum that they are in a sense "metaphysical placebos, put to use in existential palliative medicine."[23]

A belief in god, promising emotional security and protection through love, may have quite comprehensible psychological reasons we empathise with. We also take pleasure in seeing that a child believes in Santa Claus or Father Christmas, the Easter Bunny, or in a most general sense in an order of the world in which there are natural and supernatural beings that care for our enjoyment of life, maintain order, and ensure that good will always triumph over evil in the end. If we find such beliefs in adults, we are not so pleased, but, on the contrary, we feel prompted to doubt their ability of unbiased observation, their strength of mind, or, at least, their will to apply their intellectual powers consequently. Freud expressed himself unequivocally on the matter: "Am I to be obliged to believe every absurdity? And if not, why this one in particular? There is no appeal to a court above that of reason."[24]

As early as in the first half of the 19th century August Comte already moves along the boundary of a psychological explanation and a sociological and historic positioning of religion with his law of the three stages, in which he assumes that human knowledge necessarily passes through a theological-fictive stage, corresponding to childhood. That may sound like a good idea, but we have to accept that the greatest part of humanity persistently remains in this stage and that it can be overcome only very slowly even in enlightened societies. This shows that metaphysical historicist concepts reckoning on an overcoming of religion, as later the Marxist one too, fall short. To a certain degree they interpret history adequately, but by their assumption of a historical necessity that will lead to the disappearance of religion they please the needs for superiority of their intellectual creators more than they contribute to an adequate analysis of religion. It is telling that Comte himself has later made an attempt to found and establish a religion of humanity. (7)

With Marx the sociological explanation of religion becomes an economical-political one. Religion appears as an instrument of consolation and empty promises bound to disappear by itself as a consequence of the abolition of the wrong, "alienated" social conditions, and therefore there is no need to attack religion directly – though human beings have to give up their illusions about their situation. Marx' well-known statement about religion as "the opium of the people"[25] fails to recognise that religion cannot only be used for consolation by promises concerning an afterlife, and as a means to stabilise existing structures of power and rule, but that it may also be used to overthrow them. Marx' one-sidedness has its reason in his dogmatic philosophy of history which, due to its seemingly generally valid concept of development, fails to take into account adequately the diversity and individuality of historic situations.

Sociology of religion, which arises at the end of the 19th and the beginning of the 20th century by the work of Max Weber, Georg Simmel and Emile Durkheim, develops a more differentiated concept concerning the function of religion for society and its individual members.

Realistically, but at the same time epistemologically naïve, morally starry-eyed, and a bit unimaginative regarding future development, Durkheim justifies religion – in its social, not its descriptive function – by the permanence with which this phenomenon emerges in human societies. "A collective representation presents guarantees of objectivity by the fact that it is collective: for it is not without sufficient reason that it has been able to generalise and maintain itself with persistence. If it were out of accord with the nature of things, it would never have been able to acquire an extended and prolonged empire over intellects."[26] Instead of understanding social pressure towards conformity with all its positive and negative sanctions for more or less adjusted individuals as a sociological fact and a stabilising factor for established religious beliefs, the result of this pressure, the collective representation, is made a criterion of truth. There is only a little bit of sceptical uncertainty shining through when Durkheim explicitly continues along the same path: "We take it as an axiom that religious beliefs, howsoever strange their appearance may be at times, contain a truth which must be discovered." This gives the impression that here all of a sudden "truth" becomes synonymous with "psychosocial useful or desirable function".

Max Weber expands the sociological contribution to the explanation of religion by his ample studies on the interrelationship between religious ethics and economy. Modern approaches in sociology of religion study religion as a historic and still effective factor in the foundation of social order and social norms. They study its biographical impact, especially in »boundary situations« of human existence, they do research on sects, on market models of religion, and on globalisation and privatisation as factors that influence the social relevance of religion. (8)

Completely different approaches to an explanation of religion as a constant in the history of civilisation are pursued by comparative analysis of religion. If we shift attention from mental experience to mythological content, we can find a lot of historic relations, influences, and parallels between different religions. The historic contingency and interdependence of various concepts of god(s) can be demonstrated and relativises exclusive claims of authority and truth. (See also Topitsch[27]) Those who are inclined to do so, may see all these religious conceptions as a hint to a hidden reality underlying them. But it is much more plausible that all of them have been invented by humans and do not describe a reality beyond human psyche and culture.

Which conclusions emerge from this short survey of attempts to explain religion? Mackie has already aptly summed up the result: "First, it would be a mistake to think that any one of them, by itself, can fully account for religion; but it is very likely that each of them correctly identifies factors which have contributed to some extent to religion, whether to the content of its beliefs, or to its emotional power, or to its practices and organisation, both as originating and sustaining causes."[28]

It has to be added that some attempts to explain religion and its concrete manifestations have general importance while others depend on a specific historical situation. If, for instance, the Old Testament and the Sharia (not the Quran) impose the death penalty for homosexuality, how should a generally valid explanation of religion tell us why the Jewish and the Christian "Religions of the Book" have managed earlier (with the exception of some African states) to dismiss the practical realisation of such a moral and social anachronism?

Religion and the religions are relativised by explaining them. The explanation of the phenomenon "religion" mostly leads to distance. But distance does not necessarily mean unbelief. Let us listen once more to Mackie commenting on natural history of religion: "But, secondly, even an adequate unified, natural history which incorporated all these factors would not in itself amount to a disproof of theism. As William James and many others have insisted, no account of the origin of a belief can settle the question whether that belief is or is not true."[29] Accordingly, Vaas and Blume, in their excellent critical survey on the state of the research on the evolution of religion, present a negative variant in the same line of thought: "Though it is probable, after all, that religions have a psychological, social, and evolutionary benefit … it is valid nonetheless that usefulness is not the same as truth."[30] And, with regard to the anachronistic conflicts religions still produce or fuel in our modern world, one has to add that we must ask ourselves whether a human inclination to religiosity, that was possibly evolutionary and at least culturally useful time and again, might by now have become dysfunctional and a negative influence on the future development of humankind.

After all this we come to the actual philosophical question: What are the arguments for the truth of religion and a belief in god(s)?

Certainly no valid argument is the statement, insistently proposed by Küng, that the explanation of religion and the critique of religion have not proved atheism.[31] Plausible explanations of religion make the question of good reasons for its truth more urgent. Belief in god and religion are the "richer", less parsimonious propositions and those who propose them bear the burden of proof. It is easy to present propositions that cannot be refuted or that are difficult to refute. Propositions deserve credit only if there are good reasons for their truth. At this point in the history of thought it is outdated to allocate the burden of proof in a way that one has to argue against the existence of god or a certain conception of god. Today the burden of proof lies with the theologians and believers. They have to present good reasons for their ideas. Alleged revelations and authoritative historic scriptures do not count among such good reasons, nor does the mere appeal to religious experience. Subjectively convincing as it may be: thereby you can "justify" everything.

In place of the traditional proofs of god, refuted many times (9), I will examine just one of the many arguments that want to proof the existence of god or are at least supposed to serve as a hint to the existence of god. It goes like this: The principle of cause and effect (10) demands that everything must have a cause. Thus, the world must have a cause too, and a cause that has no cause itself: god. God is to be accepted as the first cause, the beginning.

Schopenhauer has criticised the deficiency of such an argumentation with powerful eloquence: "Thus the law of causality is not so obliging as to allow itself to be used like a hackney cab, which one can send off after one reaches one's destination. It is much more like the broom brought to life by Goethe's sorcerer's apprentice, which once set in motion will not stop running and drawing water … ."[32]

If god can just be there, why not the world itself? Both is equally unimaginable or imaginable. It is likewise unimaginable or imaginable that once there has been nothing. "Why nothing should have been first? That is namely what you suppose, if only tacitly. What gives you the legitimation to do so? Why nothing must have been the original, the actually ›natural‹ condition which once had to be overcome and surmounted by the creation of something?" (Anders[33]) In the same line of thought Barbara Smoker rightly formulates: "It is less complicated to suppose that particles of matter and waves of energy have always existed than to suppose that they were made out of nothing by a being who had always existed."[34]

What applies to the cosmological argument on the origin of the world applies analogously to all assumptions of an "Intelligent Design", a fine tuning of the universe friendly to humans, and a divinely supported lawful structure of the universe. Whether as a first cause or a regulatory force god is the more complicated and more redundant idea. That the world exists, and that exists in the way we can experience and realise it, gives us no hint as to the existence of a god or gods. Feelings of gratitude for existence and of admiration for the existing or read in order of the world can be included among the psychological reasons for religiosity. They do not hold up as an argument for belief in god and religion. (11)

I am convinced that all more detailed conceptions of god, which put more into this idea than a cipher for our, despite all progress in physics and cosmology, perhaps perpetually insufficient capability to understand the origin or the eternal existence of the world, are an expression of a basically (at least in this respect) childlike state of mind, governed by emotional desires. To be unable to stop asking: this is an aspect of a childlike state of mind worth preserving which has taken us quite far. But a mature humankind should be able to accept that not necessarily all questions can and have to be answered satisfactorily. This does not mean that we should stop to ask them and to push the boundaries as far as we can.

In light of the fact that a naturalistic explanation of the world has proven to be of increasing and consistent success, a recourse to a spiritual being as creator of the world appears as strange and inadequate. The divine seems dispensable even where we reach the limits of our imagination and our ability to explain. Furthermore, the question arises which emotional or moral benefits the idea of a mere creator deity might involve that never interferes later on with the course of the world once set in motion and determined by the laws of nature. What does it mean if we do not enrich a conception of god by properties that are logically contradictory and in stark contrast to how we experience the world? A rationally defensible (though not justifiable) conception of god will lack much of what most god seekers (and alleged god finders) expect of god. The most defensible conception of god is deistic, and it yields neither morals, nor a significance of individual human destiny, nor personal immortality. And if one enhances one's conception of god and believes in arbitrary interventions in the course of events by one or several gods the problem of plausibility becomes aggravated because such an assumption should be verifiable.

If one wants to maintain a last agnostic reservation as to the existence of one or several gods in this situation, this does not mean that all conceptions of god would stand on an equal footing. Conceptions of god that are logically inconsistent must not even be taken into consideration as more or less probable or improbable possibilities.

Among those is a Christian conception of god as far as it claims that god is both omnipotent and wholly good. The proof that a god who is both omnipotent and wholly good cannot exist is provided by the evil in the world lying before our very eyes. A both omnipotent and wholly good god should not allow undeserved suffering and even with suffering meant as an impulse for further moral development, a test, a penance, or a punishment such a god would have to be moderate, give a chance to the affected persons, and preserve a comprehensible relation between guilt and punishment.

Even in the face of the suffering of the most innocent child one may argumentatively resort to some fault of the parents and grandparents, right up to an original sin. But then it is beyond me, first of all, whatever might be morally reprehensible in the fictitious "original sin", the Fall, as it appears in Christian faith. To me this would mean the emergence of humans from immaturity. Curiosity, striving for knowledge and sexual pleasure turn against a prohibition that is not rationally comprehensible and serves the sole purpose to establish and emphasise divine authority by unacceptable moral diktat. Apart from that, an original sin would have to ascribe guilt to all children equally. Furthermore, kin liability is morally reprehensible and is – at least since the New Testament – no part of the conception of »good« prevalent in our culture. And it is especially incomprehensible how it might be reconcilable with divine omnipotence and omnibenevolence that human behaviour during a short lifespan in this world could decide on eternal damnation or bliss and that all misdeeds and atrocities (even, for instance, those of a Hitler) could be compensated by true repentance before death whereas the decision against the belief in god during the earthly life would be eternally unforgivable. This is an old and striking argument of Enlightenment that can already be found in Hume and d'Holbach in different versions. (12) In its most sharpened version it goes like this: Would eternal damnation of just one human being not be worse than all human atrocities as a whole because the suffering caused by human beings is of limited duration?

One may try to evade the problem by alleging that it is beyond the power of human reason to understand divine omnipotence and benevolence. But what do we state after all if we blur our notions like that? Instead of "god is good and omnipotent" might we not say, then, "god is ping and pong"? The conception of a god that is as well benevolent and almighty is either wrong or devoid of content.

Now, somebody could conceive the idea to use the previous statement that there is no objective moral standard of comparison (see 2.2. and 3.3) to defeat the argument against this logically inconsistent conception of god. But there is no need for an objective moral standard of comparison, nor for a recourse to one's own or the predominant morals of the respective society. It is perfectly sufficient, as a rule, to refer to the morality of the respective religion itself, in this case the Christian. If, however, a completely different, and not even more closely describable morality should apply to god than to us humans the reproach of meaninglessness is back. If we strip the notions "good" and "omnipotent" of their usual meaning when applying them to god, they do no longer describe anything comprehensible and are reduced to a mere cipher for the conception of god, hold by people who are – for whatever reason – able to somehow imagine a god "good" and "omnipotent" as well, contrary to all objections of reason.

The argument of Leibniz' theodicy (appealing to theologians up to our days) that god has seen the higher good in creating human beings with reason and free will and, therefore, had been forced to accept the emergence of evil as well, is not convincing. First, it requires the utmost philosophical hair-splitting to contend that all evil is of human origin, and second, god could have created human beings with a disposition to always freely choose the good (leaving aside the fact that in a naturalistic world view there are no good reasons altogether for a metaphysical concept of free will). God could have spared human beings from sadistic and cruel inclinations, thus at least limiting "moral" evil. The moral status quo of human beings, their moral imperfection, the wide span they show between moral greatness and monstrosity provide strong arguments that their morality is of evolutionary and cultural origin. Compared to a naturalistic explanation of the state of the world it sounds rather far-fetched too if modern theologians even expand Leibniz' argument a little bit and allege that god does allow evil to exist because circumstances that cause suffering in our world make it also possible to realise certain values.

The evil in the world is the final nail in the coffin of any moral conception of god. Stendhal comments all theological harmony sermons shortly and pointedly and in the same breath puts an end to the Christian conception of god: "God's only excuse is that he does not exist."[35] (13) In view of the predominant religion of his social environment Wilhelm Busch states more generally but not less aptly: "Whoever asks reason in questions of belief gets unchristian answers."[36] (14)

There is another point that makes a belief in the traditional religions appear a completely unreasonable demand (as aptly remarked by Hitchens[37]): it is the historically late appearance of the great book religions.

178

After having watched the misery of humankind for more than a 100 000 years the Jewish Christian god is supposed to have suddenly taken it into his head, 5000 years ago, to cement a pact with a single tribe of humans in the Middle East, and 2000 years ago, again in the same corner of the world, to send and sacrifice his son as a saviour. And the Muslim god is supposed to have given revelations to Muhammad some 1400 years ago, conveniently fitting well in many aspects to the situation and the circumstances of life of rival Arabian tribes at the time.

Let us now turn to less obviously incredible and especially logically consistent conceptions of god – without forgetting that the consistency of assertions about a postulated being still means nothing as to its existence.

Lichtenberg remarks: "Many years ago I already thought that our world might be the work of a subordinate being, and still I can't come back from this thought. It is a folly to believe that there could be no world without illness, pain, and death in it. After all, we imagine heaven like that. To speak of a time of trial, of gradual development, is to think of god very much by human standards and is idle talk. Why shouldn't exist different levels of spirits up to god at the top and our world be the work of one who still didn't know his matter very well, an apprentice's job?" – "If I see war, hunger, poverty, and pestilence, it is impossible for me to believe that all that should be the work of a wisest being; or it must have found a matter independent of it constraining it to a considerable degree; so that this would just be the best world respectively, as has already been taught quite often."[38]

These quotations show very well which possibilities may arise if one thinks about god without giving up the consequent use of reason.

It might be that god has just created the world and given it its structure and order by the laws of nature without exerting any further influence on it, be it because the divine being lost interest in it after the creation, be it because it runs the world as a huge experiment left to itself, or be it because it was just able to create a world with an order setting limits to divine influence.

It might be that god is almighty but also arbitrary and cruel. It might as well be that god is good but unable to overcome all the evil in the world, and therefore not almighty. The divine being's power might have been sufficient to create the world but be not sufficient to govern it. For that it is not indispensable that a second god, an evil god, or a devil exists. But the Zoroastrian or Manichean teachings about a fight between a good and evil force, a fight between light and darkness, are – though completely and unfoundedly speculative as well – more plausible than the Christian version in which it remains unclear why god does not eliminate the evil in spite of his omnipotence. The Christian kind of a monotheistic conception of god wrongly conveys the impression of a greater profundity in comparison to dualistic or polytheistic conceptions which distribute good and evil on their gods. But as long as there were no well-elaborated, fact-based naturalistic concepts to explain the world, such a monotheistic conception of a god was at least a much more comprehensible temptation than it is today.

In the face of the irrefutable contradiction between divine benevolence and omnipotence modern theology has refined its argumentation more and more. It is hardly possible to make a case for the exculpation of god in a better way than this is done by Kreiner in one of the most conclusive attempts of theodicy I know: "Now let us assume that god wanted to create a universe in which human life can emerge. Then such a universe must be designed more or less like ours. And if the laws of nature constitute a coherent unity, then the following is also valid: The laws of nature that are behind our own origin are also behind the origin of natural evil. Perhaps God could not create the world in another way without creating another world, that is to say, we might not have a place at all in another world."[39] You really need a moment to see through the trick that is performed here: the allegedly omnipotent god is robbed of his omnipotence in a very subtle manner and after that one has gained a much more comfortable position to defend his moral qualities and their insufficient reach.

The geneticist Collins takes the same line by declaring that he adheres to "theistic evolution" as "the master plan of the Almighty". "God chose the elegant mechanism of evolution … to give rise to special creatures who would have intelligence, a knowledge of right and wrong, free will, and a desire to seek fellowship with Him. He also knew these creatures would ultimately choose to disobey the Moral Law."[40]

Religious belief that comprises a logically consistent conception of god cannot be refuted nor proven. Regarding such a belief Küng's (and also Kreiner's) claim that a belief in god can be justified in the face of rational critique[41] is at least not completely bizarre though there are no good reasons for such conceptions of god either, and only such good reasons could seriously provide a justification to rational critique. The arguments put forth to make conceptions of god rationally tenable are all to obviously formulated in order to make a preconceived belief rationally digestible and do not stand up to the principle of parsimony. In the attempt of bringing nature, that is devoid of all moral criteria, and god into accord, the additional assumption "god" loses its persuasiveness, not only as to causal explanation but also as an authority providing morals and meaning. The question arises inevitably why we should not give the idea a miss and simply confine ourselves to a naturalistic explanation of the world and a life orientation without "god".

I do not want to omit discussing an argument for belief in god and religion that is seldom formulated clearly but is rather common and is looked upon as quite persuasive by many people. It goes something like this: As there are musical and unmusical people – in different gradations – so there are religious and areligious people. Religiosity is supposed to be regarded as a special gift not given in equal measure to all human beings. Often some pity for areligious people is combined with this argument as they are allegedly unable to perceive a certain significant part of reality – being kind of spiritually deaf and therefore unfortunately excluded from important experiences in life.

Now, it comes as no surprise that human beings have a great variety of more or less common special gifts, be it for music, mathematics, languages, physical performance, motion sequences, and so forth. Quite rightly we admire those fellow human beings who have such positive particular talents and commiserate with those who fall short of average concerning abilities we (or our respective society) consider important. We are astonished at what some people can do with a number of sounds or notes, some mathematical symbols, their own body, or some sports equipment. In these cases, we do not doubt, as a rule, that these gifts have to be regarded as an ability to deal in a particularly skilful manner with certain parts of reality. In other words: The substrates of these special abilities, for examples sounds, mathematical symbols, et cetera, appear to us as a part of our reality and are perceptible and comprehensible for all of us, at least in principle, no esoteric talents required.

It must not be doubted that there is a special talent for spiritual experience as well (a fact that does not necessarily imply that a religious meaning is ascribed to this experience). But in all probability such experiences are nothing more than mental processes within the brain of people with such a special ability. (See the quotation from Lewis-Williams, p. 170) These experiences can become a motivation for creating certain cultural products: cults and religions, for instance, and the works of art related to them. The particular talent for spirituality (which may lead to religiosity) is in fact just a special inclination to altered states of consciousness, namely meditative or even hallucinatory experiences that can be associated with a special suggestibility and a special readiness to set aside rational objections if the fulfilment of emotional needs is at stake. The diversity and inconsistency of religious experience make such a judgement even more plausible and suggest that the only truth claim founded on spiritual (religious) experience we should accept is that the respective person has had such a psychological experience. (Leaving aside the fact that there are people who just pretend to have such experiences in order to take some social or economic advantage of it.)

"Must it not make a Christian wonder that he owes his religion merely to the lottery of life? If he had not been born in Berlin by chance, but in Bombay, for example, he would not be praying fervently to God now, but to Vishnu. Of course, he thinks Hinduism and the stories about Rama and Sita are mere fairy tales. But what if he met his own god and the stories of Jesus and Mary with the same scepticism? Would there be anything left of his Christianity then?" (Dahl[42])

Pointing to an alleged spiritual truth common to all religions would be much more convincing if people would concur to a higher degree in their religious experience and if the different religions were more compatible. This would make it a little bit more difficult to induce doubts. But even as a collective phenomenon religious experience always tells us something about human beings only and not about the rest of the world.

Virtuosos in music and "religious virtuosos" (Max Weber[43]) are similar in so far as both are gifted with special abilities and are able to touch upon these individually more or less developed abilities in other people. "Religious virtuosity" may impress us in a way comparable to an extraordinary ability for and passionate devotion to other intensive activities in life, for instance, some artistic or emotional commitment. But religious virtuosos raise unjustified truth claims and delude themselves into thinking that these claims are valid. They raise truth claims founded on nothing more than their subjective experience, and they do this in questions about which one can definitely examine if there are good reasons for certain assumptions – on condition that one is willing to do so. And religious virtuosos often enough raise their truth claims in a dangerous, intolerant and oppressive manner which is exclusionary, immunised against criticism and even prohibiting criticism. Any virtuosity may take its toll, but religious virtuosity takes an excessive and unacceptable moral and intellectual toll. (15)

Let's sum up. Concerning the conceptions of god of all religions known to me, including those that are less blatantly logically contradictory than the Christian, I agree with Bertrand Russell's (pre-spaceflight) judgement: "I do not think the existence of the Christian God any more probable than the existence of the Gods of Olympus or Valhalla. To take another illustration: nobody can prove that there is not between Earth and Mars a china teapot revolving in an elliptic orbit, but nobody thinks this sufficiently likely to be taken into account in practice."[44]

If we let impose on ourselves one more time, for historical reasons, a way of argumentation and speaking that regards a belief in god as »normality«, then my statement is as follows: Unwillingness to believe leads to an agnosticism that is tantamount to atheism in all practical issues. A choice of a provisional belief in god, a choice to live as if a god being the initial cause of the world and having certain (logically compatible) properties would exist, is not irrational in principle, but there are no god reasons for such a belief either. Those unwilling to believe do not need a detour via god as a foundation of philosophy of life and morality. They can justify them by deliberate decisions, by fundamental choices and choices. In a world view shaped by science there is no room left for the idea of god (at least the idea of a god or gods still interfering in the course of events after creation), it simply appears as out of place. The decision for a belief in god falls victim to the principle to exercise the highest possible restraint concerning personal decisions of belief that cannot be justified further.

"Concerning the gods, I have no means of knowing whether they exist or not or of what sort they may be. Many things prevent knowledge including the obscurity of the subject and the brevity of human life" says Protagoras.[45] (16) And Charles Darwin still follows in his footsteps: "The mystery of the beginning of all things is insoluble by us; and I for one must be content to remain an Agnostic."[46] For a long time such statements seemed to be the last possible word. But meanwhile they are relativised by the progress of modern science. "The beginning of all things" or else an eternal existence of the universe has become conceivable to us, though in the form of highly abstract physical and mathematical concepts postulating, for instance, a melting of space-time at a certain point of development of the universe or a cyclic behaviour of the universe or universes. Nevertheless, it remains improbable that there may ever be spoken a "final word" in this field of theory that comes close to other scientific knowledge in certainty. Darwin may be right for ever with an agnosticism restricted to this point. The statement of Protagoras, however, seems to agnostic for us today, at least as far as the properties of possible gods are concerned. The findings of natural, human and social sciences have sent the conceptions of god that are hold by the world religions still widespread today (and among them those of the great religions of the book) to the realm of poetry, legend, and myth, equivalent to the pantheon of the ancient Greeks. Tales invented by human beings to get their bearings in the world, to explain its order, and to find an objectifying foundation of morals. Tales, sometimes lovely, sometimes wise and rich in experience, but sometimes also ridiculous, grotesque, or horrible – and at times with consequences of the same kind.

For various reasons many contemporary thinkers and scientists still shy away from expressing such a judgement of religions clearly and openly. That looks like a noble agnosticism, but it is just a backing down kind of it.

For those unwilling to believe only a scientific conception (nowadays of course including evolutionary theory) is acceptable to explain the origin and the order of the world. Admittedly this does not include a satisfactory solution for some problems: an objective authority, independent of us humans, to provide us with guidelines for our acting, a morality, or a meaning of our life that transcends our own settings, cannot be found anywhere in such a worldview. The problem of the beginning or the eternal existence of the world is solved only insufficiently though it is a great success of human striving for knowledge that it has pushed back the borders of knowledge further and further and continues to do so by a realistic and naturalistic view on the cosmos.

That simple, uneducated people still cling to religion comes as no surprise. That some eminent scientists, be it physicists, biologists, psychologists or philosophers succeed to do so is somewhat more surprising. But what is truly astounding are those cases in which scientists stick to religion after a full passage through the history and criticism of religion. Let us have a closer look on two prominent examples of this kind at the end of this chapter.

From a rational point of view William James' classical survey of the varieties of religious experience should definitely lead to religious relativism and to the assumption that religions are human creations fed by deeply rooted psychological needs. And it is a plausible guess when James, at the end of his discussion[47], comes to the conclusion that religion must necessarily play an eternal role in human history because, contrary to the cold and impersonal scientific analysis of reality, it deals with the only absolute reality we know, namely personal destiny. But then he goes further: an inward monitor would tell him that a restraint to a scientific world view were humbug. Religious people would know that not only themselves, but all beings to whom God is present, were save in his paternal hands. Perhaps the faithfulness of individuals here below might help God to be more effectively faithful to his own greater tasks.

Our second example is Hans Küng. He wants to maintain a rational masquerade, or perhaps better: a rational self-justification, as long as possible. Therefore, he presents the decision for a belief in god as rationally justifiable without having anything else on his hands than its lacking refutability. The general compatibility of a belief in god and modernity once alleged, we are faced with a sudden turn by which Küng tries to make all the contradictions and absurdities of Christian faith plausible anew, as for example the god of the Old Testament, repeatedly appearing as extremely cruel in the Bible and supposed to be benevolent nonetheless, or, more generally, the conception of a god almighty and omnibenevolent as well. According to Küng, the decision for a belief in god in general and the Christian faith in particular is not only rationally justifiable but of great importance and recommendable as well, because this were the only way to gain a radical certainty, assurance and stability. He exculpates god for the evil in the world by the "argument" that god is simply a father, "whom man can absolutely trust and on whom he can completely rely even in suffering, injustice, sin and death."[48]

After having noticed and discussed Freud's criticism of religion, the father substitute trust in god, characterised as an essential motif of religion by Freud, nevertheless celebrates a comeback in Küng's thinking, tying in with the feelings William James expressed 75 years earlier. Santa Claus – sorry: God the Father – is back in town.

How much would we trust in a real father of whom we knew that he imposes on us all the suffering and evil the world has to offer, no matter which efforts we make, and despite being able to avoid all this because of his omnipotence?

Those unwilling to believe want to hear arguments for the existence of god and for human immortality. Trust in god, as James and Küng commend, is no argument but an emotional appeal, an appeal to override the rationally probable by desires and feelings.

If we proceed like this and conclude from the insight that any philosophical or religious life orientation must ultimately be founded on decisions that we may blithely decide for whatever makes us feel emotionally comfortable, no matter how contradictory it may be from a rational point of view, why, then, a decision for Christianity and not for some other religious offer? What may be brought forward in favour of Christianity is its long-lasting historical success, a certain moral appeal of some interpretation of the Christian teachings, and the cultural and social environment we are born into. Is any of these reasons convincing?

A theologian who argues like Küng talks at cross-purposes with many modern people who are unwilling to believe. To the questionability, to which modern people are exposed due to the uncompromising criticism by reason, he does not counterpose a minimum of decisions that just allows a meaningful orientation in life. He rather wants to convince us to an inflationary expansion of subjective decisions which seem arbitrary to the unwilling to believe (apart from their historical and cultural contingency), and by which we are expected to accept the greatest inconsistencies because they appear soothing and useful and correspond with some kind of spiritual experience (very limited in its significance about an external reality) or with the desire for a moral order of the world, independent of human setting. What Küng propounds again and again – in a broadness that may make you wonder – is basically old wine in new bottles. One more time reason is made an ancilla theologiae (an "handmaid of theology") who has to deliver the predetermined result at all cost.

The appropriate attitude for critically thinking human beings is to abide a certain degree of uncertainty and to orientate in life self-responsibly. To what extent would we actually gain a certainty of an radical quality, that could not be gained in another way, by the decision for a belief in god? The decision for such a belief remains at least as questionable as the decision against it. Consequently, any position concerning knowledge and morals derived therefrom cannot claim "absoluteness". And beyond a decision for god not only any further decision to assume that a certain reality and morality has been established by god remains questionable but one is also right away confronted with the next equally questionable decision whether to accept for oneself the morality supposedly set by god. To do so, is no matter of course at all. (See also 2.1., p. 70)

Thomas Mann did already comment adequately on "modern" theology before Küng's variation existed: "No accommodation, no concessions to scientific criticism can help. Instead, those create a hybrid, a half-and-half of science and belief in revelation that is well on the way to capitulation."[49]

Admittedly the humane impetus of reform theologians deserves respect. If they are not driven by giving themselves an air of importance but strive to reconcile religion with modernity and to make it more liveable, less dogmatic, less constricting and mutilating, more tolerant, more humane in a word, then they are much more likeable as all kinds of hardliners, be it Vatican or others, not to speak of violent fundamentalists. Even if reformers, depending on the degree of success they have, may contribute to a transient stabilisation of an obsolete philosophy of life they can make social change smoother and more easily acceptable for some people.

At the end of this section the time has come to sacrifice the question mark in its subtitle. God and Religion are unavoidable antiques, but antiques nevertheless. They are unavoidable for those willing to believe and the believers because they are unable or unwilling to realise them as antiques and still take them as modern. But they are unavoidable for those unwilling to believe as well because they have to deal with them and analyse and criticise them. To what extent this may drive out belief in god and religion of the market of philosophies of life and transfer them to the antiques fair will be shown by history. Religion finds a world-wide and transhistorical acceptance and proves to be resistant against rational criticism because it represents an illusional consciousness responding to human needs and wishes (Pfahl-Traughber[50]) and it entails a functional usefulness of various kinds – partly illusory, partly quite real - as for example concerning the preservation of hope, the foundation of identity and orientation, the support of social integration, the projection of guilt, the reading of meaning into chance and destiny, and the stabilisation, criticism or re-shaping of authority or rule. These accomplishments have to be achieved in equal measure (or shown to be expendable) by secular life orientations first of all if they want to compete with religion as comparably satisfactory and appealing to a majority of people.

"In the case of the nominal Christian, you can by the aid of logic clear from his mind the notions which his memory may have retained from the age when he learnt his catechism, but you cannot argue away to the believer the value of his inner life. And even so you prove to him a hundred times that it is all but subjective sensations, he lets you your way with subject and object, and mocks your simple efforts to overturn by the breath of a mortal man the walls of Sion, whose towering battlements he sees lighted by the radiance of the lamb and the everlasting glory of God."[51]

Friedrich August Lange

"The need to find completeness in the fragmentary nature of man's existence, to reconcile conflicts within the individual and between men, the need for a fixed point in all the instability that surrounds us, for a just purpose in and behind the cruelties of life, for unity in and above life's bewildering multiplicity, and for an absolute object toward which to direct our humility and our desire for contentment – all of this nourishes man's ideas about the transcendent sphere: man's hunger feeds these ideas. The person of absolutely pure faith does not care whether these ideas are theoretically possible or impossible; he simply feels inwardly that this yearning has found an outlet and a sense of fulfilment in his faith."[52]

Georg Simmel

"But it is also possible to live in transcendental homelessness (as Lukács once described the modern attitude towards life). And with a certain pride to have grown up."[53]

Jan Philipp Reemtsma

"I actually became an atheist because I did not find any good reasons to believe in God."[54]

Hans Albert

3.5. Nature

The indifferent and fascinating basis of life

"Ratio and objective analysis are less appreciated today than in previous times. That is especially deplorable considering the wealth of additional knowledge we dispose of in comparison with the past. Repeatedly science and technology are hold responsible for things going awry regardless of the fact that nature itself permanently comes up with lesser or greater catastrophes. Knowledge and expertise are rather frowned upon nowadays. Each new discovery first and foremost undergoes questioning on the harm it might produce. Is it not just the balance of benefit and harm we should care about?"
"There are alternative options, and we should weigh one against the other. The answers will vary in different times. We have to make sure that there is a continuous rational discussion. What is right today may be wrong tomorrow. We should never make decisions that leave us no choice in the end."[1]

Manfred Eigen

A realistic view on nature, including human nature and the human position in the universe, is a significant achievement of modernity. The fundamental consequences of this world view for philosophy of life are discussed in this book in various contexts. In this chapter I will explicitly focus on our relationship with nature.

Which insights are essential for our relationship with nature? Human beings are living things that have become possible by processes following the laws of nature. But nature is not directed towards producing us. Nature allows the origin of species and individuals by evolutionary processes at our cosmic place. But there is no instance in nature which could have an interest in their maintenance. Thus, nature is indifferent to humankind as well.

Nature is the basis of our life. We can take advantage of it in many ways. Today we have expanded our scope of action to such a degree that we can destroy a considerable part of life on our earth. This applies to our own species as well – in spite of its relatively great ecological niche.

As natural beings human beings have always been exposed and will always be exposed to dangers and risks. They have to decide permanently which part of their resources they should invest to avert or reduce specific dangers and risks and how they can make the most efficient use of their resources. These resources are then no longer available to pursue other aims.

It is not adequate to confine our relationship to nature to an ecological perspective as it is sometimes done today unreflectively as if this were a matter of course. Such a perspective is historically mistaken and does not lead us to an appropriate ideational basis for our present and future dealings with nature.

Nature is a fascinating subject of research, perception, knowledge, and also manipulation for us humans. (1)

Nature is also a source of enjoyment of life. It allows us to act out our play instinct in great variety, provides us physical and aesthetic stimulation and pleasure. This finds expression for centuries not only in the visual arts, in literature, music, and sports, but it is present time and again in the sciences as well. Walking the border between natural sciences and art entails an aestheticisation of nature, from Vesalius's "Anatomy" and later Ernst Haeckel's "Art Forms in Nature" to the provocative and as well awesome Gunther von Hagens with his "Body Worlds", to mention just a couple of prominent examples. (2) On the other hand, a naturalisation of aesthetics also happens, when, for instance, Ernst Haeckel's art forms exert considerable influence on art nouveau (and ornamental elements from nature can be found in the artistic expression of humans for thousands of years, for most diverse intentions). We will come back to the topic of "natural beauty" in a wider sense in chapter 3.10..

If we think about the position of human beings within and towards nature, it makes sense to define ourselves not only by our capabilities but also by our shortcomings. Though humans are the most complex beings biological evolution has produced on our planet Earth, we should not neglect that human beings are far from reaching the peak performances of other living beings in a variety of aspects, be it physical strength, velocity, sensitivity of sense organs, size (in both directions), or simply undemandingness regarding environmental conditions. In all these attainments other species reach the pinnacle of evolution. But the criterion of evolutionary success is not peak performance or progress to complexity but optimal adaptation for a reproductive success sufficient to survive. This means that more "primitive" living beings may be more successful if conditions change to favouring them.

Even if we consider our biggest advantage in the struggle for survival, the capabilities of our brains, we humans are still beings with shortcomings. Most of us are quite good in dealing with events within "mesocosmic" dimensions (middle dimensions that we can grasp directly with our sense organs) and our closer local and temporal surroundings. Beyond this range our brain tends to misjudge things. (3)

With regard to morals human beings are deficient as well. Evolution has provided us with a brain that still makes choices according to the »egoism of our genes« but is also able to distance from such preferences consciously. Even during the past periods of history, when its destructive potential was limited, the human species has survived under great losses only. If it will manage to cope with the extension of its destructive capabilities to a global level in the long run remains to be seen.

The success of humans as a biological species shows, nevertheless, that their shortcomings have been tolerable up to now (from an evolutionary, not a moral point of view), or that the evolutionary created specific blend of capabilities and shortcomings may even be constitutive to a considerable degree for the success the human species has had up to now – evolution being a procedure to develop the best compromise (again: in terms of survival).

This is the situation we have to start from when discussing how to deal with human and extra-human nature. If we neglect these fundamental facts and harbour illusions about an ideal state of nature or a divine imprint on or a divine guidance of nature, there is a considerable probability to make inappropriate decisions.

It cannot be derived from the concept of evolution what we ought to do (as already discussed in chapter 3.3.). Statements on our position in nature do not readily justify value judgements. Since we have been equipped with such a complex brain with considerable degrees of freedom, and we have established ourselves as the most powerful biological species on this earth, able to interfere with evolution in many ways, we have to decide on our goals ourselves. Our scope extends to self-destruction, be it caused by inability or even strived for consciously. Many other biological species have gone extinct before us. If we destroy our species and our planet, nobody will be there to regret this. Perhaps the universe will have lost its only actual observers then. Or evolution produces at another time in some other "corner" of the universe another kind of higher living beings, be it similar ones or even ones of more long-lasting success (able to avoid that their biological dominance, their intraspecies rivalries, and their destructive impulses lead to self-destruction).

Science and technology allow humans to gain independence from nature to a certain degree. It cannot be denied, however, that they produce their own risks and bring about unforeseeable and unforeseen side effects that have to be identified, require an adequate reaction, and should, if possible, be avoided from the very start. This is a good reason to be cautious. But it is no good reason for a general attitude of mistrust and hostility to science and technology in the first place, or for an opposition against any human intervention in »creation«, respectively against any amendment of their natural situation by humans (to choose a more appropriate wording).

While we have to emphasise harmony between human beings and the non-human nature to a greater extent today, we should not forget that humans have to struggle against nature as well and that this aspect has understandably dominated decisions in former times if we take into account the conditions prevailing then. Whereas the interests of humans have been given too much priority for some time, we now face the risk of a new bias, a bias that – consciously or unconsciously – blames humans to be guilty and to deserve punishment as sinners against the environment that would best disappear again from nature. There is no reason to play down the destruction of nature by humans that has already been done and that is impending. But a denigration of humans, a contempt of their cultural achievements, sometimes even enriching nature, and an idealisation of a nature without humans is completely inadequate as well and will not help us in coping with the challenges of the future. (4)

Especially European ecological movements show traits of a (nature) religion nowadays. It is also popular to reform the old religion in an ecological way and accordingly not to speak about the environment and about other living beings but about "creation" and "fellow creatures". If it is intended thereby to express that life, and non-human life as well, is seen as a high value, I feel connected to this way of thinking, regardless of the fundamental differences in philosophy of life and mode of expression. But religious or secular ideological expectations of salvation, prejudice, precepts and restrictions on thinking, and the intolerant and rigid morality often linked to this, which absolutises single values and moral attitudes, often distort the perception of the world and hamper and impede appropriate approaches to problem-solving.

Religious zest is not to be trusted, for whatever it may be and even if it is for the conservation of nature. New dangers and definitely totalitarian

192

tendencies are emerging here: the danger of a new irrationalism with a very biased one-sided system of values and a distorted and unrealistic interpretation of social cost-benefit and benefit-risk or chance-risk relations, the danger of inadequate simplification in assessing problems, the danger of intolerance against all those people who weigh up the interests of human beings and non-human nature in their decisions and thus live up to responsibilities resulting from a more comprehensive system of values.

Mind how the bearing, speech and behaviour of some representatives of conservation organisations recalls preachers of repentance, feeling certain of their enlightenment and mission of salvation and prepared to restrict the freedom of their fellow citizens in an unhesitating and intolerant way. Or look how some environmental organisations rush their juvenile members into perilous actions of protest in an irresponsible manner (sometimes a comparison to the catholic church during the time of the crusades does not appear far-fetched to me).

Ecological one-sidedness and ideological preconceptions may entail a considerable loss of individual and social liberty and the squandering of a significant amount of resources, be it through inefficient use of means or through unproductive bureaucracy. And would it not be a good idea to think a little bit more about the alternative between restraints and chicanery on one side and adequate incentives on the other side (leaving a choice to the affected people)? Does it make sense, for example, to penalise the (often relatively poor) users of older, less eco-friendly goods and products (houses, cars etc.) if one considers the amount of energy and other environmental load caused by forced premature replacement or renovation?

Responsible decisions on environmental problems require a thorough assessment of the relevant facts which often means to make up a balance. On such a basis only, the right conclusions can be drawn that allow a well-founded rational weighing up. This is about the efficiency in using resources on the one hand, and it is about rationally founded risk assessment with regard to the probability of occurrence and the severity of the consequences in case of occurrence on the other hand. In a highly emotionalised atmosphere, under pressure of a propaganda shaped by prejudice that is spread by media and opportunistic politicians currying favour with the zeitgeist, inadequate assessments of effects and risks are made which lead to bad decisions that may cause a wrong use of great financial resources then no longer available for other important social tasks. To mention just two examples, which are almost historical meanwhile and caused considerable but still relatively limited costs, think of the hysteria to remove amalgam or asbestos that was safely in place.

A much bigger waste of resources impends by all kinds of panicky measures to avoid carbon dioxide emission no matter the cost and how inefficient they may be. No doubt it is important to reduce and in the long run even stop the global warming caused by humans, but this goal too is competing with other important goals and the relation between the amount of resources deployed and the effect that can be reached has to be assessed critically regarding this goal as well. Take the idea that decentralised ways of energy production would always be preferable: for some this has already taken the character of a dogma. Yet it seems highly questionable if the extent of forced promotion and funding of solar energy, with all its aesthetically ugly side effects (spoiling landscape and architecture all too often) and causing elevated cost for the consumer, did and does really make sense ecologically and economically in a country with geographic preconditions like Germany, at least as long as the possibilities for storage are very limited. Regarding wind energy it has to be critically assessed as well where this kind of energy production is effective and acceptable and if it is justified to build an increasing number of wind turbines in midst of landscapes of aesthetical value and at the price of considerable damage to nature (like high losses of bats, birds and insects). And if we discuss energy saving measures, the problem of diminishing marginal utility has to be observed. All this may easily be pushed aside if reducing carbon dioxide becomes an absolutely predominant goal. (5)

Climate protection activists often feel and present themselves as morally superior ignoring or hiding the blind spots of their attitude. These are, for example, their fundamentalist opposition to nuclear energy (especially in Germany) or the underestimation of the effects of global population growth.

Without limiting the human population on earth, climate change cannot be controlled efficiently. Alongside to protesting against irresponsible, ecologically damaging aspects of our economic system it would be consequent to protest as well against irresponsible actors who still further population growth for reasons of ideology and striving for power (as done, to mention just one example, by the catholic church with its still considerable influence in Africa and Latin America).

But even a world population of ten billion people (likely to be reached at least temporarily even in a favourable course of events), can hardly be supplied with the amount of energy that allows an acceptable level of civilisation

194

for all in an ecologically and economically responsible manner without using nuclear energy, given the current state of technology.

And in view of the relatively low level of engagement in denouncing the environmental damage caused and accepted in the pursuit of their goals by corrupt and imperialist leaders and systems, uncompromising demands for a sudden radical change in the economies of Western democracies appear even more as completely disproportionate.

Besides an irrational risk assessment wrong regulatory ideas constitute our greatest problem in dealing with complex dangers and risks. Though the ecological record of the former communist countries was disastrous and concepts of a socialist overall control by the state, planned economy and paternalism have failed time and again in the long run in a multitude of social sectors, and have not been able to solve problems satisfactorily despite of inacceptable losses of freedom, these concepts are nevertheless held in high and even newly growing esteem, especially concerning environmental problems and politics, and it is now attempted to advertise and enforce them under a green label. The problem of climate change threatens to become the source of a monstrous national and international bureaucracy with expenditures that could produce much more benefit elsewhere and that are many times higher than what we spend as aid for developing countries.

A more active politics of developing aid enabling the poorer countries to solve their misery problems, control their increase in population, and put in place a more environmentally friendly technology would very likely bring about much more benefit than a forced precipitous reduction of carbon dioxide emission in countries with an already advanced technology and politics of energy saving. Investments for furthering education, equality of women, and wealth can certainly have better effects to limit climate change than costly measures of marginal utility to reduce carbon dioxide emission directly. If a wrong allocation of resources is already very regrettable with regard to unsolved tasks within our own society, it appears all the more irresponsible in view of the problems faced by the poor countries of the world and the people living there (lacking the fulfilment of basic needs like pure water or reliable electricity).

Though eco-austerity will not solve the world's biggest problems, rich countries with a much higher per capita energy consummation than others with a comparable standard of living, above all the Unites States of America, should considerably increase their efforts to reduce the consumption of energy to meet their responsibility for the further development of our world. Exaggerated energy consumption is not only a problem with regard to climate change but also because of other environmentally negative side effects of energy production and transport and the creation of international imbalances.

While there is no lack of important tasks, wasting resources and restricting personal freedom in order to minimise marginal or marginally influenceable risks has become a considerable problem in modern affluent societies, Germany being a prominent example for this. On the other hand, there is much less willingness to consequently reduce really relevant risks for people, like speeding in road traffic, overeating and unhealthy dietary behaviours, abuse of drugs, nicotine and alcohol (or in the U.S. also the firearm violence epidemic) though these factors could be influenced at relatively low cost in many a way. But in contrast to ecological commitment such efforts lack the religious-ideological appeal.

There is also tendency to pretend (and to promote a public mood in this direction) that it would be principally illegitimate to include costs in considerations on reducing environmental, health or safety risks. It goes without saying that everybody includes economic aspects in personal risk assessment in private life, and, for example, most people do not buy the safest car they could afford if they would refrain from pursuing other interests and wishes. But when assessing risks in the fields of industrial production and social and political institutions it is suggested that economic considerations should not be allowed to matter. This is nothing more than hypocrisy. But it is a hypocrisy with very concrete political effects: it deludes the citizens into thinking that they do not have to pay for the expense caused by minimising risks in these sectors or that their personal contribution is minimal due to the great number of affected people. As this procedure becomes more and more common the costs get higher and higher for everybody and people are forced to expenditures for minimising marginal risks, risks marginal to a degree that they would never spend money for minimising them further in the realm of their private life if they would have to leave behind other interests instead. Funds can be spent only once. This holds for companies, social institutions and states as well. If they want to use their funds to minimise marginal risks, the money is lacking elsewhere, or the costs have to be passed to the citizens. This must be clearly stated in political debate.

Often the impression is conveyed that science and technology make our life less safe and riskier overall while in reality they have led to a degree of safety and control over natural conditions and risks in modern affluent societies that existed never before in human history. To take a single example: Hypothetical or at least relatively low risks of food additives and modern food production are talked up in general awareness while former risks by malnutrition, lack of possibilities for food preservation and lacking food control are ignored or denied. Of course, we should reduce food risks, and, in some details, modern food production is unreasonable and in need of improvement. Cost pressure and striving for maximum profit sometimes lead to bad decisions and make regulation unavoidable. At the same time we should think about possibilities to motivate people to adopt healthier dietary habits. And we should think about how to address the problem that parts of the food industry manage to produce food of poor palatability and nevertheless succeed in driving culinary diversity and quality out of the market.

Today's green »nature religion« does not necessarily contribute to an adequate solution of these problems. It is deficient in recognising and accepting important chances for the future of humankind as created by genetic engineering, for example. We need an ecology without natural religious prejudice, developing a rational basis for decisions on the use of our resources soberly and guided by the fact, without carelessness but as well without horror scenarios motivated by propaganda strategy. (6) Only with this kind of ecology our decisions in concrete cases will really be in accordance with the underlying preference and value decisions that are important to us.

Instead of such an approach regretfully the dictatorial tendencies of the environmental movement become more and more prominent. This starts with social pressure to bring different ways of life into line to an ecologically correct uniform level and can reach direct coercive measures or even violence against insubordinate citizens denounced as ecological sinners or against detested technologies. The ecological reasonableness of certain coercive measures has no longer to be proven as one feels confident to possess a doctrine of salvation. Competing values, be it beauty, liberty, or joy of life, do not matter anymore. The resurgence of a guilt culture threatens, similar to the one once implemented by Christianity, but now with an ecological stamp. We have to reject this and oppose the inclination of many politicians to flatter the zeitgeist by generously passing ever more detailed ecological regulations and restrictions which put considerable financial burdens as well as losses of freedom on the citizens, often enough without sufficient democratic discussion and factual justification. (7)

The job of the expert scientists is to present us the facts in a way that we can get an idea of the problems as realistically as possible while not being steered in a certain direction by a biased selection or extrapolation of facts. Regretfully also the critics of ecological mainstream ideas ignore these principles time and again in order to get more publicity.

The task of philosophers is to participate in the debate on the consequences that should be drawn from the facts and to argue the case for really drawing the adequate, morally defensible consequences.

> "'Sins against the environment' or 'ecosin', which so reminds us of the sin economics of the late Middle Ages and the early modern period, is meant not as a scientific term but as a religious metaphor."... "The trope of divine retribution for human sins has not yet faded into oblivion, even today in the twenty-first century."[2]
>
> Wolfgang Behringer

> "Even if they are not prepared to reduce historical progress of civilisation as much, green fundamentalists and all the other fundamentalists in the world are essentially alike as two peas in a pod ....
> The basic idea is always the same: If my group is in possession of the ultimate truth about salvation, truth, and life, this cannot be negotiated taking into consideration the decisions, opinions, and interests of a majority. The willingness of others to compromise, to self-limitation, and open discussion about the best solution is just a sign of their ignorance and weakness."[3]
>
> Thomas Meyer

> "Future apocalypses are as bad a vision as distant, unreachable paradises. It is a big enough challenge to make the best of the present."[4]
>
> Josef H. Reichholf

3.6. About Life and Death

Dogmas in retreat

"It would be a wrong conclusion, however, to regard a quarrel erupting about fundamental convictions hitherto stable in an everyday culture as a sign of cultural weakness of the quarrelling society, of its normative disorientation, and of the erosion of its fundamental norms. Probably, quite the opposite is true:

... In such a quarrel we come to an understanding about the norms we do not want to live without, about their content, their scope, their power, and their future."[1]

Winfried Hassemer

3.6.1. Dying, Death, Immortality

Intellectual integrity and the joy from a blackbird's song

"What counts is the whole life, and everybody may get along with it the way he believes best. We live for life and definitely not for the hour of death."[1]

Josef Popper-Lynkeus

"We know neither mind nor soul without body, but we know that our skin, our brain, our eyes, our heart decay. Everything is in harsh contradiction to a belief in immortality. Nevertheless, the thought of an end of life is unbearable for a majority. Most of the crowns of all creation are by far too much in love with themselves. Even as a pile of bones, or less than a bone remnant, one wants to be John Smith or Jane Bloggs and remain it for all eternity."[2]

Karlheinz Deschner

"All this fuss about the idea of immortality is for people of rank, and especially women, who have nothing to do. But an able man, who has something to do here, and must toil and strive day by day to accomplish it, leaves the future world till it comes, and contents himself with being active and useful in this. Thoughts about immortality are also good for those who have small success here below …"[3]

Johann Wolfgang von Goethe

I go along with Goethe in considering idle all speculations about immortality and especially the details of an alleged hereafter. Nevertheless, the question "What comes after death?" is a fundamental question humans will probably never stop to ask and be concerned about. We find strong motives to assume our immortality in our self-preservation instinct, in our hope not to lose beloved people irrevocably, and in our wish for justice being restored in an afterlife.

Still more than the decay and death of the body, the destruction of a human person, the destruction of its mental existence is offensive, striking, and even somehow inconceivable.

But these motives and feelings, this inner resistance against mortality and transience are no justification for cherishing illusions.

From the perspective of those unwilling to believe there is every indication that our individual existence and personality come to an end when our body and our brain die. For a short period of time some of our individual traits may still be recognisable by what we have passed on to our descendants on a genetic and social level. Especially in the memory of other people our individuality finds more or less lasting and more or less positive or negative reverberations.

There are no good reasons to support the assumption that mind might exist independently of a functioning brain. To the contrary, all evidence suggests that mind is a function of the corporeal organ brain. If we consider the changes the personality of a human being may undergo before she or he dies (not seldom finally *can* die), I am rationally unable to understand how one may still believe that the personality of a human being (what else should »soul« mean) could resurrect in another world. Which personality after all? The »personality« of a new-born, the personality of a five-, twenty-, fifty- or a (perhaps mentally heavily impaired) eighty- – or ninety-year-old? Or some kind of super-personality created by death, whatever that might mean? An analogous question arises if even the resurrection of the body is suggested. Should we be allowed to choose in which age we found our body most attractive? (I know, an "astral body" spares us this kind of "stupid questions" – human power of imagination does not shy away from anything.)

200

If all human beings would be born and die in full possession of their mental faculties, a life after death would appear somewhat more plausible. When assuming an immortal soul not only the question arises whereto it goes after death (Christianity offering the relatively modest number of alternatives hell, purgatory and heaven, while others reach seven heavens) but also the irrefutable question where and what the soul was before taking possession of its present brain.

Especially the great Indian religions (but not only them) offer transmigration, reincarnation or rebirth to deal with this problem, while Christianity needs an ever new divine act of creation for every soul. These concepts seem so plausible to me from a rational point of view that I cannot abstain from letting compete with them an old family wisdom about the origin of the soul. When the conversation turned to something what had happened before we children had been born, we were told: "Back then you still were in Abraham's sausage kettle!"

It is possible, admittedly, to put forward such considerations in a slightly more serious manner. David Hume: "Reasoning from the common course of nature, and without supposing any new interposition of the supreme cause, which ought always to be excluded from philosophy, what is incorruptible must also be ingenerable. The Soul therefore if immortal, existed before our birth; and if the former existence no ways concerned us, neither will the latter." "When it is asked whether Agamemnon, Thersites, Hannibal, Varro, and every stupid clown that ever existed in Italy, Scythia, Bactria or Guinea, are now alive; can any man think, that a scrutiny of nature will furnish arguments strong enough to answer so strange a question in the affirmative? The want of argument without revelation sufficiently establishes the negative."[4] (1)

Near death experiences and hereafter experiences at the brink of death, especially the experience to look upon oneself virtually from outside, prove (if reported objectively at all) nothing more than the fact that some people can have this kind of mental experiences in such situations. Interestingly such experiences are sometimes also reported by people whose brain undergoes an acute lack of oxygen under less dramatic circumstances, making it highly probable that this factor is as at least one trigger for this kind of experiences. There is no rational justification to take them as an indication for a life after death. Horst Jaedicke phrases this with unsurpassed irony in his pleasurable guide to the extension of life and transience: "Now there are people who by an error of nature were able to return after a short trip to the hereafter. But their

accounts are even more wobbly. Over and above limited by the irrefutable observation that dead people can hardly testify unless they have never been dead. No wonder all these accounts are dreamily murky. There is much talk of a separation of the mind from the body. Some people feel like having been in a tunnel with a radiant light at the other end. And quite a few have difficulties to express their experiences at all as our language does not provide words for what does actually not exist"[5] (even though in delivering this punchline he underestimates the fictional power of language – from Snow White to God).
(2)

Apart from other people's rather ephemeral direct memories of a certain person there is a relative immortality for material and mental products of human beings. Our ability to preserve certain parts of our brain activity in complex symbol systems and to transfer certain mental and cultural achievements to storage media (today highly reproducible) enables us to considerably extend the local and temporal limits of communication and especially of our own individual lifespan. Thus, we can transfer certain mental and cultural achievements and even an image of our personality as a whole to the mind of other people independently of the further existence of our own brain and beyond our own death. This way mental content becomes part of the cultural heritage of humankind accessible to all human beings living on or coming later, at least in principle. But this content does only have meaning if there are brains able and willing to realise and process it.

That some of us are able to wrest a longer period of time from transience and oblivion by significant contributions to human culture does not make this much of a difference (at least in relation to the time scales of earth history or even the cosmos). Furthermore, relative immortality is not necessarily the decisive criterion for the value of a cultural or social achievement. Regretfully, monstrous crimes can also provide relative immortality.

The metaphysical realm of ideas remains physically bound, on the one hand to sign systems, images, symbols and their carrier media as a storage for cultural products of humans, and on the other hand to human (or comparably capable) brains able to transform these material substrates of culture into other material processes in themselves allowing the mental and cultural content to arise anew. Mind always existed and exists only in such brains though no single brain is able to think and realise all that has been recorded in different storage media and lots of it is not thought about or realised by any brain in a certain moment.

202

It appears especially intriguing that there are cultural achievements, as for example the laws of logic and mathematics, that ultimately have to be accepted by everybody dealing with the same problems and structures, like logical propositions or perfect geometrical surfaces and bodies. But the existence of stable, invariant mental objects and relations (as a subject of formal sciences) is no reason to postulate a platonic world of ideas independent of the existence of complex brains.

There are no scientific reasons that would make probable any other way of immortality or afterlife. However, could there perhaps be philosophical and moral reasons that should prompt us to a more far-reaching belief in immortality? What are the psychological and social consequences of a belief in immortality and of overcoming it?

The Christian idea of a day of judgement after death when we have to justify for our deeds is psychologically understandable but otherwise so implausible that it does hardly deserve any discussion today. Let me just mention that it cannot be taken as a matter of course that such a judgement had to be fair. The assumption that an imagined beyond has to be better than the world we live in is no more than a habitual way of thinking wedded to our cultural and religious tradition. There is no good reason for this assumption as Bertrand Russell has made impressively clear by one of these striking allegories that deal a death-blow to what time-honoured theological prejudice takes for granted (theologians then try to talk their way out somehow, for instance by calling the allegory "trivial"): "Supposing you got a crate of oranges that you opened, and you found all the top layer of oranges bad, you would not argue: 'The underneath ones must be good, so as to redress the balance.' You would say: 'Probably the whole lot is a bad consignment'; and that is really what a scientific person would argue about the universe."[6]

It is unsatisfactory, of course, to accept that people like Hitler will never be hold accountable for their deeds but it is nevertheless highly probable. We should not allow our desire for retributive or restorative justice to skew our perception of the world. (But we may still deem the life of a Hitler as wholly wasted – the worst thing we may say about a human life.)

Even if an afterlife seems unlikely beyond all reasonable doubt, a minimal amount of uncertainty has to be admitted. Does this mean that the unwilling to believe would have to await death with anxiety or fear? In principle, uncertainty is neither a cause for hope nor for anxiety. Nevertheless, it cannot be disputed that people often react to it with anxiety. But if we face death after a life in which we have seriously struggled to put into practice our moral attitudes and values, I think we can do this without anxiety even if we accept a rest of doubt that death constitutes the end of our individual existence and thus of all our toils and sufferings (though of all our joys as well). It may sound arrogant and presumptuous to religious believers but those who have lived in harmony with themselves and seriously strived to realise their moral attitudes and values, will, all possible mistakes that may have happened notwithstanding, hardly take it into their head to fear a divine judgement.

However, fear in a real and even acutely occurring life-threatening situation can only be mastered to a limited extent by philosophical thinking, and most likely if this kind of thinking has become an emotionally anchored attitude. It makes sense and is a logical consequence of a realistic coping with life to prepare dying while living. But it would be presumptuous if one would venture a prediction on how oneself will really behave when facing death. "But as for death, we can try it only once: we are all apprentices when we come to it." (Montaigne[7]) And it would be even more appropriate to say: We cannot experience death at all, only dying. And in this we are all apprentices indeed. "I do not believe that I have to be afraid of my hour of death. If I will be afraid in my hour of death, I do not know." (Lessing[8]) Even if one is not afraid of death, one me afraid of dying. I do not want to reason away the old and ever new human fear of dying. I just want to do my bit that people do not let determine their philosophy of life by fear or untenable desires or hopes for compensation.

If the attachment to life of the unwilling to believe and to everything she or he believes to be important in life rests upon choices philosophically (for lack of a better alternative), this does not mean that it would be weaker than an attachment that is founded in another way (apart from the fact that philosophical considerations contribute only partly to our anchoring in life: it is mostly determined much more by our predisposition, our biography, our personal relations, and our current life situation as a whole).

I do not deem it right to let the knowledge of transience constantly interfere with one's life as if one would wear mourning a little bit all the time. In case of concrete losses I want to allow spontaneous feelings instead of immunising myself by practising a stoic attitude and by the books of consolation from the history of philosophy. To follow a doctrine that we should avoid all strong feelings which just bind ourselves to the transient impoverishes the world. "Do not envy those who are free of suffering, the idols of wood for whom

204

nothing is lacking because their souls are so poor, who care nothing about rain and sunshine because they have nothing that needs cultivation." (Hölderlin[9]) We should not belittle transience and death by accepting them all too lightly.

Next, let's examine the question whether it leads to a general moral decay if more and more people believe that an afterlife and a judgement after death are unlikely. This is an empirical problem. And Birnbacher is undoubtedly right when he writes: "Not every truth about the world promotes decent behaviour, and not every illusion is entirely harmful."[10] I do not want to deny that the loss of a traditional religious bond may pose a threat for the morality of a person until she has found a new basis for her morality. (3) And I do not want to deny either that a belief in the hereafter may have morally positive effects on some people and that there may be people who can be discouraged to commit crimes only by the threat of a Last Judgement or for whom such a threat is at least the best way to keep them from committing crimes.

But if we undertake an overall assessment of the effects of different philosophies of life, we do not find convincing evidence from human history up to now or the present state of the world that a belief in an afterlife would have or would have had morally superior effects. On the contrary, it has frequently encouraged intolerance and fanatism and is still doing so in many places. If church leaders deplore a relationship between impiety and moral decay in modern Western societies, the question arises why these societies are doubtlessly amongst the most peaceful and freest that have ever existed on this earth. It suggests itself that one of the reasons is to be found in the decreased influence of religious ideas and institutions on social and public life. The abuses within the churches that have been uncovered on a large scale in recent years are also anything but an argument for the moral superiority of the doctrines of faith they represent.

A great positive moral influence of a belief in the hereafter is quite improbable from a psychological point of view too, as Hume already saw: "The inference is not just, because finite and temporary rewards and punishments have so great influence, that therefore such as are infinite and eternal must have so much greater. Consider, I beseech you, the attachment, which we have to present things, and the little concern which we discover for objects so remote and uncertain."[11]

To further a belief in the hereafter contrary to one's own convictions would be the last resort if all examples of a secular humanism would fail in practise in comparison to a religious foundation of morals (what would be tantamount to a severe defeat for all those unwilling to believe). Fortunately things do not look like that. There is, to the contrary, no indication that the loss of a belief in the hereafter might be a danger for morality on the whole. Religion is unnecessary and inappropriate as a "prothesis of morality". (Albert[12])

Even if one of the traditional religions, even if a religion comprising a belief in an afterlife providing compensatory justice, would really predominantly be a doctrine of salvation (and not, as almost ever, a doctrine of mischief to a considerable degree as well), even then it would be mandatory to try to overcome it and to achieve its salutary consequences on a different philosophical basis. Why that? Because of its lack of plausibility.

From the point of view of an unwilling to believe an adequate answer to moral deficits cannot be found in the conservation or restoration of the old religious ideas. "What is needed is to base moral training on a less precarious foundation than myth – in other words to replace a religious by a Humanist ethics." (Margaret Knight[13])

> "Enjoy the good in life and reduce its evils to the best of your ability! Believe that it can be better on earth than it is; then it will really become better. Do not expect the better from death but from yourselves! Do not eliminate death, eliminate the evils – the evils that are eliminable, the evils that are grounded in nothing else than human idleness, wickedness and ignorance – and just these evils are the most dreadful!"[14]

> Ludwig Feuerbach

> "Nine days before his death Immanuel Kant was visited by his physician. Old, ill and nearly blind, he rose from is chair and stood trembling with weakness and muttering unintelligible words. Finally his faithful companion realized that he would not sit down again until the visitor had taken a seat. This he did, and Kant then permitted himself to be helped to his chair and, after having regained some of his strength, said, 'Das Gefühl für Humanität hat mich noch nicht verlassen' – 'The sense of humanity has not yet left me.' The two men were moved almost to tears. For, though the word *Humanität* had come, in the eighteenth century, to mean little more than politeness or civility, it had, for Kant, a much deeper significance, which the circumstances of the moment served to emphasize: man's proud and tragic consciousness of self-approved and self-imposed principles, contrasting with his utter subjection to illness, decay and all that is implied in the word 'mortality'."[15]

> Erwin Panofsky

"They don't hope for immortality but the thought that the people close to them will fondly remember them after their death fills them with joy. They reject any kind of superstition and obscurantism. In every phase of their life they consider only intellectual integrity as compatible with human dignity."[16]

Joachim Buhl (4)

"… Now
I managed to enjoy
The song of every blackbird after me too."[17]

Bertolt Brecht

"Death is not an experiment: There is nothing to report. Minds do not exist disembodied."[18]

Gerald M. Edelman

"Death is not an experience; it is befalling us and cannot become an experience anymore."[19]

Silvia Bovenschen

3.6.2. Death and Brain Death

Beyond personality

The possibilities of modern medicine have created situations in which death is occurring in two steps: brain death and death of the rest of the body, also called "clinical death". At the outset there was a broad agreement among all scientifically trained participants in the discussion that brain death had to be looked upon as equivalent with the "actual" death, thus being relevant for all substantial moral, social and legal deliberations. But during the last decades there has been a noticeable problematisation of brain death by some theologians, humanities scholars and also physicians.

There is no doubt that after the irreversible loss of higher brain functions and especially those of the cerebrum the body ceases to be the bearer of a human consciousness and a human person. Even for theologians this statement should be generally acceptable today. Within their conceptual world of faith they may say: The soul has left the body. But when brain death has occurred it is not justified to still speak of a "coma egressum", as proposed by the cardiac surgeon Unger[1] (he eschews speaking of a »coma transgressum« as this would damage all too much the scientific aura). And it is unjustified as well to classify the donation of organs as an act of social solidarity of a brain-dead "dying" person because there is no longer a person who could carry out such an act of solidarity. An act of solidarity is carried out by living people who agree to a possible donation of organs in case of their brain death. If brain death has occurred, only the relatives can carry out such an act of solidarity. But even if we imagine the soul of a dead person looking down from a cloud: she would have to think that the donation of organs is an indubitable moral duty.

Admittedly, there is more to a human individual than its consciousness. We can bring this to our mind most clearly by thinking about people whose celebrity – rightly or not – has or had to do a lot with their body. Let us imagine a Marilyn Monroe lying braindead in an intensive care unit (you may substitute any more recent male or female icons of body idealisation). Would we easily say that she is completely dead as long as we see her ventilated body with intact circulation and excretory functions? The example may seem superficial. But it may be more suitable, even for those of us who are trained to think scientifically, to foster empathy for the imposition that the concept of brain death constitutes for an everyday understanding of death and the unmediated apprehension (such an example may perhaps accomplish this better than the dreadful imagination to experience this situation with a beloved person).

In braindead human beings where the rest of the body is kept alive by intensive care the occurrence of death is doubtlessly less clearly recognisable, making it counterintuitive to denote them as dead. This may be accentuated even more by special situations, as for example when an unborn child lives on and grows in the body of a braindead mother.

The concept of brain death, as a definition of death essentially based on the irreversible loss of consciousness, should nevertheless have precedence for all moral, social and legal considerations. (1) Human life has to be taken into account as a moral value only until the brain death of a human individual has occurred. Compared with the possibility to help a – often critically – ill person through the organ of a braindead human being what may be the moral significance of clinical death, of the death of the rest of the body? Can the interests of a braindead human being or its relatives in the integrity of the body and in a gradual farewell by witnessing the clinical death, in a close experience of death, or, finally, in reverence and maintaining the peace of the dead even remotely measure up to the moral obligation to help a living person in need? (2)

The statement of some theologians and philosophers that brain death would be only a precondition of death but not death itself shows – though justifiable in principle – a wrong focus. From here it is only a small step to a slogan like "One's own dying is inviolable" (in a sense extending beyond brain death). And such a slogan is irresponsible because it encourages wrong moral judgements and decisions. It is an exaggerated backlash against the – for years admittedly all to obvious - equation of death and brain death. Transplant surgeons, to whom the whole pointless seeming philosophising about brain death is a nuisance now, have had a (small) contributory fault in bringing about this backlash. But it can only find a broader appeal against the backdrop of a (con)temporary tendency to a hostility towards science and to an overdrawn suspicion and a latently aggressive fundamental attitude towards science and technology in general. This attitude coalesces with old religious convictions and prejudices, namely that humans are not allowed "to play god" and would have to accept their destiny (even where they do not have to accept it yet). We meet with a double-faced attitude here. On the one hand, it may invite us to consider reasonably which part of the feasible should be really done because it is in the interest of the people concerned. On the other hand, this attitude may lead to a high degree of egoism and may have a sadomasochistic component.

General philosophical doubts about the extent to which the living conditions of modern civilisation and especially the modern affluent societies and the life-extending possibilities of modern medicine make people happier on the whole can be discussed back and forth with a wide variety of arguments and examples. But it is indubitable that these developments have increased average life expectancy, that they allow to reduce, avoid or postpone quality of life impairment by illness in many cases and that they extend the human scope for decision-making in many situations. Undoubtedly negative aspects for a counterbalance can be found. But let the people concerned take their own decisions wherever possible! Philosophical doubts on progress give nobody a right, anyway, to deny a young person requiring dialysis the possibility to get a kidney transplant opening up an opportunity for many years of life worth living to her or him while braindead donors and their relatives do not have to sacrifice anything which might have any comparable weight in a comprehensible moral weighing.

I consider it in the interest of the patients in need of transplants – at least in Germany for the time being – that people have the possibility to contradict organ donation after their death. The donation of organs in case of one's own brain death is a moral duty. Considering the interests in conflict here, it would be justified in principle to also enforce it legally, and a mere obligation to inform the relatives would be a morally adequate solution of this conflict of values, even in the face of a contradiction against organ donation during the lifetime of the deceased or their relatives post-mortem. But such a legal regulation would foreseeably provoke a detrimental distrust towards transplantation medicine as matters stand now. However, every citizen can be expected to decide on a potential post mortal donation of organs after having had the possibility for thorough information and explanation and, if possible, after being asked explicitly (for example when applying for or extending an ID document). By such a regulation a society makes clear that the donation of organs is morally appreciated and regarded as a moral duty. If a person has not contradicted organ donation while alive, this should be taken as consent and the relatives should no longer be granted the right to refuse organ donation. This kind of opt-out solution has proved successful in several countries without evoking significant conflicts and has contributed to a higher number of organ transplantations compared to Germany. We should confront the reality that other solutions do not sufficiently account for the inertia and indecision of many people.

However, when the goings get tough and it comes to concretely and immediately saving a human life, organ removal from a braindead donor is undoubtedly morally justified even if there is an explicit objection by braindead donors or their relatives because a weighing of interests and values clearly speaks in favour of the organ recipient, and jurisdiction should also consider it justified as a defence of necessity. If physicians commonly refrain from removing organs without consent or in the case of an actual objection, then this is morally justified by pragmatic considerations concerning the acceptance of transplantation medicine. Though one would help the concrete organ recipient one would, taking into account the social status quo, harm a greater number of potential organ recipients. Furthermore, jurisdiction is de facto divided over accepting a defence of necessity in this situation, albeit because of a wrong moral weighing, and thus a physician takes a considerable legal risks by removing an organ without consent. Considering the moral weighing at stake, one may discuss if physicians should show moral heroism here, but in my opinion the already mentioned considerations concerning the general acceptance of transplantation medicine speak against it.

By the way, I lack any understanding (we should generally break the bad habit again to show understanding for even the least justified standpoints) that some theologians, philosophers, jurists and even physicians disapprove of the completely justified and adequate considerable moral pressure in favour of a donation of organs, proclaim the refusal of organ donation as morally equitable and speak up for the "courage" to claim publicly a inviolability of one's own dying beyond brain death. That one may find oneself in an outsider position today in certain discussions when declaring organ donation a moral duty is grotesque given the weighing of interests at stake. If there is even a drivel about what a braindead human being might feel and it is maintained that a braindead human being would be unconditionally alive from a biological point of view and nobody could make a reliable statement about ist consciousness, well, then it can definitely only be regretted that such nonsense can draw considerable attention to its authors instead of disqualifying them.[2]

A positive valuation of organ donation and transplantation medicine and their social acceptance and integration are very important. It is paradoxical and inconsequential if theologians and philosophers, who often readily deplore a tendency towards selfish behaviour, act as conceptual smoke launchers in this respect and create or support mistrust without any serious justification. One can only guess what moves them. Does it originate from an insufficient examination and assessment of scientific facts, from problems to accept one's own mortality, or just from striving to put on an air of importance?

If a society manages to avoid accidents more or less satisfactorily and increasingly better, there will always be a shortage of organ donors given the possibilities of modern medicine as long as we depend on human organs (which may possibly be no longer the case in the foreseeable future.) (3) We can only reduce but not remedy this shortage. For the moment, the greatest challenges and the greatest chances to reduce this shortage lie in organisational improvements in hospitals, especially by sufficient staffing and motivational support. We should not expect all too much from legal regulation, but we should at least demand that it does not hamper transplantation medicine without good reasons. This would happen in the most extreme way by a legal regulation that would exclusively accept an explicit consent of the donor during his lifetime, and it happens quite concretely, for example, by the unjustified prohibition of a living donor cross-over organ transplantation of unrelated people in the German Organ Transplantation Act (requiring an undignified bending of facts to circumvent this).

We need the concept of brain death (or alternatively the criterion of an irreversible loss of consciousness which is still afflicted by some problems in practical application) not only for the sake of transplantation medicine. We will still need it even if we should no longer need it for this purpose because it is one plausible possibility to define the moment when intensive care measures can and should be stopped as they have no longer any prospect of success, do not serve the affected person anymore and their prolongation would be an irresponsible misallocation of resources and, furthermore, undignified (these are situations where it makes sense to refer to a proper sense of "reverence" in the sense of respect for the patient, but not for calling into question organ donation).

Perhaps a society less influenced by distrust in science and technical medicine will someday move away from an unconditional confirmation of brain death or clinical death as a prerequisite of organ removal. It would be morally justifiable and nothing else than consequent to accept patients as organ donors (if medically possible) in whom all treatment is abandoned as a sequel of the hopelessness of their medical condition and their own advance directive or their relatives' directive in fulfilling their presumed will or in whom even an active euthanasia is requested and justified because of their suffering. When a patient's death is intended for good reasons, it appears morally plausible and highly estimable if the patient or her or his relatives want to help other people even by the process of dying if this is medically possible and sensible. (4) Such a development may also be promoted by new technical possibilities concerning organ donation after cardio-circulatory death (DCD), by which it is possible due to new technical aids to remove even the heart after the cessation of circulatory support measures and mechanical ventilation and a five-minute cardiac arrest and the cerebral death thereby ensured, and to treat it outside the body in such a way that it can be used for transplantation. Like so many well-justifiable approaches in bioethics, this method is predominantly rejected across the board in Germany (in contrast to, for example, Switzerland and the UK where 46 percent of organ donors in 2022/2023 were DCD-donors). If the death of the donor is intended on the basis of an appropriate declaration of will and a hopeless situation with regard to the recovery of consciousness or a life seen as worth living, then hair-splitting discussions about, for example, the required length of a cardiac arrest prior to organ removal are out of place.

3.6.3. The Value of Life and the Right to Life

Controversial moral weighings

The following sections will be dedicated to a discussion about the value of different forms and stages of life in a wide variety of situations, including also those newly generated by the development of modern life sciences.

I will discuss these question in relatively great detail – compared to other important issues – because they partly raise extraordinarily difficult and differentiated weighings, especially if one wants to proceed according to commonly accepted moral attitudes and values in a comprehensible and consistent manner and avoid ad-hoc-decisionism as far as possible, that is, decisions based on mere situational moral intuitions or pragmatic considerations. However, the social relevance of some of these problems should not be overestimated. It may be much lower than their fundamental significance because the respective situations occur relatively rarely in comparison with other moral dilemmas.

A sufficient knowledge and a realistic consideration of scientific facts is an indispensable premise for acceptable moral judgements about the problems to be discussed here.

We humans have to set ourselves the principles for our attitude to life and our dealing with life. Creating illusions of objectivity by taking our standards from a cultural tradition, and especially a religion, does not change this. However, what we can set is subject to restrictions that do not exist in principle but are inevitably demonstrated by reality in the course of time. Thus, some social regulations, especially a too far reaching repeal of the ban on killing are simply incompatible with long-term social stability and an advanced state of human society, and certain ways of dealing with non-human life would eventually destroy the basis of our own existence.

Life, and human life too, is no absolute value. Life, or a life with the least possible amount of suffering, is not the only and not necessarily the highest value. The value of an individual life, though it deserves a high level of protection especially if it is the life of a human person, has to be weighed against the right to life of other living beings and against a variety of other values. A "monolithic view of values" is not adequate. This statement seems trivial at first glance, it appears almost impossible to contest it consequently and de facto everybody somehow proceeds accordingly. Nevertheless, to accept it consciously is already an essential step towards a stringent, rational discussion of the questions addressed in the next sections.

In my considerations I will pay special attention to the positions of the Australian philosopher Peter Singer and his colleague Helga Kuhse. Both of them confront us with the inconsistencies of traditional and widely used ways of argumentation concerning the value of life and the right to life and elucidate morally significant alternatives. It is good advice for everybody who wants to reach consequent standpoints in this field to pass through the purgatory of their argumentation which is based on a wealth of concrete and thoroughly researched examples. However, to avoid inconsequence and inconsistency is not sufficient as a justification of the advocated moral positions. Often enough I agree with Singer concerning his results. But I advocate an ethics of values and that means also and foremost an ethics of weighing up values. I consider a mere utilitarian concept just a heuristic means in ethics, comparable to claims of universalisation after the manner of Kant's imperative. Preferences and interests represent values too (even if they seem to be morally negligible, they have significance at least because of the value of personal freedom). Neither the assessment of concretely given preferences and interests nor a consideration about the consequences the universalisation of maxim's of actions would have can substitute weighings of values and decisions on values. (1) In anticipation of a more detailed discussion of specific issues I will emphasise some aspects I consider important in the discussion about the value of life and the right to life in the following part of this section.

I am convinced that human life in a morally significant sense depends on the possibility that the respective human being has, or can develop, or can regain some sort of at least rudimentary self-awareness or ego consciousness.

As soon as human life in this sense has passed the newborn period and a human person has come into existence we should at least fulfil the basic needs including an oral diet sufficient for survival even under circumstances that make the quality of this life for the individual itself seem low (but not clearly negative). ("Fulfilment of basic needs including oral diet" as a minimum

214

obligation provides a sufficiently clear demarcation, better than the quite differently interpreted distinction between "extraordinary" and "normal" therapeutical efforts; we will return to this point when discussing the issue of "prolongation of life".)

We should only terminate human life in the above mentioned sense intentionally (leaving aside self-defence, defence of victims and justifiable acts of war) or aid and abet a person in the termination of life if we are asked explicitly and seriously by her to do so because of a comprehensibly unbearable situation making life worthless for herself, be it in consequence of a hopeless agonising disease or of progressive age-related degeneration (or if we have at least convincing evidence that the respective human being would ask us for such help if she or he would be able to do so). In other words: We should terminate or help to terminate human life only if the respective person herself has no longer any interest to live on for understandable reasons but quite on the contrary wishes to die.

The state should only enact restrictions concerning new techniques dealing with human life, as provided for example by genetic engineering or reproductive medicine if otherwise a grave violation of the interests of human beings must be feared, but not in order to establish ideal demands. In judging new possibilities of reproductive medicine the possibilities a traditional family can ideally offer to children are often taken as a yardstick, especially in Germany. Given the fact that the reality of traditional family structures often falls considerably short of this ideal too, such a yardstick appears inadequate and exaggerated, and the more so, as many constellations rendered possible by modern reproductive medicine that look unusual and questionable at first glance will hardly occur in large numbers.

The state should set a legal framework and legal boundaries concerning the preservation or termination of life and the dealing with life that express a moral minimum consensus, but it should not require by law to obey particular moral norms of traditional religions or other social groups. We should distinguish, as a matter of principle, between what we consider to be morally questionable or objectionable with good reasons after thorough weighing and what requires legal prohibition. A tendency to an anticipatory legislation against risks that cannot even be assessed and estimated concretely has spread fatally and it deserves deep suspicion and sometimes firm resistance.

In Germany the discussion on bioethical problems to a considerable part neither fulfils the demand for well-founded moral evaluations nor for a separation of moral and legal evaluation. It often stays embarrassingly super-ficial and is dominated by arguments that are either morally irrelevant or of minor importance. In many cases we witness the last defensive battles of a religiously shaped thinking though the arguments are partly presented under the guise of secular philosophical phrasing. The representatives of the large Christian churches and politicians who are still predominantly determined by religiously shaped thinking (and be it in the form of the trendy green nature religion) feel very well the danger that arises for their positions of power and their influence as soon as people doubt the inevitability of their destiny ("God-given", "natural") of unlucky and unhappy life situations, make their own moral considerations, demand comprehensible moral weighings and are no longer content with an appeal to religious dogmatic formulas or their secular descendants (here in first place "human dignity", often used as nothing more than a catchword).

On the other hand, social peace is an important value and conflict minimi-sation is a substantial presupposition to achieve it. For that reason Birnbacher has made a proposal worth heeding: "the piety principle".[1] It was suggested particularly with regard to embryo protection, but it makes sense and can be applied concerning many other controversial moral issues. Its essence is that one tries to avoid to offend prevailing feelings and sensibilities. Such a piety principle has a genuine moral content because of the values to whose realisa-tion it contributes, and it cannot be dismissed as mere opportunism.

But even if we accept this principle, we do not get around the fact that often enough substantial weighings of values make it inevitable to argue out and decide conflicts. Religious positions supposing an ensoulment of human be-ings in the moment of conception, or likewise a secular concept of human dignity ascribing the full rights of protection of human persons to a human being already from this moment forth, lead to fundamentally different conse-quences in many questions concerning the value of life and the right to life compared to a naturalistic-humanistic standpoint assuming that human beings develop into a human person only gradually and that they become human be-ings with full value and full rights of protection only when reaching the status of personhood. Only then they attain human dignity in a full sense with the consequence that, at least under the conditions of a peaceful civil society, it is unconditionally forbidden to subordinate their right to life to the interests of other human persons how wellfounded they may ever be. Such differences of opinion must clash inevitably in social dispute and will remain irreconcilable
216

to some degree.

Though a common moral basis is not always possible, a society has to find a common legal basis to live with. In the future this legal basis cannot be dominated by religious or religiously influenced conceptions to the same degree as hitherto. Secular citizens can no longer be expected to accept severe restrictions and paternalism for the sake of a piety principle towards religious views. On the other hand, religious citizens are still free to adhere to their own moral rules. For reasons of minority protection, this principle should have applied to secular citizens long-since, but it becomes all the more indispensable when religiously bound citizens are increasingly becoming a minority.

At this point I want to make a short remark on the notion of "human dignity". If this is meant to be more than cheap talk and is supposed to have a concrete meaning, one may follow Kant and state as its essence that human beings are "ends in themselves" and shall not be made mere means for achieving other ends or that they should not merely serve the interest of other human beings, but that an intrinsic worth has to be ascribed to every individual human existence. Thus, the right to life, to development, and to liberty may be subsumed under one notion (though it is of very limited use to do so as such a subsumption impedes a clear consideration). In principle this changes nothing for the discussion from which stage of development on human beings should be conceded certain rights of protection. Nevertheless, the notion of human dignity is (mis)used to suggest that an all or nothing decision at the very beginning of human existence, that is at the moment of conception or nidation, would be mandatory. But human dignity as a value cannot mean the protection of mere existence regardless of the circumstances of life to be expected and regardless of the dignity of other human beings. It is not for nothing that we also speak of an "inhumane existence". A total protection of life beginning with conception looks like an easy solution for a legal system (though it is already hardly conceivable how to implement it consequently in legal practice). From a moral perspective such a standpoint appears acceptable just as long as one refuses to consider the consequences in some detail.

As to the behaviour of physicians, their own philosophical orientation will inevitably influence their decisions concerning life and especially at the border between life and death. But they should, as far as not constrained by legal boundaries or unconditionally obliged by personal decisions of conscience, just clarify the existing alternatives to the people concerned and orientate their own behaviour according to the explicit or presumed will and interest of the patient which should be assessed also with the help of relatives if necessary. Only if no sufficient guidance can be found thereby, should physicians make a decision according to their own philosophical principles. In some cases it may also be preferable to refer patients to another physician with more closely related philosophical attitudes instead of confronting and dominating them by one's own philosophical convictions.

For non-human life the presence of sentience and an ability to suffer, of consciousness, of self-awareness and of conscious individuality or ego consciousness (for this there are reasonable indications in primates only) are significant criteria for delimitation that should only be used, however, for the ascription of graduations in value. The ranking arising as a result corresponds only partly with the degree of resemblance and the genetical relatedness to us humans for what reason the latter criterion does not have a moral significance independent of other considerations. Furthermore, I do not think that »primitive« animal life lacking a central nervous system or plant life would be worthless (even if we leave aside its possible benefit for us humans). To me the following principle appears to be a reasonable and adequate guideline for our dealing with life: The lower a form of life is to be ranked according to the above-mentioned criteria the more we are allowed to direct our respect for this life less towards the individual than towards the preservation of the species.

Today it appears obvious that species conservation is a good thing. But a justification of this standpoint is all but trivial. Evidently the conservation of a species of living beings can be more valuable to us than that of individuals, and it may appear more valuable to us to conserve a species than to create or preserve ever more individuals of another species of living beings, even if these possess higher, more differentiated capabilities of consciousness. So how can we argue for species conservation and the preservation of biodiversity?

There are various good reasons: moral reasons reaching beyond us humans and selfish reasons as well. An important moral reason going beyond selfish human interest lies in the irreducible value "life" by which any sort of life is seen as morally significant, though with a reasoned ranking done by us (which is why we will hardly hesitate to eradicate pathogens completely, or with the sole exception of laboratory remnants, if we are able to do so). An expansion of human population so excessive as to lead to an extinction of other highly differentiated species will be judged morally wrong if we cherish respect for

218

life in conjunction with the moral attitude of moderation. But the weighing of interests following therefrom may be extremely difficult in concrete cases. And such considerations should not mislead us to idealise nature and an environment without or almost without human influence. Aesthetical and psychological aspects also play a role for moral considerations to justify species conservation: the beauty and joy of life which we experience through other living beings have an intrinsic moral value.

Thereby we have already arrived at selfish reasons that should move us humans to species conservation. We are not able to estimate which amount of species loss the ecosystem of our planet will tolerate before suffering severe damage or even a collapse that would massively harm or destroy the conditions of life of our own species. We cannot foresee which already known or even still unknown species could be useful for us in which way in the future. Thus, species conservation is also an imperative of responsibility towards our descendants, as a moral obligation to them on the one hand, and as a selfish undertaking with respect to the survival of our own species on the other hand. Finally, species conservation may very concretely produce more benefit for the population of a certain area than species extinction (and this is surely its best chance in a number of cases). The foreign exchange revenue from wildlife observation may better support the population of poor countries than leaving the last habitats of endangered species to a direct, displacing use by humans.

We experience today, caused by us humans, a period of species extinction on a large scale. Though there have been various periods of extensive species extinction throughout evolutionary history, and these have not only eliminated life but have also created room for new phases of evolution and a multitude of new species, the current period of species extinction is probably the fastest and definitely the greatest since the beginning of human history. This is unsettling. Even if it will not be that easy to destroy life on earth, we could bring it to the point where the conditions of life for our own species deteriorate radically. One of the most threatening factors at least for the next generations of us humans is the growth of population still insufficiently brought under control in many countries of the world.

Nevertheless, there is also reason for hope. Today the idea of conservation and preservation of nature has spread among humans like never before. Contrary to this, humans have committed overexploitation of natural resources and wiped out animal species already during former centuries but without realising any significant problem. With the expansion of our scientific knowledge and of our technical possibilities our acting has greater and faster effects. These possibilities can be used in a destructive manner but also to make the earth a relatively pleasant place in historical comparison. We are able to find the right way today if we refrain from a ruthless exploitation of nature, on the one hand, and avoid to build up the veneration and preservation of nature into a religion and constrain any room of development for ourselves and our fellow human beings, on the other hand.

3.6.4. Unborn Life, Newborns

Life is precious, not holy

The discussion about moral and legal aspects of abortion is a "playground" for the fanciers of "sharply" drawn lines. According to catholic religious teaching the development of human life should not be contracepted even if it is nothing more than the ability of a married couple to have a child. From the moment of conception human life would deserve an absolute protection and to terminate it intentionally would be immorally with just a few exceptions. At the other end of the scale there are standpoints like those of Hoerster, who argues that the right to life of human beings should deserve protection only from the moment of birth onwards, or Singer, who even wants to subject it to the decision of parents and doctors for up to four weeks after birth.

Regarding human life (and the life of the most highly developed animals) Singer advocates the view "that life only begins in the morally significant sense when there is awareness of one's existence over time."[1] As one consequence human newborn infants should not be considered as beings with an intrinsic right to life, the same claim to life as a person, during the first one to four weeks after birth. The difference between killing a severely disabled and a normal newborn is not to be seen in some presupposed right to life the latter would have, and the former would not have, but in the fact that killing a healthy newborn infant normally hurts the feelings of the parents in a dreadful manner or that one could at least find adoptive parents caring for a healthy newborn while that will often not be the case for a disabled newborn infant, depending on the degree of its disability.

To deny human newborn infants an intrinsic right to life indubitably defies the moral intuition of many of us. However, moral intuitions are very unreliable. Might it be that we are on the wrong track too following this intuition? Is it just a religiously, philosophically, and socially informed prejudice? Or does Singer neglect an important aspect?

I think the latter is indeed the case. The special value of human life does not only arise when specifically human manifestations of self-awareness, rationality and emotionality are actually present, it arises already from the potential to develop these characteristics, which human life has from its very beginning.

Singer is quite aware of this objection and counters that there is no general rule to ascribe the rights of X to a potential X.[2] Why then should we proceed like that concerning human beings? There is, however, no general rule either that we should not ascribe all the rights of X or some of the rights of X to specific kinds of potential XX's, and at least more rights than to an Y that can never become an X. And I do not propose either that we should grant the same right to life to an embryo that has just come into being that we grant to human beings equipped with self-awareness, emotionality and rationality. But I think that, when establishing morals standards for dealing with human life, it makes sense and is justified to ascribe a graduated value to it, depending on its stage of development, and already before reaching the stage of self-awareness, emotionality and rationality, and, as a consequence, also grant it a graduated degree of protection.

Singer wants to convince us by his argumentation that acquiring self-awareness and having reached the status of a person is suitable for and even asks for drawing a sharp line concerning the value of life and the right to life and, as a consequence, also concerning a moral and legal prohibition on killing. Admittedly, the question whether there is a person and whether their interests, their right to life, their autonomy and their right to a free development of personality are violated by a certain way of acting is of great importance. This is comprehensible from very different basic philosophical tenets. Thus, it is, for example, also of central importance for the Texan Catholic H. T. Engelhardt in his attempt (worth reading) to outline a secular framework for a conflicting, pluralistic society.[3] In my opinion too, the status of being a person (personhood) is an especially important and comprehensible moral and legal line of demarcation.

Nevertheless, it is just one possible line of demarcation, one possible moral weighing, a particular moral decision (whose social significance depends on conventional agreement). In the following I will try to make clear that this criterion of demarcation needs to be supplemented, that it does not suffice for a secular morality as well, neither in the personal realm nor for an agreement on a framework for a pluralistic society. A gradual extension of the protection of life and the right to life and appropriate qualifications concerning the prohibition of killing that are not based on the personhood criterion of demarcation alone lead to more acceptable and practicable standards.

As we will see, it is hardly possible to argue against killing healthy newborn infants on the basis of Singer's proposal if parents would like to do this (or have this done) for social reasons. And one may, contrary to Singer (and me), take the view that a six-weeks-old human embryo deserves a higher protection of life than an adult chimpanzee. Chimpanzees can learn simple sign languages and we know from several experiments that they obviously have a certain degree of self-awareness and perceive themselves as beings with a past and a future. But the human embryo will become a human being with all its considerably more developed mental and emotional capabilities (though not always used for something good) within a short lapse of time if its development is not disrupted by extraordinary events. To ascribe a higher value to the human embryo is not contradictory to the view that we should not unnecessarily inflict harm and suffering on chimpanzees, should protect their natural habitat as good as we can, should offer them the most possible species-appropriate environment if keeping them in captivity at all and that we should struggle against an excessive human population growth.

The reproach of "speciesism", rightly made by Singer when criticising cruel animal experimentation with no or only highly dubitable benefit for humans, is off the mark with respect to the mentioned comparison. The question whether to prefer life with an actual self-awareness as it can be found in the highest developed primates or life that will, if undisturbed, give rise to the development of a human person (possibly the personality of a philosopher of Singer's skills) cannot be decided by logical argumentation but only by a value judgement. If we decide for the human embryo, this does not mean that we would see the mere belonging to the human species as a paramount criterion valid under all circumstances. Instead, we ascribe a higher value to living beings that will later have considerably greater mental abilities than to those that already actually have lesser, though not insignificant or negligible abilities. Thus, I would judge it morally acceptable to inflict suffering on some chimpanzees or even to kill them if otherwise impossible significant progress

222

for the treatment of human diseases like AIDS could be expected therefrom, or even significant progress in reproductive, pre- and neonatal medicine. This might mean to kill some chimpanzees even for potential human persons under certain circumstances.

These deliberations show that Singer is right when he criticises the use of potentiality arguments in the sense of an equalisation argument between X and a potential X. But nevertheless, a potentiality argument can suffice to concede a special value and special rights to a potential X in comparison to an actual Y that can never become X.

If, on the other hand, progress in reproductive medicine could be reached alternatively by experiments on already born chimpanzees and on human embryos, I would judge it preferable to do the experimentation on human embryos because they have, if at all, a much lesser capacity for suffering and certainly no self-awareness. And I do not generally share the opinion that a human embryo deserves a higher degree of protection of life than a fully developed chimpanzee. When taking such a stance one could fell called to advocate a far-reaching prohibition of abortion, a morally mistaken position leading to a multitude of untenable consequences.

To ascribe a lesser value to potential capacities and characteristics than to actual ones may appear reasonable and adequate in many cases. Nevertheless, it is not a matter or course for a secular morality either but is part of the respective moral decisions and thus a moral decision in itself.

Let us proceed to other aspects now. I consider it wrong to conceive moral and legal constructions that generally reduce the protection of human life in certain situations, especially during pregnancy and the neonatal period, just to avoid the reproach of discriminating disabled life. We do nothing morally wrong or inconsequent if we allow rules for abortion for embryos and fetuses suffering from severe hereditary diseases or severe incurable developmental defects different from those for healthy ones or if we »discriminate« heavily disabled newborns in so far as not taking all possible efforts for life saving treatment going beyond basic care we would take in newborns with a prospect of life without severe permanent disease or disability. On the one hand, unborn or newborn children may be so severely disabled that even they themselves could have no interest in living on if they would be able to do the respective weighing and state their view. On the other hand, severely disabled unborn or newborn children impair the interests of other people, especially those of their closest relatives (and here de facto still mostly those of their mothers) in such a serious way that this cannot be morally insignificant.

So again: Which rules should we adopt for our dealings with unborn and newborn life? Which legal protection should we grant it?

As a matter of course, I do not see any reasonable argument against contraception, except the wish of parents to have a child. On the contrary, there are lots of reasons for contraception. This appears as a truism in our society. A different standpoint is only taken with respect to religious dogma, and even religious believers do hardly comply now with the precepts of their hierarchs. Responsible, farsighted contraception is morally completely sound and indubitably the best way for people who do not want to have children at the moment or permanently or who do not want to have more children.

The next way of interfering with the natural course of reproduction is emergency contraception by impeding ovulation or possibly the implantation of an already fertilised ovum in the uterus ("morning-after pill"). From a secular point of view this is a minor moral issue even if the implantation of a blastocyst is impeded, as this is just a well-ordered aggregation of cells which would, admittedly, evolve to become a human being if undisturbed but still has no similarity with the later human being. Furthermore, implantation is prone to a high degree of uncertainty without any external influence too. Nevertheless, this should not be a routine procedure of contraception (and it will hardly ever be regarding the frequent, though transient side effects for women because of the relatively high intake of hormones or drugs, the cost and the ever new uncertainties associated with it).

What should hold for the further course of pregnancy beyond conception? Is it justified to frame and establish different rules for abortion and protection of life depending on the stage of pregnancy and prenatal development? The right of the woman (or of both parents) to self-determination is opposed here to the right to life of an unborn human being and these rights have to be weighed against each other in an adequate and practicable manner. Good reasons can be adduced that this is best done by a graduated extension of the protection of life.

Abortion means to kill developing human life. Therefore it should not be a routine method of family planning. But I cannot see any good in forcing or just persuading women at all cost to bring children into the world they do not want or feel unable to bring up in a decent way. In particular it seems unreasonable to me to demand from a woman, who does not want this herself, to carry a child to full term from an early stage of pregnancy just to give it up for adoption (unreasonable for emotional and social reasons and for the physical strain and medical risks associated with pregnancy). And it seems definitely wrong to me that the right to self-determination of a woman who has become pregnant because of rape should be attached less importance from the beginning than a right to life ascribed to a developing human being. It also seems inadequate to me that a women should be impeded to decide if she wants to have a child or not by a mere inattentiveness or even carelessness with contraception (so this would not be laudable for both partners, especially if happening time and again). But it seems as well inacceptable to me that a healthy human being that has not passed the threshold of birth but is already viable outside the womb should be killed just because the attitude of the mother or the parents to having a child has changed during a late stage of pregnancy (even if this happens very rarely in real life).

Birth as a significant dividing line for distinctions concerning the protection of life has (as belonging to the human species as well) the advantage of a relatively high clarity for citizens, doctors and jurists and that is why it makes still sense to use it for this purpose. It serves legal certainty if a human being and even more a born human being enjoys a high degree of protection first of all without having to qualify for that by further characteristics (like actually present or potential self-awareness). Then one can still consider and establish to what extent this protection should be reduced under strictly defined conditions in certain cases.

But as a moral dividing line birth has only a minor significance in contemporary modern affluent societies because premature infants have a high probability to survive under the conditions of modern medicine during the last third of pregnancy and the risks for death during childbirth are very low to the point that a healthy fetus shortly before birth has only insignificantly lower prospects to become a healthy adult than a newborn infant.

Hoerster's proposal that an independent right to life should only begin with birth[4] exaggerates the significance we should ascribe to this event. This proposal would entail that we principally allow the killing of healthy unborn children already viable outside the womb and at most confine it by auxiliary constructions like refering to a greater risk for the mother through abortions in a late stage of pregnancy. And this proposal leads to the very implausible consequence that Hoerster wants to grant a right to life to a premature infant (so in later publications, impressed by the problems of rearing extremely preterm infants, only from 28 weeks of pregnancy onwards[5]) while he denies a healthy fetus of the same age or even older the same right just because it is still in the womb though it has much better prospects to grow to a healthy human person.

Singers above mentioned proposal, which wants to grant an unqualified right to life only from 4 weeks after birth onwards, needs similar auxiliary constructions to justify any moral and legal protection of newborns, for example by refering to a violation of the feelings and rights of the parents normally caused by killing a newborn. But how could we argue on the basis of Singer's dividing line against, for example, a practice still common in Asia to kill female newborn infants immediately after birth (be it for expecting dowry problems or because of a preference for male descendants under a one-child-policy as it existed in China)? We have a strong protective »instinct« towards newborn babies, which is generally a sound feeling, and attacking babies has always been considered an extremely vile breach of morality in our culture, from king Herod to Nazi cruelties. So if you present the idea of generally diminishing the protection of life for newborn babies to anybody not acquainted with philosophical discussions, and especially women, you will not earn much understanding and sympathy and this can be comprehended by moral philosophy as well.

Proposals like Singer's will only convince some philosophers whose desire for a clear and consequent dividing line outweighs their unease when considering such "solutions". All to simple and "consequent"dividing lines in questions concerning the protection of life and the right to life principally deserve our mistrust. They press continuous and gradual processes of nature into an all too saltatory scheme. But if we modify Singer's proposal so that the *maximum* protection for human life begins only at the end of the newborn period, we get a very convincing dividing line in my opinion.

So which gradations concerning the protection of life are adequate? A period of 12 weeks after conception appears adequate to me as a timeframe for the mother, or the parents, to exercise their right of self-determination and decide for or against a developing child (though any dividing line safely away from viability outside the womb, say up to 20 weeks, would not make a difference morally). But we should be clearly aware of what we do by an abortion at the end of week 12: we kill a human being of about six centimetres in length that already shows a human shape, in which the organs of the body are completely distinguishable, basic functions of the central nervous system have begun and involuntary movements are visible. Admittedly, any dividing line within the biologically gradual and stepless development of unborn life is a

226

disputable human positing (as are all other moral norms). Anyhow, an abortion within the above mentioned period seems legally and in some circumstances also morally acceptable to me (though I see a certain amount of moral guilt in an abortion even within this period if it is caused by carelessness).

This kind of dividing line is practicable. It leaves time for careful consideration and, as the case may be, carrying out the abortion. It makes sense from a medical point of view because doing an abortion early leaves more options for the procedure and carries less strain and risks for the pregnant women. The alternative would be an uncompromising protection of life from conception onwards and that would mean to value the right to life of the unborn child higher than the right to self-determination of the pregnant women already from the very beginning of its development. This would be a consequent standpoint to take but I think that it is neither adequate nor morally right. It seems hardly convincing without believing either in a certain variety of absolute natural law, an absolute religious foundation of values or a religious idea of ensoulment.

A mandatory independent counselling within the posited timeframe for abortion, if possible for both parents, seems reasonable and desirable to me, not only in the interests of the best possible protection of life but also in the interests of the future well-being of the women or the couple who have to decide. This counselling should not be slanted towards the continuation of pregnancy as this is not the best solution in every case. But it should inform about social support that can facilitate the continuation of pregnancy and it should explain the biological facts mentioned above, including an adequate use of photographs (not for abortion deterrence, by abusing, for example, the pioneering work of Lennart Nilsson, as it has already happened, but to illustrate the state of development at a certain stage of pregnancy). It does nobody any good if the people who have to decide on an abortion do not have a clear idea of what they are doing, and least of all themselves because they have to live with their decision in the future.

If there are significant genetic defects or disabilities in the unborn child, the situation changes. To me it is beyond doubt that one is morally allowed (and as a rule even should) terminate an early pregnancy in such a situation. In most cases it becomes possible thereby to have a healthy child later. There is no doubt that a healthy child has better prospects for a content and fulfilled life than a severely impaired one. Surely, some severely impaired children might have become a genius in some field, and some children looking perfectly healthy become felons or develop a severe chronical disease later. But such remote assumptions and exceptions should not determine our acting. Healthy children do not have worse prospects to develop extraordinary abilities just because they are healthy. There is also a romanticising of disease and disability and, no wonder, great achievements are even more impressing if they have been reached coming from a disadvantaged starting position.

A healthy, active and interested child is a great joy. A disabled child can also bring great joy and enrich the life of the other family members. It may even stabilise a marriage by the joint parental care. But a disabled child may also be a heavy burden for a family with severe privations and restrictions for the other family members lasting for decades. It may impede the opportunities for development of sisters or brothers, and it may even sometimes destroy the love of the spouses. As far as the somewhat precarious data can be assessed, marriages with severely disabled children have a higher divorce rate (with the possible exemption of mongoloid children), there are more single mothers, brothers and sisters are more frequently inflicted by mental disorders, and there is a considerable reduction of friendships outside the family.[6]

It is my firm conviction that parents who decide to terminate the life of a severely disabled embryo or fetus that is still not viable outside the womb and does not have consciousness or self-awareness make a responsible, far-sighted decision in the best interest of the whole family (including possible future healthy children). They do certainly not make a morally debased or only inferior decision. Quite the opposite: I consider it morally wrong to deliberately bring a child into the world that is burdened with a severe incurable disease or is heavily disabled. (1)

But we should not pretend that we necessarily act in the best interest of the developing unborn child too if we decide for an abortion because of an expected severe disease or disability. This may sometimes be the case, namely if its life would be agonising to a degree that it would wish itself to live no longer. But principally every living being has an urge for self-preservation first of all even if it is considerably disabled or impaired. Thus, if we decide for an abortion as a consequence of findings by prenatal diagnostics, we act in most cases against the interests the unborn child would have later (even if it does actually have nothing more than a vegetative urge to survive and no awareness of any interests whatsoever). We value the interests of the parents, of perhaps already existing or later conceived sisters and brothers higher than the right to life of the significantly disabled unborn child (even if it might wish later to have been its own younger healthy sibling). In many cases I consider this the right way of weighing up values and interests. But we should be clear about what we are doing, and we should call it what it is. Only then will we be able to correct in the long run the social prejudice prevailing in our societies that it would be morally superior to bring a severely disabled child into the world and to impose on oneself and others the associated irrevocable burdens and sacrifices concerning the realisation of a variety of other values that are anything but morally irrelevant.

To hide the so-called eugenic indication within a social or medical indication for abortion is a hypocritical way to maintain the fiction of non-discrimination also for human beings who are still not persons. The women and parents concerned mostly decide for a "discrimination" of disabled embryos and fetuses and use the social or medical indication (if a more sincere solution is not available) to terminate these pregnancies. For good reasons they prefer a healthy to a severely disabled child and use their leeway in decision-making as long as they can do so without harming a human person. It is unjustified to insinuate and to put into these parents' mind that they make morally inferior decisions for "convenience". Regrettably the cross-party tenor at least in the German debate on late-term abortions is just this. If mostly not personally affected theologians and politicians behave as if they were morally superior to a majority of citizens (and, to make matters worse, they do so in a conspicuously conforming way), we should definitely become very suspicious about the moral justification of their position.

A further remark has to be made at this point. Kurt Baier rightly points out that it is one thing to want to go on living rather than terminate one's life or have it end now; and it is quite another thing to decide that one would want once again to enter a life burdened by severe disabilities rather than not live it at all, if one could choose.[7] Or to phrase it still more pointedly: It is entirely possible that one wants to go on living now, having become a person, but at the same time be of the opinion that one's parents would have made a better choice if they would have done an abortion at the time when they became aware of the expected severe disability and when one was not a person still, and that they would have better tried to get another healthy child later.

In such a situation a timeframe of 12 weeks after conception is often too short. More time is needed to assess the relevant facts and make a decision based on them. For this cases it is reasonable to establish at least a timeframe for abortion coming close to viability outside the womb, as it had been done by German legislature with a 22 week dividing line in its second last reform of abortion law. But in my opinion it is defendable and even more adequate to allow abortion and thus the killing of an unborn child throughout the whole pregnancy in case of severe disability or impairment.

However, the inclusion of the so-called eugenic indication into a general »medical« indication extended throughout the whole pregnancy, as it was done in the last revision of German abortion law, is unsatisfying. It reduces the protection of healthy unborn children in an inadequate manner by extending the medical indication even to healthy unborn children viable outside the womb if a "severe physical or psychological disturbance of the pregnant women" can be confirmed. This ruling originates from an exaggeration of the principally right idea of anti-discrimination by already applying it to severely disabled human beings who are still not persons and have no self-awareness. In the case of a severely impaired unborn child, however, a completely different weighing of values arises compared to a healthy unborn child. As already said, it is insincere to hide an eugenic or embryopathic (which in reality more often is a "fetopathic") indication in an extended medical indication. A "severe disturbance of the pregnant woman's physical or mental health" is generally not the predominant, and not even a substantial reason to terminate the pregnancy in the case of a severely impaired fetus. Such a decision is, as we have already seen, rather a consequence of some completely different, and entirely justified, weighing of values. As our society widely accepts such decisions as a matter of course, it seems quite odd that a philosophical deliberation on their moral justification is still often enough seen as a red rag and answered by efforts to marginalise and even try to silence the respective philosophical protagonists.

Singer argues against ascribing significance to viability outside the womb as a moral and legal dividing line because that would mean that it would depend on the respective medical, historical and social situation at which stage of pregnancy this dividing line would be drawn. But what is so special about the fact that such changes of the situation also change our moral dividing lines? Just remember to what degree this was done by the birth control pill. Should the viability of foetuses outside the womb in modern affluent societies shift much further into the earlier stages of pregnancy (which is unlikely in the foreseeable future given the high costs and medical risks), one could still introduce calendar-based limits at a certain gestational age drawing upon criteria of costs and benefits. Is it adequate for a rational philosopher unbound by religion to ask for "eternal" dividing lines that are independent of the respective situation in questions concerning the value of life and the right to life? Our dividing lines should enable us to do an adequate weighing between different morally significant interests without weakening the protection of life unduly. This aim may require different dividing lines at different moments in history. For instance, in a modern affluent society where enough people willing to become adoptive parents can be found, no justification for killing healthy newborn infants is recognisable. For "primitive" people with very limited resources and no technical abilities to do abortions, or at least to do abortions safely, this may look different. The killing of healthy newborns sometimes observed here may be morally justified if this is the only way to ensure the survival of the other members of the community who are, contrary to newborn infants, already persons.

Another argument of Singer against using viability outside the womb as a dividing line is that we do not hold in other circumstances that a complete dependency on other people entitles them to decide on our living on or our death. This is indubitably correct. But he is turning the argument upside down. For persons dependency does not diminish their moral status, but for (still) non-persons a higher degree of independence may increase their moral status. One may pose the question whether the remaining dependency on the mother of a child already viable outside the womb can alone justify that she decides on its living on or death even during the newborn period. I think that few of us would like to concede this to the mother. To find a morally acceptable dividing line, it makes much more sense to formulate the question whether reaching a stage of development that allows to live on outside the womb without extreme medical measures should not justify a higher level of protection of life even if the status of a person has still not been reached. In my opinion it is adequate to draw a dividing line here.

However, I agree with Singer in so far as, though I do not consider viability outside the womb as morally irrelevant, I ascribe a far lesser significance to it as a moral and legal dividing line than to the presence of ego consciousness and the status of personhood. As a consequence, if weighing up between human beings is unavoidable, I would always unhesitatingly decide for a human being who has already developed self-awareness and become a person and against one who has only the possibility to do so, even if it is already viable outside the womb. To come back to a traditional example from the discussion of moral theology, I would always decide for the mother if her life is in danger because or during pregnancy and birth. Under the conditions of modern obstetrics, this example is, fortunately, of practical importance almost only in countries where legislation is dominated by religious fundamentalism (as in Poland where a legislation under the unholy influence of the catholic church led to the death of young and expectant mothers even in the 2020s as a consequence of such a mistaken moral weighing[7]).

Admittedly, if anyone can claim a particularly high degree of consistency for their dividing lines, then it is the radical pro-life proponents. But they pay for their consistency with consequences that hardly anyone, who faces reality, can defend in good conscience. Attaching the same value, the same »sanctity«, to human life under all circumstances leads to unacceptable consequences. As one would not be allowed to prefer one human being to another, one would, in the situation mentioned above, either have to accept the death of the mother and the child or at most draw lots. And how reasonable does it appear to demand in all seriousness that even the most severely disabled and malformed newborn infants, for example babies without a cerebrum, should be kept alive with all the means at our disposal as long as possible?

Now, what to do if a severe impairment of a child occurs or is recognised but in the last stage of pregnancy or during birth when the child is already viable outside the womb, at least if intensive care measures are deployed? What to do in cases of extreme premature birth when we have to expect considerable impairments of the surviving children in a high percentage? In principle, these questions already belong to the next section on prolongation of life and euthanasia but for the thematic connection I will treat them here.

According to the principles stated in the section on the value of life and the right to life, as well as above here, you may already guess the answer that seems adequate to me. In such a situation the decision should depend to a high degree on the wishes of the parents concerned who should be provided with all relevant, especially prognostic information as a basis for their decision. As the child still is no person, has no self-awareness and cannot have any wishes going beyond the moment and elementary needs, its life may be weighed up against other values, especially the interests of the parents and sisters and brothers. In cases with a high probability of severe impairment we should not begin intensive care measures (2), and in borderline cases where the probability of severe impairment is still considerable we should not urge for such measures or deploy them against the will of the parents. In premature births the involvement of parents in decision-making may be difficult or even

232

impossible because of time pressure. But if one is really willing to assure a say for the parents a shared decision-making on an informed basis will often be possible because such situations are foreseeable or imminent.

Is it justified to let die severely disabled newborn babies who might have a normal, close to normal, or at least decades-long life expectancy by providing comfort care only (feeding them water and possibly sedatives, among other basic measures) as it is evidently clinical practice to some extent in Great Britain?[9] We are talking about, for example, babies without some or all limbs, (perhaps only a crippled hand directly attached to the chest) and similar cases but also about babies with Down syndrome. Is it justified to kill such human newborn infants by omissions or acts?

Newborn human beings with Down syndrome have ego consciousness later, mostly have a mild to moderate intellectual disability and are able to experience pleasure and enjoy their life. Children with limb deficiencies are intellectually completely unimpaired.

Just feeding water and sedatives makes no moral difference as far as the final result is concerned compared to a deadly injection. Singer/Kuhse rightly criticise that in medicine there is often unjustifiably seen a difference between a causation by omission and active action.[10] There is such a difference if imponderabilities concerning the prognosis arise because of the omission. But if the omission inevitably leads to the same result as an action there is no moral difference first of all (though the psychological and legal difference may be considerable). A moral difference between an omission and an action leading to the same result with certainty exist only if the people concerned are able to show and have shown a preference, be it for the omission or the action, or if we can assume such a preference with sufficient plausibility and thus become obliged in one or the other direction by such a determination of the will.

A child with Down syndrome or a "only" physically severely disabled child can no doubt be a considerable, perhaps even heavy or unbearable burden for the family concerned or - if the family is not able or willing to care – a considerable burden for society. Therefore the decision to kill significantly impaired respectively disabled human beings at their parent's wish as long as they have no self-awareness and thus have not yet become persons in a well-founded moral understanding, which is the case for the newborn period, cannot easily be dismissed as immoral. Such a decision may well be the result of a moral weighing that has to be taken seriously (as it may particularly imply that the same family will have a healthy baby a short time afterwards). In a society that has proved to be disability friendly in the longer term, in a society where an excellent support and integration of disabled people has become a matter of course, that is in a society that proves continuously that it does not discriminate disabled *persons*, the killing of severely impaired newborn babies may become morally acceptable and legal.

For Germany it is – at least from the political point of view – still too early to seriously consider such a framing of the law. Our efforts for a disability friendly society are still too recent and too sketchy and the shadows of the murder of disabled persons by the National Socialists are still to close. That even the British still do not really feel at ease with this kind of decision can be seen from the fact that they do not dare to kill severely impaired newborns actively although letting them die by comfort care only and just feeding them water and possibly sedatives until death is coming is not any different from active killing as far as the result is concerned but is morally much more questionable because the newborn baby is possibly exposed to a period of dying by malnutrition and infections lasting for several days, putting a burden on relatives and medical staff too. The unexceptional maintenance of an emotional and social barrier against a direct killing of human beings by doctors provides no sufficient justification for such a proceeding, that may even be called cruel with some justification (at least with respect to the parents and the caregivers who have to witness such a process), even if the human beings concerned are still not persons with self-awareness. Therefore, it is socially and legally accepted in the Netherlands to kill severely disabled babies actively in certain cases if the prognosis regarding life expectancy and quality of life is poor and considerable suffering in the further course is foreseeable. This proceeding, which is morally better justifiable, is discussed there openly regarding its presuppositions and the details of implementation. In Belgium a majority of neonatologists has spoken out for proceeding in the same way. (3) It will still last long for such a morally adequate practice to spread around the world. Advocating a general reduction of the protection of life and the right to life for all newborn babies, as done by Peter Singer, does a disservice to the respective efforts for psychological reasons (see p. 226) though it is philosophically defendable.

Anyhow, we will be constrained to face up increasingly to the problem of severely disabled newborn babies. This can be seen, for example, from the fact that since the last revision of the legal rules for abortion in Germany that allows abortion in cases of severe disability until immediately before birth (though under the questionable labelling of a "medical indication") several obstetricians have changed over to kill such fetuses by injections of salt solution into the heart before beginning the abortion (which in these cases is tantamount to birth) because if not doing so they might face the problem that a viable child could come into the world who would have to be kept alive. Such situations which may cause inacceptable dilemmas for doctors (4) show how questionable birth has become today as a dividing line and that is has become inept at any rate as a paramount and exclusive criterion for ascribing a right to life.

If we arrive at the moral judgement that neonates, as yet lacking personhood, should not have the same right to life and the same protection of life as human persons, we must answer the question which reasons should be accepted as a justification for killing newborn infants. One consistent position is to accept the same reasons as for terminating a pregnancy at a point in time when the fetus is already viable outside the womb. Giubilini and Minerva use the term "after-birth abortion" to advocate this.[11] I agree with this proposal, but, in contrast to these authors, I consider the killing of healthy fetuses viable outside the womb in late pregnancy, as well as that of healthy newborns, to be an inappropriate weakening of the protection of life. It is undoubtedly consistent to give priority to the interests of persons over the interests of human beings that are not yet persons. But we should not follow this principle without reservation. When human beings are only a small step away from achieving personhood and can then presumably lead independent lives without foreseeable considerable suffering or undue burden on their relatives and society, we should protect their right to life and no longer leave it to the discretion of other people. I do not consider psychological problems of the mother, for example, because she loses her partner, suddenly no longer feels capable of caring for a child and cannot bear the thought of giving it up for adoption, as burdensome as these problems can be, to be sufficient grounds for killing healthy, viable fetuses or newborns. Surprisingly, however, such reasons are quite often morally and legally accepted as reasons for a late-term abortion, while any discussion of the killing of newborn infants for much more justifiable reasons is taboo or leads to an outcry.

Now the question is brought up quite rightly if accepting the killing of severely disabled babies would mean that we would also have to allow or be allowed to kill older severely disabled human beings who are impaired so heavily that they have lost self-awareness and no longer fulfil the criteria for

235

being a person. Here several new aspects are of importance. In spite of the fact known meanwhile that there are psychosomatic relations between the mother and the unconscious unborn child that may also have an influence on the later psychological development of the child, it can hardly be disputed that a newborn baby has no self-awareness and, therefore, is actually no person either. Contrary to that, human beings on later stages of development and age have these capacities as a rule and, accordingly, also an actual conscious interest to survive. This leads to a shift in the burden of proof. Thus, we would have to proof as convincingly as is humanly possible that just this concrete severely disabled human being has actually no self-awareness and personhood and will never regain it in order to question their right to life or weigh it up directly against the interests of other human beings. Even the simplest signs of pleasure or unpleasure connected with basic everyday life activities would have to make us doubt if this might really be the case.

And even if we could assess with a certainty leaving no reasonable doubt, that a certain human being beyond the newborn age has permanently no self-awareness and personhood, a ponderous reason remains why we should not get ourselves into adopting this kind of dividing line. This reason is the fear of other and especially significantly disabled people that their right to life might be endangered and could become subject to a weighing up against the interests of other people, how unsubstantiated such a fear may ever be. For the sake of this fear, we should not consider the killing of even profoundly disabled human beings beyond the newborn age just because we are convinced that they have no (or no longer have) self-awareness and personhood. To kill profoundly disabled human beings should only be considered if life for themselves consists of nothing more than persistent suffering and they obviously have not only no interest in living on but even an interest to be allowed to die. (See 3.6.5. and the precautions described there to avoid an abuse of euthanasia)

After this digression let us return to the moral and legal problems that can arise concerning newborn babies. If we decide that the state and the legal system should already guarantee a right to life to severely impaired newborns too, we should at least not unduly claim that the affected family should bear this burden mainly alone, and we should not raise the claim that the child may grow up at home as a matter of course. Though other members of the family may become more morally mature and develop themselves by interacting with and caring for a severely disabled child, nobody should be forced into such a

236

situation. A state that guarantees a right to life for severely disabled newborns should, as a consequence, also allow for enough facilities that provide a satisfactory care for them, that support the families concerned and can step in temporarily or permanently if a family cannot (or can no longer) cope with the situation. Moral and legal theorists should think things through very thoroughly and have very good reasons for imposing extremely heavy, long-lasting and even lifelong burdens on other people. And politicians who are responsible for such a legal framework should feel obliged to alleviate the burden of the people concerned as far as possible.

To gain more clarity about the dividing lines we may and should choose, we shall have a look on some further exemplary situations. A mongoloid child is born with a bowel obstruction that makes oral feeding impossible and would lead to death without an operation but can be removed with high chances of success by a relatively simple operation, so that we would do this surgery without hesitating in any otherwise healthy newborn. Or: A mongoloid child acquires a pneumonia during the newborn period which we would treat by antibiotics without hesitating in an otherwise healthy newborn. Singer/Kuhse speak of morally irrelevant coincidences in such cases and hold that, if one advocates a right to life guaranteed by the state for newborn infants, one also has to advocate an obligation for doing the surgery or applying the antibiotics. I do not share this position. Which causes in a causal chain we consider morally significant and which consequences we draw therefrom, is already a part of our moral weighing. Even if one wants to guarantee severely disabled newborns a right to life in principle, I consider it a practicable and reasonable dividing line to leave the decisions whether to take extraordinary measures or not to the parents in cases where a further disorder occurs in addition, requiring procedures exceeding basic care like oral feeding (though there is, admittedly, also a moral choice in seeing a morally significant difference between ordinary and extraordinary measures). The parents should get all the information relevant for their decision as far as possible and should not be urged in one direction or the other, because they will have to live with the consequences of their decision in the first place, not doctors, caregivers, psychologists or theologians. And I also hold that we may leave it with a clear conscience to doctors and parents in such situations to decide whether a disability is so severe (or the risk of a severe disability appears so high in pre-term newborns) that foregoing treatment is justified. If it comes to such difficult discretionary decisions we should refer to the idea of non liquet or nonjusticiability and not overindulge in the idea that anything and everything must and can be regulated down to the details of the specific case.

But we should be entirely clear that, if we choose the proposed dividing line, we make a difference in the value of life we ascribe to severely disabled and to healthy newborns. We would never let die an otherwise seemingly healthy newborn just because of a bowel obstruction that can be surgically removed rather easily. To the contrary, we would do the surgery immediately as a matter of course. To concede the decision for foregoing treatment to the parents in such cases can, at least in some cases, expand their freedom of choice even in societies (still) not prepared to generally confine the protection of life for severely disabled newborn infants.

If parents and doctors decide against the antibiotic treatment or the surgery they accept to cause the death of the newborn child by omission. But there is a significant difference to the situation discussed earlier (and that is why I disagree with the moral evaluation of Singer/Kuhse at this point): If we refuse to provide basic care and oral feeding to a mongoloid newborn without further significant disease, we initiate the causal chain leading to death by our omission only. In the cases discussed later we just refrain from stopping a causal chain that was started without our intent. (5) But there are differences even here: to refrain from an antibiotic treatment carries considerable imponderables because the child might survive, nevertheless. Thus, this kind of omission is still quite different from an action of active killing. However, if we refrain from doing surgery in a mongoloid newborn baby with a complete bowel obstruction, our way of acting only differs from a deadly injection as far as the time factor and the circumstances of dying a concerned but not as to the result that will occur with certainty.

To summarise this discussion: Whatever may be the details of the legal norms established to protect newborn babies, I consider it morally justified to still make a difference concerning the value of life and the protection of life between seemingly healthy and significantly disabled children during the newborn period when a human individual has not yet developed self-awareness and personhood. Once the newborn period is passed and a human being has developed – to which extent ever – self-awareness and has become a person, its own interest to survive must be absolutely paramount in all decisions about prolongation of life. I hold that the proposal of Singer (and others) to take the presence or absence of self-awareness and personhood as the most important criterion for dividing lines concerning the right to life and the protection of life is well-founded and reasonable. But I hold also that this criterion should not lead us to weaken too much the protection of seemingly healthy human life during late pregnancy and the newborn period. And I hold as well that the honest striving for non-discrimination of disabled people should not go so far as to demand the same duty to sustain life in severely disabled human embryos, fetuses and newborns as in healthy ones. As we will see in the following, hardly any convincing secular argument is conceivable for such a demand. If such a duty is postulated, it ultimately traces back to a religious conception of ensoulment. We should no longer accept that legal standards derived therefrom are imposed on all citizens (with possibly serious and long-lasting impact on their lives) whatever their philosophy of life may be.

Coming closer to the end of this section I want to discuss a problem that, regrettably, cannot be dismissed. The possibilities of prenatal testing available today and a ruling leaving more choices open to parents of severely disabled newborn babies according to the above mentioned proposals indubitably involve the danger that the inclination of people to intolerance and ruthlessness may find a new focal point and that disabled children may be considered as a principally avoidable affliction and fault of the parents. Already now disabled people are complaining about having to overhear comments uttered behind their back like "Today such a child would no longer come into the world!".

Such comments are indeed more than just grossly impolite and callous. Rightly we already consider it as scathing and offending common decency to demean a person for physical shortcomings, especially when doing so to the face or within earshot. How much more of an affront is it, then, to give human beings the impression that their existence is regarded as pitiable. Left apart the fact that such comments reveal a deplorable lack of knowledge concerning the prenatal recognisability and the possible origins of severe disabilities. But are disabled people right, on the other hand, to view such stupid, improper and violating utterances as an attack on their right to life and the value of their life? In most cases hopefully not.

I am able to comprehend psychologically and I am able to understand that for people who have been born with severe disabilities, recognisable today by prenatal diagnostics, the thought that they might no longer come into this world now is an affront at the first moment. This is a principally sound and natural expression of self-esteem and the will for self-preservation (and a comprehensible psychological reason for a spontaneous, inconsiderate, fierce

239

opposition to somebody advocating views like those of Peter Singer). But why should anybody worry about coincidences or even conscious choices deciding on our existence at a point in time when we still had no self-awareness? All of us could not have come to the world if some coincidences had not occurred or different coincidences had occurred. As far as this is due to the conscious choices of other people, they have decided against a human being who could have become a human person like us later, but they have not decided against that person because it did not exist when they made the decision and they do not compromise the right to exist or the dignity of any other person.

Today in many cases not disabled younger sisters or brothers of severely disabled fetuses come into the world and they would not have been conceived if the parents would not have decided for an abortion before. I cannot recognise anything morally wrong in this development. These later conceived children have indubitably better preconditions for their life (though that does not necessarily mean that they will lead a happier and better life as the disabled child would have done against whose life the parents have decided). To deny existence to a future child also has moral significance and an abortion may well be justified if it increases the probability of a future pregnancy with much more favourable preconditions for the child born then. (Hare) (6) It is understandable and adequate that families in which a severely disabled child has become a human person and a family member cannot imagine and do not want to imagine that this human being would not be there. But families that have chosen an abortion because of a foreseeable severe disability and have got another child later instead can imagine just as little that this later born child would not be there.

We should get straight in our mind what it means if we justify a demand to refrain from an abortion in cases of recognisable severe disability of the unborn child by the interests of already born disabled persons. So that human beings who have to cope with a life burdened by disability and disadvantages feel possibly psychologically more comfortable, such a life with similar burdens and disadvantages should be imposed on other people (and their relatives). One misses the Kantian figure of argumentation here, otherwise quite popular among pro-life activists, that a human being (Kant referred to human persons by the way) should never be treated as mere means in the interest of other people, or be instrumentalised, as one would perhaps say today. Why should it be justified to inflict serious avoidable burdens and disadvantages on human beings in order to support other human beings psychologically in

240

coping with already existing unavoidable burdens and disadvantages?

If one formulates the statement in a neutral discourse situation that, for example, children with malformations like completely missing limbs are seldom born in the age of ultrasound scans during pregnancy because such serious disabilities are recognised before birth as a rule and most parents decide for abortion in such a situation, then this is nothing more, first of all, than a correct description of the facts. If a drug would be applied today causing such serious malformations as thalidomide, far less children disabled to such an extent would come into the world. Now, we have to make a moral valuation of this fact. Together with many other people I consider it a clear progress. It is my firm conviction that parents make the right decision as a rule if they decide to have an abortion in such a case. This does not demean in the least those fellow human beings who have to live with a disability like those caused by thalidomide and who often do that in an admirable manner.

I want to leave no doubt that behaving responsibly means to me to acquaint oneself with all the information available at the respective state of the art of medicine and seeming adequate given the individual risk (which includes, as a matter of course, taking into account risks originating from the diagnostic measures themselves). Fatalism and blind faith in god are no acceptable arguments against prenatal testing. And the conviction that human life would be »holy« from the beginning is a bad argument against prenatal testing. It should not be forgotten, by the way, that prenatal testing already makes for prenatal therapeutic measures in some cases and that it is no longer – so still more often – about the consequence of doing an abortion or not.

Let us now proceed to the most difficult question that arises in the context of abortion and disabled newborns. Must we always accept, and should we always accept the decision of parents to bring a foreseeable severely disabled child into the world or keep a severely disabled newborn baby alive? Certainly insufficient is the answer of some neoliberal theorists who want to push back claims to social solidarity and who believe that nearly all social problems might be solved best by economic nudges. In my opinion it is wrong to demand that those of us who consciously decide to bring a severely disabled child into the world or keep a severely disabled newborn alive should be left alone as far as possible with the financial consequences. It is not justified to break down social solidarity and to exert pressure in the direction of the more economic decision thereby if difficult moral questions are at stake with serious reasons for very different choices. Furthermore, such decisions made by the parents are irreversible and to quit social solidarity would directly concern various human persons: the disabled human persons themselves (having had no influence whatsoever on the foregone decisions) and their relatives. Thus, we should continue to accept the decisions made by the parents within wide limits even if we hold that their decision is morally wrong, and we would have made a different choice ourselves.

But should we always leave the decision to the parents alone? Could they be unable to cope adequately with such a decision in some situations? Let us assume the following case for clarification: In a child, whose parents reject modern technical medicine and have not done ultrasound screening during pregnancy as a consequence, it is found in late pregnancy or even as late as immediately after birth that it has no arms and no legs. The parents want to keep alive the child by all means for religious reasons (for not to say: religious fanatism). And they do not want to care for it themselves but give it to an institution. In this case there is a rather great probability that the human being concerned might later, after having become a human person, reproach her or his parents – and us who let them do what they wanted to do – for having kept her or him alive and not having had the possibility to become her or his younger sister or brother without such a severe disability.

What is morally adequate in such a situation? I definitely feel uncomfortable with the thought that the killing of a severely disabled newborn should be done as the result of a decision made by an ethics committee, possibly against the will of the parents. But I feel equally uncomfortable with the thought that the decision should be left to the parents alone in such extreme cases. I think that we should leave the decision to the parents alone in all cases where a human being will in all likelihood be able – and be it with considerable sup-port – to live a satisfying life without tantalising massive limitations of its possibilities for action and movement. This would apply to mongoloid chil-dren, for example. Whereas in such extreme cases as the one assumed above the decision should indeed be made by an ethics committee, with participation of the parents and considering all the aspects of the specific case but also the authority to make a decision against the parents in exceptional cases. A deci-sion against the parents should be possible as well in cases where an abortion during a late stage of pregnancy or the killing of a newborn baby appears to be inadequate because of a just minor disability.

Such a standpoint, conceding a wide freedom of choice to parents, is also very convincingly advocated by Swiss neonatologist Christian Kind. He rightly points out that adult patients differ widely in what they consider a fair chance of success that is worth to undergo a severely burdensome therapy. Thus, there is no reason either in preterm children with a high risk of permanent disability to prefer the opinion of the attending doctors on what a "fair chance" might be in comparison to the opinion of the parents. "To the contrary, the fact that the parents have to bear the consequences of such a decision for life is a strong argument that the parents should, if they want to, make this decision themselves within certain limits or should at least have a say in it. The parental freedom of choice is limited downwards by a very low probability to survive without a disability that turns a therapy into a pointless torture and upwards by the probability with which a refusal of treatment - in spite of good chances to survive without disability - would have to be considered as a violation of parental responsibility for the best interests of the child."[10]

One thing we should never forget in all of this: To be entitled to form an opinion on the behaviour and the decisions of the respective parents one should definitely have a very precise knowledge of the circumstances of the specific case. And even if one is of the opinion, then, that the parents should not have kept alive a child, that they have made a wrong decision, and that oneself would have decided otherwise, this does still not justify to speak out such an opinion referring to a concrete case to the parents afterwards or even in earshot of a disabled person who could understand this as an attack on her or his right to life and value of life. We owe equal respect to human persons independent of the degree of a possible disability, and this respect includes that their right to life is beyond any discussion. Only if life has obviously lost its value for a person herself the weighings valid for the prolongation of life and euthanasia come into effect.

But back to the worries of disabled people that their right to life and the value of their life might be progressively less esteemed and that they might be progressively less accepted. Why should the change that has occurred and will occur further by medical progress in prenatal testing contribute to such a development? Why should the fact that most people decide for an abortion in case of a severe disability of their unborn child mean that disabled people who are already born, who are born nevertheless, or who acquire a disability later will be less respected and supported? One should expect, on the contrary, that a society having to care for a smaller number of severely disabled people will be the more so prepared and able to provide the best possible support for them. This would at least be consequent and this is what we should act for.

Admittedly, it is not a matter of course, given the proneness of human beings to intolerance and ruthlessness. However, the results of several surveys and also the concurrent spread of prenatal testing and better integration of and support for disabled people indicate that there is, fortunately and reasonably, no relevant tendency to hostility toward disabled people in modern affluent societies that would go beyond isolated cases and fringe groups. There is, on the contrary, a development striving to avoid disability, on the one hand, and to compensate the limitations caused by unavoidable disability as far as possible, on the other hand. (7) It is quite safe to say that, despite of all remaining shortcomings, never before as much attention and support was given to disabled persons as today in modern Western societies. This is not counterbalanced by a few stupid and blinded characters who complain if people with disabilities spend their holidays at the same hotel. And it is neither counterbalanced by some criminals who offend or even attack disabled fellow human beings. Society has to deal with them in the same way as with other comparable inhumane delinquents.

That and how and where we come into the world is beyond our command, it is fate (here the term is really appropriate though our parents have much more influence on this fate by their decisions today than in former times). And when we have made it to the world of as a person we have a claim to be respected. To every human being, and the more so to everybody who has passed the newborn period and has become some kind of person, we owe protection and help. And we owe special respect to the achievement, the courage and the enjoyment of life of disabled people who can often enough be an inspiring example to others. (How many healthy people having much better preconditions make far less of their lives?) We will never create paradise on earth, and we should never glance down at fellow human beings who do not fulfil our idea of perfection or normality.

I am also convinced that we should not use prenatal testing and abortion for a mere selection of traits. (As it is possible already today concerning gender and will be increasingly possible concerning a multitude of traits and predispositions for diseases, also of minor significance, in the future.) Such a proceeding underrates the value of life and the right to life of the fetus and, moreover, one can hardly expect "better" offspring from it, given the complexity of inheritance.

Disabled people are right when they make themselves felt and speak up for their interests and rights in society. They are not right if they believe that they should, in doing this, also oppose prenatal testing and abortion as a consequence drawn thereof in cases of severe disabilities or the possibility of limiting treatment in severely disabled newborn babies or of even killing them. And they are absolutely wrong if they call for intolerance against those who, like Peter Singer, want to raise a responsible discussion on the value of life and the right to life or if they even want to render impossible such a discussion by brute force (especially as they possibly vilify somebody, as in the concrete case of Singer, who indubitably advocates for the concerns of disabled *persons*). If we try to avoid or to remove disabilities wherever it is possible, this does not mean that we appreciate disabled persons less than non-disabled fellow human beings.

3.6.5. Prolongation of Life, Euthanasia

To the bitter end?

> "The core of the dispute on euthanasia is the fundamental question if and to what extent human beings are entitled to decide on their own lives."[1]

> Eric Hilgendorf

> "In an enlightened, pluralistic, democratic state power over and interpretation of self-determined dying should not be left to fatalists submissive to authority (be it church representatives, presidents of medical associations, jurists or politicians) just because these people believe they would be 'the strongest' ..."

> Anton Wohlfart (1)

To the old human fears of death and dying a new one is added today: not to be able to die in dignity at the right time. The possibilities of modern medicine and the use made thereof sometimes indubitably justify such concerns. When an otherworldly orientated religiosity no longer exists, a lot less often a meaning can be seen in physical suffering without a realistic prospect of recovery or in living through a phase of old age associated with pronounced restrictions until the end, or also in abiding progressive dementia.

Religious people do not necessarily insist on a duty to sustain life by use of all possibilities, partly they do it even less than people who have an exclusively secular orientation and who hold that death is the end of everything. But many religious people, or at less their representatives in public, still reject any kind of direct life-shortening measures at human hands, even in case of incurable and agonising illness. Life is seen in God's hands and humans are not allowed to rush ahead of God's decree and to violate the unconditional sanctity of life. A religious meaning is given to suffering (for example as an anticipated purification), even if we humans may be incapable of comprehending the unfathomable will of God.

To give meaning to suffering in such a way is out of question for those unwilling to believe. According to the value system advocated here, life is a high value, but a value that should be seen, nevertheless, as competing with other values and that can be less important than other values in certain situations and can be rejected by the individual for good reason, for example, considering the quality and the perspectives of life that can still be expected. For a secular humanism suffering has a meaning only in so far as the person affected is able to put a meaning into it, as by living more consciously or giving help and example to others even by the way she or he deals with the suffering.

If we want to find an adequate position concerning the prolongation of life and euthanasia, there is one principle that should be at the forefront in my opinion: The perspective of the person whose life is at stake must be paramount. Sometimes burdens for family members or informal caregivers will inevitably find a place in these personal considerations. But from what perspective soever, the burdens for relatives and the society should always be of secondary importance in questions concerning the prolongation of life and euthanasia (as much as a society is able to afford such a position). Nevertheless, it is justified to include such aspects in our moral weighings in extreme cases, for example in dealing with some patients with long-lasting syndromes of unresponsive wakefulness (no longer called "apallic syndrome" for good reasons (2)) who have no chance to regain awareness even as a minimally conscious state. With the exception of a few cases like this, in which there a no prospects that the person concerned might be able to return to a life worth living, considerations of social utility or convenience should not have an influence on our respective decisions.

Often we have to decide whether and when certain life-prolonging measures should be implemented or continued. The most frequent error in considering this is the idea that the omission of life-prolonging measures would be a more serious and morally more questionable intervention in the course of life than implementing them. In critical illness, however, the people concerned, and especially doctors, do not become arbiters of life and death only when deciding for omissions. Today they become such arbiters anyway, whatever they do. Whether they decide for active acting or for omissions - both has to be justified considering the prognosis, the interest and the explicit or presumable volition of the person concerned. The decision to implement all available measures is not at all more morally unproblematic than the decision to omit such measures.

If the decision to implement technical measures for the prolongation of life today suggests itself more easily to many doctors and seems more unassailable to them morally and legally as the decision for their omission, then this is a grave error, in any case as far as moral unassailability is concerned. Regrettably, there is still, at least in Germany, an overemphasis among doctors, and especially among their leading representatives, of a duty to prolong life (often combined with a moral dismissal of any form of directly intended assisted dying), an attitude which may be understandable for historical reasons but does not become more appropriate therefore.

In our contemporary society doctors certainly incur guilt more often by implementing and continuing measures to prolongate life excessively than by an unjustified omission or premature termination of such measures. The reasonably assumable interests of the person concerned should be the paramount criterion for the beginning and the continuation of life-prolonging treatments. This principle is defied often enough by doctors under the assumption of abstract moral and legal duties to prolong life, and for lack of willingness to take on the toil and the responsibility of differentiated individual case decisions. I think that social change will bring about a situation where inadequate life-prolonging measures will be considered as physical injury more often than today and also lead to legal sanctions (for example, if such measures, as it still happens, alas, are implemented in critically ill patients with a very poor prognosis who can no longer express themselves but have explicitly declined such measures before, or if their relatives have declined such measures in place of them). (3)

In making the decision when which measures should be still applied errors can occur, as in other comparable difficult decisions, and such errors may also occur to the effect that one gives up on a patient too early. But this risk does not justify a thoughtless maximal therapy in all cases. If we were able to spare a thousand people a considerable amount of unnecessary suffering and had to accept that we shortened the life of one person because we arrived at an unjustified negative result concerning the prognosis and have therefore given up on this person too early, we have done right, nevertheless. In other weighings we value far less important goods than the avoidance of suffering higher than the maximal protection of life.

And even if this should only be a subordinate point of view: Maximal therapy in cases with very low prospect of success takes and uses up resources that could be deployed with much greater utility for people elsewhere. The decisions for what to deploy our resources are ultimately moral decisions and we always make them somehow by the way we act. We may skilfully hide this fact to ourselves, but it is an error to believe that we could duck out of it.

We should advocate a deliberative, moderate attitude to medical prolongation of life. Even then we will not be satisfied with our decisions in every case. In spite of all technical possibilities an individual course of disease is foreseeable only to a limited extent, and we will be confronted, time and again, with the situation that our modern possibilities of treatment impose a long, distressing existence as care dependant on some of our fellow human beings that may make us regret our efforts to prolong life in hindsight or at least may let appear these efforts as highly questionable.

It is rather easy to reach a consensus that people suffering from an advanced malignant disease with desperate prognosis should not be subjected to intensive measures to prolong life. Practically much more problematic are those cases, becoming ever more frequent with increasing life expectancy and growing medical possibilities, in which many diseases, that would be manageable taken separately, summarise to an overall situation with a prognosis as hopeless as that of an advanced malignant disease, with the only difference that at the end of treatment there may not be death yet but a "minimal life". For some time a human being survives who is bedridden, permanently care dependant, hardly contactable, and possibly just kept alive by a feeding tube.

Can we really want this? Is it in the interest of the people concerned? If an eighty-year-old patient with circulatory disorders in the brain and an earlier history of temporary disorientation acquires heart failure and has to be put on artificial ventilation and he or she does not improve after some days despite intensive care, but develops a pneumonia and a kidney failure, should we really begin haemodialysis then? The answer must not always be »no«, it has to be guided by all the relevant circumstances of the individual case, that is, among other things, not to make a hasty judgement according to the
248

chronological age but to take into account an overall impression of the biological age of the respective patient. I am convinced, however, that the answer should be »no« more often than it is today.

That nobody among the responsible doctors and the relatives wants to engage seriously in such considerations and finally also assume responsibility for the omitted escalation, the limitation or even the termination of treatment, is certainly no satisfactory reason for applying or continuing it.

Conceivable legal problems with family members because of a limitation or termination of treatment are often nothing more than a pretextual argument of doctors to spare themselves decisions experienced as burdensome in such situations. Relatives who have been able to follow such a course of disease, have been adequately informed about the situation, and have finally also been involved in the decisions on a limitation or termination of treatment, are helpful to doctors as a rule and not a danger for them. Only lonely decisions of doctors are legally dangerous, and they should be avoided anyway whenever possible. And, admittedly, from time to time you come across certain relatives who are indeed legally dangerous; these are those who, for a variety of reasons want to demonstrate special efforts, be it because of feeling guilty towards or having neglected the critically ill patient somehow and wanting to compensate for that hurriedly before it is too late, at least unconsciously. They may even look for a scapegoat for their own failures or qualify as worthy heirs. However, doctors who talk to the relatives will rather reliably recognise this type of relatives. In this case doctors have no choice for reasons of self-protection but to extend their efforts of treatment to a point beyond possible reproach. You can only hope not to have such relatives when you get in such an ultimate situation.

The living wills or advance directives recommended nowadays, by which, for example, certain treatments and especially intensive care measures are refused in advance in case of a critical, probably hopeless disease, make sense, but they can only have limited significance. They are helpful because they signal that the person concerned has explicitly addressed the problem and wanted to set a reasonable limit to the prolongation of life. Our decisions are facilitated significantly if we have convincing indications from earlier expressions of the will that a person, now in a hopeless situation and possibly suffering from it considerably, would not have wanted to live on in this situation and would have refused any further treatment or certain life-prolonging treatments. Living wills or advance healthcare care directives become more convincing and morally and legally more binding if they are not confined to general formulations or a standard text distributed by some organisation but refer to the specific life situation and course of disease of the individual patient and to foreseeable situations that may arise from it. Jurisdiction and legislation in Germany and other modern societies show a gratifying tendency to ascribe a high degree of binding force for doctors to such advance directives, a development that should be supported.

The limited significance of earlier expressions of the will is due to the fact that it is often impossible to foresee exactly the situation between life and death into which one may fall and thus also the decisions one would make then. With or without individual expressions of the will of the person concerned we have to consider as well, therefore, how an average, reasonably weighing, contemporary person would probably decide in a given situation. Such considerations are justified and necessary in spite of the sometimes quite different individual preferences of human beings. The less we know about expressions of the will of the person concerned, applicable on the concrete situation, the more such considerations will be the best guidance we have. (4)

Problems concerning the prolongation of life do not only arise as far as acute medical treatment is concerned. Very problematic are also, for example, those situations in which we get by the achievement of percutaneous feeding tubes (indubitably advantageous for certain patients). Thereby the nutrition of patients unable to take in food and beverage by themselves becomes a lot easier and less afflicted by complications. Among other things life-threatening pneumonias occur much more seldom than with the previously common nasal feeding tubes. This technical progress brings us a formerly unknown number of long time care-dependant patients with severe brain damage who are sometimes completely disorientated, often cannot speak, do not or at best to a small part understand what is told to them, cannot or almost not move the limbs of one half of the body, are bedridden or can be sat at most in an invalid chair for a part of the day. They deteriorate slowly, what may mean over years, may develop bedsore with deep, foul, purulent defects of tissue (so less frequent now due to technical progress in care), partly suffer from considerable pain when moved or lifted. Some of these patients obviously experience their situation as severely distressing even though they are not able or nearly not able anymore to speak about it.

It is understandable and justified to consider if we do something good by this kind of long-term care. That we thereby enable the persons concerned to still live a life worth living may be doubted for good reasons in many such cases. Unfortunately they themselves mostly cannot tell us at all or only in a very limited way what they think about it. So, should we only give the necessary amount of liquids to avoid dying of dehydration in such cases and not do anything more to prolong such a life, that is to say, should we starve these human beings to death if no further complication will accelerate dying? For those who are frequently confronted with such situations in their everyday life, there is indubitably a certain temptation to advocate such a proceeding, as it would obviously shorten the suffering of the people concerned. But this is nothing else than a protracted form of directly intended euthanasia. Omissions that entail no noteworthy imponderables but lead to the same result as an active action with a probability bordering on certainty, just differing in a delay of the result, are morally equal to the respective active actions. (From a legal point of view omission and active action may be classified differently, especially refering to legal duties.)

If we consider euthanasia for human beings who cannot signify unambiguously that they want to end a life experienced as unworthy and unacceptably agonising, we have to apply particularly strict standards. The principle that the perspective of the person concerned has to be paramount for our considerations must not become shaky.

If we just presume that life may have lost any worth for a person and that she or he wishes to end it as soon as possible, but we are not absolutely sure, then it is better to just alleviate suffering and to refrain from life-prolonging measures like therapies with antibiotics as far as they do not make sense for alleviating the suffering and would indeed only serve the prolongation of life.

But if we are sure, we should consider directly intended euthanasia observing the provisos described later on, be it by completely terminating the supply with nutrition and liquids via a feeding tube or by a direct act of killing. If we are convinced that the person concerned would have refused nutrition through a feeding tube in the given situation, it is inconsequent to stop nutrition but continue to give liquids, as, for instance, tea via the tube to delay death thereby, possibly for weeks. (5) Such inconsequence follows from an insufficient socio-legal discussion and convention building on this issue, as this is still the case, for example, in Germany up to now. At the same time we must be aware that the wish to abandon all life-prolonging treatment and the wish for euthanasia by also stopping the supply with food and liquids or by a direct act of killing are not identical. Abandoning treatment and even stopping tube feeding do not lead to death directly, they do not even lead unfailingly to the expected consequence of an imminent death of the person concerned in all cases. (Some persons are able, contrary to all expectations, to take a certain amount of food or at least beverage by the normal way and stabilise again for some time.)

An important decision aid for relatives and doctors concerning the prolongation of life and euthanasia (as generally in recommending and considering medical measures) can certainly be found in a concrete application of Confucius' Golden Rule in a positive form: What would I want if I or a person close to me, my wife, my husband, my mother, my father, my child would be in the same situation?

As an example for a concrete application of this way to think let us come back again to the just described problems with tube feeding. What still happens quite frequently today, is the following: The situation is not completely explained to the relatives who have to consent to the implantation of a feeding tube leading through the abdominal wall. Instead they are put under pressure to give their consent with the argument that this would be the best way to care for the patient and basically inevitable. (Actually "inevitable" it is often enough only with regard to keeping the hospital stay as short as possible and to be able to send the patient home or to a nursing home.) A detailed consideration on the probable prospects for the further life of the patient and the possibility to refuse the implantation of such a feeding tube frequently does not take place. It does not become clear to the relatives who have to make the decision that, given a poor prognosis, it would be a tenable (and certainly often more humane) alternative to continue care for some more time with a conventional nasal feeding tube. Though care is made somewhat more difficult thereby, the course is left open to a much greater extent. On the one hand, a distinct tendency to improvement may be seen and one may think anew about the necessary and adequate long-term care, on the other hand, the patient has a much better chance (which is sometimes definitely the right word here) to die from a complication, especially a pneumonia, that may be left untreated.

And often it becomes even less clear to the relatives and is not explained sufficiently to them that one could confine treatment to comfort care only and do without feeding tube or infusion bottle altogether. Even we as doctors are now hardly aware of the fact anymore that such a proceeding was normal not long ago for lack of other possibilities. And we should choose such a proceeding still and again today when thorough consideration leads us to the

252

conviction that a patient can no longer have an interest in living on with a probability bordering on certainty, for example, after extensive destruction of higher cerebral structures has occurred. It is not a must that an infusion bottle should hang beside every dying patient in a hospital, and surely not if it is just a tokenism. A feeding tube or an intravenous hydration or nutrition are already invasive measures clearly going beyond basic care with intake of food and beverage in a normal way.

At this point I want to make some short remarks on the distinction between "extraordinary" and "ordinary" methods of treatment which is used time and again in a variety of formulations to find guidance concerning the question how long and to which extent we should apply life-prolonging measures. If we leave apart that our prima facie obligation should always be to provide basic support with comfort care and supply of food and beverage for intake in the normal way, I think that this kind of distinction does not contribute a lot to clarify such situations in most cases. We should always make the decision as to which measures we carry out dependent on the interests of the person concerned, i.e. on the prognosis, the prospects of success, the quality of life that can still be expected and his or her individual attitudes and wishes. Even antibiotic therapy for pneumonia in persons in great need of care, who are suffering to a considerable degree and who no longer have any prospect of a significant improvement in their overall situation, can be morally irresponsible and wrong. On the other hand, it goes without saying that we should offer a heart transplant to a 45-year-old patient with an otherwise insufficiently treatable cardiac insufficiency, if this option is available to us, and it goes without saying that we should offer dialysis treatment to an 85-year-old mentally fit patient, if this makes it possible to prolong a subjectively worthwhile life and the patient accordingly wishes such a procedure (and we should rather save on other, less vital things for younger or less ill patients - such as massages, travel vaccinations financed by general insurance contributions, etc. - or forego the pointless continuation of treatments without any realistic prospect of success).

However, in applying life-prolonging measures there are also undesirable proceedings which are caused less by scruples about giving up the patient too early or by legal safeguarding considerations than by a highly questionable enthusiasm for what is possible. When, for example, a heart transplant is carried out on newborn babies, a life of highly uncertain duration and quality of life is forced upon a human being who, at the time of the treatment, does not yet have an ego consciousness, is not a person in the philosophically relevant sense, and this is done by consuming great material resources. I consider this to be inappropriate, all the more so when a society - such as that of the USA, where the first such operations were carried out - is unable to ensure even remotely equal health care for all its ego-conscious members and partly permits abortion of viable healthy children right up to the final stage of pregnancy.

If we decide on the use of the means available to us on the basis of a sensible weighing of the interests and prospects of success present in the specific situation, then we also make a significant contribution to a meaningful use of the available resources and to avoid rationing and the exclusion of people from receiving substantial benefits in medical care.

Now to euthanasia in the narrower sense or, to put it another way, to assisted dying brought about by direct life-ending measures within a short period of time. Should society permit direct life-ending measures for severely suffering, incurably ill people if they insist on them, and should doctors (and usually only doctors?) carry out or enable people to carry out such measures? The request for this kind of euthanasia may arise less frequently in practice, depending on the situation in the respective society, than the question of the right degree of prolongation of life. However, we have to take an adequate stand on the matter given the great significance for the people concerned on the one hand and its fundamental importance on the other. Accordingly this discussion is led in all modern, secular states. Moreover, the frequency of the desire for direct life-ending euthanasia is underestimated as long as a legal system is restrictive on this issue. This is demonstrated by the numbers of respective requests in countries which allow such possibilities. Many terminally ill people who would like to shorten their lives in the final phase consider it futile to express such a wish in a restrictive legal system, or do not want to ask their doctor to break the law.

Since the ruling of the Federal Constitutional Court of 26 February 2020[2] declaring the ban on regular organisational assistance in suicide to be invalid, Germany is basically one of the progressive countries in the world as far as the right to self-determined dying is concerned. Despite of the progressive ruling of the Bundesverfassungsgericht a socially integrated self-determined dying is still more difficult than it should be. Assisted suicide continues to be socially tabooed and scandalised to a considerable extent in an unjustified manner, especially as a possibility of medical practice. Other countries are much further ahead in terms of the concrete enabling and social integration of self-determined dying (availability of sodium pentobarbital, integration of euthanasia into regular medical and nursing care).

There are two different approaches to deal with assisted dying. In some countries only assisted suicide is accepted, others also allow the termination of life on request by physicians under certain conditions (and may nevertheless have a more restrictive regulation in some respects). Some countries allow only doctors to perform euthanasia under certain conditions that are specified in detail by law, whether it be as an assisted suicide or as a termination of life on request. The Netherlands is the prime example of this. Other countries assign only an evaluating and, to a varying extent, supportive role to doctors. This applies in particular to Switzerland and now also to Germany where the rules have been created by the activities of organisations for dying in dignity and by jurisdiction in want of a respective legislation.

Let us consider the pros and cons of these different approaches.

It is often argued that it would be desirable to leave the final decision, the ultimate control, to the person who wants to die, wherever possible, i.e., to favour assisted suicide over euthanasia performed directly by a doctor, since this represents the best way of verifying the determination of the wish to die and confirms it one last time. However, experience in the Netherlands shows that the people concerned decide differently when both alternatives are available to them: only a little more than 2% opt for assisted suicide (which, however, is also only allowed in the presence of a doctor) and almost 98% choose the direct termination of life by a doctor.[5] [(p.12)] This suggests that, for the most part, assisted suicide is a stopgap solution for those countries that do not allow killing on demand by a physician. In a country with a long-established euthanasia regulation[3,4,7] that is generally trusted and shows no tendency towards abuse (even if there will always be individual decisions that need to be discussed or are even questionable), people overwhelmingly decide against assisted suicide. They do this because there are good reasons for doing so. Even though assisted suicide by ingesting a sufficiently high quantity of pentobarbital is rapid and unproblematic in the vast majority of cases, there are occasional cases in which, despite appropriate preparation, vomiting occurs, or the process is delayed due to reduced absorption of pentobarbital. When the choice is left open, evidently few people who are willing to die want to take this risk. Even with the intravenous administration of medication, most people who wish to die obviously prefer to have it given by a doctor if this is permitted.

The Dutch system, with its detailed documentation requirements, strict binding of the physician to certain procedures, including the detailed specification of the permissible medications and the monitoring of all cases by control commissions, has significant advantages: The population has a very high level of trust in the system, the availability of data is incomparably better and more detailed[6] than in other countries, and positive side effects arise that are hardly possible anywhere else, such as organ and tissue donations by some people who have died by euthanasia.[5 (p.20)] Furthermore, the detailed legal regulation in the Netherlands has led to the fact that euthanasia by physicians has been integrated into the standard care of general practitioners and family medicine to an extent not found anywhere else in the world, and that patients are only relatively rarely dependent on doctors they have not previously known. However, the price for this system is a certain degree of bureaucracy obviously not impeding the functioning of the system) and a relatively high dependency on doctors concerning the acceptance of the wish for euthanasia and right up to the immediate dying process. Buijsen rightly notes that the regulations in the Netherlands are characterised more by the moral attitude of compassion than by the moral value of freedom and the right to a self-determined death derived therefrom.[7]

In contrast, the advantage of drinking a solution containing pentobarbital, which is the predominant method in Switzerland, is that a physician is not necessarily required to be present during the procedure. The physician's role can then be limited to verifying the patient's capacity of free decision-making and to assess that are grounds for prescribing the medication causing death that are sufficient for the respective physician. The advantage of greater independence from the physician, which in the Netherlands is already eliminated due to the mandatory presence of a physician during assisted suicide, is questionable, however, since the presence of a physician, given the appropriate legal conditions, offers the option of immediate intravenous life termination by her or him in the event of problems. Though only assisted suicide is allowed in Germany, a similar dependence on doctors for the immediate execution of the self-determined dying process as in the Netherlands currently exists, due to the lack of availability of pentobarbital and the necessity of preparing an intravenous drip.

Assisted suicide does not necessarily require special, detailed legal regulation. Unfortunately, it has to be feared, especially in Germany, that the relevant legislative procedures are being abused by fundamental, and in particular religiously motivated opponents of the right to a self-determined dying, to undermine this right by setting unreasonably and impractically high hurdles under the pretext of safeguards against abuse (waiting periods, qualification requirements for consultants, etc.). It is therefore sufficient for the time being that a legal system guarantees the right to a freely responsible and self-determined death, as is the case in Switzerland and, definitely since 2020, also in Germany. Apart from an amendment to the provisions of the German Narcotics Act, which are aimed exclusively at combating addiction and providing pain relief, and which prevent access to sodium pentobarbital, and thus to the most suitable substance for a self-determined suicide without the direct involvement of a physician, no new statutory provisions are definitely necessary in Germany at present with regard to assisted suicide. Nevertheless, a statutory clarification to determine the capacity of free decision-making would be desirable in principle and could contribute to the acceptance of self-determined dying as a possible option at the end of life and to its integration into the standard care of general practitioners and family medicine.

In contrast, the prevention of abuse is not a reason for a special legal regulation. Other existing legal norms already provide sufficient protection. In Switzerland, for example, this is the punishability of inducing or assisting suicide for selfish motives, in Germany the punishability of failure to assist to a person in danger as well as the relevant offences of involuntary manslaughter and manslaughter (and the Swiss restriction on the impunity of inducing or assisting suicide could be adopted in addition). As has been shown in particular by decades of experience in Switzerland (and meanwhile also by the intermediary services of the DGHS in Germany), civil society organisations offering support for assisted suicide are very well able to give themselves appropriate and fully sufficient guidelines to ensure that the wish to die is the result of free decision-making. Such guidelines can be modified much more flexibly in correspondence to changing societal developments, for example, if the acceptance of advanced multimorbidity in old age or of therapy-resistant mental illnesses as understandable reasons for assisted suicide changes. It has to be said, however, that the Dutch system shows some adaptability in this respect too.

Without special legal regulation, assisted suicide has become a socially accepted and largely unbureaucratic option (often mentioned gratefully in obituaries), especially through the EXIT association founded in 1982, which now has over 165,000 members, and later also through Dignitas. (For comparison: the DGHS has 38,000 members, with a population almost ten times as large in Germany.) EXIT, for example, conducts detailed counselling on possible alternatives prior to any assisted suicide and then requires a minimum of documents including a medical diagnosis from the attending physician, a confirmation of unimpaired decision-making capacity by a physician and a medical prescription for the anti-death drug sodium pentobarbital.[3] With this procedure, there have been no indications of misuse of assisted suicide over several decades.

The rules for accompaniment of assisted suicide by the German Society for Humane Dying (DGHS) additionally require an assessment by a jurist and their presence as a witness during the assisted suicide.[4] In view of the Swiss experience, this already amounts to an overregulation. However, given the special historical situation in Germany and the fact that the admissibility of assisted suicide has only been definitively clarified here since 2020, this solution appears sensible, at least for a transitional period. And a four-eyes principle when assessing free responsibility remains an appropriate security measure in the long run too before providing assistance in obtaining means of suicide.

The best social regulation for the problem of euthanasia would be a combination of the Dutch and Swiss models: on the one hand, a comparably detailed legal regulation of termination of life on request by physicians, since this is probably a prerequisite to make it part of standard primary care, and on the other hand, legal freedom for assisted suicide with a relatively reduced role for doctors, who can limit themselves to assessing responsibility and exercising responsible discretion when prescribing death-inducing drugs. The people who want to die can and will then decide which path they want to take. Statutory provisions should respect the various proven ways of euthanasia, even if they have understandably been and are influenced by different national traditions. In the Netherlands, for example, the establishment of euthanasia was driven forward to a large extent by medical professional organisations too[7] (which unfortunately represents an exception), while in Switzerland civil society organisations were decisive. In Switzerland, EXIT has shied away from calling for the legalisation of assisted suicide for tactical reasons, and the organisation and politics as a whole continue to avoid explicitly seeking legislation on euthanasia because a divisive social debate and a step backwards for the practices attained by civil engagement is feared.

Despite the great effectiveness of well-organised euthanasia organisations, as demonstrated in Switzerland, it will be difficult to do justice to the actual, comprehensible wishes for help in dying in a self-determined manner without legal regulation of physician-assisted euthanasia and the resulting integration of this help into standard primary care. In the Netherlands, 9,068 cases of euthanasia were reported in 2023, which corresponds to 5.4% of all deaths. This figure is continuously rising due to the ageing of the population and the increased acceptance of euthanasia.[5 (p.12)] Converted to Switzerland, with 72,000 deaths, this would correspond to 3,900 cases of euthanasia. However, all Swiss euthanasia organisations together only provided assisted suicide in around 2,000 cases in 2023. In Germany, with just over one million deaths per year, the Dutch percentage would result in 55,000 cases of euthanasia per year. The German Association for Human Dying has arranged help in assisted suicide in a little more than 600 cases in 2024. Thus, it seems completely illusionary, even in the long term, that assisted suicides carried out by euthanasia organisations alone and without the integration of euthanasia into standard primary care, could come somewhere close to meeting people's wishes in terms of numbers.

The Dutch statistics inevitably also raise the question as to why the euthanasia figures are comparatively high here. The main reason is likely to be that people more often express a desire for euthanasia when it is recognised and offered as an option in standard primary care, and that they do so in a significant number of cases as an alternative to palliative care or, in any case, from a certain point in time, as an alternative to continued palliative care. This should give pause to conservative circles that pit palliative medicine against euthanasia instead of seeing both together as mutually complementary forms of support for suffering people.

The situation of persons suffering from a variety of old-age ailments, who may also have lost many of their social relations and attachments and conclude that they have lived long enough and that it is time to go, is particularly difficult. However, assisted suicide or termination of life on request by physicians may be justified in such cases too. Especially in this situation, but also when personal preferences are against these options, voluntary stopping eating and drinking (VSED), "fasting to death", is another possibility to end one's life in a socially integrated, non-violent manner. With expert care-giving and medical support, this can be a good and dignified way to say goodbye to life. (6) As an individual way of self-determined dying and as a last resort to be able to decide on the end of one's life even in countries with restrictive euthanasia legislation, it is also suitable for other situations in which a premature self-determined ending of one's own life comes into question. If we want to realise a humane culture of dying, "fasting to death" should become an accepted option in outpatient and inpatient palliative and hospice work, about which those people who want to end their lives in a self-determined way get also adequately informed.

Voluntary stopping eating and drinking cannot be a general substitute for other forms of euthanasia which do not cause death by omission but by directly effective medication, since not everyone will want to accept such a protracted dying process once they have decided for good reasons to end their life. The burden on relatives can also be considerable and even be perceived as unacceptable. "Fasting to death" is, in a not explicitly declared form, a well-known traditional last resort at the end of life, and one that has been tacitly practised even in religiously authoritarian societies. In modern societies that enable access to assisted suicide and termination of life on request by physicians this approach will, due to the relatively burdensome process, certainly remain a form of self-determined dying chosen by only a small minority.

We should always reject euthanasia if there is any realistic possibility that life could still have value for the person concerned. For example, it is conceivable that people who are permanently bedridden and in need of care, and incapable or barely capable of responding to their surroundings, may have memories of their former life that still give value to their life (at least as long as they are not dominated by constant severe pain). We should also reject euthanasia if only the relatives are no longer able or willing to bear the condition of the persons concerned, but we cannot be completely sure that they themselves have lost all interest in survival and would refuse to continue living in their condition. It speaks for the responsible handling of euthanasia in the Netherlands that the number of cases of euthanasia in nursing homes is very low there.[9]

However, at the same time we should respect advance directives of people who demand the cessation of all treatment, including food and fluid intake, for the onset of such advanced states of deterioration (as seen mainly through progressive dementia).

Euthanasia in the sense of a deliberate termination of life by doctors should also be allowed in any case where severely suffering incurably ill persons have asked the doctor to end their life if their situation deteriorates further and they themselves can no longer take the deliberate situational decision due to the deterioration of their physical powers or disturbances of their consciousness. Similarly, the termination of life by doctors should be allowed if the relatives or guardians ask the doctor to do so on behalf of the person concerned, without any previous statement on this subject being known from the latter, in a situation where is no reasonable doubt that the persons concerned suffer severely, because an incurable, hopeless illness makes further life worthless for them and that they would wish their life to be ended if they could make a statement on the matter (as, for example, in the case of prolonged unconsciousness as a result of severe irreversible brain damage caused by an advanced tumor with permanent seizures or extensive destruction of the brain by hemorrhage).

Under no circumstances should considerations of social utility play more than a subordinate role in decisions about prolonging life and euthanasia in modern civilised societies. The primary concern must always be the interests of the people affected. In 1920, Binding and Hoche softened this principle in their book "Die Freigabe der Vernichtung lebensunwerten Lebens" (Allowing the Destruction of Life Unworthy of Life) and, with a legal-philosophically flawed theory of norms and many unfortunate to inhumane, emotionally-suggestive formulations, became (inadvertently) the masterminds of the National Socialist murders of the handicapped and mentally ill (although the National Socialist practices are covered by the considerations expressed in this book only for a small part of the people affected; for example, it is emphasised that even the sickest and "most useless" people have a right that their will to live be respected). (7)

Though there were similar publications and currents in England and France, for example, only the National Socialists implemented a Social Darwinist "euthanasia" concept. An appropriate discussion of euthanasia was thus made impossible in Germany for decades to come and is still hampered today. This is also shown by the massive hostility and the denial of discussion shown towards the Australian philosopher Peter Singer, even though he (who, by the way, lost several close relatives in concentration camps) can only be associated with the National Socialist "euthanasia" murders by considerable blindness or malice. Singer and the other serious contemporary advocates of euthanasia under certain conditions are concerned with the interests of the people affected, with preserving their right to self-determination and avoiding unnecessary suffering. What this is supposed to have to do with the murder of the handicapped and mentally ill by the National Socialists, which was determined by social ("völkischen") and eugenic considerations of utility and regarded the people concerned as inferior beings whose interests, expressions of will and social relations were irrelevant, remains the secret of those who keep rehashing such parallels. Already the use of the word "euthanasia" by the National Socialists is a usurpation, since their concern and objective never was a "good death" for suffering people or people who were tired of life. The "euthanasia" extermination measures were carried out without a legal basis and were concealed and covered up from the population. The criminal law and the criminal law commentators, on the other hand, continued to adhere to a ban on euthanasia during the National Socialist regime.

The National Socialist atrocities have also made it almost impossible in Germany to this day to discuss the fact that the costs to society at the border between life and death represent a morally relevant problem, which in extreme cases can also justify direct euthanasia, namely when, at great expense to society, the chances of a life worth living for the person concerned are zero or at any rate infinitesimally small. For example, I consider a time limit on the treatment of people with a syndrome of unresponsive wakefulness to be morally appropriate, depending on prognostic factors that determine the chances of regaining consciousness and a life worth living in some way (such as the cause of the brain damage, duration of the syndrome, age and, in the future, probably also the results of communication attempts using functional magnetic resonance imaging and brain/computer interfaces as a firmly established component in the diagnosis and care of such patients. (8) Each of us deserves a fair chance if we find ourselves in such a situation. However, societal resources are necessarily always limited, and if the probability of benefit for the respective human being is exceedingly low, it is morally better to use them elsewhere.

We should develop a more humane culture of letting die and euthanasia, especially in the field of medical responsibility. This need not in any way diminish trust in doctors as advocates of life, quite on the contrary. Doctors are credible as advocates of a life worth living for the person concerned (and this as long as there is even a small but still realistic chance of a life worth living at present or in the future from the point of view of this person), not as advocates of life under all circumstances and at any price. (9) Where assisted dying is comprehensively desired, it should be possible in the social environment of the respective person and ideally be realised on the basis of a previous doctor-patient relationship.

I do not see any convincing arguments why we should not give terminally ill people who no longer see any value in their life, but only experience it as a hopeless, unacceptable path of suffering, the opportunity to determine the time of their death themselves in the environment of their choice and then also to bring about this death in a planned, calm and painless way in the presence of their family, or in whatever social surroundings otherwise desired by them. I fully agree with the observations made by the Nobel Prize-winning physicist Percy Bridgman before killing himself at the age of 79 because of metastatic cancer, fearing severe pain and, above all, a loss of intellectual integrity: "I would like to take advantage of the situation in which I find myself to establish a general principle, namely, that when the end is as inevitable as it now appears to be, the individual has a right to ask his doctor to end it for him." On the day of his suicide he then left the following note: "It isn't decent for Society to make a man do this thing himself. Probably this is the last day I will be able to do it myself."[10]

Why should persons in this situation, for example, have to hang themselves from the gallows of their hospital bed with the belt of their bathrobe (as I have experienced myself as a doctor) or have to choose a similar violent way of dying that makes the social embedding of dying almost impossible and often considerably traumatises other people? I do not believe that we have to fear a breach of taboo with regard to the protection of life if we allow and socially accept assisted suicide or even direct euthanasia in some special cases in such situations.

Especially in societies with sufficiently elaborated health and welfare systems, I consider fears to be largely unjustified that social pressure in the direction of euthanasia could be exerted on the seriously ill and those in need of care because they are a burden. I regard it as unlikely that the doctors providing care and the person whose life is at stake would take such a wrong path together. However, in health care and welfare systems with a pronounced lack of solidarity, as in the US, the probability of such a constellation increases considerably and can become a serious argument for a more restrictive regulation of assisted suicide and euthanasia and for additional advisory hurdles. It is a difficult and increasingly important task of social politics to avert that the costs of illness and care become unaffordable and can lead to impoverishment.

On the other hand, it is also a misjudgement to pretend that the burdens elderly, seriously ill persons can impose on their families are morally irrelevant and would and should play absolutely no role in a person's own deliberations about the value of his or her further life. (10)

It must be admitted that wherever we humans have to make decisions, there are also wrong decisions and opportunities for abuse. Today we also have wrong decisions in questions of prolonging life, and in some cases we have an abuse of medicine for a pointless prolongation of life despite of a hopeless prognosis. I believe that such wrong decisions and abuses will not become more frequent, but rarer, if euthanasia is permitted within reasonable limits.

Good pain therapy and humane end-of-life care can certainly make that the desire for euthanasia is pronounced less frequent than it would be otherwise. The palliative care units and hospices that have emerged and are emerging for some years now offer the possibility of a more humane dying, especially for those for whom adequate home care in the last phase of their lives or end-of-life care by people close to them is not possible. The care-oriented attitude of these facilities should also be increasingly cultivated in the traditional hospital departments. However, nice declarations of intent are of little help in this regard. The most important prerequisite for bringing about an improvement here is sufficient room and staffing to provide peace and intimacy for dying people and - especially if this task cannot be taken over by relatives – the possibility of a temporary allocation of staff for end-of-life care or of care by staff specially trained for this purpose.

However, it is an illusion to believe that the wish for euthanasia can be eliminated with such improvements. Some of those people who have the possibility to die at home in the company of people close to them can and will have the understandable wish as well to end their lives at a certain point in time (in a non-violent and painless way) and to decide on this end themselves. As experience in countries shows that already allow assisted suicide or the termination of life by doctors on request for quite some time, seriously ill people experience relief simply by having this option open to them, and to a considerable extent eventually do not use it.

If people whose wish to die is understandable because of a progressed incurable disease are forced to suffer for a longer period of time by referring to humane end-of-life care or letting die in the sense of "passive" euthanasia, although they themselves would like to actively end their life, then this is morally wrong and cruel, because there are no sufficient generally understandable reasons for justifying this prolongation of and increase in suffering. Such situations are so clearly ascertainable and definable that the argument of the slippery slope with regard to a softening of the protection of human life does not apply here. As a rule, this argument is only a pretext. What is really at stake, is the religious view that human beings are not allowed to preempt divine decisions by determining the end of their lives themselves. Every religious believer is free to live and die according to this conviction. However, it is completely unacceptable to impose it on all people through the legal system. Incidentally, there are also quite different opinions from the theological side, which grant terminally ill people the right to decide on the end of their lives on their own responsibility. (11)

> "Making someone die in a way others approve, but he believes contradicts his own dignity, is a serious, unjustified, unnecessary form of tyranny."[11]
>
> Ronald Dworkin

However, it cannot be the task of doctors and society to assist people in suicide for whom life no longer seems worth living on the basis of their subjective balance, without irreversible, considerable restrictions on their quality of life being objectifiable and clearly comprehensible to other people. On the contrary, doctors and society have the task here of doing everything in their power to prevent suicide. The moral irresponsibility of initiatives that propagate suicide and often questionable methods of performing it without personally dealing with the individual case is shown by the fact that 80 to 90 percent of saved suicides do not attempt it again. On the other hand, counsellors who responsibly offer help in euthanasia repeatedly report that the mere possibility of having recourse to it if necessary causes up to 70% of potential suicides to refrain from it.

A better culture of euthanasia will still have its limits. If, for example, some people consider the mere limitations of old age to be so debilitating that they no longer want to live, without suffering from an agonising, incurable, hopeless disease, a pronounced multimorbidity, or an objectively present and subjectively unacceptable, substantial loss of autonomy, it may be difficult, depending on the individual case, to understand this valuation and to accept socially integrated euthanasia. Some situations of weariness of life can exceed the limits of what is suitable for euthanasia under medical co-responsibility, because sufficiently clear demarcation criteria are lacking with regard to the dependence of such wishes on the social situation and remediable temporary depressive developments. Those who reject life under such circumstances may only be able to expect and claim the assistance of a close person, but not that of society, if they decide to commit suicide. The same applies to the rare cases of philosophically motivated suicide, in which people decide against continuing to live though the balance that leads them to do does not reveal generally comprehensible reasons. But in these cases too assistance in suicide should remain exempt from punishment, provided that selfish motives or negligent failure to render help in a recognisable and treatable state of mental illness do not prevail. In contrast, I consider the idea of some activists that people should generally be given easier access to suicide methods, whether in the form of a "last will pill" or physical-mechanical suicide methods, *without any examination* of the comprehensibility of the wish to die, to be misguided. The risk of abuse is too high. Availability lowers the threshold for abuse, analogous to liberal gun control laws. However, it should be expressly emphasised once again at this point, that not only hopeless single conditions can justify socially integrated euthanasia, but also the pronounced restriction of the quality of life due to a summation of multiple old-age diseases. (12)

If we can develop a better culture of dying and letting die based on an open-minded, rationally comprehensible weighing of values, we can look forward with confidence to the societal boundaries that will develop from this. A better culture of dying and letting die also means that it is characterised not only by the moral attitude of compassion but also by the moral value of freedom and the right to a self-determined dying that is derived therefrom.

We should strive for a society that cares for its elderly in such a convincing way that it can in good conscience also accept a euthanasia regulation for those who at a certain point want to escape the decaying symptoms of old age without suffering from a serious, hopeless illness.

The "gentle" or at any rate sudden death at the right time after a life lived to the full but not marked by incurable, agonising illness will nevertheless remain a stroke of luck.

Nor will it ever be possible to completely eliminate lonely and violent "balance sheet" suicides, since not everyone will be willing to discuss and justify their decision with their family or, more generally, in accordance with social regulations - whatever these may be.

3.6.6. Reproductive Medicine

Against the power of habit

As in other sections of this book dealing with questions of bioethics, the aim here is not to provide as complete an examination as possible of all the essential detailed problems, but rather to clarify only a few points which seem to me to be essential to the respective topic, and especially with regard to the prejudices frequently encountered in this field. On the one hand, I do not want this book to become a casuistic treatise. On the other hand, it makes sense to describe a certain number of concrete moral considerations in order to clarify the consequences of a secular, relativistic humanist morality and to show what its position can be on problems that have newly arisen in our time.

More than in many other countries, in Germany the discussion about reproductive medicine is characterised by mistrust of new possibilities and of the people concerned and their doctors. It is still considerably influenced by an idealisation of the social reality of traditional family structures and their effects. This is the basis for a restrictive attitude which, under the pretext of protecting the interests of children, curtails or wants to curtail the freedoms of minorities. In an unholy alliance, moral apostles on a traditional religious basis and people fearing progress as a consequence of natural-religious ideas come together. It is true that there are advantages to not immediately bursting into euphoria for everything that is possible. However, reservations must be justified in a detailed and comprehensible manner if they are to go beyond mere prejudice and resentment.

If we consider, for example, that at least one third of all marriages are divorced and that in a considerable number of the remaining things are not going well with regard to the care and upbringing of children, what justifies us then in denying people who want to live in other ways the right to have children? The traditional family also provides good conditions only in favourable cases.

In the enthusiasm for what is feasible, mistakes have undoubtedly been made and are still being made here. Particularly in the early phase of reproductive medicine, the fulfilment of the desire to have children was at the forefront and sometimes it still is today, especially for commercial reasons. There is a mentality that disregards the needs of people born through reproductive medicine for information about their origins and identity, according to the motto "They should be glad that they were brought into the world and shouldn't make such a fuss!". This mentality can be seen, for example, in the fact that the sperm of sperm donors was mixed, no records of the identity of the sperm donors were kept (long-term) or the sperm of individual donors was used for many fertilisations at the same institution, regardless of the fears of the conceived children of later meeting a half-sibling as a partner.

On the other hand, many constellations, the pros and cons of which can be discussed but which should be a matter of personal choice, were initially ruled out in principle by medical or legal regulations. There is no doubt that the interests of children should be our primary concern and we should not sacrifice them to questionable self-fulfilment projects of some people. But why should, for example, two intelligent and educated lesbians who have entered into a long-term partnership not be able to raise a child that one of them conceives through artificial insemination (possibly from the sperm of a carefully selected man among their acquaintances) just as well (or unfortunately just as badly) as parents in a traditional family? There are more and more concrete examples of such new kinds of family structures. The fact that psychologically problematic situations can arise for the children, even if the surrounding society accepts such constellations does not justify prohibition. Whether one should really strive for such family structures depends on many factors and requires thorough consideration in each individual case.

Let's have a look on a few more examples to illustrate what is at stake.

An Italian couple decided to create embryos by artificial insemination outside the body because of an unfulfilled desire to have children. After some embryos had been implanted into the wife without success, she died in a traffic accident. The husband's married sister carried one of the embryos as a surrogate mother and gave birth to a girl. She is to grow up with her aunt and uncle and the biological father wants to take on the role of uncle.[1] I cannot see what is readily condemnable about this. It may not be easy one day to explain all this to the child, and one can debate whether the father would have done better to rather raise his child himself, he would not have been the first widower to have to accomplish this. But he may have had good reasons for deciding as he did. What is important is that the child grows up in an orderly and loving family and with a clear legal status.

We should also be aware of the fact that the procedures of modern reproductive medicine are predominantly used within the framework of traditional family constellations. The sensation caused by exceptional cases easily gives a false impression of their frequency. And it is precisely those unusual and novel cases that happen basically within traditional family structures that are perhaps best suited to show how difficult it is to justify a total opposition even to seemingly particularly questionable reproductive medicine procedures, such as surrogate motherhood.

What convincing reasons can be given against a healthy mother (and prospective grandmother) in her fifties carrying a child to term for her daughter and son-in-law because the daughter was born without a uterus or had to have it removed? Where would we end up if we were to take the mere possibility of physical or psychological complications in the use of certain medical procedures as a general reason to declare a total ban and to patronise the people directly affected? The prohibition of altruistic surrogate motherhood is an unjustified paternalism by the state.

And even in commercial surrogacy, in which the restrictive position seems spontaneously more plausible, a complete, unqualified ban appears as highly questionable. I too have serious doubts about whether a couple should go so far as to pay another woman to carry a foreign child conceived outside the body through artificial insemination. But do such doubts justify a state ban? Let us be clear about the interests involved. Certainly, the surrogate mother takes a certain health risk in exchange for payment. But this risk is not particularly high. If we compare it with the health risk that a Formula I racing driver a professional boxer or various other sorts of extreme athletes take for money, for much lesser motives than helping a couple with an unfulfilled wish to have a child, then the state would have much better reasons to ban this kind of modern gladiator fights. The whole moralising fuss about paid surrogacy seems far exaggerated. Possible risks to the child through surrogacy are to be considered, but they are largely speculative in nature; in any case, they do not exceed the usual risks to unborn children to an extent that they would justify a ban on surrogacy. A serious impairment of children's interests is hardly recognisable if the child's legal position is clear and it is unambiguously established from the outset that it is to grow up with its genetic parents, that they have all parental rights and duties and that the surrogate mother cannot make any claims on the child. The fact that the surrogate mother can develop an emotional bond with the child she has born, out of which she then no longer wishes to give the child away, is - if the legal relationships have been clarified - not a problem serious enough to justify a prohibition. The widespread social consensus regarding the prohibition of commercial surrogacy is in striking contradiction to the efforts to give the sale of sexual services as "sex work" the appearance of a service that would be comparable to many other social services, although it can be very understandably argued that the sellers here market something much more intimate that should be withdrawn from commercial exchange and that they do this (under often violent and exploiting conditions) in order to satisfy needs whose importance is considerably less than the desire for one's own offspring (if we leave apart their own often precarious economic situation).

It is not inappropriate to ask whether it is very reasonable for modern reproductive medicine to enable women over the age of sixty to still have children. On the other hand, it has rightly been argued that a hundred years ago, when the average life expectancy of women in Western Europe was around fifty instead of around eighty, no one was bothered by the fact that women were still having children at the age of thirty.[2] Moreover, hardly anyone has ever been seriously bothered by men having children at an advanced age. Well, then at least the woman is certainly younger. But basically it depends on the constellation in each individual case whether it is responsible to have children at an advanced age. If one feels healthy and biologically still relatively young and if family structures are in place that give reason to expect loving care for the children by other family members in case one should get health problems and die, such a decision can be quite defensible. In any case, I see no justification for the state to interfere with the individual's freedom of choice by imposing massive restrictions. It would be much more justifiable to prohibit people who smoke two packs of cigarettes a day from having children. Nevertheless, while still more should be done against nicotine abuse, our society will not improve but become a nightmare if it is determined by comprehensive

270

prohibition, regulation and control).

It must be admitted that the new and unusual constellations made possible by modern reproductive medicine make life more complicated for the people directly affected as well as for reproductive physicians, for lawyers and politicians. Those directly affected have to account for the possible, also long-term, psychological and social effects of their actions. Reproduction doctors cannot, as in the case of a rigid restriction of their procedures to the traditional family pattern, take a back seat and reassure themselves that formal requirements are fulfilled, but must examine the seriousness and justification of their patients' wishes in each individual case and may also find themselves exposed to social and legal difficulties and hostility. Jurists must come up with regulations that shape and secure the position and rights of children in such constellations. Politicians have to enforce such regulations against all kinds of resistance (in many European countries, for example, against the still not inconsiderable influence of the Catholic Church in particular).

In any case, the state should primarily confine itself to safeguarding and securing the interests and legal position of children in the new situations made possible by modern reproductive medicine, and otherwise leave the moral considerations to the people concerned and their doctors. If the state, as happened in Italy after the above-mentioned event (and already codified in Germany in an overzealous manner with the Embryo Protection Act of 1991), knows nothing better than to impose strict restrictions on reproductive medicine, then it makes itself the bailiff of the bearers of ultimately religiously influenced prejudices, who cannot stand the fact that people expand their scope of action into areas which, in their world of imagination, are reserved for divine rule and providence.

It is not my intention here to discuss exhaustively all the constellations that arise or can arise through modern reproductive medicine. However, I would like to emphasise once again that the possible psychological and social problems for the partners involved (married or not) and the children conceived through such procedures do not represent anything fundamentally new (in contrast to the impression usually given by those who mainly appear to have reservations about such procedures). Very similar problems arise with the adoption of children, with divorces or the remarriage of people who already have children - without anyone coming up with the idea that these ways of conduct should be prohibited by the state in order to prevent such problems from the outset (instead of leaving them where they belong, namely in the sphere of responsibility of the people concerned).

Most people have a strong, evolutionary originated desire to reproduce, the expression of which is influenced by social circumstances and the resources available to them. There are many historical examples of powerful and economically strong individuals having produced more offspring than less well-off fellow human beings. And these descendants were and are often presented publicly, if only to convey dynastic continuity. Today, a large number of children has predominantly become a characteristic of poorer classes and countries. In the use of modern reproductive medicine, however, we find a continuation of the historical examples mentioned, even if it is no longer a question of many children, but rather of the possibility of reproducing at least with a part of one's own genetic heritage. Just as many earlier "multiple procreators" hardly had the welfare of the procreated children in mind as a priority (and some "normal" parents do not either), those who make use of modern reproductive medicine procedures may also have considerations in the foreground for which the welfare of the children is secondary, such as an exaggerated need for self-realisation or inheritance considerations. In some cases there is undoubtedly considerable family and social pressure on those involved, especially women, which can lead to stressful and risky measures being undertaken without the desirable detached and critical consideration of whether these measures are really in the best interests of oneself and the intended child. This can and should be considered, addressed and discussed on a case-by-case basis. Responsible reproductive medicine also means giving the impetus for such considerations as well as providing the necessary information for this and not being carried away by enthusiasm for one's own technical skills or being guided by financial interests. Even if reproductive medicine may not always be practised so responsibly, this is not an argument for generally restrictive regulations.

I would like to discuss another situation which, although beyond the field of reproductive medicine according to the customary use of the term, is best placed here within the framework of this treatise: It is the cases where a pregnant woman suffers brain death and then receives further intensive medical treatment to enable the further development and survival of the unborn child. This situation, which became known in Germany in particular through the case of the "Baby of Erlangen"[3] is - despite its rarity - well suited to once again illustrate some of the conflicts and principles presented in the section "The value of life value and the right to life" by way of example. In this situation, too, the decision should not be based on the idea of an absolute value of life and an absolute right to life, but on a careful consideration of the interests of the child and the relatives concerned. In this specific case, it also became clear what an important role psychologically understandable but morally insignificant, zeitgeist arguments can play in the debate (as we have already seen in the discussion of brain death).

The initial situation was as follows: An 18-year-old woman, four months pregnant, had suffered brain death as a result of a traffic accident, and the question now arose as to whether her body should be kept alive by intensive medical measures so that the child could possibly be saved. The doctors in charge took the position that (although they were asked about this) the consent of the unmarried biological father of the child as well as the child's grandparents was basically irrelevant, since the child had an independent right to life, which the doctors were obliged to preserve as far as possible. In the public debate, and especially from the feminist side, the argument was often put forward that the human dignity and peace in death of the mother would be unjustifiably violated by maintaining intensive medical measures after brain death.

Let us first clarify the specific problems of such cases. What distinguishes them from a situation in which an abortion is being considered in a pregnancy of the same age?

A first essential difference is that the mother, since she is brain-dead, is no longer the bearer of substantial interests. If a woman is expected to carry an unwanted pregnancy to term only in order to give the child up for adoption, this is undoubtedly a heavy burden for her. The brain-dead mother, on the other hand, whatever her attitude to the pregnancy may have been during her lifetime, is no longer burdened by the continuation of the pregnancy after her death. The mother's peace in death and other considerations related to the dead mother cannot seriously be placed in competition as a value with the survival interest of a developing human being. If this does happen, then women's feelings of oppression towards a medicine and politics still partly determined by male dominance, are expressed in the wrong place.

A second essential difference to an abortion at the same gestational age lies in the fact that, in contrast to an abortion, we do not ourselves initiate the causal chain leading to the death of the foetus when we forego intensive medical care for the brain-dead mother in order to maintain the pregnancy; rather, this causal chain has already been initiated by the event which caused the brain death of the mother. We should keep this difference in mind, but it does not justify the abandonment of intensive medical care for the brain-dead mother in order to maintain the pregnancy. And once the intensive medical care of the brain-dead mother for the purpose of maintaining the pregnancy has been started, there is no longer any difference between an abortion by discontinuing these measures and an abortion by other means.

A third important difference lies in the experimental character of maintaining a pregnancy in a brain-dead mother (which is more pronounced the lower the gestational age). Since only a few such cases with different outcomes have been described so far, a substantial damage to the child in such a pregnancy cannot be excluded, and the risk involved is difficult to estimate because of the limited experience. (In addition, there is the possibility that the event which led to the brain death of the mother could also have caused damage to the unborn child). And it is this third difference - and only this difference - that should prompt us to grant the father or other remaining close relatives more extensive rights of co-determination in the pregnancy of a brain-dead mother than we would do in any other pregnancy with an apparently healthy embryo or foetus. They are the ones who have to bear the consequences of such an experiment in the first place, not the doctors in charge and not the jurists. Therefore, they should be allowed to decide on the continuation of intensive medical care for the brain-dead mother and thus the maintenance of the pregnancy as long as the child is certainly not yet viable outside the womb (and if there are indications of serious damage to or disability of the foetus, they should have the same rights as parents would otherwise have in such cases, see the discussion on this under 3.6.4).

On the other hand, the physical and possibly also psychological risks for the unborn child resulting from the mother's brain death should not be over-emphasised. If one considers, by comparison, the risks to which many unborn children are exposed through the irresponsible lifestyle of their mothers, for example through their alcohol and nicotine abuse, then it seems by no means irresponsible from the outset to maintain a pregnancy in a brain-dead mother. And if, in the longer term, greater experience with such situations should show that the probability of a healthy child (if it survives at all) is not significantly lower than in a normal pregnancy, then I would no longer see any justification for deviating from the otherwise applicable rules for abortion.

It cannot be denied that the interests of the relatives are affected to a considerable extent by such a situation. The father becomes a single parent. Or if we assume that he has also died in an accident and there are only frail grandparents left or no close relatives at all, it may be that the child has to be given up for adoption. But all this does not justify foregoing the continuation of intensive medical measures and letting the unborn child die without further consideration. For if the mother or both parents die two months after the birth of a child, the situation is no different and yet no one would propose the idea that the infant should be killed or allowed to die because of this.

Next, I would like to discuss the problem of reducing multiple pregnancies by selective feticide. How should and may we proceed when certain procedures of modern reproductive medicine (hormonal treatment, multiple transfer of embryos produced in vitro) result in multiple pregnancies?

If we accept the right of women to decide for themselves whether to continue or terminate a pregnancy, for example during the first twelve weeks, I see no convincing reason to deny them the right to opt for a partial abortion by killing one or some of the multiple embryos or fetuses during this period. To be distinguished from this is the moral judgement of such procedures and situations. Here, first of all, it falls within the moral responsibility of the doctors concerned to avoid the occurrence of multiple pregnancies by careful monitoring and management of the treatment to the extent that seems reasonable and possible with regard to the desired outcome of the treatment. Furthermore, the attending physician and the woman or the parents should discuss the risk of a multiple pregnancy with each other before the beginning of the treatment and should be clear about the extent to which there is a willingness to carry such a pregnancy to term or to select embryos for in vitro fertilisation or to partially terminate multiple pregnancies by killing part of the developing embryos. State paternalism has no place in these decisions. In view of the risks of multiple pregnancies, which can result in serious burdens for the parents and the children, it is wrong to restrict the possibilities of reducing multiple pregnancies through embryo selection by means of morally patronising legal provisions, as is happening in Germany as a consequence of a bioethics debate predominantly influenced by Christianity and natural religion. A selective reduction of multiple fetuses may have to be justified in Germany via the hypocritical diversions of a medical indication refering to health problems of the expectant mother, regardless of whether there are indications of a significant disability of one of the fetuses or not.

If a multiple pregnancy has developed following a reproductive medical treatment procedure, it is not possible to make unambiguous, universally valid determinations in advance regarding the appropriate moral decisions. The individual situation of the pregnant woman must be taken into account as well as medical facts. Twins, despite somewhat increased risks, have a good chance of surviving and surviving in good health, and the social task that falls to the parents appears to be manageable. But in older pregnant women a pregnancy with twins already carries considerably higher risks. And with a triplet pregnancy, the risk of a significant handicap is about 30 percent, which means that about half of all families have to reckon with a handicapped child. From a quadruplet pregnancy onwards, the number of disabled children increases drastically and at the same time the risk to the mother increases significantly. In this situation, I consider it an appropriate consideration if the attending doctors and the parents concerned only accept a multiple pregnancy up to twins. If one decides on a procedure that involves the risk of a multiple pregnancy, then it seems to me, unless there are special reasons against it in the individual case, that it is worth considering (but not compulsory) from a moral point of view to take on the additional burdens that a twin birth entails for the mother and the rest of the family.

At the end of this section, I would like to briefly discuss the problems of research on human embryos and the use of embryonic cells and tissues in medicine (although these issues are only partly related to reproductive medicine).

Just as abortion should not be used as a routine method of birth control, research on human embryos should not be carried out for the sake of mere curiosity. However, if there is a well-founded interest in knowledge, I believe that time limits for such research, up to those that apply to abortion, are justifiable. Important for transparency and confidence-building vis-à-vis science is the prerequisite that the donors of the egg and sperm cells or the zygote, the "parents", give their consent.

A well-founded interest in embryo research may be given in several respects, for example to improve artificial insemination techniques by directly introducing sperm into the egg cell, to obtain blood stem cells for blood cancer treatments or to cultivate organ tissue cultures that can be transplanted. The hasty total ban on embryo research, which in the German Embryo Protection Act already protects embryos with a few cells much more strictly than unborn children in later and even late stages of pregnancy, is completely excessive and morally untenable from a secular point of view.

Among other things, this law has impeded pre-implantation diagnostics for

276

serious hereditary diseases with a high probability of occurrence for twenty years in Germany. The right to life of embryos in early stages of development with only a few cells, many of which are afflicted in addition by serious hereditary diseases because of the genetic disposition of the parents, was given higher priority than the interest of the parents in having a healthy child with a high probability. The probability of success of in vitro fertilisation, which is associated with considerable stress for the woman due to the removal of the eggs, was reduced by the ban on preserving embryos instead of eggs. It is still uncertain whether the easing by the later jurisdiction of the Federal Court of Justice[4], which could not recognise any criminal use of human embryos in pre-implantation diagnostics, will survive political efforts for a renewed, even stricter prohibitive legislation. At least there is a persisting cross-party reluctancy to revise the outdated embryo protection law though there are high-level scientific proposals to do so. (1)

Nor can I see any good reasons why, for example, in vitro fertilisation with donor sperm should be prohibited on principle. It is also incomprehensible that egg donation is prohibited in Germany, but embryo donation is not. The additional risks compared to sperm donation are not so serious as to justify a legal ban.

All in all, this is no longer just about Germany's threatening or already existing backwardness in some areas of science and research, but about very concrete, serious paternalism and impairments of affected fellow citizens without the underlying considerations being consistent and comprehensible in any way. Despite the fact that we are a pluralistic society, we still partly cling to a Christian-religious legal system in which the beliefs of a religious group are made binding for all citizens using criminal law.

The use of embryonic cells for therapeutic purposes or research seems to me to be morally unobjectionable if the life of the embryos had been terminated by an abortion irrespective of the subsequent use of their cells or they would have been disposed of as unused embryos from in vitro fertilisation. The doctors who advise the woman on the abortion or reproductive procedures and perform them should not be directly involved in the use of embryonic cells and, in particular, should not have any economic interest in it. Moreover, for reasons of transparency and confidence-building, the consent of the mother or the parents of the embryo should be made a prerequisite for such use of their cells. The moral problem, however, lies in the decision on abortion or the respective reproductive procedure and not in the decision on the use of embryonic or foetal cells.

And if the only way to cure a life-threatening or severely debilitating illness of an ego-conscious human individual, a human person, is to create a genetically identical embryo and kill it after a few weeks to obtain certain cell or organ cultures, this can be morally justified. Admittedly, it is by no means morally trivial to instrumentalise a human being in this way for the benefit of another, even if it is in an early stage of development. But the interests of a human person in continuing to live or in the healing of a serious illness are morally higher than the right to life of a human embryo, which could indeed become a human person, but in its current stage of development only has a vegetative urge to survive and not yet any consciousness and especially no awareness of any interests.

In various mammalian species, chromosomally identical individuals can already be produced by micro manipulating embryos at an early stage and, meanwhile, also by transferring genetic material from body cells of already adult animals into oocytes, and there are good reasons to use such procedures in animal breeding.

Nature also produces identical twins in humans with a frequency of three to four per thousand births, which means that in Germany there are about 300,000 identical twins (not to mention the rare cases of higher-grade multiples), although due to mutations picked up in the womb, different gene activation (especially of the two X chromosomes in females), other epigenetic mechanisms and a different distribution of mitochondrial hereditary material, these individuals are not completely identical from a genetic point of view already early in their life and before later different biographical influences.

One can certainly take the view that the deliberate creation of genetically identical or almost identical human persons would be a manipulation that violates the individuality of human beings, worthy of protection. At least as long as there is no concrete danger that such a procedure is intended on a large scale (i.e. in considerably larger numbers than the natural rate of monozygotic multiple pregnancies), a legal ban on creating multiple identical embryos through cloning or embryo splitting can hardly be justified. Who would seriously claim that several hundred thousand of our fellow citizens, namely all monozygotic multiple births, suffer from a deplorable lack of individuality and human dignity, and even a lack even would make one wish that they had better not been born? One rarely sees as clearly as in this train of thought how inconsiderately things that are simply scary to people are often branded as a

278

violation of human dignity. If, for example, a woman's only chance of having her own genetically related child is to carry a child cloned from her own cells, and if the production of such a child does not involve any risks for the child that go significantly beyond those involved in natural pregnancies, where are the morally relevant arguments against such an undertaking? (2) From experience with cloning animals from somatic cells, however, there are at present serious safety concerns about the use of this method in humans. Damage to future persons who would be created in this way is not unlikely given the current state of technology, and it is irresponsible to transfer this procedure to humans before it has been proven to be highly safe in animal experiments.

In the case of some reproductive medical procedures already in use today or conceivable in the future, one can justifiably question whether it is appropriate and reasonable to go to such lengths to remedy the problem of childlessness, or in any case to argue against the costs for this being borne by the health insurance system. If the objections are serious enough, however, to justify a legal ban, is a different question that has to be answered separately for each procedure after thorough examination.

3.6.7. Genetic Engineering

Misconceptions at the root of a phobia

Genetic engineering is one of the most controversial branches of science and technology today, especially in Germany. Quite a few demonise it and would prefer to ban it altogether. Is there a rational basis for this rejection or for a ban?

First of all, it should be noted that nature itself is constantly changing genetic material. On the one hand, this is the prerequisite for evolution and thus also for the existence of us humans. However, the harmful and neutral changes predominate, which then either disappear through selection or do not spread because of a lack of selective advantage. And even those changes that bring an advantage for certain living beings repeatedly give rise to - sometimes catastrophic - threats for other living beings and species. Under favourable local conditions, nature allows the development and, under certain circumstances, even a high degree of differentiation of life. However, to attribute to it an interest in the survival of certain species or some tendency towards peace or harmony is a romanticisation that lacks any scientific basis.

Furthermore, humans have been changing the genetic makeup of animals and plants since Neolithic times, through breeding measures in the sense of selection and also through the eradication of species. After preliminary work in the 18th and 19th century - and in particular the formulation of Mendel's rules - human intervention in the genetic material of plants and animals has taken on new dimensions since about 1900 in the form of breeding on a scientific basis.

Migratory movements of plants and animals are also an integral part of evolutionary history. Since the modern age of exploration and the resulting global trade, humans have transported living organisms to other parts of the world on a large scale, in some cases significantly changing the local flora and fauna - with both desirable and undesirable consequences.

Changes to the genetic material and the local biotopes were made by humans long before modern genetic engineering. However, this technology works in vitro on isolated genetic material or (in a broader version of the term) on early cell division stages of developing organisms and allows more extensive changes of the genetic material. Such changes can now be carried out many times faster and in a more targeted manner, individual genes can be inserted into the genome of other organisms and take over certain control functions there, species and genus boundaries can be broken down in previously unimaginable ways and the ever more precise genetic scissors can now alter the genetic material of living beings in such a way that, without corresponding information from the genetic engineers, in many cases the results of genome editing can no longer be distinguished from genetic alterations not caused by humans or caused by breeding. With these possibilities, a new dimension of human access to the genome has undeniably been created.

With the expanded possibilities come new opportunities and new risks. They must be carefully weighed against each other in the individual case, in relation to the respective project. There can be no doubt that there will be mistakes. The future may teach us (possibly painfully) that our impact assessment was inadequate, as it has been for so many other scientific and technical projects in the past.

On the other hand, exaggerated fear and scaremongering about such risks is completely inappropriate. Such behaviour is based on various irrational motives: (non-human) nature is idealised and it is not recognised that, apart from its orientation towards reproductive success, it is teleologically indifferent and in any case has no moral orientation whatsoever. Genetic engineering interventions by humans are perceived as sacrilege, as the transgression of human boundaries into areas reserved for a divine power, even if the god is only a divinised nature. If nature were good (for us) the way it is, then we would not be justified in interfering with nature in any other way either. We should rather let people die prematurely of pneumonia or peritonitis due to perforated appendixes, instead of using antibiotics and operating. Why interventions in the natural genome should have a fundamentally different quality than other interventions in nature is not justifiable on a rational basis. Many other, earlier interventions in nature have also left lasting consequences, be it the extinction of animal species or the exploitation of natural resources, for example for energy production (to stick to a biased presentation and mention only negative consequences). And conversely, interventions in genetic material will not always leave lasting consequences, just like many other interventions in nature.

In contrast to earlier interventions in nature, genetic engineering is accompanied from the outset by an intensive discussion of the risks and by (sometimes even considerably exaggerated) social regulation. This offers good prospects that it will be accompanied by fewer undesirable effects and unforeseen risks than earlier interventions in nature. However, it is illusory to assume that one can make use of promising scientific or technical procedures without learning the hard way when applying them. This would only be possible at the price of a ban on innovation.

Thus, there is no reason to be particularly suspicious of genetic engineering. It is undoubtedly justified, however, to set some broad limits for genetic engineering interventions, of which a few examples are given here:

- Certain types of chimeras, especially crossbreeds between humans and animals, should be taboo - at least with the aim of rearing. If such mixed creatures were viable (which, however, is very unlikely), they would bring us into unforeseeable moral conflicts.
- Manipulations in the human germ line should be subjected to a high standard of justification with regard to the research goals pursued in this context. At present, there is hardly any justification for such manipulations or at least not for advancing the development of human beings with such manipulations to viable stages. However, this does not justify a complete ban on research in this field. If germ line therapy should ever appear to be feasible with sufficient safety, it will first of all be justified from the point of view of individual therapy. Eugenic concepts are not suitable as an

argument for genetic engineering at the present stage of development. However, it cannot be ruled out that future developments could also make such approaches responsible (in the sense of avoiding disease, not of creating an "ideal human being"). There must be no prohibitions on thinking and weighing in this respect either. In this context, however, it should be pointed out that the widespread prejudice that we have to reckon with a deterioration of the genetic make-up of humankind because modern medicine makes it possible for more carriers of hereditary diseases to reproduce is based on information deficits and is scientifically untenable. There are also many genetically positive factors that result from modern medicine and lifestyle, such as the greater mixing of the genetic make-up due to increased geographic and social mobility or (in wealthy countries) the concentration of the birth of fewer offspring at an age of the parents that is still quite favourable from the point of view of mutation (despite the higher average age of first-time mothers), to name just two of many examples. The overall effect of the various factors on the genetic make-up is difficult to survey. (1)

– The use of genetic testing for predispositions of diseases requires a careful consideration of the resulting consequences for the persons concerned, their relatives and society. In those cases where the benefit for the persons concerned is not indisputable and clear (e.g. because there are no prevention and treatment options), their consent is required after careful information about the possible consequences (whereby parents must not generally be granted the right to decide on the use of such tests on their children before they themselves can grasp the consequences and make the decision; rather, depending on the disease predisposition in question, the decision must be made that is in the best interests of the children). Among other things, tendencies towards a lack of solidarity, as we could observe in part with AIDS, is a real danger as a consequence of such tests that must be contained. However, this is not a specific problem of genetic tests, but also concerns other diagnostic procedures. (2) A general ban on the use of genetic tests in the insurance industry, as is sometimes demanded without much thought, does not make sense, since such tests can also be used, for example, to enable members of families with hereditary diseases, who previously could not insure themselves or could only do so with high surcharges, to obtain normal insurance conditions if tested negative.

– Genetic diagnostics and therapy in humans should always be applied from an individual therapeutic or prophylactic point of view in the best interest of the affected individuals and families and should not pursue eugenic goals with regard to society as a whole, apart from the possible elimination of genetic disorders. "Breeding humans" with a view to promoting or avoiding certain characteristics, analogous to animal breeding, would be technically conceivable but entail unacceptable moral and social costs and risks.

The production and cultivation of genetically modified plants, for example with resistance to total herbicides, is fraught with question marks and requires critical examination (for example, the initial benefit can be lost again through the cross-fertilisation of resistance to weeds, and herbicides with few side effects can become ineffective as a result). The dependence of farmers on large corporations and the negative effects on small-scale farming structures in developing countries (analogous to the consequences of subsidised food exports to these countries) must be prevented by appropriate regulatory measures. In addition, there is a risk of impoverishment of the crop diversity, which would reduce the possibilities of resorting to other varieties in the event of epidemics. Such problems can be exacerbated by green genetic engineering, but they are not specific to it and arise similarly from the protection and marketing of conventionally bred plant varieties.

However, genetic engineering that leads to changes in food can cause further problems. It has been shown that the genetic code for allergenic proteins can also be transferred during the genetic manipulation of food plants. This can be a life-threatening danger for people suffering from allergies, since it is then impossible for them to avoid a known allergen now appearing unexpectedly in a food that was previously harmless to them. Such modifications therefore require compulsory labelling with an indication of the type of gene transfer, if their desirable effects are so pronounced that they cannot be avoided altogether. The new, more precises methods of genetic engineering by genetic scissors reduce risks of this kind.

The problem of adequate labelling of the ingredients of food, cosmetics etc. does not arise from genetic engineering and is also not a problem specifically connected with it, but only comes in a new variation here. And in the case of genetic modifications it is much better possible to describe precisely what happens than in the case of breeding-related changes or exposure to new foodstuffs through more intensive trade exchange between different parts of the world.

Genetic changes in plants and animals have been achieved for a long time by conventional breeding measures without causing much (or then mostly positive) excitement and, above all, without ever leading to uncontrollable, catastrophic effects. The consequences of such breeding measures were and are much more difficult to assess than those of genetic engineering, in which defined genes with a precisely known structure and function are transferred. It is true that in genetic engineering, too, factors of uncertainty remain with regard to the result of the genetic manipulation, for example due to the complex interplay of different genes ("position effect"), which also includes the possibility of activating previously inactive genes in the genetically modified cell, as well as due to the frequent, technically induced transfer of further genetic material, beyond the gene whose transfer is actually aimed at or due to remaining inaccuracies of the work of genetic scissors. No fantastic horror creatures are to be expected anyhow, but as a rule only a lack of gene expression and stability, i.e. a failure to achieve the desired effect.

Different applications of genetic engineering are at different stages of development and involve different opportunities and risks - from food and drug production to the different variants of gene therapy in the narrower sense. The effects of new possibilities for genome editing are still incalculable. possible Ever faster and more precise interventions in the genome become possible and are likely to increasingly extend to influencing epigenetic processes. Partly the genetic modifications are no longer detectable without the relevant information from their creators. Here, as in other issues, we need careful risk assessments and ecological, social and moral evaluations, not emotional, prejudiced guesswork. If we strive for an appropriate, rational cost-benefit balance, it is irresponsible if the safety, bureaucratic and liability requirements, for example for genetic engineering production plants or the approval of experiments with plants to which resistance genes against certain plant diseases have been transferred, are raised to such an extent that they take on an almost prohibitive character and favourable developments are massively delayed or even made impossible. An outright rejection of genetic engineering in agriculture and livestock breeding without detailed study is not justified, since more environmentally harmful methods may be replaced and substantial increases in yield may be achieved. There is as yet no reason to regard the risks of genetic engineering research and development as so threatening that a ban or excessive restriction should be derived from this. Countries and regions that do so will fall behind and face severe disadvantages.

We are facing a host of serious problems: We have to create humane living conditions for a strongly increased and still growing world population in a way that is as environmentally friendly as possible. To do this, we must first of all ensure that alle people are fed. For this, we need crops that are as productive as possible and are adapted to different climatic zones and to climate change. We must fight new diseases, such as AIDS, and find more effective means against old diseases that become available to more people. I am convinced that it is irresponsible to reject the contribution that genetic engineering can already make to solving serious human problems today and promises to make in the future (even if this contribution may be relatively small compared to solving political-organisational questions) because of reservations that are often not well thought out and because of a one-sided emphasis on the risks. (3)

3.6.8. Sexual and Gender Minorities

The lengthy farewell to »unnaturalness«

Discussing and attacking the paternalism and discrimination of people through social prejudice and legislation determined less by comprehensible considerations than by ideological dogma is a concern that plays an essential role in the various chapters of this whole section 3.6. devoted to bioethical issues. That is why sexual and gender orientation have their own chapter here. For the purpose of example it deals first of all rather extensively with homosexuality as (together with bisexuality) the most common sexual minority orientation.

Homosexuality appears at first sight to be hostile to procreation. This is undoubtedly one of the reasons why homosexual people were and are particularly affected by the prejudice and paternalism mentioned above.

When I speak of homosexuality in the following, I basically mean male and female homosexuality in equal measure. Much of what is discussed here with regard to homosexuality also applies analogously to transsexuality, which, with a certain delay, is going through a similar social history, namely from rejection and discrimination to heightened, fashionable attention, already exaggerated in relation to its numerical importance, and further on to acceptance and a personal characteristic more or less regarded as a matter of course.

Let us first deal with the still popular statement that homosexuality is "unnatural". What does that actually mean?

If it is meant as a moral condemnation, it can be answered simply by stating that nature is morally neutral, that the equation of "natural" and "morally good" or "unnatural" and "morally bad" is unjustified and represents a misjudgement, by now only to be described as naïve. (See also 3.3.)

If the statement that homosexuality is unnatural is meant as a factual assertion, it refutes itself. If homosexuality were unnatural in this sense, it would not exist. This leads to the interesting question: Why does homosexuality exist, and why does it manifest itself in a relatively high percentage of about two to four (if one includes bisexuality) or even ten (if one includes occasional homoerotic inclinations and contacts) percent of the population?

It is not very plausible to explain a trait that is evolutionarily stable in the long term with such frequency as merely maladaptive (or even as just socially caused). Among other things it was the further development of evolutionary theory in the form of sociobiology that has enabled us to find approaches for a better explanation. Sociobiology has given us the insight that the success of genetic programmes is also largely determined by the behaviour of genetically closely related individuals who do not reproduce themselves directly or who accept reduced chances of reproduction for themselves if this improves the chances of reproduction of their genetic programmes via genetically closely related individuals. With this concept, many apparently altruistic behaviours can be explained in terms of evolutionary biology. (1) And it can also be used to explain that having homosexual relatives can mean an evolutionary advantage: They forego their own reproduction or at least have fewer offspring of their own, but care for the offspring of genetically close relatives and can thus increase their reproductive success. This could explain why the genetic predispositions for homosexuality persist in the gene pool in the percentage mentioned. In evolutionary biology, homosexuality could be understood as a genetically anchored disposition to and kin selection. However, such an explanation would also favour asexuality and the question remains unanswered why evolution should lastingly preserve such a detour which ultimately leads to less reproductive success.

As homosexual and asexual individuals would nevertheless have a diminished reproductive success and it is hard to imagine how their sexual orientation could be firmly established as a contribution to the inclusive fitness of their genes such an explanation remains doubtful. The same applies to various other suggestions, such as a genetic link between homosexuality and a tendency towards more sexual partners, which could have been maintained by the fact that it could also have benefited heterosexuals, inheritance of homosexuality in the maternal line, the genetic basis of which could simultaneously have favoured increased fertility in women, an improved ability to resolve social conflicts and cooperate through homo- or bisexuality.... Ultimately, there is still no conclusive and convincing evolutionary explanation for homosexuality.

Twin studies and the widespread distribution of homosexuality in animals indicate that there is a considerable genetic influence in the origin of homosexuality, while genetic studies carried out in recent years on the localisation of genes significant for male homosexuality have so far only yielded unclear and controversial results. In genetically male individuals, sexual behaviour is apparently also influenced by the temporally critical effect of testosterone and stress hormones during embryonic development. At least in the borderline area of heterosexuality, bisexuality and homosexuality, the development of sexual disposition is certainly also dependent on social factors (such as different acceptance of homosexual behaviour, lack of opposite-sex sexual partners or availability of sexual partners with similar inclinations) and cultural shaping processes. On the other hand, to regard homosexuality as decisively determined by an early childhood developmental process, as is done in the psychoanalytical explanatory model of drive-fate, is a highly speculative theory for which only a few supporting findings could be produced and which therefore should no longer be upheld. It is true that various findings show that a high percentage of us have a disposition for same-sex inclinations and same-sex sexuality, which comes to the surface to a greater or lesser extent depending on social conditions. However, this does not justify the assumption that in principle every human being can become a homosexual through early childhood imprinting. In that case, evolutionary development would not primarily have produced a clear predominance of heterosexual disposition, but would merely have ensured that the imprinting processes leading to heterosexual behaviour take place more frequently. Arguments for such a "diversion" would still have to be provided. And above all, the psychoanalytical "explanation" of homosexuality owes us the answer to the question of why the postulated early childhood development to homosexuality would happen at all in a certain, not insignificant frequency. The conjectures about typical family structures for this are not very convincing. But whatever the case may be, homosexuality would remain just as natural as heterosexuality, even if psychoanalytical and other psychological concepts on its causation were correct.

An excessive spread of homosexuality would obviously be detrimental to reproductive success (and is therefore prevented by the evolutionary process). This might also be part of the explanation why the "normal", numerically predominant, heterosexually oriented individuals, who actually benefit from homosexuality, often reject it so strongly. Another motive for this may lie in their own homosexual inclinations, which are to be suppressed. Apart from this, people's attitudes towards homosexuality are determined to a large extent by religious and ideological ideas and social conventions that differ greatly in different societies and historical epochs.

With the current state of knowledge, it can be considered certain that the development of homosexuality, bisexuality and transsexuality are complex processes that defy a monocausal explanation. Whatever the details of a scientific explanation of homosexuality may look like in the end, it is already clear by now that the talk of the unnaturalness of sexual minority orientations is inadequate and nothing more than a mere unreflective prejudice. A prejudice for which earlier times at least had the excuse of less knowledge. (2)

But are there perhaps nevertheless negative moral, health or social consequences of homosexuality?

There is no justification for a morally different judgement on various sexual orientations. To ask whether homosexuality or heterosexuality is morally better is just as inappropriate as wanting to make a moral judgement on different eye colours. Even if a simple explanation of homosexuality as a maladaptive variant with regard to reproductive success were biologically correct, this would not provide any justification for morally devaluing this sexual orientation. All forms of sexual orientation can bring us humans great joy and great suffering. The same moral ideals should apply to all forms of eroticism and sexuality (equality, mutual respect, consent, renunciation of violence). These ideals are basically no more and no less realised or disregarded in heterosexual relationships than in homosexual ones.

Since the advent of AIDS, the idea of negative health consequences, especially of homosexuality, seems obvious. However, this is merely a mental bias. Many diseases were and are transmitted through heterosexual contact. Before the discovery of effective antibiotics (and especially penicillin), syphilis was just as dangerous to humankind as later AIDS. The fact that the spread

288

of AIDS affected homosexuals as a main risk group earlier and more strongly than heterosexuals (undeniably favoured by the promiscuity of male homosexuals in the USA who had just been freed from social restrictions) is a mere fact which in no way devalues this type of sexual orientation. Whether homosexual or heterosexual, health risks of sexual practices are promoted by lack of knowledge, lack of education and illusionary misjudgement of realities, and all this in turn by the normative ideas and taboos of an often religiously motivated moral dogmatism and rigorism.

But what about overall negative social consequences of homosexuality? They do exist and unfortunately still do. Homosexuals were and are in danger of becoming outsiders, with consequences including social ostracism and physical persecution. Especially in rural areas where church influence remains strong, this is still true to some extent even in liberal western societies. There it can still be difficult to openly show homosexuality and still be socially accepted and remain integrated. Discrimination and prejudice are still anchored in the law as well. Why do different legal norms for the protection of minors still apply to homosexual contacts than to heterosexual ones, even in Germany? Why has our legal system only recently come up with a (still disputed) institute for establishing and protecting long-term relationships between homosexual people (as if possible children were the only reason for such a legal institute)? Long-term homosexual relationships are a social reality in such considerable numbers that a state-protected legal safeguard for this form of partnership should be a matter of course. (3) The cause of negative social consequences of homosexuality lies predominantly in the prejudices and discrimination with which society treats this sexual orientation. And here, even in modern Western societies, some long overdue changes still need to be implemented. It is true that we can rejoice that we no longer live in Victorian England, that Oscar Wilde's fate and E. M. Forster's novel "Maurice" seem to us today like stories from a bygone era. But the long farewell to "unnaturalness" and the moral and social discrimination based on it has not yet come to an end in our countries either, not to mention the situation in most parts of the world outside the Western cultural sphere and especially in many African and Islamic states.

In western countries, discrimination against homosexuals has fortunately decreased significantly in recent decades. Instead, there are now sometimes bitter debates on the topics of intersexuality and gender incongruence. We need to find our way back to a culture of debate in which the natural sciences, such as biology, and the social sciences once again come together in a joint endeavour to gain knowledge in the best interests of the people concerned and society as a whole, and in which the biological or social aspects are given appropriate consideration depending on the context. Fighting slogans from one side or the other will not help. When biologists shout "There are only two sexes!", one wonders how they want to categorise the many biologically determined forms of intersexuality? If, on the other hand, social scientists claim that gender identity is only a social attribution, one wonders how far scientific fashions can move away from the facts without their protagonists exposing themselves to ridicule?

Intersexual people and people with gender incongruence should lead a life equal in rights in society with the best possible prospects of personal happiness. At the same time, people who have a sexual majority orientation must not be unfairly disadvantaged.

An appropriate discussion and assessment of the facts is not just a theoretical endeavour, but has concrete practical implications. For example, premature, irreversible gender reassignment therapies at a young age must be avoided (which particularly affects girls in puberty, whose gender dysphoria may prove to be a temporary episode and not a permanent gender incongruence). Or another example: In competitive elite sports, injustices occur in relation to people who clearly belong to the female sex biologically when intersex people who are only women from a social point of view, but who have male characteristics genetically or hormonally, are allowed to compete as women (because people do not want to check or take note of the biological facts, sometimes deliberately for political reasons). Such people must be either categorised as men in competitive sports or need their own category. Sacrificing competition fairness in elite sports is the wrong way to further social integration of intersex athletes. It is also unacceptable that biological men, who only define themselves socially as women, demand access to protected areas for women, invoking protection against discrimination. Anti-discrimination efforts, as honourable as they are in principle, must not create new injustices and endangerments.

3.6.9. Humans and Animals

Beyond self-deception and evasions

> "The question ist not, Can they reason? nor Can they talk? but, Can they suffer?"[1]
>
> Jeremy Bentham

Jeremy Bentham´s statement of 1780 is still fundamental to the moral consideration of animals. But meanwhile there are more ambitious modern approaches on animal welfare and animal rights. What significance do they have? Which ways of treating animals can be acceptable?

The discovery of biological evolution and the massive, continuing growth of knowledge about animal behaviour and animal capabilities in the last decades have made our attitude towards animals a major concern of ethics and personal morality. Today we are aware of many astonishing achievements in consciousness, memory and intelligence in the animal world. And we know that such achievements are not only found in vertebrates and mammals but also in animals that are genetically very distant from us, such as cephalopods, for example squids and octopuses. As the theory of evolution would lead us to expect the distinction between humans and animals meanwhile seems less clear-cut and more gradual in many respects. Great apes apparently even recognise themselves as (mortal) individuals, have self-awareness and are capable of empathy. Well, great apes are not, or at least not to any significant extent, among the animals eaten by humans (even if our treatment of them still has many other questionable aspects). But many other higher animals are undoubtedly at least capable of suffering and have consciousness and memory.

Self-awareness appears as a plausible criterion for ascribing particularly far-reaching rights, but the other abilities mentioned, above all the existence of the capacity to suffer, prompt us to regard the fate of living beings as morally relevant and to spare them unnecessary suffering and grant them considerable rights of protection.

Important differences remain between animals and humans, for example the exclusively human capability to make life plans and have fears or hopes for a more distant future. And we can take the quite plausible position that there can be no animal rights that are equivalent to the rights of humans and human rights as animals cannot have duties corresponding to rights and cannot make moral considerations. But all these qualifications should not be used to deny that we have considerable moral obligations towards animals.

Let´s have a look on the most important modern approaches on animal ethics. There is Peter Singers "equal consideration of interests", demanding us to leave behind "speciesism", presented, for example, in one of the most influential books on the matter, "Animal Liberation". It is a must-read, also for bringing to mind historical and present cruelties towards animals we humans are responsible for. Taken strictly "equal consideration of interests"[2] comes to vegetarianism or even veganism. The question is if we are really morally obliged to an equal consideration of animal interests or if some kind of "adequate" consideration of animal interests (to be discussed in detail) can also be acceptable.

Another interesting approach is Christine Korsgaard`s neo-Kantian concept. She proposes to ascribe sentient animals a dignity similar to human dignity and to extend Kant´s imperative that we should not use other people as mere means to our ends but consider them as ends in themselves to animals.[3] Taken strictly this comes to vegetarianism or even veganism as well. The problem is that we do not even accept this principle without exceptions and qualifications when other people are concerned. The more so I do not find the idea convincing that Kant´s imperative should be extended to animals without further qualification. But there is some truth in Korsgaard´s approach as well: It seems morally wrong to use animals *just* as means to our ends while ruthlessly neglecting there suffering and their interests in a life adequate to their species.

Martha Nussbaum extends the "capability approach" of justice to animals and tries to convince us that we have to give all animals (sentient animals at least) the possibility to develop and live up to their capabilities and realise the respective "functionings" (i.e., the "beings" and "doings" that are the outgrowths of the capabilities).[4] There is some plausibility in this concept as well. Taken strictly it also comes to vegetarianism or even veganism. But here again the question is if we really have the moral obligation to give all animals whose life we can influence the possibility to realise all their possible capabilities as far as possible. It seems morally wrong if animals cannot unfold any of the typical behaviour of their species and lead no worthwhile life at all, as, for example, in the case of chickens in small or crowded battery cages where they cannot express even a minimal amount of normal behaviour. But is it unacceptable to limit the unfolding of animal capabilities and functionings to a certain degree by the way we keep them or by causing their premature death? Is it morally unacceptable, for example, to breed and kill calves (which are an unavoidable by-product of dairy production) if they are kept in conditions which allow socialising and the expression of other behaviours typical for the species (though during a relatively short life)? Or is it necessarily wrong to keep animals in zoos if we manage to provide surroundings emulating natural habitats and undertake efforts to relieve boredom in species with more complex cognitive capabilities?

Even if you believe, as I do, that there is no "objective" morality, but that morality is a cultural achievement based on individual decisions and social conventions, all the philosophical proposals mentioned above have a considerable heuristic value to find an acceptable and adequate moral attitude towards animals. How could it look like if we do not want to adopt vegetarianism or veganism?

First of all, we have to get clear about our situation. Our status as omnivores and our ability to use animals in other ways (for example as a means for transportation) has undoubtedly been an evolutionary advantage and may still be a question of survival in precarious nutritional and economical situations in poorer countries. But in modern affluent societies the use of animals mostly just serves our pleasure (with some exceptions, as in well justified and irreplaceable animal experiments or testing). The fact that eating and being eaten occurs frequently in nature cannot (any longer) be used to justify human behaviour. Humans can, and in this respect they are indeed different from all animals, make decisions about their diet based on moral considerations. From a medical point of view too, there is no longer any doubt that a varied vegetarian diet and also a vegan diet can generally be a fully adequate form of nutrition even if it needs some more planning than the ordinary mixed nutrition. Apart from special life situations like infancy, childhood, adolescence and pregnancy, about which there is some controversy, only vitamin B_{12} is required as a regular dietary supplement. These special situations may require medical or dietetic supervision but additional supplements that may be necessary like vitamin D or trace elements can be provided without having to resort to products from dead animals. However, some people feel fitter and stronger when adding dairy products and fish to their diet (as even Martha Nussbaum describes for herself[5]).

Furthermore, the breeding of animals and the exploitation of natural animal populations for human consumption produces increasing environmental problems in a world of between 8 and 10 billion people that will be the reality we have to face at least for the next decades to come.

This situation puts vegetarians and vegans in a relatively comfortable moral position. They can salve their conscience by justly claiming that they are not personally responsible for the environmental problems and the suffering and the cruelties imposed on animals through eating meat and other uses for human ends. If vegetarians and vegans make additional efforts to protect animals their moral balance becomes even better.

For the rest of us who stick to eating meat and eggs, drinking milk, using leather etc. things are much more difficult. Our pleasure must always appear as a relatively weak justification for imposing suffering and premature death on animals even if many animals we breed would never exist if we would not want to use them for our ends. Mind that the latter aspect alone is not enough as a justification: We are not obliged to bring animals into existence but if we do so we are responsible that they have a decent life, and only then the aspect that we make their existence possible can mitigate our moral burden to a certain degree.

A moral weighing that prioritises our pleasure over the lives of animals appears more justifiable if we succeed in making the keeping and killing of animals largely free of suffering. Furthermore, such a trade-off is easier to justify if we at least refrain from the thoughtless consumption of animals. If animals have to suffer or die for fast food or cheap disposable fashion items that could just as easily be made from other raw materials, this is much less of a justifiable value judgement than if they are used to prepare a meal of culinary value or to produce a high-quality handicraft product, i.e., things that are part of a long tradition, the discontinuation of which would be a considerable loss for human culture.

If we omnivores and animal users want to make our position morally defendable to some degree we have to open our eyes and realise what really happens to animals for our consumption. Transparency is key and the first step on the way to an at least acceptable moral stance. We must know and must insist on getting the information on what happens in breeding, transport, slaughtering or hunting of the various animals we consume. The second step is to work on improving these procedures or to reject them in cases where no adequate improvement is possible.

This means to do hard, difficult and long-lasting work in detail and to reject again and again the attempts of lobbies to lull us. The difficulties are diverse. One great problem is that the animal business is international and the attitude towards animals varies substantially from country to country. Thus, we cannot just raise the standards for treating animals in one country as would be desirable without running the risk that the local farmers are going out of business or without implementing a high degree of protectionism which may impede economic exchange as a whole. Likewise, we have to keep in mind economic feasibility for farmers and should change regulations at a pace that does not overstrain their economic adaptability. But all the difficulties, of which these are just two examples, are no justification for doing nothing and leaving things unchanged.

Many improvements are possible, even if some "ideal" procedures like keeping animals free range and farm or pasture slaughtering can only be done in small numbers or with limitations. Solidly informed people tend to agree to a considerable degree on what appears acceptable in breeding, transporting, slaughtering or hunting animals.

Thus, stables were milk cows can walk around unhindered and possibly outside at least for some periods of their life or keeping chicken with sufficient space or even free range, procedures that are feasible even on a relatively large scale, appear acceptable to many consumers while small cages for chickens or fur animals leaving nearly no possibility for species specific behaviour do not.

Transport of animals appears acceptable if the transport of life animals is restricted to an unavoidable minimum in time and adequate sustenance is provided for the animals.

Slaughtering procedures appear acceptable if they minimise fear and pain and effectively provide a quick death. Slaughtering processes can be improved if we work on technically better slaughtering methods and insist on the obligation of slaughterhouses to employ well-trained staff at attractive conditions instead of contract workers with a high fluctuation doing piecework often leading them to have little commitment to minimise the suffering of animals and to produce, for example, an unnecessary high percentage of insufficient stunning.

Hunting and fishing appear acceptable if animals are killed quickly and without much suffering as a rule and not just for fun. Especially in commercial fishing there are still big problems regarding the protection of the animals as the capability of fish to suffer and to learn has been denied or underestimated for a long time. Commercial fishing has to be sustainable. The problem, often encountered in our relation to animals as well as in other context, of foregoing maximum short-term profit for an economic process that is stable in the long run or morally preferable, presents itself in an especially urgent way here. There are various approaches to make commercial fishing more animal friendly: measures to reduce bycatch, restrictions on areas and periods of fishing, measures to reduce the duration of capture and to reduce stress and injury during catching and landing, minimizing time out of water before applying considerate methods of stunning and killing. Some practices should be abandoned altogether because they expose fish to a suffering that appears unacceptable, like deep-sea fishing causing decompression with, for example, stomachs or eyes forced out of their bodies. On the whole the efforts for animal welfare in commercial fishing lag significantly behind compared to land animals.

Meaningful and really informative animal welfare labels can and must be become a rule in food retail trade in order to facilitate animal friendly buying decision for customers.

We must accept that many improvements can only be brought about if we reduce and limit our consumption of animal products and are prepared to value these products higher and pay more for them. This must not be tantamount with turning them into luxury products for the rich. But a certain degree of such a constraint in consumption is unavoidable as well for the preservation of the environment as for increased animal welfare.

Furthermore, we should abandon some practices of dealing with animals although they have a cultural or even religious tradition and a locally cherished social context: the bloody version of bullfighting in Spain, whale and dolphin hunting on the Faroe Islands, ritual slaughter in the Jewish or Muslim way, force-feeding of ducks or geese … We should not support these practices by consuming the respective products, attending the respective events or doing long-distance shipping of live animals to states insisting on ritual slaughter. But the important thing in these cases is that change is approved by a majority of the respective group of people following better information and progressing ethical discussion. Some foreign pressure, pointing out the damage to the international reputation of a region, country or religion if practices remain unchanged or even building up some kind of economic pressure, may be helpful. And it must not be accepted that progressive voices from inside those groups are neglected or silenced. But finally, change has to be accepted by a majority of the people whose tradition is at stake. Otherwise there is the risk that conservative forces abuse pressure from outside to present themselves as defenders against threats to group identity and tradition and thus obstruct desirable change.

Animal experiments have to be limited to cases where the research interest or safety considerations for humans are really is in an adequate relation to the restrictions and damage done to animals. In spite of the undeniable progress of knowledge that has been obtained by animal experiments there is also a regrettable tradition of inconsiderate and unjustifiable ruthlessness against animals in science. Having every student of medicine decapitating frogs just for demonstrating long known electrophysiological facts, a common and obligatory part of education during my time of studies, is just one example. "Mere damnable and detestable curiosity" as the only or predominant motive for animal testing was already denounced by Charles Darwin[6] and the same should be valid for a mere pleasure in experimenting, for personal ambition or striving for profit. For a collection of further monstrosities in this line see Singer's above mentioned Book, chapter 2, as well as some of his earlier publications in defense of animals. Many of these unjustifiable cruelties have been approved by publicly funded research facilities and scientists to their disgrace.

Sometimes it is said that we should not concern ourselves too much with the situation and welfare of animals as long as large parts of humanity still suffer from malnutrition and inhumane conditions. This is one of those arguments (along the lines of: no money for art, no money for luxury as long as not everyone has enough to eat) which, if followed, would make life on earth highly unpleasant; and it is also one of those arguments with which we like to shift responsibility away from ourselves. We must, of necessity, pursue a wide variety of goals at the same time and constantly weigh up what level of resources we want to invest in which goal, and for which goals we are most likely to be able to do something through our personal behaviour. Animals cannot wait until we have solved all important problems of humans, because otherwise they may have to wait forever for their interests to be morally taken into account and, to a significant extent, they will no longer exist until we deem the time has come to take care of them.

Animal protection, efforts to improve animal welfare, limiting meat consumption and vegetarianism or veganism are part of a cultural development of humankind that seeks to curb violence and extend protection against avoidable suffering.

In the future cultured meat from cells may also contribute to this development if the problems of high energy consumption and high cost can be solved and the products are tasty enough to find acceptance.

Then there is also the argument that (rightly) points out to us that the greatest danger to animals (leaving farmed animals apart) comes from the excessive proliferation and spread of the human species. This is correct and for the sake of favourable living conditions for us humans alone, we must make the most decisive efforts to limit population growth and thereby preserve the habitat of as many animal species as possible and promote their survival. But in calling for the limitation of population growth, especially in view of the fact that modern affluent societies only have a minor, if not negative, share in this, we are once again to a considerable extent moving in the dangerously thin air of general postulates, which easily remain largely inconsequential and hardly demand anything concrete from us as individuals (even if, in the case of the population problem, there is an obligation for the wealthy states as a whole to provide more resources so that conditions can be created in the poorer countries that make it possible to limit population growth).

3.7. Law

Rules for a better life

The following sections will deal with some fundamental problems of the philosophy of law: How can the moral bindingness of positive law be justified if we presuppose unwillingness to believe? When does one no longer have to obey positive law or even have a moral duty to resist? What is the relationship between the foundation of the moral bindingness of law and its political assertiveness? What is to be done when it is required to subject actions to a legal judgement which occurred while a fundamentally different legal system was or appeared to be valid law? To what extent should the demands that a majority or the dominating groups of a society make on individual morality be made into sanctionable demands on the individual citizen through legislation? What other limits of a regulation of behaviour through legislation should be observed?

The aim of law should be to establish rules for social coexistence that allow the members of a society to live in freedom and security in humane conditions and to resolve conflicts in a rule-based and relatively non-violent manner. However, we should be aware of the fact that this idea of law as "rules for a better life" is an ideal. Law is also an instrument for exercising power, which can unfortunately be used or misused to stabilise any kind of rule and thus also totalitarian systems of any kind, be they religious, secular ideological or kleptocratic-oligarchic.

3.7.1. The Basis of Law: from Existence to Moral Bindingness

Laying the foundations

"Though presenting themselves as irreconcilable enemies absolutist positions of natural law and of positive law come close to each other in a decisive point: both base law on an authoritarian foundation."[1]
"After all that has happened in modern dictatorships, the proposition that law and morality have nothing to do with each other can hardly be

maintained anymore."[2]

"If we think the majority decision wrong, we must make up our minds about how gravely it is wrong."[3]

Peter Singer

In order to gain clarity about the foundations of law, I propose to distinguish between mere existence, acceptance, validity and moral bindingness of law. These distinction do better justice to this difficult problem than just the terms legality and legitimacy.

Legal provisions exist, are positive law, if they are formulated with a minimum claim to generality (as opposed to the mere arbitrary decision of a potentate in an individual case) and if a power stands behind them that can ensure their enforcement - even if only for a short period of time. (1)

Legal provisions become accepted law if the way of legislation and, at any rate, a substantial part of the legal norms are largely recognised by the respective society or at least by the holders of state power.

Existing and accepted law can still be statutory injustice.

Legal norms become valid law if, in addition, a minimum of formalisation and deliberative reference to pre-existing legal traditions is observed in its creation and if basic demands of individual and social morality are respected.

So we should not even grant validity to a law that disregards minimal moral claims - it never has more than force and power on its side, it can exist and be accepted and thus be enforceable, but never valid. By its very existence it can still offer an advantage of legal certainty over sheer arbitrariness, and by its acceptance it can prevent complete anarchy, but that is where its justification ends. These distinctions will be clarified later by concrete examples (as in section 3.7.2.).

But what about the normative justification of law, which already underlies its validity and then also its more far-reaching moral bindingness? The question of the justification of the moral bindingness of law, whether it concerns human and civil rights, criminal law, civil law or other areas of law, is linked to the question of the justification of morality. The difference lies in the fact that law is not an individual morality, but a social morality of the kind that violations of it can result in more than just disapproval and possible social disadvantages, namely by leading to certain sanctions of the community in the form of punishment or other coercive measures.

Through the fundamental choice of unwillingness to believe a religious justification of law becomes impossible, and recourse to a natural law is also out of question. It has already been stated in the discussion of ethics and morals (3.3.) that morality cannot be derived from nature. Neither can a natural law be derived from it. This is illustrated here in more detail with a quotation from Zippelius:

"In our world there is, for example, polygamy and monogamy. From mere existence, either one can be justified as much, i.e. as little, as the other. Precisely because there are factual alternatives, the problem of making the right choice between them, the problem of justice, arises. The criterion for the rightness of this choice, however, cannot lie in the facts as such.

This is why theories of natural law tend to single out certain facts from the abundance of what exists in which 'true nature' is supposed to present itself. In this way, however, a judgemental selection has already been made, i.e., certain ethical standards have been placed in the natural order to then read them out as the 'true nature' of the human being, the institution or the matter. This procedure is nothing else than circular reasoning.

Therefore, one can 'derive' very different, even contradictory principles of justice as natural law, depending on the presupposed ethos and the image of 'true nature' determined by it. Thus we have found that there are - depending on the facts which are emphasised - justifications for equal rights and for the right of the stronger based on natural law. Private property as well as communism of goods, monarchy as well democracy have been justified by natural law.

Behind what are considered compelling conclusions drawn from human nature, there are often the author's traditional ideas of justice or simply his own sense of justice."[4] (2)(3)

As a consequence of the failure of natural law thinking, legal positivism emerged. Its core principles are: The concept of law is to be formally defined, law can in principle be given any humanly possible regulatory content. There are no recognisable absolute norms as standards of the right law.

These statements are first of all a plausible description of reality. In contrast, the view that valid and even binding law is everything that is set as law by a law-making authority which also has the power to enforce the norms it sets, if only certain minimal formal requirements are observed, is only the opinion of a part of the "legal positivists", who should better be called "legal totalitarians". This view completely undermines the basis for moral objections to law. The inadequacy of such a legal philosophical position has been made especially clear to us Germans, because it was used to justify or excuse the participation of many representatives of the German judiciary in the crimes of National Socialism (and their insufficient prosecution and continued service in the judiciary after the war) and to omit or delay the legal rehabilitation of their victims.

Whenever legal positivism believes that it has already settled the problem of the justification of law with a mere description of reality, it in fact opens the floodgates for a determination of law by any inhumane ideology.

The "totalitarian" positivist conception of law was then equated with legal positivism in general by the post-war restoration of West Germany (4) and thus used to build up a one-sided propagandistic bogeyman that served to discredit all critical approaches to the justification of law that tried to avoid dubious metaphysical and philosophical assumptions as far as possible. At the same time, paradoxically, members of the judiciary in a misunderstood collegiality often continued to cling to a legal-totalitarian variety of legal positivism when the legal investigation of judicial crimes would have been due.

There is no doubt that a "totalitarian" positivist conception of law played its part in the unjust legal system of the Third Reich. However, there is also another tradition of legal positivism which recognises that law gains its validity and binding force through reference to moral principles though without knowing yet how to deal with this insight. Kelsen even thinks (wrongly) that a moral principle, namely that of tolerance, can be derived from a relativistic philosophy of law.[5] But why should one not want to enforce a point of view that is recognised as subjective or historically conditioned in an intolerant, totalitarian manner too? The fact that ethical relativism and tolerance often go hand in hand is a psychological and intellectual phenomenon, a fact of experience. This does not mean, however, that this must always be the case or that the moral position of tolerance can be inferred from a relativistic ethical position in the sense of a normative justification.

Moreover, tolerance alone is not sufficient to judge the moral bindingness of law. Actually, the legal positivists leave a vacuum after successfully excoriating the idea of natural law. In this situation, an idea for the normative justification of law is to look for legal rules that are constant in the overwhelming number of all legal systems and to declare them to be the core of law that is valid and binding in any case. At first glance, this would almost reintroduce a kind of natural law, since one would have to assume that legal norms that occur in all, at least all long-term stable, human legal systems, arise from human nature (however, the inclinations that make these legal provisions necessary in the first place obviously do so as well). Such a doctrine could also be called positivism, since it wants to base the bindingness of law on empirical conditions, if not necessarily on the legislation of a concrete legislator, then at least on longer-term phenomena of human legal reality.

The problems of such an approach to the normative justification of law will be discussed below using the example of the doctrine of interests as impressively advocated by Hoerster (who by the way also attempts to justify morality in this way).[6] Legal provisions are to be justified intersubjectively by proving the indisputable interest of an overwhelming majority of the members of a society in a certain norm, for example – and above all - the prohibition of killing. With a few extreme exceptions, everyone has a greater interest in their own survival than in (occasional) killing and can realise their survival interest in society as permanently and safely as possible only by renouncing their (comparatively inferior) interest in killing. Such a norm thus becomes a prerequisite for a long-term stable society and can thus be justified intersubjectively.

Several serious objections can be raised against this conception, even and especially if one has recognised the inadequacy of objectivist theories of morality and law and shares the effort to overcome them. Firstly, it must be justified that an interest in survival is not only to be observed in the majority of people but that this interest in survival is also valuable and deserves to be respected and that its protection should then also belong to the essential goals of a legal order. This alone requires a moral decision that cannot be rationally justified. It is quite possible without contradiction to reject life, to consider it of little value or worthless, to sacrifice it or put it at risk for the sake of some experience or goal, or to assume that an interest in survival is justified only for selected individuals. Thus, someone can also claim unlimited special rights for himself and prefer to be a tyrant rather than a citizen of a reasonable society based on equality (and consciously accept the possibly higher personal risk, including a possibly shorter life). The fact that tyrannies are transitory does not imply a moral evaluation. That the Hitlers, Stalins and Putins of this world act reprehensibly cannot be justified rationally alone (because rational argumentation always presupposes a certain morality) but only through moral decisions. Wanting to live is not a matter of course (see 1.3.) and wanting to let live is either.

Another problem is that even elementary legal norms, such as the prohibition of killing other people or of stealing, which are most likely to be found in some form in every human legal system and seem most likely to be justifiable by a doctrine of interests, are undermined by the admission of different, quite essential exceptions and to the extent that they may be hardly comparable anymore: Here the killing of female newborns is not punishable, there the killing of disabled people or people of a different ethnic or religious affiliation, in the third legal system at least the killing of the enemy in war remains unpunished.

Even the prohibition of killing can be broken on a fairly large scale without a society necessarily becoming unstable. Homicides that occur in accordance with social conventions and are directed, for example, against outsiders about whose inferiority, undesirability or dangerousness there is widespread agreement in the respective society, can be exempted from external and - depending on the homogeneity and stability of the society - also from internal (conscience-related) negative sanctions. This can lead to a restriction of the prohibition of killing which changes this norm to such an extent that it hardly deserves the designation "general prohibition of killing".

Stalin's and Mao Zedong's regimes of terror were, after all, so stable that they themselves died in bed and their successors were able to avoid a revolutionary overthrow for decades with only minor reforms. The same would have been true with some probability of National Socialism if it had confined itself to terror against the Jews and had not at the same time taken on the whole world in boundless expansiveness. Terror regimes, anarchies, systems of domination and oppression can obviously remain stable in the long term even when implementing a rather far-reaching abrogation of the prohibition of killing, provided that this only affects minorities or relatively powerless groups, be they definable sociologically (e.g. Jews, opponents of the regime) or geographically (e.g. inhabitants of a civil war country, inhabitants of developing countries). Even before the great mass exterminations of the 20th century (Mao is probably responsible for the deaths of up to eighty million people), events such as the pogroms against the Jews in the Middle Ages, the extensive extermination of the North American Indians in the 19th century, or the Turkish genocide of Armenians (just to mention a few more relevant atrocities from human history) show us that under certain circumstances an abrogation of the prohibition of killing can affect millions of people without necessarily having a destabilising effect on the society concerned.

In a society that does not protect minorities there is a certain risk for everyone to become (be defined) unexpectedly a member of such an unprotected minority. This risk will, nevertheless, (realistically) seem very small to the members of the majority as a rule. Or to ask more generally: Why should we take into account the interests of those who can very likely at most impair our own interests but hardly promote them according to a doctrine just relying on mere interests?

How should one convincingly argue against the death penalty, for example, if law is merely justified in terms of interests? On the contrary, one could very well - completely rationally - put forward the following considerations: The death penalty admittedly entails the disadvantage of no longer correctable miscarriages of justice. But the relatively low risk of the citizen who behaves according to the legal norms to fall victim to such an error in a state under the rule of law is far outweighed by the advantage of reliable, definitive and inexpensive protection against serious criminals (whereby the cost saving may only be ostensible, depending on the "long-windedness" of the respective criminal justice system, and even considerable extra costs may be generated, as in the US). (5) And what should count more: the greatest possible protection of the integrity and survival interests of peaceful citizens - for example, by eliminating murderers through execution and thus preventing further threats to life by the same perpetrator - or the survival interests of the perpetrators? If one wants to counter this argumentation of a "devil's advocate", one needs a minimum of value ethics, one needs a moral decision for the high rank of individual human life, which admits to legally kill human persons only in self-defence and emergency situations.

The analysis of interests does not suffice to provide a guideline for our actions. To give another example: In certain cases of advanced, hopeless diseases it will be possible to reach a general agreement that the person concerned no longer has any interest in survival. However, this still allows for a wide variety of views on what is appropriate and morally right behaviour in such a situation.

A theory of interests suggests that one makes it dependent on the concrete social and historical situation what degree of respect should be accorded to the (survival) interest of the individual (an observation that is not to be misunderstood as a mere reproach). People have to decide which value they attach to which interests, and these decisions are always made differently at different times. A theory of interests is therefore realistic. A normative content, however, does not result solely from interests that can be stated, but from the weighing of values between the respective interests and the moral decisions required thereby.

If we want to use constants of factual norms or even certain constants in people's interests to suggest the validity and bindingness of certain legal norms, then this procedure is only somewhat convincing for those partial contents of some important legal norms without which the coexistence of a larger number of people over a longer period of time hardly seems conceivable. But what is the use of a legal-philosophical concept that can only help in the intersubjective justification of norms to the extent that it sets broad limits, for example, for the excessiveness of terror regimes, the extent and permanence of anarchies or the extent of our overexploitation of the environment? Such limits are more or less quickly demonstrated to us by reality, even without such philosophical efforts.

A doctrine of interests differs from legal positivism in a legal-totalitarian sense in that it is less short-sighted and time-bound, because it is not, or at least not only, oriented towards the concrete legislation of the respective legislator but towards realities that crystallise in a longer-term consideration of human history. The analysis of interests can give us some indications of the status quo of human coexistence to be expected in the longer term. But: Why should we elevate the resulting meagre constants of the factual to the normative that is binding for us? What speaks in favour of making the moral decision necessary for this (without which we would only be advocating a form of positivism, would only be committing the is-ought fallacy once again)? The constants of factual norms would have to be clearer, more detailed and morally more convincing in order to suggest to us the decision to use them as a normative foundation of law.

A theory of interests can contribute to the clarification of the respective problem by guiding us to look as completely as possible at the interests that are present and affected, are being pursued and could be pursued in a given situation. We can thus gain a more solid basis for decision-making. A theory of interests may even tell us something about how certain interests can be enforced most effectively or how their consideration can best be ensured. However, a theory of interests does not tell us what rank we should assign to specific interests, how we should value them and weigh them up against each other.

Another possibility is to make the validity and bindingness of positive law dependent on the conformity with the sense of justice of a majority or a significant part of those affected by the law. "Because one often does not arrive at a conclusion, especially in practically important value decisions, that can be comprehended by all people and times one must of necessity be content with basing value decisions that are important for the legal community on at least a qualified partial consensus: for example, on the sense of justice of the majority or on that of a leading group that does not necessarily have to coincide with the majority." (Zippelius[7]) Unfortunately, however, it does not solve our problem once and for all if one decides to refer to a general or authoritative sense of justice in cases of doubt in judicial decisions or even to regard the decisions of the law-making institutions as valid law only on the condition that they agree with such a sense of justice.

Firstly, it will not always be possible to clearly establish conformity with a general sense of justice. More important is, however, that even law which agrees with a general sense of justice can contradict the morals of the individual and that such law can also be morally wrong. A majority can take a path which the individual cannot reconcile with his or her conscience and which may later also be regarded by a majority as an erroneous path. "Cruelties are practised in accordance with acts of senate and popular assembly", says Seneca.[8] And Bertrand Russell shows us the problem of majority decision-making in a more general form, whether it is a question of the justification of law or epistemological questions: "Even if all are of one opinion, all can be wrong."[9]

Thus, not only a normative foundation of law by a "general sense of justice" proves to be insufficient but also the attempt to derive the validity and bindingness of law solely from the way it was created, for example by declaring only democratically created law to be valid and morally binding. However, it is less probable - at least in a society that allows for open discussion - that many people together will be seriously mistaken in the long term than that this will happen to individuals.

For reasons of expediency, for the assertiveness and enforceability of law, it is undoubtedly desirable that jurisdiction does not stray too far from a general sense of justice, but on the other hand, proximity to such a sense of justice does not yet establish the validity and bindingness of law. And if one considers it desirable that law comes into being democratically (see 3.8.1.), and if one generally wants to recognise law that has come into being in this way as valid and binding, this does not mean that law that has come into being in another way could not be just as valid and even binding and neither that law that has come into being democratically could not also lack bindingness and even validity.

Conventions supported by an authority as convincing as possible, such as the Universal Declaration of Human Rights by the United Nations, are important because they establish standards that can be invoked by individuals and supranational jurisdictions, also against local law (and especially against dictatorial bending of law). Such conventions are a convincing and honest way of constituting human rights as an internationally valid legal norm and giving them a legal reality that can be based on more than the moral conviction of individuals. (6) Because of the insurmountable fundamental dubiousness of majority decision-making, however, even a convention that has come into being in an undeniably democratic way, no matter how convincing it may be, can only suggest the validity and, above all, the moral bindingness of law which is ultimately based on the moral convictions and decisions of the individuals (i.e., also of those who have participated in bringing about the convention or who endorse its contents for good reasons).

"Where even the prevailing ethos fails as a basis for decision-making, the search for the just decision is left only with recourse to the personal sense of justice in all its relativity. And beyond that, decisions are also conceivable that do not even find support in an unambiguous subjective holding-to-be-true, cases in which the decision about justice cannot even be won out of supposed insight, but only in a legal-ethical venture." - "The search for the just decision can also lead to the situation that existential philosophy places at the centre of its consideration: the plight of highly personal decision-making, in which the problems can only be solved in radical subjectivity, out of which no effort at knowledge directed towards objective truth can help." (Zippelius[10]) What applies to the judge in his search for a just decision applies to the citizen in general when he first questions law for its validity and then its bindingness. From its validity follows a considerable and from its bindingness the strongest possible moral bindingness of law. Validity justifies obedience to the law, bindingness demands obedience to the law. And not only does morality influence the law, the law also influences morality.

The deliberations in the following sections will show that we do not have to get into a subjectivist chaos with such a concept. Nor is it the intention here to advocate a decisionism which, in the style of some existential philosophers, believes that the compulsion to make a decision, which we are ultimately confronted with, relieves us of the obligation to explore the pros and cons of the various alternatives and to weigh them up against each other in a rational manner as carefully as the respective situation allows before we face up to the decision.

Ultimately, the bindingness of law can and must be measured against the standard of the individual's morality. Law is binding when it is compatible with one's own morality, the morality of the individual, or is even demanded by it, but at least does not seriously contradict it. I do not see any alternative to this standpoint for those who are unwilling to believe, and I cannot see any other way in which a philosophy of unwillingness to believe could overcome legal positivism as far as personal philosophy of life and morality are concerned.

In the search for the right morality and the right moral decisions the heuristic and argumentative achievements of the philosophical tradition can help us. In the search for the right law, we draw on the history of morality and law and especially the essential codifications that document and record the progress of law achieved in human history - from the Bill of Rights to the Constitution of the United States and the Universal Declaration of Human Rights of the United Nations to the many constitutions of modern democracies that guarantee human and civil rights. Anyone who wants to fall short of this loses any right to decide on law. In order to make this clear and to fight for this again and again, moral and political decisions are needed, but not a seemingly absolute, objectivist basis of law. The morality of the individual is not found in a detached space of arbitrariness. This is all the more true for the social conventions of law and morality, which - apart from local relapses into pre-modern times, phases of general blindness and temporary setbacks - offer the prospect of absorbing and implementing the moral and legal achievements of humanity, at least in the long term. Traditional legal principles and the jurisdiction developed by precedents are an important part of these conventions.

If people, according to their different philosophies of life, disagree on the justification of the basic requirements of social morality, which they have nevertheless agreed on as constitutional content, then this should be a reason to formulate such basic requirements in law only substantially, but not to justify them with a particular philosophical or theological doctrine - or even a general reference to God. In particular the constitution of a state, but also other subordinate legal norms, should be acceptable for as many citizens of different philosophies of life as possible, as to their justification as well. Such a justification should refer to the history of philosophy and law, but should not disguise its ultimately conventional character with illusory claims. The legal culture that has emerged and been consolidated in the development of liberal democratic states is anything but arbitrary and represents a (and at the same time the only) good and sufficient basis for fundamental conventional legal formulations. There is subjectivity in the recognition of this legal culture as well. However, this can be described with good reason as subjectivity objectified by cultural history. Human and civil rights can also be regarded and declared as irrevocable if one recognises that they have a subjective moral and a conventional social basis.

What has been said in this section about the validity and especially about the moral bindingness of law will not satisfy many who, as in the case of morality, demand an "objective" justification. However, all the seemingly objective justifications of the validity and bindingness of law can be traced back to subjective moral decisions in the end. Subjectivity does not become greater by openly admitting it. And this is, in any case, much more honest or testifies to a higher level of reflection. (7) (8)

3.7.2. Right and Duty to Resist

How far and no further?

What should happen when law and morality are in contradiction? The answer will have to differ depending on the basis and source of the respective law and on how significant the contradiction is.

In the case of a relatively minor contradiction, obedience to the law is to be considered, not only because of the threat of coercive measures, but also from the point of view of legal certainty, even if this, at least in its effects in the concrete case, contradicts one's own moral conviction, one's own sense of justice. Here - but also in the case of more serious contradictions between the law and one's own morals - one can come to the conclusion that disobedience to the law would entail a more significant violation of one's own morals in its consequences than the fulfilment of what is legally required. (1) Legal certainty will play an important role particularly if one knows that the general sense of justice is against one, if one is dealing with not only existing and accepted but also valid law, and if one fundamentally agrees with the given

310

legal and state system - apart from the concrete conflict at hand - and does not strive for, expect or hope for an overthrow that would fundamentally change law and state. Thus, out of respect for the democratic decision-making structures which have produced a certain law, one will time and again have to recognise legal provisions as binding which do not agree in detail with intersubjectively justifiable moral concepts or one's own morals. The importance of legal certainty is also shown by the fact that totalitarian states often have to break through their own legal systems in order to be able to proceed against their opponents in the desired manner. Even in an undemocratic state, it is more difficult to institutionalise moral injustice in legal form than to exercise it through arbitrary acts. The insistence on legal certainty obviously makes even those legal systems better that contain injustice in the moral sense to a considerable extent. Considering the value of legal certainty, obedience can also be justified towards a part of the regulations of a law that merely exists and is accepted, but cannot claim any validity.

In the face of more serious contradictions of law and morality, the next possibility is to disregard certain legal provisions or to refuse to cooperate in the enforcement of a certain legal provision or decision and thus possibly sabotage its enforcement. One can also feel obliged to act in this way towards democratically legitimised law. The law set by a majority can also be in such clear contradiction to one's own morals that it no longer seems sufficient to stand up for a change of this law according to democratic rules but that one feels obliged to refuse to obey this law.

In such a situation the question arises as to whether one may and should disregard certain legal provisions secretly or at least tacitly or else demonstratively. In particular, the personal consequences to be expected but also the importance and acceptance of a certain legal provision in society play a role here. Let us take, for example, a doctor who is considering actively assisting the dying of a severely suffering incurable patient who seriously requests it. If a society is still far from allowing active euthanasia in its legal system and it would almost certainly mean the end of the doctor's professional career and possibly the destruction of his civil existence if he admitted to having performed active euthanasia, it may be morally right to do so secretly. However, if a society is already on the threshold of a corresponding reform of the legal system, demonstrative violations of the law still in force may be morally justified because they can help to accelerate the change at an acceptable personal risk.

Another possible situation: A person who in principle submits to the existing law and accepts a conviction for a criminal offence in accordance with this law may be faced with the question of whether she or he should also accept the sentence imposed. In general - that is, if there is not, according to one's own moral judgement, a blatant disproportion between culpability and sentence - one will have to acccpt a sentence for reasons of legal certainty, provided that one regards the sentence as justified at all and the legal remedies have been exhausted. Even then, however, I would see, for example, a sentence to archaic punishments - such as cutting off hands - or a sentence to death as a possible moral justification for escape and aiding escape. To grant jurisdiction even the direct decision on the physical integrity and on life and death of persons (whatever they have committed) is a concept of retribution that we have overcome through our cultural development (with the sad exception of, among others, considerable parts of the US), and it does not seem justified to me according to my moral convictions.

These examples also illustrate once again the difference between existence, acceptance, validity and moral bindingness: A law that provides for the cutting off of hands as a punishment for theft can exist and be accepted, but it can never be valid, let alone binding, since it disproportionately violates a human being's minimal claim to physical integrity. The same applies if democratically legitimised institutions (even if only by orders on the executive level) systematically allow interrogation methods of prisoners that violate human rights, as has happened, for example, by the US with the method of simulated drowning (waterboarding) which must be classified as torture. (2) A law that provides for the death penalty for murder, on the other hand, can still be valid because this punishment still occurs in the tradition of modern constitutional states and its outlawing has not yet become a generally recognised part of international human rights codifications. As soon as the death penalty is declared to be contrary to human rights in this way, the day is foreseeable when no one in the world will be able to invoke the validity of local law that continues to provide for it. For anyone who participates in its implementation, the protection against retroactive prosecution will then cease to apply. Until then, the death penalty is "only" morally wrong and a law that provides for it is not binding, since the criminal justice system is morally obliged to respect the right to life in the perpetrator as well. Thus it is morally justified to oppose the execution of the death sentence by any means that do not in turn endanger the lives of other people.

There is no doubt that even in a democratic constitutional state there can be situations of conflict between law and conscience which entitle individuals to disregard the law or to refuse to cooperate in the enforcement of certain legal provisions and legal decisions (in our German state they can partly invoke the freedom of conscience guaranteed in the Basic Law for this). A right to resist in the sense of a right to refuse is still relatively easy to accept from the point of view of legal policy, since it only allows for individual convictions of conscience but does not impose personal convictions on others.

Finally, the answer to a severe contradiction between existing, accepted or even valid law and one's own morals is open resistance in its various forms, i.e., the attempt to change the distribution of power, at first without or ultimately also with violence, in such a way that another law becomes possible. "When guaranteed law and justice come into conflict, action must be taken to bring about a change in guaranteed right. Justice requires personal commitment." "The ultima ratio to resolve the conflict between guaranteed law and extra-legal norms is revolution. The German Peasants' War, the North American War of Independence and the French Revolution were all undertaken in the name of 'natural law'. The dynamics of such a conflict of norms, the fact that it cannot be resolved by conceptual-normative means, is illustrated better than by anything else by the different outcomes of these undertakings." (Zippelius[1])

Outright resistance that goes beyond demonstrative pressure is not already justified by an individual act of injustice that takes place on the part of legislation or jurisdiction (for here the thought of legal certainty still predominates and induces obedience to the law) but only by systematic acts of injustice, by the establishment of a regime of injustice.

The fate of resistance fighters in the reality of the moment and in people's memories is, among other things, also decided by the philosophical-ideological justification of their resistance. In certain power struggles contending that the law one wants to bring about already exists as natural law can be a weapon. Its effectiveness is based on the fact that one conjures up the illusion that what one demands is actually already law. Recourse to natural law ideas only has practical value if one's own supporters and/or opponents accept this kind of philosophical justification. For those unwilling to believe, such a recourse means in any case a serious violation of the moral attitude of truthfulness. For them, therefore, if they find it necessary to stand up against the existing legal order, it is more appropriate to do so by invoking philosophical and cultural tradition as well as their own morality. If they can refer to existing heuristic principles of ethics, legal traditions or widely recognised conventions (such as the aforementioned Universal Declaration of Human Rights) to strengthen their position, all the better. If in a certain society no convincing justification for resistance can be achieved in this way, those unwilling to believe can come to the conclusion in a moral weighing that, for the sake of a better chance of success, they should refer to a justification for resistance, for example to natural law, that is more convincing for the respective society even if they do not accept it themselves. In all this, however, one must not overestimate the importance of the question of how resistance to a particular legal order is justified philosophically. This is only one of many aspects that decide a power struggle.

Regardless of their reasons for doing so, those who decide to resist an existing legal order must expect that resolute action will be taken against them on its basis as long as a power stands behind it. This cannot be otherwise. A right to resist the law cannot be anchored in the law, otherwise it gives itself up, suspends itself.

To be sure, a legal system can itself provide for mitigating regulations within the law in the event of a possible conflict between the law and demands of conscience, as is generally the case with the fundamental right to freedom of conscience in our German Basic Law and specifically, for example, with the admission of conscientious objection. However, this does not establish a right of resistance in a more comprehensive sense.

If a legal system does indeed explicitly speak of the right of resistance, this does not refer to resistance within itself but to resistance to attempts to overthrow or fundamentally change the existing legal system (see for example Article 20 (4) of the Basic Law of the Federal Republic of Germany). The revolutionary situation can only ever be envisaged in law as a situation of defending the law, otherwise it would agree to its own abolition in advance.

That the state has a monopoly on violence respectively the legitimate use of force as a rule is a great cultural advance worth preserving. It allows for the security of the individual and a lawful solution of conflicts. Just like any other legal system that wants to survive, a democratically legitimised one cannot tolerate morally justified, violent resistance. It also has the least reason to tolerate violent resistance because it offers the possibility of peaceful expression of opinion without existential risks and of peaceful political implementation of essential changes. The democratic state should therefore also act resolutely

314

against perpetrators using politically motivated violence, since their violence amounts to coercion against the state and thus against the majority of citizens, and consequently counteracts democracy (and this also applies to the sometimes so belittled "violence against property"). The democratic state has a duty to the majority of its citizens who abide by the democratic rules to ensure that decisions are taken by the democratic institutions they have commissioned or by institutionalised plebiscitary mechanisms and not by vociferous, violent minorities. If violence is justified as counter-violence against the violence threatened or used by the democratic state to protect the legal order, this usually means, at least when fully considering the consequences, that one rejects this state and either wants a fundamentally different form of state or no state at all which would ultimately lead back to the law of the strongest.

In a democratic state governed by the rule of law there is hardly any moral justification for resistance with the active use of force, with the exception of an immediate, present, unavoidable threat to one's own or another human life by majority decisions. However, it can happen that majority decisions made by democratic institutions are for other reasons so severely opposed to the morality of the individual that he or she feels obliged to use passive violence in the form of so-called passive resistance. I see a respectable moral justification for this in majority decisions, for example on questions of armament, which considerably threaten one's own life, the life of a large number of citizens of one's own country and/or other countries or even the existence of humankind, at least indirectly and in the long term. In such cases, the democratic state should live with the conflict and not try to criminalise those who engage in passive resistance with a morally respectable and comprehensible justification. In particular, actions of passive resistance that are mainly demonstrative in nature should not be treated lightly as coercion.

With regard to "nonviolent" action, however, a fundamental misunderstanding must be cleared up: the means of so-called non-violent action are not justified for their own sake but must always be justified in a moral weighing of the individual case considering the aims pursued and taking into account the situation in which they are applied. And the more these means actually amount to coercion of others the more they must be justified. If one crosses the line between political debate and protest on the one hand and outright resistance on the other hand, even with methods of "non-violent" action, then there is a danger that democracy will be undermined and that the state will become ungovernable in the struggle between conflicting group interests.

3.7.3. The Foundation of Law and its Political Assertiveness

No permanent retreat to an as if

What is the relationship between the foundation of the validity and binding-ness of law and its political assertiveness? Or more concretely: Does a law that explicitly builds on convention and whose validity and bindingness are ultimately founded on subjective moral decisions lack political assertiveness compared to legal systems that are based on other philosophical foundations? Does such law have worse prospects of becoming and remaining law?

What was said under 2.2. on the subject of choices and morality applies analogously here. For those who think they can give a better foundation for the validity and bindingness of law, for example in the form of belief in a natural law, recourse to the morality of the individual and to conventions will be unconvincing. The opposite is true for those who are unwilling to believe because their trust in a philosophical foundation of law is shaken precisely by unjustified claims to objectivity.

The consequence of these considerations for those unwilling to believe can only be that they try to spread their philosophical views and thus give them increasing political effectiveness. If this is not possible or not promising in a society, they can, as we have already seen when discussing the problem of resistance, decide with a heavy heart to subordinate truthfulness to other moral attitudes and values and, for the time being, propagate another reason (of which they are not themselves convinced) for the validity and bindingness of the law they desire.

If we imagine, for example, people who are unwilling to believe in a strictly Christian, medieval society and who would have wanted to achieve any significant changes in the existing legal order, they would certainly have been in this position. But even today, such a situation is conceivable in many societies around the world, at least in times of crisis even in Western democracies. Here, however, it should actually be sufficient to attack invalid positive law with reference to history and the traditions of philosophical ethics and secular philosophy of law, without having to resort to untenable speculative con-structs and illusory belief systems.

History will show whether a foundation of law without the illusion of ob-jectivity can assert itself or prevail in the political debate. To date, such a

316

foundation of the validity and bindingness of law has been fought for far too little.

3.7.4. Universally Valid Law and Retroactive Assessment of Law

Crossing borders

"Democracy, separation of powers, secularity of the state, tolerance, human rights and gender equality are principles that have emerged in the West over the last centuries but have universal validity."[1]

Navid Kermani

"There are all kind of laws to protect human rights everywhere. They're not very well enforced, but we have courts, including the ICC. Is it satisfactory? Of course not. Will it be satisfactory eventually? Of course it will."[2]

Benjamin Ferencz

What is to be done when actions are to be and have to be subjected to legal judgement which occurred while such a fundamentally different legal system was existing and accepted law that the now recognised elementary moral demands did not occur in it or were in any case suspended to a considerable extent (the situation of, for example, the Nuremberg Trials)?

If one rejects objectivist, i.e. in particular religious and natural law foundations of law, the constitution in force at any given time and the human and civil rights guaranteed by it or by international declarations are also based on convention. (1) By creating such a convention, an important step has been taken to gain acceptance for them, to give them validity and to suggest that they have moral bindingness.

For a retroactive annulment of the claim to validity of law, it must suffice, if need be, to refer to the philosophical, cultural, social and political state of development of the respective epoch - as well documented as possible. However, it is much easier to retroactively annul or contest the validity of law if the basic moral demands mentioned have already been laid down as legal norms in international conventions, as is the case today in particular for the universal human and civil rights.

If one wants to achieve a retroactive legal assessment of acts, taking into account at least the human and civil rights laid down in the currently valid constitution or in international declarations, then one has no choice but to declare such human and civil rights - not in letter, but in moral content - to be universally valid as to place and time and to derive from this the lack of validity of contradictory positive law, even if this fulfils or had fulfilled the criteria of force and formalisation defined as further prerequisites for the validity of law at a certain point in time. From such a declaration of general validity, the punishability of violations of human and civil rights can then be derived, even if these acts did not constitute a violation of local positive law at the place and time where they were committed or were even required by such law. Such a declaration of general validity will be all the more convincing if it can also be based on the power of an international judicial and police organisation which, at least in a part of the cases, shows itself capable of actually prosecuting and punishing the corresponding violations of law and of thus demonstrating the risk of such violations to potential perpetrators.

Apart from the situation in which two legal systems with completely different moral foundations supersede each other, the prohibition of retroactive legal provisions should be upheld for the sake of legal certainty. If only basic moral requirements are affected by a retroactive legal provision, then, at least if one remains in the same cultural sphere and does not go back further than one human age, it is usually not the case that the perpetrators did not know these basic moral requirements but merely did not accept or follow them and did not see themselves directly confronted with them as positive law. However, the fundamental moral conventions that shape a culture do not necessarily have to be positive law in order to be authoritative, also in a legally valid sense.

It is certainly more satisfactory to be able to prosecute someone according to the rules of the legal system which, at the time of their actions and, if possible, also at the place of their actions, was undoubtedly and clearly recognisable to them as the posited law. However, if legal systems with a substantially different moral basis supersede each other, it will not always be possible to completely dispense with the retroactive overruling or even enactment of legal norms, if one does not want to leave unpunished events that are now judged to be serious crimes or if one wants to be able to annul unjust convictions. In this situation, it is appropriate and sometimes unavoidable to retroactively enact a law oriented towards human rights and fundamental civil liberties and rights or to retroactively extend the scope of such fundamental legal norms or even to claim their universal validity (and thus, if necessary, to retroactively repeal contradictory positive law). If one does this, one should not rely on the outdated and untenable legal-philosophical construction of a natural law but instead openly admit that one is making moral decisions here, decisions that are not arbitrary, however, but are based on a long cultural development and a multitude of conventions that have already arisen from it.

Law is a cultural achievement of humans which they have developed, among other things, with the intention to reduce the use of violence, or at least arbitrary violence, in the regulation of cohabitation, the enforcement of certain norms of behaviour and the settlement of conflicts. There is no convincing evidence that there is a point of reference outside of human culture and morality for the foundation of law including fundamental legal norms such as human rights.

In the retrospective judgement of the behaviour shown under a morally fundamentally different legal system, some special principles should apply, which also take into account possible predicaments of the perpetrator: The individual would have been obliged to refuse to cooperate in the enforcement of a right that contradicts basic moral requirements (according to the basic requirements of the new legal system). And he or she would have been all the more obliged to do so, the less they would have had to accept personal disadvantages and dangers with this refusal and the more they exercised command over others. In this respect, their actions are judged according to the new law. However, no one is prosecuted for not actively resisting in order to remove the old legal system. What should be punished is the disregard of basic moral demands which, as fundamental legal goods, are part of the new legal system, but not the absence of heroism. Here should be applied, analogously, what is proposed below as restraint of the legislator in criminal law for certain situations within a stable legal system. Moral demands and legal obligations are not identical.

As far as the current status of human rights is concerned, they have fortunately been codified to such a sufficient extent internationally that they no longer have to be put into effect retroactively anywhere in the world. No politician and no averagely educated citizen of a modern state can claim today not to know them. The fact that they do not want to recognise them for some reason or believe that they cannot do this, does not exempt them from the risk of legitimate prosecution by national or international bodies. Thus, the reference to a postulated natural law is also superfluous if contradictory positive law has to be retroactively declared invalid. In its place, reference can be made to national legal provisions of democratic legislators concerning civil rights and to international legal provisions (se for example the case law of the Federal Court of Justice and the Federal Constitutional Court of Germany and the European Court of Human Rights on the fatal shootings at the inner-German border). (2)

Violations of human rights remain illegitimate even if the perpetrators can refer to a democratically established law. However, they can then claim mitigating circumstances to a certain extent with the argument that they could have trusted that the validity of the corresponding legislation would also endure in retrospect due to its democratic origin.

The prohibition of retroactivity in Article 103 of the German Basic Law should be explicitly limited by reference to the European Convention for the Protection of Human Rights and Fundamental Freedoms. If this had been done earlier, the judicial processing of GDR crimes would have been much easier and would not have required the creation of morally adequate case law.

There is still a long way to go before human rights can be enforced globally. An important step on this path is the establishment of a permanent human rights and criminal court in 2002, after important preparatory work had already been done by international criminal tribunals of the United Nations with limited temporal and local jurisdiction, such as for the former Yugoslavia and Rwanda. Even if the effectiveness of the executive power at the disposal of the International Criminal Court. leaves much to be desired due to its dependence on the willingness of the State Parties to co-operate, this is the first time that civilian international criminal tribunals have been established that are not tainted by the odium of victor's justice. It is to be hoped that the International Criminal Court, despite the various restrictions imposed on it, will acquire increasing prestige and competence through its work, so that the contracting states will find themselves under increasing moral pressure to act as executives to enforce its decisions and non-contracting states will find themselves under increasing pressure to join. (3) Even if the project of the International Criminal Court comes under pressure at times due to politically motivated influence and acts of sabotage by powerful and less powerful state actors, it must nevertheless be driven forward undeterred. The decisive factor here is that the great powers USA, Russia, China and India will also become State Parties at some point.

For reasons of legal clarity, the adoption of an international criminal code is also desirable in the long term, the content of which would then not only define, as is now the case with the Statute of the International Criminal Court, the offences for which such a court is competent, but would also lead to a further consolidation of internationally recognised international criminal law by defining the sentences and their appropriate range for each level of seriousness of the offences. The national adoption of international criminal codes, as was done in Germany in 2002, can only be an intermediate step in the process of progressive international codification which improves the status of human rights and advances them further and further on the path from norms refering to declarations, which are incorporated into national law and national jurisdiction only in some states, to concretely applicable international law implementing the principle nulla poena sine lege (no punishment without law) with regard to human rights violations still better than before.

Insofar as the permanent International Criminal Court is not competent for offences or is insufficiently equipped in terms of personnel and organisation or does not have a sufficiently effective executive, the prosecution of crimes relevant under international criminal law by national constitutional states, as recognised in the principle of universal jurisdiction and accordingly embodied in § 6 and 7 of the German Criminal Code, remains a sensible and necessary supplement. This expresses the unconditional insistence on the universal validity of certain rights (which are concretely enforced by the corresponding national legal norm as a substitute).

Even a permanent International Criminal Court will not be able to enforce equal global respect for human rights in the foreseeable future. Apart from the lack of a corresponding executive, the main obstacles to this are the gross economic underdevelopment but also the backwardness in cultural development of large regions of the world (I stand by the wording "backwardness in cultural development": even great cultural achievements in the history of a people are no compensation for the lack of respect for human and civil rights in the present). However, it would be much more difficult, for example, to shake hands again at the highest political level with a Chinese prime minister who is responsible for a massacre against unarmed students, or who is at least largely responsible for it, if he were convicted of this massacre by an international criminal court of the United Nations and was wanted with an international warrant of arrest. Even countries that cannot be excluded from political contacts at the highest level in the long term because of their size and economic importance would be much more likely to be forced to remove at least highly compromised politicians from leadership positions (which in itself could create a not inconsiderable additional pressure in favour of respect for human and civil rights).

The argumentation pattern popular with the rulers of those states that systematically violate the human and civil rights of their citizens, invoking the sovereignty of their own state and the principle of non-interference to reject protests from abroad against these violations, must no longer be accepted in the future. States that systematically or in a particularly blatant way disregard human and civil rights temporarily forfeit the full claim to respect for their sovereignty. (See also 3.8.3., last section)

However, we must not narrow our perspective to an International Criminal Court or Human Rights Court. A more efficient United Nations Court of International Law, which overcomes the shortcomings of the current conception of the International Court of Justice in The Hague, would also be of great importance for a better international legal order and the prevention of human rights violations on a large scale. The basis of international law and the competences and sanctioning possibilities of international jurisdiction must be expanded, even if we are only making progress on this path in laborious small steps (at least there is this small progress again and again, such as the creation of the International Tribunal for the Law of the Sea in Hamburg in 1996). In the further development of the Court of International Law, the deficiencies from which the current International Court of Justice in The Hague suffers must be eliminated. The consent of the states concerned to submit to proceedings and to recognise the judgment must no longer be required. States which are not directly affected and which see a violation of international law and a threat to peace by another state must also have the right of action. The International Court of Justice should be assigned a prosecuting authority which - according to the principle of an official offence - can bring disputes between states that have led or threaten to lead to a violent conflict before the Court on its own initiative. In the longer term, the UN or temporarily first of all a confederation of democratic states must consistently see itself as the executive branch of the International Court of Justice.

But let us return to the problem of human rights violations, and now with a dilemma that would also fit into the next section: If one thinks about the enforcement of human rights and the prosecution of crimes committed under a prior regime, one comes up against the question of whether and when such prosecution should be dispensed with for pragmatic reasons, born of

322

necessity, and preference given instead to another form of coming to terms with the past, for example through "truth commissions". Refraining from bringing all significant crimes to justice appropriately is always an affront to the victims and also contains great dangers for the moral legitimacy and the consciousness of justice and injustice of a society. Such a path may nevertheless appear advantageous or even vital for the development of a newly won democracy. This can only be decided on the basis of the circumstances of the individual case.

3.7.5. The Limits of Law

When law is not the answer

We will first deal with the question as to which extent the demands made by the majority or the dominant class of a society on individual morality and social behaviour should be imposed on the individual citizen through their formulation as legal provisions enforced by sanctions. This question must ultimately be answered separately for each individual moral demand, but the fundamental tendency results from the choice of tolerance with the content discussed in 1.4.5.. The application of tolerance to the law is expressed in the doctrine of restraint of the legislator concerning criminal law, as presented, for example, by Kaufmann: "The immoral, the sinful as such, does not affect criminal law, for the latter serves solely to protect those legal interests which are indispensable for the maintenance of the human community and which cannot be effectively protected in any other way than by criminal law."[1] (1)

What is considered indispensable for the maintenance of the human community, depends, however, as well on the morality of the individual. If one presupposes the choice of tolerance, then one will certainly reject all those legal provisions which seek to regulate the private life of the citizen down to the last detail. Examples of this are the rigid rules of conduct in strict confessional states or totalitarian secular dictatorships - or just the often seemingly convincing demands of a majority morality which, with a little distanced reflection, prove to be fundamental to society in no way.

The demand for moral restraint on the part of the legislator follows above all from the choices of the moral attitude of tolerance and the value of freedom. In terms of the legal system, it can be derived to a certain extent from the civil liberties mentioned in the catalogue of fundamental rights.

Considerations as to what limits should be set for the regulation of behaviour by legal provisions lead, however, beyond the demand for liberality and tolerance. We also come up against the question of whether one should try to determine decisions in moral borderline situations through legal standardisation, for example, the decision of a doctor who can save only one of two patients because of the limitations of means and must somehow decide, or the decision of the parents of an unborn, severely handicapped child for or against an abortion. Here we come across the concept of a "law-free area" or "restraint in law". It is based on the insight that, in view of the diversity and individuality of possible situations, an overly detailed, foresighted standardisation is, if not impossible, then at least inappropriate, and that there are moral borderline situations in which opposing decisions can be morally and socially justified (even if one assumes a broad agreement on certain basic values), which is why it would be inappropriate to oblige or even force the individual by law to make one or the other decision. I agree with Kaufmann that such a concept of a law-free space has its justification and that we should therefore advocate "that in borderline situations of the kind described, the legal order, in the absence of a rationally understandable, generally binding standard of decision, refrains from standardisation and thus leaves it to the free decision of conscience of the individual as to what is to be done here."[2] The renunciation of standardisation is not to be understood as a complete withdrawal of the legal order from a certain problem area, but only as a widening of the individual's scope for decision-making in such questions.

On the other hand, law should also find its limits where the issues at stake are simply too insignificant for the community to require legal regulation and the parties concerned can be expected to settle their disputes through discourse, or at least to reach an out-of-court settlement. The legal system should not allow itself to be harassed with every neighbourhood dispute (the courts should more often be allowed to strike down proceedings on grounds of triviality and impose financial sanctions on the initiators). The legal system should only allow itself to be obliged to intervene to bring peace in the most diverse trivial conflicts when the opposing parties violate essential legal interests by the way of their dispute. Overburdening the legal system with trivialities prevents citizens from receiving answers to essential legal questions in a timely manner.

Limits of law - this should mean a limitation of law-making in the case of moral aporias and a limitation of jurisdiction in the case of the trivial. And in the area of individual morality, it should mean a limitation of the appeal to law and the enforcement of law, as already described and proposed by Aristotle as the moral attitude of goodness, fairness or equity: The equitable man is one "who is not apt to press the letter of the law on the worse side but content to waive his strict claims though backed by the law: and this moral state is equity, being a species of Justice, not a different moral state from Justice."[3]

Equity is also one of the roots of the legal institution of mercy. Mercy is not only generosity and forgiveness on the part of the person whose right has been violated, or on the part of the state as the guardian of the law. Mercy in the legal sense takes into account the fact that even law that is just in principle can lead to injustice for various reasons: because the law cannot always do justice to the diversity of the circumstances of the case, because there are miscarriages of justice, because not everyone has the same means at their disposal to assert themselves in a legal dispute, because the exercise of discretion and the granting of exceptions that the law allows are handled quite differently, sometimes deliberately (for example by knowing the right people, pressure of public opinion or manipulation of opinion). The application of mercy can then create a certain compensation for the one against whom the law was applied with undue harshness. However, the granting of mercy itself also carries the risk of undue arbitrariness.

At the end of these remarks on the limits of law, it should be pointed out that we should not commit ourselves to the basic attitude that we have too much law in all areas. Legal norms enacted to a reasonable extent by the legislator guarantee legal clarity and equality before the law in principle better than a case law with all its imponderables, and they show the ability of the legislator to shape the law. It is true that today we tend to suffer from a regulation frenzy on the part of the legislature which in many cases also legislates where it would be dispensable. On the other hand, it is not a good tendency when the legislature shirks from or proves incapable of adopting appropriate standards on essential issues for political reasons. To give just one example: It is no credit to the German legislature that it has so far proved incapable of enacting provisions on the international role of the Bundeswehr in the Basic Law that are fit for the future and that subordinate laws or the Federal Constitutional Court have to fill this gap in a makeshift manner.

3.7.6. On the Justification of Punishment

Defending values without illusionary metaphysics

"Criminal culpability means subjective imputation of unlawful conduct. It cannot be understood as the misuse of freedom of choice in the indeterministic sense, but pragmatically, on the basis of experience, as falling short of the degree of behaviour expected of the citizen under normal conditions, as the misuse of a skill that we mutually attribute to each other for the practice of our individual and social lives. Such a concept of culpability remains below the insoluble alternative of determinism and indeterminism ... it does not presuppose freedom of will, which is in any case incapable of individual determination in criminal proceedings, but merely a normal determinability of behaviour by social norms."[1]

Hans-Ludwig Schreiber

"Why should it not be sufficient for the concept of culpability in criminal law to state that the convicted person cannot invoke one of the statutory grounds for exclusion of criminal responsibility?"[2]

Winfried Hassemer

"Otherwise than with the imputation of culpability and the imposition of appropriate punishment ... the peaceful order of a free society (free as to action!), that is a society primarily controlled by norms and not by physical power, is not conceivable."[3]

Reinhard Merkel

If one is forced to make a statement that must leave aside reservations and differentiations, then the following applies: The alternative of determinism and indeterminism has been scientifically and philosophically decided in favour of determinism, even if we understand it, as I myself also do, in a compatibilist way. However, the alternative of determinism and indeterminism will remain unsolvable for a long time to come, in so far as no social consensus can be reached. Therefore, a concept of culpability is important that is acceptable to both indeterminists and determinists. Moreover, even a society of determinists will hardly be able to do without a concept of personal responsibility and culpability for practical purposes.

The concept of culpability is not dependent on a metaphysical-idealistic concept of free will. Culpability means that moral, social, legal norms have been violated in a way for which there are no justifying reasons or excuses that an individual or the respective society can recognise and which lead to a reduction or cancellation of culpability through a weighing of goods or to diminished or cancelled criminal responsibility. The individuals who became guilty were not determined in their behaviour by social norms to a degree acceptable for the respective society, although no excusable reasons are recognisable that would comprehensibly contradict a sufficient determinability of their behaviour by social norms. This does not make any statement about the range for decision-making that was available to a certain person under the given circumstances. "Here we no longer have the claim that an agent could have acted otherwise. The claim here is only that an individual has fallen short of a standard and his behaviour is attributed to him personally because this makes sanctions effective. Attributing responsibility is a social strategy for getting people to behave according to standards." (Walter[4])

This attribution of responsibility will always be based on time-bound social norms. However, these should find their limits in universally applicable law. (See 3.7.4.)

On the basis of such a concept of guilt and culpability, which is compatible with the current state of neurobiological knowledge, it is important for the practical application of criminal law to distinguish illness in the narrower sense from illness in the broader sense, i.e. to differentiate between rather clearly definable psychiatric clinical pictures and psychosocial deviation. Such a distinction has considerable consequences for dealing with offenders in criminal proceedings and also for subsequent decisions on the suspension or continuation of punitive and therapeutic measures or on preventive detention.

For those people who need psychiatric therapy and for whom such therapy promises to be successful, it is unnecessary and inappropriate to impose a sanction that goes beyond the obligation to undergo therapy. On the other hand, those sick people who pose a considerable danger to society and who, on the basis of current knowledge, cannot be adequately treated, must be kept in lasting preventive detention for security reasons. Furthermore, there are borderline cases that, although they require psychiatric/psychological/socio-therapeutic therapy, can still be influenced by criminal sanctions.

For those people whose tendency to violate norms is caused by psychosocial deviation, attempts at therapy are also sensible and desirable. For social purposes, however, the main question to be answered is whether they can be influenced – be it by therapeutic measures or by punitive sanctions in the sense of education or "dressage" - in such a way that they can be reintegrated into society after therapy and punishment.

Since the desirable psychological therapy for all offenders (as far as they are at all willing) will realistically hardly be feasible in the foreseeable future, we must try to concentrate the use of available capacities and resources on those people for whom success in the sense of a possible reintegration into society can most likely be expected.

Reasonable jurists are already trying to realise the described assignment and the necessary consequences of it as well as possible with the instruments and procedures of today's criminal law and penal system. Unfortunately, one often has the impression that this still fails to succeed adequately. There are still too many morally charged attributions of guilt in sentencing and the formulation of verdicts. It is noticeable that the training of the jurists with regard to a neurobiologically based conception of humans and their awareness of the state of the discussion on freedom of will are still insufficient in many cases. Far too many metaphysically detached concepts and ideas remain present in the minds and in the discussion, and a consistent naturalistic approach to explanation and understanding is still too little widespread and accepted. Even more than in Europe this is true for the US legal system which is still overly shaped by the concept of retribution.

On the other hand, some modern criminal law theorists, who have abandoned the concept of a metaphysical-idealistic free will, have therewith completely or largely abandoned not only revenge and atonement, but also retribution as the purpose of punishment; some even fundamentally doubt the justification of punishment. (1) Let us clarify the central argument in this regard, which is derived from determinism. It reads as follows: Harm to the victim (even irreparable harm) does not justify that we now also inflict harm on the offender who basically has become blamelessly (in the sense of inevitably) guilty. Inflicting harm on the offender who is also only a victim of unfortunate circumstances should not be done unless for the sake of a better future for victim, offender or society as a whole.

As we have already seen, a metaphysical-idealistic conception of free will, which can no longer be maintained today, is by no means necessary for the justification of criminal law. Criminal law can be justified to a large extent by its protective function for society (in the form of deterrence and security

328

through imprisonment or, if inevitable, permanent or long-lasting preventive detention of offenders) and by its educational or treatment function for offenders independently of the discussion about their free will. The threat of punishment and the punishment imposed are influencing factors that can and do change people's decisions and actions. If one renounces the belief in free will, this does not have the consequence that criminal justice would only have to serve the detention of people who have necessarily committed a crime and threaten to commit it again.

A completely different question is whether the current form of criminal law, the current level of custodial sentences and the current design of the penal system are appropriate and efficient. There is still a lot to be done here, be it in the therapy and re-socialisation of offenders, be it in the application of victim-offender mediation and compensation for damages suffered between victim and offender, be it in the appropriate structuring of the threat of punishment and the sentencing for offences with financial damages on the one hand and offences against the person on the other.

Moreover, even in liberal societies governed by the rule of law, the discussion about which types of behaviour should be punishable cannot be considered closed. Admittedly, these societies have got rid of many criminal offences in the last hundred years which we now look back on with more or less awe, such as adultery or homosexual relations. But there are still some highly questionable relics, some of them largely insignificant in practice in modern societies, for example blasphemy paragraphs, others of great social and economic significance, such as the currently prevailing form of criminalisation of drug use and distribution, which fosters and maintains inhumane criminal structures and economic and moral corruption on a huge scale worldwide. (2) In the course of historical development, not only the socially prevailing views on the reprehensibility and punishability of behaviour and facts change. The appropriateness of criminal law norms and their enforcement must also be reevaluated in part with regard to their social consequences depending on the situation.

Even if social conditions are much better than they are today in the prosperous countries of the world, and even if criminal law and therapy for offenders are optimised, there will still be people (and by no means only those with clearly definable mental illnesses (3)) who have to be securely detained for many years and in some cases for life in order to protect society (the considerable problems associated with this will be discussed in detail later). Those who claim the opposite reveal an unrealistic image of humans, which in particular fails to recognise that humans were not created according to an ideal model and blueprint (in the traditional words of the Bible: "made in the image of God"), which are only spoiled by adverse circumstances, but, like other biological species, "only" represent beings that have been sufficiently successful for survival up to the present day, with a wide range of variation of more or less socially constructive or destructive individuals even within the normal distribution of those who are sensibly described as healthy (whereby the boundaries for "healthy" and "sick" are also again fluid). (4)

Those who work in the therapy of offenders and in resocialisation more often have a certain tendency, for psychologically understandable reasons, to see criminal justice and the penal system more from the perspective of helping the offenders, since they are their patients and clients. They see the deplorable personal fates these people also have in many cases, while they usually have no personal relationship with the victims. They therefore tend to overestimate the interests of the offenders and to neglect the interests of the victims.

On the one hand, it is sensible to use mechanisms of victim-offender mediation and compensation more than hitherto. But it must be noted that this has its limits if the victim has suffered permanent damage or has been killed so that the damage cannot be made good or cannot be made good adequately, or if the offender is unwilling or unable to provide compensation.

Particularly in the case of offences against life and limb, a disproportionately and unjustly low sentencing can be observed in our jurisprudence due to the overvaluing of the offenders' interests (disproportionate in comparison to offences with pecuniary damage and unjust with regard to the severity of the impairment of the victims' interests).

There are crimes (even if they are fortunately relatively rare) that can only be answered morally and socially appropriately with the demand for retribution, since only in this way can norms central to the maintenance of social order be protected and their validity re-emphasised. To ensure this, the respective sanctions must be proportionate to the importance of the respective norm and the severity of its violation.

If someone, acting as a concentration camp warden, sadistically tortures and murders a multitude of people, if someone, out of ideological-religious fanaticism, blows up an aeroplane with hundreds of people on board, if someone stabs a walker he does not know out of a general hatred for people, or kills a random motorist by throwing a stone from a motorway bridge, to name just a

330

few examples, it would be completely inappropriate to release such perpetrators from prison after a few years, even if they had credibly distanced themselves from their moral blindness during this time, shown remorse and tried to dissuade others from committing similar acts. It would be inappropriate, even if one takes into account that in the case of excessive offenders, fanatics and other severe psychological aberrations, a deterrent effect of the sentence on others can hardly be expected (so that in the examples given, all the other purposes of punishment mentioned above, namely deterrence, security, education/treatment for the offender could cease to apply or, in the favourable case, would have resolved themselves after a few years).

Whatever social and personal circumstances may have caused a person to commit such a serious crime: anyone who (without lacking criminal responsibility due to a generally comprehensible, serious disturbance of consciousness or mental illness or being able to claim a reduction of guilt due to exceptional circumstances) has killed other people under the elements of the crime of murder and thus deprived them of all possibilities should have to put up with serious restrictions on their own possibilities of self-unfolding for many years (and in this way also be given the opportunity to reflect on their crimes for a long time). Even without a metaphysical-religious concept of freedom of will, this is a demand of justice, justice understood here not as a presumptuous ideal of the judging but as an indispensable basis of a satisfactorily ordered society and a free constitutional state. Justice is a moral concept that is characteristically unloved by the above-mentioned school of modern criminal law theorists and is usually regarded as a relic of unenlightened times - although they have their own version of it: they believe that offenders should not be subjected to any compensatory harm, no retribution, but should be treated exclusively from the point of view of their reintegration into society and the future protection of society.

Just imagine that someone close to you, a loved one, had died as a result of such an act. Would you find it appropriate to meet the perpetrator on the street again after only a few years even if it seemed credible that he or she had matured and been rehabilitated? Serious crimes against life and limb with irreversible consequences for the victims must not be allowed to become a short biographical episode for the perpetrator, one that can be overlooked and then, under certain circumstances, also calculated. We will hardly ever see a cured fanatic with the same eyes as a treated psychotic, because we judge the thinking of the latter as confused and that of the former as morally wrong, even if the fanatic also could not get out of his skin in his respective concrete circumstances and incidents. Merkel quite rightly states that one of the conditions of a credible normative protection for all law-abiding citizens "is the 'obligation to pay', which gives the non-insane perpetrator a burdensome sanction also for the past deed and not only for a law-abiding future." "If sentences that would have to forego a culpability-based punishment for mentally healthy criminals because of the impossibility of acting otherwise could guarantee the protection of society from future crimes of these offenders with preventive measures, no matter how secure and humane, there would always remain an unfinished business: the past deed." "... without the offender having to 'pay' somehow for the violation of the norm, a credible restitution of the validity of the norm is not possible."[5]

Even if criminals could not have acted otherwise due to personal disposition and social circumstances, it is inappropriate in the interest of the protection of norms, at least in the case of serious crimes and especially those against life and limb, to keep their burden as low as deemed necessary with regard to the protection of society and their own re-education, and not to put it in relation to the severity of the norm violation and the resulting harm suffered by the victims.

That is why I also consider the efforts to abolish life imprisonment to be misguided. After all, the victims of a murder have lost the whole life they would have had before them, while the perpetrators in prison at least retain their lives with a certain, albeit severely limited, range of self-unfolding. A prison sentence with no upper time limit, which can be suspended after 15 years at the earliest on parole, depending on the biographical and social history, the motives and circumstances of the offence and the remorse and further development of the offender, is entirely appropriate to the seriousness of such a crime. However, life imprisonment should no longer be the mandatory sentence for murder without any possibility of considering mitigating circumstances. On the other hand, the differences that occur in conceding parole (as inevitably in the application of any law, beginning with the classification of the offence) must be endured by the offender in view of the seriousness of the norm violation for which such a sentence is possible. It is, however, appropriate to limit them in the case of life imprisonment by the fact that the convicted person is entitled to a judicial decision on the suspension of the remaining sentence after serving at least 15 years (as has been stipulated in the German Penal Code since 1981). However, if some mass murderers or particularly

332

cruel murderers who show no remorse are indeed imprisoned for life, this is not revenge, but a reasonable and appropriate reaction of society in the interest of maintaining a desirable system of norms (see also below: "positive general prevention").

In modern criminal law doctrine, the view is sometimes held that the sentence must always be finally determined in the court proceedings, taking into account the seriousness of the offence or of the guilt, and that these may not be reassessed in the later decision on parole. The decision on parole should also - apart from the necessary prognosis assessments - not be made dependent on the subsequent behaviour of offenders during the serving of their sentence (i.e. on remorse and distancing from the offence).[6] This point of view arises from an overvaluation of the striving for legal certainty and equal treatment under the law which neglects both the protective interests of society and the aforementioned justice criterion. This disregards the fact that repentant offenders through their repentance (apart from the fact that the social prognosis can be hoped to be more favourable as a result) introduce a moral element that speaks for a stronger consideration of their interests (even if hypocrisy may sometimes be rewarded in the process). We must not forget, moreover, that a legal system can only preserve the state's monopoly on the use of force and punishment, avoid self-administered justice, private vendettas and never-ending spirals of violence to a large extent, and that it can only channel people's need for retributive justice in an orderly and moderate manner, if it meets it to a sufficient degree - however much this need is modified by the respective level of knowledge and state of culture of a society and the degree of enlightenment that goes along with it, and however far it can fortunately move away from a blind need for revenge (to which the adoption of an illusory concept of free will undoubtedly makes an essential contribution). In the limitation of conflict, in the possibility of ordering and moderating retribution, lies a further justification of state punishment. Appropriate punishments not only serve to maintain the normative order of society as a whole but also serve social peace directly.

This is still not a general statement on the justification of the norms an offender has violated and thus still not a statement on guilt in the sense of a moral valuation, although in the end no legal system can avoid - at least implicit - moral affirmations and thus neither the problem of the justification of law and morality discussed earlier in this book.

If a legal system wanted to get by without a concept of guilt, this would ultimately amount to a considerable expansion of the concept of illness to include social deviations. But how should we deal with a concept of illness that, for example, classifies murder out of greed as pathological without further ado? What concrete therapy should there be for greed, for example, and what time frame and success control for such a therapy? The absence of further murders by the same perpetrator as a test for the success of the therapy? And what if the perpetrator had the intention and the chance to satisfy his greed for his whole life by a single murder and to be a peaceful and useful member of society in the future, and if he might have succeeded in doing so if the crime had not been discovered, and if he is now, as a result of his failure due to the discovery of the crime, finally dissuaded from such a course of action and regrets it (i.e., he is no longer a danger in the future)? The appropriate answer of society and the just compensation for the victim in such cases is not the sole and allegedly self-evident classification of the perpetrator as a sick person, but first of all retribution in the form of life imprisonment, in practice at least for many years (even if one assumes that personal disposition, social circumstances and factual circumstances of the crime have inevitably led the perpetrator to his act).

However, adherence to the concept of guilt must not mean that the offender who is deemed to have committed a crime in a state of culpability is deprived of psychological and psychotherapeutic care, or that efforts are stopped to eliminate social conditions that encourage crime. In criminal proceedings and in the penitentiary system, the constitutional and developmental reasons that lead to a person becoming a criminal should be intensively investigated, and appropriate psychotherapeutic and sociotherapeutic consequences should then be drawn from the knowledge gained. In individual cases, it may be difficult to correct the developmental deficiencies caused by a person's disposition and development, especially those that occurred during childhood and adolescence. But the utopia of a therapy individually tailored to each offender, their personality and their crime within the framework of the imposed custodial sentence must be thought of and conceived as a goal, even if the state will find it very difficult to realise this in the foreseeable future. As soon as such a utopia would become reality, it could, for example, become appropriate in some cases to say: "A socio-therapeutic measure of at least 15 years is imposed for murder" instead of simply talking about the imposition of a prison sentence of 15 years. We will rightly see a further gradual psychiatrisation of the penal system. However, this can become hypocrisy that discredits the whole approach if it is pushed without a sufficiently precise description of illness entities, especially concerning individual personality disorders which can so far be only insufficiently differentiated in psychiatric assessment. Only a sufficiently precise description of illness entities allows therapy options to be determined and then to be implemented and, if necessary, to convincingly present reasons for detention. (5)

Realistically, we also have to realise and acknowledge that the origin of a whole range of criminal offences can be assigned to the borderline area of illness and social deviation, as is the case, for example, for a considerable part of sexual offences. And it is then quite appropriate that society with its legal system also reacts ambivalently to these offences and, if the offenders' lack of culpability is not sufficiently clear, sentences them - and thus determines an appropriate minimum period of imprisonment - but on the other hand also subjects them to psychiatric-psychotherapeutic treatment and, if necessary, orders further therapy and supervision or even continued preventive detention after the end of the sentence. In the case of a considerable risk of repetition, it should not only be possible to order this preventive detention in the course of the criminal proceedings after a crime but also in subsequent judicial proceedings, in which the development of the offender during the sentence or therapy can be taken into account. With the introduction of so-called reserved preventive detention and subsequent preventive detention in juvenile criminal law, the right steps have been taken in this direction. In adult criminal law too, it should be possible that the correctional authorities apply for preventive detention of offenders in a new formal court procedure if this possibility was not reserved in the criminal proceedings but the development of the offender during the term of imprisonment makes preventive detention appear necessary. Moreover, preventive detention should not be excluded in principle for first-time offenders. There are extreme offences which indicate an extensive or complete lack of empathy and responsibility. In such cases, it is not justifiable to demand one or even two further serious offences as proof of the offender's continuing dangerousness which then justify preventive detention. Similarly, there are extreme offences which are rightly treated under juvenile criminal law on the assumption of a delay in maturation, but where it cannot be sufficiently assessed whether, in addition to the delay in maturation, there is not a serious permanent personality disorder as a result of which the offender poses a prolonged or permanent danger to society even after reaching adulthood.

In the application of preventive detention, however, it must be taken into account that the associated deprivation of liberty unlimited in time can also represent a danger to legal certainty. The legally comprehensible, pre-announced connection between the offence and the threat of punishment, the principle of legal punishment, is weakened. The offender is permanently or at least for a longer period of time excluded from the community of people capable of responsibility and is assigned to the psycho- or sociopaths. This instrument should therefore be used with moderation and purpose and not be misused to serve an extremely exaggerated need for security in society. There can be no such thing as an absolutely safe society, and risks to life through crime should be seen in relation to other risks to life that are generally accepted. In the case of serious offences against life and limb, however, it is appropriate to give higher priority to victim protection in case of doubt. That in Germany as of 2023 about 600 particularly dangerous offenders (among them 2 women) are subject to preventive detention (which has to be judicially reviewed every two years) indicates that this most serious instrument of criminal law is not handled lightly. The fact that in the mid-eighties of the 20th century there were still fewer than half as many people in preventive detention can rather be attributed to a very offender-oriented reform phase in criminal law policy than to an excessive use of preventive detention in later years. The biographies of the perpetrators speak for themselves for the most part. However, the European Court of Human Rights has rightly raised the claim that preventive detention must differ decisively from the normal penal system. Such serious encroachments on legal principles as the de facto resulting partial abrogation of the prohibition of double punishment and a deprivation of liberty which is not clearly limited in time from the outset can only be justified if preventive detention actually has the character of a therapeutic and/or preventive measure and not that of a punishment, i.e., if the persons concerned are offered appropriate therapy to a sufficient extent and are granted all the alleviations which are compatible with the aims of a preventive measure. (6)

Ultimately, every investigated and punished offender suffers the consequences of unfortunate personal (and that does not only mean: social) circumstances and is in this respect a victim himself or herself. But: The victims of the crime and their relatives also suffer from the consequences of these unfortunate circumstances, and in a just normative order they have a moral claim for compensation against the offender depending on the severity of the norm violation and the consequences of the crime. This claim is reduced to the extent that the offender was incapable or insufficiently capable of feeling guilt due to clearly definable and comprehensible circumstances and thus lacked criminal responsibility or could not recognise it fully and it should also be reduced by the extent to which offenders show insight and remorse and make successful social reintegration probable through their later behaviour.

The distinction between offender and victim is most blurred in the case of crimes committed by the offender out of sheer necessity or provoked by the victims through morally irresponsible behaviour and especially their own cruelty. This, however, does not justify a general discrediting of the distinction between offender and victim. The justified principle that protection, care and solidarity of society should, as a rule, be given primarily to the victims of crime (including potential victims) and only secondarily to the offenders is otherwise easily called into question (which has already repeatedly led to considerable undesirable developments and wrong decisions in the administration of justice). The social priority of victims' interests is justified insofar as the offenders violate individual and social moral attitudes and values protected by legal norms and impair individual and common welfare.

Punishment is one of the means by which society defends its values and norms, by which it defends the rights of its citizens and, in particular, the rights of those citizens who have been victimised. Punishment towards the guilty has as much justification as the law and the political system whose defence it serves. Feelings of guilt and punishment can also be misused for ideological purposes and to stabilise false or highly questionable objectivist moral and legal systems.

To the extent that the respective legal system has moral justification, the punishment can also have a moral meaning from the offenders' point of view, as far as they are capable of moral development. If offenders consciously accept their punishment, they can again be members of society who are not only tolerated but persons who can accept themselves and have regained their self-respect.

The intuitively plausible considerations discussed here about the significance of the victim perspective and retribution for criminal law were also convincingly introduced into criminal law theory through the concept of "positive general prevention". It is succinctly explained and summarised by Reemtsma: "The measure of punishment is oriented towards the idea of retribution insofar as a community makes it clear in the threat of punishment how high it considers the violated legal good to be - in other words, to what degree its members would consider life unbearable in a society in which the norm in question did not apply. Through the goal of norm clarification, it is easy to justify why a crime must be punished, even if there is no risk that the offender will re-offend again, nor a deterrent signal effect can be assumed."[7] At the same time, these considerations lead to a clear demarcation from what is conveyed in the conventional sense by the terms revenge, atonement, retribution, reparation: "For the victim of a crime, the punishment of the offender is not reparation but the averting of further harm. It is this kind of individual as well as social harm from which, within the framework of the theory of positive general prevention, the notion of 'right' returns to social technology. The victim's right that the perpetrator be punished arises from the state's duty to limit the social harm that a crime causes."[8] The concept of retribution stands today for the proportionality of punishment and violation of norms, for a socially acceptable response to people's sense of justice and their need for justice, and for an offer to the offenders for moral reintegration into society, even in cases where they are denied the opportunity to reintegrate into its everyday life in the long term. Above all, however, the concept of retribution stands for the protection of the normative system of society as a whole.

In the end, however, it remains to be said that there can be no justice for criminals in the strict sense, especially when they have committed serious crimes against life and limb with irreversible consequences for the victims. Society can do justice to the sick by trying to compensate for their disadvantages caused by unfortunate circumstances in the best possible way. Already here, this effort for justice will at some point, always to be renegotiated, come into conflict with other interests that the members of society also want to pursue. The situation vis-à-vis the offender is different from the outset: his or her behaviour, which is also the result of unfortunate circumstances, collides with the prevailing and, at least ideally, also rationally justifiable values of society and its order based on them. The defence of these values and the maintenance of this order must have priority over the effort to compensate for the disadvantage of the offender caused by unfortunate circumstances. This does not release society from the obligation to regard offenders as a kind of sick persons in need of help as well and to orientate its behaviour towards them according this idea as far as it appears compatible with the maintenance of the social value system and the social order. We will have to live with the unresolvable tension between these opposing obligations and objectives in perpetuity.

"We should have no illusions about the fact that a justification of punishment depending on guilt can only be obtained from the point of view of the protection of norms and thus ultimately the protection of society, but not solely with regard to the wrongdoing of the offender. Whether he as an empirical human being really deserves what is imposed on him by the punishment as a legal person, we do not know. "[9]

Reinhard Merkel

However, we should keep one more point of view in mind: The punishment of guilt also serves to protect the offender's freedom. This may seem paradoxical for a moment but it soon becomes plausible: a purely psycho- and sociotherapeutic system of forensic commitments would consequently mean a success- and prognosis-dependent dissolution of the assignment of certain sanctions to certain norm violations, whereby in extreme cases a life-long deprivation of freedom would be conceivable even without a clear serious psychiatric diagnosis and proven danger to society. In contrast, the offender who is classified as normatively responsive may rely on the fact that, after serving a clearly defined sentence provided for in the penal code and pronounced in the criminal proceedings, he will be given the possibility, or at least the chance, to return to society as a citizen free to act.

3.8. Political Order – National and Transnational

How much Leviathan?

3.8.1. State

A friendship founded on business, not a love affair

"I do not love the state, I love my wife! "[1]

Gustav Heinemann

"I propose to argue that States are not gods, and no State should be worshipped, and that the good of the citizens should not be sacrificed to the good of the State. "[2]

Richard Robinson

"We need freedom to prevent the state from abusing its power, and we need the state to prevent the abuse of freedom."[3]

Karl R. Popper

"I don't love democracy, and I allege that other people don't love it either. It is the least evil. Why should one not be annoyed by this evil?"[4]

Theodor Eschenburg(1)

"I do not know how to involve myself so deeply and so entirely. When my will gives me over to one party, it is not with so violent an obligation that my understanding is infected by it."[5]

Michel de Montaigne

For those who are unwilling to believe, there is no "objective" justification and aim for the state, that is to say, none that exists before the setting by humans, would it be as a divinely ordained institution or an institution necessarily following from a fictitious state of nature or from the demands of a forthcoming ideal utopian society. The state is a cultural product of humans which they can shape according to their needs and preferences. By the way they shape it they also show a more or less felicitous handling of their evolutionarily acquired behavioural dispositions. Whether and to what extent one considers a state to be necessary depends on one's philosophy of life, on the moral attitudes and values of the individual and on the historical and social situation. If one regards some fundamental interests as justified and worthy of protection, in which an overwhelming majority of people agree, an intersubjective justification of the state and also of the democratic state (at least as a historical goal) does result from this.

The state is necessary to ensure the enforcement of civil and human rights as codified in the wake of the Enlightenment. It is necessary in order to guarantee the security and freedom that individuals need to unfold their interests in life, to protect them (especially if they belong to a social minority) from some of their fellow human beings, to limit conflicts and to establish a framework to decide them in an orderly manner and to set boundaries to the behaviour of the individual in the interest of the community. In addition, we need the state to take over certain public tasks that cannot be or are not adequately fulfilled by self-interested behaviour according to the rules of the free market and or by the private social initiative of individuals or social groups. At the very least, it is the task of the state to ensure the completion of such tasks by creating suitable incentive regulations.

An organisation of social life without an actual state is in principle conceivable even for modern civilised societies, for example on the basis of smaller, cooperating groups or also through supranational, oligarchic power cartels. However, apart from all the practical difficulties to be expected, this does not seem to me to be a desirable goal, above all because it would reduce the control (or at least the democratic control) of the striving for power and thus, after a short time, of the power of individual people - even if, at first glance, the opposite seems to be the case. That the control of power has been arduously increased in the course of historical development to the level found in democracies with separation of powers represents a significant historical advance (although this control of power is, on the one hand, endangered time and again and, on the other hand, still needs improvement even here, which is by no means meant only in the sense of a further restriction of power but can also mean, for example, the temporary transfer of greater personal responsibility and power for a certain area of responsibility).

Those unwilling to believe will not be able to see any objective justification for a certain form of state. Just as a certain law cannot be derived from the nature of humans a certain form of state cannot be derived from it either. To consider the state as such or a form of state or even a concrete state as a value for its own sake is far from my mind. Nor should one recognise the power of a state as a value and goal for its own sake. Accordingly, I am not in favour of the mere prestige of a state becoming the driving force behind political action without reference to other values behind it. (2) The worship of power and prestige of a state for its own sake has caused many wars and much suffering and continues to do so.

Democracy in the sense of the democratic constitutional state with separation of powers seems to me to be the best form of government. Even if I do not consider democracy itself to be a value, I do consider it to be valuable (this corresponds to the view of the state as a means, not an end in itself), because as a rule it still makes it possible best to realise the moral attitudes and values that I accept and value, especially the attitude of tolerance and the values of peace, freedom and justice. (3) This is a conviction based on experience in the form of contemplating and experiencing history. The decision in favour of democracy therefore does not result directly from my morality, but follows from an evaluation of the experience with different forms of state on the basis of my morality. Interest-based and historical arguments interact with subjective moral convictions to justify democracy.

However, there are very different types of democracy. If one looks at the development in the large representative democracies, one notices an increasing degree of disappointment with politics. Citizens see their interests less and less represented and feel powerless. Members of parliament have to decide on complex legislative projects under - at least de facto – whipped vote and sometimes under great time pressure, and their democratic legitimacy suffers considerably as a result. Often the deputies no longer have an overview of the considerable burdens they impose on the citizens. The citizens themselves consider many of these burdens ill-considered or absurd and accept them only grudgingly and of necessity. Power is increasingly being shifted from the legislature to the executive in the form of bureaucratic apparatuses. Milton Friedman's statement loses more and more its polemical emphasis and becomes a description of reality: "... we have government of the people not by the people but by a largely faceless group of bureaucrats."[6] However, this undesirable development is only possible because the legislature is working insufficiently and confers too much power on the bureaucratic executive by overregulation and bad laws in the first place. As an extreme pendulum swing into the opposite direction, reckless and ruthless populist deregulators then appear on the scene.

What response does this situation require? I believe, meanwhile, that the large democracies would really need more direct influence by the electorate along the lines of Switzerland. Overall, the decisions taken in Switzerland refute the dangers of populist-demagogic influence that are repeatedly painted on the wall. (4) Citizens who can not only express a very undifferentiated, rough preference for a party at long intervals with their ballot paper, but can also decide on very concrete issues, such as tax burdens, age limits and pensions in the statutory pension system or setting the course in energy or environmental politics are much less at risk of distancing themselves from their system of state and government and falling for anti-democratic conspiracy theorists and demagogues. The more grotesque effects representative paternalistic democracies produce, the more important becomes the Swiss countermodel which is supported by a long tradition. Why it shouldn't work in countries with a considerably higher population is beyond me.

Despite all the caution required in this respect and the immense risks of abuse and the often bad historical experiences, one must also admit that even in a democracy such chaotic situations can arise that another form of state seems appropriate as a temporary solution to guarantee the elementary rights of the citizens, to satisfy their basic needs and to enable the establishment of a reformed democracy. And one must also admit that the level of development of some countries - and especially the level of education of large parts of the population there - may make an enlightened dictatorship (as rare as it is) seem reasonable as a temporary solution. Democracy does not guarantee human and civil rights best under all circumstances.

However, such exceptional cases must not be misused to justify authoritarian tendencies in democracies that are far from experiencing a breakdown in public order and are very well capable of solving their problems while adhering to democratic rules. In such circumstances, authoritarian aspirations are nothing more than an attempt by egotistical and often narcissistic politicians to secure power and unfair economic advantages for themselves and their cronies. Typically, such authoritarian aspirations go hand in hand with attacks on the separation of powers, and even democracies with a long tradition are not immune to this. All those who bear responsibility in state institutions, and ultimately all citizens, are called upon to oppose autocratic and oligarchic distortions of the democratic state.

Let us now look a little closer at some of the tasks of the state mentioned above.

If we set the state the goal of enabling its citizens to lead their life in the greatest possible freedom and security, i.e., to offer them the most favourable conditions possible for satisfaction and happiness, then we should at the same time emphasise that the state should not directly concern itself with the satisfaction and happiness of its citizens and in particular should not dictate to them how they should become satisfied and happy – at least as long as they do not harm others through their behaviour. The state should not want to force anyone to be happy - or to become happy in a certain way determined by the state - and should only exert coercion on persons for the sake of their own well-being in a few extreme situations, namely when there are good reasons for assuming that the persons concerned are considerably impaired in their power of judgement (as will apply in a considerable part of the cases of suicide attempts or in the case of severe intoxication and addiction problems or mental illness), or if they at the same time substantially impair the interests of other citizens by their self-endangering behaviour. Even if one accepts these principles, however, there will still be quite different opinions about the preconditions for satisfaction and happiness to be created, depending on the philosophy of life and preferences of the individual.

The obligation of the state to be tolerant is once again expressed in the words of R. Robinson: "The state may not interfere with the individual merely on the ground that his action is morally wrong." - "What gives the State a right here is the possible harm to others, not the immorality of the act."[7] An essential component of state tolerance are the concepts of restraint of the legislator and a "law-free area" already discussed in 3.7.5.. And where the state has to or believes to have to restrict the freedom of the individual for the sake of other citizens, it should first try to convince, wherever the balance of interests at hand allows this, and not issue regulations and exercise coercion from the outset.

The state should be philosophically neutral, apart from fundamental moral and legal principles. (And one should agree on these fundamental principles without giving them a veneer of objectivity that goes beyond inter-subjective communicability.) Philosophical neutrality does not only mean that citizens may belong to the religious community to which they wish to belong, but also that they can give up or change their affiliation at will and may engage in religious activities in the way they wish, as long as this does not violate the rights of others. Philosophical neutrality also means that the state does not identify itself with certain religious communities (for example, by displaying their religious symbols in public institutions which are supposed to serve all citizens, regardless of their respective philosophy of life, or by using religious oath formulas as the "normal" variant and the like). Accordingly, the state should not make itself the administrative and executive organ of religious communities (for example, through collecting church taxes by the state) and should not support religious communities in activities that are not primarily about social services for citizens regardless of their religious or philosophical affiliation or about cultural services of general importance but about the propagation of the respective religion or philosophy of life. (5)

3.8.2. Economic and Social System

Fresh fish for as many as possible

"It is not from the benevolence of the butcher, the brewer, or the baker, that we expect our dinner, but from their regard to their own interest."[1]

Adam Smith

"It is no coincidence that in the past all political systems that despised human dignity and trampled on intellectual freedom also showed a tendency towards the strongest interventions economically. (...) Those who see this only as a coincidental phenomenon misjudge the inner logic of a system of governance, which finds it impossible to remain calmly in the form it has once attained, but which, fleeing from its own absurdities, must resort to ever stronger means of coercion. (...) This connection between command economy and intellectual and political lack of freedom must be particularly observed in Germany, since here, in view of the predominance of a state-oriented way of thinking, a lively tradition of liberal attitudes is extremely weak."[2]

Alfred Müller-Armack

"The policy of laissez-faire mobilised the forces of self-interest so that the public interest would be promoted. It underestimated the danger that individual interest could turn against the public interest."
"Thus the criticism of the policy of laissez-faire leads to a negative and a

positive result. It becomes the great task of economic policy to direct the forces that arise from individual interests in such a way that the public interest is promoted, that is, that a meaningful coordination of individual interests takes place."[3]

Walter Eucken

The state should only take care of things that citizens cannot do at least as well on their own initiative. For many areas of economy and society the belief in the necessity and superiority of state regulation and organisation has proven to be unjustified. Nevertheless, it persists for these areas as well because it has its roots not only in righteous anger about shortcomings but also in the vice of envy and an illusory striving for "absolute justice" as well as in the striving for power of politicians and functionaries. After all, a state-dirigiste social order can best guarantee the greatest possible equality of a large majority of people at a low level. Richard Robinson aptly writes: The demanders of equality in wealth "imply without realizing it that they would rather have everyone undernourished and equally undernourished, than have everyone well nourished and some very rich." - "Stale fish for all is better than fresh fish for coastdwellers only."[4] Robinson found this incompatible with his morality and I feel the same way.

Time and again there are attempts to convey the impression that the value of freedom can be upheld in a democracy independently of the organisation of economic life. This is by no means true. Not only the right to elect one's rulers and the traditional human and civil rights are an essential part of social freedom, but also the possibility for citizens to develop private initiative, to realise their own forms of organisation in economy and society to the greatest possible extent and to decide for themselves on the use of the greater part of their wealth and income. The expansion of state regulation and power comes at the expense of freedom, even though the democratic system is preserved (and thus also the basic possibility of a non-violent change of conditions), whereby in many cases this loss of freedom is not compensated or outweighed by the promotion of other values. Even democratic legislation can develop a particularly insidious mechanism for restricting freedom: Citizens' rights to freedom, such as the rights to the free development of personality and to the free exercise of one's profession, are restricted in small steps by invoking (in an often not even factually justified way) community interests. Such a dismantling of freedom in small steps is only insufficiently counteracted by

346

constitutional control, because the Constitutional Court rightly shies away from interfering with the legislature's ability to shape policy by constantly intervening in relatively small legislative steps and shifting political decisions from parliament to the courtroom. The preservation of freedom is therefore highly dependent on the love of freedom of the political class in democracies too (and especially in distinctly representative ones). Unfortunately, since the political class is often more interested in power than in freedom, freedom always remains at risk. If the liberal character of the state is not to be lost too much, in view of the rampant regulation, especially in the social sphere and in environmental protection, at least the German Federal Constitutional Court will not be able to avoid subjecting legislative encroachments on fundamental rights to a stricter need for justification, even if these seem relatively insignificant in the specific case.

Due to the progressive automation of the production of goods and of administration and the associated release of labour, a tendency to monopolies threatening competition, the globalisation of markets and the aggravation of environmental problems, the regulatory intervention of the state will in future be necessary in some areas to an even greater extent than before (at least temporarily - to mitigate adaptation problems). If we do not want to keep outdated, labour-intensive structures alive and thus forfeit the opportunities offered by technical progress because of an inability to reorganise society, and if, on the other hand, this progress is not to lead to a destabilisation of the social security systems in the developed countries, it is of great importance to constantly question the unavoidable regulatory policy of the state with regard to whether the desired goal cannot be achieved with less dirigiste, more liberal means. (1)

Moral appeals, which call on people to act explicitly against their self-interest, have at best only a marginal influence on the development of the economic and social system. Combined with an unwise regulatory system that shapes the regulatory conditions of economic activity in such a way that the honest, decent and socially oriented people often get the short end of the stick, these appeals even cause increasing annoyance, especially when they are voiced from privileged positions.

Socialism and communism seem to have been largely overcome as state-supporting ideologies. On the other hand, the shortcomings and crisis manifestations of capitalism are obvious. This form of economy and society also has major problems with a reasonably fair distribution of work and resources.

In capitalist systems too, accomplishments are often not valued and supported in proportion to their social usefulness and to the efforts and needs of those concerned. Increasingly, the rarity and attention getting value and the income opportunities that result from this for others are used as a yardstick for the financial reward of occupations.

To name just two (almost infinitely multipliable) examples: Top sporting achievements in popular disciplines, that are socially useful only to a very limited extent, are rewarded grotesquely higher than, for example, even the most dedicated work in caring for the elderly and the sick. Or top performances by prominent artists are remunerated with salaries that can also only be described as grotesque when one considers that at the same time highly qualified but less promotionally effective actors, singers or ballet dancers from the ensemble are expected to content themselves with salaries that are often somewhere between the earnings of cleaning staff and stagehands. The economic conditions for young academics also often defy description. The market, uninfluenced or inadequately regulated by the state, does not provide sufficient economic justice. It does not bring enough staff into care homes, it does not provide sufficient resources for a humane penal system, it does not create largely equal educational opportunities for all, and so on.

The capitalist system offers people who get into the right place in society, or who manage to get there and then show some skill, excessive earning potential which is completely disproportionate to the income from many years of often socially more useful activities. Company executives, top sportsmen or film actors believe that they have in principle unlimited percentage claims to a share of profits generated with their help, without reference to average earned income. However, it is an illusion to believe that the prospect of thirty million euros per year motivates more than that of three million euros. This is all about power and prestige games played by international oligarchic groups who create their own "market" at the expense of social cohesion. Whereas in the mid-1980s, CEO pay in the USA was still around 40 times that of a production worker, it has fluctuated between 200 and 400 times since the turn of the millennium. There is no recognisable increase in performance for companies and society that would justify this.

Determining the position in in a hierarchy and power structure, for example in the field of management, is not necessarily dependent on an excessively accelerating income scale. The attractiveness of much lower-paid political leadership positions shows that this is also possible to a considerable extent directly through the allocation of decision-making powers. Excessive salaries for economic leadership positions are not only unjust with regard to the rewarding of life and work achievements, but are also damaging because the interest of executives in the long-term development of the company decreases. Capitalist societies need to develop rules and practices that on the one hand reward executives according to the long-term success of companies and on the other hand guarantee a noticeable personal participation in losses - analogous to what applies to entrepreneurs who use their own capital or manage with loans for which they are personally liable. (2)

Reservations about high corporate profits, on the other hand, are much less justified. Companies that offer innovative products and services must be rewarded for the risks taken in order to preserve the willingness to take risks and must also be able to acquire the capital to supply the population efficiently and on a large scale with their products. The alternative is a stagnant, inflexible, undynamic and then also psychologically depressing society. If we expect pharmaceutical companies, just to mention an example from my professional field, to make their products available with only a small mark-up on their costs because of their humanitarian obligation, then we pay a high price: we largely forego therapeutic progress. How many innovations were created in the decades of socialist economy behind the Iron Curtain? On the other hand, in view of the large number of high-priced innovations that place a considerable burden on the social system, society also has a right to disclosure of the underlying calculations and profit margins in this sector, and there must be public negotiations on what is appropriate and acceptable.

The market is an effective, indeed undoubtedly the most effective means of ensuring the satisfaction of needs. However, the market should not be an end in itself, it is not a value in itself. It has the positive property of leaving it up to the individuals to a large extent to decide how much individual needs and desires are worth to them, how much they want to spend to satisfy them. In this way, it ensures a wide range of choices for the satisfaction of the most diverse needs and desires and serves the value of freedom in particular. The market, however, cannot replace social objectives that ultimately provide a morally justified balance in favour of those people who, for various reasons, are disadvantaged and less efficient or who have less striving for power and assertiveness (in negative terms: dog-eat-dog personality), but perhaps other pleasant and socially useful skills and traits. The market therefore does not sufficiently serve other essential values, especially justice (which at the same time also means freedom, namely freedom for the economically weaker).

The capitalist economy today shows a worrying tendency to regard profit maximisation as the primary or even the only really serious goal of economic life. Other goals, such as job satisfaction or providing citizens with high-quality goods or essential, socially and individually desirable services as well as jobs that provide a livelihood and personal development opportunities, are pushed into the background. It is true that this development is exploited and driven by the economy. However, one must not lose sight of the fact that it is essentially shaped by the behaviour of citizens as consumers. Feuilletonistic criticism of capitalism in the manner of critical theory is off the mark. As consumers of goods and services, everyone has the opportunity to orientate themselves not only towards the lowest price and to counteract poor quality mass production and anonymous treatment.

The providers of goods and services will not be able or willing to live with the above-mentioned undesirable developments in the long run. Let us take an example from the field of media, where the deformation of work through the primacy of profit is particularly obvious: The programme director of a private channel who broadcasts only "sex and crime", voyeuristic-exhibitionist talk shows and the like all day long, may reassure himself at the end of his working hours that he is only earning his money with this activity. The programme director of a cultural channel or a station that devotes at least part of its broadcasting time to more demanding and meaningful programmes, on the other hand, can go home with the feeling that he has done something valuable, useful or really pleasing for his fellow human beings.

For particularly indolent people, the reassurance that "after all, one is only earning one's money" may last a lifetime. However, many of those who work exclusively for profit will one day look in the mirror, ask themselves about the meaning of their occupation and envy those who have done and do their work not just for the sake of money. (3)

Business enterprises must work profitably in order to survive. But at some point, people will get out of the habit of smiling at the head of a company who is satisfied with an annual profit of 10 per cent and in return maintains the on its own unprofitable supply of citizens in a remote area, instead of striving for 20 per cent and more and in return liquidating all unprofitable or not maximally profitable individual activities of his company without social and moral considerations. In some fields, such as essential social services like health insurance, annual profits of 10 per cent may already be unacceptably high.

Unsocial behaviour of a company must affect its image and the personal reputation of the responsible managers to a sufficient degree to seriously damage their social position and also bring clear disadvantages in business terms. Then one will not be able to live with such behaviour even if one wanted to.

Not only through our consumption behaviour, but also through the contribution we make to the social climate, we all have it in our hands to a certain extent to bring about a change. Economic justice is ultimately a question of the prevailing consciousness of a society. State intervention will only ever be able to make a limited contribution. Even proposals that sound reasonable at first glance, such as limiting the tax deductibility of executive salaries to an acceptable multiple of an average worker's income, are likely to be very difficult to implement in a globally connected economy without doing more harm than good to the respective economy (some such proposals would nevertheless be worth a try, as long as they do not require excessive control and bureaucracy).

When we criticise undesirable developments in the capitalist system, we should, however, generally bear one thing in mind: in the balance sheet as well as in the regulation of the vast majority of social sub-areas, all socialist systems attempted so far have fared much worse. This should cause us to approach with the greatest mistrust all those who commend further attempts of this kind.

Extensive concentration of economic power in the hands of the state leads to negative effects on society even if this is or appears to be associated with better democratic control of economic power. Economic and cultural life (including charitable and humanitarian undertakings) are only flexible and diverse to a desirable extent if, in addition to institutions controlled by bodies of the state or institutions close to the state, there are still centres of power in which individuals or small groups, for example according to family interests or personal preferences, can make quick and unusual decisions which would not come about in formal, institutionalised processes because they would fall victim to the obligation to justify them.

However, the state should intervene with a sense of proportion and with careful consideration of counterproductive side effects of its measures in order to counteract the undesirable developments of the capitalist system. This includes, for example, measures against increasing inequality in the distribution of income and wealth, which impairs economic development and social stability, against cartels which endanger or destroy competition and against

351

excessive concentrations of economic power, and it also includes certain measures to regulate the financial markets, such as a ban on opaque financial products or risky trading mechanisms which involve incalculable risks for the international financial and economic system. On the other hand, state influence should be restrained and pushed back wherever it is not absolutely necessary. In the search for the right middle way, we should be clear about the following: What a society spends its resources on is always determined by political decisions, be they for intervention or abstinence. The state is usually overburdened if it arrogates to itself too detailed a regulatory competence in specific issues, and in doing so it easily stifles social progress and the freedom of citizens. However, it can decisively promote the development of a just and free society by sensibly shaping the regulatory framework of economic and social action.

State intervention should, wherever possible, take the form of an incentive-based rather than a regimentation-based policy. (4) This too is - or at least should be - a form of consistent regulatory policy by the state, in contrast to the exaggerated confidence of some neo-liberals in the free play of forces. The character of this regulatory policy, however, is then still shaped to a large extent by the political decisions as to which incentives should be set for what. Even under the regulatory paradigm of an incentive-based policy, certain mandatory regulations cannot be avoided, but they are primarily directed at shaping the framework for behaviour and avoid, wherever possible, detailed paternalism. This is also the approach of "libertarian paternalism", which aims to make it easier for people to make decisions that are in the best long-term interest of both themselves and society by skilfully presenting alternatives, i.e., by smartly choosing the architecture of decision-making. At the same time, the costs and burdens of divergent decisions should be kept low, which on the one hand manifests the value of freedom and on the other hand the awareness that even the experts and politicians who choose the direction of the desired influence can make wrong decisions or be guided by selfish or lobby-driven motives. With its approach of libertarian paternalism, behavioural economics, which is based on psychological mechanisms, proves to be in the humanitarian liberal tradition of Adam Smith and distances itself from the misuse of its findings, in principle also possible, for the mere maximisation of profit. (5)

As important as the motive of economic self-interest is, it should be kept in mind that for many people psychological aspects - especially job satisfaction

- and moral aspects also play a role (i.e., they are part of their self-interest in a broader sense). An incentive-based policy is particularly promising if it smartly relies on a combination of these motives. Economic profit is more enjoyable for most people if they also have the feeling that they are doing something useful and valuable.

The distinction between incentive-based and regimentation-based policy characterises, even if it may come down to a catchphrase with limited discriminatory power, very different ways of practising politics. The social security fraud investigator may amount to regimentation policy, a reduced wage during sick leave is an incentive policy, a levy for companies not providing company-based apprenticeship is regimentation policy, limiting non-wage labour costs and wage and income taxes to a reasonable level is incentive policy, mandatory car-free Sundays or exhaust emission limits for entire fleets of certain car manufacturers are regimentation policy, while an emissions-based tax burden is more of an incentive policy - and so on along these lines (although exaggerations can also turn measures that should actually be regarded as incentive-based policy into regimentation-based policy). One should not underestimate the extent to which even in a democratic society the more or less free atmosphere (and thus also the long-term economic success and satisfaction of the citizens) depends on which side the ruling policy predominantly takes. In particular, only an intelligent incentive-based policy will succeed in financing a social security system of desirable proportions in the long term and in financing it in such a way that it works to the advantage of the entire national economy instead of strangling it and thus ultimately destroying itself.

An intelligent incentive-based policy should especially take into account that production and services in the social sector are also best provided if they are paid properly and according to performance. There is – at least in Germany and other European democracies – a strong tendency to grant, for example, car manufacturers or banks good profit margins, but to expect that the manufacturers of vital medicines, the operators of old age care homes, physiotherapists, care at home services or doctors should be content with covering their own costs with a small wage supplement and derive their motivation mainly from the social usefulness of their work. However, since people working in these areas are not ascetics as well for the most part, this basic attitude is extremely counterproductive for a good supply of society with the corresponding services. Since the individual cannot decide on the use of social services

353

with the same freedom of choice as in matters of consumption that go beyond basic needs, but rather is often existentially dependent on the use of social services, profit margins for such services as with luxury goods are undoubtedly out of the question. On the other hand, a society should not accept demotivating underpayment in the social sector – if not out of a sense of justice, then at least in its own interest. In the long run, social services obey the same economic mechanisms as consumer goods or other services. If the price is too low, there will be a shortage of supply and at the same time a high demand. Moral and socio-legal coercion of the people working in this field can mitigate and delay this process in the social sector for some time but cannot permanently override it.

So what is it that makes the path of regimentation policy so regrettably attractive time and again? It meets the state's need - specifically, the need of the politicians who shape the state - for the exercise of power and direct control. It also springs from a perfectionist ideal of the greatest possible justice that does not consider its consequences. This ideal then gives birth to rules, regulations, which – if they do not miss the desired goal of the greatest possible justice in their complexity anyway - only achieve it with disproportionate bureaucratic effort and thereby waste resources that would be better used to realise other values than to approach maximum justice. The pursuit of maximal justice leads to a sprawling welfare state in which private initiative and self-responsibility are made unattractive and are suppressed, and in which everyone is ultimately worse off. A social system should compensate for serious disadvantages that arise for individuals due to relatively low personal capacities for work or due to strokes of fate; however, it should not attempt to completely compensate for all such disadvantages, as this would remove the incentive for individuals to provide for themselves to the best of their ability and tempt them to exploit solidarity systems. In Germany, as a result of such perfectionist thinking about justice, an all-providing state has already developed in some areas, whose designation as a social market economy must be called a fraudulent label, since market mechanisms are ignored and overridden on a large scale, which contributes considerably to crisis developments that endanger the social security systems.

It should also not be underestimated to what extent overregulation arises from the political compromises of party politicians who do not have a consequent concept of how regulatory policy should look like. Instead of: "If you renounce your regulation, I will renounce mine!" they say: "If you accept my umpteenth exemption and complication in tax or social law, I'll accept yours too! " Thus, everything gets worse and worse.

The legal complication goes hand in hand with excessive control thinking which is supported by a culture of mistrust towards the citizen in general and the service providers in specific areas in particular - a culture in which the insinuation of incompetence, dishonesty or even malice is always present, at least subliminally. Ever more perfect controls, however, mean an ever more pronounced shift of resources from the area of performance to the area of control of society. If, instead of spot checks, one wants to control every single case, if instead of intelligent surveys that are specifically aimed at identifying errors and undesirable developments and improving processes, one wants complete monitoring of processes, one wastes resources to an extent that even a rich society cannot cope with without a significant deterioration in performance.

Any increase in bureaucracy - for the citizen as well as for the state - should be subjected to a high degree of justification. Politicians should see one of their main goals in sparing citizens unnecessary bureaucracy or freeing them from it. Giving back to the citizen the time of life stolen by excessive bureaucracy for more rewarding and enjoyable activities is - at least in societies like Germany's, suffering from a bureaucratic overload - not only an economic necessity but is increasingly becoming an essential moral, humanitarian task of politics.

On the one hand, the state should guarantee social security to a much greater extent than is the case in the unjust system of the US, which is social Darwinist or shaped by ideas of divine providence in many aspects. On the other hand, the state should attend to this task in a much more efficient way than, for example, the National Health Service in Great Britain, which is unfortunately increasingly becoming a model for other countries. It corresponds to a regrettable extent to Robinson's fish example and cannot even guarantee stale fish for all. Think, for instance, of the rationing of cost-intensive treatments such as hip replacement or dialysis. To avoid such inefficiency, one must make far better use of self-interest and private initiative.

Let us give some more thought to the example of the health care system. I think that the frequently expressed fears that, due to the cost-intensive treatment options of modern medicine and the increasing ageing of the population, we will inevitably be forced in the future for financial reasons to provide certain life-prolonging, expensive treatment methods only to some of the patients who would benefit from them, are in principle largely unjustified as far as the rich, economically highly developed countries are concerned. If something like this happens here, it is mostly the result of organisational-political mis-developments.

Such undesirable developments, which concern solidarity-based health and illness insurance (inevitably always in some form subsidised), are, however, quite avoidable if, in addition to the previously discussed sensible use of the available life-prolonging measures, we take into account a few other essential points: Affluent people must participate appropriately in the health care of the population as a whole. Excessive profits from health services must be avoided, as well as demotivating underpayments, flat rates, restrictions and regimentations. In the case of extremely expensive therapies, compromises must be negotiated with the pharmaceutical industry that do not stifle research on the one hand and prevent excessive profits at the expense of solidary social insurance arrangements on the other. Funds for services that may be pleasant but do not belong to the core area of health care must be cut, because otherwise the financing of vital services is no longer secured with increasing life expectancy and medical possibilities.

Social and health policy must give considerable importance to the aspect of preventing abuse as effectively as possible, but to this end it should rely less on control systems and more on psychologically skilful incentives which directly address people's self-interest. In any case, it must not be based on an unrealistic, idealistic, euphemistic image of humans.

A waste of social insurance funds or tax revenues for scientifically unproven methods or for minimising at best marginal risks must be avoided, even if such misdirection of funds meets the zeitgeist needs of considerable parts of the population. In these areas we see how much money can still be mobilised even in times of scarcity, and also how much money a misguided and insufficiently informed population is willing to spend on ineffective or almost ineffective nonsense. We should advocate that this money should rather be used for sensible and efficient prophylactic measures.

It must be discussed more openly and without politically motivated cowardice what the available resources should be used for. The decisive criteria must be comprehensible needs, not the loudest protest or the least resistance. If this is not done, we will be confronted more and more often with the misallocation of funds: For example, health insurance companies will then pay for all kinds of often very dubious treatment measures for either self-limiting or

356

permanently largely uninfluenceable complaints in the area of the musculo-skeletal system but no longer for suitable visual aids for severely defective vision. Or they stubbornly resist the coverage of costs for innovative diagnostic and therapeutic measures of undisputed and sometimes decisive value for the patient, because they are not prepared to free up the necessary resources, for example by consistently excluding from reimbursement medicines that are ineffective or of highly questionable effectiveness.

Decisions limiting costs must be made at the political level. This can be achieved by excluding certain measures and therapies that are considered less important from reimbursement by the solidarity community or by setting maximum amounts for certain therapies that allow the most cost-effective therapy in accordance with the current state of medical science. Coercive measures against individual doctors that force them to accept flat-rate cost limits are to be rejected. Such coercive measures also include models that transfer budget responsibility to doctors for a certain number of patients and allow them or entice them to profit from savings in the care of the patient. Such structures poison the doctor-patient relationship because the patient rightly has to fear that medical decisions will be overridden by socially or privately motivated - or forced - cost limitation considerations instead of the search for the best individual treatment. If rationing is unavoidable, it must be supported by democratic political decisions after an open discussion.

It is the task of politics, admittedly not always easy, to create a regulatory framework that ensures that neither societal rationing interests nor the profit interests of the individual doctor displace the well-being of the patient as the primary goal of the doctor-patient relationship.

Finally, one essential aspect must not be forgotten: If we want to maintain and make possible high-quality medicine for all with increasing life expectancy and increasing medical possibilities, then we must exert more pressure than before on people to behave sensibly with regard to their health. This includes, for example, consistent protection of non-smokers in everyday life. Harassing and harming others through the use of stimulants has nothing to do with the proper exercise of freedom. Experience has shown that the most effective (and most liberal) way of exerting pressure towards healthy behaviour is through the purse. For example: taxes on social drugs or unhealthy foodstuffs as high as possible without provoking a problematic black market development; percentage surcharges on health insurance contributions to the extent that the normal weight is exceeded. Many such measures can be implemented without great cost and bureaucracy if there only is political will.

But back to more general considerations. It is important to repeatedly call on the state to limit its expenditures in a reasonable way and to discuss state or state-induced waste and misinvestment of resources on the one hand and the abuse of social security systems on the other, and to look for ways to avoid such undesirable developments. However, in view of the chronic shortage of funds in the public sector and in the social security systems, there is a tendency to overestimate the discussion on the need for economy and fighting misuse and waste and to make wrong decisions on the basis of this approach. The well-known pattern of looking for scapegoats comes up again, for example in the form of xenophobia, which makes the - admittedly quite real and not insignificant - burdens on the social system caused by immigrants and asylum seekers, for example, the main cause of difficulties in the social security systems beyond all realistic proportions. This neglects the fact that the appropriate and desirable level of state tasks and social security, even with optimal organisation, requires high resources and that the essential, the decisive threat to our state order and our social systems emanates from the fact that the tax system and the financing of the social systems have so far only insufficiently been adapted to the profound change in the population pyramid and the production and work structures, although the necessity of corresponding measures has at least been recognisable or should have been recognisable since the 1970s to reasonably far-sighted analysts and politicians.

For a long time, however, the positive effects of simply reducing working hours were overestimated in an all too naïve way. In view of automation in production and administration, reductions in working hours and increased part-time work are undoubtedly necessary to a certain extent and also desirable because of the associated gain in freedom. However, reductions in working time have complete effects that need to be analysed and observed closely. Here I would like to draw particular attention to the following two aspects: Entrepreneurs will always try to pass on to their customers on the one hand and to the workers on the other hand only a part of the increase in productivity that can be achieved through rationalisation and automation and to keep a more or less large part of it for themselves, which is quite legitimate and, moreover, quite human in view of the burdens and investments associated with constant, rapid and far-reaching structural change. In times of international competition for jobs, the mechanisms of the free market are at the service of the customers here, but they may do more harm than good to the workers.

On top of that, a reduction in working hours in sectors that have relatively large possibilities for economisation and automation means that, quite understandably and justifiably, employees in other sectors of the economy, especially in the service sector and in relatively small-scale craft or trade business, where these possibilities are comparatively very limited, accept their constant disadvantage only to a certain extent and at some point demand at least a partial equalisation of their working hours or financial compensation. Without corresponding changes in the system of taxes and social a contributions, the consequence will be that the above-mentioned labour-intensive sectors will be increasingly burdened and stifled, or at least their growth will be severely hindered, even though an increase in employment in these sectors would be urgently desirable, because it is predominantly about meaningful and necessary work which, on top of that, is largely locally bound and a desirable compensation for the job losses caused by economisation and automatisation. In the service and craft and trade business sectors meaningful work remains undone on a large scale or is carried out with great delay only, or done, often more badly than good, by moonlighting or private improvisation, without taxes and social security contributions accruing or being paid. This exacerbates the financing problems of the state and the social security systems. In societies that suffer from a labour shortage, particularly in the service and skilled craft and trade sectors, the order of the day is not to reduce working hours, but to create incentives that once again offer greater rewards for more and longer hours of work.

There is no silver bullet, there are no simple solutions for the structural problems of modern societies. In addition, the great difficulty lies in the political implementation of sensible measures against short-sighted objectors and short-term interests as well as ideological biases. Having said this, I want to consider a few more ideas for sensible reforms in the following.

We need an intelligent and imaginative employment promotion policy that tries out measures changing the regulatory conditions in the most diverse areas with a certain willingness to experiment, be it tax law or social insurance.

In the future, a higher proportion of the state's tax revenue should come from consumption taxes and turnover, sales or value-added taxes, while wage- and income-based taxes must be reduced at least for income still predominantly acquired by personal work. This will make personal work and job creation more attractive again and give citizens more freedom in the use of their income. In addition, intelligent and non-excessive consumption taxes are a contribution to tax justice because, while not immune to tax fraud with high criminal energy, they are less prone to tax evasion and tax avoidance. However, since consumption taxes impose the heaviest burden on those citizens who are forced to spend the greatest part of their income on consumption, justice then demands that transfers for the needy be sufficiently high and that modest incomes be exempted from taxation, either entirely or to a large extent.

If consumption-based taxes can at the same time achieve steering effects that are desirable for other reasons - such as environmental or health policy - all the better. However, such objectives should only be pursued through the tax system if they cannot be achieved more rationally by other means and do not lead to disproportionate complication and bureaucracy.

The tax burden should be shifted more from lower and in particular middle incomes to the really high incomes and the really wealthy. If the maximum tax rate on income already applies to all better incomes that can be earned through personal, socially desirable and useful work, then this is absurd and counterproductive for a society. Wealth taxation must take into account the overall tax burden in a country and the problem of capital flight.

The taxation of companies should favour labour-intensive companies depending on the relation between the wages and salaries sum and the profit. In addition, "small" employment-promoting measures must be consistently tested and used (example: the tax deductibility of domestic workers).

In the longer term, social insurance contributions must be levied more in relation to turnover and less in relation to the employed persons, for example by levying the employer's share of social insurance contributions as a kind of social tax in relation to turnover and only charging the personal contribution of the employee on a personal basis because it is needed later as a measure for the respective personal claims.

However, the implementation of such proposals is delayed and limited by possible negative effects on the international competitiveness of certain branches of production. It should be borne in mind, however, that although this is an important consideration, it is by no means the only decisive factor in political decisions, even in an export-oriented country. The stability and quality of a society are only partly decided by the conditions for industrial production; factors such as the unemployment rate and domestic demand also play a major role. By gradually shifting labour to the service sector, unemployment can be reduced, domestic demand generated and society made more humane. And in the medium and long term at least, all highly industrialised societies will increasingly face the same structural problems.

_In the short and medium term, it will probably only be possible to avoid an extension of working hours in the wealthy countries at the price of a significant reduction in income expectations or, conversely, a reduction in working hours will only be possible at this price. A relatively lower pay for workers will thus hardly be avoidable. It will require skilful political decisions on regulatory conditions to at least mitigate these effects. This situation is a consequence of the pronounced differences in wealth both on a global scale and already between closely neighbouring countries. In Europe, it is also a legacy of decades of socialist mismanagement, for which the wealthy countries must now inevitably pay in a longer transitional period of wealth equalisation. On the one hand, this is unfair, since these countries are not responsible for the wrong way the socialist dictatorships took. On the other hand, from the perspective of the people of the countries of former state communism, who have been restricted in freedom and forcibly disadvantaged for decades, it may with some reason also be regarded as compensatory justice. In the longer term, everyone will benefit from an equalisation of prosperity. A similar development can be expected in the long run with regard to the developing countries. However, the pressure from these countries towards equalisation of wealth (leaving aside a moral point of view) is temporarily less because the geographical and cultural distance and, in many cases, the political instability and the reduced implementation of workplace and environmental standards in these countries limit the transfer of goods and labour. These factors also make it easier for rich countries to find excuses to close off their markets. The rich countries thereby alleviate their adjustment problems, but on the other hand the urgently needed overcoming of the misery structures in the poor countries is made more difficult.

But let us turn once again to fundamental questions of democracy. It has not yet been made sufficiently clear and has not yet been sufficiently understood that democracy is not only threatened by fanatics and totalitarian ideologies but also by very gradual undesirable social developments. Freedom can also be massively endangered in democratic states without civil rights being formally restricted or abolished. Capitalism, in the form of the social market economy, has led to a historically unprecedented degree of widespread prosperity and personal freedom. However, such a system is not an unlosable achievement; it can undergo very unpleasant developments even without a fundamental change of system.

A great danger lies in a laissez-faire capitalism which, if not making them appear as exemplary, at least allows shameless profit and salary maximisers, who basically follow early capitalist ideas, to determine the social course of events. In their materialistically oriented, oligarchically organised strategies of enrichment, social responsibility plays at best a subordinate role and hardly goes beyond mere charity, and even this is in the end mostly calculated in their own interest. The consequence is an increasing inequality and economic disadvantage of large population groups. We need to develop more ingenuity to counteract the incentive to maximise profits and accumulate capital at the expense of jobs (for example, through stronger incentives to reinvest profits).

Another great danger lies in a levelling state of functionaries, regulations and surveillance that blocks economic as well as social and cultural dynamics and creativity. For each individual, naturally always well-intentioned regulation a number of arguments can always be put forward, at least from a bureaucratic-perfectionist point of view, and the citizens' room for manoeuvre is increasingly restricted. The individual measures appear to be quite insignificant and only more or less annoying, in any case they remain below the threshold that triggers sufficient resistance to prevent them, but when added up, the freedom-restricting effect is fatal.

Insidiously, the construction of the regimentation and surveillance state is largely contributed to regardless of a specific ideological affiliation across the boundaries of the political camps. Even if one political party is somewhat more inclined to do so than the other, all of them always find enough seemingly good reasons to push this process forward. And unfortunately, one does not feel obliged to look for an old regulation that has become superfluous and could be abolished for every new one that is implemented. On the contrary, restrictions and bureaucracies that have been introduced once prove to be extremely persistent, even if their harmfulness or at least their dispensability has long since become clear. A plethora of regulations, which in their totality considerably restrict the freedom of the individual, are enacted without being able to be justified by a convincing social benefit. To a large extent, they are produced without sufficient democratic legitimacy by bureaucrats who are given too much leeway by the elected politicians or whose democratically no longer sufficiently controlled spheres of power these politicians have created in the first place through bad, bureaucracy-laden laws. This creates understandable disenchantment with the state and the political system and is, for example, one of the most important factors at the European level that support reservations against European integration. Environmental policy in particular is increasingly proving to be an area in which insufficiently reflected zeitgeist currents can establish almost eco-dictatorial detailed regulations even within democratic societies.

The expansion of the power of functionaries and of regimentation and surveillance in the state is accompanied by a renaissance of authoritarian thinking (however well this is concealed behind modernist-emancipatory empty formulas). Instead of reforms from below with the participation of the people concerned, reforms are often imposed from above (6), which rightly leaves people with a feeling of powerlessness and often causes them to distance themselves from the reform process - and often even worse: to exercise their actually valued professional activity only with limited commitment because it is hindered by inappropriate regulations conflicting with the demands of everyday reality. (7)

An important instrument for the expansion of state power is excessive absorption of the private property of citizens, as we can observe in high-tax states. Instead of letting citizens make their own decisions as far as possible and only fulfilling subsidiary social tasks, the state seizes economic power by expanding transfer payments high frictional losses. In the process, the tax system can take on a form that no longer has anything to do with an appropriate social obligation of property and contradicts fundamental civil liberties. If - to give just one example - the inheritance of already taxed assets between siblings is taxed at 30 to 50 per cent with only small tax allowances, the point is reached where the citizens are morally entitled to draw on civil resistance in various forms. Since open legal and political resistance can be associated with disproportionate burdens on private lives and, on top of that, brings only questionable prospects of success, civil disobedience, for example in the form of simple concealment of assets, is also justified in the case of such excesses of state intervention. Even with democratic legitimacy, the state undermines law-abidingness and legal certainty through excessive confiscation of the income and assets of its citizens (and thus also weakens the rule of law in other areas). What is lawful can nevertheless be unjust and is indeed sometimes unjust in political reality. If the citizen tries to correct this according to his own comprehensible value weighings, then this is worse than a good policy that makes such behaviour dispensable, but it represents - limited to exceptions - a response to political undesirable developments that does not endanger the state order as a whole and can even rather be seen as a preventive against disenchantment with the state.

Every individual is called upon, as best he or she can, to oppose both the radical capitalist denial of solidarity as well as the renaissance of the authoritarian state and the octopus-like proliferation of the welfare state - and to accept a certain degree of personal disadvantages for these efforts if necessary. This resistance can be made in any social position and will have to take place to a considerable part in a grassroots democratic way outside the encrusted parties and associations. The fact that they can attribute their power to a democratic legitimacy does not give politicians and functionaries the right to make their decisions without taking into account the wishes of the individuals and to strangle their freedom more and more. With such a line of action, they abuse their power, undermine democracy and create disenchantment with the state. A liberal social order can also be gradually carried to its grave without it being properly noticed beforehand how far the disease process has already progressed. (8)

> »We should develop the practice of examining both the benefits and the costs
> of proposed government interventions and require a very clear balance of
> benefits over costs before adopting them.«[5]
>
> Milton and Rose Friedman (9)

Situations of financial and economic crisis, such as in the recent past the financial crisis of the years of 2007–2009, which arose because the state did not sufficiently exercise its control functions and market participants were seduced like lemmings into financial operations and financial products with an unsound basis - partly also through state encouragement and support - do not change the correctness of such liberal basic rules. On the contrary, such crises harbour a considerable risk for future undesirable developments if they are misused not only to correct the underlying mistakes and to develop protective mechanisms against their repetition but also to unjustifiably expand state power.

On the other hand, the Friedmans' motto must be taken more seriously than they themselves have done, for propagandistic reasons. If the advantages of state intervention outweigh the disadvantages, then it should take place. And where the state is needed, we should call things as they are. "The confidence in the self-healing powers of the economy has not been able to assert itself in the face of economic crises." (Müller-Armack[6]) It is contradictory when Friedman, on the one hand, correctly states that the crisis of 1929 assumed its fatal proportions not only due to a misguided deflationary monetary policy, but above all due to the lack of state refinancing and support for banks in a situation of panic-like loss of confidence while claiming, on the other hand, that this situation was created and aggravated not only by wrong, but by too much rather than too little state intervention. (10) Fortunately, however, policymakers seem to learn something from the analysis of historical crises even when analysts inappropriately reinterpret their findings.

In view of the risks involved in special crisis situations, the Friedmans' motto does not contradict the inclusion of Keynesian tools of demand support in dealing with them, even if the dispute over their effectiveness has not been settled. Measures supporting demand can also be designed as sensible incentive policies and do not have to lead to an increase in state power and the expansion of a regulatory state. However, the Keynesian repertoire should not be played out lightly, because another economic truth has been confirmed so often that it should be completely indisputable by now: The state finds it very difficult to consistently reduce the benefits it grants and the debts it incurs in good times, and what it imposes on itself and thus on its citizens considerably restricts future political room for manoeuvre. That one should consistently reduce debts and government ratios in good times in order to have room for manoeuvre in bad times unfortunately often remains only a laudable intention. At some point, there is no way around financial recovery at the expense of the citizens, be it through drastic measures at a certain moment, such as currency reforms, or through protracted devaluation of the citizens' assets, for example through a longer-term low-interest policy.

The fundamental question of how much state intervention, control and regulation the economic and social system needs is and must be discussed again and again. This is a play which is primarily about the appropriate relationship between the values of freedom and equality and at the end of this section I will try to consider it once again with as much critical distance as possible. Admittedly, there are some timeless truths in this debate (which here means social experiences that have been confirmed again and again). These include Adam Smith's insight, quoted at the beginning, that to be successful an economic and social system should take people's self-interest into account and use it for social purposes. Regulatory conditions that are unsuitable for using people's self-interest for social purposes, and which are either based on an illusory, moralising image of humans or on the enforcement of social behaviour against self-interest, neither promote social commitment nor do they serve the protection of nature or the interests of future generations in an efficient way.

That a strong middle class and a not too high degree of economic inequality are of great importance for a desirable society and a stable constitutional democracy is also one of these simple lasting truths. Those who want a stable democratic and social constitutional state must also accept that, as a rule, such a state can only exist and fulfil its tasks if it receives a substantial share of its citizens' income for this purpose. Assuming the acceptance of such truths, the extent to which state intervention is promising or tolerable depends to a large extent on the respective historical situation. Likewise, how observers view and evaluate such interventions depends to a large extent on the society they come from and on their social situation and biography. (11)

> "Standing up for the market economy must not be understood as a renunciation of subjecting our way of life to cultural standards: On the contrary, we believe that we can see in it a means of implementing certain ideals of shaping human culture, such as social reforms in particular, in an especially realistic and effective way."[7]

> Alfred Müller-Armack (12)

Market economy and a democratic constitutional state are not necessarily linked. Market-oriented autocracies or oligarchies can, under certain circumstances, at least temporarily ensure economic and social stability more successfully than democracies. This can be the case, for example, in the economic catching-up of less developed states and especially in regions where there are no or hardly any democratic traditions. The improvement of the economic living conditions of the population then initially makes the claims for respect of human and civil rights recede into the background.

This challenges not only the economic foundations but the entire concept of the democratic constitutional state and of its connection with a social market economy. It cannot be taken for granted that this challenge will be met. To do so, on the one hand, a constant renewal of awareness of the value of human and civil rights is required and, on the other hand, a reflection on the basic principles of a social market economy, that means to keep economic structures adaptable and flexible and to reward performance and individual initiative in the most diverse areas of society in such a way that sound economic foundations are created and maintained for the desirable equalising measures through compensatory taxation and transfer payments. Historical experience shows that a solid economic basis is a decisive prerequisite for the defence of the democratic constitutional state.

3.8.3. Beyond the Nation State

Globalisation for human and civil rights

"From this time onward, the danger of mankind perishing by human action will always be with us – it will never vanish again."[1]

Karl Jaspers

"World domestic policy is no less controversial than any form of internal politics, but it sees its conflicts as differently localized and as resolvable by means other than those of classical foreign policy."[2]

Carl Friedrich von Weizsäcker

"The picture of international relations today is chaotic because there is too much military force – and because there is too little of it where it would be needed."[3]

Wilfried von Bredow

"The subsidiary and federal world republic stipulated here is ... the utopia of a 'not-yet', an ideal which humanity has a legal-moral obligation to implement. Fortunately, humanity is already headed in this direction."[4]

Otfried Höffe

It is an already trivial observation that our world has become "small" due to the development of modern transport, information and military technology and due to the increasing global effects of human behaviour (as a result of increasing technical possibilities and an increasing population leading to an overexploitation of natural resources). As a consequence people all over the world belong together and are dependent on each other for better or worse to an extent that was previously unimaginable.

Moreover, the idea of general human and civil rights, to which not only the citizens of a particular nation, but in principle all people are entitled, has been developed and already spread to such a high degree that it can no longer be suppressed in the long run by any authoritarian state conception of a religious, ideological or just oligarchic nature. And this has not only idealistic reasons: Democracies - and to an even greater extent cooperating democracies - are not only best able to realise these rights, but are also the most economically successful state structures for the majority of citizens created so far. However, even democracies are not immune to movements calling for nationalist isolation and egoistic defence of possessions and interests or enrichment at the expense of others. In the long run, however, all more radical programmes of this kind will fail because of their practical and moral untenability.

Today and in the future, the nation state is no longer sufficient as the largest political structure of the human community. Neither the continuation of nation-state policy at the international level in the sense of a policy of alliances and balances, as promoted in the 19th century in particular, nor the pacification of a world region through incorporation of states into the sphere of influence of a hegemonic power can meet the requirements of the modern world in the long term. We need a world domestic policy[5] on a federalist basis.

The plan for a federation of states, even if initially "only" with the aim of securing lasting peace, was already conceived in the 18th century, especially by the Abbé de Saint-Pierre. Kant went beyond his predecessors by declaring a federation of republican states to be necessary, by which he understood not democracies, but constitutional states. (1) The catastrophe of the First World War then brought about the first, imperfect political institutionalisation of such a world confederation in the form of the League of Nations. (2) However, the League of Nations already saw its task not only in conflict resolution and peacekeeping, but also pursued - rightly and in part with considerable success - a wealth of humanitarian goals. This development has been augmented in the successor organisation, the United Nations, which came into being after the next world catastrophe. But central problems, such as the prevention of war and peacekeeping or the removal of inhumane dictatorships (by force if necessary), the overcoming of which is an essential prerequisite for the guarantee of human and civil rights and for economic, social and cultural development and cooperation, have unfortunately not been solved or only been addressed very unsatisfactorily hitherto by the United Nations as well.

What can be done in the future to come closer to a solution of these fundamental problems?

The United Nations will continue to have problems with its democratic legitimisation for the foreseeable future. A large proportion of the member states are not democracies themselves, and the principle of "one state - one vote" is also questionable because it does not take into account the size of the population and other factors that are important for the international significance of a state. On the one hand, these factors are taken into account to a certain extent by the right of veto in the Security Council, which is itself undemocratic. On the other hand, however, the veto power is regularly abused, particularly by the totalitarian members China and Russia, thus paralysing the United Nations. The UN Charter's demand that member states provide the United Nations with troops and other forms of military support at the request of the Security Council for coercive measures necessary to secure peace or even to enforce the rights guaranteed in the Universal Declaration of Human Rights is largely unrealistic and ineffective in view of the presence and veto power of dictatorships in the Security Council and the high number of authoritarian member states. And even the authorised UN peacekeeping missions have repeatedly proved to be a fiasco, just think of the genocide in Rwanda or the massacre in Srebrenica.

Nevertheless, the existence and structure of the United Nations and the declarations it has adopted, especially the Universal Declaration of Human Rights, the United Nations Charter and the adoption of the Responsibility to protect (R2P) commitment in 2005 exert a clear pressure towards democracy and an international order based on the rule of law. Despite all the frustration about the shortcomings of the United Nations, we must not forget that the idea of a global federation of states is just four hundred years old and that the first concrete attempts to realise it are just over a hundred years old - a very short period of time compared to the history of humankind.

For the time being there is no alternative to the UN as a global supranational organisation. The United Nations can only exist as a - despite everything - highly significant and forward-looking global political bracket if the aforementioned restrictions on its democratic legitimacy are still accepted in the longer term.

There are many good ideas for reforming the United Nations: recognised democracies should be allowed to send more voting delegates to the General

Assembly and Security Council than other states, the right of veto should at least be granted only to democratic member states of the Security Council, the number of voting delegates in the General Assembly should in some way reflect the size of the population, for example by giving states with less than 1% of the world's population one vote and more populous states two. Only democracies should be admitted to the United Nations Human Rights Council. In order to promote a reform in the direction of more democracy, a second chamber of a world parliament, a world citizens' chamber, could be set up in addition to the United Nations Chamber of States (following a suggestion by Höffe[6]) whose members would initially be delegated by the national parliaments, but would later be directly elected.

Unfortunately such reform proposals are largely utopian and a democratisation of the UN will at best only be achieved in the very long term and with great effort against the authoritarian member states.

The democratic states must therefore think about other ways to create the necessary structures that allow human and civil rights and the democratic state model to be enforced. This can only succeed if, in addition to the UN, a community of democratic states is institutionalised that can stand up for democracy and human and civil rights worldwide on a civil and military level without the obstruction of authoritarian regimes that exists in the UN.

We find ourselves in a historical situation in which democracy, human and civil rights are under pressure in many ways: by a Chinese regime that is consistently realising the nightmare of Orwell's 1984 with a total surveillance of its citizens, the restriction and control of access to information and a language regime that distorts reality as well as by the consistent repression of any opposition; by an aggressive Russian dictatorship that lacks any moral standards, undermines the European peace order and supports criminal regimes all over the world; by the inhumane Islamist religious dictatorship in Iran, which is doing its utmost to undermine a possible modernisation in the Islamic world; by individual criminal regimes such as North Korea, which are dangerously armed; by serious efforts to bring the democracy of the United States under the control of evangelism and capitalist kleptocracy and to shape the global economic order through ruthless selfishness instead of co-operation in the interests of all ... . The new possibilities for hybrid warfare using coordinated cyberattacks on critical infrastructure and influencing public opinion and elections through fake information in internet portals and social media and AI-generated reality distortion pose additional dangers to the stability of democratic states beyond military threats. (3)

All these developments make a closer global cooperation of democratic states an urgent political task, striving in the long run for a confederation of democratic states besides the UN which will be needed until the UN itself become a confederation of democratic states.

On the civilian level, this is particularly about promoting an education system that enables people to think critically. On the economic level, democratic states must avoid or reduce excessive dependence on authoritarian states and protect their own economic capabilities against state-subsidised market distortion by authoritarian states. The various forms of collaboration between actors in democratic states in laundering assets acquired in autocracies must be combated by consistent measures to increase transparency regarding the origin of funds and ownership. Emergency aid in the event of disasters must be concentrated primarily on democratic states or made dependent on authoritarian regimes contributing an appropriate amount of their own resources, allowing monitoring of the use of aid and making concessions regarding the promotion of democracy and human rights.

The attempts of authoritarian states to undermine the universal validity of human and civil rights by invoking sovereignty, non-interference, cultural plurality or a multipolar world order must no longer be accepted. Ensuring unhindered access to uncensored information, and in particular to an uncensored Internet, should be a high-priority goal of democratic states that is worth investing considerable resources in.

At the military level, it is a question of conflict prevention through the convincing threat of superior military force. A community of democratic states must be able to intervene at short notice and with superior military force if this is unavoidable to secure peace and, in particular, to defend democratic states against attacks by authoritarian states, so that the duration of the conflict and the loss of human life can be kept to a minimum. This is an essential contribution to achieving a state of world peace in the long term, which in turn is an essential prerequisite for being able to solve other problems of humankind. Anyone who dies in such a peacekeeping operation has truly died for world peace and the future of humankind and has not sacrificed his or her life, as in so many wars in human history, for the glorified power interests of some nation or some national potentate or oligarch.

The democratic states need a standing intervention force of several hundred thousand soldiers, available at all times, which is equipped in such a way that it can not only fulfil tasks of mediation, conflict settlement, securing cease-fires and the protection of humanitarian operations, but can also intervene quickly in local conflicts in war and civil war zones in an emergency and with a low risk of loss to its own forces. This intervention force can be made available to this alliance of democratic states by ensuring that each member state that maintains military formations equips a sufficient percentage of its troops as internationally deployable collaborative forces and keeps them permanently available for call-up by a central command structure. The member states would not have to incur any long-term additional costs (in practice possibly the most important counterargument against such a concept), apart from initial reorganisation costs, as they have to maintain the respective troop contingents anyway as part of their own security concepts. And to the extent that additional costs are incurred - for example for the corresponding transport facilities and special equipment - the economic benefits of the global security gains achieved would undoubtedly outweigh these by far.

In the event of serious human rights violations, the task of a permanent international armed force of democratic states can also be the forcible removal of dictatorships and terrorist regimes if all other means fail and the deployment can be expected to be overwhelmingly accepted by the population of the affected country or threatened population groups. However, the bad experiences with previous interventions, such as in Iraq, Libya or Afghanistan, must be analysed.

If an intervention is considered, an idea of the further political development of the respective country should always be conceived consistently and with foresight, just as at least the Western Allies did relatively well with regard to Germany during the Second World War, and an attempt should be made to implement this concept in the wake of military operations as skilfully and decisively as possible, taking into account local circumstances and, in particular, respecting local culture as far as possible. Due to the lack of pre-conditions for this in ethnically and religiously divided and administratively desolate countries, especially in the so-called Third World ("burdened societies" in the sense of Rawls[7]), it will not always be possible to initiate a truly satisfactory democratic development or to guarantee it in the long term, and in some cases one will have to be satisfied with the interim goal of at least achieving an elimination of chaos and anarchy.

NATO is the largest and most successful peacekeeping alliance in history. It was initially based on a primarily geographic idea of defence, which made sense for practical reasons and remains sensible to a certain extent. However, it should not be swept under the carpet that NATO also owes the dark points in its history to this geographical idea of defence, namely the temporary stabilisation and support of dictatorships for strategic reasons. Fortunately, there has been a clear convergence in the longer term within the NATO states in the sense of democratic development of the member states. The Greek, Portuguese and Spanish dictatorships have been overcome. With certain limitations with regard to Turkey, which still has clear deficiencies and setbacks in its democratic development and must be patiently but consistently influenced in this respect, all NATO countries are now genuine democracies in which respect for human and civil rights is guaranteed in principle and, where it is imperfect in practice, can mostly be demanded publicly without serious personal threat. This is true despite temporary authoritarian tendencies and attacks on the separation of powers and freedom of the press in some countries. Future-oriented consequences should be drawn from this development for NATO's self-image and strategy.

NATO should be renamed DENTO, Democratic Nations Treaty Organization. It is no longer just the countries bordering the North Atlantic that have to be defended, no longer primarily a geographical region, but a form of state and life with a long-term global claim, namely pluralistic democracy. The original NATO treaty already contains a considerable number of statements to this effect. In the meantime, however, the time has come to further weaken the geographical principle in relation to this content, for example, by soliciting the joining of long-term stable democratic states in other regions of the world, such as Australia, Japan and New Zealand, to which the Alliance can credibly guarantee support in the defence of their democracy internally and their state integrity externally. On the other hand, the geographical principle continues to make sense in a modified form, because the gradual admission of further "democratically emerging countries" (along the lines of Turkey) which are geographically adjacent to the already existing territory of this democratic protective community can promote the democratic development of such countries, and in geographically adjacent regions the defence of a still imperfect democracy by the community can most credibly be guaranteed both internally and externally. However, such democratically emerging countries should only be admitted gradually in limited numbers so as not to compromise the democratic legitimacy and structure of DENTO too much.

Changing the name to DENTO would also increase the pressure on member states, whose democracies are still shaky and at risk of backsliding, to develop into fully-fledged and stable democracies. However, a mere change of name is not enough: the NATO Treaty must be supplemented by a graduated sanctions procedure for member states that undermine their own democratic order (the lack of an infringement procedure in this respect and corresponding concrete options for sanctions is a birth defect of the NATO Treaty). The membership of states that develop into autocratic or dictatorial states can be temporarily maintained for reasons of regional defence, but this must then only be a second-class membership with clearly restricted rights.

The geographical principle should also remain important insofar as DENTO should quickly and decisively end a war or civil war in countries bordering on its territory, if necessary also through massive military intervention, and force the conflict parties to the negotiating table (at least if the UN proves incapable of doing so). DENTO should feel obliged to undertake such local and regionally limited pacification tasks in its immediate border area - again provided that adequate acceptance by the population of the respective region can be expected - even if no or only conditional or unstable democratic structures exist in the countries concerned.

Just as there was a historical window of opportunity for the realisation of the German reunification, there would also have been a historical window of opportunity for the further development of NATO into DENTO after the overcoming of the Southern European dictatorships and the joining of formerly totalitarian Eastern European democracies, as long as at the same time the leading power, the United States, was led by presidents who felt committed to democratic ideals. Unfortunately, this window of opportunity has passed unused due to the lack of correspondingly far-sighted politicians. On the one hand, this makes it more difficult to exert pressure on member states with increasing autocratic and dictatorial tendencies, such as Turkey, and on the other hand, it also impairs NATO's possibilities to distinguish itself even more clearly from its external opponents as a defensive alliance of democratic states.

In view of the global threat to democracy, these failures should not lead us, however, to consider the work on a treaty organisation of democratic states to be hopeless or to underestimate the urgency of this task. Preparations should begin now, so that a possible new favourable window of opportunity in the future does not pass by unused once again. With regard to the constitutional foundations, the DENTO can largely refer to the fundamental UN documents mentioned above. The UN is exemplary as far as the paperwork and the moral standards and the development of international law in its fundamental declarations are concerned, but unfortunately the implementation is completely inadequate.

In particular, the DENTO also needs its own Human Rights Council, which can document and disclose violations of human and civil rights and support and promote their prosecution by the International Criminal Court or, if necessary, by special tribunals for regionally committed serious crimes against humanity.

The UN's intervention policy to date, which has failed to a considerable extent, impressively illustrates that the value of security and assistance guarantees depends decisively on their credibility. And only credible guarantees of this kind will lead to the disappearance of warlike conflicts and to a gradual reduction of national armament efforts, and thus of the unproductive use of resources for armament in general, in confidence in a common security system. In this way, the member states of DENTO should also reduce their nuclear armament to such an extent that the common nuclear weapons potential is sufficient for secure protection against those nuclear weapons which are still in the hands of undemocratic states and "countries on the threshold to democracy". In the long term, only the quantity of nuclear weapons (or later also only the material necessary for their short-term construction) should be kept in stock which is necessary to protect against possible blackmail by dictators, terrorists or other criminals, taking into account whether and to what extent they could secretly acquire nuclear weapons.

Unfortunately, it is unavoidable in the near future that democratic states will strengthen their military structures and significantly increase their defence spending. The old Roman principle "Si vis pacem, para bellum" (if you want peace, prepare for war) has been carelessly neglected, as most recently demonstrated by the criminal Russian war of aggression against Ukraine. Without a decisive change of course, further avoidable losses of human life and prosperity on a large scale by aggressions of imperialist autocrats are to be feared, and not only in Europe.

The long-term goal should be that DENTO and the UN can coincide in a federal world union of democratic states. In realising this, we will have to find a middle way between a confederation of states that "only" fends off war, civil war and serious systematic violations of human rights, and a world republic that interferes in too many things and destroys freedom. (4)

In the transition phase to more effective and powerful federal structures of a world republic or world community of democratic states, we will still have to deal time and again with the problem of wars that have to be justified morally and under international law. The strong position of the sovereignty of the individual state under international law can no longer apply in the traditional form. In a world of nation-states, most of which were not genuine democracies and could not be clearly distinguished in terms of the respect for human and civil rights that prevailed in them, and which, moreover, were always inclined to attack their neighbours for reasons of power politics, an important step towards the pacification and juridification of international relations was to make the sovereignty of nation states the predominant protected right in international law. This historical period extends roughly from the end of the Thirty Years' War to the end of the First World War. But as early as 1625, Hugo Grotius, an international law scholar with a natural law orientation, sympathised with a humanitarian right of intervention (not yet a duty to intervene) under certain conditions. (5) And in any case, the founding of the League of Nations marks the beginning of the modern development towards the gradual relativisation of state sovereignty in international law. In a world that has in mind and can realise the goal of making the democratic constitutional state the only globally accepted form of state, a further development of international law that is appropriate to this goal is sensible and necessary.

No dictator, at least not one under whose rule a country is being economically destroyed or human rights violations are being committed on a large scale, should be able to hide behind the appeal to the sovereignty of his country. If the UN or regional associations of states prove incapable of putting an end to large-scale human rights violations (e.g. because various member states are acting on the basis of fearing precedent or following considerations of economic advantage or power politics), then every state or alliance of states that is willing and able to do so should have the right to take on this task and, if other means fail, to use armed force to do so. However, such military interventions should comply with the principles of the UN Charter in order to support with the desirable historical development towards a reliable international legal order.

There is a historical trend of international law towards a more positive assessment of humanitarian interventions. The fact that the principle of responsibility to protect was unanimously adopted in the final document of the so-called United Nations World Summit in 2005, which assigns responsibility for the protection of human rights not only to individual states, but also to the United Nations as a substitute in the event of their failure, is already a major step forward in international law that was achieved surprisingly quickly. Unfortunately, however, it also shows that such codification still means little if in concrete cases there are too many states that torpedo its practical implementation for the sake of their own interests or if there are no states that are actually willing to commit to its implementation (as for example in the Syrian civil war that has become a nightmare of many years). (6)

Therefore, the path of creating customary law with regard to humanitarian interventions, as lengthy and problematic as it may be, is likely to be more successful for the time being. In addition to the spirit of the UN Charter and the UN Declaration on Human Rights, one can now also refer to the "responsibility to protect" decision mentioned above. Every successful humanitarian intervention on this basis of international law, which is no longer so feeble, helps to prepare for a later, formally higher-ranking and then also increasingly effective codification at the level of the DENTO and someday also at the UN level. The fact that Russia and China are for the time being once again uncompromisingly invoking the principle of state sovereignty under international law to cover their crimes and their imperialist policies and therefore are consistently combating the responsibility to protect principle through their right of veto must not be accepted and must be counteracted in an imaginative way.

For the time being treaties between democratic states or the members of regional alliances and security organisations of states can create a more solid basis in international law for humanitarian interventions (for example, within the framework of the charter of a future DENTO). (Stromseth, Buchanan (6)) Another alternative is to excuse humanitarian violations of the right to state sovereignty merely on the grounds of emergency. However, this is a morally highly unsatisfactory legal fallback construction, which can hardly be the last word in the long run, because it makes far too little clear that a humanitarian intervention can not only be legally excusable but also morally imperative and should therefore also be legitimate. What is legitimate must not be considered illegal and only excusable in the long run.

Deciding when and to what extent military intervention is appropriate and wise remains an extremely difficult and responsible task of practical politics, even with a corresponding interpretation or further development of international law. The chances for a new order based on the rule of law must be weighed against the danger of anarchic chaos in the wake of an intervention. The extent of the necessary means and the willingness of one's own population to bear the resulting burdens, possibly also over a longer period of time, must be thoroughly and critically examined.

Furthermore, it must be considered to what extent an intervention hurts the national feeling of the affected people and whether the desire to be freed from an inhumane dictatorship actually promises to outweigh such a violation. One has to ask oneself whether the dictatorship in a country is really only supported by a small stratum of society around the ruler or rulers or whether it has managed to connect with the cultural, national and religious self-image of a considerable part of the population to such an extent that an intervention from outside to remove the dictatorship is not seen to a sufficient degree as a liberation and a chance for a new beginning, but is perceived as an occupation and threatens to meet with prolonged resistance in the form of widespread terrorism or guerrilla warfare. In such a case, the risks of intervention may seem incalculable and unreasonable, and it may be better to continue to watch the evil of the dictatorship from the outside in for a while longer, merely supporting the reform forces of the respective country from the outside as best as possible, as well as assisting refugees and the harassed population with humanitarian actions.

If economic interests also play a role in humanitarian interventions, this is not fundamentally reprehensible. What counts in the end is the humanitarian outcome. What is reprehensible, on the other hand, is when interventions are not carried out despite the fact that the effort required is foreseeable and manageable because the country in question is considered too insignificant economically, as happened, for example, with the genocide in Rwanda in 1994.

When calling for intervention, however, the following must also be taken into account: The democratic constitutional states of the West, in which respect for human and civil rights is largely guaranteed, are the result of a historical development that has required great sacrifices. It is an excessive demand on the population of these states if they are expected to make these sacrifices once again in the interest of other peoples in which these ideals are not yet aspired to by the majority or meet with considerable violent resistance. Democracies must defend their system of political order and at the same time they should support democratic movements around the world. The direct burden of the struggle against dictatorial regimes, however, must be borne largely by the peoples concerned themselves.

It is understandable and justified that the population in democracies accustomed to peace is very reluctant to military interventions. For this reason, the leading politicians in most democratic states will hardly decide on such interventions lightly. In individual cases, however, this can also result in too long, inappropriate hesitation, which costs the lives of a large number of people, whereas a swift, consistent intervention would only have cost a few lives (as in the Bosnian civil war).

If intervention forces acting in the name of democracy and human rights do not find the support of the majority of the population in a country in the foreseeable future, but are rather regarded as detested occupiers, it will only be possible to convince the population of the countries of origin of the sense of considerable sacrifices in the long term if the country in question actually poses a great danger that cannot be controlled in any other way. In the case of countries without a democratic tradition, where the totalitarian claims of religions or secular ideologies still find support among the population on a large scale, it can make much more sense to choose limited "police" operations instead of large-scale interventions, even if these must resemble war operations in individual cases.

Justifying interventions to combat terrorism should be viewed extremely critically. This objective may require individual military strikes but hardly justifies large-scale military action and rather requires police and intelligence measures and undermining the ideological justifications of terrorism and addressing its social and political causes.

If an intervention can be justified under international law, this does not mean that it is also wise and responsible under political considerations or with regard to the sum of its humanitarian consequences. "But truly unworldly people are those who think that good intentions and a strong arm are enough to put the world to rights." (Purdy[8])

The greater the geographical, but above all the cultural distance, the more sceptically we should judge interventions. Sad results, such as those of the UN missions in Somalia from 1992 to 1995, the invasion of Iraq in 2003 or the NATO airstrikes in Libya in 2011 teach us that rash interventions without a sustainable, long-term concept can in the end contradict the moral convictions that prompted or justified them. And this is unfortunately true even if, for once, they were actually undertaken not primarily by economic and political power interests, but predominantly out of understandable and honourable humanitarian outrage and humanitarian motives (which may well be assumed, at least for the UN's Somalia operations).

When it comes, for example, to conflicts in countries that were formerly under colonial rule, it is primarily troops and police units from countries that were not involved in the colonial system of rule and exploitation, albeit with the support of DENTO or the UN, that should ensure order there in view of this past. In extreme cases, however, the international community should not shirk its humanitarian obligations and should push aside such considerations. That an extensive, brutal genocide was possible in Rwanda in 1994 using the most primitive means under the eyes of the world public, although it could in all probability have been prevented with relatively little military effort, remains a disgrace for the international community that should not occur again.

The fact that a humanitarian intervention policy based, if necessary, on military force will, firstly, be overlaid by power interests and, secondly, will continue to be plagued for a long time by inconsistency determined by considerations of expediency based on the concrete circumstances of the individual case, should cause us to examine every such proposal with suspicion and care. On the other hand, this is not a good reason to reject humanitarian interventions in principle. To renounce intervention altogether, to always want to stay out of it, is a declaration of humanitarian bankruptcy. (8)

It makes perfect sense and is also politically feasible to set very specific peace-promoting goals in the respective historical situation. One such goal, for example, is that war and warlike conflicts are no longer accepted in Europe in the 21st century. With a clear objective, the corresponding consequences can then also be advocated and implemented - such as, in the concrete case of the Balkan, a joint military deployment of the European states with the necessary scope and duration required to achieve this objective or, in the case of the Russian war of aggression against Ukraine that began in 2022, such consistent military support for Ukraine that the criminal Russian attack against the European peace order is repelled and thwarted and a convincing deterrence of further similar aggressions is achieved.

The boundaries between humanitarian intervention and strategic support to protect democracy and human rights can be indistinct.

Unfortunately, we also have to accept that there are historical phases in which the democratic states can only support the spread of the democratic form of government to a very limited extent and in which they have to concentrate on defending their own democratic achievements internally and externally in order not to overstretch their resources.

380

"Beyond the nation state" – this development must not be narrowed down to a common security policy. If ever larger parts of humankind are to enjoy a high degree of prosperity and freedom, this will require the dismantling of small-scale economic barriers through the creation of large, federal, supranational economic and living communities along the lines of the European Union, which also aim at a convergence of social security systems and economic regulatory conditions, for example in the field of environmental protection.

In the specific case of Europe, the cultural and economic commonalities of many European states have now reached an extent which makes an even closer union in the form of a genuine common federal state, i.e. a further development of the European Union into the United States of Europe, at least in its core area, appear entirely appropriate and possible. The United States of Europe are not only appropriate and possible, but also desirable in order to secure both the economic well-being of Europe and the influence of European cultural traditions in the world for the future. However, these United States of Europe should have a strongly federal structure in which the regulatory competence is only shifted upwards for those issues where this is really necessary and advantageous for living together on a European level. Only with such a strongly federal structure will a European federal state be accepted. The feeling and the experience of being remote-controlled and patronised by a centralist and unrealistic Euro-bureaucracy is the greatest danger to European unification.

The nation states have the essential advantage that they can test and choose a variety of different legal regulations, for example in bioethical questions. We should retain this advantage even beyond the nation state: another good reason for a strongly developed federalism.

If one strives for a genuine European federal state, the creation of a common defence policy of the European Union is also necessary (for which the transfer of the treaty contents of the Western European Union to the EU makes sense). Consequently, the European Union as a whole and no longer the individual federal states would act as members of NATO or DENTO. Such goals must not be abandoned despite the current swing back to nationalism. The more substantial integration achievements succeed, the more difficult it will be to push through new backward movements in the direction of particularism.

At the global level, in addition to the security structures already discussed, the long-term goal must be a global economic area without protectionist trade barriers aiming at unilateral advantage and not justified by genuine qualitative criteria. In addition to fair trade conditions, international pressure is needed on commodity-exporting countries to invest the revenues generated in improving the infrastructure and the economic and social situation of the population at large instead of in the excessive enrichment of small ruling classes. At the same time, excessive demands for short-term compliance with demanding social and environmental standards must not be misused by the wealthy countries as a pretext for new protectionism. Transfer payments from the wealthy countries alone are not suitable (and in some cases even counterproductive) for stabilising state structures and achieving socio-economic progress. All in all, there is no promising alternative to globalisation, even if it brings with it problems of adaptation and dangers, such as ecologically unreasonable transport costs or the destruction of local economic structures with serious social consequences. These dangers can and must be counteracted by setting the right regulatory conditions at the national and international level and by a reasonable behaviour of consumers.

> "Experience from many countries shows that economic progress is the only guarantee for an improvement in living conditions. Human rights and the market economy are inextricably linked, even if they do not always develop at the same pace. ... The consistent commitment to both values throughout the world is the contribution we can make to peace and prosperity."[9]

> Otto Graf Lambsdorff

> "... political philosophy is realistically utopian when it extends what are ordinarily thought to be the limits of practicable political possibility and, in so doing, reconciles us to our political and social condition."[10]

> John Rawls

3.9. History

The splendour and misery of utopia

"The selectivity of perception and the forgetting of details lead to the fact that people only have fragmentary information about the past at their disposal. If they are supposed to remember a certain situation, the gaps between the remembered facts or data are closed by new (invented) intermediate pieces in such a way that the situation remains or becomes 'logical', free of contradictions and coherent in itself."[1]

Walter Schönwandt

"Historiography is always perspectival, and it is always a construction that incorporates a variety of factors. But it does not follow from this that historical accounts cannot be rationally evaluated." - "Some prove to be more appropriate and plausible than others in inner-scientific discourse. The relation to reality is thereby established by reference to the existing historical data, which any interpretation that is to be taken seriously must integrate."[2]

Jens Pape

"As a historical being, man always lives in the face of death and decay, and he is constantly determined to master them by extending memory into seemingly infinite pasts and by looking forward to the future. Ultimately, the will to live into the future and to shed light on the future is thus one with the will to make the past surveyable."[3]

Theodor Schieder (1)

»It almost looks as if historicists were trying to compensate themselves for the loss of an unchanging world by clinging to the faith that change can be foreseen because it is ruled by an unchanging law.«[4]

Karl R. Popper

"The same giving of meaning with hindsight as is consolingly practised regarding the accidental changes of power in history also serves to make the disparity of lucky chances, courses of life and destinies comprehensible and acceptable." "A legitimate distribution and order of destiny, lot, fortune, happiness and pleasure is not a given but a task of man."[5]

Theodor Lessing

"By stating as a façon de parler that history teaches us to know from tales who we and others are, it is eo ipso clear that such 'teaching' and such knowledge have not at all a direct normative character. Notwithstanding this, identity-relevant historical assessments can have considerable practical consequences under certain conditions."[6]

Hermann Lübbe

"Historical studies should help us to better understand phenomena in our present through knowledge of their genesis. It should help us to orientate ourselves in the present and the future by showing us how all cultural phenomena can be changed, by pointing out alternative possibilities for the realisation of human existence and, finally, by providing us with exemplary insights into political, social or economic interrelationships. Furthermore, historical studies should enable us to rationally criticise the instrumentalisation of history for political or economic purposes. In this function, they serve the critique of ideology and the debunking of historical myths. "[7]

Jens Pape

"Thus it could happen that an old relation once again comes into force: the greater the experience, the more cautious one is, but also the more open the expectation."[8]

Reinhart Koselleck

"While unlimited foresight to base our judgement on is impossible, we face the necessity to take steering action."[9]

Manfred Eigen

A critical stance towards history begins with leaving behind illusory notions about the degree of objectivity that our historical insights and assessments can reach, even with we make an honest effort.

Furthermore, in the field of philosophy of history too, we have to deal with the urge of humans to extend the boundaries of their knowledge by faith beyond the degree of those fundamental decisions of faith necessary for any scientific activity, until they believe to recognise an order that allows for moral criteria in some way, thus providing a feeling of comfort or at least a feeling of superior insight into the course of the world. This urge is expressed in the doctrines of divine providence, but also in all the teachings of a secular faith that claim that the course of world history is predetermined and inevitable. The more presumptuous versions of such doctrines also claim that humans can reliably predict the course of history on the basis of recognisable laws that it follows. If one ascribes a necessity to history, then the following consequence described by Koselleck is not inevitable, but nevertheless plausible: submitting oneself to history, "to defer to it in order to promote a supposed necessity. This assumed necessity injects meaning into history that disenfranchises human agents."[10]

If there were a preordained or inevitable meaning of history arising from its course, assessing this would not mean disenfranchisement but knowledge. Under the presupposition of unwillingness to believe, however, there are no good reasons for such an assumption.

But this is not to say that it is impossible to work out certain tendencies and long-term trends of historical development with some plausibility and to adequately understand and explain essential characteristics of individual epochs or causal connections of certain historical developments by observing and analysing history.

In addition, "constants", typical constellations, modes of behaviour and courses of events found in examples from the past may allow us to consider certain developments more likely than others when similar situations arise in the future (although a very critical view is always advisable with regard to a postulated similarity of historical situations). (2)

Since historical situations can only be compared to a very limited extent and especially the behaviour of "the human factor" can only be foreseen very unreliably, all attempts to predict the course of historical events in a similar way as a specific course of events in extrahuman nature are not promising. Furthermore, there is a high degree of unpredictability in natural history as well, since we are not sufficiently able to survey the complexity of the factors at work and their temporal coincidence.

In addition, we humans like to forget unpleasant things and do not like to accept historical lessons if they contradict our wishful thinking. Historical situations hide their similarities behind different appearances, which can be emphasised all the more strongly the less one wants to perceive the similarities.

Despite all these difficulties, however, we should not give up our aspiration to want to learn from history. Unfortunately, the memory of historical failures cannot exclude the repetition of similar undesirable developments, as can be seen, for example, in the desire for authoritarian forms of government or socialist forms of economy, which is reawakened again and again in different variations. Nevertheless, recollection can reduce the risk of similar things happening again or at least improve the chances that undesirable developments will not take on the same proportions again.

For the unwilling to believe, neither the course of history can be reliably foreseen, nor can a meaning or a goal be recognised in it. (3) But those unwilling to believe can give history meaning and purpose following their convictions and can try to influence it accordingly – within the scope of their personal possibilities. For me, the meaning and goal of history is to bring about a world more in keeping with the moral attitudes and values advocated in this book than the present one. In the individual realm, this means in particular that people increasingly seek to justify their moral attitudes and values, and the weighings between them, through rational deliberation. In the social sphere, it is about a better realisation of human and civil rights for an ever larger part of humankind. At least in those parts of the world that are shaped by the concepts of government that we owe primarily to the European Enlightenment, there is historical progress in this respect. This progress is a fact, but not a necessity, and it is an achievement that is always endangered and to be defended anew.

Hope is a sentiment neither unfamiliar to those unwilling to believe nor neglected by them. However, in contrast to religions and secular religions, it is not of central importance for the philosophy of life of those unwilling to believe, no matter how much such a "lack" may hinder the spread of this philosophy of life - at least for the time being. The unwilling to believe is promised neither a this-worldly nor an other-worldly paradise. He can only hope (and fight) that the good sides of us humans will gain the upper hand.

Various influential thinkers of the 19th century highlighted the dangers of an orientation towards an otherworldly paradise. The events of the 20th century have taught us how disastrous the absolutisation of this-worldly "paradise" dreams can be. Nowadays, the idea is emphasised that present people should not live at the expense of future generations. It is rightly demanded that present people should take into account the life prospects of their descendants and also of non-human life on earth, and that they should accept restrictions for this purpose. The other side of the coin, however, is - and this is to be held against the totalitarian utopias of secular substitute religions (including radical ecologism) - that the desired happiness of future people does not justify sacrificing the happiness or even the lives of present people. The (abstract) love of future people is not to be trusted if it can be reconciled with (concrete) hatred of present people.

A positive utopia is made difficult above all by the excessive growth of human population. The dream of life chances for all people that come close to those that existed in earlier societies only for a thin upper class can hardly be realised already with a population density like in Germany, even with an optimal organisation of society. "For a *prosperous* civilization even the Western population density is already well beyond its optimum. This was not obvious so long as only a very small fraction of the population could travel, but now millions can afford it, and it is pitiful to behold the masses which are ushered as fast as possible through the Piazza San Marco or the Louvre, or who try to enjoy themselves in the seaside places, in rows upon rows of deck chairs, with hardly a glimpse of the sea." "The modern suburb is certainly better than worker's slums, but a population housed in the modern version of stately homes, in large country houses with ample grounds, is something to fire the imagination." (Gabor[11]) Dennis Gabor made this assessment in 1963, when the world population was 3.2 billion. If we were to follow his thinking, then the long-term global population target would be perhaps in the region of 2.5 billion people, or about a quarter of what is currently expected to be the peak before a gradual population decline is likely to occur.

Yet the situation in the economically underdeveloped countries of the world is incomparably worse, and there it is a matter of bare survival rather than a more or less individual, diverse and culturally rich life.

In many places, people are crowding excessively, displacing and driving to extinction other living beings and overusing nature. Defending an individualistic way and concept of life against an "ant existence" with all its limitations enforced by overpopulation, is becoming an increasingly serious problem, morally and practically. The degree of solidarity that can and should be expected from the rich and wealthy I see in the effort to create fair conditions for economic activity and exchange as well as in a reasonable degree of self-restraint and in the use of the resources thus released for aid and development assistance, at least to the extent that the elementary needs of life of all people can be satisfied and the vicious circle of underdevelopment and population growth can be broken.

On the other hand, equalising all people at the same low level, as sometimes demanded by radical moralists, would be a nightmare. This would one-sidedly overemphasise the value of "equality" and thereby sacrifice many other values, but fortunately it is also quite unrealistic. What is realistic for the future unfortunately, are considerable struggles over distribution, which can also take on violent forms. Here it is necessary to urge voluntary sharing and equalisation, above all through better equality of opportunities. We have to give more attention to other people's basic needs and to strive for improvement patiently, without losing sight - however unrealistic and distant it may seem temporarily - of the long-term goal of better, individualistically shaped living conditions and a culturally superior life for the individual in a world with a smaller number of people.

Even if we manage to shape the future more sensibly than the history of humankind so far, we will still have to bear the heavy burden of past undesirable developments for a long time to come.

Historiography should analyse and criticise myths, stereotypes and discriminations and not provide the material to facilitate their formation and instrumentalisation in political life. In doing so, historians should not only feel obliged to the project of enlightenment in describing and analysing the past as accurately as possible, but should have an independent critical ambition that goes beyond this and is directed towards the conflicts of the respective present: "We must resist the *formation* of national, ethnic and other myths, as they are being formed. It will not make us popular." (Hobsbawn[12]) This not only counters the ideological-historicist instrumentalisation of history, but at the same time formulates a clear opposition to narrative, truth-indifferentist conceptions of history, such as those that with their feuilletonistic, seemingly emancipatory, intellectual-superiority pretending appeal found a completely inappropriate attention and spread especially during postmodernism. (4)

An important prerequisite for a good future lies in a differentiated historical thinking that knows and respects origins and traditions, carries forward the elements worth preserving and those that are rewarding for the future, and at the same time resolutely stands up for freedom and democracy. We should neither glorify nor condemn the past, regard the present as a task and an opportunity, preserve hope for the future and work for it without indulging in airy dreams, but also without resigning ourselves lightly.

"History teaches us about the uncertain limits of our scope of power."

"History demonstrates to us that our plans lack resistance to intervention by chance."[13]

Hermann Lübbe

"One must never stop imagining the world as it would be most reasonable."[14]

Friedrich Dürrenmatt

3.10. Aesthetics

There can be rational disputes in matters of taste

>»If there are no standards for works of art and hence none for criticism (in the sense in which there are standards of measurement), there are nevertheless criteria in judgement, so that criticism does not fall in the field of mere impressionism.«[1]

John Dewey

>»But in reality the difficulty of finding, even in particulars, the standard of taste, is not so great as is represented.«[2]

David Hume

Aesthetics has a descriptive and a normative aspect. This should always be kept in mind, even if these two aspects are not treated strictly one after the other in the following, but rather joined together again and again.

The heretical question of whether a normative aesthetics is needed at all is answered in a clearly positive way by the life practice of aesthetically interested people.

Aesthetics needs a grip on reality. A mere theory of art is not a sufficient aesthetics. In descriptive aesthetics, this grip on reality comes not only from cultural history, but also to a considerable extent from evolutionary approaches of explanation. For normative aesthetics, it is not only the state of art history and philosophical reflection on aesthetics that is important but also people's everyday aesthetics.

On the one hand, Nietzsche is right when he writes that man believes that the world itself is filled with beauty and forgets that it is he who has created it.[3] On the other hand, the world is the cause of the existence of the human sense of beauty.

The fact that humans with their entire perceptual apparatus and their brains that process, structure, interpret and judge these perceptions are evolutionary beings has great significance for aesthetics too. The ability to perceive colours and patterns has already brought evolutionary advantages to animals. These abilities have therefore developed more and more in the evolutionary process and influenced it considerably. This created the prerequisites for the development and significance of aesthetic perception in humans. It is a concomitant and part of their evolutionary characteristics and accomplishments, which then also make a culture possible, which in turn shapes the aesthetic sensibility and aesthetic judgements. The ability of human beings to recognise and create structure is closely connected with their aesthetic sensibility and this in turn with their emotional and communicative differentiation and responsiveness and the development of their social structures in general. However, the aesthetic sensibility of human beings is not a side effect of the evolutionary process in the sense of a mere extra or luxury product. It reinforces the development of emotional, social and cultural competence and thus contributes to the historical success of humans.

Aesthetic sense is an aspect of the human ability to give structure to the world, to order it according to idealising criteria and thereby to make first of all one's own perception more successful, but later also to make and communicate conscious, theoretical calculations and generalisations with the help of the most varied (initially pictorial, then increasingly abstract) symbolic codes. Important idealisations with the help of which we can better understand and handle our environment are perceptual criteria, mental and linguistic general terms and finally increasingly detached structural scientific abstractions, such as proportions, symmetry and ideal geometric bodies, which we can analyse mathematically and create in approximation in the model. Some structures of order also serve directly as signals in a verifiable way, such as the symmetrical physique of living beings as an indication of health and presumably good reproductive success.

However, the fact that our structural thinking is so successful presupposes that the world actually has a certain degree of order. This may appear to some as an indication of a divine hand. The simpler, agnostic-atheistic or naturalistic version of this is that a certain degree of order in the world is a prerequisite for its, and thus also for our existence, and that we are not able to find any further "explanation" for this order which would be more than wild speculation.

The aesthetic sense is also an aspect of the human ability to form differentiated preferential tendencies and interests that go beyond the mere satisfaction of basic needs. Aesthetic sensation simulates and opens up alternatives and thus contributes to human adaptability and flexibility. This is also how the intertwined connection between aesthetics and utility can be understood. The seemingly abstruse can lead to the rational of the future.

The scientific analysis of aesthetic perception means, on a fundamental level, neurobiological research into the processes that take place in the brain. In recent decades, thanks to new technical research methods, it has become possible to obtain the first detailed information about the way in which aesthetically relevant perceptions are processed in the brain, and to show, for example, that when abstract images are viewed, there is a different activation of certain functional structures in the brain than when representational images are viewed. This research is still in the early stages. We already know a lot about the perception of colours, basic pictorial structural elements or faces, but very little about integrative processes of aesthetic perception, by which an emotional evaluation and a connection to the individual biography and to the social, cultural and historical context is established. (1)

An essential part of descriptive aesthetics is the description of the natural, evolutionary developed dispositions of our aesthetic perception and sensation. (2)

Descriptive aesthetics shows us different evaluation criteria for different areas of perception. There is a large body of work on evolutionarily explicable beauty criteria in mate choice, their connection with indications of good reproductive success and sexual attraction based on this. (3) On the other hand, these beauty criteria are to a considerable extent influenced by cultural and contemporary preferences and fashions. Both together can take a back seat to individual reasons for decision-making, such as those that make us find a valued or beloved person beautiful because of his or her nature and certain personal characteristics, even if he or she does not or does no longer meet the prevailing beauty criteria (for example, due to age-related changes). But also the strong need for security and comfort on the one hand and the need for differentiation, experimentation and provocation on the other hand (especially in youth) have a considerable influence on aesthetic perception. The most diverse social signals are reinforced by aesthetic elements, both in everyday life and in festive enhancement. Aesthetic preferences, signs and symbols serve social identification, the experience and representation of group membership and rankings as well as territorial demarcation.

If, due to the complexity of the influencing factors that determine our aesthetic sense, we can only ever state probabilities for alternative individual decisions in this area, this nevertheless has considerable significance as soon as we move far enough away from random probability and at least achieve useful statistical statements (one only has to think of some economic decisions for which, for example, assumptions about a prevailing sensation of beauty play a major role).

The aesthetic sense enables people to make greater use of their imagination to gain knowledge. It is at the same time one of the regulating elements in the boundlessness of theoretical approaches. However, the influence of aesthetic motives on the process of cognition can also promote misconceptions, wishful thinking and fantasies and thus lead us astray. In other words, the beautiful does not have to be true, the aesthetically unattractive or ugly does not have to be false. Aesthetic evaluations are no more a sufficient criterion of truth than they are a sufficient moral criterion. Addressing the aesthetic sense can make creations of meaning more successful, but it does not privilege them in a normative sense.

Descriptive aesthetics must not be narrowed biologically despite all justified efforts to pay attention to neglected aspects of evolutionary biology. The evolutionary developments in human history that later made art possible lie far in the past, so that all assumptions that would attribute significance to human artistic activity in the history of evolution are extremely questionable. The account and analysis of the cultural shaping and development of aesthetic sense and artistic expression is more fruitful and more interesting in the long run because of its greater differentiation and more pronounced historicity and openness. Individual predispositions and biographical factors further complicate the analysis.

Descriptive aesthetics does not only consist of cultural history, but also to a considerable extent of statistics, in that it describes a frequency distribution of aesthetic criteria or more or less conscious tendencies towards certain preferences and also individually different degrees of aesthetic sensibility, whereby this description applies in some respects across time and cultures, but in other respects only to a specific historical situation.

In the historical sequence (4) the oscillation between symbolism and naturalism is particularly striking. Not only among "primitive" peoples, but even today religious art serves magical purposes to a certain extent. Even as more and more differentiated aesthetic criteria come to play a role, art continues to fulfil a wide variety of other purposes at the same time. For example, it serves to convey religious content (especially to the illiterate), is important in religious cult or serves, more generally, to exert ideological and political influence, to legitimise claims to power, to impress the subjects or, in democracy, the fellow citizens and citizens of a state, or serves the self-expression (or self-glorification) of the purchasers, patrons and creators (and, not to be forgotten, the livelihood of the latter). Art serves in many ways the individual and socio-cultural memory, the representation, symbolisation and influencing of human feelings, systems of interpretation and belief, institutions and relationships. Sometimes it also or even primarily serves social criticism.

Even in its beginnings, in the Stone Age cave paintings, art proves to be a complex phenomenon that can neither be adequately explained by hunting magic nor by personal needs for beauty, but rather fulfilled differentiated social functions for individuals and groups within the framework of shamanistic cults. (5)

In ancient Egyptian culture, we are confronted with a symbolising art that, in accordance with religious viewpoints, is oriented towards ritual gestures and a representation of the perceived world that is as complete and vivid as possible but not primarily realistic.

Insofar as art has realistic elements, it does so first for the sake of a magical, then a religious function.

It was only much later, in classical antiquity in Greece, that artists were able to detach themselves to a considerable extent from a mastering of the world according to religiously prescribed criteria and, despite the continuing symbolic value of the works of art, also direct their attention and ambition to depicting the world as realistically as possible for the sake of this-worldly ideals of knowledge, depiction and beauty. This has been preserved in many works of sculpture, which represent the realistic, albeit initially still ideal-typical moment with its physical activity (in a multitude of movement variations) and the intentions and emotional states expressed in it. Later, Hellenistic art already reached the individual portrait and, in the painting influenced by it, as it has been preserved for us, for example, in Pompeii and the neighbouring cities, depicts the perceptible world in an unrestricted variety of aspects (only the exact knowledge of the laws of perspective is still missing). Roman art intensifies realism, whether in portraiture or in the depiction of war.

The craftsmanship associated with the artistic achievements of classical antiquity could, however, also have been developed by the ancient Egyptian masters during the long period of the flowering of their culture, if they had not been prevented from doing so by their religious presuppositions and the interests of depiction following from them, which caused them to apply, for example, the composite pose or twisted perspective and the "perspective of importance", which depicts figures in a size corresponding to their religious, iconographic and social significance.

Later, over long periods of Christian art, and much later, in modernity, artistic symbolic languages develop again, some of which are not very interested in a representation of an external world - be it by completeness, idealisation or realism (although they still want to react to or influence this world). In a way, this is a return to pre-classical beginnings. Early Christian art has similarity to the ancient Egyptian art in its concentration on the religiously essential and in the standardisation of artistic means, but it integrates some of the achievements in craftsmanship and creative motifs of classical antiquity. In medieval art, the depiction of - especially religious - events, feelings and attitudes becomes a motif that has priority over realistic depiction and is new in this form, allowing - right down to the colouring - a detachment from the imitation of nature and thus completely new possibilities of composition. The "perspective of importance", which now sometimes already integrates an artist's subjective elements of significance, creates distance to realism here again. Art now also has the important function of pictorial religious instruction for illiterates.

Since the Renaissance, and ultimately up to Impressionism, Expressionism and Surrealism, the artistic representation of various aspects of the world has been perfected and differentiated in ever new ways, with increasing emphasis on subjective experience, including dream worlds. This includes the creation of illusions, the often surprising resolution of which is not necessarily made easy to the viewer.

With the transition to abstraction in modernism an effort appeared on the scene to create something aesthetically valuable and artistically significant that can claim an intrinsic value without reference to tradition, similar to the beauty of nature. Later, Pop Art followed with the artistic transformation of everyday objects to the point of simply charging them with meaning through the way they are presented ("readymades") and the creation of a new context of interpretation. The significance of aesthetical beauty and of craftsmanship as a characteristic of art is fading away, a development that continues in action and performance art. (6)

Uniformity is now lacking, both with regard to formal aspects and certainly with regard to an all-embracing, generally binding conceptual or ideological basis. Experiment, provocation, crisis as a permanent state, or at least a relatively short-term change, the accelerated succession of novelties - this may be the notions for sketching something like a common denominator of modern art in the best way. But one can also express this in a much more positive way: The artistic situation of the present also means freedom, allows for an interesting variety of forms and means of expression, makes it possible to keep finding new aspects and to convey meaning in ever new ways without still being under the pressure of a certain style or predominant expectations in a way comparable to earlier epochs.

As far as normative aesthetics is concerned: "In matters of taste, there can be no disputes" - as hackneyed as this saying is, it is not bad as a provocation for philosophers. It concerns them how and to what extent and for what purpose taste can be argued about and should be argued about.

There are undoubtedly many aesthetic questions where philosophical reflection does not help much. What philosophical contribution could be made to the question of whether a Romanesque, Gothic or Baroque church is more beautiful or at least aesthetically more meaningful, or whether a swan is more beautiful than a spider, and similar questions. Such aesthetic decisions between things of indisputably individual character and value are - as far as they are not completely dispensable, which in my opinion is often the case - in fact purely questions of taste and valuation that are bound to time and personality. For example, the fact that the best Baroque churches clearly surpass the best Gothic churches in the complexity of their ground plan, their handling of space and their technical and artistic means can be proven rationally in detail. However, this in no way implies a certain ranking in the aesthetic evaluation. We can trace the historical development, explain and understand the thinking and feeling that led to a certain style, and we can sympathise with it to varying degrees - an aesthetic criterion hardly results from this.

Many other aesthetic questions, however, and especially those that are important for decision-making, can be discussed on the basis of rationally comprehensible criteria, even if these must first be accepted through subjective decisions. There are no objective aesthetic criteria, just as there are no objective principles of morality. However, it is possible and sensible to analyse one's own aesthetic perception and the aesthetic perception of one's fellow human beings and not only to examine its evolutionary and cultural roots, but also to question its justification. Through this criteria can be found that are subjective and provisional, but nevertheless rationally discussable and that can serve aesthetic orientation. These criteria can help in the majority of cases, but none of them applies without exception, and counter-examples for which they do not apply can be found for each of them. Although aesthetic criteria are not universally valid and binding, they can be interesting and useful for oneself and for a larger circle of other people. Rationally comprehensible and discussible aesthetic criteria demarcate unavoidable subjectivity from mere arbitrariness. Aesthetic criteria and judgements are essentially shaped by the philosophy of life of the respective person. However, they can transcend religious and ideological boundaries and build bridges.

Positive aesthetic criteria can be worked out to a considerable extent by a devious route via negative questions: "What is boring, tasteless, ugly, aesthetically unsatisfactory?"

The following negative criteria seem to me to carry relatively far (try to find your own examples for them): Boring, tasteless, ugly, but in any case aesthetically unsatisfactory are

- Lack of uniformity, arbitrary compositions without comprehensible principles of form and design,
- schematic and seamless pursuit of principles of design at the expense of expression,
- desperate attempt at originality and narcissism on the part of the producers,
- reduced or lost functionality,
- functionality under obvious indifference to aesthetic impression,
- the insincere, the mimicry, the surrogate - or in short (a beautiful achievement of the German language): kitsch,
- historicising traditionalism with political intent,
- the repetition of the once aesthetically significant to the point of weariness,
- the suppression of diversity and individuality (without substituting a creative idea for them that could possibly justify such suppression, at least from an aesthetic point of view),
- uprooted poverty that is perceived as suffering and imposed restriction, misery.

(The last two points describe not only violations of aesthetic criteria but often also depressing and outrageous violations of human and civil rights).

In the following I give some examples of the concrete application of these criteria, examples that I see myself confronted with (you will, depending on your personal environment, think of enough others - some of them certainly more essential). Often several negative criteria combine or overlap.

Examples of a lack of uniformity are provided by large parts of post-modern architecture, namely when they resort to the arbitrary decorative accumulation of quotations instead of building convincing bridges between styles and cultures.

Much more perceptible on a broad scale are the small, in themselves insignificant violations of lack of uniformity that a large number of fellow citizens afford themselves. Architectural styles from completely different landscapes, cultural and building traditions are imported and mixed together in a crippled way, or stylistically completely incoherent elements are added to existing residential buildings, be they rustic or modern foreign bodies, for example in the form of balconies or conservatories. On the one hand, one tries to find ostensible solidity, security, comfort or "cosiness" in an indiscriminate eclecticism or in a bygone, pseudo-ancestral culture that never actually existed as such or, on the other hand, to realise functional needs without taking aesthetic considerations into account. As far as one encounters a fairly uniform "rustic" style, from the exterior design of the houses to the furnishings, this style, even if it radiates a relatively harmless complaisance, nevertheless belongs to a considerable extent to the category of "the insincere, mimicry and surrogate" to be discussed below - somewhere between farmhouse parlour and aristocratic country house. If one is looking for a more benevolent expression, one can also speak of careless, naïve cosiness. (Incidentally, the misguided need for security and comfort that underlies all this - in addition to a considerable degree of unimaginativeness or, at any rate, circumscribed mental laziness - is also one of the most important guarantees of the existence of conventional religions.) You can already see that the aesthetic "sins" mix where thoughtlessness reigns.

The buildings of some postmodern (star) architects also reveal more vain self-reflection than respect for the fulfilment of a set task and the users' needs and possibilities of development. The decorative arbitrary, also in the version of being conspicuous or provocative at all costs, is one of the most common aesthetic sins of our time. In "postmodern" architecture, this sin is often the last vestige of "uniformity".

Today, unfortunately, obsessive striving for originality and vain self-reflection on the part of the producers can often be found in theatre directors who deform plays from the traditional stage repertoire to a point beyond recognition and use them as mere associative stimuli for their own conglomerate without any respect for the historical situation and the intentions of the authors and their verbal art.

In the meantime, however, it has become clear that the term "postmodern" has conveyed an overestimation of itself. Thus, many good examples of modern architecture continue to emerge that do not need arbitrary citations to show individuality. And at least the decorative-arbitrary architecture that has spread even to the backcountry is often less ugly than the worse, aesthetically often completely undemanding products of the preceding, thoughtlessly or reductively functionally oriented period, a phase that - despite its almost exclusive orientation towards the functional - was often not even able to take into account in a differentiated way the functions that a building should fulfil, misled by the idea of a definitive predictability and determination of the users' needs.

Unfortunately, the reductive functionalism of modernism does not only have the merit of having reduced and concentrated the language of form to the simple and essential. It has often slipped into schematic boredom and coldness and has also ruthlessly ignored traditional experience, reduced the functional needs of the user to the imagination of the planner and thus confined and patronised the user to an unpleasant extent (which is then repeated - with the poorer justification of mere attention-seeking originality - in the narcissism of some postmodern architects and star architects). Regrettably, the building sins of the fifties, sixties and seventies of the 20th century are already inherent in classical modernist architecture like the Bauhaus style. This should not be glossed over, despite all the enthusiasm for the innovative power of the Bauhaus formal language and for the comprehensive concept of design of this movement and the liberation it achieved.

In particular, the uncompromisingly consistent extension of Bauhaus principles to the interior has something dictatorial about it and, above all, is almost completely ahistorical. The comprehensible desire of people to collect and accumulate, to insert themselves into a cultural tradition and to demonstrate their origins and to live with them is hardly given any room here. The valuable idea of setting creative principles against arbitrariness becomes a shackle in its extreme enforcement and creates sterility. Incidentally, even classical modernity can become a convention once it has proclaimed its new and liberating message. Then the lack of reference of such buildings to the individuality of the landscape, the respective culture and the inhabitants or users becomes a weakness. They deny that measure of security and cosiness that we can find in a cultural continuity beyond all misguided traditionalism, promote anonymity and isolation and can - especially when applied to large buildings (whether in housing or institutional buildings such as schools or universities) - hinder the development of a desirable measure of communication and sense of community. (7)

Other examples of a lack of functionality are the fashion of round silhouettes in car design that has broken out in recent years and that is not sufficiently justified by aerodynamic aspects, but also various products by furniture designers and architects who sacrifice the interests of the user to a desperate striving for originality.

Examples of functionality where a prevailing indifference to the aesthetic impression leaps to the eye (which then often amounts to a reduced, insufficiently thought through functionality) are offered by the reconstruction architecture and urban planning of the post-war years, but also by many architectural and urban planning products up to the seventies of the 20th century. To stay with examples from architecture, one must also mention those numerous single-family houses that show that the position of their window openings was determined only by the interior layout, without any interest in the proportions or the design of the façade.

A new, epidemic variant of functionality with prevailing indifference to the aesthetic impression is the often unimaginative energy-saving architecture characterised by the unbroken monotony of cubes and cuboids, shying away from opening and connecting the buildings to the surroundings, avoiding any reference to local building traditions and no longer being able to use building materials in an interesting and differentiated way.

Mimicry exists as the aping of other times, other styles, other social classes, other countries, personal idols. Mimicry can take the form of inferior copying or (often exaggerated and deforming) imitation, but it can also take place by using high-quality details, for example when people decorate their own living space almost exclusively with originals of a past time, another culture or different past times and foreign cultures. Goethe's somewhat ruthless condemnation gets to the heart of the matter: "It is a sort of masquerade, which can, in the long run, do no good in any respect, but must, on the contrary, have an unfavourable influence on the man who adopts it. Such a fashion is in contradiction to the age in which we live, and will only confirm the empty and hollow way of thinking and feeling in which it originates."[4]

The aesthetic quotation, the selective representation of the culturally foreign or historical within the framework of a self-confident culture of one's own, is to be distinguished from mimicry. Such quotations are justified and have their own aesthetic appeal if there is a connection to the motivation and statement of the respective craft or artistic product and a more than arbitrary reference to the current design project can be recognised. Otherwise they lead, especially in their accumulation, to a slide into the decorative arbitrary, a special form of mimicry, which at the same time violates the already mentioned principle of uniformity. The more self-confident a culture is, the more creative power it has, the more quotations it may allow itself (and then it does not overdo it anyway).

Most readers will be able to think of enough examples of the insincere, mimicry, surrogate, kitsch. "Socialist realism", for example, has provided us with plenty of examples of the insincere (at least this applies to most of its products after an idealistic initial phase), and the visual arts in the service of National Socialism no less so. The hollow aesthetics of the usurpers of power are often not only insincere but they also love the historicising surrogate: from Ceausescu's monster palace to the monstrous replica of St. Peter's Basilica in poverty-stricken Ivory Coast to the pompous palatial terminal station of the Tibet railway in Lhasa. The totalitarian and autocratic rulers are often clumsy and cannot hide their primitiveness and backwardness when they try to create their own aesthetics. The most insidious of all their efforts is the frivolous appeal of elaborately and skilfully staged mass events. Apart from that, however, dictators usually fare better and can more easily feign respectability when they adorn themselves with "borrowed", actually historical aesthetics created by others (when, for example, the mass murderer Putin stages himself in the Kremlin like a Tsar).

A few more harmless examples on the subject of the insincere, of mimicry, surrogate, kitsch: city dwellers, who no longer have anything to do with rural life and are often hardly aware of its historical realities, are enthusiastic about sterile folk music, idealised and idealising in terms of technique and motifs. Mimicry and surrogate also meet in the production of period furniture or in all the "gold and silver" decorations of fashionable new hotel buildings and a considerable part of private home furnishings that are reminiscent of bygone palace decorations.

Not to be confused with the surrogate are illusionary means used for the purpose of entertainment or in the service of a creative design, as in illusionary painting or scenery in the theatre.

Examples of the suppression of diversity and individuality (without a creative concept that could promise at least partial aesthetic compensation) are provided by the decline of the most diverse cultural areas under the socialist regimes (one only has to think of the neglect of buildings and the culture of building or also of culinary culture).

Uprooted poverty and misery could be found in the industrialised countries most pronouncedly in the workers' and poor quarters of the 19th century, and today they can be seen even worse and in larger dimensions in the slums of the developing countries. In a materially less pronounced, but mentally and culturally applicable sense, they can also be found in the social hotspots, especially in big cities, of rich industrial nations. The fact that uprooted poverty and misery are also an aesthetic negative criterion seems insignificant, however, when one considers the moral affront they represent for violating other values.

With all these aesthetic negative criteria, the dependence of the aesthetic impression on the point of view must be emphasised. For example, with sufficiently detailed and individualised or sufficiently distanced, personally unaffected observation, there is still much beauty to be found even in poverty and misery.

However, material confinement and scarcity, even if it is not yet actual poverty, makes the consideration of aesthetic criteria and the fulfilment of aesthetic demands (even if only in the form of artisanal or industrial product quality) much more difficult. It is better to respond to insurmountable material meagreness with forced asceticism than by lowering one's standards of quality. But this is neither consistently practicable, nor is it pleasing.

Compared to the negative aesthetic criteria mentioned above, meaningful positive criteria remain relatively blurred (on the other hand, as the history of human culture and art shows, it is possible - at least at some distance in time - to reach an astonishing degree of agreement, or at least a prevailing opinion, as to whether and in what order they are fulfilled). (8) Some such positive criteria already result indirectly from the negative criteria already mentioned. Traditional positive criteria, which originate from a beauty-oriented aesthetics, still carry a certain weight and are by no means obsolete - especially in everyday aesthetics: shapeliness, balance, harmony, regularity, rhythm, symmetry and exciting violations thereof, variety from a (possibly quite simple) common structural principle, complexity, subtleness, differentiation, perfection, mastery. To the extent that one approaches this and a high level (at least achieved by some) becomes usual and a matter of course, the simple, the "primitive", the "original" and new productions inspired by this often regain aesthetic interest and appreciation and new inspiration is drawn from reduction. Neither technical perfection nor beauty can be equated with artistic value. They can go hand in hand, but they do not have to. Not only criteria for beauty are positive aesthetic criteria.

This is also shown by the following essential positive aesthetic criteria or quality criteria for art: consideration of a given frame of reference and exciting violations of it, originality, enabling a new perspective, provocation, holding up a mirror to us, breaking entrenched structures of perception, sensation and thought, expanding our imagination, confronting us in a contemplative way with things that are not directly purposeful, transcending the immediate necessities of existence. This is where artistic and scientific innovation meet.

Further substantial aesthetic criteria are: emotional and conceptual adequacy and significance and also philosophical meaningfulness and giving of meaning (especially in addressing fundamental and liminal experiences as well as formative historical experiences of human beings or in the symbolisation of a certain attitude towards life).

By fulfilling these criteria, ugliness can also become aesthetically productive. In addition, ugliness (or even the aesthetically indifferent, the insignificant) can acquire aesthetic appeal through artistic transformation, for example through the manner and circumstances of presentation, by gaining an unusual perspective, by ironising and exaggerating or by working out or creating entirely new structures. This can be achieved, for example, by approaching or distancing, by singling out sections, by concentrating on details or blurring details, or by using new techniques and technical aids, by creating historical references and allusions, sometimes simply by taking objects or the viewer out of their usual everyday contexts. The way of representation or presentation alone can sometimes elevate the trivial to the status of the exemplary and characteristic. Rosenkranz, who as early as 1853 made the ugly an unavoidable object of aesthetics, even if still fixated on the contrast to an idealistic-absolute beauty that was assumed to be self-evident, did not for nothing give a lot of space to the bridging function of the comic and here especially to the discussion of caricature.[5]

The representation of the trivial, the ugly or even the terrible need not itself be ugly or trivial. Paradoxically, ugliness or horror can be depicted by the artist in such a way that it makes sense to call this depiction beautiful in contrast to its object. In addition, some works of art baffle our concept of beauty.

For example, when confronted with Alberto Giacometti's busts and figures, deformed according to traditional criteria, we no longer know whether we should call their dignity or peculiar form of dynamic elegance simply beautiful nonetheless. The artistic representation of the ugly or the terrible also gives the viewers – without softening or diminishing it – a reflexive freedom and autonomy that they do not possess in the face of real ugliness. If necessary, the viewer can withdraw from this experience "by averting his gaze from the illustration, closing the book or leaving the museum." (Pauen (9))

This reflexive freedom and autonomy of the viewer and spectator is still expressed (even if often paired with a certain sensationalism) in the shuddering interest that we, as established members of society, take in precarious artists' existences, driven by all kinds of debauchery, addictions and excessive passions, which in part lead to their early perdition. With their transgressions, they have a representative function for us, because we can perceive and empathise as a possibility what we ourselves cannot or do not want to experience, or fortunately do not have to experience.

Regarding the unity between form and content a strong mistrust is advisable, as already briefly mentioned in the discussion of the influence of aesthetic aspects on our cognitive performance. The morally good is not necessarily aesthetically significant or beautiful or produces beauty, just as the morally evil does not always have to be aesthetically insignificant or ugly or produce ugliness. And tragic, terrible, cruel and gruesome events as well as ugliness, no less than beauty, often serve as impetus, theme and reference for important artistic achievements. The unusual, the liminal situation, the shocking or simply the exciting and surprising often provoke the artist more than the well-ordered and good, which is interesting as a goal but can easily and quickly appear boring when realised.

An "aesthetics of evil" is dependent on the existence of moral norms and the violation of them - but can only be justified if these violations remain imaginary and fictitious. Peter-André Alt elucidates this with a focus on literature: "The reader can only cope with the challenges posed by the excesses of evil if he situates them as elements of literary invention and sees through their fictitious character as an art product. Only the aesthetics of distance makes it possible for the aesthetics of evil to trigger the contradictory impulse that activates moral consciousness, but at the same time tempts us to leave its security systems. This explains why immoral literature also activates a mixed programme in terms of reception theory by activating a combination of identification and distancing in the reader."[6] (10)

At this point, it is appropriate to mention the association between art and heightened perception or even ecstasy, as can be achieved through meditative procedures, through rites or the consumption of drugs and intoxicants. Such states can, on the one hand, stimulate artistic production and, on the other, lead the persons who have put themselves in such a state to perceive their own inner experience and also an otherwise meaningless, trivial or in any case relatively charmless environment in a kind of artistic exaltation. This goes as far as a feeling of "becoming one" with the universe, in which not only one of the roots of religion lies. Even some fellow human beings who are distanced from traditional religions uncritically want to see more in it than a mere psychic phenomenon of the human brain and are able of building a surrogate of philosophy in the sense of an areligious esotericism on it. (11)

In some products of modern art it becomes clear that there can also be an aesthetically completely or largely empty art, at least in the sense of traditional aesthetics, which is only or almost only concerned with a political statement or a general statement on the human condition or with stimulating associations somehow. Such art is concerned, for example, with getting people to deal with the problems, suffering and crimes of our world more effectively than a merely factual documentation and information may do. Such a criterion of efficiency can also be declared an aesthetic criterion. However, if ugliness is used all too ubiquitously as a provocation, the attention-getting effect associated with it quickly deadens, as with other repetitions too.

Positive criteria that capture the complex phenomenon of natural beauty pose a particular problem. What, for example, constitutes the beauty of a pristine (or a culturally shaped) river landscape, what the beauty of a waterfall or a dragonfly? Those beauty criteria concerning some natural phenomena, which are directed towards reproductive success and thus seem relatively easy to explain, have already been mentioned above. Furthermore, once the ability to feel aesthetically has been recognised as a product of our evolutionary history, it seems hardly surprising that we humans tend to be aesthetically captivated by certain natural phenomena, such as the sun, light, water or green plants, which are the precondition of our life and survival and which appeal in a variety of ways to our senses that have been developed to perceive them. The preferences for the respective local landscape, on the one hand, and for landscape characteristics that have proven to be favourable for the survival of humans (half-open, park-like landscapes; vantage points that allow exploration and protection), on the other hand, are also well comprehensible from the developmental history of the individual and the species. Finally, striking, surprising landscape impressions, even if of rather human-unfriendly landscape types, at least meet human curiosity and urge to explore or carry the attraction of solitude, especially for people who are otherwise confronted with the impression of narrowness and overpopulation.

Furthermore, one may try to use some of the aesthetic positive criteria mentioned above also for natural beauty and especially for the beautiful combination of nature and culture. An essential reason for an aesthetic disposition towards nature also seems to lie in the astonishment at the dimensions of natural phenomena (both small and large) and at their mere existence. The fact that nature is and will remain largely beyond the reach of human influence (all the more of the individual, but also of humanity as a whole), its uncontrollability, also plays a role in this. The confrontation with nature points us to our individuality and loneliness, makes us aware of our relative individual insignificance and powerlessness, our being at the mercy of nature and our transience, and admonishes us to modesty (and also to solidarity with our fellow human beings, but this is only of marginal importance in the context of aesthetic considerations, when one notes, for example, that people who rejoice or those who devote themselves to helping others can exude their own kind of beauty). The distinction between the (pleasing) beautiful and the sublime (which triggers a movement of emotion), which goes back to Burke's classic text[7] written in exemplary Anglo-Saxon readability and which was so influential in Kant[8] and in the further aesthetics of the 19th century, seems rather inaccessible to us today at first glance, but it is still essential for understanding our emotional relationship to nature.

Like other phenomena that are aesthetically significant to us, however, nature can also appear ugly to us. However, the negative criteria listed above cannot be applied here, as they all refer to human failures. What appears ugly to us in nature is often what is sensually unpleasant, what is uncanny or truly hostile to life and threatening and what deviates too much from our notions of normality or is all too alien. (12)

The traditional approaches to philosophical aesthetics predominantly attempted to find objective, absolute, or at least sharply divisive definitions and criteria - for beauty, for example. In contrast, useful aesthetic criteria that are differentiated enough to do justice to the reality of our aesthetic perception, "only" lead to graded evaluations, for example between "beautiful", "ugly", "significant" and "aesthetically insignificant, indifferent", even if we decide to use one or the other term at some border. Our opinion within these conceptual gradations is also influenced by whether our aesthetic sensation and evaluation capacity became active spontaneously or on request, i.e., whether our judgement is immediate or delayed and reflected.

The aesthetic impression we feel, and especially the effect of a work of art, can be full of contradictions. Often enough, the objects, configurations, structures that trigger aesthetic impressions fulfil some aesthetic criteria and at the same time violate others, and it is then up to the perceivers to deal with this contradictoriness, either to analyse it or to play it over, to endure it or to overcome it in an overall evaluation according to what is primarily decisive and significant for them.

Art can also be contradictory in that the impression the artist wants to make and the impression that remains in the long run - at least when we look at a work more than superficially - can be very different. Furthermore, the work can point us to the opposite poles of what the artist explicitly wanted to communicate or recommend to us, even if she herself was not animated by contradictory intentions.

For a long time, philosophical aesthetics was characterised by approaches that sought to domesticate and subordinate art. Depending on the epoch, the most diverse demands were made, from the fulfilment of aesthetic ideals to social relevance. This was followed in modernity by a kind of self-disempowerment of philosophical aesthetics, which in the final consequence would have had to lead to mere silence. Against these exaggerations, I take a third position proposed by Wolfgang Welsch for the aesthetic analysis of art, "one which shifts the hermeneutic structure of works themselves into the centre". "It is important to come to terms with a double finding: art must be understood in its own right - but it never speaks from itself alone." "Works take shape in the midst of semantic contexts from the start. They are nourished by them, take up their stance within them. They don't, however, simply adopt these contexts and pass them on unaltered, but intervene in their constellation and amend this - through continuation, reorganisation, transcendence, or in whatever other way. Their reference to their surroundings is receptive and productive at the same time."[9]

A few more remarks on the widespread opinion and complaint that we are living in an end time of art and culture; that nothing essentially new can be expected from art as a whole, or at least from various art forms such as music and painting. This view falsely equates the supposed end of significant artistic possibilities of expression with the correct realisation that in many fields a periodic succession of relatively closed, time-defining styles comparable to the past can hardly be expected any more, and with the correct observation that many art forms have been explored to extreme poles, for example of differentiation and perfection of craftsmanship on the one hand and simplification and reduction of the means of craftsmanship and design on the other, or also of adaptation and provocation. Even if the concept of art has long since gone beyond the beautiful, the talk of the end of art is in a certain way a modern continuation of the motif of "mourning the beautiful"[10] that has recurred in aesthetics since Plato, claiming, for example, that the beautiful were only accessible to us to a limited extent in comparison to earlier cultural epochs or due to the deformation of nature by culture.

Artistic creation has "always" included more reproducing and interpreting activities on the one hand and more original creative activities on the other. The latter, however, are now becoming increasingly individualised in the absence of a style shaping the era (although there have also "always" been relatively strongly individualised, non-reproducible or hardly reproducible artistic creations on the one hand and well-reproducible ones on the other hand). Now the new arises more from the individual personality of the artist. Increasing individualisation makes artistic production less surveyable, but this does not mean the end of significant art. People do not stop responding as artists to their respective historical and life situations. Highly individualised artistic creations often cannot be reproduced or can only be reproduced imperfectly or hardly be used as a medium of their own artistic interpretation by other "performing" artists. But on the other hand modern technical processes make it possible to reproduce them and keep them alive to an extent previously unimaginable.

It is true that the 20th century has probably not brought forth any composer who will still be played to the same extent as Mozart or Beethoven two hundred years later. Some of them, however, are unlikely to be completely forgotten and adequately express the feelings and world view of our time. And whole genres of music, such as jazz and rock music (and the experimental extremes like minimal music), have been added. In addition, today not only what can be recorded in notes (or passed on in direct transmission) is here to stay. Would it not be a loss - to name just a few (at least for my generation) relatively broadly agreed examples - never to have heard the voices of Louis

Armstrong and Ella Fitzgerald, never to have heard the trumpet of Dizzy Gillespie, never to have seen a performance by Frank Sinatra or Sammy Davis jr. (which is now possible for everyone in the recording)?

Many new artistic means of expression have been added, such as photography, which was undervalued for a long time.

In the relatively young art form of film, we are also direct contemporaries in the creation of masterpieces. We are so little at a loss for examples that any selection inevitably remains highly subjective and unsatisfactory: Woody Allen's "Crimes and Misdemeanors", but also some of his other films, some by Hitchcock and Truffaut and many others, often enough by directors who, though some of them very productive, only succeeded in making one really great movie, such as Michael Curtiz with "Casablanca", a film, by the way, that belongs to a kind of artworks that could be called the "A Little Night Music Group", ubiquitous and - be it from the beginning or through our handling of it - on a knife edge between great art and kitsch.

After all, film is not just a continuation of stagecraft with new, more perfect and richer technical means and more "action". The film can use nature and landscape to give time to the happenings and to deepen moods. And sometimes the medium of film, which at first glance seems "loud", succeeds in creating drama and the highest emotional involvement even and especially when the external drama is low and the protagonists behave in a realistic, differentiated and reasonable manner (think of Clint Eastwood's "The Bridges of Madison County", for example). Contrary to the impression from superficial mass production, film is a differentiated representational genre that can rival literature in terms of quiet tones. In both film and theatre plays, agonising or provocative monotony can also become a design principle. In contrast, opera, for example, usually needs the fairytalelike story or the mythological, historical or personal catastrophe (apart from exceptions such as Mozart's late, timelessly modern psychodramatic masterpiece "La Clemenza di Tito").

So what is the point of whining about the end of true art? The artistic activity of humankind will not degenerate into nothing more than crafts or mere reproduction, reception and more or less individual interpretation. Human beings will not cease to respond as artists in ever new ways to a constantly changing world and thus in turn participate in this change. Who would seriously wish to return to an earlier, relatively homogeneous and be it "classical" epoch and renounce everything that has emerged since then and can still emerge even in our own lifetime?

From time immemorial, one of the basic motives of artistic activity has been to resist transience for a more or less long lapse of time (up to the extreme, the striving for eternity, as it characterises, for example, the religiously motivated creations of the ancient Egyptians). And the last hundred years have brought forth a wealth of new means to realise this goal, futile as it is in the long run, especially by new technical possibilities for multiplication, distribution and preservation. The diversity of artistic forms of expression has grown enormously. Think, for example, of the use - linked to personalities such as Tàpies - of the most diverse materials and material mixtures, which have expanded the repertoire of visual art since the invention of modern collage. (13)

So art doesn't really need a defence (unless you have to argue with politicians about funds for artistic purposes). Nevertheless, let me say a few more words about its extraordinary function and significance, which - even if one includes the ugly as an antipole in aesthetics - cannot be adequately described with aesthetic criteria alone. Only the most detached of art apologists will deny that art is in part quite simply enjoyment, entertainment, pastime, also a distraction from pressing everyday problems and as such a contribution to the enjoyment of life (though sometimes also to manipulation, numbing or stupefaction). But art is also a medium of emotional self-assurance and philosophical self-reflection, a medium through which insights that (at least in principle) can also be formulated rationally can become emotionally significant and an integral part of the personality. Art allows insights of great complexity that can often only be (or could only be) rationally comprehended in a laborious, circuitous and slow way.

Rationality is only one of the interwoven layers of human nature. In art, the other layers can also be expressed, addressed and used - and this without demanding unreasonable sacrifices, a sacrifice of the intellect, as is the case with religions. Art can hold up a mirror to us humans and make us think in a way that direct appeal or rational argumentation cannot. "Today as well, it has … one of its most important tasks in its turning to what is hidden, in the exploration of what has become imperceptible, or is excluded or deviant." (Welsch[11])

Art can strive to grasp the complexity of mental life as a whole, but on the other hand it can also approach analytical thinking again by picking out and illuminating one of the layers of human nature more or less clearly. It serves, by language and non-verbal means, the confrontation of the individual and the society with history, the present and the future in their pleasing,

410

depressing, suppressed or just their characteristic aspects. Art can help us to distance ourselves from our respective biographies and historical situation and to preserve or regain a sense of the essentials.

However, art also has a potential for seduction and the justification of its contents must be subjected to rational criticism. (14)

Art therefore also has a cognitive value. And it facilitates differentiated and wide-ranging communication, sometimes even makes it possible in the first place or makes communication more enjoyable. Art promotes communication (even where the individual artist largely refuses it), it promotes community, even if it is sometimes "only" - or initially only - for more or less elitist or avant-garde small groups in society, whose members can be outwardly quite isolated from one another. With these references to the function of art in promoting knowledge and communication as well as in creating community, we finally come back to the considerations made at the beginning about evolutionary explanations for the development of an aesthetic sense in humans.

The phenomenon of art is complicated. But that does not mean that only what is complicated were art. And even if many works of art have something enigmatical about them and this is an essential part of their appeal and an essential reason for the (lasting) interest in them, Adorno nevertheless exaggerates when he declares enigmaticalness to be constitutive for works of art and claims that artworks that unfold to contemplation and thought without any remainder are not artworks.[12] (15) Such an absolutisation would largely exclude not only agitational art, but also the large field of commercial art from art - i.e. crafts, or in a modern term: design - which would be completely inappropriate. Even if we are moving at the boundaries of the concept of art: functional beauty of form in everyday life may claim to be part of art, especially if it is also inventive. On the other hand, the various varieties of arts and crafts that only convey worn-out forms and ideas (and often even in a distorted manner) are more adequately seen as cultural and social props.

The object of aesthetics are not only those phenomena that are commonly subsumed under art, nor only natural beauty as a counterpart to it. Our perception and everyday life are constantly influenced by aesthetic sensibility and aesthetic criteria, albeit in individually and culturally very different degrees. And a certain aestheticisation of one's own life, also of one's basic needs, of everyday life and of the immediate environment accessible to individual shaping, is one of the essential characteristics, possibilities and pleasures open to human beings. It only becomes a negative phenomenon when it pushes other essential values and moral attitudes too far into the background and degenerates into a superficial panting to follow every fashion, a thoughtless consuming aestheticism, or cold perfectionism or pedantry and compulsivity. When Welsch, for example, writes: "Aren't we treated like sheep led to a green pasture when they want to please us with a 'feast for the eyes'?"[13] this justified wake-up call yet contains another exaggerated polemic against "everyday aestheticisation".

4. The Unwilling to believe in Society

A barren kind of philosophy of life?

"The cultivated man, in sum, is repelled by the unimaginative and sterile 'ideologizing' of modern agnosticism, which seems to offer no occasion for aesthetic creation or aesthetic pleasure."[1]

Gerhard Szczesny

"Thus, especially the venereal disease, the plague of the pleasure-seeking modern bigots, poets and aesthetes is incurable, who, measuring the value of things only according to their poetic charm, are so dishonourable and shameless that they even come to the defence of the illusion recognised as illusion, because they consider it beautiful and beneficent, who are so devoid of character and truth that they no longer even feel that an illusion is only beautiful as long as it is not considered an illusion, but truth."[2]

Ludwig Feuerbach (1)

"*Art makes the thinker's heart heavy.* – How strong the metaphysical need is, and how hard nature makes it to bid it a final farewell, can be seen from the fact that even when the free spirit has divested himself of everything metaphysical the highest effects of art can easily set the metaphysical strings, which have long been silent or indeed snapped apart, vibrating in sympathy; so it can happen, for example, that a passage in Beethoven's Ninth Symphony will make him feel he is hovering above the earth in a dome of stars with the dream of *immortality* in his heart: all the stars seem to glitter around him and the earth seems to sink farther and farther away. – If he becomes aware of this condition he feels a profound stab in the heart and sighs for the man who will lead him back to his lost love, whether she be called religion or metaphysics. It is in such moments that his intellectual probity is put to the test."[3]

Friedrich Nietzsche

"... it is a mistake to think that unbelievers are all insensitive Philistines with no appreciation of beauty, no respect for tradition, no capacity for wonder and reverence, who would like nothing better than to pull down the cathedral at Chartres and erect a public washhouse on the site. I do not want to pull down Chartres any more than I want to pull down the Parthenon; but I should like to see them treated rather more on one level. One can feel awe, and wonder, and reverence before the Parthenon without believing in the Greek goddess Athene to whose worship it was dedicated; and one can have similar emotions at Chartres without believing in the God of Israel."[4]

Margaret Knight

"One should ... not confuse the cognitive respect that religions certainly do not deserve with regard to their dark contents with the cultural-historical respect that one certainly owes to ecclesiastical buildings because of their age and aesthetic value. Miguel de Unamuno ... expressed this difference very well: 'En la iglesia me quito el sombrero, pero no me quito la cabeza.' So one can certainly enjoy a performance of Ludwig van Beethoven's Missa solemnis in St. Stephen's Cathedral in Vienna ... without accepting the truth claim of the mass text. Such aestheticising respect for these cultural products is certainly not in conformity with the intentions of the creators of the buildings and works of art, but the creation of cultural value is not necessarily dependent on the acceptance of the integrated metaphysics."[5]

Bernulf Kanitscheider

"The process of disenchantment, which indeed accompanies atheism, frees the world from all humbug, but does not touch the real enchantment inherent to it."[6]

Joachim Kahl

"How trivial the opinion seems to me at present that with the abandonment of so-called religious ideas all poetry and elevated sentiment would disappear from the world! On the contrary! The world has become infinitely more beautiful and deeper to me, life is more precious and intense, death more serious and critical, and only now prompts me with all its might to fulfil my task and purify and satisfy my consciousness, since I have no prospect of making up for what I have neglected in some other corner of the world."[7]

Gottfried Keller

414

4.1. Belonging to a Religious Community

Leaving behind wrong labels

> "'Käthe', Luther called into the adjacent room, 'Käthe, come in quickly, come and look at this person. He is neither a Jew nor a Christian nor a Turk, nor does he believe in God.'"[1]
>
> Joseph Popper-Lynkeus

> "The will to believe is, strangely enough, often valued more highly than the striving for intellectual integrity and the will to be honest ... "[2]
>
> Hans Albert

Those who are unwilling to believe often live outside the religion that used to be theirs without renouncing membership in their religious community socially, as would be desirable in the interest of truthfulness. What are the reasons and possible justifications for the absence of this separation?

One reason is consideration for the social environment. It can be of very different weight, depending on its tolerance.

In a tolerant society it is perhaps a matter of not hurting relatives. Such a consideration is to be taken seriously and need have nothing to do with cowardice, for example, when it comes to elderly relatives who one wants to spare a serious injury to their feelings in the last years of their lives. However, I do not think it right to permanently put off the separation from a religious community whose faith one no longer shares for the sake of other people's feelings.

As tolerance decreases, the reasons for the individual to show consideration for society become more serious: threats to reputation, economic existence, and ultimately life and limb. Under such circumstances, those who are unwilling to believe may for the time being see their task less in publicly professing their convictions than in striving for greater tolerance in society. "I will follow the good side right to the fire, but not into it if I can help it." (Montaigne[3])

Unfortunately, even in modern pluralistic democracies, it can still be observed that many people are very shy about professing atheism because the social standing of religious people is still far higher in many places than that

415

of atheists (accordingly, only a few top politicians are prepared to profess themselves as atheists or even as agnostics, whereas many are eager to flaunt their Christianity). Atheism is still almost as badly regarded in contemporary German society as astrology and communism (Allensbach survey 1989). And in the USA, which is exemplary for the separation of church and state - even if only on a constitutional-principled level - President Bush senior could still afford to say during his election campaign that a good American must believe in God, and that he was of the opinion that an atheist could not be a true patriot. A bon mot by Richard Dawkins is recommended against disparagement of this kind: "We are all atheists about most of the gods that humanity has ever believed in. Some of us just go one god further."[4] And meanwhile there are at least in countries with pluralistic democracies, and depending on the proportion of atheists, already relatively high approval rates for the statement that it is possible to act morally and have good values as an atheist (90% of approval in Sweden and even as much as 73% in the US in 2019/2022, compared to only 5% in Kenya and 2% in Indonesia).[5]

A second, in practice very significant reason for those unwilling to believe to remain in a religious community is indicated by Szczesny's sentence quoted at the beginning. People become aware of the usefulness of religion and the religious community for aesthetic mediation and aesthetic enjoyment (even if it is only to create comforting vibes) and as a mediator of some contemplation at least on certain solemn occasions. The birth of a child, the transition of a person from childhood to adolescence and adulthood, a wedding and finally a funeral are arranged with the help of religion and by the religious community in a romantic and/or dignified way, as the case may be. With their tradition-mediated competence for this, religions succeed in shaping rites of passage in a way that continues to appeal to many people. They manage to convey a sense of significance and importance, or at least spare people the difficulties of an unconventional approach to a rite of passage and the need to justify this, which can understandably mean an excessive demand, especially in a situation of personal strain or bereavement.

Many people stay in a religious community mainly because they cannot imagine or do not trust themselves to organise such occasions in a way that is at least equally satisfying, or because they consider it too tedious. However, I consider this reason weak, indeed morally unacceptable. To live before the world in the forms of a faith one does not share is a violation of truthfulness that calls for a more convincing justification. Those unwilling to believe

416

should shape the mentioned occasions themselves in accordance with their views. Otherwise, Feuerbach's bitter sentence applies to them, with which I have prefaced these reflections. However, I do not consider the attitude described drastically, but in substance correctly, to be completely incurable, but I rather believe that it should be possible to convince many more people that it is morally questionable to remain a member of a religious community only for aesthetic reasons (in the broadest sense). We are not dependent on religion for contemplation, sensibility, meaningfulness, emotionality, aesthetic enjoyment and an 'aesthetic' shaping of certain situations in life. (1)

It is true that everyone can realise this individually for themselves or be individually supported in doing so - as is increasingly happening, for example, through non-denominational, free speakers and celebrators at weddings or funerals. Nevertheless, it is desirable that people are offered an organised alternative for the organisation of the rites of passage of human life that corresponds to the ideas of secular humanism. This is done, for example, by the Norwegian Humanists, who have gained more than one hundred thousand members for this reason among others.[6] In the Netherlands, humanist counsellors are an established part of psychosocial care in hospitals or the military, a development meanwhile spreading to other countries, though at a snail's pace.

In Germany there are good initiatives too that enjoy considerable popularity locally, for example, the association for youth ceremonies ("Verein Jugendweihe"). But generally a sufficient organisational basis is lacking up to now. Unfortunately, non-denominational people, members of religious communities of free faith, free thinkers, agnostics, atheists, secular humanists, people who are unwilling to believe, and whatever other terms are used for adherents of philosophies of life that want to minimise metaphysics, are currently organised only in various small associations (which are often at odds with each other). Therefore a political advocacy organisation for people who are non-denominational in the religious sense corresponding to their proportion of the population is also lacking. Unfortunately, neither one of the older nor one of the newer associations has been able to establish itself as a nationwide force in recent decades. And an umbrella organisation, meanwhile established as "Central Council of People Free of Denomination in Germany" (Zentralrat der Konfessionsfreien in Deutschland), has only insufficiently managed to attract adequate public attention up to now. (2) "People free of denomination", as the literal translation would be, evokes more positive associations than "non-denominational people" and expresses the fact that the goal is not primarily to criticise religion, but to reject religious claims to control society that impair the interests of people free of denomination and restrict their scope of action in the name of claims to universality of religious norms. Nevertheless, it is problematic to use a term that merely refers negatively to a lacking or revoked membership in a religious institution. The originator of the Central Council idea himself, Schmidt-Salomon, rightly proposes that in the field of social services, positive value orientation must take precedence and that there should therefore be a "Humanist Welfare Association" and not a "Welfare Association Free of Denomination". Good ideas - and (with Ludwig Marcuse) Schmidt-Salomon justly states that it is better than nothing that good ideas exist at least on paper (and meanwhile in modest practical approaches). The "only" problem that remains is to find a sufficient number among the strongly individualistic people free of denomination who have enough organisational talent and willingness to commit themselves to putting these ideas into practice. Enough intellectually incorruptible and socially respected people would have to be willing to get involved to bring the whole enterprise out of the atmosphere of backroom activism. Flat anti-clericalism will only do harm. The situation will only be satisfactory when a degree of broad social acceptance has been achieved that makes a commitment to and for these institutions appear as natural to society as is the case today with church institutions and which makes it equally easy to get involved at the local level as today with traditional Christian denominations. Unfortunately, this is not yet foreseeable, and for the time being one must admit that the diagnosis of Thomas Meyer's readable analysis of the relationship between state and religion in Germany at the beginning of the 21st century is correct: "The asymmetry in the readiness for socialising or institutional affiliation between the two-thirds of German society registered as Christians and the one-third of non-Christians is structurally entrenched."[7] Even if the proportion of members of Christian denominations has now fallen to around 50%, with a clear trend further downward, this diagnosis is still basically correct. However, the Norwegian example shows that it is possible in principle to motivate a much higher percentage of people with an areligious and secular humanistic orientation to become a member in an association representing their interests than is currently the case in Germany and many other countries.

The reason why non-denominational people have such a hard time organising themselves is not only due to their individualism, "which tends to emphasise the differences to similar positions and to understate the common-alities." (Meyer[8]) Many people free of denomination devote themselves to philosophical questions through art, literature and philosophy to such an ex-tent that they rarely lack the help of an institutionalised community of like-minded people for their intellectual self-assurance and their social life (the shaping of some rites of passage in life being a possible exception). In addi-tion, the majority of people in most Western countries today no longer find the restrictions imposed by religious dogma and the social conventions, regu-lations and legal provisions derived from them - which still exist in some es-sential respects - particularly burdensome. The large Christian religious com-munities are often relatively tolerant in modern pluralistic societies and thus reduce the points of attack and conflict. The group of people who suffer spe-cifically from the continuing social dominance of Christian religious moral claims is too small and too fragmented to be significantly effective as a social force. Drastic reduction of career options in some regions and professions as a consequence of religious demands, continued discrimination against women and sexual minorities, psychological and social pressure through mandatory celibacy, religious paternalism in questions of bioethics (e.g. regarding eutha-nasia or reproductive medicine) - all this no longer carries enough weight to give sufficient impetus to organised counterforces to the religious communi-ties and to decisively take the wind out of the sails of those communities in a largely secularised and, in historical comparison, very liberal society. Indeed, sexual abuse scandals have done a lot of damage to the churches. But never-theless many people are more worried by the rapid change of traditional social structures and moral standards than by the moral paternalism of religions. In light of this even some non-believers see religion rather as a desirable stabi-lising factor.

Thus, some people who are unwilling to believe remain in a religious com-munity because they believe that faith in God and a compensatory justice after death are necessary to motivate a large proportion of people, though not themselves, to adhere to certain moral norms. They therefore do not want to weaken faith in God by publicly displaying their own unbelief. In this regard, I just want to point out once again that religion makes neither a necessary nor a sufficient contribution to the preservation of or the approximation to a desirable moral state of society. (See also 3.6.1.) Therefore, I am principally opposed to such a philosophy of as-if with the associated loss of truthfulness.

(See also note 1.2. (6)) I can only imagine compromises in this respect in very extreme situations.

Many who remain in a religious community despite being unwilling to believe also lack clarity about their own worldview and a sufficiently thought-out attitude to those important questions that are not only traditionally answered by religious faith but necessarily require at least a provisional answer for a philosophical way of life. These people therefore do not yet lead a bad life. They make decisions about the shaping of their lives and experience meaning, values and moral attitudes without consistently thinking about their foundations. In their innermost being, they still harbour the thought that religion is not entirely dispensable for the justification and realisation of what they consider good. The lack of resoluteness in thinking leads to the fact that they cannot decide to openly separate from a religious community whose faith they actually no longer share.

Finally, can the endorsement of the charitable activities of religious communities serve as a justification for remaining a member as an unwilling to believe and for contributing to the preservation of these communities? In my opinion, one should not support an institution whose philosophical principles one does not share only because it has also positive sides. For the churches, social commitment (without denying that they also have moral motives for this) is a factor that gives them social influence and guarantees that they retain power. In Germany, for example, large parts of the social service sector and the charitable sector are organisationally and ideologically dominated by the churches (in particular, there are also local and regional monopolies, or dominance close to that, which have considerable consequences, such as the already mentioned regionally drastically restricted opportunities for people not affiliated with the church to work in certain professions). At the same time, 85 to 100 per cent of the funding for church-run institutions is almost always provided by the state or collective insurances.

To be fair it has to be said, however, that society is mostly quite pleased and willing with the churches filling gaps in the social sector, because this is convenient and often still appears relatively economical. The structures to replace the churches' activities in this area would still have to be created to a considerable extent. For various reasons, which will not be discussed here, the state alone will not be able to do this adequately, but non-denominational private organisations will also be needed for these tasks. Such a process of change will not be easy, and it is certainly desirable that the role of the churches does

420

not dwindle too suddenly, but gradually. On the other hand, it is not accepta-ble in the long run that the churches guarantee and control a much larger share of social services than is commensurate with their remaining followers. This variant of wrong labelling, which ignores the philosophical status quo of so-ciety, is unacceptable and will increasingly lead to conflicts in the longer term.

People who are willing to help will not disappear from society with the de-cline of religious faith. What is likely to disappear, however, is a self-sacri-ficing shared humanity that goes beyond committed help. Only people who believe in an Hereafter are likely to take on a life in larger numbers that is entirely oriented towards altruistic service. The loss of such sacrificing hu-manity, which I - without wanting to disparage its achievements - do not re-gard as a desirable attitude to life (see also 1.4.2. and note 3.6.3. (1)) would then be the price we would have to pay for unwillingness to believe and truth-fulness, a situation that is anything but exceptional for human beings, not be-ing able to have the advantages of two attitudes and avoid their disadvantages as well. However, the distance to self-sacrificing humanity should not prevent us from recognising the social commitment of some religiously bound and motivated people as impressive and from seeing in it a demand on ourselves.

Those who are unwilling to believe should distance themselves from reli-gious communities for the sake of their fundamentally different world view. However, they should by no means be hostile to them in general and consider the following insight of Montesquieu: "It is a false way of reasoning against religion, to collect, in a large work a long detail of the evils it has produced, if we do not give, the same time, an enumeration of the advantages which have flowed from it."[9] Justice must also be done to religions. However, this is not to be confused with indifferentism and neutrality. On the whole, I agree with the verdict succinctly expressed by Bertrand Russell: "I am as firmly convinced that religions do harm as I am that they are untrue."[10]

4.2. The Attitude towards Religious Customs, Festivals and Holidays

The hobgoblin of little minds

"To be ignorant, to observe religious holy days exactly, to honour old customs, to prepare old familiar food on certain feast days, to bake the sweet cakes in exactly the same form as the great-grandparents, to kiss the priest's hand, to take off one's cap in the evening when the bell rings and to say a prayer down - all this, usually called piety and honesty, does not make a good and ethical person."[1]

Joseph Popper-Lynkeus

"And for those to whom the Christian Christmas means nothing or nothing anymore, the custom of mutually giving and receiving gifts could give their celebration a new meaning. - So Christmas can be celebrated as a kind of Thanksgiving Day, as a festival in which people become more aware of social ties and thank each other for closeness, help, partnership and love. But then one should also be consistent enough not to retain Christian motifs like fairy tale backdrops. (However, where the dividing lines between Christian and non-Christian understanding of Christmas run right through the family, everything depends on mutual tolerance!)"[2]

Ernst Emrich

"Each year, I reflect on the nascent stage of Christmas's evolution beyond its Christian roots, recognizing that cultural transformation cannot be rushed or artificially created. They evolve gradually, demanding numerous trials across various contexts over many years.

Learning to celebrate festivals, and Christmas in particular, is an art. The commercialization of Christmas often overshadows its deeper significance, leading many, especially the younger generation attuned to the hollowness of certain traditions, to withdraw from its observance.

However, Christmas remains a resilient celebration, born out of a genuine need to symbolize light and warmth with a rich array of symbols and practices during the coldest and darkest season. It serves to provide spiritual guidance and orientation, transcending the immediate, material aspects of existence."[3]

Joachim Kahl

"I attach no religious significance to Christmas, but I find it a pleasant custom and in no way see the need to avoid celebrating it because I grant it no ritualistic importance ...."[4]

Bertrand Russell

"A foolish consistency is the hobgoblin of little minds ..."[5]

R. W. Emerson

"Our life is too short to escape as far as we might like to from what is usual – from the existing mores, customs, traditions – into the absolute, or wherever else."[6]

Odo Marquard

As already discussed, one reason for the lack of separation of those who are unwilling to believe from their religious community is that they lack the determination and strength to independently shape the social occasions on which one usually calls upon one's religious community. However, this does not only refer to important, socially significant events in individual human life, which can be relatively easily organised independently of a religious tradition, but also to the large, annually recurring festivals with their customs shaped to a great extent by religion. (1)

Social traditions in Europe are, after all, strongly characterised by Christianity. It is therefore not surprising that distancing oneself from this brings with it certain problems in social life. In other parts of the world, the same applies to other religions and the customs and constraints derived from them, except that the consequences of a manifest distancing are often much more serious. But therefore those who are unwilling to believe cannot and will not become willing to believe and believing again and go back on their decision to be unwilling to believe.

According to my cultural background, the examples in this section refer to Christianity. However, a secular festive culture involving and assimilating other religious traditions is just as conceivable and seems equally feasible in principle. The problems that arise when distancing oneself from the respective traditional religion are basically the same for all cultures.

The most consistent way to avoid hypocrisy and untruthfulness is surely to stop celebrating festivals that are predominantly shaped by religion altogether and to treat the festive days as ordinary days off. This is consistent, but there are many other arguments against it. If we simply ignore the major religious festivals, we break with our history and our traditions in an excessively radical way. (2) We lose a festive culture that has grown over the centuries and which by no means contains only religious elements and we thus suffer a bitter loss. Even if the moral attitudes and values traditionally emphasised, for example, on the occasion of Christmas, can be realised without this festival and the desires expressed in this festival could also be satisfied in another way, we are depriving ourselves of a lot of joy and forcing ourselves without necessity to tear apart our emotional ties to traditional forms and time-honoured customs. In doing so, we also lose those playful and fairy tale-like traits that still penetrate into the adult world with some religiously shaped festivals - and this is especially true for Christmas. (3)

All this seems to me not only personally unpleasant; it certainly does not have a favourable effect on the spread of a philosophy of life that emphasises rationality, appearing overly intellectual to many people anyway.

However, we should also not celebrate the festivals whose basis of faith we no longer share as if nothing had happened and as if we continued to hold the religious beliefs they once predominantly represented. We must not fall into an uncritical traditionalism.

Instead, the religiously, i.e. in our culture area, Christianly shaped festivals must gradually be assimilated by a secular humanism. In this process, we can and should make our contribution to the development of a secular festive culture by increasingly renouncing explicitly Christian traditions, rituals and symbols, or by allowing them to play only a minor role as a kind of cultural quotation, and instead gain our own festive traditions. In this way we can bring philosophical orientation and customs back into better harmony and promote a gradual move away from the Christian character of the major social festivals in the course of the year. Simply escaping from Christian festivals - be it to the South Seas or elsewhere - does not contribute to this (although in certain personal life situations there is no reason why this should not be done once in a while).

If the dividing line in terms of religious belief still runs through the family, the efforts of those who are unwilling to believe to reshape traditional religious festivals according to their own convictions are made more difficult. With a certain degree of willingness to accommodate on both sides, however, it is possible to live with this quite well.

If we stay with the example of Christmas, it is conceivable for the future that non-specifically Christian elements will pass over to a secular festival of joy, a festival of light, colour and warmth, a festival of joy, love, peace, shared humanity, helping and thanksgiving. There is enough meaningful content linked to grown traditions, for a secular humanism as well. Such a festival should sensibly coincide in the calendar with the Christian festival of Christmas (and the older festival of the winter solstice), thus taking into account the historical development and maintaining a common, unifying festival across the different world views. The other Christian festivals will then also lose significance as religious events, but - like their pagan predecessors - will leave some secularised traces in our social life.

With increasing secularisation of society, the question will arise more and more as to whether Christian holidays should not be abolished in favour of new secular holidays that could have significance for the whole of society, bridging the differences in philosophies of life. Such secular holidays could, for example, mark important moments in the course of the year, such as the beginning of the seasons, or significant cultural achievements. A Day of Democracy or a Day of Human Rights, for example, would be appropriate and meaningful occasions.

A change in traditional customs will follow the intellectual distancing from the old religious views only gradually and with considerable delay, if the development is allowed to run its course. If one tries to force a secularisation of customs in the short term by means of an intellectual vanguard or an ideology trying to substitute religion with a claim to supremacy, passing over the world view or only the traditional ties of the overwhelming majority of the population, then this is just largely unsuccessful in the favourable case, in the unfavourable case it produces downright ridiculous results. The socialist states have provided an example of this (for example, in the GDR, where the Christmas angel was renamed the "winged figure of the end of the year", and this was in earnest). To the extent that a secular interpretation and assimilation of the major formerly Christian festivals gains ground in society, there will be a gradual transformation and displacement of Christian motifs in customs without such awkwardness, even if this will take generations and will not be without some temporary ups and downs. In other cultures with other religions, an analogue development is conceivable and desirable, even if from today's perspective it can only be expected with a considerably longer delay. The psychological "rewards" offered by religions are so great that the more than three-hundred-year process of enlightenment to which Christianity was subjected will be almost impossible to catch up with in fast-forward even in a global culture with modern information technology.

Sometimes tolerant church institutions also show us what the secularisation and social opening of festivals can look like. A successful example of this is when Protestant kindergartens celebrate St. Martin's Day as a lantern festival for all philosophies of life. In this way, they ensure that this festival of lights in the dark season and the associated joy for children and adults is preserved and that the festival with its reminder of the obligation to share with the needy becomes acceptable not only for all Christian denominations, but also for people with other world views, be they Muslims or those who are unwilling to believe.

Certainly there will be no way back to the old abundance of living customs and traditions. For such customs, the shaping of the whole life by a religion was just as much a prerequisite as a much greater dependence of humans on a largely incomprehensible and overpowering nature, on the change of seasons and weather. If customs no longer have to remind us of religious events and no longer have to serve to address and at least seemingly control inscrutable threats, they have lost essential functions. "Those who in the evening, by pressing a button, produce bright light in their room, are necessarily in a different relationship to life than those whose candle barely reached the walls of their narrow room with its light." (Schlechta[7])

On the one hand, the study of traditional customs is historically interesting and we can also gain ideas for our own contemporary festive culture from it. On the other hand, it is inauthentic and hollow to strenuously keep alive traditions that no longer have any reference to the modern situation of life, for instance, by ascribing the traditional farmer's way of life an importance in society that it has long since lost. In the same way, a great part of the new production of dialect literature and folk music, to which everything degenerates into sentimentality or criticism of modern times romanticising the past, is insupportable and simply nothing more than kitsch. It is understandable that, for example, an Anatolian peasant who has suddenly found himself in the modern world clings to peasant and traditional religious customs and seeks security and orientation in them. It is much less understandable for a European

426

from a modern western society. A large part of old customs deserve to be cultivated only with a museum-like intention and the appropriate distance, and over time most of the population may look on religious customs in general in this way, just as today on the customs of traditional peasant communities.

The distancing from church and religion in other areas of social life, as well as a resolute stand for the separation of church and state, is much more important, by the way, than a narrow-minded striving for consistency as to festivals and customs.

But festivals should and will remain. Festive interruptions of the daily routine will continue to exist, they will develop further and take on new forms again and again. Festivals are an essential enrichment of human life. A society without common celebrations, at least among larger groups of the population, is not desirable and hardly imaginable (and it will be difficult to find a historical example).

> "... it is important to make clear to oneself and to others that there has been and still is not only a religiously motivated festive joy, but also a millennia-old tradition of purely secularly based festive joy, joy in the festive yes to life itself. "[8]

Joachim Kahl

> "The life without festivity is a long road without an inn."[9]

Democritus

4.3. The Future Prospects for the Spread of a Philosophy of Life with Emphasis on Rationality and Metaphysical Parsimony

Is the recipe of the species hopelessly corrupted?

> "For faith there are causes, not reasons."[1]

> "Certain things are attacked as vainly with words as ghosts are with weapons. The sabre breaks, the bullet falls feebly to the ground."[2]

Wilhelm Busch

"I, who, by reason of my obligations to my State, know many specimens of the species of the unfeathered bipeds, predict to you that neither you nor all the philosophers of the world will cure the human species of the superstition to which it clings. Nature has added this spice to the mixture of this species; it is fear, weakness, credulity, a hasty judgement, which seduces men, out of a common inclination, to the system of the miraculous.

Rare are the philosophical souls who possess sufficient strength to destroy deep within themselves the roots which the prejudices implanted by education have struck in them."[3]

Frederick II of Prussia (1)

"As is now well known, convictions that in no way correspond to reality – the inadequacy of which is readily apparent to a critical observer – can prove extraordinarily stable if they are supported strongly enough by the society. *Correspondence to reality* can be extensively replaced by *social anchoring*. The loss of stable anchorings for a world view, and the associated condition of uncertainty, absence of norms, and disorientation, on the other hand, seem hardly bearable."[4]

Hans Albert

"The Empire of Philosophy extends over a few; and with Regard to these too, her Authority is very weak and limited."[5]

David Hume

"Each one lets into his head only so much light as is compatible with his sense of self and the peace of his heart."[6]

Ludwig Feuerbach

The question already posed in section 3.4, to what extent belief in god and religion are to be regarded as inevitable, is to be addressed here once again in more practical and prognostic terms.

On the one hand, enlightenment and secularisation are powerful historical tendencies that have increasingly prevailed - despite all the phasic setbacks and counter-reactions (such as the recurring waves of esotericism and irrationality or even periods of a more serious, but still temporary renaissance of religious life orientation). Once positions criticising religions and ideology have been convincingly formulated and have achieved at least a minimum of dissemination, they become - at least in the long run – part of the intellectual heritage of humanity that can no longer be suppressed. On the other hand, a realistic look at the situation so far gives little cause for confidence regarding the future social and especially global spread of a philosophy of life with emphasis in rationality and metaphysical parsimony. At the most, one can express expedient optimism here.

The basic positions of a morally sustainable agnostic or atheistic and naturalistic secular humanism have been formulated in ever new and impressive variations since at least the end of the 19th century. Despite certain inadequacies and the possibility given even here of turning into a totalitarian, fanatical, inhuman ideology, first of all the ability of these philosophical concepts to criticise themselves has increased. On the other hand, their spread is still very limited even in modern liberal and pluralistic societies, at least measured by the willingness to profess and stand up for them in social life. Unwillingness to believe remains and probably will remain for the foreseeable future, perhaps even permanently, the attitude of a qualified minority. Even among natural scientists, the proportion of religious believers remained about the same in surveys in 1916 and 1996, at around 40 per cent (although among top scientists 90 per cent were non-believers in a 1998 survey, and among biologists as many as 95 per cent).[7]

In the religious and ideological sphere certain firmly established thought patterns as well as social conventions and institutions prove to be regrettably uninfluenceable or at least influenceable only very slowly by rational considerations. Hoerster has described the situation very succinctly: "Religious convictions are usually not only not arrived at by rational means, they are usually not changeable by rational means either. In other words, most people, for psychological reasons, seem unwilling or unable to seriously question their religious beliefs and to change them substantially on the basis of rational thought. Therefore, any rational consideration and argumentation in the religious field can only be limited in its effect from the outset."[8]

Hoche (2) has already described this problem vividly: "The attempt at an objective, serious discussion about God, immortality and the like with an interlocutor of average comprehension has a typical curve: for a while he goes along with interest, a little further out of politeness, but then the phase of rejection sets in, accompanied by a superior smile; words slide off the armoured attitude: you talk what you want, I cannot refute you, but my inner self says something else.

This is the decisive point; the power of religious conviction does not rest on facts or logical grounds, but in the energy of a feeling, and thus it moves out of the field of fire of rational evidence; at this point the fork in the road becomes clear, the separation of men into those who believe only what is proved to them, or at least made highly probable, and those who believe what satisfies their desires and hopes."[9]

Unfortunately, even Hoche's restriction to "interlocutors of average comprehension" cannot be upheld. Rather, his considerations in some cases apply to Nobel Prize winners as well as to Jane Bloggs. (See also the last part of section 3.4.). The satisfaction of psychological needs, especially the needs for social inclusion, security and comfort, is important for people with the most diverse intellectual abilities. The modern world is experienced as a world full of change and uncertainty – which is indeed true, despite objectively significantly lower personal life risks in affluent countries compared to the past. The life partner (who was also often lost in the past, but mostly through death and not through personal decisions) is often replaced by subsequent temporary cohabitations, many people have to change their job and place of residence again and again, negative side effects of science and technology as well as the dissolution of traditional social structures are increasingly perceived. Religion, whose seeming power of explanation promises an objectivist way of "giving meaning to the meaningless", can be perceived as a more attractive help in the imponderables and adversities of personal life than secular humanism, which is only able to interpret many strokes of fate in life as unfortunate coincidences that follow natural, biographical and historical processes and which, if it can only refer people to their own power to find meaning, sometimes overstrains them.

It may seem paradoxical at first, but the essential prerequisite for the rationally emphasised attitude of unwillingness to believe - unjustifiably dismissed by some as "rationalistic" - is a relatively high emotional security. This security is necessary in order
- to be able to question and change religious beliefs as a consequence of rational considerations,
- to be able to deal with the needs underlying these beliefs (such as for comfort) in a way that does not require intellectual sacrifice,
- to still be able to act rationally even in situations of severe personal strain,
- to be able to distance oneself from the prejudices of the respective society without falling into a quasi-religious sense of mission.

430

Providing such emotional security is one of the most important tasks of education. And unfortunately, education often fails to be up to this very task because the parents or psychological parents themselves lack emotional security or the family situation is not intact. This is one of the reasons why the efforts of enlightenment to spread a rationally emphasised worldview have not been more successful so far.

The ability of religion to stimulate artistic production and to provide aesthetic pleasure, which has been so often impressively demonstrated in history and has not yet been exhausted in the present, is also likely to prove to be one of its essential supports for a long time to come. In contrast to other, less pleasing aspects of religion, this has the advantage that even the unbelievers and those unwilling to believe can profit from it. However, the fact that religion has also contributed and continues to contribute to the disfigurement of the world through unspeakable quantities of kitsch of a more or less evil variety is worth mentioning in this context, but does not derogate its merits for art. After all, one can overlook this stuff, and besides, it probably helps many simple-minded people to get through life better, and from this point of view it deserves not to be ridiculed too much.

The importance of religion for art has diminished drastically in the modern era. Art is not dependent on religion. It is not surprising that the art of past centuries is to a large extent religious art, since at the time there were almost only religious artists and commissioners for art. No other orientation towards life existed, or not in a socially perceptible way. Dawkins also rightly points out that artists need a livelihood and clients and that the church was able to fulfil this function in a prominent way for a long time through its material resources.[10] However, the opportunities for certain artistic talents to develop depend on the socio-cultural circumstances of the time and not everyone who could create a great work in a religious environment could do so in a secular one - and vice versa. (Great) works of art remain historical strokes of luck - under whatever premises.

Whether a large number or even a majority of people will ever be able to accept a rationally emphasised, minimally metaphysical philosophy of life and to shape their lives and living together accordingly remains questionable. (3) This does not mean, however, that we should give up the struggle for it. Even an enlightened minority (but unfortunately also a deluded one) can have a significant influence on the quality of a society, indeed on the course of human history. And the thinking and commitment of those who themselves have a rationally emphasised view of the world would not have been in vain or worthless even if humanity were to perish one day because of a predominant inability to be guided by reason. Striving for truth and reason have their own value.

Enlightenment values are largely an achievement of Western culture. The population ratios on earth will continue to shift to its disadvantage for a longer period of time. Religiously oriented people and religiously influenced societies generally have higher birth rates, as has been demonstrated by a large number of example, which is mainly due to the lack of equal rights for women. (4) Nevertheless, there is a glimmer of hope in the fact that a rationally emphasised, low-metaphysical worldview has become much more common in modern pluralist affluent societies and that in these societies, even more than such a worldview itself, there is always positive and negative freedom of religion and belief, tolerance and freedom from social constraints and conventions to an unprecedented degree (even if these achievements are always endangered and have so far only applied to a small part of the world - and even there with restrictions; think, for example, of the fate of the British citizen Salman Rushdie and, less prominently but even more terrible, the 39 deaths and numerous serious injuries resulting from attacks on translators of his "Satanic Verses"). (5)

Unfortunately, Islam in particular is increasingly proving to be a problematic religion, not only for the people in the Muslim-majority countries themselves, but also for pluralistic democracies, and not only because of the meanwhile disturbingly long list of Islamist acts of violence. The fact that some Muslims exert social pressure on others to observe religious rules, whether it be a religious dress code, religious rules for interaction between the sexes or strict observance of the fast during Ramadan, requires a differentiated response from pluralistic societies in order to enable also Muslims to live their religion in a liberal way or to abandon it altogether. If the threat of violent fanatics makes it impossible even in a pluralistic society to live liberal views of a traditional religion, then some restrictions may be accepted here temporarily so as not to endanger human life. However, this cannot be a situation that is accepted permanently. At some point, Muslims will also have to accept that there are mosques where men and women pray together and where people with openly lived minority sexual orientations are welcome. Demanding religious tolerance from all religions is a task that must be tackled in the most diverse areas of society, but above all in politics and education. For this to succeed, the problems caused by traditional religious beliefs must first be clearly recognised and addressed, and it must also be stated which religions are causing the greatest problems at a particular historical moment in a particular society. And in most pluralistic democracies, this is undoubtedly Islam at the present time. However, after such a clear analysis of the situation, appropriate measures must also be consistently implemented, such as compulsory, joint, critical ethics lessons for pupils of all world views.

Religiously-minded people and their descendants are also confronted with the achievements and efforts of the Enlightenment and are more receptive to them as they become more affluent and educated. However, we should not rely on this to automatically solve the problems associated with authoritarian and intolerant religious views, if we do not address them consequently.

> "There is no reason to despair - and none to be confident of victory. Cultural pessimism, thus delimited, blends in with an active life that is not endangered by scepticism and resignation when they are taken as a matter of course from an early age."[11]

Ludwig Marcuse

Finally, this kind of "cultural pessimism", which is actually cultural realism, includes the realisation that the spread of a rationally emphasised, minimally metaphysical worldview does not easily bring about the rational management of personal, social and political issues. Behaving as we think requires a continuous effort.

In terms of intellectual history, there is no alternative to the Enlightenment project. Nevertheless, it could fail in the historical development. We should work to ensure that Enlightenment thought retains its dynamism, prevails in the struggle for intellectual leadership and decisively shapes our cultural development. (6)

Agnostics, atheists and secular humanists must show themselves and make themselves felt in society and work for appropriate integration and participation. For example, in the wake of fatal disasters and attacks, public mourning and remembrance are often still disproportionately dominated by church events (even when, as in the new federal states of Germany, the proportion of church members in the population is no more than between 10% and 15%). Today, at least in Germany, the predominant form of such events is an ecumenical service, often also involving non-Christian religions, which is already a significant step forward. However, it does not do justice to areligious people. The large, awe-inspiring churches in the city centre are very appropriate places for mourning and remembrance and the traditional religious rituals can relieve people in crisis situations of the effort of shaping their own ceremony. However, in the long run this cannot justify imposing the forms of religious belief on those who no longer share it. Significant religious monuments are a cultural heritage of society as a whole and should therefore increasingly be available and used for events which truly accept and integrate different philosophies of life.

Omega

An end before the end

"To quarrel with the uncertainty that besets us in intellectual affairs, would be about as reasonable as to object to live one's life, with due thought for the morrow, because no man can be sure he will be alive an hour hence. Such are the conditions imposed upon us by nature, and we have to make the best of them."[1]

Thomas Henry Huxley

"Philosophers and house owners always have repairs."[2]

Wilhelm Busch

"Indeed, if from history one learned nothing else than the variability of views, it would be invaluable."[3]

Ernst Mach

"… for one strives to come to an end, before the end comes, albeit one knows that the incompleteness of our thought is as sure as death."[4]

Jean Améry

Francisco Farreras, Relieve madera (wood relief) N.°750a, 2005

Acknowledgements

I would like to thank all those who have encouraged me by discussing my thoughts. I would especially like to thank: Detlef Zander for his suggestions and detailed proposals for improvement as well as for his meticulous proofreading of early versions of the manuscript of the second edition, Wolf Pohl for his rewarding suggestions and references to interesting literature, especially in the fields of neurobiology, neurophilosophy and cosmology, Vito von Eichborn for his co-operation on my book "God and the Chinese Teapot". I learnt a lot from this semi-fictional project, and it contributed significantly to making this book more readable and interesting too. In particular, Vito von Eichborn has sharpened my sensitivity to generalities, as unavoidable as they sometimes are in a thematically broad philosophical book. Thanks to the work of my dedicated publisher's reader of the second edition, Diane Zilliges, this book has gained considerably in both form and content. While working on the third edition, I benefited from many discussions with and suggestions by Christian Walther. Finally, I would like to thank all those who, through their human attention and the creation of favourable external living conditions, have helped me to develop the emotional security that is an essential prerequisite for trying to see the world as realistically and without illusions as possible, and for being able to admit how much one is "building on sand" in philosophical questions. This is just one of the many background influences that I owe especially to my wife Margret and our decades of life together. Among other things, she reminds the philosopher at her side, time and again, tacitly or explicitly, that philosophy should not stray too far from common sense.

Suggested Further Reading

Albert, H., Treatise on Critical Reason, translated by M. V. Rorty, Princeton University Press 1985, Reprint 2014 (Traktat über kritische Vernunft, 1968, 5. verbesserte und erweiterte Auflage, Mohr Tübingen 1991)

Baggini, J., Atheism. A Very Short Introduction, Oxford University Press 2003

Camus, A., The Myth of Sisyphus, translated by J. O'Brien, 1955, Reprint Penguin London 2005 (Le mythe de Sisyphe, 1942)

Greene, B., The Fabric of the Cosmos, Alfred A. Knopf New York 2004

Dawkins, R., The God Delusion, Bantam Press London 2006

Höffe, O., Democracy in an Age of Globalisation, Springer Dordrecht 2007 (Demokratie im Zeitalter der Globalisierung, 1999, 1., überarbeitete und aktualisierte Neuausgabe, Beck'sche Reihe, C. H. Beck München 2002)

Jaspers, K., Way to Wisdom: An Introduction to Philosophy, translated by R. Manheim: Yale University Press 1954, Second Edition 2003 (Einführung in die Philosophie, 1949, Neuausgabe, Piper München 1971)

Jauch, U. P., Jenseits der Maschine (Beyond the machine). Philosophie, Ironie und Ästhetik bei Julien Offray de La Mettrie, Hanser München/Wien 1998

Krauss, L. M., A Universe from Nothing, Free Press New York 2012

Kahl, J., Weltlicher Humanismus. Eine Philosophie für unsere Zeit (Secular Humanism. A Philosophy for our time), 2005, 4. korrigierte Auflage, LIT Verlag Münster 2009

Lamont, C., The Philosophy of Humanism, Sixth Edition, Frederick Ungar New York 1982

Lichtenberg, G. Chr., The Waste Books, translated by R. J. Hollingdale, first published as *Aphorisms*, 1990, New York Review Book 2000, original German text: Sudelbücher, 1800, modern German editions: Aphorismen, ed. M. Rychner, Manesse Zürich 1958, small and nice; Schriften und Briefe, ed. W. Promies, 4 Volumes, Carl Hanser München 1967 – 1972, the big scientific thing, and, nevertheless, equally a pleasure for bibliophiles

Montaigne, M. de, The Complete Essays, Book 3, Chapter 13, Of experience, translated by Donald M. Frame, Stanford University Press 1958, Printing 2016 (Essais, 1580)

Robinson, R., An Atheist's Values, 1964, reissued Blackwell Oxford 1975

Russell, B., Autobiography, 1967 – 1969, Routledge Classics New York 2009

Russell, B., The Conquest of Happiness, 1930, Allen & Unwin London 1975

Safranski, R., Schopenhauer and the Wild Years of Philosophy, translated by E. Osers, Harvard University Press 1991 (Schopenhauer und Die wilden Jahre der Philosophie, Hanser München/Wien 1987),

Singer, P., Practical Ethics, 1979, Second Edition, Cambridge University Press 1993

Stein, G. (Hrsg.), The Encyclopedia of Unbelief (2 Volumes), Prometheus Buffalo 1985

Szczesny, G., The Future of Unbelief, translated by E. B. Garside, George Braziller New York 1961 (Die Zukunft des Unglaubens, 1958, Mit dem erweiterten Briefwechsel Friedrich Heer – Gerhard Szczesny, List München 1965, 1972,)

Vollmer, G., Evolutionäre Erkenntnistheorie (Evolutionary Epistomology),
8. Aufl., Hirzel Stuttgart 2002

Weischedel, W., Skeptische Ethik (Sceptical Ethics), Suhrkamp Frankfurt a. M.
1976

Zippelius, R., Das Wesen des Rechts (The Nature of Law), 3. Aufl., Beck München 1973 (The third edition is a good blend of conciseness and spiciness while the fifth edition of 1997 is shortened to a mere introduction, considerably reduced in favour of the author's Philosophy of Law.)

Zuckerman, P., Living the Secular Life. New Answers to Old Questions, Penguin Press New York 2014 (sociological facts and personal experiences concerning a secular humanist coping with life)

Notes

Introduction

(1) Without a doubt, it is useful and sometimes fruitful and stimulating also for non-religious people to reflect on religiously motivated moral arguments and positions (and for the sake of social coexistence alone a discussion of such positions is necessary and desirable). However, even in modern, relatively largely secularised Western societies, this takes place against the background of the political dominance of positions shaped by religious thinking and the pressure still exerted on non-religious people to decide and act against their own moral convictions in essential questions of life and possibly to have to take on considerable burdens throughout their lives for this reason. In view of this, it seems somewhat strange and a complete distortion of today's conflict situation when a prominent contemporary philosopher, Jürgen Habermas, calls for a "non-destructive secularisation" of religious positions instead of advocating a philosophy that engages in unprejudiced, rationally comprehensible discussions of values. His example is symptomatic of what we have to expect when we adopt such a proposal: instead of the divine Creator, nature is offered to us as a Creator that has to be respected in questions of reproductive medicine and genetic engineering, as if we did not yet know that nature is morally "blind" - that is, completely indifferent to human interests and moral considerations. The mere fact that nature has allowed human beings to come into being and to survive so far hardly justifies to give our conception of nature a meaning that would avoid an "emptying secularisation". Habermas goes on to praise the "inspiring, indeed indispensable semantic contents" of religious languages, which still await translation into justifying discourses. Only in a certain sense is he right in all this: in so far as he succinctly describes the central illusion and the central deficit of his way of doing philosophy. The illusion is that one can almost completely avoid moral and philosophical decisions and permanently hide behind a mask of sterile scientificity. And the deficit is not to profess a life-determining, albeit revisable, secular worldview as a philosopher, a secular worldview that constitutes a commitment in conscious and emphasised contrast to the theological and secular-ideological mode of argumentation: no appeal to authorities, no blind decisionism, rather rational argumentation for decisions, which nevertheless remain decisions and are not simply compulsory results of logical and scientific thinking. And this commitment should, please, be communicated in a generally understandable, not unnecessarily

encoded language. If you want to be considered a philosopher, do you really have to speak of an extreme stratification of world society instead of simply denounce the all too great contrast between the rich and the poor? While this is "just" a formality, the exaggerated respect of Habermas for a religiously founded morality is no accident: Discourse as a fundamental principle of ethics is likeable and certainly often a good idea in private and public matters but it is at the same time morally "empty" to a similar degree as universalisation principles like Kant's categorical imperative. Both do not produce moral attitudes and values, rather these must be presupposed if desirable consequences are to be reached. We will come back to this problem in chapter 3.3.. See: Habermas, J. , Glaube und Wissen. Friedenspreis des deutschen Buchhandels 2001, Suhrkamp Verlag Berlin 2016, especially pp. 19, 20., translated by H. Beister and M. Pensky: Faith and Knowledge, Peace Prize of the German Book Trade 2001, in: id., The Future of Human Nature, Polity Press Cambridge 2003, pp. 101–115, especially p. 114. With a similar, but somewhat mitigated tenor later also in extenso in: id., Zwischen Naturalismus und Religion. Philosophische Aufsätze, Suhrkamp Frankfurt a. M. 2005, translated by C. Cronin: Between Naturalism and Religion, Polity Press Cambridge 2008. And, as a trenchant criticism of Habermas' position: Paolo Flores D'Arcais, Eleven Theses against Habermas, 2007, available online: https://www.the-utopian.org/d%27Arcais_1, retrieved 3 January 2023 (translated by G. Donis). Besides the criticism of Habermas, the Italian philosopher clearly sorts out the conflict between a secular and a religious worldview still persisting even in the modern Western orientated democracies and advocates that religious views should no longer rule the lives of citizens that do not share them.

(2) Some examples of the revival of the critique of religion, each worthwhile:

Julian Baggini, Atheism, 2003, see Suggested Further Reading. A short but intense reading pleasure.

Richard Dawkins, The God Delusion, 2006, see Suggested Further Reading. A book for the island, substituting if need be, no, not only if need be, a philosophical book on proofs for the existence of God, a physics book on cosmology, a biology book on evolutionary theory and "intelligent design", a history book on religion and atheist totalitarianism. And the man can write! However, compassionate understanding for the psychological needs of those in need of faith is not his thing.

Sam Harris, The End of Faith. Religion, Terror and the Future of Reason, 2004, The Free Press London 2006. Not always balanced, but refreshing.

Norbert Hoerster Die Frage nach Gott (The Question of God), Beck München 2005. A meritorious German enlightener.

Michel Onfray, Traité d'athéologie, Grasset Paris 2005). Not much new, but a defiant book that dares to mock religion.

Christopher Hitchens, god is not Great, Twelve New York/Boston 2007.
A condensed criminal history of religions, based not primarily on historical sources but on personal experience.

(3) Against all the euphemism regarding a traditional-conservative interpreted Islam which (still) refuses a tolerant reinterpretation along the lines of the European Enlightenment the exciting and touching autobiography of Ayan Hirsi Ali is an impressive remedy: Infidel, Free Press New York 2007. She strives for the greatest objectivity in spite of the personal attacks she had to suffer and to survive. Less exciting, but more analytical, is her examination of the serious conflict between prevailing Islamic views and modernity in: The Caged Virgin. An Emancipation Proclamation for Women and Islam, Free Press New York 2006 (Originally in Dutch 2004). Regretfully, Ayan Hirsi Ali announced a "political" conversion to Christianity in 2023 on the grounds that it is needed to defend Western civilisation.

(4) »So to me the important challenge is not to debunk religion, but to address its issues in better ways«, is the conclusion of the Nobel Prize winner in physics in his answer to the Edge annual question 2008 about what one had changed one's mind about and why: The Science Formerly Known as Religion, https://www.edge.org/responses/what-have-you-changed-your-mind-about-why, retrieved 5 January 2023

(5) Two kindred spirits or forerunners of this kind of crossover philosophy worth reading: Joachim Kahl, Weltlicher Humanismus. Eine Philosophie für unsere Zeit (Secular Humanism. A philosophy for our time), Richard Robinson, An Atheist's Values, see Suggested Further Reading.

(6) The useful distinction between partial truths and half-truths is elaborated very well by Günther Patzig in his essay "Objektivität und Wertfreiheit. Zwei Grundprobleme der Wissenschaftstheorie" (Objectivity and value freedom. Two fundamental problems of the philosophy of science), in: id., Gesammelte Schriften (Collected Writings) IV, Wallstein Göttingen 1996, pp. 82–98, in particular pp. 90, 91.

(7) Wolfgang Kersting recommends this in his reflections on the relationship between contemporary philosophy and the art of living: Über ein Leben mit Eigenbeteiligung - Unzusammenhängende Bemerkungen zum gegenwärtigen Interesse an der Lebenskunst, in: id., Gerechtigkeit und Lebenskunst. Philosophische Nebensachen (Justice and the art of living. Philosophical side issues), mentis Paderborn 2005, chapter 18, pp. 179–210, here especially pp. 205, 206. Kersting's keeping distance from all too zeitgeisty adaptations and derivatives of the art of living tradition is, however, very justified.

1.1.

(1) Wilhelm Weischedel also builds on fundamental choices (»Grundentschlüsse«), some of them similar, in his "Sceptical Ethics" (see Suggested Further Reading).

1.2.

(1) The French sceptic Francois de La Mothe Le Vayer placed this saying at the end of his "Dialogue sur le sujet de la divinité" (Dialogue on the subject of the divinity). First published probably in 1630, in: Deux dialogues faits à l'imitation des anciens (Two dialogues in the manner of the ancients), Éditions Bossard Paris 1922, p. 153.

(2) Of course, a certain degree of provisional belief in authority, of belief in authority with reservations, is an essential prerequisite for the successful pursuit of knowledge and especially for a successful scientific practice. If everyone always wanted to check and repeat everything themselves, humans would not get very far as cultural beings. Such a revocable belief in intellectual authorities, however, is merely a credit of trust granted to certain personalities regarding their transmission of tradition, their abilities to gain knowledge and the reliable application of scientific methods. It has little to do with authority as a criterion of knowledge and truth in the (book-)religious, theological, scholastic, ideological sense.

The tendency to believe in authority, however, may have very primal roots in our species, whose evolutionary success rests very largely on its extraordinary abilities to pass on information and experience, namely as a survival advantage, especially for children. For Richard Dawkins, this is an essential aspect for an evolutionary explanation of religion as a "by-product": "Natural selection builds child brains with a tendency to believe whatever their parents and tribal elders tell them. Such trusting obedience is valuable for survival. ... An automatic consequence is that the truster has no way of distinguishing good advice from bad. The child cannot know that 'Don't paddle in the crocodile-infested Limpopo' is good advice, but 'You must sacrifice a goat at the time of the full moon, otherwise the rains will fail' is at best a waste of time and goats." And some authorities use this superiority for their own purposes: "Religious leaders are well aware of the vulnerability of the child brain, and the importance of getting the indoctrination in early." In: The God Delusion, see Suggested Further Reading, pp. 176, 177. In addition to their intuitive plausibility, Dawkins' reflections find some experimental support in the famous Milgram experiments of the 1960s, which showed how much difficulty we have in rebelling against the demands of even weakly founded authority on the basis of rational considerations and moral principles.

However, belief in authority primarily offers a good way to explain why religious ideas are successfully passed on and persist. It does not sufficiently explain why religious ideas arise in the first place and why certain contents (such as a theistic concept of god and a continuation of life after death) are favoured.

For evolutionary explanations of religion see also 3.4. and for literature suitable as an overview especially note 3.4. (1).

(3) One can say with some justification that William von Occam's "razor" or "principle of parsimony" ("It is unjustifiable to explain with greater effort something that can also be explained with less", see 3.1.3.) is hereby transferred from ontology and philosophy of science to ethics and morality (by analogy, replaces "explain" with "justify").

(4) The right balance between thinking and feeling is, on the one hand, a goal of a philosophical conduct of life (the concept of reason brings both together). In addition to this moral, normative aspect of the relationship between thinking and feeling, the findings of modern neurological research, especially on patients with prefrontal brain damage, have now added a functional aspect: We are - at least in the area of personal and social decisions - unable to use our intellect in a sensible way that enables us to cope with everyday life without the help of feelings. See Antonio Damasio's book "Descartes' Error. Emotion, Reason and the Human Brain", 1994, Avon Paperback New York 1995

(5) The obvious differences already begin with the fact that in the Priestly Scriptures of the Genesis man stands at the end of creation, but in the "Jahwist" paradise narrative at the beginning. See on this in brief: Westermann, C., Welt und Mensch im Urgeschehen, Deutsche Bibelgesellschaft Stuttgart 1999, or: Westermann, C., F. Ahuis, Calwer Bibelkunde, 14th edition, Calwer Verlag Stuttgart. The part on Genesis can be found in more detail in the large Biblical Commentary by Westermann: Biblischer Kommentar I/1, 3rd edition, Neukirchener Verlag Neukirchen-Vluyn 1983, translated by J. J. Scullion: Genesis 1-11: A Continental Commentary, Augsburg Publishing House Minneapolis 1984. See also the more topical Wikipedia article on the "Genesis creation narrative" which states rightly: "Consistency was evidently not seen as essential to storytelling in ancient Near Eastern literature. The overlapping stories of Genesis 1 and 2 are contradictory but also complementary ..." https://en.wikipedia.org/wiki/Genesis_creation_narrative, retrieved 14 January 2023, modified later, in a version retrieved 11 April 2025 see Note f.

(6) That is why I generally do not think much of the recognition of any religious and cultural fictions in the sense of an as-if, as the positivist Vaihinger wants to make palatable to us in his "Philosophy of As if" (Vaihinger, H., Die Philosophie des Als Ob, 1911, 10th ed. 1927, translated by C. K. Ogden: The Philosophy of "As if", Harcourt Brace New York 1924, new editions Routledge London and New York 1968 and 2021). In order to commit such a serious violation of truthfulness

that one retains ideas, which one believes to have recognised as fiction, for the sake of some consequences considered desirable, as if they were knowledge, one should definitely have very convincing arguments. History does not provide such arguments, at least not to the present day - or at best for special, temporary historical situations.

Why still talk about Vaihinger, some may say, who still remembers him? Among philosophers, perhaps not too many, but in the educated classes of Western countries, Vaihinger's approach plays an important role, often tacitly, rarely explicitly formulated (even more rarely with a mention of his paternity), and contributes significantly to the stabilisation of outdated traditional guarantors of norms, be it the concept of natural law in legal doctrine or, more generally, the traditional, institutionalised religions in society.

(7) See for example: Der Garten des Menschlichen (The human garden), 1977, Fischer Taschenbuch Verlag Frankfurt a. M. 1980, especially pp. 350–355; or: Die Tragweite der Wissenschaft (The scope of science), 6th edition, Stuttgart Hirzel 1990, pp. 405–433.

(8) Someone who has a faith in revelation, but also the Marxist with his dogmas that are dependent on authority and only glossed over by pseudoscientific rationales but are in reality presupposed as irrefutable beliefs (for example, that there is a necessary, predictable direction of the course of history) can in principle be a doubter in the sense of the first principle of unwillingness to believe in contexts that do not touch his or her fundamental beliefs. For the adherent of a secular ideology, see Bertolt Brecht's beautiful poem "Der Zweifler" (The Doubter) as an example: His doubter doubts many things (and we can still learn something from him in the process), but not that there is a necessary stream of happening, at least one that can be predicted in its essential direction, nor that it is important to be "in the stream of happening" ("im Fluß des Geschehens"). Gedichte 1933-1938, in: Gesammelte Gedichte, Suhrkamp Frankfurt a. M. 1976, vol. 2, p. 587, translated in: Poems 1913–1956, edited by J. Willett and R. Manheim, Methuen London 1976, revised edition 1987, reprinted by Routledge New York, pp. 270, 271

(9) "It is no coincidence that religious persecutions are the monopoly of objective theorists", says P. H. Nowell-Smith (Ethics, Penguin Melbourne/London/Baltimore 1954, p. 47). Although this may not be entirely true (or at least it would be conceivable that a "subjectivist" would become a persecutor), a strong connection is nevertheless correctly observed here.

(10) I want to point out here that a fundamental choice of scepticism (as proposed by Weischedel in his Skeptische Ethik, p. 181, see Suggested Further Reading), which is explained as a fundamental choice to radically question everything

except this fundamental choice itself (although its questionability is accepted), may appear more comprehensive and profound than the fundamental choice of unwillingness to believe. The fact is, however, that to a sceptic - even if she or he keep doubt alive in themselves and reconsider everything again and again - the different kinds of knowledge usually appear to be credible to quite different degrees. Therefore, the fundamental choice of unwillingness to believe, as it is formulated here, is clearer and of more binding content. However, it is by no means intended to forcibly bring up a contradiction between these formulations: despite these principled objections Weischedel's fundamental choice of scepticism means, at least in his understanding, something very similar to the fundamental choice of unwillingness to believe.

(11) I want to mention explicitly how the position of the unwilling to believe differs from positivism: Positivists forbid certain kinds of knowledge by calling the terms used in them meaningless; unwillings to believe prohibit (themselves) certain ways to knowledge which they consider unreliable, but they acknowledge that the terms used in them (such as "god") have a meaning as constructs of the human mind, irrespective of their questionable or lacking descriptive function. Positivists do not accept the fact that their statement on knowledge also includes a belief (or in any case convictions that cannot be justified by reason only), but unwillings to believe do.

(12) I have relegated the following lovely saying to the notes instead of prefacing this section with it as a motto because, while there is much truth in it, it lacks empathy for people who need religious faith for a variety of reasons. In other words, as pretty as it is, it exaggerates arrogance somewhat.

"Zum Adler sprach die Taube:
Wo das Denken aufhört, da beginnt der Glaube.
Recht, recht, so sprach der Adler,
Mit dem Unterschied jedoch,
Wo du schon glaubst, da denk' ich noch."

"To the eagle spoke the pigeon:
Where thinking ends, begins religion.
Right, right, the eagle spoke,
With the difference, however,
Where you already believe, I still think."

The saying is quoted here in German too because its rhymes can hardly be translated without a loss in attractivity into English. It is attributed to the now almost forgotten poet, playwright and publicist Ludwig Robert (1778–1832), Rahel

Varnhagen's brother.

1.3.

(1) Gerhard Radnitzky aptly says: "To murder oneself is just as logically impossible as committing adultery with one's own wife. The semantic mischief of 'selfmurder' seems to be a German speciality ... ." Zur Sterbehilfe in Deutschland (On euthanasia in Germany), Aufklärung und Kritik, Schwerpunkt: Selbstbestimmtes Sterben (Focus: self-determined dying), Sonderheft (Special Issue) 11/2006, p. 64. Only in the case of suicide assassins the German word 'Selbstmordattentäter' (self-murdering assassin) makes some sense in most of the cases because there are base motives for the suicide too.

(2) An impressive personal testimony of a comprehensible rational suicide is given by Chris Hill in his suicide note, "an open letter to anyone who wants to understand why I've checked out." (Hill, C., The Note, 10 February 1993, in: Kuhse, H., Singer, P. (Ed.), Bioethics. An Anthology, Blackwell Oxford 1999, pp. 323–326). In this note he describes an active and rich life lived full of joie de vivre, the manifold humiliating restrictions and deformations that were unbearable for him due to the paraplegia he suffered, and the resulting, well-considered decision to end his life despite the loving care he received from people close to him. He emphasises that this is a very personal decision and that for him, with his biography, his interests and his expectations, life is no longer worth living under these circumstances.

1.4.1.

(1) At this point, I want to mention a very good, concentrated introduction to the problem of experiments with humans or on humans, in which the value conflicts and weighings that arise here are made clear: Günther Patzig, Ethische Aspekte des Versuchs mit Menschen (Ethical aspects of human experimentation), in: Gesammelte Schriften II, Angewandte Ethik (erroneously called "Grundlagen der Ethik" by an oversight on the part of the publisher), Wallstein Göttingen 1993, pp. 86–105.

(2) Helpers and politically active persons can also get into an analogous undesirable development.

1.4.2.

(1) However, this is not to deny that the wealthy countries bear some blame for the misery in the developing countries. Examples can be found quickly and in large numbers: the heavy burden placed on poor countries by adaptation to climate

change, though this is mainly attributable to the wealthy countries is in its current phase; the cooperation of corporations and states with corrupt dictators, which can often be described as complicity, in order to obtain raw materials without ensuring that a substantial share of the revenues reaches the population of the respective country; the destruction of traditional livelihoods when, for example, modern industrial fishing fleets empty the fishing grounds; unfair trade barriers – there is still a long way to go towards a more just world order. But there are rays of hope, such as the UN Convention against Corruption of 2003: it is no longer so easy and almost a matter of course for dictators to make off with their stolen billions.

(2) Instead of "shared humanity", I originally used "fraternity", a term of Christian origin (all human beings children of God, brothers and sisters in Christ; for the history of the term fraternity or brotherhood see Kamlah, W., Von der Sprache zur Vernunft. Philosophie und Wissenschaft in der neuzeitlichen Profanität (From language to reason. Philosophy and science in modern secularity), Bibliographisches Institut Mannheim/Wien/Zürich 1975, pp. 37, 38). See also a compilation of Bible verses about "Brothers in Christ": https://www.openbible.info/topics/brothers_in_christ, retrieved 3 February 2023. Contrary to a suggestion made by Detlef Zander as early as 1994, I have held on to this secularised Christian term for a long time. Why? "Fraternity" has a long history of impact and an emotional and appealing content that I did not want to do without at first. "Shared humanity" (Mitmenschlichkeit), on the other hand, can also be understood as a mere trivial description of the status quo. (Incidentally, I also have a strong aversion to the misguided "politically correct" feminist suggestion to undertake a consequent language purification avoiding all male or originally male-related general terms).

Over time, however, I have changed my thinking and now I would rather describe the emotional and appealing content of fraternity, which used to be assessed positively, as idealistic pathos, and I feel it is precisely positive that "shared humanity" is more realistic. We feel love or brotherly, sisterly or family affection and obligations only for very few close or genetically related people. The moral imperative of necessary - but also necessarily limited - solidarity with all other human beings is much more appropriately understood by "shared humanity" than by "fraternity" or "brotherhood" or even the Christian principle of "loving" thy neighbour as yourself. I do not think that we should proceed in morality in the same way trade unions sometimes proceed in wage negotiations, i.e. demanding double so that one gets at least half. In morality, a lack of realism easily becomes a cheap excuse for declaring its claims as unrealisable. If too great a sacrifice is demanded, a reasonable one is gladly spared as well.

(And despite my previous remark: of course it is preferable to use a gender-neutral term, as long as one does not have to spoil language in the process, does not bureaucratise it and does not diminish its expressive power too much).

1.4.4.

(1) However, communication should not degenerate into an end in itself without significant content; it should not be pushed to the fore too much in our lives and take up the last reserves of time. With the multitude of modern means of communication, their negative aspects also become clearer: we pay for the facilitation of communication with a considerable expenditure of time for the attention to and the feeding of the various communication means, we are put under pressure to respond promptly and have to fight harder for undisturbed time against various claims of permanent availability.

(2) Power as a means, not as an end in itself: an ideal. As a rule, only those will play a significant role in politics for whom power is also, at least to a considerable extent, an end in itself. Only for them, only for those who also enjoy power, does it outweigh all the deprivations and burdens, sacrifices (for example, concerning personal relationships with close people or the possibility of a relaxed, "purpose-free" interaction with other people) and the self-denial that tend to be associated with it. And: in order to gain power, it is useful not to be too far away from the prevailing views of those over whom or among whom one wants to exercise power, even if one exaggerates their views to the extreme (ideal or frightening). Those who are convinced themselves, are more convincing. They don't have to pretend and betray their principles as much.

(3) This means approximately: "above all the turmoil or mess or above the battle" - a metaphor worth considering whether in reference to historical turmoil or to that of individual life. Originally this was the title of an article by Romain Rolland in the Journal de Genève of 15 September 1914. Rolland was critical of the war and calling for understanding among the great European cultural nations and considered the general enthusiasm for war, shared and supported by a large part of European intellectuals, as a contagious epidemic. Later, the entire series of articles was also published as a book under this title: Paul Ollendorff Paris 1915, reprinted by Nabu Press 2010. Translated by C. K. Ogden: Above The Battle, Open Court Chicago 1916, available online: https://archive.org/details/abovebattle00roma/page/n7/mode/2up, retrieved 7 February 2023

(4) Here I would like to draw attention to a very beautiful essay by Bertrand Russell in which he takes up the cudgels for "useless knowledge": "'Useless' Knowledge", in: Russell, B. , Let The People Think, The Thinker's Library, No. 84, Watts London 1941, pp. 80–91. Russell emphasises in particular the value of "useless knowledge" for a contemplative habit of mind, which protects against

action without adequate previous reflection, for a profound apprehension of the universe and human destiny, for preserving serenity in misfortune and peace of mind among worries, and for the enjoyment of life.

5) By the way, when a philosopher of Montaigne's kind says something like this, it is only partly an observation and expression of opinion, but likewise an exhortation, above all to oneself, and this completely removes the touch of arrogance that may suggest itself to the casual reader.

(6) For the origin of the German version quotation see Büchmann, Geflügelte Worte (Dictums), keyword "Dort, wo du nicht bist". The source that comes closest is a line from Schubert's song "Der Wanderer" after "Des Fremdlings Abendlied" (The Stranger's Evening Song) by Georg Schmidt von Lübeck: "Dort, wo du nicht bist, dort ist das Glück!", translated by R. Wigmore: The Wanderer, available online: https://www.oxfordlieder.co.uk/song/1542, retrieved 8 February 2023. Quite similar before other sources also Shakespeare: "For what thou hast not, still thou striv'st to get, and what thou hast, forget'st." Measure for Measure, 1623, Act 3, Scene 1, for example in: The Complete Works of William Shakespeare, Henry Pordes London 1977, p. 90.

(7) About happiness and contentment: These terms are very well suited to stimulate reflection on one's own life and to take stock of one's own life, but in the end their concrete meaning can only be given by the individual and often enough not even then in a reliable and lasting way. "Happiness" and "contentment" are first of all descriptions of psychological states. Whether we consider the respective circumstances as a comprehensible cause of happiness and contentment and as worth striving for, is, however, something on which we can make philosophical comments.

"All men seek happiness ... This is the motive ...even of those who hang themselves", says Pascal (Pensées, 1670, Le Livre de Poche Paris 1972, Section VII, La Morale et la Doctrine, Pensée 425, p. 186, English text available online: https://www.gutenberg.org/files/18269/18269-h/18269-h.htm#SECTION_VII, retrieved 8 February 2023). And there is some truth in this, even if most people who hang themselves do so because they have had enough of unhappiness, which one will only call tantamount to the search for happiness if one has a very philosophical disposition.

But without a doubt: people react very differently and often seemingly paradoxically to the situations they find themselves in (which has a lot to do with their character disposition). Humans can still be content and happy when they are ill, poor, lonely or unfree (indeed, under certain circumstances they can even be more content and happy than before); on the other hand, they can be discontent and unhappy, although outwardly they seem to lack nothing. This was already stated

by one of the clearest and most modern thinkers of the 18th century Enlightenment, La Mettrie, in his treatise on happiness ("Anti-Seneca"), which is still very
worth reading: "I have known happy characters like this: often, the sick were even
in better humor than the healthy, and the poor than the rich ..." (Anti-Seneque ou
le Souverain bien, several editions 1748–1751, the 1750 Potsdam edition is available online: https://gallica.bnf.fr/ark:/12148/bpt6k1523675n/f19.item, p. 9, retrieved 8 February 2023; translated by K. Watson: Anti-Seneca, Or On Happiness, in: The Hedonist Alternative: Anti-Seneca, The System of Epicurus, and
Other Texts, Independently published 2014, p. 15).

However, we should take the ideas of a majority of our fellow human beings
about contentment and happiness very seriously. That they cannot be an absolute
measure is no reason to view them with condescension or to disregard them
lightly.

How should we distinguish between "happiness" and "contentment", and what
is their relationship to each other? For me, "happiness" is a term that rather describes moments of great instantaneous fulfilment, which for this reason rather
applies to short periods of time and is less suitable as an aim of a philosophical
conduct of life. (A state which, by the way, can now also be characterised quite
well neurophysiologically.) "Contentment", on the other hand, is a state of agreement with oneself and one's life situation on the whole. But this has nothing to
do with stoic detachment. There is much wisdom in the classic German fairy tale
ending "And they lived contentedly and happily ever after ..." - for those who are
happy and content can consider themselves truly fortunate. Only the calm sea of
contentment or only stormy moments of happiness - both are already worth a lot,
but only both together are truly happiness in the philosophical sense of a happy
life, where happiness and contentment then flow together again, in the sense in
which Bertrand Russell felt his life was happy (see the sentence quoted at the
beginning of this chapter) or in which Karl Popper said of himself in his autobiography that he was probably the happiest philosopher he had met. (Unended
Quest, 1974, Fontana/Collins Glasgow 1976, p. 126) And to describe such a degree of contentment this word is then even too restrained, it deserves the word
"happiness", even if it is not just about the happy moment here, but rather about
a deep contentment in life.

Both happiness and contentment are descriptions of mental states. They only
gain moral content through the way in which one seeks to achieve these states,
through the moral attitudes and values on which one bases one's conduct of life.

For those who want to look more closely at the philosophical and psychological
tradition on happiness and contentment, an excellent, concentrated article by Di-
eter Birnbacher is recommended: Philosophie des Glücks (Philosophy of Happiness), e-Journal Philosophie der Psychologie, No. 1, March 2005, http://

sammelpunkt.philo.at/id/eprint/2588/1/BirnbacherD1.pdf, retrieved 28.2.2010), slightly defaced in detail by abridgements, but substantially intact also in: Information Philosophie 1/2006, March 2006, pp. 7–22. Towards the end of his essay, Birnbacher very aptly warns against burdening the concept of happiness with morals instead of postulating moral standards independently of it: "It remains questionable whether the concept of happiness has a sufficiently large stomach and can tolerate such heavy fare." This is an interesting parallel to the inadequacy of too extensive moral values that I will explain at the beginning of section 1.4.6.. Another essay by Birnbacher is a very good addition regarding the psychology of happiness: Glück – Lustempfindung, Wunscherfüllung oder Zufriedenheit? (Happiness – Experience of Lust, Wish Fulfillment or Contentment?), Aufklärung und Kritik, Schwerpunkt: Glück und Lebenskunst (Main topic: happiness and the art of living), Sonderheft 14/2008.

(8) But anyone who thinks today that they can and should produce thoughts "only in their own workshop" is merely aggrandising themselves – something that already Brecht's Mr K. rightly could not stand.

At the end of this section, which is particularly rich in quotations, is the right place to expand a little on the defence of quotations, for which I have already used Walter Benjamin and Bertolt Brecht (Stories of Mr Keuner, "Originality", translated by M. Chalmers, City Light Books San Francisco 2001, p. 13, online: https://monoskop.org/images/6/69/Brecht_Bertolt_Stories_of_Mr_Keuner.pdf) in the motto and in the conclusion to the commentary volume of "God and the China Teapot". Some may be offended by the great number of quotations. One "doesn't do" such things – certainly not in the academic world – lest one be suspected of not having enough of one's own to offer. But the quotations have their justification and even programmatic significance. Beyond a more or less unstructured eclecticism on the one hand and a desperate striving for independence and originality on the other, thinking that seems essential is to be integrated, and here and there explicitly, not only in terms of content. Sometimes this is also a bow to the felicitous rhetorical form of a statement, or to the intellectual significance of the author, or a suggestion to the reader to read further. And there is the intention to make the intellectual web on which this book is grounded accessible to the readers and thus to enable them to use it for their own connections and expansions. Sometimes the quotations are also meant to provoke or to unfold a field of tension in which the discussion moves. The quotations give the book a richness that cannot be achieved otherwise – and this is nevertheless not a stolen richness. The eloquent defence of quotations that Wilhelm Schmid makes for Montaigne is one I also invoke for this book: "The aphorisms that are quotations create interstices in the text, pauses for somebody else to speak, breaks where one can halt to catch one's breath. They are fruits of reading that intersperse and break up the writing and bear witness to the long interludes that M. spent with the books, from which he picked up a sentence, walked around with it, let it gaze out of the window for a long time, confronted it with his long experience, rejected it or incorporated it into his own work ..." "These aphorisms ... are literally the dynamite of discourse, used to blow up continuity. ... They can have the function of an authority, a maxim, a proof, a mnemonic, an example or a bon mot." (Der Essay als Lebenskunst bei Michel de Montaigne (The essay as art of living in Michel de Montaigne), Schwabenakademie Irsee 1993, pp. 7, 8).

At this point it is almost impossible to miss another quotation: "If scientists copy from someone else's work, it is called plagiarism; if they copy from the work of several others, it is called mediocrity; if they copy from the work of many, it is called research" (copied by me from Volker Sommer, Wider die Natur? Homosexualität und Evolution (Against nature? Homosexuality and evolution), Beck München 1990, p. 158, who in turn has also copied it from at least two others).

1.4.6.

(1) At this point, I would like to expressly suggest two books, which have been cited several times in other context and in which very inspiring and reasonable thoughts can be found on many of the moral attitudes and values mentioned below: Wilhelm Weischedel, Sceptical Ethics, and Richard Robinson, An Atheist's Values (see Suggested Further Reading).

A more feuilletonistic, now and then somewhat redundant, on the other hand sometimes a little shorthand, in some chapters (such as the one on "purity") rather questionable, but overall quite successful and above all humane contemporary summary of and treatise on the philosophical teaching of virtues is given by André Comte-Sponville: Petit traité des grandes vertus, Paris 1995, translated by C. Temerson: A Small Treatise on the Great Virtues, 2001, Holt Paperbacks New York 2002. The fact that a contemporary philosopher writes such a breviary of virtues at all, and exposes himself to the sometimes unavoidable tightrope walk on the edge of triviality and masters it with some bravura, deserves respect. The greatest advantage of this book is its relativism (but not indifferentism), which is exemplified again and again by specific weighings – today a sine qua non for moral-philosophical reflections that want to be taken seriously. Incidentally, this book also demonstrates once again the vagueness of philosophical terminology: one can approach similar results in the discussion of philosophical content (much more so than in any of the specialised sciences) in quite different conceptual ways.

And even if not all of the virtues discussed by Comte-Sponville actually belong to the "great" virtues, it is worth reflecting a little on this choice of words. The "great" virtues or primary virtues usually have to do directly with the realisation of moral attitudes and values, or at least represent them. Take fidelity, for example: the virtue "fidelity" realises the moral attitude or value "fidelity" or at least represents its claim to moral consideration. Secondary or social virtues, such as politeness, on the other hand, are "only" indirectly related to the validity and realisation of moral attitude and values. This does not mean, however, that they are morally insignificant. What has considerable significance for our interpersonal relationships cannot be morally irrelevant. Tellingly, Comte-Sponville's book begins with a detailed, highly ambiguous discussion of politeness.

(2) The fact that moral attitudes and values are in competition with each other and must not be absolutised is of particular importance with regard to truthfulness.

Being honest does not mean giving in to a fanaticism about truth. Not deceiving other people does not mean imposing parts of the truth or what one believes to be the truth on them when one can foresee, or at any rate seriously has to fear, that they will have decidedly negative, destructive effects on the respective people (and their social relations) in the given life situation. Truth can be a positive provocation, but it can also develop destructive power or mean unnecessary cruelty. It must sometimes take a back seat to other moral attitudes and values. In general philosophical considerations, the striving for truth and (even if already somewhat subordinate and relativised) the truthfulness of expressed opinions have a very high value. In concrete individual life situations, on the other hand, youthful impetuous truthfulness or an (age-independent) exaggerated zeal for truth are signs of immaturity that can cause a lot of damage. Especially when it comes to central problems of human life, such as love or death, we should carefully consider which degree of truth is beneficial to the respective persons and best suits the totality of our moral attitudes and values.

(3) Transience is a fact. Readiness to depart is the philosophical attitude to deal with it appropriately. This also includes – but is not limited to – the "Carpe diem!" and the "Memento mori!". Horst Jaedicke provides an outlook on less widely publicised aspects of readiness to depart between ironic distance and indignation: Von der Kunst, das Leben zu verlängern. Sterben ist doof. Alles andere ist Lüge (On the art of prolonging life. Dying is stupid. Everything else is a lie), Edition BoD, ed. Vito von Eichborn, Books on Demand Norderstedt 2007.

(4) On a specific aspect of fidelity: I consider fidelity to a joint life plan and joint journey through life in a relationship of husband and wife (or other long-term partner relationships) to be an essential part of this moral attitude. But this does not have to be synonymous with sexual fidelity without exception. Only to some people the latter appears to be a natural consequence of great love. In general, exclusivity is neither a necessary nor a sufficient characteristic of fidelity.

The commitment to sexual fidelity without exception has its advantages and disadvantages. If one follows it, one avoids various risks: the risk of excessive, even life-threatening acts of jealousy, the risk of emotional conflicts that can go as far as despair, and the risk of losing mutual love through a sexual or erotic relationship with another partner. Medical risks aside, one also avoids the social risk of destroying and having to give up a jointly built way of living, and this too by no means concerns only material values. On the other hand, such a relationship can bring joy and variety. It can strengthen one's self-confidence by making one feel that one is still attractive to other people (this does not necessarily have to be so negative and exclusively self-centred that a relationship only serves to flatter one's own vanity). And it can contribute to the clarification of one's own feelings and save one from the feeling of having missed out on something, and can thus even strengthen the love for the permanent life partner. Nevertheless, exclusive intimacy remains one of the hallmarks of great love. This exclusive intimacy can only be shared to a very limited extent and certainly not many times.

The extent to which polygamous or monogamous inclinations occur statistically more or less frequently in men and women depends to a large extent on the respective social conditions. In any case, women can, under certain circumstances, increase their reproductive success through "extra-pair copulation", so that - contrary to earlier, simpler ideas of evolutionary biology - this can also be an evolutionarily meaningful strategy for them to a considerable extent (see: Hrdy, B. S., Mother Nature. Maternal Instincts and the Shaping of the Species, Vintage London 2000, especially pp. 245–257. And for an overview: Menninghaus, W. Das Versprechen der Schönheit (The promise of beauty), 2003, Suhrkamp Taschenbuch Wissenschaft Frankfurt a. M. 2007, pp. 180–183). Nevertheless, with regard to reproductive success and the investment made for this purpose, it remains plausible as a prevailing behavioural tendency that men tend to be more promiscuous and at the same time find it harder to forgive sexual infidelity, while women tend to concentrate more on one or a few successive partners and at the same time find it harder to forgive emotional infidelity than merely sexual infidelity. Evolutionary biology, however, can at best help to explain some of the difficulties in relationships between men and women. For the respective partners, it is important to find a way to live together, given their individual inclinations, without poisoning their relationship.

The right degree of sexual fidelity can be debated, and even people who really love each other will go different ways here. Fidelity to a joint life plan and joint journey through life, on the other hand, is a much more important and indisputable value for a lasting life partnership based on love. Without it, one runs a great risk of deeply hurting oneself and others and at some point finding oneself quite lonely. As illustration take the rather desperate struggle against loneliness that many of the protagonists in Woody Allen's films fight. To always live one's life according to the most intense or even the most recent feeling of love is a very questionable idea. Honesty is not the only moral attitude that matters, and even great, yearning love competes with other values, is not the only value that matters. On the other hand, there are undeniably relationships in which the common ground is lost - or never really existed - and whose continuation is only a torment or a life lie for those involved. My impression is, however, that, while in the past the maintenance of such relationships was often enforced by social pressure, today there is more of a danger that couples give up on relationships to hastily and thoughtlessly and that the importance of fidelity is underestimated. This is often connected with a wrong understanding of what really constitutes great love (that it does not depend on the attraction of the new) and also a wrong weighing of different moral attitudes and values.

Thus, in the process of the (undoubtedly necessary and gratifying) emancipation of individuals from social conventions and the accompanying, sometimes downright unconditional glorification of romantic love between man and woman, it was sometimes completely forgotten that fidelity also refers to joint children. In a whole series of films since about 1950, the great passion that strikes like a bolt of lightning is portrayed, and the children of the participants and the family conditions under which they grow up appear almost completely secondary, as something not worth considering. This looks good in the dramaturgy of films, but in reality it is just as inappropriate as the demand that a partnership must be maintained at all costs because of the children. A classic example of this genre is "Les amants" (The Lovers) by Louis Malle, 1958. The fact that the German distributor at the time felt obliged to cut out all scenes showing that the couple in question had a daughter documents the social narrowness of the 1950s, but in this case it does not speak against the moral evaluation that was assumed to prevail. The permanent relationship between two people, in institutionalised form: the monogamous marriage, is of course not the only possible core structure of the family and form of living together between man and woman (or same-sex partners), or the one that is absolutely morally preferable or even demanded by a "natural moral law". However, if one considers that under the conditions of modern civilised societies, with far-reaching and at least formal equality of the sexes and a high degree of personal aspirations in life, at least one third of traditional marriages, and in large cities as many as 50 percent, are divorced, this does not seem to me to be an argument that living together with more than two partners will be successful in the longer term in more than some individual cases. With more than two partners, it is much more likely that the problems and the risk of failure will increase considerably compared to a relationship of two people than that additional partners will have a redeeming effect. Well, lasting success is not the only standard of value for a love relationship and a partnership, but most people - me included - see it as a worthwhile goal, one of the essential sources of contentment and happiness in life.

Is it even possible to live the truly great love more than once at the same time? It may be that a few people manage to live and live out great love without the desire for exclusionary intimacy more than once during the same phase of their lives. If this is possible – and I remain quite sceptical about this – it is at least a very rare event. In the meantime, I believe that the mature decision for those people to whom great love happens twice at the same time – or better: who have the luck to experience it twice – is in the vast majority of cases to live the love that came along later as a friendship without a sexual relationship, or at least to make a decision and to stay committed to it in the future. Anything else carries a high risk of destroying the older and the newer love and of deeply hurting at least some of the people involved and, in the worst case, even destroying their physical existence.

In the long and often painful (and highly necessary) struggle against being constrained by religious and societal conventional restrictions, the great importance of self-chosen renunciations for a satisfactory shaping of human relationships in some situations has been pushed too far into the background. Sometimes such self-chosen renunciations are the only acceptable alternative.

(5) Even if the meaning of the concept of reasonableness cannot be defined in a generally valid way, reasonableness deserves to be mentioned as a comprehensive virtue that represents the necessity of the right, i.e. "reasonable" weighing of various moral attitudes and values (and also the consideration of people's natural inclinations, i.e. the renunciation of illusionary, unrealistic, and thus "unreasonable" excessive moral demands).

(6) The personal fundamental choice to live does not yet mean that life is generally regarded as a significant value.

(7) Justice is not only a moral attitude for the individual, but also a value for the shaping of society.

(8) Few terms are used with such different meanings as "equality". Absolute equality of all human beings in every respect is hardly desired by anyone. R. Robinson specifies the desirable degree of equality in a way that I largely agree with (in: An Atheist's Values, pp. 173–187, see Suggested Further Reading). The essential statement here is that equality should not be realised as levelling at a low standard. See also 3.8.2, 3.9.

(9) Moral attitudes in general could also be subsumed under values. However, the characteristic of a personal quality, virtue or objective associated with these

attitudes justifies a conceptual separation. Some of the examples mentioned here show that a differentiation of meaning can also be expressed in this.

Finally, I would also like to explain why I do not mention some terms that are often considered to denote values and may be missed here.

First: dignity, and in particular: human dignity. I do not believe that dignity is suitable as an independent value. Even the Kantian prohibition of the use of human beings as a means to an end is not able to give dignity a content that is reasonably undisputed in its essential meaning in a way comparable to that of other values. We constantly use other living beings and other human beings as means to ends and whether this is justified is decided by the values and moral attitudes that are pursued or disregarded in the process, but not without further ado by the fact or the extent of the use as a means. An example: If we consider the Allied soldiers fighting in the invasion on D-Day, they were undoubtedly used as a means of ending Nazi rule and little consideration could be given to their individual right to life. Nevertheless, given the values that were at stake, this kind of use as a means does not constitute a violation of human dignity.

But dignity is a heuristically (and also rhetorically) useful concept. Thinking about it can help us to find appropriate weighings between different values and moral attitudes. Peter Bieri exemplifies this excellently in his book "Eine Art zu leben. Über die Vielfalt menschlicher Würde", Hanser München 2013 (translated by D. Siclovan: Human Dignity. A Way of Living, Polity Press Cambridge and Malden 2017). In this function, the concept of dignity and human dignity has a rightful and important place in philosophical discussion and social debate as well as in law and especially in declarations of human and civil rights and in constitutions, even if its content remains blurred and it can only fulfil its function in connection with further and more concrete setting of values.

Property, too, may be missed as a value: Personal property, as necessary as a certain amount of it seems to me for a free and lively society, can, depending on its use, serve the realisation of the moral attitudes and values I cherish, but it can also stand in the way of it. That is why I do not list it as a value in its own right, but I do see it as an essential prerequisite for the realisation of a variety of moral attitudes and values.

And when I think about "home", I realise that the things that come to mind are already part of my morality (for example, through the choice to enjoy life, through the moral attitude of fidelity, through the values of life, freedom, love and beauty). In my consciousness, the term "home" summarises things that seem valuable to me without bringing anything fundamentally new. What seems valuable to me in my homeland also seems valuable to me on other parts of the earth's surface; it only seems particularly valuable to me in my homeland because I am familiar with it, know it from childhood or long habit and therefore feel secure.

Jean Améry convincingly describes the uprootedness and insecurity of those driven from their homeland. "The mere fact that one could not decipher people's faces was frightening. ... Faces, gestures, clothes, houses, words (even if I half-way understood them) were sensory reality, but not interpretable signs. There was no order for me in this world. Was the smile of the police official who checked our papers good-natured, indifferent or mocking? Was his deep voice resentful or full of good will? I did not know. ... I staggered through a world whose signs remained as inscrutable to me as Etruscan script. Unlike the tourist, however, for whom such things may be a piquant form of alienation, I was dependent on this world of riddles. ... Home is security, I say. ... One feels secure, however, where no chance occurrence is to be expected, nothing completely strange to be feared." (Jenseits von Schuld und Sühne. Bewältigungsversuche eines Überwältigten, 2. Aufl., Klett-Cotta Stuttgart 1980, pp. 82, 83; translated by S. Rosenfeld and S. P. Rosenfeld: At the Mind's Limits. Contemplations by a Survivor on Auschwitz and its Realities, Indiana University Press Bloomington and Indianapolis 1980, pp. 46, 47).

Home is an essential element for a person's psychological constitution, and all the more significant for those who have lost it. Philosophically, however, in a discussion about values, the term has primarily a heuristic role ("What is really important to me?").

If we have to say "I want to defend my country!", this should not be a manifestation of an enthusiastic and ill-conceived patriotism. Only when we are clear about the concept of homeland can we associate clear ideas with this statement: We then want to defend the possibility of living on a certain part of the earth's surface, to which we have become accustomed through long residence and perhaps especially through our childhood and youth, or to which we feel particularly attached because of certain personal inclinations and which we have become particularly familiar with, in the manner to which we are accustomed and which we and our fellow citizens value, while preserving our cultural and especially linguistic identity. Such (sober) reflections on the subject of "homeland" lead one to be a patriot and a cosmopolitan at the same time and not to regard these attitudes as incompatible in any way.

Accordingly, Gregor von Rezzori answered to the question "What does homeland mean to you?": "In any case, it's not what patriotic associations and songs convey, it's not deep emotion, it's very sober: I am more at home here than in Burma. The term homeland has nothing sentimental for me at all." ("I am a living anachronism", interview, Süddeutsche Zeitung, 26/27 November 1994, p. 19; see also: https://www.nytimes.com/1998/04/30/arts/gregor-von-rezzori-83-chronicler-of-a-lost-europe-dies.html, retrieved 13 February 2023)

This goes against all phoney, corny, merely nostalgic glorification of home.

But it excludes by no means that one associates feelings with one's homeland, with what this term represents and summarises, for example, about homely things, homely language, homely familiar tone or homely idioms, the various reminiscences of home in a foreign country or the return to home, the feeling of sadness when one loses one's home, the feeling of security that home conveys, for example through the ability to grasp and to evaluate immediately details and nuances of language, idiom and social interaction as described by Améry.

A sober analysis of the concept of homeland can protect us from a blind commitment to our country and also from having a love for the state or a party foisted on us under the pretext of love for our country. The state can (and should) preserve our homeland, but it can also destroy it.

And: Those who really love their homeland will not want to destroy other people's homeland.

Finally, home does not have to evoke positive feelings and associations for everyone. Some people will feel that their home and their homeland is oppressive, or that it is a place of misery and permanent conflict, and will be glad to leave it behind or to have left it behind and to find a new home somewhere else, or at least to be able to look for one.

2.1.

(1) Interesting reflections on this, especially from a historical-social-psychological perspective, can be found, for example, in: Gerhard Szczesny, The Future of Unbelief (see Suggested Further Reading).

(2) A very stimulating and worthwhile discussion of the problem of the "naturalistic" or rather: is-ought fallacy, combined with a fundamental critique of moral philosophy from a naturalistic-evolutionary-biological point of view, is offered by Eckart Voland: Genese und Geltung - Das Legitimationsdilemma der Evolutionären Ethik und ein Vorschlag zu seiner Überwindung (Genesis and validity - the legitimation dilemma of evolutionary ethics and a proposal to overcome it), in: Philosophia naturalis 1/2004, pp. 139–153, also available online: http://sammelpunkt.philo.at/id/eprint/2603/1/voland1.pdf, retrieved 15 February 2023. An essay that contains much intellectual explosive. Here are some samples: "Moral autonomy is illusory and remains a philosophical fiction. ... Morality is the execution of evolutionary programmes within the socio-ecologically limited room for manoeuvre given in each case." (p. 149). "...the biological genesis of morality simply means that nothing comes of the question of validity." (p. 150) With all due respect to naturalism and to avoiding illusions: by this kind of evolutionary reductionism Voland underestimates the discursive and deliberative capacities of our brain, which not only serve to rationalise after the fact, but can actually change our decisions, even against evolutionarily traceable motives. Under certain

circumstances, we can explicitly decide against what we recognise as biologically useful for ourselves. Evolution has given us a decision-making apparatus that is so differentiated that we are no longer completely dependent on what is evolutionary predefined, neither individually nor culturally.

(3) An interesting precursor of this thinking is Hugo Dingler. However, he is still in the tradition of classical rationalism and has not yet been able to free himself from a high-sounding, objectivist philosophical system claim. See, for example, Das System. Das philosophisch-rationale Grundproblem und die exakte Methode der Philosophie (The system. The philosophical-rational fundamental problem and the exact method of philosophy), Ernst Reinhardt München 1930, especially pp. 42-44.

(4) The formulations presented here are inspired by an excellent article by Wolfgang Prinz: Kritik des freien Willens. Bemerkungen über eine soziale Institution (Critique of free will. Some remarks on a social institution), Psychologische Rundschau 55 (2004), Issue 4, pp. 198–206, available online: https://www.studgen.uni-mainz.de/files/2019/02/Prinz_27.10.04_Manuskript.pdf, retrieved 16 February 2023

2.2.

(1) Today one would rather say: "... because ecclesiastical proposals of faith no longer prove convincing." Apart from its content, which remains fundamentally true, the Huxley quotation is interesting from an intellectual and historical point of view: the relationship between science and theology in the 19th century finds expression in it. More than today, theological statements were readily regarded as hypotheses in accordance with the methodology of modern science and could thus be easily dismissed from the point of view of scientists. This approach later lost its persuasive power the more one thought about the foundations of science itself and the more the theologians themselves interpreted many of their statements as metaphorical. Today and in the future, the contrast - here a scientist or a person oriented towards a scientific world view and there a believer - looks somewhat different. It is a question of what kind of belief people find convincing, what kind of belief they choose, whether they want to fall back on and trust a spiritually experienced, allegorically understood (revelatory) religion beyond the realm of science (that is no longer open to serious fundamental doubt), or whether they also demand good reasons for assumptions of philosophy of life and as a consequence reject a religious orientation in life and want to set their own moral attitudes and values.

And Huxley's diction is not that outdated: even in extreme metaphorically interpreted retreat positions, religious faith usually still contains hypotheses about the world for which there are no good reasons at all. It hardly makes sense, for example, to call a faith Christian if it does not contain the assumption (completely implausible for those unwilling to believe) of divine providence and divine intervention in the course of the world also between the act of creation and the last judgment.

(2) Jean Paulhan has provided a nice illustration of this unfortunate aspect of human nature in his "Entretiens sur des faits divers" (Conversations on Mixed News), which are well worth reading:

Me: "But thinking correctly means first and foremost giving the secret its place...

R. M. (René Martin): ...and introduce a zero, as it were, into our calculations about humans.

Me: So common sense is also prepared for atrocities and crimes.

R. M.: Have you seen those buildings in Italy that so proudly call themselves Palazzo della Ragione (that is, in a sense: Palace of Reason)?

Me: If I am not mistaken, these are the palaces where the patricides, thefts, rapes, and extortions of the kingdom are tried at appointed dates?

R. M.: Yes. All mixed news."

Entretiens sur des faits divers, Gallimard Paris 1945, p. 156, available online: https://archive.org/entretiensurdesf0000jean/page/156/mode/2up, retrieved 20 February 2023

(3) On the subject of individual morality, social morality and the justification by the will, the following text by Hans Reichenbach is also worth reading: The Nature of Ethics, in: id., The Rise of Scientific Philosophy, University of California Press Berkeley and Los Angeles 1951, pp. 276–302, especially pp. 294–302.

2.3.

(1) This is not only about self-numbing and escape, but also about a vague hope, about the longing for a different, more meaningful life that could be granted to one in the rush forward after all.

On the other hand, the modern prevalence of a relatively turbulent life should not be talked up too much in psychological and philosophical terms: it is often the result of compulsions that we have built up individually and socially because modern technical possibilities allow us to do so. Or it is about curiosity, the fear of missing out, the desire not to miss out on anything that can be packed into a life today. If we see exaggerations here and sometimes the focus seems to be set wrongly, this does not mean that we are numbing ourselves and fleeing from inner dreariness and emptiness. The possibilities open to people in the wealthy countries of the world today are also rightly fascinating.

(2) For German-speaking readers: An excellent overview of the knowledge relevant to our current worldview and the position of humankind in nature and the

universe is provided by Wolfgang Welsch in his Jena Anthropology Lecture of 2006/2007. Available on audio CDs: Anthropologie, 12 CDs, Auditorium Netzwerk Müllheim-Baden 2007.

(3) Such considerations have been made in cosmology for some time. As early as the beginning of the 1990s, the respected astrophysicist Dennis W. Sciama, for example, gave good reasons why such a consideration is not just wild speculation, proposing "that the hypothesis of the existence of many universes leads to verifiable statements and is therefore a physical hypothesis." "Whether it is also true will become apparent." (Sciama, D. W., Ist das Universum einzigartig? (Is the Universe Unique?) in: Börner, G., J. Ehlers, H. Meier, Hrsg., Vom Urknall zum komplexen Universum Die Kosmologie der Gegenwart (From the Big Bang to the complex universe. The cosmology of the present), Veröffentlichungen der Carl Friedrich von Siemens Stiftung, Piper München 1993, pp. 183–194, here p. 194). Progress made in recent years with regard to some of the difficulties of string theory makes such considerations seem increasingly attractive, even if the descriptive value of these mathematical models is not yet clarified, experimental confirmation is pending and even its possibility is uncertain. A good introduction to this discussion can be found in: Susskind, L., The Cosmic Landscape. String Theory and the Illusion of Intelligent Design, Little Brown New York 2006; Smolin, L., The Trouble with Physics: The Rise of String Theory, the Fall of a Science, and What Comes Next, Houghton Mifflin 2006. And for an overview of different views: Universe or Multiverse, ed. by B. Carr, Cambridge University Press 2007, available online: https://archive.org/details/bernard-carr-universe-or-multiverse/page/n1/mode/2up retrieved 22 February 2023

(4) A nice overview of the wealth of variants of such cosmological models including their respective prominent protagonists is given in a paper published 2004 by Rüdiger Vaas: Time before Time, available online: https://arxiv.org/ftp/physics/papers/0408/0408111.pdf (25 pages), retrieved 22 February 2023.

(5) This chain of improbable coincidences begins with the fact that "shortly" (in astronomical time scales) before the formation of our sun, a supernova exploded nearby, which gave the emerging solar system chemical elements that are indispensable for biochemical processes. In the 4.5 billion years that have passed since then, no such event has occurred in our cosmic realm. The resulting X-rays would have destroyed all life. Furthermore, our sun is not bound in a binary star system, like half of all stars in the universe, which therefore cannot bind planets to themselves. It also has a mass from which it should not deviate by more than 20 per cent, because otherwise either burning time or gravitational field would make the formation of life on a planet impossible. The fact that a planet orbits the central star on an almost circular path at the right distance so that water can exist in liquid

form may still be considered relatively probable. On the other hand, it is much more improbable that another planet got such an unusually large moon in relation to its own mass because it, like the Earth, was hit by a huge asteroid while still in a liquid state, which tore out this moon. Without the stabilisation of the Earth's axis by the moon, there would be no Earth atmosphere to make life possible. Finally, the conditions on Earth are also stabilised by the fact that the planet Jupiter, which is three hundred times heavier, is located in our solar system and reduces the probability of a comet impact on Earth through its deflecting force. A good, concentrated summary of astrophysical arguments for the 'uniqueness' of the Earth is given by: Illinger, P., Kein Platz für Außerirdische (No Place for Extraterrestrials), Süddeutsche Zeitung, 7 May 1998, p. 21. Similarly too: Dawkins, R., The God Delusion, see Suggested Further Reading, pp. 135–138.

(6) Franz M. Wuketits has critically dealt with the idea of evolutionary progress in various publications. Briefly summarised and concentrated, for example, in: Wuketits, F. M., Evolution und Fortschritt – Mythen, Illusionen, gefährliche Hoffnungen, in: Aufklärung und Kritik, 2/1995, pp. 39–50. A good paper on this topic in English was published in 2012 by N. A. Johnson, D. C. Lahti and D. T. Blumstein: Combating the Assumption of Evolutionary Progress: Lessons from the Decay and Loss of Traits, in: Evolution: Education and Outreach 5, 2012, pp. 128–138, available online: https://evolution-outreach.biomedcentral.com/articles/10.1007/s12052-011-0381-y, retrieved 23 February 2023.

7) Richard Dawkins makes this impressively clear in his "World History of Evolution" (written somewhat in the manner of historical fiction): The Ancestor's Tale: A Pilgrimage to the Dawn of Evolution, 2004, revised and expanded edition, co-authored by Y. Wang, Houghton Mifflin Harcourt Boston/New York 2016

(8) Paul Kurtz has written a differentiated and concentrated statement on the question of meaning of life with which I largely agree: The Meaning of Life. Ethics minus God, in: The Humanist, January/February 1975, reprinted in: Kurtz, P., In Defense of Secular Humanism, Prometheus Books New York 1983, pp. 153–168.

(9) Thomas Mann lets his narrator say it very well in "Doktor Faustus": "'Questionable' (bedenklich) is a splendid word; I have always attached a great philological value to it. It calls up a desire both to pursue and to avoid, or at any rate a very cautious pursuit, and it stands in the twofold light shed by what is noteworthy and notorious in a thing – or a person." Doktor Faustus, 1947, translated by J. E. Woods: Doctor Faustus: the life of the German composer Adrian Leverkühn as told by a friend, Alfred A. Knopf New York 1997, p. 119, available online: https://archive.org/details/doctorfaustus00thom_0, retrieved 24 February 2023, p. 118 of the pdf

(10) Briefly and aptly about fate or destiny, chance, custom: Odo Marquard in his

acceptance speech on the occasion of the award of the Sigmund Freud Prize for Scientific Prose in 1984: Skeptiker, in: Marquard, O., Apologie des Zufälligen, Reclam Stuttgart 1986, pp. 6–10, translated by R. M. Wallace: Sceptics: a Speech of Thanks, as 1.[2], pp. 3–7

(11) This also applies to all attributions of meaning or meaninglessness that we make about other people's lives – but such attributions are equally justified or unjustified as other value judgements we make.

3.1.

(1) See: Maturana, H. R., Varela, F. J., The Tree of Knowledge. The Biological Roots of Human Understanding, 1987, originally 1984 in Spanish: El árbol del conocimiento, revised English edition, Shambhala Boston and London 1998; and as an excellent literary illustration: Süskind, P., Die Taube, Diogenes Zurich 1987, translated by J. E. Woods: The Pigeon, Alfred A. Knopf New York 1988

(2) Reservations of subjectivity with regard to human ability of knowledge have been a recurring motif of thought since Bacon. Here are two more examples with slightly different nuances:

"With some self-discipline and self-observation we can all find out for ourselves that what we call seeing is invariably coloured and shaped by our knowledge (or belief) of what we see. ... If we look out of the window, we can see the view in a thousand different ways. One time we look at that, then at something else, and our sense impression is completely different when we look out for the postman or when we want to estimate whether it is going to rain." (Last sentence my translation from the 16th edition in German, differing from the English edition.) "It the sober truth that our feelings about things do colour the way in which we see them, and, even more, the forms which we remember. Everyone must have experienced how different the same place may look when we are happy and when we are sad." Gombrich, E. H., The Story of Art, 16th edition, Phaidon Press New York 1995, pp. 562, 564.

"People cannot say how something happened, but only how they think it happened." Lichtenberg, G. Chr., The Waste Books, Notebook C, German text: Aphorism 375, Sudelbücher I, Promies edition, p. 223, Rychner edition, p. 141, not included in Hollingdale's translation, see Suggested Further Reading.

The German word "Wahrnehmung" (perception) conveys a double meaning worth thinking about which is lacking in the words for perception of other languages that are derived from the Latin 'percipere' and are merely concerned with the reception of sense data. Taking the German word literally means, on the one hand, that we perceive something that we become aware of, but also that we take as true something that we perceive or believe or want to perceive.

We should be aware of the fact that the criterion for evolutionary success of perception and its interpretation is not truth but expediency in terms of survival and reproductive success ("differential fitness").

3.1.1.

(1) Popper's three worlds concept is an ontological structuring that can adequately comprehend this area of knowledge too. However, one should be aware that world 3 (which, in addition to objective formal scientific knowledge, includes all cultural concepts regardless of their truth content) is incommunicable without world 1 (the physical facts) and meaningless without world 2 (the mental contents). If this is neglected, one is in danger of slipping into groundless speculation, for example about hitherto unknown physical forces that cause spiritual force fields. In order to understand the power of cultural concepts, one should rather use history, sociology and psychology instead of trying to overthrow physics. (For a short overview of Popper´s three worlds concept see: https://en.wikipedia.org/wiki/Popper%27s_three_worlds, retrieved 10 March 2023.)

3.1.2.

(1) Although it has already become trivial and is used, among other things, as an advertising slogan for travel guides, Goethe's saying "We see only what we know" undoubtedly contains an essential partial truth about our ability for knowledge. (Goethe's original wording: »Was man weiß, sieht man erst!" Schriften zur Kunst, Propyläen, Einleitung, Artemis Gedenkausgabe, Zürich und Stuttgart 1954, Band 13, S. 142, dtv Gesamtausgabe, Band 33, 2. Aufl., dtv München, 1974, p. 77, translated by J. Gage: Goethe on Art, Introduction to the 'Propyläen', University of California Press Berkeley and Los Angeles 1980, p. 7. And: »Man erblickt nur, was man schon weiß und versteht.« You only see what you already know and understand. F. v. Müller's diary entry of 24 April 1819 about a soiree at Goethe's, Artemis Gedenkausgabe, as above, 2nd ed. 1966, vol. 23, p. 52).

This applies equally to the everyday and scientific use of our ability for knowledge: "It is the theory which decides what we can observe", Einstein said to young Heisenberg in 1926. Heisenberg, W. , Der Teil und das Ganze. Gespräche im Umkreis der Atomphysik, 2. Aufl., dtv München 1975, p. 80, translated by A. J. Pomerans: Physics and Beyond. Encounters and Conversations, Harper & Row New York 1972. p. 63, available online: https://archive.org/details/physicsbeyondenc00heis/page/n5/mode/2up, retrieved 10 March 2023, p. 62 of the pdf

(2) Consequently, special emphasis should be placed on the teaching of scientific thinking in education in fields of science that are particularly at risk in this respect, such as medicine. Unfortunately, just the opposite happens. Especially in medicine, unscientific practices are promoted politically time and again and are

also represented at universities to an astonishing degree. Not a few people consider alternative medicine at least a form of psychological care that should be tolerated or even promoted where scientific medicine no longer offers any chance of a cure. Although a fanaticism of veracity about the individual condition and prognosis has no place in the care of the terminally ill, this does not justify uncritical thinking, pseudoscientific procedures (which always set a bad example and the promotion of which represents a misuse of economic resources), self-deception or systemic fraud against the patient. Patients may expect physical and psychological help given to the best of one's ability, but they cannot have a claim to the application of scientifically unproven or even demonstrably ineffective procedures. (This is not directed against a placebo therapy that is applied in a well-considered situational manner with the therapist clearly understanding its character as such: this is indeed a scientifically proven therapy.) Leaving the individual patient in the dark about his or her situation or even sugar-coating it can be justified under certain circumstances. However, that doctors systematically deceive themselves and their patients about the effectiveness of healing methods is not acceptable at all. The fashionable tendency to make the patient's wish, rather than the medical appropriateness, the primary criterion for the application of medical procedures is an aberration, which is made even more unpleasant by the fact that it is used by certain therapists primarily for economic self-interest and even unashamed interest in enrichment (sometimes, however, it is also driven by economic need or at any rate to compensate for unjust economic disadvantage, a case for which one may muster a certain degree of sympathy).

Placebo therapy may even be more effective if therapists themselves are not aware that they are doing this kind of therapy. So one might say: Let the "alternative therapies" go about their business as long as they do not use harmful methods and as long as they know when time has come to use a scientifically justifiable medical procedure. But the matter is not that simple: apart from the fact that alternative medicine leads to a regrettable misdirection of financial resources, especially in times of scarcity, a very considerable danger that goes along with it lies in turning away from a scientific way of thinking and neglecting the education to it.

Through their behaviour and their many personal contacts doctors can (at present, unfortunately, one has to say too often: could) make a significant contribution to spread a scientific way of thinking among the population, more than other (scientifically) trained experts. Instead, many of them nowadays blur the boundaries to quack and charlatan medicine by applying and thereby enhancing such unscientific methods themselves; they participate in initiatives to combat marginal, and in some cases completely unproven and questionable risks, instead of advocating a rational risk assessment among the population in accordance with statistical risk comparisons, consistently directing attention to the main risks (which largely lie in the area of personal behaviour and lifestyle) and demanding appropriate political decisions as well as a rational use of the available means to reduce them. The failure of the medical profession to promote a scientific way of thinking is all the more regrettable because our education system has also proved to lack efficiency in this respect.

3.1.3.

(1) "Pluralitas non est ponenda sine necessitate" (Plurality is not to be posited without necessity). On the history and formulations of "Occam's razor", see, as a source in German, Enzyklopädie Philosophie und Wissenschaftstheorie, ed. Jürgen Mittelstraß, Metzler Stuttgart Weimar 1995, unchanged special edition 2004, vol. 2, pp. 1059 and 1063/1064. And in English: William of Ockham, Philosophical Writings. A Selection, translated by Ph. Boehner and revised by S. F. Brown, Hackney Publishing Indianapolis 1990, especially Introduction, pp. XX, XXI, and also Russell, B., History of Western Philosophy, 8th ed., Allen & Unwin London 1975, pp. 462, 463.

For a detailed discussion of the epistemological significance of simplicity or parsimony and its importance in the history of science see Elliot Sober: Ockham's Razors. A User's Manual, Cambridge University Press 2015. I agree with Sober's approach that the weighing of probabilities is and should be the core content of the criterion of simplicity or parsimony. But if he treats essential philosophical questions only with the formal tools of probability theory, this not only becomes tedious in the long run, but it is also inappropriate because conceptual clarification and the weighing of probabilities are closely related and must be applied together. Disregarding this, Sober claims that it makes sense to assess the probability of a simultaneously omnipotent, omniscient and omnibenevolent God. In his view, such a God could exist if he allowed evil to exist for reasons we cannot understand. But "these reasons we cannot understand" are tantamount to the complete dissolution of any meaningful concept of simultaneously all-powerful, all-knowing and all-good. If these qualities are understood to mean something entirely different from what we humans usually associate with them, the concept of a simultaneously omnipotent, omniscient and omnibenevolent God becomes empty talk and we simply no longer have any idea of what we are still weighing a probability for.

(2) And what theologians deem simple(r), even prominent ones, can be quite striking anyway. Some fine examples of this (especially with regard to Swinburne's views) are given by Richard Dawkins in 'The God Delusion', see Suggested Further Reading, pp. 147–151.

(3) A good overview of the intricacies of the principle of simplicity can be found in an article by S. Fitzpatrick in the Internet Encyclopedia of Philosophy:

https://iep.utm.edu/simplici/, retrieved 12 March 2023.

3.1.4.

(1) This interaction and the haziness between invention and discovery is nicely outlined by Lorraine Daston in the introduction to her book "Biographies of Scientific Objects", The University of Chicago Press, Chicago and London 2000, especially pp. 3, 4, 13.

(2) Convincing arguments for a critical and hypothetical realism do not only result from the scientific process of knowledge. Only at first glance do the different ways of seeing the world in the history of art (and in particular in representational art) appear to be an argument in favour of constructivism. On closer examination, however, they provide a strong argument against it: Basically, the many and varied artistic ways of looking at the world, shaped by very different cultural backgrounds and motivations, lead to an increasingly self-critical, complementary way of looking at the world in their historical sequence, as we perceive them today in retrospect and can experience them in a parallelism not accessible to earlier cultures.

3.1.5.

(1) Provided that the theological faculties are fully supported by the churches as independent universities, the faculties of the respective religions historically established in a society can still be granted a right to remain in association with the corresponding universities for reasons of cultural tradition, if they attach importance to this.

However, if Islamic faculties dependent on religious confession and denomination are to be newly established in countries like Germany, this is a decidedly negative development. For a country like Atatürk's Turkey, and even for Turkey today, it is politically wise to bring theology and the training and funding of religious teachers under state control. A secular central European democracy in the 21st century, on the other hand, brings shame on itself when believing that it needs to take such action in the fight against religious extremism.

(2) This remark is reported by Lee Smolin in his book »The Trouble with Physics: The Rise of String Theory, the Fall of a Science, and What Comes Next«, Houghton Mifflin 2006, p. 297, p. 367). The reference to Lakatos' book »Proofs and Refutations« is not specified and could not be tracked. By the way: Part IV of Smolin´s book (»Learning from Experience«, pp. 261–355) is also a worthwhile reading on the real and the desirable course of action in science.

(3) A concentrated and clear summary on the subject of verification/falsification is provided by Mario Bunge in: Dictionary of Philosophy, Prometheus Books Amherst 1999, headwords "falsifiability" and "falsificationism" and the cross-

references there. In general, this philosophical dictionary is a worthwhile and refreshing, clarifying read (even if there is a little bit of forcible simplification under one or the other headword).

(4) This "internal consensus" has become notorious, especially in German social and pharmaceutical law, as a prerequisite for the authorisation of scientifically unfounded therapeutic procedures (this legal provision of 1976 is still valid in spite of increasing criticism). However, it is a widespread pseudoscientific argumentation. A concise and entertaining read about this is a book by Martin Lambeck: Irrt die Physik? Über alternative Medizin und Esoterik (Is physics wrong? On alternative medicine and esotericism), 2nd ed., Beck München 2005, especially pp. 35, 36.

(5) Both the very different uses of the term "understanding" and the errors and misuses associated with it are very well analysed by Günther Patzig: Erklären und Verstehen. Bemerkungen zum Verhältnis von Natur- und Geisteswissenschaften (Explaining and understanding. Remarks on the relationship between natural and human sciences), in: Gesammelte Schriften IV, Wallstein Göttingen 1996, pp. 117–145 (also a good introduction to the history of the "Verstehen-Erklären" controversy).

(6) To me the most likable, and, depending on the historical situation, more or less good excuse for maintaining one's attachment to a religious community as a scientifically minded person is the social one. It is nicely illustrated by the bon mot with which Phil Zuckerman quotes his father: "Shlomo goes to synagogue to talk to God. I go to synagogue to talk to Shlomo." (Living the Secular Life, see Suggested Further Reading, p. 64)

3.1.7.

(1) A worthwhile read on this is an essay by Theodor Ickler: Zum Diskurs von Para- und Pseudowissenschaften (On the discourse of para- and pseudosciences), in: Aufklärung und Kritik, 1/1995, pp. 29–56, regretfully not digitised and not translated

3.1.8.

(1) An instructive as well as amusing discussion of the importance of intuitions is offered by Gerd Gigerenzer: Gut Feelings. The Intelligence of the Unconscious, Viking New York 2007. However, the advantages of intuitions are emphasised somewhat too one-sidedly here. Some nuances are probably somewhat different shortly before a global economic and financial crisis than afterwards.

A worthwhile read on the misjudgements of human intuition (and human thinking) is offered by Dietrich Dörner's book "Die Logik des Mißlingens", 1989, translated by R. and R. Kimber: The Logic of Failure, Henry Holt & Co New York

1996

3.1.9.

(1) A very good overview of the philosophical discussion of language is given by Günther Patzig: Die Sprache, philosophisch befragt (Language, a philosophical survey), in: as note 3.1.5. (5), pp. 146–168. He maintains an appropriate balance between a critical deliberation of language and the acceptance and appreciation of natural language.

The extent to which our view of the world and our behaviour are influenced by our respective language is a highly interesting question. A worthwhile and very readable account of the history of science in this field and the current state of knowledge is provided by Guy Deutscher: Through the Language Glass. How Words Colour Your World, William Heinemann London 2010. An interesting text on this topic is also Patzig's contribution in the same volume as above: "Wilhelm von Humboldts 'kopernikanische Wende' in der Sprachbetrachtung" (Wilhelm von Humboldt's 'Copernican Turn' in the Consideration of Language), pp. 230–247.

(2) Kant not only attacked the philosophical foundations of contemporary society, but also made very concrete, eminently political statements, for example, he delivered a sharp critique of colonialism, see his book "Perpetual Peace", which in many points outlines a programme that is still utopian even for today's politics, but nevertheless highly necessary.

And on Kant's linguistic self-criticism: Letter to Christian Garve of 7 August 1783, Akademieausgabe, Vol. X, pp. 336-342, here p. 337, quoted by me giving the general sense of it from: Patzig, G.. 200 years of Kant's "Critique of Pure Reason", in: as note 3.1.5. (5), pp. 209–229, here pp. 213, 214. The letter was translated by A. Zweig: Immanuel Kant, Correspondence. Cambridge University Press 1999, pp. 196, 197, available online: #https://prussia.online/Data/Book/co/correspondence/Kant%20I.%20Correspondence%20(1999).pdf, retrieved 22 March 2023, pp. 216, 217 of the pdf

(3) I don't like Heidegger. But that is not only because of his language. I do not see any acceptable contribution by him to the important tasks of philosophy of criticising ideologies and providing orientation in life. Instead of distancing himself with sufficient clarity from his initial promotion of national socialism and his actions during his rectorate in Freiburg, he has only ever tried to excuse his conduct. I particularly resent the fact that he – just like Ernst Jünger, whom I dislike equally, especially for this reason – claims a position for extraordinary human beings that relieves them of the moral obligation of justification that applies to others. Both are of the opinion that above a certain level of intellectual excellence (which is, of course, exceeded by themselves) one no longer has to justify oneself

for one's mistakes in the same way as ordinary people have to. If they exist at all, the fog of unclear, romanticised thinking prevents feelings of guilt from coming to light. Nevertheless, I grapple with Heidegger more than with many other philosophers in whose work I see a more essential contribution to human thinking. This also has to do with the fact that I see in Heidegger a very German example of bad philosophy, whose roots go back to Romanticism and whose consequences still manifest themselves today in the great influence that an irrational, religious ecologism exerts in Germany.

3.2.

(1) Observations of identical twins who grew up separately provide remarkable findings on the significance of genetic predispositions. Even if they differ in many respects and no reliable conclusions can be drawn from the behaviour of one twin to that of the other, the similarities range from everyday trivialities such as a preference for the same toothpaste to professional interests, views on death penalty or the degree of religiosity or, more precisely, spirituality. A brief summary and further references can be found in Steven Pinker, The Language Instinct, William Morrow and Company New York 1994, pp. 335, 336, available online: https://archive.org/details/languageinstinct0000pink_d1h2/page/336/mode/2up, retrieved 27 March 2023. pp. 334, 336 of the pdf.

(2) With Sven Walter, I find "banal", or at least morally irrelevant situational unconscious influences particularly problematic if they lead us to "demonstrably deciding and acting on the basis of motives with which, had we been aware of them, we would not have been able to identify, that is, we would not have been able to recognise them as 'ours' and approve of them against the background of our profile of preferences and values." (On the debate about free will: a conclusion, in: Information Philosophie 3/2011, August 2011, pp. 42–49, here p. 45) Such influences have been demonstrated by social psychology in many ways, for example in the form of the well-known responsibility-inhibiting "bystander effect" or of experiences influencing mood or else altering our sensory perception (even if only in the form of simple haptic experiences) immediately preceding our decisions (situationism). An overview of this discussion can be found here: Upton, C.L. Virtue Ethics and Moral Psychology: The Situationism Debate. J Ethics 13, 103–115 (2009). https://doi.org/10.1007/s10892-009-9054-2, retrieved 14 April 2025.

If one strives for a philosophical conduct of life, one will have to try to become aware of such influencing factors to the best of one's ability in order to be able to control and correct them through well-founded considerations. The fact that we will undoubtedly only succeed to a limited extent in this remains a humiliation for reason.

(3) Fortunately, we humans relatively rarely realise destructive psycho-pathological

impulses and behaviours, whether in the private sphere or on the societal level - and if we do, we rightly have to reckon with therapeutic, criminal or, in extreme cases, martial sanctions. The fact, however, that we take considerable pleasure in imaginary and fictitious rule-breaking, just think of all the criminal cases, horror and sadomasochistic stories in literature and the visual media, could also be explained in part (the more positive one) as our brain's constant experimentation with behavioural alternatives and thus as an expression of the degrees of freedom we have evolved to have. Edgar Allan Poe was already aware of this part of our nature, made ample use of it in his stories and explicitly exaggerated our tendency to realise it in order to heighten the horror: "Yet I am not more sure that my soul lives, than I am that perverseness is one of the primitive impulses of the human heart – one of the indivisible primary faculties, or sentiments, which give direction to the character of Man. Who has not, a hundred times, found himself committing a vile or silly action, for no other reason than because he knows he should *not?* Have we not a perpetual inclination, in the teeth of our best judgement, to violate that which is *Law,* merely because we understand it to be such?" The Black Cat, 1846, for example in: Complete Stories and Poems of Edgar Allan Poe, Doubleday New York 1984, p. 65.

(4) That these findings – admittedly anti-intuitive for pre-scientific thinking – are not really anchored in people's minds, however, is shown by the extent of the reaction to Benjamin Libet's experiments published in 1983 and the intensified controversy about freedom of the will since then. (For a description and discussion of the Libet experiments see: https://en.wikipedia.org/wiki/Benjamin_Libet, retrieved 27 March 2023) From a naturalistic point of view it is not at all surprising that our intentions are preceded by measurable brain processes that correspond to them but only reach our consciousness after a short delay. Obviously, even in the scientific community, enough people are still surprised by what is to be expected, so they still seem to flirt with a dualistic-metaphysical concept of the mind.

(5) Even according to a traditional deterministic, "mechanistic and reductionist" view of brain function, the described diversity of the preconditions pertaining to different individuals and the complexity of the influences acting on them are sufficient to make a reliable prediction of human behaviour impossible.

At this point, a short digression is made for readers who are inclined to be distracted for a moment from the main line of argument on the subject of free will: Those who celebrate deterministic chaos with all too much enthusiasm as a new scientific paradigm and place it in sharp contrast to previous thinking, especially in the natural sciences, must ask themselves how this natural science could be so successful by investigating only the regular exceptions, "an artificial world of the simple".

Mathematical models of "deterministic chaos", with their inherent unpredictability of the results achieved after a certain runtime of the model, can possibly help us to better understand certain sub-structures and functions of the human brain. As a global brain model, however, they are only a new inadequate simplification. Chaos theory is just as suitable as quantum theory before it to spout fashionable gibberish without explanatory value.

Results of chaos theory must not be transferred lightly to real systems and misused as arguments. This applies, for example, to the "butterfly effect". If the smallest deviations or changes in the initial state in a computer model cause large deviations in the subsequent states after some time, this can only be transferred to systems in nature or society to a very limited extent. If systems in the real world are at all stable in the long term, then this is precisely an indication that they have a considerable tolerance or possibility of correction with regard to changes in the environmental conditions. In environmental discussions, for example, references to butterfly effects are rather harmful because they create diffuse fears, lead to the minimisation of marginal risks and distract from much more massive influences that can actually change our environment in a way that is highly unfavourable for humans.

Leaving aside the system-theoretical aspect, the possible effects of butterfly effects are, moreover, in no way more impressive than the effects that initially seemingly insignificant punctual coincidences or chance can have more or less immediately. Because of a traffic jam someone misses an aeroplane which then crashes, or a dictator shortens his speech because he does not feel well and thus escapes an assassination attempt, with the consequence that under certain circumstances hundreds of thousands of people have to die in a war he has instigated, or a comet or a large meteorite that was deflected long ago passing a star in the depths of space hits the earth or does just not hit it, and so on - a well-known point of view for which there are many concrete examples with more or less serious consequences.

But back to the problem of scientific theories and models. We obviously need different models for different questions. If the coastline of Great Britain is infinitely long in fractal terms, this insight may be of much less use to us for certain tasks than a concrete number resulting from a simplifying approach. In the same way, classical physics is not only completely sufficient for many practical problems, but also much better applicable, and only for the understanding of atomic or subatomic processes do we need quantum theory or for the understanding of processes in the range of the speed of light the theory of relativity. The models of deterministic chaos can help us to better simulate and understand certain processes in nature and in human society. They can further our understanding of complexity and the limitations of our predictive capabilities. This can also generate an appropriate and desirable degree of humility. And it may help us to better achieve the goals we set for the future. But we should not construct too much of a contradiction to previous scientific thinking out of this. And above all, we should not allow the chaos paradigm to be used to undermine scientific quality standards and to support the fashionable tendency of hostility towards science and technology.

With reference to quantum theory, we have already been served up enough pseudo-scientific talk, especially in connection with the topic of "freedom of will", partly even with the support of renowned physicists. The hundredth birthday of quantum theory in 2000 provided examples in abundance. The physicist Wolf Pohl briefly and succinctly summarised what needs to be said: "For the micro events in the area of atoms and elementary particles the principally indeterministic quantum theory applies, which only specifies probabilities for the possibilities of future events. ... What does the limitation of determinism by quantum theory mean for the problem of free will? Nothing. For the processes that are of significance for human life are so macroscopic that any quantum events have no significant influence. This certainly also applies to the neuronal processes in the brain that are decisive for the problem of free will. Apart from that, the fact that quantum processes could have an influence on neuronal events would not mean anything good for the problem of free will. For what would be gained if our so-called acts of will, insofar as they do not proceed deterministically, were controlled by random quantum processes?" (Pohl, W., Determinismus und Willensfreiheit (Determinism and freedom of the will), unpublished lecture manuscript 2000, p. 1).

A very good, detailed discussion of the instrumentalisation of chaos theory and quantum physics in the discussion of free will is provided by Daniel C. Dennett: Freedom Evolves, 2003, Penguin London 2004, Chapter 4, A Hearing for Libertarianism, pp. 97–139, with references and starting points to study the history of this whole discussion.

Gerhard Roth also deals shortly and succinctly with this topic, pointing out that there are also deterministic physical processes – of a much lower complexity than our brain functions – whose behaviour cannot be calculated or predicted: Hume, Willensfreiheit und Hirnforschung (Hume, freedom of the will and brain research), Aufklärung und Kritik, 1/2011, Schwerpunkt: David Hume zum 300. Geburtstag, pp. 167–183, in particular pp. 169, 170.

The decisive résumé against all these instrumentalisations of different theories in favour of freedom of will is, with Reinhard Merkel: "... that everything that is determined allows no alternative and everything that is indeterminate allows no control." And: "With excursions into the difficult areas of quantum physics, chaos theory and other natural sciences, one may assert rather than prove some kind of emancipation of the mental from the neurophysiological. But then one is hopelessly confronted with the problem of having to draw the just abolished determination of the will by the brain from some other source, in order to prove it to be controllable and manoeuvrable ..." (Willensfreiheit und rechtliche Schuld. Eine strafrechtsphilosophische Untersuchung (Freedom of the will and legal guilt. A treatise on the philosophy of criminal law) Nomos Baden-Baden 2008, pp. 77, 78).

At this point, let me make a comment on our dreams of artificial intelligence (in a sense that really deserves the name). If we can mimic certain brain functions (and provide some of them even faster and more reliably than our brains can), whether with digital machines in the traditional sense or with new generations of computers and robots, this is fundamentally different from the task of researching and understanding how our brains actually produce such functions - although such machine simulation and mimicking may help us, or even be indispensable, in order to make progress in understanding our brains. Gerald Edelman: "Computers are not appropriate models of brains, but they are the most powerful heuristic tools we have with which to try to understand the matter of mind." (Bright Air, brilliant Fire: on the matter of the mind, Basic Books New York 1992, p. 194). This book is still recommended for anyone interested in the discussion of the analogy or discrepancy between the brain and the computer and in science's efforts to simulate brain functions.

On the other hand, the function of the nervous system and especially of the brain is capable of giving us ideas for the development of ever more sophisticated hardware and software.

It is difficult to estimate how far we will be able to make progress in understanding our brain and reproducing its functions in the future (and how much we will want to do so). Today's computers and robots already show us that we can imitate partial functions of our brain with machines and algorithms that are built completely differently from this brain. No one knows where the limits lie here, but we have certainly not reached them by a long shot. After all, we have also learned to fly with machines that function completely differently from a bird. Even if the analogy may be lame and refers to a much simpler function, it still shows us that one can arrive at similar results in completely different ways.

In any case, artificial intelligence opens up a wealth of new, previously unattainable possibilities for us. Many applications are already emerging, for example when it comes to fatigue-free pattern recognition. And as so often in the history of technology, the new possibilities are used constructively, for example in medicine, as well as negatively and destructively, for example for the ever more perfect surveillance of citizens in dictatorships or new methods of warfare.

Efforts to technically imitate and emulate the brain will continue. A relatively early, well-founded optimistic assessment of possibilities in this regard is given P. M. Churchland: The Engine of Reason, the Seat of the Soul. A Philosophical Journey into the Brain, 1995, Paperback Edition, Sixth Printing, The MIT Press Cambridge 1999. Meanwhile research burgeons in the fields of artificial intelligence, neuroengineering and cognitive science. For an overview on fundamental problems and the wealth of research approaches see: Norvig, P., Russell, S., Artificial Intelligence: A Modern Approach, Fourth Edition, Pearson Harlow 2022.

Since the brain is a physicochemical structure, it seems possible in principle to reproduce this structure and its functions artificially. However great the practical difficulties are: so far, none of the fundamental objections that have been raised against such a possibility have been lastingly convincing. (Like many earlier erroneous predictions about the limits of what is scientifically achievable, they could also be based on a lack of imagination.) Even if this still seems very unlikely at the moment, it cannot be ruled out that with the acquisition of the ability to artificially imitate and possibly exceed the personality-relevant performances of their brain, humans will face another of those humiliations they have already incurred as a consequence of other scientific triumphs (which in this case would be connected with serious new moral problems concerning the status of such artefacts).

On the other hand, it is also quite possible that the idea of artificial persons is based on fundamental errors and will remain forever unrealisable: Human thought and action appears in many ways to be inseparably linked to our evolutionary and individual developmental history, our social relationships, our diverse sensory and bodily experiences, our interests, longings, desires and appetites, our memories, which, moreover, are not lexically fixed, but can be modified and reevaluated again and again in the course of our lives. These arguments are impressively presented by Siri Hustvedt in her book "The Delusions of Certainty. Reflections on the Mind-Body Problem", Sceptre London 2016.

(6) The threats to human freedom also include mental illnesses, in the most extreme form psychoses and drug addiction. Here, our social action and our legal system are, at least in Germany, still determined far too one-sidedly by the idea of protecting the freedom of those affected, although their free will is more or less suspended due to their illness. It is easy to focus primarily on protecting the freedom of the sick, because this requires intervention only in the case of the most obvious threats to others. However, this approach has serious negative and sometimes fatal consequences for the sick themselves, their relatives and society. In the long run, one will have to recognise at some point that a morally and socially justifiable approach does require compulsory treatment or at least pressure under threat of sanctions to agree to treatment in certain appropriate cases as one of the possible measures. It is wrong to restrict the concept of self-harm of mentally ill persons

to the most serious immediate dangers, such as the risk of suicide, serious self-injury or a restricted food and fluid intake insufficient for survival. The concept of the risk of self-harm, which is relevant with regard to compulsory treatment, should also include progressive social decline and personal neglect, if these are recognisable as illness-related and appear with considerable probability to be avoidable through adequate therapy. Otherwise, we are abandoning people to misery who are incapable to make free choices.

3.3.

(1) This scientific discipline owes much to logical empiricism and the early analytic philosophy that succeeded it. The language of morality, concepts, thought structures and modes of argumentation are examined much more precisely than before. Thus a specification and clarification of the questions at hand is achieved. Some contributions to this line of thought that are particularly worth reading should be explicitly mentioned here: Stevenson, C. L., Ethics and Language, Yale University Press New Haven and London 1944; Hare, R. M., The Language of Morals, 1952, Oxford University Press London/Oxford/New York 1964; Nowell-Smith, P. H., Ethics, Penguin London 1954; Frankena, W. Ethics, Prentice-Hall Englewood Cliffs 1963, second edition 1973, available online https://dor-shon.com/wp-content/uploads/2018/03/Ethics.pdf, retrieved 28 March 2023.

However, when it comes to normative philosophical questions, at least those beyond the norms of philosophical communication, this school of thought largely refrains from taking a stand. The questions of whether and why we should obey a certain morality and what it should be like are usually left unanswered. They are either avoided by claiming that the conceptual clarification in this part of philosophy has not yet progressed far enough to be able to answer them, or else they are banished from the philosophy that one is interested in and wants to pursue and relegated to the sphere of personal decisions that cannot be discussed philosophically any further. At best, quite decrepit rationalist moral constructions are offered (for example, in Frankena, when he presents a critical, rational approach to moral questions as a sufficient justification for a moral judgement. (As above, Chapter 6: A Theory of Justification, pp. 111, 112, pp. 123, 124 of the pdf)

The price for this philosophy, which only appears to be free of a philosophy of life, is high: it means to abstain mostly from suggestions for coping with practical life. Such a (self-)limitation of philosophy is wrong and disastrous. This kind of highly one-sided selection of interest, aptly called an "existential deficit of philosophy" (see also Introduction) is at the same time provocative and unattractive – this is how I experienced analytical philosophy in the seventies of the 20th century during my studies at German universities.

However, the self-restraint described above is by no means synonymous with a life in the ivory tower, ideological disinterest or ideological indifference. Various members of the Vienna Circle, for example, were politically and socially very committed, although they did not believe they could give any philosophical justification for this. And Wittgenstein, for example, considered the questions about which he believed he could not speak philosophically to be the most important ones in life (Letter to Ludwig von Ficker, probably end of October 1919, available online: https://edition.ficker-gesamtbriefwechsel.net/#/briefe/nach-jahren/50ce1a03-9af3-442b-b86e-8a0d8e29d01b, Datierung 1919-10-31; an English translation can be found in: Tejedor, Ch., The Ethical Dimension of the *Tractatus*, in: Doubt, Ethics and Religion. Wittgenstein and the Counter-Enlightenment, ed. Perissinotto, L., Sanfélix, V., Ontos Heusenstamm 2011, p. 85, the passage from the letter is also available online: https://www.degruyter.com/document/doi/10.1515/9783110321883.85/html?lang=en, both retrieved 28 March 2023).

Although such an attitude contains a potential for a critical evaluation of ideologies and philosophies of life, it nevertheless results in leaving terrain to restorative or untenable conservative lines of thought.

But essential problems can only be suppressed for a while. In contrast to the perception I had during my studies, philosophers in the tradition of logical empiricism and analytical philosophy very soon began to deal with questions of the philosophical orientation of life and to make their personal standpoint clear enough. A good compilation of representative sections from such works can be found in: Fehige, C., Meggle, G., Wessels, U., (eds.), Der Sinn des Lebens (The meaning of life), dtv München 2000. A smaller but also worthwhile reader in English is: Klemke, E. D., Cahn, S. M. (eds.), The Meaning of Life, third edition, Oxford University Press 2008.

Nevertheless, even today, many philosophers regard a personal statement on the philosophy of life as suspicious and as a violation of a kind of scientific purity law of philosophy. Wrongly so: A philosophical conduct of life should indeed mean that one clarifies one's concepts, argues for certain positions with well-founded arguments and points out where personal decisions are necessary and unavoidable. Provided that, however, the description of such decisions and the argumentation for certain such decisions is then also a legitimate and important part of philosophy. Philosophers should always be aware of the fact that they cannot gain ground with too much nobility in the face of far less reflective and reserved religious or secular ideological orientations of life. In other words, philosophers should have the courage to present us not only with their ethics, but also with their morals.

(2) A good, readable summary of what evolutionary biology, evolutionary psychology and developmental psychology have contributed so far to the description of

our moral status quo is given by Marc D. Hauser: Moral Minds. How Nature Designed Our Universal Sense of Right and Wrong, HarperCollins New York 2006. The book has an optimistic undertone, the justification of which further human history will hopefully prove. To complete the inventory of our moral status quo, a comparably good book on the socio-cultural aspects of our morality would have to be written, including both the psychology of historical moral catastrophes and that of the great events of progress in human history.

(3) Based on an insight by Hume (A Treatise of Human Nature, Book III, 1740, Fontana/Collins London 1972, p. 208), the derivation of the ought from the is became also known as the "naturalistic fallacy": "It is impossible, therefore, that the character of natural and unnatural can ever, in any sense, mark the boundaries of vice and virtue". This is also an interesting example of what may happen to concepts in the history of philosophy: It was G. E. Moore (Principia Ethica, 1903, Cambridge University Press 1922, Chapter 1, pp. 10–20) who explicitly coined the term "naturalistic fallacy", which is predominantly used today to describe a viewpoint such as that put forward by Hume. Yet Moore used the term in a clearly different way, namely in the sense of the "indefinability" of the term "good" by other properties. Therefore, conceptually and in terms of philosophical history, it is better to speak of the "is-ought fallacy" when referring to the naturalistic fallacy in Hume's sense. This is, however, difficult to push through against the tradition that has been created in philosophical debate. On the is-ought fallacy see also 2.1, pp. 73, 74 and note 2.1 (2).

Searle (Speech Acts, Cambridge University Press 1969, pp. 175–198) has shown that it is not impossible in a linguistic-analytical, logical sense to derive a proposition of ought from a proposition of being, that there is at any rate a more than coincidental relationship between these propositions and even a consequential relationship can exist or be established. This, however, does not eliminate the critique of the is-ought fallacy as essentially for ethics, namely that kind of critique that is expressed in Hume's quoted formulation. Even if there is a logical and linguistic connection between propositions of is and propositions of ought, it is still true that no recommendations for certain moral attitudes and values and the morally appropriate balancing between them can be derived from the mere description of reality. Nor can such recommendations be derived from speech acts that express obligations. Such speech acts can describe norms, communicate them and call for their observance, but they do not provide a justification for norms.

(4) In morals too, as with feelings or the question of free will, the separation between humans and even the most highly developed animals, especially chimpanzees and bonobos, can no longer be justified in such a strict way as it was assumed for a long time. Some observations now suggest that at least the behaviour of

these great apes cannot always be adequately understood by a sociobiological theory that explains supposedly morally analogous behaviour through hidden genetic self-interest of the individuals. Chimpanzees and bonobos apparently occasionally show situational altruistic behaviour that cannot be explained in this way, behaviour which may also be determined by earlier contacts and experiences with special individuals of their own species or of another species (humans). And they also apparently show preliminary stages of sadism, which we otherwise only know from humans.

It should not seem so surprising to a thinking shaped by evolutionary theory that these animals could already show preliminary stages of our morality (and that always also means: our immorality). After all, they also show preliminary stages of our ability to develop concepts. They can understand human language to such an extent that they can comply with everyday requests for action, even if the objects to which they refer are not visible, they can learn and use a few hundred symbols of a sign language and also have their own sign system.

The genetic difference between chimpanzees and humans is small (about 1.6 per cent of the genetic material). However, such an - albeit impressive - finding alone does not explain very much. There are other biological measurements that make the considerable difference in brain performance more expectable. For example, the quotients brain volume/brain stem volume and brain weight/body weight are twice as high in humans as in chimpanzees.

A balanced, solid presentation of the various connecting and differentiating aspects between humans, apes and other animals can be found in: Lethmate, J. Die Besonderheiten des Menschen (Uniquely human traits): Schiefenhövel, W. , Chr. Vogel, G. Vollmer, U. Opolka (Eds.), Der Mensch in seiner Welt. Anthropologie heute, Vol. 1, Vom Affen zum Halbgott. Der Weg des Menschen aus der Natur, Trias Thieme Stuttgart 1994, pp. 13–41.

A good summary of primatological research and the pertinent literature at that time is also given in the book "The Great Ape Project", edited by Paola Cavalieri/Peter Singer, Fourth Estate London 1993. One can doubt one or the other interpretation given here of the behaviour to be observed in these animals and attribute it to the political intention of the authors. But enough remains to show that the differences to humans are more gradual than previously assumed and that a demarcation can no longer be maintained with the sharpness to which we were accustomed in the past. Even if one may regret or reject some of the one-sidedness of the aforementioned book, such findings undoubtedly make the demand for a high degree of respect and protection particularly for apes more plausible and urgent.

And of course Frans de Waal must be mentioned here, who has enlivened the discussion about analogies and differences between apes and humans with a wealth of detailed observations. Particularly rewarding for our topic is the discussion with various philosophers – including Philip Kitcher and Peter Singer – in: Frans de Waal, Primates and Philosophers. How Morality Evolved, University Presses of California 2006. De Waal tends to idealise the behaviour of the great apes somewhat and prefers not to mention observations in which the moral abysses of humans already announce themselves. He underestimates the problem of the wide range of individual moral (and also immoral) dispositions, extremes also being compatible with the survival of the species as long as they do not become too frequent and the negative/destructive deviants do not have too much power at their disposal.

Both our moral achievements and our moral failures are based on evolutionary heritage and cultural developments. We should not succumb to the temptation to attribute the achievements or the failures to only one of the two factors. But: Since we cannot significantly change the evolutionary heritage (at least such considerations seem unpromising and unjustifiably risky so far), moral progress can only come from cultural development. That is why I find it unconvincing to seek this progress under the label of an "evolutionary" humanism. The now trivial observation that all our cultural achievements are ultimately based on our evolutionarily acquired traits and abilities does not justify characterising a philosophical life orientation we deem essential for the shaping of our future by the concept of evolution.

When discussing preliminary stages of morality in highly evolved animals, it is important to clarify the terms sufficiently. From a philosophical point of view, it does not make sense to interpret the mere existence of even quite complex, evolutionarily developed systems of rules and norms for social behaviour in the sense of morality. It is true that human moral systems can also be explained to a considerable extent as evolutionary originated systems of rules and norms, the observance of which improves reproductive success. However, it would be wrong to interpret cultural development, which plays such an important role in humans and overrides the biological presets, only as the extended arm of these presets. And morality in the philosophically significant sense only comes into existence when living beings are able to make conscious, value-weighing decisions and, under certain circumstances, also decide against their genetic self-interest, without this being able to be adequately described as a disease or deviant behaviour. On the other hand, this does not mean that it is a criterion for the morality of a course of action whether it serves genetic self-interest or not. It is only that actions which actually contradict genetic self-interest can make it easier for us to draw conclusions about the existence of morality.

It is possible, and some observations suggest it, that highly evolved species with complex brains, and most likely our closest relatives, the great apes, do produce individuals who, at least in certain situations, are capable of making conscious decisions that run counter to their genetic self-interest, and that this is where we see the beginning of morality. It seems, for example, that these apes sometimes put their lives on the line for the life of someone emotionally (but not necessarily genetically) close to them, even if they probably do not see the consequences in the same way as a human being doing the same thing. But it seems that only humans are capable of self-sacrifice (but unfortunately also ideologically motivated self-destruction) in full awareness of their actions.

In humans too morality consists partly of spontaneous, predominantly emotional reactions, the rational justification of which can be difficult even in retrospect. But it does not only consist of this. And it by no means consists only or even predominantly in the "solution" of trolley problems (which often cannot be dealt with in a morally satisfactory way, but can only be handled in a more or less unsatisfactory way when there is a real pressure to make a decision). Such partial aspects of morality must not be overrated, even if they are interesting objects of analysis.

Vogel is right when he simultaneously relativises and resolutely maintains the demarcation between highly developed animals and humans in the question of morality. For only humans can establish abstracted moral norms, discuss them, accept or reject them, consciously violate them and impose sanctions for such violations that reach far beyond the immediate situation. Only humans have a distinct, far-reaching ability to imagine the past and the (possible) future and can thus assess the consequences of their actions to a far greater extent than any other living being known to us (which, however, does not yet mean that they also use this ability to the desirable extent and then also behave in accordance with the results). Only humans can develop value systems that are far off immediate biological necessities, and only they can pass on value systems beyond immediate personal contact. Only humans have the appropriate and necessary language for this. Only in humans do we have clear indications of shame and conscience. (See especially pp. 98–104 in Vogel's cited book) It may be that he has still underestimated the empathic capacity of our closest relatives, the great apes, but nevertheless his considerations remain essentially correct.

However, it is plausible that also a reciprocal altruism that goes beyond living beings in the immediate environment and even the - albeit quite rare - occurrence of individuals who are actually selfless to a high degree are predominantly not by-products or cultural luxury products of the human brain, which has so much complexity, but have been developed and spread to a certain extent because this has brought humans essential evolutionary advantages (which, however, is not to reduce the morality of the individual to an evolutionary phenomenon). Even if there is an enduring dispute in evolutionary biology about the extent to which group selection is an essential factor in evolution, there is some evidence that it begins to play a significant role when evolutionary mechanisms effective at the level of the individual have already produced creatures with such highly developed abilities to communicate and cooperate as humans. (For the ongoing discussion on the evolutionary mechanisms of the emergence of altruism see E. O. Wilson, The Social Conquest of Earth, Liveright New York 2012, in which "the father of sociobiology" doubts or relativises the importance of the mechanisms traditionally postulated by his discipline.) It undoubtedly plays an essential role in the spread of humans that they can join forces in large, complexly organised groups (and thus also military organisations and alliances), that they can form differentiated cultural traditions and develop them in the long term, and that they can pass them on with the help of language and writing far beyond the sphere of their immediate environment and even of their contemporaries. And from a certain historical stage, it is obviously also important for the spread of humans that they can show altruism towards conspecifics they have never seen (today, for example, by providing funds for medical care in far-away poor countries). However, it is not yet clear whether the simultaneously great and, on the other hand, imperfect and very limited capacity for altruism humans show is really successful in the long term, or whether they have developed a mixture of ability and inability that will cause the human species to go extinct already a long time before the end of its cosmically possible lifespan.

As far as the emergence of such far-reaching altruism (which also transcends one's own species) is concerned, as we partly observe in humans, the concept of "dual function" seems to me to offer the best explanation for this, a concept with which other complex and highly differentiated results of evolution can also be best understood. This concept assumes that even small individual steps on the way to the finally observable complex result offer evolutionary advantages and thus structures arise which can then take on ever new additional tasks (see on this Vollmer, G., Was können wir wissen? Die Erkenntnis der Natur (What can we know? The knowledge of nature), Volume 2, second edition, Hirzel Stuttgart 1988, pp. 21–29). Just as the eye has developed via light sensitivity, directional and motion vision to the complex lens eye, altruism could also have developed via advantageous bartering in the immediate vicinity and reciprocal altruism at a greater distance to the actual unselfish altruism towards strangers and individuals of other species that can be observed in some humans.

However, the distinction between success factors in actual biological evolution and socio-cultural success factors in historical development remains problematic in these considerations.

(5) On the occasion of the never-ending attempts to derive morality from nature, I want to criticise incidentally a naïve antithesis here, which in many cases still or

once again dominates thinking: What nature produces is considered good, and what humans produce is considered bad or in any case inferior. It is often overlooked that "naturalness" is in many cases a relative term that only characterises different degrees of human influence and modification. There is another reason why the discriminatory power of the term "natural" is overestimated: Humans, with all their actions and products, are also a product of nature and in this respect everything they cause is "natural". Even if one considers this to be hair-splitting and wants to refer "natural" to nature that has not been created or substantially changed by humans, this delimitation does not provide a useful criterion for valuation. For example, the poison of the death cap is also a product of nature, and on the other hand, many substances newly created by humans have indisputably beneficial effects and can be superior to pre-existing similar natural substances. It is not only in the case of morality that the contrast between the good natural product and the bad artificial product is untenable (as well as its currently less popular inversion). Naturalness is neither a useful moral argument nor otherwise a measure of quality. A very good, concentrated critique of the "sanctification of nature", with various trenchant examples, is given in an essay by Günther Patzig: "Kann die Natur Quelle moralischer Normen sein?" (Can nature be the source of moral norms?) In: Daecke, S. M., Bresch, C., Gut und Böse in der Evolution (Good and evil in evolution), Hirzel Stuttgart 1995, pp. 85–98.

(6) Marc D. Hauser points out that neighbouring groups of people have different languages, dress codes, marriage customs, rules for punishment (which in itself seems to be at least largely a human phenomenon) and beliefs about the supernatural and the afterlife. In contrast, the differences between neighbouring animal groups are trivial and are more on the level of the difference between countries with right-hand and left-hand traffic. Moral Minds, as note 3.3. (2), here pp. 415–416.

(7) One more word on the opposition between duty and inclination, which plays such an important role in Kantian moral philosophy. The character of an action as moral and its moral value are not determined by the fact that we follow our sense of duty or our inclination, but by the moral weighing we make. Altruism does not become morally inferior because it is mixed with self-interest. The fact that parents take care of their children does not become morally inferior because they want to pass on their hereditary dispositions and hope that their children will take care of them in their old age. We should show special respect for those who, against their inclination, follow their sense of duty and who, without any recognisable self-interest, act in a way they consider altruistic, if we also consider their actions to be morally acceptable. However, there is no reason to show them special respect if we consider their dutiful or altruistic action morally reprehensible, for example, because they impose their values and their way of life on others.

485

Sense of duty and altruism are only moral attitudes worthy of esteem if they are related to other well-founded moral attitudes and values. They can do a lot of harm if they take on a life of their own in the service of questionable or reprehensible goals.

Kant himself, however, should not be misunderstood. He turned the concept of duty over in his mind again and again, and the more passages one reads about it, the better one understands that, firstly, he naturally never understood it to mean anything like 'corpse-like' obedience and that, secondly, he was quite concerned with reconciling duty and inclination. For example: "Now if we search we shall find for all actions that are worthy of praise a law of duty which *commands,* and does not leave us to choose what may be agreeable to our inclinations. This is the only way of representing things that can give a moral training to the soul, because it alone is capable of solid and accurately defined principles." (Translated by T. K. Abbott: Kant´s Critique of Practical Reason, Longmans, Green and Co. London 1927, p. 179, available online: https://archive.org/details/in.ernet.dli.2015. 222115/page/n5/mode/2up, retrieved 3 April 2023, p. 246 of the pdf. German text: Kritik der praktischen Vernunft, 1788, Reclam Stuttgart 1973, p. 138, original edition p. 153).

Kant's concept of duty is – despite some of the formulations he chose, which make it comprehensible that he is often understood in this way – not a kind of philosophical masochism, but it represents his call for a consistent moral weighing and a philosophical conduct of life.

(8) In this book I want to single out only some aspects on universalisation in ethics and morality that appear important to me personally. Those who want to deal more comprehensively with this problem, to which Hare, Hoerster and Mackie, among others, have made interesting contributions, will find good starting points here: In German: Keyword "Universalisierung", Enzyklopädie Philosophie und Wissenschaftsgeschichte, ed. Jürgen Mittelstraß, Metzler Stuttgart 1996, 2004, Vol. 4, pp. 413, 414; or also: https://en.wikipedia.org/wiki/Golden_Rule, retrieved 3 April 2023.

(9) Unfortunately, many publications on discourse ethics are characterised by a scientific jargon that is often difficult to digest. Habermas, for example, can write amazingly well and clearly when he addresses the public in speeches and newspaper articles. But as far as his books are concerned, consider the readability, size and content of these volumes and compare them from this point of view with Singer's "Practical Ethics", for example. Habermas, Jürgen, Theorie des kommunikativen Handelns, 1981 (The Theory of Communicative Action, 1985, 512 pages) Vorstudien und Ergänzungen zur Theorie des kommunikativen Handelns, 1984/1995 (Preliminary studies and addenda to the theory of communicative action, not translated into English, 607 pages), Erläuterungen zur Diskursethik,

1991 (Justification and Application: Remarks on Discourse Ethics, 1993, 336 pages), Faktizität und Geltung, 1998 (Between Facts and Norms, 1998, 676 pages).

The question arises as to why this overflow of a not uninteresting, but basically simple approach is tolerated, even enthusiastically celebrated. Suggestion for an answer: You don't have to read all this, especially not outside the academic field, where scientific careers can be founded on this kind of terminology-burdened redundancy. What is important for its success is above all the integrative, social effect of this communication philosophy. No one's ideological ideas are insistently questioned as long as they are dutifully participating in the discourse. And so this harmony philosophy of pluralistic democracy also takes the outdated traditional religions under its large wings. That a predominantly procedural philosophy, which largely tries to get by without clear decisions for certain moral attitudes and values, is inadequate, is now demonstrated by the helplessness of discourse ethics in the face of autocratic attacks on pluralist democracy and a rule-based world order.

3.4.

(1) In the book cited, Daniel Dennett gives a detailed overview of the multitude of approaches that have been proposed in the meantime to explain religion on the basis of its evolutionary and cultural benefits. Also very good in condensed form is an article by Rüdiger Vaas: Die Evolution der Religiosität. Gehirne, Gedanken, Gruppen und Gott (The evolution of religiosity. Genes, brains, thoughts, groups and God), Universitas November 2006, 61 (2006) 1116–1137. And later in more detail: Vaas, R., Blume, M., Gott, Gene und Gehirn. Warum Glaube nützt. Die Evolution der Religiosität (God, genes and brain. Why faith is useful. The evolution of religiosity), Hirzel Stuttgart 2009.

(2) In this respect, Pascal Boyer, for example, takes the easy way out for long stretches in his book: Religion Explained. The Evolutionary Origins of Religious Thought, Basic Books New York 2001. After a somewhat know-it-all frontal attack on all previous approaches to explain religion, he himself wants to explain it by saying that religious ideas and behaviours are a little better than other ideas and behaviours at activating certain mental systems and eliciting certain conclusions. If he relies especially on the attention value and the power of counterintuitive descriptions and explanations, he produces at least another psychological hypothesis for the explanation of religion, which appears somewhat far-fetched, but is quite original (see especially pp. 325–326). However, it seems to be supported by some evidence only in (pre-)adolescents.

(3) A short, readable discussion of the connection between intentionalism, animism, dualism and religion can be found in Edgar Dahl: Wer zur Hölle will schon in

den Himmel? Ein Brevier für Ungläubige und solche, die es werden wollen (Who the hell wants to go to heaven? A breviary for unbelievers and those who would like to become one), BoD Norderstedt 2010, Nachwort (Epilogue), pp. 151–155.

(4) For a good overview of the history and developmental trends of the psychology of religion, see: Henning, C., Murken, S. , Nestler, E. (eds.), Einführung in die Religionspsychologie (Introduction to the psychology of religion), Ferdinand Schöningh Paderborn 2003. And for a short overview in English: https://en.wikipedia.org/wiki/Psychology_of_religion, retrieved 11 April 2023. For an overview of newer publications on religious conversion see: Stelling, L., Recent studies in Religious Conversion, English Literary Renaissance, Volume 47, Number 1, Winter 2017, available online:
https://www.journals.uchicago.edu/toc/elr/2017/47/1, retrieved 23 August 2024

(5) Georg Simmel has pointed to this aspect, for example, by relating monarchical or hierarchical-aristocratic worlds of gods to the constitution of the respective societies: Simmel, G., Die Religion, 1912, 9.–11. Tausend, Rütten & Loening Frankfurt a. M. 1922, especially pp. 61–62, edited and translated by H. J. Helle: Essays on Religion, Part 5, 11 Religion, Yale University Press 1997, pp. 180, 181.

(6) A very good overview of the cognitive, biological and neuro-scientific approaches to study religion and their problems and limitations is given by the theologian Oviedo in the Interdisciplinary Encyclopedia of Religion and Science of the Pontifical University of the Holy Cross: https://inters.org/religion-scientific-study (as of 2019, retrieved 11 April 2023). However, his hope that the scientific study of religion could contribute to the human mind's dealing jointly and harmoniously with the scientific and religious domains seems neither realistic nor desirable to those unwilling to believe.

(7) Comte presents the three-stage law in his Cours de philosophie positive (The Course in Positive Philosophy), Paris 1830-1842. For a brief summary of Comte's teaching see: https://en.wikipedia.org/wiki/Law_of_three_stages., retrieved 12 April 2023. Comte later acts as a founder of religion with his Catéchisme positiviste, 1852, Garnier-Flammarion Paris 1966, translated by R. Congreve: The Catechism of Positive Religion, 1891, reissued by Cambridge University Press 2009

(8) A good overview of the history and the development of sociology of religion gives: Knoblauch, H., Religionssoziologie, de Gruyter Berlin New York 1999 (regrettably not translated into English). Here you find good summaries of the contributions of Max Weber, pp. 39–57 (not limited to the famous "The Protestant Ethic and the Spirit of Capitalism"), Georg Simmel, pp. 65–68, and Émile Durkheim, pp. 58–65. https://en.wikipedia.org/wiki/Sociology_of_religion (retrieved 12 April 2023) can also be used as a starting point.

(9) A good insight into the discussion and refutation of the traditional proofs of God can be gained, for example, in: Hoerster, N. (ed.), Glaube und Vernunft. Texte zur Religionsphilosophie (Faith and reason. Texts in the philosophy of religion) Reclam Stuttgart 1985, Chapter 1 and 2: Die traditionellen Gottesbeweise, pp. 16–93 (proofs of God and their refutations in original texts by eminent philosophers from Anselm of Canterbury to John Leslie Mackie). Küng's already quoted book "Does God exist?" (3.4.[31]) is also quite useful for this purpose, explicitly pp. 529–588, as well as earlier in the discussion of individual thinkers. More detailed is Mackie's worthwhile book "The Miracle of Theism" (3.3.[1]). Norbert Hoerster's book "Die Frage nach Gott" (The question of god), Beck Munich 2005, is also a good and compact read.

(10) In this book I shall not discuss the problem of causality in detail. However, even if this does not bring any new points of view with regard to the problem of the first cause, a concept should be pointed out here that leads beyond Hume's critique of the human understanding of and need for causality. To reduce causality to a regular succession of events (if A, then B) is unsatisfactory, however advisable it is to always ask oneself whether there is really more to apparent cause-effect relations than a mere succession or juxtaposition. In contrast, it seems convincing and fruitful to characterise causality by a transfer of energy as a link between cause and effect and to demand proof of a transfer of energy as a necessary condition of a causal relationship (see on this Vollmer, Mesokosmos und objektive Erkenntnis, 1.2.[3], pp. 77–83). In particular, onetime causal events can then also be explained without problems. The objections raised against such an approach (see Birnbacher, D., Tun und Unterlassen, Reclam Stuttgart 1995, pp. 96–99) do not seem conclusive to me. In particular, I also consider the classification of causality by omission as the absence of a plausibly possible energy transfer to be quite appropriate (even if it admittedly seems somewhat contrived at first glance).

(11) A nice little satire – unjust, a little ludicrous and yet, as it is in its nature, accurate – on perhaps the best-known protagonist, at least among the famous philosophers, of a doctrine determined by such sentiments is provided by Anton Kuh in his "Lexikon berühmter Sachsen" (Dictionary of famous Saxons): "Leibniz. Known in wider popular circles as a tasty biscuit. Invented, as to the philosopher, the so-called monad system, a borough and district division of infinity, in order to bring order into the cosmos. By the discovery of 'preestablished harmony' (the cosiness of the spheres) he acquired the merit of inspiring the most important satirical creation in world literature: Voltaire's 'Candide'." In: Der Querschnitt 10 (1930) 331–332, reprinted in: Hans Nebbich in Glück, Feuilletons, Essays und Publizistik (1913–1940), Diogenes Zurich 1987, p. 204.

And for those who want to read instructive excerpts from the original text of

Leibniz's theodicy (originally in French, 1710) and not the whole thing: Hoerster, N. (ed.), Glaube und Vernunft. Texte zur Religionsphilosophie, Reclam Stuttgart 1985, pp. 109–115, or as a source in English: The Best of all Possible Worlds (from Theodicy), https://rintintin.colorado.edu/~vancecd/phil1020/Leibniz.pdf, retrieved 14 April 2023.

By the way, not even Leibniz's monadology is completely dead, as it appears congenial to some modern constructivists.

(12) David Hume (ascribed): Essays on Suicide, and the Immortality of the Soul, London Smith 1783, Essay II., On the Immortality of the Soul, II., p. 33 (available online: https://ota.bodleian.ox.ac.uk/repository/xmlui/bitstream/handle/20.500.1 2024/K001770.000/K001770.000.html?sequence=5&isAllowed=y; D'Holbach, P.-H. Th., Système de la Nature, Étienne Ledoux Paris 1821, II, Chapitre XIX, p. 460, available online: https://books.google.de/books?id=JxMpAAAAYAAJ& printsec=frontcover&source=gbs_ge_summary_r&cad=0#v=onepage&q&f=fal se; translated by H. D. Robinson: The System of Nature, Volume II., originally published 1868, Batoche Books Kitchener Ontario 2001, Chapter XIX. Absurd and Extraordinary Theological Opinions, available online: https://historyofeconomicthought.mcmaster.ca/holbach/Volume2.pdf, p. 180 of the pdf, all three retrieved 16 April 2023

(13) Not quite as laconic, but no less trenchant, Silvia Bovenschen formulates: "Problem of faith. For an ageing impaired multimorbid person, belief in a creator of all things is multiply impaired. One must either have a bad opinion of oneself or of the creator." Älter werden (Growing older), 2006, Fischer Taschenbuch Verlag Frankfurt a. M. 2008, p. 90.

(14) Those interested in a more detailed discussion of the theodicy problem and the excuses put forward in this context are referred, for example, to: Hoerster, N. , Zur Unlösbarkeit des Theodizee-Problems (On the unsolvable problem of theodicy), Theologie und Philosophie, Heft 3, 60 (1985), pp. 400–409. A more detailed discussion with reference to some recent theological evasions can be found in his book on the question of God recommended in note (9), pp. 87–113. An excellent, concentrated summary and critique of the arguments advanced over time on the problem of evil and divine existence and power is also given in P. H. Hare, Evil, Problem of, in: Stein, G., The Encyclopedia of Unbelief (see Suggested Further Reading), Vol. I, pp. 187–195.

(15) Whether an impaired musicality and a reduced religiosity coincide more often than not would be an interesting topic for psychological or sociological studies. Conjectures that musicality and religiosity could be connected in the evolutionary history of humans have some plausibility. (See Vaas/Blume, as note (1), pp. 143, 144) If, however, such a coincidence could be proven, the question would still

remain open then - beyond evolutionary considerations of usefulness - whether the lack of religiosity of human beings with some kind of amusia represents a second impairment or rather an advantage, a special talent for clear thinking (which I would then decisively assert - that something is useful does not mean that it is also desirable or worth striving for morally).

Be that as it may: if a well thought-out areligious worldview is written down, the content will be little influenced by whether the author is musical or suffers from some kind of musical disorder – but it may be different as to the form. (And as an excursion into the personal: Of course, everyone is free to regret that I suffer from some aspects of amusia. I regret this myself, but not because of the possible effects of this fact on my philosophical texts).

Moreover, musical disorders must not be confused with a lack of interest in the arts. For example, the inability or below-average ability of the person with a musical disorder to remember and reproduce sounds and melodies or to stay on a beat (disorders of musicality are varied and complex) and the inability (often also unwillingness) of the person lacking interest in the arts to attach value to artistic expressions and to understand art are two different defects. They can be present in the same person, but do not have to be. The person with some kind of amusia, who does not lack interest in music, can also be quite capable of distinguishing good and bad music and of understanding the essential expressions of music and art in general. In contrast, there are highly musical people who are more or less artistically »tone-deaf«, to whom music means no more than pleasant or artistic sequences of notes, or who in any case have a highly conventional taste in music and the arts that perceives or appreciates only a small part of what is possible as artistic expression in music and the arts.

Neither amusia nor lack of religiosity mean that human beings have to be disinterested in art and that the differentiated medium of expression and communication of art, which goes beyond rationality and certainly beyond explicit rationality and includes and addresses other layers of a person, would thus elude them.

Apparently there is a genetic disposition or "gift" for spirituality/religiosity just as there is for musicality. And certainly religiosity can be furthered by practice to a certain extent, just like musicality. Religions have known this for a long time, and they also know that for religiosity, too, it is more successful to start this practice in childhood, which is why they are so concerned about the religious education of children. But while it is undoubtedly regrettable if one did not have sufficient opportunity as a child to improve and develop one's musicality through practice, this is not at all true of religiosity: I can see nothing positive in practising an illusory and often dogmatic view of the world. The emotional rewards that can be gained in this way are also accessible to humans in other ways. Fortunately, religious education often provides educational "by-products" - historical, cultural and humanitarian education (and yes - also spiritual education, which can later bring psychological enrichment and benefit if it does not impair critical faculties). And a good religious education will even inevitably confront their recipients with religious criticism at some point, at least if they have eyes to see and ears to hear. That is why secular humanism should not develop an exaggerated bogeyman out of an education based on »strange« premises, on premises that one considers to be false. Rather, The real enemy rather is deliberate indoctrination.

Extreme rationality and artistic "craziness" can go well together, by the way. One example: The Bavarian doctor, songwriter and musician Georg Ringsgwandl. For his rational part see for example: Georg Ringsgwandl über Altern (Georg Ringsgwandl on aging), interview by Stefan Klein, Süddeutsche Zeitung, SZ am Wochenende, 6/7 January 2007, p. VIII.

(16) I do not want to refrain from a remark in honour of the Sophists (at least some of them), since they are terribly belittled in most histories of philosophy. In contrast, let me quote Bertrand Russell here: "To a certain extent – though it is impossible to say how far – the disrepute into which the Sophists fell, not only among the general public but also among Plato and later philosophers, was due to their intellectual merit. The search for truth, if it is done wholeheartedly, must neglect moral considerations; we cannot know in advance that truth will turn out to be something that is considered constructive in a particular society. The sophists were prepared to follow a train of thought wherever it might lead them. Often it led them to scepticism." And Russell highlights yet another point of view about the criticism of the Sophists: "Plato himself had sufficient private means and was obviously unable to notice the hardships of those who were not so fortunate. It is strange that modern professors, seeing no reason to reject a salary, have so often repeated Plato's sharp criticism." History of Western Philosophy, 1946, 8th edition, Allen & Unwin London 1975, pp. 95, 94.

3.5.

(1) This fascination runs through the entire history of science and jumps out at you time and again when you deal with it. If you want to follow this development by using a single book (though meanwhile somewhat historical in itself), you can't do this lightly – in the case of the German edition you should be able to hold 1.6 kilograms, the English version might be a bit lighter. In return, you get a wealth of solid texts and beautiful illustrations. English edition: Peter Tallack (ed.), The Science Book, Cassell London 2001, also as a paperback: Weidenfeld Nicholson London 2006

(2) Andreas Vesalius, De humani corporis fabrica libri septem, 1543, translated by W. Richardson and J. Carman: On the Fabric of the Human Body, Norman Publishing Novato 2009; Ernst Haeckel, Kunstformen der Natur, 10 Hefte 1899–1904,

Bibliographisches Institut Leipzig und Wien 1904, available online: https://archive.org/details/KunstformenDerNaturErnstHaeckel, retrieved 24 April 2023. New edition Prestel Munich New York 1998, 2004 (with two worthwhile essays on nature and aesthetics/art/craft by Olaf Breidbach and Irenäus Eibl-Eibesfeldt), translated by M. Schons: Art Forms in Nature, 1998, available online: https://archive.org/details/artformsinnature0000haec/page/n5/mode/2up, retrieved 14 Januar 2024; Franz J. Wetz, Brigitte Tag (eds.), Schöne neue Körperwelten. Der Streit um die Ausstellung (Beautiful new body worlds. The controversy on the exhibition), Klett-Cotta Stuttgart 2001 (with a contribution by Gunther von Hagens and illustrations). Even if many conservative resentments resonate in the criticism of von Hagens: one cannot help feeling that he is by no means driven by an enlightened impulse alone, but also wants to serve exhibitionism and places a high value on economic interests. To get a good impression of the merits of and the controversy over Gunther von Hagens see also: https://en.wikipedia.org/wiki/Gunther_von_Hagens, retrieved 24 April 2023.

(3) The consequences of our mesocosm-oriented evolutionary development have been investigated by Gerhard Vollmer in various publications: I recommend in particular the two chapters "Probleme der Anschaulichkeit" (Problems of visualisability) and "Jenseits des Mesokosmos. Anschaulichkeit in Physik und Didaktik" (Beyond mesocosm. Visualisability in physics and didactics) from his book "Was können wir wissen?" (What can we know?) Volume 2, Die Erkenntnis der Natur. Beiträge zur modernen Naturphilosophie (The knowledge of nature. Contributions to a modern philosophy of nature), Hirzel Stuttgart 1988. There is also a paper in English in which he sums up his views concisely: How Is It That We Can Know This World. New Arguments in Evolutionary Epistemology, in: Darwinism & Philosophy (eds. V. Hösle and C. Illies), University of Notre Dame Press Indiana 2005, pp. 259–274, available online: https://archive.org/details/darwinismphiloso0000unse, retrieved 24 April 2023

(4) The ambivalence of nature and our relationship to it is rewardingly and entertainingly elaborated by Joachim Kahl in a meditation on René Magritte's painting "Hegel's Holiday" (1958), 2007, available online: https://hegel-system.de/de/v33 1331magritte.htm or https://www.kahl-marburg.privat.t-online.de/kahl_magritte.pdf, retrieved 14 January 2025.

(5) We are in the fifth or sixth ice age of the last 3 billion years of the history of Earth and thus in an extraordinary climatic state. Iced polar ice caps have only existed during short periods (in geological terms) of the history of earth, see for a brief overview https://en.wikipedia.org/wiki/Paleoclimatology (retrieved 26 April 2023) or also Behringer, see below, pp. 20–22. In the case of short-term climate changes, we humans have considerable adaptation problems and adaptation costs (although in other regions we also have adaptation gains). Since the current

warming period within the still ongoing fifth or sixth ice age is very likely due to a considerable degree to human activities, a reasonable level of effort to slow down climate change is basically in our interest. However, given the growth of the world population, further human-induced global warming will be unavoidable for some time to come, even with considerable technological advances, unless unexpected changes in the history of Earth or man-made catastrophes counteract this development. Thus, we are certainly doing well to also invest in adapting to the unavoidable climate change, just as people in other historical epochs have done in other circumstances. Instructive on this and on a differentiated discussion of climate change in general is a book by Wolfgang Behringer: Kulturgeschichte des Klimas. Von der Eiszeit bis zur globalen Erwärmung, 6th edition, C H. Beck München 2022, translated by P. Camiller: A Cultural History of Climate, Polity Press Cambridge 2010.

Since the rich countries are in relation to their population responsible for a disproportionate share of greenhouse gas emissions and thus of climate change caused by human activity, they have a special obligation to help developing countries solve or mitigate their adaptation problems. However, these adjustment problems cannot be solved only by transferring money and technology from the richer to the poorer countries. Mismanagement, corruption, ethnic conflicts and educational deficits in these countries must also be clearly identified and combated, without being dissuaded by the killer argument of colonialism.

(6) A good plea for such a "secularised" ecology is made by Josef H. Reichholf: Die falschen Propheten (False prophets), Verlag Klaus Wagenbach, Berlin 2002.

Good food for thought against contemporary eco-conformism and the regulatory idea of state-socialist planned economy of complex systems, which is harmful here as elsewhere, is also provided by the material-rich polemic by Dirk Maxeiner and Michael Miersch: Die Zukunft und ihre Feinde. Wie Fortschrittspessimisten unsere Gesellschaft lähmen (The future and its enemies. How pessimists about progress paralyse our society), Eichborn Frankfurt a. M. 2002. Unfortunately, however, the authors of both books resemble some of their opponents in that they do not always observe the desirable scientific strictness in the presentation of facts.

A very readable, comprehensive, more up-to-date examination of the one-sidedness and the inconsistencies that can be found all too often in the environmental movement was published by environmental activist Michael Shellenberger: Apocalypse Never: Why Environmental Alarmism Hurts Us All, HarperCollins New York 2020.

(7) In democracies, too, dictatorial structures can develop, at least in certain segments of society, if the majority of elected representatives allow themselves to be carried away by interfering with civil liberties without sufficient reason (whereby

democratic legitimacy often suffers not only from the neglect of the protection of minorities, but also from the extensive prescribing of decisions by an expertocracy, the shifting of essential encroachments on civil liberties to the level of ordinances or directives of democratically only very indirectly legitimised expert committees or the requirement to vote in accordance with party policy). In order not to remain too abstract, let us mention an example - still relatively harmless and now already historical, but characteristic of the underlying way of thinking, in which environmental legislation is already turning into eco-dictatorship: the European Community's ban on incandescent light bulbs. If it is considered ecologically sensible to reduce the use of such light bulbs, and if it is believed that consumers would not comply quickly enough by themselves because of the savings by lower electricity consumptions, a justifiable price surcharge could have been imposed. In the chosen proceeding, however, works of art that depend on incandescent light bulbs or lamps in which they are an integral part of the design can only continue to be operated unimpaired because of old stock or precautionary buying of museum directors and private people. The nuisance of paternalism persists and fraudulent labelling is provoked, as not uncommon under dictatorship: the light bulb returns to internet shops as a heating device instead of a lamp, because it thus seemed to evade the prohibition regulations (which was then, at least in Germany, also forbidden by court ruling). The same kind of proceeding is no repeated by the intended unexceptional prohibition of new registrations of cars with traditional combustive engines, concerning for example classical sportscars which are also a kind of cultural achievement. Considering the small percentage of these vehicles in relation to the miles driven by all cars this is quite evidently more about exploiting feelings of envy and clinging to principles than about any ecological benefit worth mentioning. The extent to which a partial dictatorship can lead to undesirable developments and hypocrisy can then also be seen in the social sector, with much more serious consequences, see 3.8.2.

3.6.1.

(1) A good summary of substantial arguments against an afterlife and personal immortality can be found in Corliss Lamont, The Philosophy of Humanism (see Suggested Further Reading), pp. 81–107.

(2) A summary of relevant literature and a critique based on the authors' own research can already be found in: Demling, L., S. Strobel, S., Blick ins Jenseits (A view into the hereafter), Fortschritte der Medizin 97 (1979) 1831–1833.

Lewis-Williams points out the similarity of such sensations of being underground or under water, or passing through a vortex, or tunnel, with trance experiences in shamanism and ubiquitously in the mystical strand of religious traditions: The Mind in the Cave, Thames & Hudson London 2002, especially p. 145.

On this book see also 3.4., p. 168 and note 3.10. (5).

(3) The representative validity and significance of some of Woody Allen's best films (and perhaps, in some respects, of his own life) lies, among other things, in the fact that he shows how difficult it is, even for intelligent, educated and responsible people, to find their own standards when they are suddenly – within one or two generations – forced to do so (because not only the religious, but also the previously valid social-conventional standards have rapidly lost their binding force).

(4) These sentences should not only speak for themselves here, but also represent the whole impressive plea for "cheerful" composure in death (whether "cheerful" is really appropriate here is debatable), which the young philosopher Joachim Buhl wrote facing his own, much too early death: "How a free human being dies", see the reference.

I admit, however, that such an attitude has its limits. In the face of the death of children or of people whose intellect or personality does not allow them to overcome childlike needs for security, an attitude of as-if regarding an afterlife and immortality may be appropriate. One should let them die in peace and let them have their heaven (just as sensible parents let their children have other fairy tale ideas as long as they spontaneously believe in them and enjoy them). As far as children in particular are concerned, however, their ability to face the world realistically and truthfully, especially in personal crisis situations, is and was often underestimated. Just as with adults, we should not hastily offer or even impose allegedly gentle untruths on children (which is often only the more convenient solution for relatives and carers), but try to find out how they want to and can deal with the truth in individual cases. However, the truth should not be forced upon them, and that refers also to the truth that they are about to die. My paternal grandmother, for example, never forgave the church for the fact that a priest administered the last rites to her terminally ill eight-year-old son against her will, thus making it clear to him that he had to die.

Moreover, the deathbed is no place for any ideological confrontations. One should take a back seat, respect the ideological and religious convictions of the dying person and only bring in one's own to the extent that one cannot build on the convictions of the dying person in helping her. We should strive to let a person die according to the philosophical or religious orientation that has determined his or her life. Attempts at conversion at the deathbed and conversions on the deathbed, in favour of whatever worldview, leave an unpleasant aftertaste: such influences and decisions in a state of diminished judgement and/or dwindling strength of personality bend the true self of the person concerned.

3.6.2.

(1) In medicine brain death is not just a short, more comprehensible term for irreversible loss of consciousness but generally means more precisely: brain stem death, which, in addition to the loss of the functions of the cerebral cortex, also involves in particular the loss of the patient's own respiratory activity. Although many patients in a persistent vegetative state respectively a state of unresponsive wakefulness suffer an irreversible loss of the functions of the cerebral cortex as well, it is often only the chronological sequence that allows a more and more certain statement about the irreversibility and thus the prognosis. In many cases, at least up to now, death of the cerebrum alone cannot be determined with the same certainty beyond all reasonable doubt as death of the brain stem. Patients in a persistent vegetative state are therefore not yet considered as organ donors. However, it is reasonable and justified to limit life-prolonging measures in people in a persistent vegetative state respectively unresponsive wakefulness syndrome (for the terminology see note 3.6.5.[2]), since the prospects of regaining consciousness are then increasingly close to zero and, in addition, advanced defective states in the musculature and soft tissues would massively restrict the quality of life even in the extremely unlikely case of regaining consciousness, and it is therefore justified to assume that life-prolonging measures are no longer in the interest of the person concerned.

It must be admitted, however, that the concept of brain stem death also has weaknesses. When we speak of "brain death", we are making a simplification insofar as the "dead" brain can still show neurohumoral activity. However, this simplification does not cause any major problems, because it does not change the reliable statement that consciousness and the functions of the brain representing personality have irreversibly ceased. Much more difficulties arise with patients in a state of unresponsive wakefulness, in whom the cerebral functions and thus consciousness and personality are demonstrably irreversibly lost, but the brain stem functions and thus spontaneous breathing have been preserved. If we also want to call these patients brain dead, the concept of brain death becomes counterintuitive and contradictory to the spontaneous impression to a much greater extent than in the previous brain death definition. Consequently, we would then have to define the time of death as the point in time at which the irreversible failure of the cerebral functions was determined and not as the point in time at which the patient "dies" through the cessation of spontaneous respiration. So there would be "dead people" who still breathe on their own. If we apply the determination of brain death used today (and the same would be valid if the definition of death would be extended to an irreversible loss of consciousness) and state the time of death as the time at which death was determined according to the criteria laid down for this purpose, then this time of death remains to be a social and legal fiction, since we do not state the time at which the irreversible failure of the higher brain functions actually or presumably occurred. Strictly speaking, we would often have to make similarly vague statements about the time of death as in the case of a person found dead, whose time of death can only be narrowed down to a certain range on the basis of circumstantial evidence. Such considerations make Singer's proposal seem consistent and reasonable that in the longer term the concept of brain death should be abandoned again and decisions on the termination of treatment and the release of organs for transplantation should instead be made dependent on the criterion of demonstrably irreversible loss of consciousness, and otherwise the definition of death should return to irreversible circulatory arrest (although the essential event in the process of dying remains, of course, cerebral death). (Singer, P., Is The Sanctity of Life Ethic Terminally Ill? in: as 3.6.6.[2], but pp. 292–301, especially p. 300).

First of all, however, it must be remembered that the concept of brain death has proven to be practicable and successful, and has made it possible to deal appropriately with many problematic situations in the medical, social and legal spheres. It is now anchored in the consciousness of many people and has found its way into guidelines and legislation. People should be given time to get used to the new situations created by modern medicine before they are forced to undergo another process of rethinking and thus become insecure.

Moreover, Singer's philosophically consistent considerations are also premature because there are as yet no generally accepted, sufficiently reliable criteria and procedures for determining cerebral death in case of preserved brain stem function that are practicable for all coma patients in everyday medical practice. A very good overview of the problem is given by Steven Laureys: Death, unconsciousness and the brain, Nature Reviews Neuroscience 6, 2005, 899–909, available online: https://www.nature.com/articles/nrn1789, retrieved 10 June 2023, and also: Eyes Open, Brain Shut, Scientific American, Vol. 296, No. 5, May 2007, pp. 84–89.

(2) A stringent presentation of these considerations of interests is given by Norbert Hoerster in his excellent essay "Definition of Death and Organ Transplantation", Universitas 52 (1997), January 1997, pp. 42–52. Among other things, he rightly points out that in the case of a forensic autopsy, for example, society considers interventions in the 'peace of the dead' to be legitimate without the consent of the persons concerned during their lifetime or of their relatives after their death, although the interests of other people are only affected in a much more indirect way here than in the case of ill persons dependent on – possibly live-saving – organ transplants.

(3) There are various promising approaches that could make us increasingly independent of human organ donations in the foreseeable future. For example,

intensive work is being done to provide animal organs which, as xenotransplants, take over the essential functions of the corresponding human organs and are no longer rejected by the human immune system (which could be achieved by genetic modification of the animals and/or by subsequent treatment of animal organs - and is already a reality in the case of heart valves, for example). Other research projects deal with the production of organ replacements from cell cultures and the further development of technical implants that can take over certain organ functions.

(4) The formalised determination of brain death, as customary in clinical practice today, could be dispensed with if severe brain damage and other hopeless disease states, which make a return to a life worth living impossible for the person concerned with a probability bordering on certainty, were permitted as a prerequisite for organ removal, provided the person concerned has made a respective advance directive or the relatives acting in accordance with his or her presumed will want to make such a decision. However, this does not change the fact that the currently valid concept of brain death contains the essential content of the term "death" and ensures its safe determination, because it means the irreversible loss of the status of a human person and thus also of the personality associated with this person.

If one considers a societal change in attitudes towards organ donation in the direction addressed here to be desirable and would like to initiate it (as this also applies to me), one should do so without talking up the concept of brain death, otherwise one is working into the hands of the fundamental opponents of organ transplantation. Unfortunately, some advocates of "generous" attitudes to organ removal have failed to understand this because they are too impressed by the counterintuitive aspect of brain death, such as: Miller, F. G., Truog, R. D., Rethinking the Ethics of Vital Organ Donations, Hastings Center Report 38, no. 6 (2008). Their misjudgement of brain death is already announced, as are their other morally justifiable intentions, in the subtitle of their article: "Accepted medical practice already violates the dead donor rule. Explicitly jettisoning the rule – allowing vital organs to be extracted, under certain conditions, from living patients – would expand the pool of eligible organ donors."

There are undoubtedly justified critical comments on transplantation medicine, such as the question of whether more emphasis should not be placed on reducing the need for transplants through better prevention or doubts about the justification of the extraordinary use of financial resources in individual cases. The discussion about the brain death concept, on the other hand, does not lead to justified objections against transplantation medicine.

3.6.3.

(1) Singer's "principle of equal consideration of interests" is a very useful and

productively provocative means of ethical discussion. As the sole moral standard, however, it amounts to a very limited system of values, in which de facto values such as individuality, enjoyment of life and beauty – and thus an essential part of human culture – would have to be largely sacrificed, since they only count when the elementary needs of all people are satisfied. Singer's appeal to the relatively rich of the world to take the interests of the poor into account to a greater extent than before and to share more with them is honourable and necessary but a world in which, for example, opera houses could only be operated after no one is starving anymore would be boring and sad. Against that Singer argues by the example that we would hardly consider the behaviour of a doctor defensible who, faced with hundreds of victims of a train crash goes to the opera after treating fifty of them on the grounds that going to the opera is part of a well-rounded life (Singer, Practical Ethics, as 1.4.2.[1], but p. 244). Sure, we would rightly disapprove of this doctor's behaviour, but no doctor comes to a train crash every day. If, however, we wanted to satisfy the vital needs of all human beings before we afford to go to the opera, we would not go to the opera all our lives and there would be no opera houses at all. We would be in the situation of a doctor who is constantly confronted with one catastrophe after another, which means that cultural activities that are not immediately vital would have to be suspended for an unforeseeable period of time. I consider this value judgement to be wrong. I would find life in such a world much less worth living, and I doubt that humanity would still have the strength and motivation to improve its situation as a whole under these conditions, at least in the long term. (Moreover, a certain amount of luxury also has very positive economic consequences, gets people into "work and bread", to use a somewhat historical expression, which is – though later discredited by its use as a Nazi slogan – not out of place here, because Bernard Mandeville already took into account this aspect at the beginning of the 18th century in his "Fable of the Bees, or Private Vices, Publick Benefits", 1705/1714. A commented edition of by B. F. Kaye, Clarendon Press Oxford 1924, is available online as a reprint: http://files.libertyfund.org/files/846/0014-01_Bk.pdf, retrieved 31 January 2023.

A differentiated examination of what he called the "Singer Principle" conducts Appiah, Cosmopolitanism, as 1.4.5.[4], Chapter 10, Kindness to Strangers, pp. 155 –174. Singer himself presents his plea for ascetic altruism in even greater detail and more impressively than in his "Practical Ethics" in: The Life You Can Save. Acting Now to End World Poverty, Picador London 2009.

Briefly and aptly on this part of Singer's moral claims also Edgar Dahl: Der unbarmherzige Samariter. Ist es moralisch vertretbar, zu Weihnachten eine Luxusuhr zu schenken? (The unmerciful Samaritan. Is it morally justifiable to give a luxury watch for Christmas?) NZZ Online, Neue Zürcher Zeitung, 30 November 2007, available online: https://www.nzz.ch/der_unbarmherzige_samariter-ld.4487

18, retrieved 31 January 2023). The editorial title of his essay does sound a little like a concession to specifically Swiss, pre-Christmas economic and consumer desires. The content and the concise summary are no less appropriate for that reason: "From the duty to save a drowning child you cannot deduce the duty to save the entire world."

3.6.4.

(1) A well-argued case for such a judgement is presented, for example, by Laura M. Purdy in her essay: "Are Pregnant Women Fetal Containers?" in: as 3.6.6.[2], but pp. 71–81.

(2) In contrast to the previously sometimes extremely pro-life stance in perinatal medicine, which often failed to recognise the appropriate critical self-restraint, there is now a fairly broad, cross-national consensus in affluent countries on the appropriate approach and the involvement of parents, even if the definition of the grey area for the decision between palliative and active therapy still varies somewhat from country to country. See, for example, the Austrian recommendation from 2024: Empfehlung zur Versorgung von Frühgeborenen an der Grenze zur Lebensfähigkeit (Recommendations for care of premature infants at the limit of viability, with references in English): https://www.springermedizin.de/das-frueh-geborene/neonatologie/empfehlung-zur-versorgung-von-fruehgeborenen-an-der-grenze-der-l/50097340, retrieved 15 April 2024). That the preservation of the lives of premature babies with extremely low gestational age and/or birth weight is boastfully publicised in the popular press without any trace of justification for the risk taken (and the extreme use of resources) can hardly be seen anymore.

(3) On the Dutch practice, which is anything but inconsiderate and rather strictly limited, see Verhagen, A. A. E., Sauer, P. J. J., End of Life Decisions in Newborns. An Approach from the Netherlands, Pediatrics 116 (2005) 736–739.

For those readers, and especially those German fellow citizens, who consider the question of whether it is permissible to kill severely damaged newborn infants to be completely immoral and out of the question, it should be pointed out that this question has been answered in the affirmative time and again in human social and cultural history, even by societies which we consider to be culturally advanced, indeed the cradle of our culture. Not only did many primitive peoples develop such a practice (here one can still say: by necessity), but it was also common practice in classical Greece and ancient Rome. Plato, Aristotle and Seneca handed down and advocated the practice of killing malformed newborns (Kuhse, Singer, as 3.6.4.[8], chapter 5, Infanticide: A look beyond one's own borders, pp. 135–159, here especially pp. 151, 152; with sources). For example, Seneca explicitly in De ira (First Book, section 15, original text and good translation in

Prosperi, as below, pp. 187/492). Of course, this is no moral justification for such a procedure (one could point out that we do not take the bloodthirsty "games" and gladiator fights of ancient Rome or other cruel practices from history as a model). But if culturally advanced societies and serious thinkers saw nothing morally wrong or objectionable in the killing of malformed newborns, this should at least be one more reason to allow a serious discussion on the subject, without silencing or morally defaming those who consider such a procedure or advocate it under certain circumstances.

The religious historian Adriano Prosperi has presented a highly interesting study on the historical change of ideas regarding the "ensoulment" of unborn children and the worthiness of protection of newborns in Christianity: Dare l'anima. Storia di un infanticidio, 2005, English translation (Bilingual edition): The Giving of the Soul. The History of an Infanticide, or: Infanticide, secular Justice, and Religious Debate in Early Modern Europe (Europa Sacra, 10), Brepols Publishers Turnhout 2016. It is also a contribution to the role of women in Christianity and – though without explicit intentions in this direction – to the criminal history of Christianity. Thus, downright sadistic treatment of women who had committed infanticide and were often executed in the cruellest way for it is documented in detail (esp. pp. 84–96). The fact that caesarean sections began as a practice that was propagated and carried out on women who had just died or who appeared doomed to die, in order to save the child and especially its soul, sometimes forcing the mother to have her abdomen slit open while fully conscious and thus find certain death, also deserves to be snatched from oblivion (pp. 292–297).

This is the appropriate place for a brief digression on the criminal history of Christianity. It should protect us from arrogance when we look, for example, at today's fundamentalist Islam. For this part of history too, there are of course other good reasons to keep it in memory, such as the avoidance of fatal repetition or at least posthumous reparation to the victims. And there is no doubt that the criminal history of Christianity severely damages its moral qualification, which is still claimed quite penetratingly (even as special) today. On the other hand, we should abandon the ritual of constantly reproaching today's Christianity for its criminal history, a ritual that is repeatedly reheated in discussions and has only limited fruitfulness. Ultimately, it is the positions that Christianity takes today that matter: their justification and social claims must be discussed and argued about.

(4) This was impressively illustrated by a supreme court decision of the German Federal Supreme Court (BGH) of 10 November 2020. The BGH felt compelled – despite explicit denial of criminal energy on the part of the defendants – to confirm the conviction of two obstetricians for manslaughter who, at the mother's request, had killed a severely brain-damaged twin child by injecting potassium chloride into the umbilical vein only after opening the uterus to give birth to the

healthy twin child and who had chosen this procedure because an earlier intrauterine killing of the severely damaged twin could have harmed the healthy twin. (BGH - 5 StR 256/20) For a detailed discussion of this case and the unresolved issues it raises, see my essay on it: Strafbare Kindstötung: der BGH und die fragwürdig gewordene Geburtsgrenze (Prosecutable Infanticide: the BGH and the now questionable dividing line of birth), Aufklärung und Kritik 1/2022, pp. 180–185.

(5) This kind of distinction between doing and allowing is of considerable general importance. Without it, one could reach the absurd conclusion that it is justified to kill a healthy person if one could save several terminally ill people. Seems farfetched? Read for the surprisingly great difficulties one might have in rejecting such an argument without this distinction: John Harris, The Survival Lottery, in: as 3.6.6.[2], but pp. 399–403.

(6) R. M. Hare emphasises this in an excellent essay on the subject of abortion and thus resolutely opposes the view, which is generally taken for granted in Germany, that it makes a decisive moral difference whether a child already exists as a fertilised egg cell or an implanted embryo or even foetus or only has a probability of existence (admittedly incurring more uncertainties) in the form of an egg cell and a sperm cell and the procreative intention of the parents. (Abortion and the Golden Rule, 1975, reprinted in: as 3.6.6.[2], but pp. 58–68).

(7) This development is well documented in a nutshell and supported in particular by demoscopic comparative figures from recent decades in an article by Wolfgang Van den Daele: Zeugung auf Probe. Die nächste Bioethikdebatte: Die Präimplantationsdiagnostik (PID) ist Selektion, aber sie führt nicht zur Diskriminierung Behinderter (Procreation on trial. The next bioethics debate: Preimplantation diagnostics (PGD) is selection, but it does not lead to discrimination against the disabled), Die Zeit, 2 October 2002, p. 34.

3.6.5.

(1) This is a quotation from an excellent essay by the family doctor Anton Wohlfart in which he describes the emotional and rational confrontation with the problem of euthanasia as experienced by a doctor directly involved in patient care. He Also worth reading are his reflections there on "compassionate", rather than professional, solidary, friendly or loving care: "Seine eigenen Gefühle wahrnehmen – und dann anfangen zu denken" (Be aware of your own feelings - and then start thinking), Aufklärung und Kritik, Schwerpunkt: Selbstbestimmtes Sterben (Focus: Self-determined Dying), Sonderheft 11/2006, pp. 164–173, this quotation pp. 172, 173.

(2) For the justification of the change to the term "unresponsive wakefulness

syndrome" (UWS), see: Laureys, S. et al: Unresponsive wakefulness syndrome: a new name for the vegetative state or apallic syndrome, BMC Med. 2010; 8: 68, https://www.ncbi.nlm.nih.gov/pmc/articles/PMC2987895/. It is about avoiding devaluation and wrong factual descriptions associated with the older terms.

(3) This prospect is already presented in the excellent legal handbook by Wolfgang Putz, Beate Steldinger and Tanja Unger, which is unwaveringly committed to the patient's right to self-determination: Patientenrechte am Ende des Lebens (Patients' Rights at the End of Life), 7th edition, dtv München 2020. For the basic principles, see p. 234; for a case study in which a guiltless legal error was still granted in such a case for an event in 2002, p. 302.

(4) In some constellations, however, there are considerable pitfalls both in living wills and in other conclusions drawn from an earlier presumed will of the person concerned to his or her current presumed will, which only become apparent on closer examination. Problematic is, in particular, the following situation which is becoming more and more frequent with the increasing number of people suffering from senile dementia: A person who, in full possession of his or her mental powers, has excluded life-prolonging or life-sustaining medical measures in an advance directive in the event of the onset of senile dementia, can then, after the onset of dementia, obviously still enjoy simple pleasures of life and appears to be quite content with his or her life. The first mental reflex for the majority of people, including me, is that the advance directive must continue to apply because it concerns the same person and he or she wanted to avoid a condition that they, in full possession of their mental powers, felt to be unworthy. This point of view is also shared by renowned legal philosophers (such as Dworkin). Reinhard Merkel, however, objects convincingly that there now exists "a radically different subjectivity", "a literally different ego" in the body of the patient instead of the former person, and this new ego has far more to lose if the former order is enforced than its author if it remains unfulfilled (since the latter no longer exists as a person in the meaning of the term essential here). Even if the unquestionable continuance of a person's identity may be meaningful and indisputable for other contexts of the legal system (such as the law of inheritance), this does not apply in such a case to (advance) dispositions over one's own body. See Merkel, R., Personale Identität und die Grenzen strafrechtlicher Zuordnung (Personal identity and the limits of ascription in criminal law), Juristenzeitung 10/1999, pp. 502–511, in particular pp. 507–508. Merkel's conclusive argumentation, however, also makes it all the more clear that those who find the idea unbearable and unworthy that they could continue to exist as a demented person with a completely altered personality have no other choice than to put an end to their life in time.

A possible way out of this radical alternative, acceptable at least to some people, could be living wills that contain more detailed advance directives for the case of progressive dementia, for example by stipulating that a person wishes to end his or her life (for example by stopping the supply of food and fluids) as soon as the dementia reaches a stage that entails constant bedriddenness, the impossibility of taking in food and fluids by themselves and the inability to recognise other people and to communicate with them verbally or in another comprehensible form. In such a stage of dementia, it should also be easier to overcome the understandable inhibition of doctors, nursing staff and legal scholars and practitioners to comply with the dying wish laid down in an advance directive. Menzel offers preliminary considerations for such a concept (which, however, still seem somewhat overcomplicated to be practical): P. T. Menzel, B. Steinbock, Advance Directives, Dementia and Physician-Assisted Death, Journal of Law, Medicine and Ethics, Summer 2013, pp. 484–500.

(5) In the final stage of old-age decline or emaciating diseases, gradual dehydration has been proven to reduce pain sensitivity. As much as, on the one hand, lack of fluid intake is a frequent problem in geriatric medicine (as long as it is still meaningfully concerned with a longer-term perspective to ensure the best possible quality of life for the old person), the fear of agonising dehydration in the final stage of hopeless illnesses is, on the other hand, primarily a problem for the relatives and not for the sick persons themselves, a problem that leads to activist infusion therapies in the wrong situations time and again, which then only increase pain sensitivity and the need for painkillers without bringing any benefits to the persons concerned.

(6) Social, care-giving, legal and moral aspects of dying by VSED are described in detail, competently and in a balanced way in: Chabot, B., Walther, C., Ausweg am Lebensende. Sterbefasten – Selbstbestimmtes Sterben durch freiwilligen Verzicht auf Essen und Trinken (Exit at the end of life. Fasting to death – Self-determined dying by voluntary stopping eating and drinking), 6th, revised edition, Ernst Reinhardt München 2021
A good short overview of the most important aspects of VSED in English can be found on the website of End of Life Choices New York: https://endoflifechoicesny.org/education/resources/vsed/vsed_overview/, retrieved 8 August 2023

(7) In the meantime, the previously relatively inaccessible text by Binding and Hoche has been reprinted for study purposes, so that it is now easier to judge for yourself: Binding, K., Hoche, A., Die Freigabe der Vernichtung lebensunwerten Lebens. Ihr Maß und ihre Form, Meiner Leipzig 1920, second edition 1922, reprint of the 1920 edition, Berliner Wissenschaftsverlag 2006. There is also a translation into English by C. Modak that contains the German text as well: Allowing the Destruction of Life Unworthy of Life. Its measure and form, Suzeteo Enterprises Greenwood 2012. The translation comes with a foreword by A. Horvath, attacking especially utilitarian approaches in a questionable way that is

nevertheless worth reading. The German reprint is preceded by an introduction by Wolfgang Naucke, that is instructive, albeit wobbling around in terms of philosophy of law and unsatisfactory in its anti-secular tendency. There are also extensive references. The negative aspects of Binding's and Hoche's book have been clearly and rightly pointed out many times, for example when Hoche speaks of "ballast existences" and "empty human shells" and proclaims that the task of us Germans is going to be the most highly intensified aggregation of all possibilities and that modern endeavours "to also retain all weaklings of all sorts" stand in the way of the fulfillment of this task. (pp. 51, 52 German edition, Pos. 1072 of the kindle edition of the above-mentioned English edition) For the sake of justice, however, the following sentences of Binding are also quoted here: "Each unprohibited killing of a third party must be perceived at the very least as a relief for that person: otherwise, its permission is forbidden by itself. This, however, leads to an absolutely necessary demand: the *full respect for the will to live of all people, even the sickest and most suffering and the most useless ones . ...* The issue of allowing the killing of the most feeble-minded, who feel good about their life, is obviously out of the question too." (p. 27 German edition, italics in the original text, Pos. 747 of the kindle edition in English, translation slightly modified) That Binding and Hoche would have supported the criminal practice of the National Socialists, which was exclusively motivated by the idea of an advantage for other people respectively the society, namely the German people (Volk) as a whole, is thus an insinuation. Further clarification would only have been possible if Binding had not died in 1920. Hoche was blinded by German nationalism during the First World War and the Weimar Republic, like most German scientists. But he was married to a Jewish woman, was granted respectively forced into early emeritus status in 1933 (for which he received a very cool farewell letter from Rector Heidegger) and he never got involved with the National Socialists and never expressed anti-Semitic views. He died in 1943 and there are indications from the last years of his life that make it quite likely that after the end of National Socialism he might have been much more capable of a self-critical confrontation with earlier positions than a Mr Heidegger was. On Hoche see also note 4.3 (2).

(8)   An Insight into these new developments, but also the difficulties and uncertainties associated with them, as well as sensitive descriptions of the human and psychological burdens associated with these fates for all the people involved, gives Adrian Owen: Into the Gray Zone, Scribner New York 2017.

(9) Helga Kuhse describes very well what she thinks (and I think) a trustworthy position of doctors should look like: "If the raison d'être of morality is to allow people to live together in relative peace and security, what kind of motivation would we like doctors to have, and what kind of actions would we like them to perform? Clearly, we would like them to be motivated to primarily seek our good, rather

than their own; to keep us alive, if this is in our best interests, and to 'let' us die, or to 'make' us die, when either one of these actions serves us best." Why Killing is Not Always Worse – and Sometimes Better – Than Letting Die, in: as 3.6.6.[2], but pp. 236–239.

(10) In the Anglo-Saxon world, this is discussed much more openly and appropriately than it is possible in Germany, though, unfortunately, partly under the influence of inadequate social security systems (which, however, does not change the fundamental justification of the questions raised). In particular, the seemingly self-evident assumption (and the resulting moral and social pressure) must be questioned that it is under all circumstances a justified moral claim or a morally preferable decision for younger family members or entire families to fundamentally change their way of life and life planning in the interest of caring for elderly family members, even at the price of serious long-term sacrifices. For an eye-opener read John Hardwig: Is There a Duty to Die? in: as 3.6.6.[2], but pp. 339–348.

That old persons themselves come to the conclusion at a certain point that the prospects and quality of life still possible for them are grossly disproportionate to the psychological and financial burdens they cause for younger family members or even society as a whole, and therefore prefer to die, can be based on an understandable consideration of values and can be a morally comprehensible decision.

(11) So Hans Küng: " … the all-merciful God, who has given men and women freedom and responsibility for their lives, has also left to dying people the responsibility for making a conscientious decision about the manner and time of their deaths." German text: Küng, H. , W. Jens, Menschenwürdig sterben. Ein Plädoyer für Selbstverantwortung, second edition. Piper München Zürich 1995, pp. 1–85, here pp. 71, 72. Translated by J. Bowden: Dying with Dignity. A Plea for Personal Responsibility, Continuum New York 1995, pp. 1–40, here p. 37, 38. Available online: https://archive.org/details/dyingwithdignity0000kung/page/38/mode/2up, retrieved 23 August 2023. There you can also find references to similar positions of various other theologians.

Also worthwhile is the very thorough and well-informed study by Michael Frieß: "Komm süßer Tod" - Europa auf dem Weg zur Euthanasie? ("Come, sweet death" – Europe on the way to euthanasia?) Like many Protestant theologians, Frieß adopts a naturalistic-humanistic argumentation to such an extent that one can hardly suppress the question of whether he himself still considers the theological considerations that go beyond this to be really convincing and necessary. But in the end – unavoidable in a Protestant dissertation after all — there are nevertheless professions using theological terms (but the practical result agrees with what seems reasonable from a secular point of view): "Neither the state nor God limits sane persons in decisions concerning the time of their own death. The creature's God-given freedom is extended to all areas of earthly life." (p. 231) "Suicide and active euthanasia can be a believing letting go of oneself in devout trust in God's promise of eternal life." (p. 225)

(12) A relatively early, prominent example is the joint suicide of the von Brauchitsch couple in September 2010, for which care was taken by the Swiss organisation for self-determined and dignified dying "EXIT". Both spouses suffered from chronic, severely burdening illnesses which would, however, not necessarily have been deadly in the short run. For a report in German see: www.spiegel.de/economy/social/0,1518,716939,00.html, for a translated summary see: https://www.thelocal.de/20100911/29757, both retrieved 24 August 2023.

3.6.6.

(1) Deutsche Akademie der Wissenschaften Leopoldina/Union der deutschen Akademien der Wissenschaften (Hrsg.), Neubewertung des Schutzes von In-Vitro-Embryonen in Deutschland (A new evaluation of the protection of in vitro embryos in Germany), Stellungnahme 2021, available online: https://www.leopoldina.org/uploads/tx_leopublication/2021_Stellungnahme_Embryonenschutz_web.pdf. Though this document is not translated, there are several statements on this topic and other issues in reproductive medicine in English on the respective website: https://www.leopoldina.org/en/topics/reproductive-medicine/reproductive-medicine-22/, retrieved 29 August 2023

(2) A very good analysis of the problem is given by John Harris ("Goodbye Dolly? The Ethics of Human Cloning", in: as 3.6.6.[2], but pp. 143–152). He points out quite clearly that at the heart of the debate is the question of whether people should have the right to control their own reproductive destiny and choose their own path of reproduction, analogous to their right to live according to their own philosophical convictions, as long as they do not violate the rights of others or threaten society. (And he clearly affirms this).

His general warning against the misuse of the concept of human dignity is also worth heeding: "Appeals to human dignity, while universally attractive, are comprehensively vague and deserve separate attention. A first question to ask when the idea of human dignity is invoked is: whose dignity is attacked and how?" (p. 145) The concept of human dignity is not infrequently used as a propagandistic catchword to put opponents in the wrong and to silence them, without taking the trouble of a rationally comprehensible moral argumentation.

3.6.7.

(1) A good, concentrated insight into this topic is given in: Vogel, F., Gentechnologie und die biologische Zukunft der Menschheit (Genetic engineering and the biological future of humankind), Deutsches Ärzteblatt 86 (1989), 27 April 1989,

pp. B-878–B-882. A very sensible and solid statement on the subject of eugenics and genetic engineering as a whole is also: Flatz, B., Gentechnik und die genetische Zukunft der Menschheit (Genetic engineering and the genetic future of humankind), in: Schiefenhövel, W., Chr. Vogel, G. Vollmer, U. Opolka (eds.), Der Mensch in seiner Welt. Anthropologie heute, Vol. 1, Vom Affen zum Halbgott. Der Wege des Menschen aus der Natur, Trias Thieme Stuttgart 1994, pp. 153–177.

More recently Theodore Friedmann has written a good, critical article on genetic engineering and its possible applications for the genetic optimisation of humankind, which also takes into account the failed historical attempts to do so: Genetic therapies, human genetic enhancement, and ... eugenics? Available online: https://www.nature.com/articles/s41434-019-0088-1, retrieved 23 September 2023.

For the history and the problems of this issue see also the Wikipedia articles "Eugenics" and "Dysgenics", retrieved 23 September 2023.

(2) For a discussion of the considerations required here see, for example, Günther Patzig, Ethische Probleme der Gentechnologie, Pränataldiagnostik und Postnataldiagnostik (Ethical problems of genetic engineering, prenatal and postnatal diagnostics), as 1.4.6.[6] , but pp. 128–143.

(3) The problem of irrational reservations about green genetic engineering in particular is discussed in great detail and solidly by Johannes Bergler: Grüne Gentechnik. Eingebildete Gefahren (Green genetic engineering. Imaginary risks), Skeptiker 23 (2010) No. 1, 13–21. The article also addresses the general problem of a rational public discussion of issues that require scientific expertise in a field of tension between economic interests and aggressive, placative environmental lobbyism under the conditions of media democracy. It becomes very clear that irrational environmental activism can very easily achieve the opposite of its actual objective, i.e. cause considerable harm to people and their environment. Balancing and informative with regard to actually relevant risks and side effects of green genetic engineering is a further article by Jasmin Barmann and Johannes Bergler: Grüne Gentechnik. Berechtigte Bedenken (Green genetic engineering. Justified concerns), Skeptiker 23 (2010) No. 3, 140–45 (with literature).

And, as fun to read: the equally enlightening and amusing open letter by Nobel Prize winner Christiane Nüsslein-Volhard to the gourmet and cook Wolfram Siebeck: Genetik für Gourmets (Genetics for gourmets). Die Zeit, 19 November 1998, reprinted in: Die Zeit 65 Jahre, March 2011, pp. 19–21 available online: https://www.zeit.de/1998/48/199848.genfood_.xml?utm_referrer=https%3A%2F%2Fwww.google.com%2F, retrieved 26 September 2023

3.6.8.

(1) A well readable introduction to this problem is given by Christian Vogel: Vom Töten zum Mord. Das wirkliche Böse in der Evolutionsgeschichte (From killing to murder. On the real evil in evolutionary history), Hanser München/Wien 1989 especially pp. 29–37; see also his contribution 3.3.[9].

A further remark on sociobiology: Various sociobiological concepts that are now well documented, such as "kin support" or "kin selection" (see the respective Wikipedia article, https://en.wikipedia.org/wiki/Kin_selection, retrieved 16 January 2025) or "reciprocal altruism", have contributed to our understanding of the evolutionary process though the discussion on the significance of various mechanism and levels of selection is all but completed. As it happens so often with new scientific concepts, a host of new questions are raised. For example: How do genes make their respective phenotype recognise and weight (quantitatively and qualitatively) genetic relatedness in other phenotypes, and adjust its behaviour accordingly, with the most diverse gradations? A wealth of trait and behavioural details will certainly play a role in this (appearance, smells, movements, vocalisations) and social correlations, which normally indicate genetic kinship, are also likely to be of essential importance. In the case of highly organised organisms, especially humans, we must also not neglect common interests, desires and preferences that go beyond elementary needs, as motivations for support, cooperation and bonding that become important for reproductive behaviour and reproductive success.

(2) A good summary of modern scientific knowledge on homosexuality (to be considered as historically meritorious meanwhile) is given by Volker Sommer: Wider die Natur? Homosexualität und Evolution (Against nature? Homosexuality and evolution), Beck Munich 1990, new edition 2000. In addition to its actual subject, this book (and also the lecture recommended below) are interesting lessons on "naturalness", "natural morality", "nature and morality". A brief summary of his reflections on the subject can also be found in: Sommer, V., Vom Menschen und anderen Tieren. Essays zur Evolutionsbiologie (On humans and other animals. Essays on evolutionary biology), Hirzel Stuttgart/Leipzig 2000, chapter 4: Homosexualität. Ein Paradoxon für die Evolutionstheorie? (Homosexuality. A Paradox for the Theory of Evolution?) In English there is also an entertaining and informative talk by Volker Sommer summing up his findings (2011 at University College London). You can listen to it on SoundCloud: https://soundcloud.com/uclsound/against-nature-homosexuality-and-evolution, retrieved 26 September 2023.

Very good is also the Wikipedia article "Homosexuality" summing up, among other things, more or less all important knowledge collected by science on the origin, formation and explanation of homosexuality: https://en.wikipedia.org/wiki/Homosexuality, retrieved 27 September 2023

(3) However, this does not apply to every unusual permanent cohabitation and life partnership, for example, in our culture - at least so far - not to polygamous cohabitation. A type of relationship should already be a social reality with a certain frequency and a certain minimum prospect of long-term success in order to deserve special legal protection. Unusual types of relationships, which deserve tolerance if based on free decisions, do not necessarily need a special anchoring in the legal system. It seems more appropriate to me that the legal system follows social change (and thus also reinforces it at a relatively late stage) than to try to make itself the spearhead of such change and thereby endanger its general acceptance.

3.7.1.

(1) In addition to positive law, there is also law that has no immediate, current social regulatory force, namely historical, conceptual or postulatory law. Such law can nevertheless influence the acceptance and the judgement on the validity of positive law.

(2) Gustav Radbruch's attempt to position suprastatutory law against statutory injustice with the help of a minimalist concept of natural law reduced exclusively to the concept of justice also fails because of the problem that there is no objective, generally accepted meaning and interpretation of justice. Such an emergency anchor seemed necessary as a response to the National Socialist regime of injustice, and it still shapes the jurisprudence of the Federal Republic of Germany in its coming to terms with the injustice of the GDR and to this day. Basically Radbruch himself was already aware of the inadequacy of his justification of law when he wrote that the determination of what is just is doubtful and that one must ultimately leave the solution to the voice of God, "which speaks to the conscience of the individual only in the particular case." (Radbruch, G., Fünf Minuten Rechtsphilosophie (Five minutes of Legal Philosophy), Rhein-Neckar-Zeitung 12.9.1945, reprinted in: id., Rechtsphilosophie (Legal philosophy), Koehler Stuttgart 1973, pp. 327–329, here p. 329), translated by B. Litschewski Paulson and S. L. Paulson: Five Minutes of Legal Philosophy, Oxford Journal of Legal Studies, :Vo. 26, No. 1 (2006), pp. 13–15, available online: https://idv.sinica.edu .tw/philaw/Jurisprudence_Reading/Five%20Minutes%20of%20Legal%20Philosophy%20(1945).pdf, retrieved 23 January 2024. And at the same time, Radbruch was already very close to a truly convincing solution of the conflict between statutory injustice and suprastatutory law when he wrote that the legal

principles that deprive any law that contradicts them of its validity have been established over centuries as a solid stock and have been collected in the so-called declarations of human and civil rights with far-reaching consensus. (p. 328 of the German text, p. 15 of the translation).

If Gustav Radbruch had been able to overcome his Christian inclination and recognise that this basis is completely sufficient in the social framework (and also constitutes a better point of reference for the individual's decision of conscience than illusory divine voices), our jurisdiction could today already rely on a solid secular basis even in the judgement of statutory injustice, instead of still making reference - albeit in a rather intricate manner - to foundations of natural law and religion that have long since ceased to be sustainable.

If, however, the criticism of the belief in natural law should seem all too self-evident to someone: Scientific authorities still feel called upon to give us the impression that we can select from nature - and especially from human nature - what we like, and then pass this off in good conscience as "true nature" and draw normative conclusions from it. In 1987, Professor Martin Kriele, Director of the Department of Political Philosophy and Legal Policy at the University of Cologne and at the same time a judge at the Constitutional Court of North Rhine-Westphalia, wrote: "The law that guarantees people and nations the freedom to shape their own lives and at the same time limits this freedom in such a way that other people and nations enjoy the same freedom is the only form of coexistence that corresponds to human nature. This is the reason why the democratic revolution has a natural tendency to spread universally throughout humanity: it is the world revolution par excellence" (Kriele, M., Die demokratische Weltrevolution (The democratic world revolution), Piper München 1987, p. 12).

I share this ideal of law and state. I understand that Kriele suffers from the existential deficit of contemporary thought and its consequences, and I struggle with him against the indifferentism that is often derived from the relativism to which philosophical scepticism leads us. But good intentions and reasonable positions on many practical questions, which make Kriele's book sympathetic, do not, however, justify continuing to propagate a belief in natural law and thus replacing philosophical scepticism with philosophical simplicity. Could one seriously argue that all previous undemocratic forms of government and their law were "unnatural"? Human history, in other words, largely in contradiction to human nature!? As unconvincing as Kriele's assertion may be as an anthropological statement or as a justification of norms, it is to be hoped that it may be correct as a historical prognosis (even if one will, regretfully, see this more sceptical for the moment than at the time when Kriele's book was published).

However, even Kriele is basically cautious: he presents the above-mentioned natural law position as a doctrine of the Enlightenment and gives us the impression that it is still valid, without clearly adopting it for himself. In later publications, however, it becomes clear that this is not due to Kriele's critical distance from the idea of natural law in general, but that he only misses the religious justification in Enlightenment thinking on natural law. He does not prove to be an advocate of critical reason, but a Christian philosopher of religion of the simpler kind (under the influence of his wife, he even believes that he can communicate directly with angels). On this, see Martin Kriele, Gott und die Vernunft. Kann ein vernünftiger Mensch ungläubig sein? (God and reason. Can a reasonable person be unbelieving?) Christiana-Verlag Stein am Rhein 2008, and Hans Albert's apt commentary: Träume eines Geistersehers. Zur Kritik des Krieleschen Spiritualismus (Dreams of a spirit-seer. A critique of Kriele's spiritualism), Aufklärung und Kritik 2/2009, pp. 19–34, and Norbert Hoerster, Rechtsethik aus dem Mund der Engel? (Legal ethics by the mouth of angels?) Aufklärung und Kritik 1/2010, pp. 223–227.

(3) Even John Rawls' "Theory of Justice" that is so much discussed and very sympathetic but often overestimated in its explanatory value, amounts in essence to nothing more than a moderately sophisticated variant of the derivation of morality and law from a "nature of humans" already charged with values. Here this comes in the guise of a social contract theory of rational egoists. Even if "the principles that free and rational persons concerned to further their own interests would accept in an initial position of equality as defining the fundamental terms of their association" could be convincingly established (which is not the case), these principles would still be no more than a fiction, because the postulated situation of equality is already such a fiction - or, as Rawls puts it – "... a purely hypothetical situation characterized so as to lead to a certain conception of justice." (Rawls, J., A Theory of Justice, 1971, revised edition 1990, Oxford University Press 1999, pp. 10, 11). Now, one can ask with good reason why we should rather base our law and morality on such a fiction than on the inequality that actually exists from the beginning. Even if unambiguous principles could be derived from such a fiction, even if it were possible to derive them from a contract-theoretical ("natural") creation of law based on a social contract theory assuming the premise of initial equality, these would only be one shade in the broad spectrum of human morality and would first have to be recognised as binding by the individual through a personal decision (respectively, this hypothetical contractualism would have to be recognised by the individual through a decision as a method of finding morality and law).

One can discuss to what extent a fictitious primordial state – Rawlsian or otherwise – can or should have a certain function in finding justice as a heuristic principle, analogous to the function of universalisation principles, such as the categorical imperative, in moral considerations in general. Personally, I believe that such a fictitious primordial state can in any case have only very limited heuristic value because of the vagueness of the consequences and that we have to decide what justice is for us in weighings of interests and then of values, with a view to the reality of the world. Rawls himself introduces such values through the back door when he postulates that citizens must have "a rational moral psychology" with an aptitude for a conception of the good and for developing a sense of justice and a desire to act on it. (Rawls, J., Political Liberalism, New Edition, Columbia University Press New York 1996, esp. pp. 85–88, pp. 121–125).

(4) A collection of representatives of this morally well-intentioned but philosophically weak backslide (with only a few and then also not very convincing alibi opponents) is presented in the volume: Naturrecht oder Rechtspositivismus? (Natural law or legal positivism? ed. Werner Maihofer, Wissenschaftliche Buchgesellschaft Darmstadt 1962, second unchanged edition 1972

(5) In the US (and this will hardly be feasible differently in other states of law) the execution of the death penalty costs more than a life sentence due to specifically high costs of the criminal proceedings produced in addition to the cost of incarcerating the prisoner. See: https://www.amnestyusa.org/issues/death-penalty/death-penalty-facts/death-penalty-cost/, retrieved 30 January 2024

(6) An essential contribution to the constitution of human rights as an internationally binding legal norm, even before their adequate codification at the international level, were exemplary court proceedings, especially the Nuremberg Trials, in which - despite all the weaknesses of such proceedings - the observance of general principles of humanity and the respect for human rights was demanded as a now binding component of the cultural and legal tradition of humankind.

This remains historically correct, even if the charge of "crimes against humanity" still played a relatively (and regrettably) subordinate role in the Nuremberg Trials and was still seen in terms of legal construction as heavily dependent on the charges of conspiracy, crimes against peace and war crimes - for which there was a clearer tradition of international law, despite all the dubiousness in this regard (for example, of the charge of "war of aggression"). The victorious powers could also have put their own leaders in the dock under these other points - just think of the Hitler-Stalin Pact for the partition of Poland, British area bombings such as in Dresden or the American atomic bombs dropped on major Japanese cities. On the other hand, at a time when the extent of the Stalinist terror was not yet known, they could not yet be accused of anything in terms of "crimes against humanity" that would have been even remotely comparable to the dimensions of National Socialist atrocities.

The fact that the prosecution did not emphasise the violation of human rights more strongly at the Nuremberg Trials seems outdated today. On the other hand, the basis of the Nuremberg Trials is also extraordinarily modern. The law applicable to the Court and its legitimacy were in fact founded exclusively conventionally by an agreement of the Allies and with additional reference to earlier agreements and customs under international law and the law of war, without recourse to God, natural law or any other objectivist-idealistic construct. (See the London Four-Power Agreement and the Statute for the International Military Tribunal agreed upon in its execution, text for instance in: Taylor, T., The Anatomy of the Nuremberg Trials. A Personal Memoir, A. Knopf New York 1992, Appendix A) Thus, religious rhetoric was pleasantly dispensed with. This fact (which is undoubtedly due to the great differences in the ideological ideas of the victorious powers) could - and should - be a model for a future international jurisdiction on the basis of conventional human and international law which leaves aside the ideological and religious legal justifications prevailing in the individual nations. On the significance of the Nuremberg Trials, see also Nürnberger Menschenrechtszentrum (The Nuremberg Human Rights Center) (ed.), Von Nürnberg nach Den Haag. Menschenrechtsverbrechen vor Gericht — Zur Aktualität des Nürnberger Prozesses, Europäische Verlagsanstalt Hamburg 1996.

(7) To those who read German texts I recommend a small but substantial volume by Norbert Hoerster for thinking about problems in the philosophy of law: Was ist Recht? Grundfragen der Rechtsphilosophie (What is law? Fundamental questions of legal philosophy), Beck München 2006. However, one will notice that terms used by me are used there with partly considerably different meanings. In the philosophy of law, a different use of the same terms is particularly widespread. You have to look all the more closely if you want to compare the points of view of different authors.

(8) The discussion of legal positivism was and is particularly fraught with historical guilt in Germany. The Anglo-American discussion took a somewhat different course in detail, especially in the long-lasting and continuing Hart-Dworkin debate which is, however, ultimately also about the relation of morality and law. For a good overview of the state of affairs see: Jimenez, F., Legal Principles, Law and Tradition, Yale Journal of Law and the Humanities, Vol. 33 (2022) pp. 5991, available online: https://openyls.law.yale.edu/bitstream/handle/20.500.13051/18173/2_Jimenez_Legal%20Princples_PRINT_20220426.pdf?sequence=1&isAllowed=y, retrieved 29 January 2023

3.7.2.

(1) Socrates, for example, came to this conclusion, and this was one of the reasons why he refused to flee. In his situation, however, I would probably have come to a different result of my moral deliberations.

(2) However, Reinhard Merkel rightly points out that torture should not always be

regarded as contrary to human rights. If a criminal directly threatens other people with death, this is to be regarded as a situation of self-defence or defence of others in which the infliction of psychological and physical harm, under certain circumstances up to and including the direct infliction of pain on the criminal, is justified if this promises to be able to prevent the realisation of the death threat. Otherwise, the human dignity of the criminal is placed higher than that of the victim. "According to general principles of the attribution of actions and consequences what is necessary to defend against an unlawful attack is attributed to the attacker himself. Whoever lunges at his enemy with the intention of murder and is killed by him in self-defence has, normatively speaking, literally killed himself. This principle of imputation, however, applies to acts of self-defence even if, in the extreme, they would only be possible in the mode of torture. And now, of course, one must remain consistent: The arrested kidnapper of a child, who does not want to reveal the acutely life-threatening hiding place in which he is holding his victim, threatens himself with the torture he is threatened with in case of his continued refusal. He has it entirely in his own hands to prevent or end the procedure of inflicting pain, and he is absolutely legally obliged to do so - with the strongest duty of the citizen of all: that of not killing his fellow human being." Folter als Notwehr (Torture as self-defence), Die Zeit, 6 March 2008, p. 46.

With the reference to the right of self-defence and defence of others with its long tradition in legislation and jurisprudence, which in particular requires the existence of a present attack and the use of appropriate means to defend against it, and which threatens excessive means of self-defence with punishment, sufficient protection seems to me to be given to prevent unreasonably harsh coercive measures and the development of a slippery slope with the extension of direct coercive measures into ordinary practice of interrogation. If, on the other hand, the German Code of Criminal Procedure pushes the protection of the accused so far that he may not even be impaired by fatigue, for example (§ 136a StPO), this seems grossly inappropriate for situations (such as the well-known Gäfgen case) where there are concrete indications that the life of the victim could depend on the timely disclosure of information by the perpetrator.

3.7.4.

(1) In concrete terms this means that, for example, the basic rights established in the Basic Law of the Federal Republic of Germany are fundamental provisions of a legal order based on majority decisions, i.e. convention, that ultimately only become binding through their conformity with personal morality, but they are not philosophical truths. And the same applies at the level of an international legal order, for example, considering human rights as laid down in the Universal Declaration of Human Rights of the United Nations. The fact that human rights

represent a great cultural-civilisational advance of humankind makes them valid (and gives them a moral claim to general bindingness), but it does not make them a philosophical truth in the sense of an objective datum given independent of human positing.

(2) On the German Federal Constitutional Court's case-law on this question, which is reasonable and does not contain any untenable legal philosophical contortions, see the guidelines to the decision of the Second Senate of 24 October 1996: "2. The strict prohibition of retroactivity under Article 103 (2) of the Basic Law is justified in the constitutional state by the special foundation of trust conferred to criminal law if it is enacted by a democratic legislator bound to the basic civil rights. 3. Such a foundation of trust is lacking if the bearer of state power excludes punishability for the area of the most serious criminal injustice through grounds of justification by inciting such injustice beyond the written norms, by favouring it and thus grossly disregarding the human rights generally recognised in the community of nations. The strict protection of trust by Article 103 (2) GG must then be waived." In its judgement of 22 March 2001 on the case the European Court of Human Rights expressed the same legal conception. No one should believe therefore that they can hide behind the just existing and accepted law of a dictatorship or that they can easily invoke a superior orders plea with regard to instructions of a dictatorship that are contrary to basic civil and human rights.

A compilation of the relevant judgments with references to the original texts of the decisions can be found at https://de.wikipedia.org/wiki/Schie%C3%9Fbefehl, retrieved 2 February 2024.

(4) For a comprehensive overview of the development and status of international criminal law and international criminal justice, see: Werle, G. Völkerstrafrecht, Mohr Siebeck Tübingen 2003, 5th, revised and updated edition, Werle, G., F. Jeßberger, ibid. 2020. 4th English edition: Principles of International Criminal Law, Oxford University Press 2020

3.7.5.

(1) The realisation of this principle of moral restraint has made great progress in German jurisprudence under the influence of sensible legal scholars such as Kaufmann. In particular, the law on sexual offences has been largely freed from moralising with the abolition, for example, of the punishability of adultery and of homosexual relations between adults. How arduous it is, however, to finally accomplish this is shown, for example, as late as 2008 by the misguided decision of the German Federal Constitutional Court on the prohibition of incest, in which only the well-reasoned dissenting opinion of Hassemer did justice to the principle established by Kaufmann, while the majority of the Senate still believed that they

had to enforce an assumed majority morality by means of criminal law, using all kinds of unsustainable auxiliary arguments. For the relatively rare cases of incest which are not covered by other protective provisions of criminal law a specifically tailored criminal law norm is certainly not the right answer of society. The case that gave rise to the above-mentioned decision made this abundantly clear. See Bundesverfassungsgericht Entscheidung 2BvR392/07, www.bundesverfassungsgericht.de/entscheidungen/rs20080226_2bvr039207.html, retrieved 4 February 2024. Social assistance and not prison - that would be a humane approach here.

To date the idea of restraint in the criminal law seems to be discussed rarely in the Anglo-Saxon Philosophy of Law. Here is an exception by Patrick Healy from McGill University in Montreal, published on the website of the Government of Canada in 2022: Restraint in the Criminal Law, https://www.justice.gc.ca/eng/rp-pr/csj-sjc/ilp-pji/cl-dp/index.html, retrieved 4 February 2024.

3.7.6.

(1) A good impression of this school of thought (also substantially influenced by psychoanalysis) is given by: Lüderssen, K., Abschaffen des Strafens? (Abolishing punishment?) Suhrkamp Frankfurt a. M. 1995. However, the book would have benefited from a few more concrete examples to make what is meant clearer.

(2) A sensible drugs policy should educate about the consequential damage of drug use and reduce the social harm caused by it (even if one accepts that citizens should have a certain degree of freedom to harm themselves). It must combat the social decline of addicts, reduce the number of drug-related deaths and reduce the number of deaths caused by the struggle for the lucrative market in illegal drugs. It should reduce the waste of national and international resources through the one-sided, repressive, police-related prosecution of drug use and trafficking, which manifests itself in the largely unsuccessful fight against problematic drug use, despite these measures.

Promising approaches in this regard, which have been able to achieve a relatively large reduction in the number of drug-related deaths, are offered in particular by Portugal's decriminalising drug policy, which, however, does not yet optimally solve the problem of the continuing compulsion to obtain drugs illegally and whose innovative approach is endangered by an again increasing criminal prosecution of drug consumers (see the also basically informative paper Rêgo, X., Oliveira, M. J., Lameira, C. et al., 20 years of Portuguese drug policy - developments, challenges and the quest for human rights. Subst Abuse Treat Prev Policy 16, 59 (2021), available online : https://substanceabusepolicy.biomed central.com/articles/10.1186/s13011-021-00394-7, retrieved 21 January 2025. A good approach is also the Swiss 4-pillar policy with repression of drug trafficking, prevention of use, therapy for addicts and harm reduction for drug users). But even here, various unresolved problems remain, such as the question of substitution for some drugs, for example uncontrolled cocaine use. As a source in German see: https://www.nzz.ch/zuerich/drogen-politik-in-der-schweiz-pionier-andre-seidenberg-warnt-vor-legalem-kokain-tld.1829759, 20 May 2024, retrieved 20 January 2025.

A restrictive drug policy without sufficient harm reduction measures for drug addicts, as in the USA, on the other hand, leads to a drug-related death rate that is about 35 times higher per million inhabitants than in Portugal, not to mention the other social repercussions. For an overview of restrictive strategies (beginning with the US prohibition) of alcohol and modern decriminalisation strategies see: Fouch, P., Decriminalization: A Way Out of the Unwinnable War on Drugs, 22 Appalachian Journal of Law (2023).

Regardless of the details of the respective drug policies, international experience seems to justify at least the following conclusions: First, the criminalisation of drug users has no positive effects, neither individually nor socially. Second, if one not only tolerates the possession of drugs for personal use, but considers it justifiable to legalise the use of certain drugs (here it is primarily about cannabis), albeit with, for example, well-founded age limits because of the otherwise considerably enhance risk of psychosis, then a legal and controlled system for the distribution of drugs should also be established, instead of creating new business opportunities for the illegal drug trade, with all its negative and violent side effects. Third, for drugs that are not traditionally anchored in the respective society the question must also be answered (as for the mostly legal drugs alcohol and nicotine) what the balance should be between the individual right to freedom of intoxication and the consumption or even abuse of drugs and the protection of the population from the associated negative effects.

(3) Our ideas about clearly definable mental illnesses can by no means be regarded as complete. For example, it is to be expected that congenital and acquired frontal brain damage and damage in the limbic system, which make compassion and moral behaviour completely or partially impossible for the affected person despite preserved rational abilities, can be diagnosed more precisely in the future and are likely to play a greater role as a cause of incapacity or reduced culpability. In Germany, criminal law is already prepared for all extensions of neurobiologically and psychologically comprehensible psycho- and sociopathological deviations through the broad provision of § 20 of the Criminal Code, which declares that lack of criminal responsibility may occur not only due to a "pathological mental disorder" but also due to "a severe other mental abnormality".

(4) Once again: In the sense of the best imaginable physical, mental and moral

capacities, humans are deficient beings, even if this wording makes sense only from an ideal perspective but not for an evolutionary realism.

(5) An impressive plea for an individual analysis and individual therapy of offenders, which is not limited to the mere assignment to the usual, often still relatively unsubtle psychiatric pigeonholes, is given from the long experience of the court reporter by Hans Holzhaider: Tiefseelforscher. Kannibalen, Serienmörder, Kinderschänder (Deep Soul Explorer. Cannibals, serial killers, child molesters), Süddeutsche Zeitung, SZ am Wochenende, 6/7 March 2004, p. I., available online: https://www.sueddeutsche.de/panorama/justiz-und-psychtrie-tiefseelforscher-1.922144, retrieved 21 January 2025. The problem is that, compared to other areas of medicine, psychiatric diagnoses are often more gradual and, secondly, still much more symptom-oriented than cause-oriented. Holzhaider also objects to convenient, superficial legal attributions of motive that do not do justice to perpetrators with severe personality disorders. Even with an individualised assessment of sociopaths and psychopaths, who partly may be able to lead an adapted life but are still capable of committing the most horrific crimes, we are faced with the problem of having to penalise their serious norm violations and protect society from further crimes by these perpetrators.

(6) Preventive detention should therefore give the persons concerned much more room for shaping their lives and their environment than is the case in a prison or, if they are in need of therapy and can be treated accordingly, it should be replaced by placement in a forensic psychiatric ward. In this respect, the repeated criticism by the European Court of Human Rights of the German regulation of preventive detention as well as reserved and subsequently ordered preventive detention is justified. However, it leads to absurd practical effects if, instead of setting a deadline for improving the legal regulation and the design of preventive detention, the immediate release of obviously still highly dangerous offenders is ordered and also implemented in concrete terms in various cases (for the respective case law, see European Court of Human Rights, Fifth Section, Case of M. v. Germany, Application no. 19359 /04, Judgment Strasbourg 17 December 2009, on this in particular sections 127 and 129, p. 25; Case of Haidn versus Germany, Application no. 6587/04, Judgment 13 January 2011). In a later decision, however, due to the improved design of preventive detention in the meantime, the Court approved German jurisdiction even on the retroactive preventive detention of violent criminals who continue to be classified as dangerous. (Case of Ilnseher versus Germany, Applications nos. 10211/12 and 27505/14, Judgement 02 February 2017)

3.8.1.

(1) The quotation makes the essential and unfortunately unavoidable point that in democracy it is often not possible to gain acceptance for the most reasonable solution. It is retained here even though the role of its author during the National Socialist era and, above all, his lack of willingness to come to terms with the past honestly and self-critically later on must now be viewed very critically.

(2) A relatively harmless example of this is when competitions between members of different states in the field of sport lose their playful character and become a kind of substitute for war for which considerable material and propagandistic effort is expended by the state. Despite its relative harmlessness, this variant of states' addiction to prestige must also be rejected, as it often harms at least the health of the protagonists and means a waste of public money that could be used more sensible in other ways.

(3) K. R. Popper has extensively debated contrary views of the state in a way which largely corresponds to my convictions. See his book: The Open Society and its Enemies, Routledge and Kegan Paul London 1945/1947, available from the Internet Archive: https://archive.org/details/in.ernet.dli.2015.59272 (Vol. I) and https://archive.org/details/in.ernet.dli.2015.77661 (Vol. II), retrieved 11 February 2024

(4) Let's just take an old "knockout argument": The citizens would perhaps reintroduce the death penalty in a direct democracy. Well, which of the old democracies still has the death penalty? Not Switzerland, but the US with its decidedly representative system.

(5) The following remarks apply especially to Germany (and to other states where the separation of church and state is incomplete).

Religious instruction should be left to the individual religious communities and should not be taught by state-paid teachers as a regular subject at state schools. Instead, these schools should offer a subject dealing with philosophy, conduct of life, and religions, introducing students to different philosophical concepts and religions.

Nor is it the task of the state to fund the education of chaplains and theologians of the various religious communities.

The state should not allow church monopolies in social care institutions (and thus also prevent the regional de facto occupational bans for non-denominational people in certain social professions). Church-run and dominated institutions should not be predominantly financed by state funds. Even though the ties between church and state have already loosened considerably in the Federal Republic of Germany, there are still enough relics of a state church, in the form of a lacking separation of state and church. Some further examples: state-funded military, prison and hospital chaplaincies, concordat chairs at universities, state salaries for church dignitaries.

3.8.2.

(1) Ludwig Erhard's exemplary pursuit of this way of thinking is a lasting legacy. If today, in cursory retrospect, the economic rise of the Federal Republic of Germany after the Second World War may seem almost a matter of course due to favourable circumstances, it is worth to take a closer look back and to recognise how much staunch effort, especially on Erhard's part, and how many fortunate political decisions led to the Federal Republic of Germany not becoming a poor and grey planned economic democracy: Ludwig Erhard, Wohlstand für Alle (Prosperity for all), Econ Düsseldorf 1957, translated by E.T. Roberts and J. B. Woods under the somewhat distorting title "Prosperity through Competition", Praeger New York 1958, available online: https://cdn.mises.org/Prosperity%20 Through%20Competition_3.pdf, retrieved 13 February 2024. Despite the fact that the circumstances have changed in many respects today, there are a lot of lessons to be learned from it that could help us to better shape the future.

A good overview of the positions of the fathers of the social market economy and of the advantages and problems of this regulatory concept, also with regard to tasks that later came into focus, such as environmental protection, is provided by H. Jörg Thieme, Soziale Marktwirtschaft (Social market economy), second edition, Beck München 1994.

(2) For the comparison of the managerial position to the entrepreneur, see Ludwig von Mises: Human Action. A Treatise on Economics, 1949, 1963, Liberty Fund Indianapolis 2007, Vol. 2, Chapter 15, 10, Promoters, Managers, Technicians and Bureaucrats, pp. 303–311.

(3) A good contribution on this: Ottfried Höffe, Was ist ein "verantwortlicher" Wirtschaftsführer? Wider die Verkürzung des Konzepts "Profit" auf seine pekuniären Aspekt (What makes a responsible leader in business? Against the reduction of the concept of "profit" to its pecuniary aspect), Neue Zürcher Zeitung, 3 April 2010, p. 29. It could have been made a little clearer in the article that one should always perform one's work in such a way that it also brings a benefit to the community. Giving back profits to the community through "charity", for example by setting up charitable foundations, is an attractive but secondary way of giving meaning to one's own gainful occupation (and one's life as a whole).

(4) Worthwhile on this: Karl Homann, Vorteile und Anreize. Zur Grundlegung einer Ethik der Zukunft (Advantages and incentives. Laying the foundations for an ethics of the future), Mohr Siebeck Tübingen 2002.

(5) A good impression of this is given (although in detail very much adapted to US conditions) by: Thaler, R. H., Sunstein, C. R., Nudge. Improving Decisions

About Health, Wealth and Happiness, Yale University Press New Haven & London 2008.

(6) A typical - albeit still relatively harmless and insignificant - example of such processes is the German spelling reform. Instead of codifying the evolution of language retrospectively, making cautious simplifications and accepting alternative spellings without a predefined time limit and thus allowing and waiting for the historical development of language first of all, committees of experts and politicians try to impose an ahistorical and in many details nonsensical corset on people from above. Very similar, but often much more momentous processes can be found in school reforms and other activist undertakings of new regimentation in the social, economic and environmental spheres.

(7) In Germany, for example, since 2005 general practitioners have been forced into the role of a standardised minimum doctor, whose scope of services is defined and monitored in detail, without any consideration of personal interests and qualifications. At the same time, the doctor-patient relationship is burdened by perfidious, immoral rationing dilemmas in which the doctor is forced to make secret decisions to ration treatment under threat of financial loss (in extreme cases, even reaching bankruptcy), while the patient is made to believe that he is receiving the best possible care. Doctors are not allowed to tell individual patients that they had to choose a sub-optimal therapy for them, as otherwise the patients could claim the best possible therapy, which would destroy the doctor's economic existence. For many doctors, such predicaments give rise to a professional attitude to life of being both economically humiliated and bureaucratically bossed around lackeys of a social dictatorship with only limited democratic legitimacy. These lackeys, in turn, are increasingly only able to employ their qualified and motivated staff in underpaid jobs. The negative consequences will not be mitigated and concealed in the long term, even by moral and legal coercion and blackmail of those affected, and will not only lead to an increasing shortage of GPs, but also to a reduction in their willingness to provide services and of the range of their services.

Other professional groups in the health and social services sector are also facing similar dilemmas as a result of increased social, bureaucratic and legal demands and a simultaneous shortage of funds, which makes it impossible to fulfil all these demands. Underpayment, psychological humiliation and bad decisions from the hierarchy of the respective institutions are added to this and combine to form an overall constellation that drives motivated and qualified staff out of the social sector or keeps them away from it altogether.

The fundamental problems consist firstly in the fact that politics and administration do not see themselves in a serving role, with the aim of making the work of those who provide the actual care services easier and sufficiently attractive.

Instead, politics and administration have internalised a mentality of domination that regards the "service providers" just as cost factors and as interchangeable employees who can be ordered around at will and whose motivation is not a matter of concern. Secondly, politicians are not honest about the rationing of services they decide on (and in some cases have to decide on), but instead present the public with a mendacious promise of unlimited services, while at the same time forcing those involved in patient care to engage in hidden rationing.

We must not accept such undesirable developments as inevitable side-effects of social healthcare systems that strive to provide a high level of care for all strata of the population. In the social care and healthcare sector too, we need to return to a social market economy policy based on incentives.

(8) Still very impressive and worth reading is Hayek's insistent plea against the creeping loss of freedom through planned economy and collectivism: Hayek, F. A., The Road to Serfdom, 1944, also available online: https://nae.com.pt/wp-content/uploads/The-Road-to-Serfdom-F.-A.-von-Hayek.pdf, retrieved 22 February 2024.

(9) Anyone who takes a closer look at the book cited here and the work of the Friedmans as a whole will find that it is by no means – following in Adam Smith's footsteps in this point too - characterised by social coldness (see, for example, Friedman's concept of the "negative income tax", according to whose basic concept a sustainable, efficient social system with little bureaucracy is quite conceivable, or his commitment to a better, socially permeable school system).

Milton Friedman's restriction to economic advice in dealing with the Chilean dictatorship has understandably been held against him. However, it was a reaction to the catastrophic economic failure of the Allende government, and Friedman defended himself by saying that he had also given his advice independently of the ruling political system in other cases and that Chile's economic recovery ultimately contributed to the overthrow of the dictatorship.

The main problem with Friedman is that, with his Friedman Doctrine, which unilaterally emphasises "shareholder value", he has contributed significantly to the current phase of a capitalism that promotes and celebrates inequality. ("The social responsibility of business is to increase profits.") The fact that the economically weaker members of society and society as a whole would ultimately benefit from this without regulatory measures of the state ("trickle-down economics") has not been confirmed either now or in earlier phases of economic history. For a discussion of Friedman in this regard, see Daron Acemoglu and Simon Johnson's book Power and Progress, Basic Books London 2023, especially pp. 270–273.

(10) For Friedman's analysis see the chapter "The Anatomy of Crisis" in Free to Choose, as 3.8.1.[6], pp. 70–90. And for justified criticism on this: Paul Krugman,

Who Was Milton Friedman? The New York Review of Books, Volume 54, Number 2, February 15, 2007

(11) On the different perceptions and the different historical conditions for state intervention see, for example, Paul Krugman's compact overview of American economic history, especially since the 1920s, in: The Conscience of a Liberal. Reclaiming America from the Right, Allen Lane New York 2007.

In this book, Krugman himself is particularly impressed by the inadequate health care for significant parts of the population in the USA. This indeed unacceptable deplorable state of affairs leads him to idealise healthcare systems with pronounced state dirigisme.

The biographical influences on me personally, on the other hand, are considerably different: I experienced the demotivating paralysis of economic life, the nomenklatura society as a class society of a different kind and the dreariness of actually existing socialism from my own experience (even if, fortunately, only as an occasional visitor). Such a background of experience is very likely to lead to a different assessment of state intervention than that of people for whom actually existing socialism is only a historical narrative.

Unfortunately, this was not enough and I had to observe the increasing spread of a socialist planned economy in the German health care system at first hand, with all the typical phenomena: pronounced loss of freedom with disenfranchisement of the citizen as a service provider and as a patient, increasing demotivation of the workforce, increasing shortages and waiting lists, disproportionate privileges for functionaries who are therefore more interested in maintaining the system than in eliminating grievances.

Or a more general example of how the judgement about the role of the state is influenced by the social situation: Dependent employees or civil servants who have never been personally liable for investment decisions and loans will tend to see state dirigisme with different eyes than a tradesman, freelancer or entrepreneur.

(12) A modern elaboration of this thinking is offered by Shiller, R. J., Finance and the Good Society, Princeton University Press 2012. A 'de-demonisation' of the financial sector and a defence of the achievements of modern financial systems on the one hand, and on the other hand a critique of undesirable developments in the capitalist economic system, especially rising economic inequality, and a call to deal creatively with their correction (however practicable the proposals made may be in detail). Even if it is primarily based on conditions in the U.S., it is nevertheless of general importance.

The intellectual fathers of the German social market economy have received relatively little attention in the English-speaking world. However, the problem of a socially responsible economy and an appropriate distribution of wealth, which was close to their hearts, cannot be suppressed anywhere in the long term. (About this see, in addition to Shiller's book, for example the book by Acemoglu and Johnson mentioned in note (9)). If ordoliberalism degenerates too much in the direction of over-regulation, the appropriate response is to cut back on regulation, not to adopt a modern form of a "Manchester Capitalism".

3.8.3.

(1) See: Kant, I. Zum ewigen Frieden, 1795, Reclam Stuttgart 1984, pp. 10–20, especially p. 19 (Second Definitive Article of Perpetual Peace), translated by M. Campbell Smith: Perpetual Peace, George Allen & Unwin London 1903, pp. 120–129 and especially 128, 129, available online: https://oll-resources.s3.us-east-2.amazonaws.com/oll3/store/titles/357/0075_Bk.pdf, retrieved 26 February 2024. And as good introductions to the modern state of thinking in this field: Merkel, R., Wittmann, R., "Zum ewigen Frieden", Grundlagen, Aktualität und Aussichten einer Idee von Immanuel Kant, Suhrkamp Frankfurt a. Main 1996, and also a collection of essays in English: Perpetual Peace. Essays on Kant's Cosmopolitan Ideal, ed. by J. Bohman and M. Lutz-Bachmann, The MIT Press Cambridge Massachussetts/London England 1997, available online: https://archive.org/details/perpetualpeacees0000unse/page/n3/mode/2up, retrieved 26 February 2024

(2) Tragically, one of the main initiators of this historic step forward, U. S. president Woodrow Wilson, failed to persuade his own country to join.

(3) An impressing summary of the many dangers that threaten democracy on a global scale is provided by Anne Applebaum: Autocracy, Inc., Allen Lane New York 2024.

(4) A good overview of the most diverse considerations and approaches to the creation of a global democratic legal and state order can be found in Otfried Höffe's book Democracy in an Age of Globalisation, see 3.8.3.[4].

(5) Central aspects of the modern discussion have already been set out by Hugo Grotius: »It is another Question, *Whether we have a just Cause for War with another Prince, in order to relieve his Subjects from the Oppression under him.*« »And therefore, according to *Seneca*, I may make War upon a Man, tho' he and I are of different Nations, if he disturbs and molests his own Country … Ancient and modern History indeed informs us, that Avarice and Ambition do frequently lay hold on such Excuses; but the Use that wicked Men make of a Thing, does not always hinder it from being just in itself.« De iure belli ac pacis libri tres, Paris 1625, Book II, Chapter 25, Section 8, quoted here from the 1738 English translation by J. Morrice, edited by R. Tuck: The Rights of War and Peace, Book II, Liberty Fund Indianapolis 2005, pp. 1159, 1162, available online: https://archive.org/details/rightsofwarpeace0000grot_g6n8/page/1158/mode/2up,

retrieved 4 March 2024

(6) On the "RtoP" decision, as well as on the past record and future perspectives of UN missions, see also Wolfgang Seibel, UN-Friedensmissionen, Zwischen politischer und bürokratischer Logik (UN peacekeeping missions, between political and bureaucratic logic), Universitas 64 (2009) No. 754, April 2009, pp. 346–371, especially p. 364.

There is also a good online source recording and explaining the prospects and problems of humanitarian intervention and the R2P approach: The Rise and Fall of the Responsibility to Protect, https://world101.cfr.org/understanding-international-system/building-blocks/rise-and-fall-responsibility-protect, retrieved 4 March 2024

(7) For detailed reflections on the problems discussed here, see the anthology recommended in note 8, in particular Allen Buchanan, Reforming the international law of humanitarian intervention, pp. 130–173, and Jane Stromseth, Rethinking humanitarian intervention: the case for incremental change, pp. 232–272.

(8) The effort to weigh up the justification of interventions appropriately can already be found in Michael Walzer's work. Long before there was an almost inflationary surge of publications on the subject, at least in the English-speaking world, after Rwanda in 1994, Serbia/Kosovo in 1999 and the interventions in Afghanistan and Iraq in the wake of 11 September 2001, this author, sometimes misinterpreted as a strict anti-interventionist, wrote in his fundamental treatise: "It is not necessarily an argument against humanitarian intervention that it is, at best, partially humanitarian, but it is a reason to be sceptical and to look closely at the other parts." "Humanitarian intervention is justified when it is a response (with reasonable expectations of success) to acts 'that shock the moral conscience of humanity'. This old-fashioned language seems to me exactly right." (Just and Unjust Wars, A Moral Argument with Historical Illustrations, Basic Books New York 1977, third edition 1999, pp. 102, 107).

From the later literature, I want to recommend an excellent anthology in which the moral, legal and political aspects of humanitarian interventions as well as a further development of the concept and of the rank of state sovereignty are discussed comprehensively from different positions (including very good contributions by the editors themselves): Holzgrefe, J. L., Keohane, R. O. (eds.), Humanitarian Intervention. Ethical, Legal and Political Dilemmas, Cambridge University Press 2003, Sixth Printing, Cambridge 2008.

3.9.

(1) Unfortunately, Theodor Schieder, who later wrote so many sensible things, obviously glorified the fascist dictatorships as a young man and supported and

justified the expulsion and resettlement policies of the National Socialists without later admitting this and distancing himself from it. See on this the book by G. Aly: Macht, Geist und Wahn. Kontinuitäten deutschen Denkens (Power, mind and delusion. Continuities of German thought), Argon Berlin 1997, in which Schieder is discussed on pp. 169–183 (with sources). See also the German and (for a rather abbreviated overview) also the English Wikipedia article on Schieder: https://de.wikipedia.org/wiki/Theodor_Schieder, https://en.wikipedia.org/wiki/Theodor_Schieder, both retrieved 5 March 2024. The question of how morally burdened someone may be so that one still wants to quote him or her always remains a difficult discretionary decision (on other similar cases see also note 4.3. (2)). Where is the line between petty and arrogant censorship and self-censorship with regrettable losses for intellectual debate and intellectual honesty on the one hand and tastelessness and mockery of the victims on the other? No one would want to quote individual sensible sounding sentences from Hitler's "Mein Kampf", for example, or whoever did so would rightly be suspected of radical right-wing political intentions.

Can comprehensible criteria be worked out to decide whether an author is still quotable? I use the following questions: What is the overall level of reflection? What is the level of eloquence? To what extent do he or she later distance themselves from mistakes or at least prove themselves capable of an intellectually productive change in the further course of their lives? To what extent were they responsible for the practical implementation of theoretical aberrations and did participate in this? Applying these criteria, Schieder's quotability is borderline.

(2) On these two aspects see Schieder, as 3.9.[3], but pp. 41–43.

(3) For a detailed criticism of teleological and clairvoyant philosophy of history I refer to K. R. Popper's book "The Poverty of Historicism", already cited. However, Popper makes it too easy for himself when he presents his remarks as a presuppositionless refutation of teleological views of history, apart from the recognition of the principles of logic. For he also presupposes some contents of unwillingness to believe, without – at least in this book – recognising and acknowledging in an appropriate way the further subjectivity or pre-rational moral decision given with that (as done here by the fundamental choice of unwillingness to believe). Elsewhere, however, Popper himself refers to an "irrational faith in reason", see 2.1. and 2.1.[4].

(4) For a brief critical insight into such conceptions see: Schultze, S., Fiktion und Kritik. Hayden Whites Metatheorie der Geschichte aus kritisch-rationaler Perspektive (Hayden White's Metatheory of History from a Critical-Rational Perspective), Aufklärung und Kritik 1/2010, pp. 145–158

3.10.

(1) Visual processes and visual brain functions are already relatively well researched. What neurobiology can contribute to a detailed analysis of aesthetic perception on this basis is described by Semir Zeki in his book "Inner Vision. An Exploration of Art and the Brain", Oxford University Press Oxford/New York 1999. It is also characterised, especially in the epilogue, by the modesty to admit that our neurobiological analyses still barely reach the essence of aesthetic experience, namely its emotional significance.

(2) A relatively early overview of evolutionary biological contributions to aesthetic analysis is given in: Sütterlin, C., Kunst und Ästhetik (Art and Aesthetics) with the programmatic chapter headings: "Ein integrativer Ansatz aus der Sicht der Humanethologie" (An integrative approach from the perspective of human ethology), "Ästhetisch relevante Vor-Urteile der menschlichen Wahrnehmung" (Aesthetically relevant pre-judgements of human perception"), in: Schiefenhövel, W., Vogel, Chr., Vollmer, G., Opolka, U. (eds.), Der Mensch in seiner Welt. Anthropologie heute, Vol. 3, Gemachte und gedachte Welten. Der Mensch und seine Ideen, Trias Thieme Stuttgart 1994, pp. 95–119. A more detailed, comprehensive investigation of aesthetics from the point of view of evolutionary biology is undertaken by Klaus Richter in: Die Herkunft des Schönen. Grundzüge der evolutionären Ästhetik (The origin of the beautiful. An outline of evolutionary aesthetics), Philipp von Zabern Mainz 1999. A good impression of the basic concepts and various approaches of evolutionary aesthetics is given by: Voland, E. Grammer, K., Evolutionary Aesthetics, Springer Berlin Heidelberg 2003. In 2007 I. Eibl-Eibesfeldt and C. Sütterlin published a heavyweight (also in the literal sense), opulently illustrated aesthetics with an extensive list of further literature: Weltsprache Kunst. Zur Natur- und Kunstgeschichte bildlicher Kommunikation (Art as a universal language. On the natural and art history of pictorial communication), Christian Brandstätter Vienna. Although the evolutionary and ethological perspective is given special importance here, the view is not narrowed to this, but is fruitfully combined with a cultural-historical approach.

For an overview of evolutionary theoretical approaches to aesthetics from an "outsider perspective", or rather the perspective of a crossover scholar between the humanities and science see the books by Winfried Menninghaus: Das Versprechen der Schönheit (The promise of beauty), 2003, Suhrkamp Taschenbuch Wissenschaft Frankfurt a. M. 2007, and Aesthetics after Darwin. The Multiple Origins and Functions of the Arts, translated by A. Berlina, Academic Studies Press Brookline 2019 (both with extensive literature). Menninghaus, originally a literary scholar, views evolutionary theoretical approaches with a very fertile mixture of fascination and distance. He argues plausibly that "the human arts arose as new variants of human behaviour, as three ancient and largely independent adaptations – the sensitivity for visual and auditory beauty, play behaviour, and tool use – joined forces with, and were transformed by, the human capacities for symbolic cognition and language. (Aesthetics after Darwin, Chapter 4: A Cooptation Model of the Evolution of the Human Arts, p. 117) On the one hand, Menninghaus stands firmly by the fundamental justification and inevitability of evolutionary theoretical explanations, but questions their sometimes speculative excesses and exaggerated interpretative claims in detail and keeps the significance of cultural-historical factors in mind. Evolutionary theoretical concepts are partly similar to psychoanalytical ones in that, with a little twist, one can offer a plausible explanation for the most contradictory phenomena, but then, unfortunately, falsifiability is largely lost.

(3) The attractiveness and limitations of evolutionary concepts dealing with aesthetic criteria in mate choice are discussed comprehensively from Darwin to the present day in Menninghaus' books quoted under (2), in particular in »Das Versprechen der Schönheit«: III. Zur Evolutionstheorie attraktiven Aussehens nach Darwin (On the evolutionary theory of attractive appearance after Darwin), pp. 138–198, but also pp. 241–244 "für die Kehrseiten der Schönheit" (the downsides of beauty).

(4) As a crash course in art history probably still unsurpassed: Gombrich, E. H., The Story of Art, sixteenth edition, Phaidon Press New York 1995. In addition to this, there is an excellently illustrated casuistry, mainly from the field of painting, which lacks any verbosity and includes cultural and social history in a highly instructive manner: Hagen, R. and R.-M., What Great Paintings Say. 100 Masterpieces in Detail, translated by K. Williams, Taschen Köln 2016. This volume are also eminently suitable for proving wrong those who are inclined to the erroneous view that only evolutionary and neurobiological approaches to aesthetics are scientific in a strict sense. – For an easy-to-read, richly illustrated overview with many useful introductory morsels from philosophical aesthetics, one can also turn to Umberto Eco's volumes The History of Beauty, Seeker and Warburg London 2004 and On Ugliness, Harvill Secker 2007, and later in various paperback editions, both translated by A. McEwen. Two books, however, that are overall very descriptive and not analytical enough, which – since they deal almost exclusively with art and even here mainly with painting and illustration – demonstrate as much a narrowing of perspective as in their titles an unfulfilled, far-reaching claim. Thus, beauty and ugliness in everyday life (for example in architecture or design) are almost completely absent and the thought of evolutionary biological aspects of aesthetics is still completely foreign to Eco's books despite their date of publication. – Finally, as a kind of résumé, though anything but a last word: Danto, C. After the End of Art. Contemporary Art and the Pale of History, Princeton University Press 1997. Danto does not really mean that art is

at its end, but "only" that its history has come to an end "in a certain way" with the extreme form of serially produced readymades, for which Duchamps' fountain or Warhol's Brillo Boxes (as an artistic copy and recreation of a readymade) stand, by pursuing the spectrum of possible means of expression to an utmost end (see also his book note (6), p. VII).

(5) On Stone Age cave painting the book by David Lewis-Williams, The Mind in the Cave, Thames & Hudson London 2002, is worth reading. It is interesting beyond its specific subject as a contribution to the history of art, culture and science and also contains interesting reflections on the theory of consciousness, see (11). Lewis-Williams combines great ingenuity in his explanatory approaches with a sober reference to reality and a consistently critical spirit of enlightenment.

(6) Danto dealt with such developments under the title "The Transfiguration of the Commonplace", Harvard University Press, 1981. Ellen Dissanayake even recommends "making special" as the central explanatory term for the emergence of aesthetic experience and the arts in general: Homo aestheticus. Where art comes from and why, University of Washington Press, Seattle and London 1995. With such a comprehensive claim, however, the concept of "making special" remains too vague, all too easily including "everything", for which other motivations provide a more differentiated explanation. If, on the other hand, it is at one extreme pole of modern art a matter of the everyday object being turned into a work of art by the specific historical context of modernity by the way it is presented and by a correspondingly charged interpretation, then "making special" is a sensible central criterion. Danto circles around this transformation with the help of the concepts of expression, style, rhetoric and metaphor, which are themselves fuzzy but still useful (see his book mentioned above, for example p. 148). Liessmann's reflections on constituent speech are also worth reading: "The constituent discourse must be so powerful that, in the most extreme case, it can make a work of art out of a sensual nothingness." Serving as a means of "transfiguring the ordinary" are especially contextualisation, historicising genealogy, as well as a highfalutin elaboration and prominent placement of discourse contributions. Liessmann, K. P. , Die Schneeschaufel. Wie man mit Theorien Kunst erzeugt (The snow shovel. How to create art with theories), in: id., Das Universum der Dinge. Zur Ästhetik des Alltäglichen (The universe of things. On the aesthetics of the commonplace), Paul Zsolnay Wien 2010, pp. 64–78, here especially pp. 75, 76. Depending on the degree of primitiveness and banality or perfection and originality of craftmanship of a work of art, there are many gradations in the importance of the constituent discourse.

(7) At this point it should be pointed out that, after various exaggerations, we are now in a basically pleasing situation, especially in architecture: "Just as the uniform formal language of modernism was initially a liberation and then

531

degenerated into confinement, the postmodern vivification has now also done its duty. Today, one can design beyond it: truly specific to function, location and culture — and one should do so." Welsch, W., Das Bauhaus als Institution der Moderne – Rückblicke und Zukunftsperspektiven. Rede zur Namensgebung „Bauhaus-Universität Weimar" 1996 (The Bauhaus as an institution of modernism - looking backward and to future perspectives. Speech on the naming of "Bauhaus-Universität Weimar" 1996, in: id., Blickwechsel. Neue Wege der Ästhetik (Change of perspective. New ways in aesthetics), Reclam Stuttgart 2012, pp. 52–79, here p. 78.

(8) In his essay "Of the Standard of Taste", cited at the beginning of this chapter, David Hume already made an interesting attempt to go beyond a merely subjectivist aesthetics without making unacceptable intellectual sacrifices. In doing so, he essentially relied on this kind of considerations. What survives the ages and withstands the judgement of the knowledgeable persons is what counts: "Strong sense, united to delicate sentiment, improved by practice, perfected by comparison, and cleared of all prejudice, can alone entitle critics to this valuable character" (of a true judge in the finer arts); "and the joint verdict of such, wherever they are to be found, is the true standard of taste and beauty." (As 3.10.[2], p. 229). Not the last word on aesthetics, but still a comprehensible criterion, even if the "joint verdict" will mostly just be one of a majority.

(9) I follow here a very good, concentrated essay by Michael Pauen: Die Ästhetik des Häßlichen. Grauenhafte Probleme und eine schöne Bescherung (The aesthetics of ugliness. Atrocious problems and a nice mess) Information Philosophie 32 (2004), Heft 3, August 2004, pp. 14-21, in particular p. 21, expanded version in: Klemme, H. F., Raters, I. (eds.), Im Schatten des Schönen. Die Ästhetik des Häßlichen in historischen Ansätzen und aktuellen Debatten (In the shadow of the beautiful. The aesthetics of ugliness in historical approaches and contemporary debate), Aisthesis Bielefeld 2006, pp. 211–226, here pp. 223, 224

That there is a difference between an ugly representation and a representation of the ugly – a difference which, however, amounts to a difficult tightrope walk, especially in the case of the terrible – has also been very well understood by some filmmakers in our time. Just think of Roberto Benigni's film "Life is Beautiful".

(10) The fact that a confusion of the mind is possible which fails to recognise that evil can only be art in imaginary and fictitious form was impressively demonstrated by the composer Karlheinz Stockhausen in his statements after the attacks of 11 September 2001: "Hm. So what happened there is of course – now you all have to rearrange your brains – the greatest work of art there has ever been. Minds achieving something in one act that we couldn't even dream of in music, people rehearsing like mad for ten years, preparing fanatically for a concert. And then they die. And that is the greatest work of art there is for the whole cosmos. Just

imagine what happened there. You have people who are so focused just on this, on only one performance, and then five thousand people are blown to resurrection. In a single moment. At least the artistic-religious fundamentalist Stockhausen was still bothered by the fact that the people concerned had not agreed and had not come to this "concert" voluntarily, which is why he classified this "greatest work of art" as a crime at the same time ("Huuh!" The press conference on 16 September 2001 in the Senate Room of the Hotel Atlantic in Hamburg, MusikTexte no. 91, pp. 69–77, here pp. 76, 77). For the translation of Stockhausen's sliding into evil ways see: http://www.osborne-conant.org/documentation_stockhausen.htm, retrieved 20 March 2024

(11) A classic description of such states is given by Aldous Huxley with the reports on his mescaline experiments in: The Doors of Perception, Chatto & Windus London 1954 and Heaven and Hell, ibid. 1956. Lewis-Williams' descriptions are also very good in this respect, demonstrating such phenomena as constants of human consciousness that transcend cultural boundaries. (As (5), pp. 121–135).

(12) For evolutionary considerations of the beauty of nature and the aesthetic qualities of aspects of nature and landscape impressions in particular, see for example Richter, as (2), pp. 129–148, or Eibl-Eibesfeldt/Sütterlin, as (2), pp. 241–281.

(13) A good overview of the diversity of artistic expression in the "visual" arts (in the form of essays, artist biographies and visual material) can be found, for example, in: Tate Modern. The Handbook (ed. I. Blazwick and S. Wilson), Tate Gallery Publishing London 2000, revised edition (ed. M. Gale) 2016

(14) That we should not uncritically surrender to the suggestive power and effectiveness of art is emphasised by Bernd Schmidt in an also otherwise very stimulating and concentrated essay: Kunst, was ist das? (What is art?) Aufklärung und Kritik 2/2006, pp. 82–109, on this especially pp. 87, 88 and pp. 98, 99. Available online: http://www.alt.gkpn.de/schmidt_kunst.pdf, retrieved 9 April 2024

(15) Once again, one would wish that this highly educated man had handed down us his often stimulating thoughts, which rightly question all kinds of traditional positions, in a less pointed form and had not so often allowed himself to be carried away by feuilletonistic one-sidedness seeking significance. And in many other passages, one would also wish that he had used a simpler, less twisted and highfalutin language. Many of Adorno's truths can also be said in a simpler way, so that even those who have not gone through the initiation rites of corresponding philosophical seminars can understand them. One of those German-speaking philosophers who would first have to be translated into German, whereby the oeuvre would then also become considerably more slender due to the discovery of redundancy.

4.

(1) One would like to add: ... or at least its character as an illusion is not obfuscated.

4.1.

(1) For example, it is hypocrisy when people who are unwilling to believe marry in church. Quite apart from the inadequacy of aesthetic reasons for such behaviour, at this point consideration for the family and even for the partner no longer seems to me to be an acceptable justification, because at a church wedding (at least a Christian one) one must expressly declare one's willingness to believe, and for those unwilling to believe this means: lying.

As far as the funeral is concerned, I would as well like a form without Christian symbolism and without Christian rituals as an unwilling to believe. I don't care much for detailed regulations on the course of one's own funeral (which is not that important to me), but it is important to me that my world view is not obfuscated after my death:

> "Furthermore, the priest shall stay away from my grave;
> Though it is just words blown away by the wind,
> It does not seem right that protest
> Should be preached to what I have been,
> Whilst I rest in the spell of eternal silence."

Theodor Storm (as 1.2.[1])

Incidentally, church funerals are often impersonal enough. With a little thought, this occasion is particularly suitable for an independent arrangement that does better justice to the personality of the deceased. For example, friends, relatives (or intellectual relatives) of the deceased, despite or even because of their shock at the loss, are much more likely to be qualified to speak about the deceased than a clergyman who receives some biographical information from the family only shortly beforehand.

(2) As far as the fragmentation of the humanist associations in Germany is concerned, the separation of the two organisations that actually run a considerable number of social institutions and projects regionally is particularly regrettable, namely the Humanist Association of Germany (Humanistischer Verband Deutschland) with the focus of its activities in Berlin and the Humanist Association of Bavaria (Humanistische Vereinigung Bayern) with its focus in the Nuremberg area.

On the subject of umbrella organisations: Michael Schmidt-Salomon, Konfessionslose aller Bundesländer vereinigt euch? Überlegungen zu einem "Zentralrat der Konfessionsfreien in Deutschland" (Non-denominational people of all federal states unite? Reflections on a Central Council of the Non-denominational in Germany), Materialien und Informationen zur Zeit (MIZ), Politisches Magazin für Konfessionslose und AtheistINNen 33 (2004), No. 4/04, pp. 3–11 and https://de.wikipedia.org/wiki/Zentralrat_der_Konfessionsfreien_(Deutschland), retrieved 20 April 2024

4.2.

(1) In this context, it is interesting that the great atheist religion of modern times, Marxism, saw itself induced to attempt to fill the vacuum it had created in terms of festivals and customs through state inventions and ordinances (only few of them were successful, for example, the "youth consecration" in the GDR which evidently addresses a social need and has survived the collapse of this state).

Comte also wanted to lend strength to his positivism by assimilating religious forms, see his "Catéchisme positiviste" (the name itself is the programme), especially "Septième entretien. Culte public" (Comte, A. Catéchisme positiviste, 1852, Garnier Flammarion Paris 1966, pp. 185–198). Translated by R. Congrave: The Catechism of Positivism, John Chapman London 1858, Conversation V, Public Worship, pp. 139–159, available online: https://archive.org/details/catechismofposit00comt/page/158/mode/2up, retrieved 25 April 2024

(2) This point of view has been aptly made by Margaret Knight with regard to education: "We do not want a generation who do not know what Christmas and Easter mean; who have never heard of the star of Bethlehem or the angel at the door of the tomb. These are part of the fabric of our culture; they are woven into our literature and art and architecture … So, I suggest, let children read and listen to New Testament stories in the same way as they read and listen to the stories of Greek mythology. And when they ask if the stories are true, they can be told that they are a mixture of fact and legend." (As 4.[4])

(3) It is possible to succumb to the poetic charms of Christmas without feeling hit by Feuerbach's accusation of being a victim to "the plague of the pleasure-seeking". Theodor Storm has shown what this can look like already in 1846 in a masterly balancing act in which ironic distance lurks beneath the smoothly rhymed, at first glance sentimental surface. (In: as 1.2.[1], but pp. 10, 11)

Weihnachtslied

Vom Himmel in die tiefsten Klüfte
Ein milder Stern herniederlacht;
Vom Tannenwalde steigen Düfte
Und hauchen durch die Winterlüfte,
Und kerzenhelle wird die Nacht.

Mir ist das Herz so froh erschrocken,
Das ist die liebe Weihnachtszeit!
Ich höre fernher Kirchenglocken
Mich lieblich heimatlich verlocken
In märchenstille Herrlichkeit.

Ein frommer Zauber hält mich wieder,
Anbetend, staunend muß ich stehn;
Es sinkt auf meine Augenlider
Ein goldner Kindertraum hernieder,
Ich fühl's, ein Wunder ist geschehn.

Christmas Carol

From the sky into the deepest ravines
A gentle star is laughing down;
Scents rise from the fir forest
And subtly pervade the winter airs,
And the night becomes candle bright.

My heart is so gladly frightened,
This is dear Christmastime!
I hear church bells from afar,
Sweetly tempting me back home
Into quiet fairy-tale glory.

A pious spell holds me again,
Adoring, filled with wonder I must stand;
To my eyelids descends
A golden childhood dream,
I feel it, a miracle has happened.

4.3.

(1) What is interesting about Frederick's statement is that he equates religious faith and superstition without further ado. This is historically justified and at any rate still applies to popular faith with all its petitions and sacrifices aimed at direct divine influence. You can argue about how much distance a modern theology ultimately has from superstition, no matter how refined and despite accepting the results of science, if it nevertheless believes in a moral world order without any good reason.

(2) Hoche unfortunately played a very unfortunate role as a forerunner of national

socialist "euthanasia" and Social Darwinist ideas in general. He was a highly intelligent and educated man who, however, shows some very unsympathetic traits in the form of an elitist, authoritarian, uncompromisingly hierarchical way of thinking. On the other hand, he formulated many a good thought, and his autobiographical reflections "Jahresringe" are still worth reading, and not only for historical reasons.

The procedure of the editors of the new edition of 1969, to simply omit the deliberations about "euthanasia", the "extermination of life unworthy of life" (here also understood as essentially for the benefit of others, i. e. the society), is in my opinion a serious mistake (it may have seemed necessary to them in the situation at the time in order to make it possible for the other parts of the book to be received at all). The justification that these were only "views of the time", which Hoche himself resignedly had put aside after he had experienced the inhumanities to which doctors, to whom the right to kill was entrusted for a time, were able and prepared to do during the Nazi regime, is in any case completely insufficient for this and does not represent an adequate examination of Hoche's historical role and views on this question. Almost 25 years after the end of the war, the renowned J. F. Lehmanns Verlag should not have allowed Hoche's "Jahresringe" to be published without a thorough critical examination of his role with regard to the Nazi "Euthanasia" program. This is another example of the failure to come to terms with the past, or the failure to do so, for far too long in the restorative phase of the Federal Republic of Germany.

It was not until thirty years later that an adequate assessment of Hoche's role and biography got underway: Walter Müller-Seidel, Alfred Hoche. Lebensgeschichte im Spannungsfeld von Psychiatrie, Strafrecht und Literatur (A life between the poles of psychiatry, criminal law and literature), Beck München 1999. An informative little treatise on the intellectual history of the 20th century, which elaborates the contradictions in Hoche's personality, working life and life's work with appropriate understanding and distanced justice. Also very instructive and solid (despite the not really felicitous title): Oliver Tolmein, Der Haß kann auch die Maske des Mitleids annehmen. Der deutsche Psychiater Alfred Hoche und die Freigabe der Vernichtung lebensunwerten Lebens (Hatred can manifest itself under the guise of compassion. The German psychiatrist Alfred Hoche and the approval of the destruction of life unworthy of living). DLF, cultural feature, broadcast 29 November 2002, https://www.tolmein.de/bioethik/details/artikel/der-hass-kann-auch-die-maske-des-mitleids-annehmen-1049.html, retrieved 27 June 2024, see also 3.6.5, p. 261, and note 3.6.5. (10).

In any case, I do not consider it justified to impose an intellectual quarantine on a man like Hoche because of his blunders in discussing the justification of the killing of life unworthy to live and therefore to no longer quote any of his statements. If one wanted to proceed in this way, this quarantine would rather have to apply to someone like Heidegger, who was not only an intellectual progenitor, but temporarily a very active supporter of National Socialist politics. On the problem of historical guilt or "contamination", see also note 3.9. (1).

(3) I also refer to Paul Kurtz's sobering assessment of the spread of such a philosophy of life so far and to be expected in the future: Kurtz, P., Will Humanism Replace Theism? in: National Forum, Spring 1983, reprinted in: id., In Defense of Secular Humanism, Prometheus New York 1983, pp. 190–198. The British paleoanthropologist Richard Leakey expressed a similar opinion and it could unfortunately be quite accurate: "Although I regard religions as a great fraud (one may add that this includes self-deception, author's note), it seems obvious to me that most people need something that humanists can do without. We are in a minority and will perhaps always remain so." Quoted from Edgar Dahl, Wer zur Hölle will schon in den Himmel? Ein Brevier für Ungläubige und solche, die es werden wollen (Who the hell wants to go to heaven? A breviary for unbelievers and those who want to become), Books on Demand Norderstedt 2010, p. 102, my back translation, English source not found. For the humanist stance of Richard Leakey see for example: https://thehumanist.com/magazine/july-august-2012/features/evolution-humanism-and-conservation-the-humanist-interview-with-richard-leakey retrieved 27 June 2024.

(4) Extensive material on this can be found in in: Vaas, R., Blume, M., Gott, Gene und Gehirn. Warum Glaube nützt. Die Evolution der Religiosität (God, genes and the brain. Why faith is useful. The evolution of religiosity) , Hirzel Stuttgart 2009, Demografie: Religion und Kindersegen (Demography: religion and fertility), pp. 65–106. A good overview with a prognosis about the future was published by Pew Research Center in 2017: https://www.pewresearch.org/religion/2017/04/05/the-changing-global-religious-landscape/, retrieved 27 June 2024.

(5) The Italian translator Ettore Capriolo was seriously injured, and the Japanese translator Hitoshi Igarashi was murdered. In an attack on the Turkish translator Aziz Nesin, 37 people were killed when a fanatical mob set fire to a hotel. The Norwegian publisher William Nygaard was critically injured by gunfire. See https://en.wikipedia.org/wiki/The_Satanic_Verses, retrieved 27 June 2024.

(6) A commendable timely contribution to this never-ending task is Steven Pinker's book Enlightenment Now. The Case for Reason, Science, Humanism and Progress, Allen Lane 2018.

References

Quotations from books in German are translated by me if not stated otherwise.

Alpha

1 Montesquieu original source not traceable. This remark, probably only attributed to Montesquieu, is quoted in different variations from one author to the other. Weaker versions, which would not fit quite as well as a motto for this book, are also popular, such as: »A man almost never comes to reason by reason.«

2 Anders, G., Ketzereien (Heresies), Beck München 1982, p. 246

3 Huxley, J., New Bottles for New Wine. Ideology and Scientific Knowledge, in: New Bottles for New Wine, Readers Union Chatto & Windus London 1959, pp. 93–127, here p. 99

4 Wetz, F. J., Hermeneutischer Naturalismus (Hermeneutic Naturalism), in: Kanitscheider, B., Wetz, F. J., Hermeneutik und Naturalismus, Mohr Tübingen 1998, pp. 101–138, here p. 127

5 Dworkin, R., Justice for Hedgehogs, The Belknap Press of Harvard University Press, Cambridge Massachusetts, London England 2011, p. 86

Introduction

1 Mumford, L., The Transformations of Man, Allen & Unwin London 1957, p. 173

2 Rahner, K., Rundfunkvortrag (radio lecture), Bayerischer Rundfunk 1984

3 Buhl, J., Wie ein freier Mensch stirbt (How a free human being dies), in: Baurmann, M., Kliemt, H. (Hrsg.), Glück und Moral, Reclam Stuttgart 1987, pp. 158–162, here p. 158

4 Améry, J., Aufklärung als Philosophia perennis, in: Weiterleben – aber wie? Essays 1968–1978, Klett-Cotta Stuttgart 1982, pp. 248–278, here p. 249, translated by S. and S. P. Rosenfeld: Enlightenment as Philosophia perennis, Address given on 16 May 1977 upon receiving the Hamburg Lessing Prize, in: Radical Humanism: Selected Essays, Indiana University Press Bloomington 1984, available online: https://muse.jhu.edu/chapter/3058346#ch12, paragraph 3, retrieved 9 January 2022

1.

1 Piece of dialogue from Woody Allen's film "Crime and Misdemeanors", 1989.

With this, Woody Allen has not only created another great work of art, but also the best casuistic treatise on moral philosophy in the medium of film that I know of.

2   Marquard, O., Apologie des Zufälligen, Reclam Stuttgart 1986, p. 131, translated by R. M. Wallace: In Defense of the Accidental, Oxford University Press 1991, p. 122, available online: https://archive.org/details/indefenseofaccid0000marq/page/n3/mode/2up, retrieved 24 February 2023

1.1.

1   Epiktet, Handbüchlein der Moral und Unterredungen, Hrsg. H. Schmid, Kröner Stuttgart 1973, Unterredungen I., 6., 10., p. 57 (The Discourses of Epictetus, Book I, Chapter 6, Of providence). The quotation here is my retranslation of the obviously rather free translation of the German editor from the Greek. Though the translation does not seem to be very close to the original it probably represents Epictetus' thinking quite well.

2   Russell, B., Sceptical Essays, 1935, Allen & Unwin London 1977, p. 11

3   Sextus Empiricus, Adversus Mathematicos, XI, 165, 166, translated by R. Bury (bilingual edition): Sextus Empiricus, III, Against The Physicists, Against The Ethicist (which is Book XI of Adversus Mathematicos), William Heinemann London/Harvard University Press Cambridge, Massachusetts 1936, p. 457, available online: https://archive.org/details/sextusempiricus0003unse/page/464/mode/2up, retrieved 10 January 2023, p. 456 of the pdf

4   Montaigne, M. de, Essais, 1580, Livre III, Chapitre XIII, Garnier-Flammarion Paris 1969, p. 320, translated by D. M. Frame: The Complete Essays, Book 3, Chapter 13, Of experience, Stanford University Press 1958, Printing 2016, p. 850

1.2.

1   Storm, Th., Ein Sterbender (A dying man), 1863, Gedichte (Poems), Erstes Buch. In: Werke, Aufbau Verlag Berlin und Weimar 1986, Hanser München 1988, Lizenzausgabe Wissenschaftliche Buchgesellschaft Darmstadt 1988, p. 79

2   Russell, B., The Problems of Philosophy, 1912, Chapter II, The Existence of Matter, last two paragraphs; available online: https://www.gutenberg.org/files/5827/5827-h/5827-h.htm#, retrieved 10 January 2023

3   Vollmer, G., Mesokosmos und objektive Erkenntnis. Über Probleme, die von einer evolutionären Erkenntnistheorie gelöst werden, in: Lorenz, K., F. M. Wuketits (Ed.), Die Evolution des Denkens, Piper München 1983, pp. 29–91, in particular pp. 45, 46, English version: Mesocosm and Objective Knowledge. On Problems Solved by Evolutionary Epistemology, in: Wuketits, F. M. (ed.), Concepts and Approaches in Evolutionary Epistemology, Reidel Publishing

Company Dordrecht 1984, pp. 69–121, in particular p. 83, available online: https://archive.org/details/conceptsapproach0000unse/page/n9/mode/2up, retrieved 23 January 2025

4   Ratzinger, J., Schöpfungsglaube und Evolutionstheorie (Belief in creation and evolutionary theory), in: Schultz, H. J. (Hrsg.), Wer ist das eigentlich – Gott? München 1969, pp. 232–245, in particular p. 234. Translation: Ratzinger, J., Credo for Today: What Christians Believe, Ignatius Press San Francisco 2009, pp. 32–47, Chapter 3 "Creation: Belief in Creation and the Theory of Evolution", p. 35, this chapter available online: https://inters.org/ratzinger-creation-evolution, retrieved 23 January 2025, paragraph 4

5   Pope John Paul II, A Message to the Pontifical Academy of Sciences: On Evolution, 5., October 22, 1996, available online: https://humanorigins.si.edu/sites/default/files/MESSAGE%20TO%20THE%20PONTIFICAL%20ACADEMY%20OF%20SCIENCES%20(Pope%20John%20Paul%20II).pdf, retrieved 14 January 2023

6   Pascal, B., Pensées, 1670, Section III, De la nécessité du Pari, especially Pensée 233, p. 114, translated by W. F. Trotter: Blaise Pascal, Thoughts, P. F. Collier and Son New York 1910, Section III, On the Necessity of the Wager, 233, pp. 83–87, available online: https://en.wikisource.org/wiki/Blaise_Pascal/Thoughts/Section_3, retrieved 14 January 2023

7   James, W., The Will to Believe, 1897, available online: http://www.gutenberg.org/files/26659/26659-h/26659-h.htm, retrieved February 18, 2018

8   Weizsäcker, C. F. v., Die Tragweite der Wissenschaft (The scope of science), 6th edition, Stuttgart Hirzel 1990, p. 6

9   Weizsäcker, as 8, but p. 5

10   Rosten, L., Bertrand Russell and God: A Memoir, The Saturday Review, 23 February 1974, p. 26

11   Ayer, A. J., The Central Questions of Philosophy, 1973, Penguin London 1976, p. 55

12   Wuketits, F. M., Epilog: Eine neue "realistische Philosophie"? (Epilogue: A New "Realistic Philosophy"?), in: Lorenz, K., F. M. Wuketits (Ed.), Die Evolution des Denkens, Piper München 1983, pp. 361–367, here p. 363

1.3.

1   Améry, J., Hand an sich legen (Taking one's own life), 1976, Klett-Cotta Stuttgart 1983, V. Der Weg ins Freie, p. 153, English translation by John D. Barlow: On Suicide: A Discourse on Voluntary Death, V. The Road to the Open, Indiana University Press Bloomington 1999, p. 151

2   Camus, A., Le mythe de Sisyphe. Essai sur L'absurde, 1942, Gallimard

Collection Idées 1973, p. 15, translated by J. O'Brien: The Myth of Sisyphus, 1955, Reprint Penguin London 2005, see Suggested Further Reading, p. 1 (translation modified by me)

3   Améry, as 1, but I., Vor dem Absprung, p. 24, English translation, I. Before the Leap, p. 12 (translation slightly modified by me)

4   Joyce, J., The Dead, first published in the short story collection Dubliners, 1914, single edition, Melville House Hoboken 2004, pp. 62, 63

5   Weischedel, W., Skeptische Ethik (Sceptical Ethics), see Suggested Further Reading, p. 183

6   Améry, as 3, but p. 40, English translation, p. 40

7   Seneca, Epistulae morales ad Lucilium, Liber VI, Epistula 58, 35., 36., Moral Letters to Lucilius, translated by R. M. Gummere, Loeb Classical Library Edition, Volume 1, Harvard University Press 1917, available online: https://en.wikisource. org/wiki/Moral_letters_to_Lucilius/Letter_58, retrieved 28 February 2018

8   Kanitscheider, B., Entzauberte Welt. Über den Sinn des Lebens in uns selbst. Eine Streitschrift (Disenchanted World. On the meaning of life in ourselves), Hirzel Stuttgart 2008, p. 102

9   James, W., Is Life Worth Living? S. Burns Weston Philadelphia 1896, p. 63, available online: https://archive.org/details/islifeworthlivin00jameuoft, retrieved February 23, 2018

1.4.

1   Montaigne, as 1.1.[4], but Book 2, Chapter 6, Of practice, p. 267

2   Weischedel, as 1.3.[5,] but p. 179

3   Thiry, P., Baron d'Holbach (Pseudo: Dumarsais), Essai sur les préjugés ou de l'influence des opinions sur les mœurs et sur le bonheur des hommes (Essay on the prejudices: of the influence of the opinions on the manners and the happiness of man), Paris 1792, Faksimile Edition, Brekle, H. E. (ed. and self-published) Regensburg 1988, Tome second, p. 11

4   Seneca, Of a Happy Life (De Vita Beata), Book XX, Beginning, translated by A. Stewart, Bohn's Classical Library Edition; London, George Bell and Sons, 1900; available online: https://en.wikisource.org/wiki/Of_a_Happy_Life, retrieved 23 March 2018

5   Hume, D., An Enquiry concerning Human Understanding, 1758, 1777, Section I, Of the Different Species of Philosophy, available online: http://www.davidhume. org/texts/ehu.html, E 1.6, SBN 10, retrieved 23 March 2018

1.4.1.

1   Lessing, Th., Geschichte als Sinngebung des Sinnlosen (History as giving

meaning to the meaningless), II. Buch, Psychologie der Geschichte. Der Geschichtsoptimismus, Beck München 1919, here quoted from the new edition Matthes und Seitz München 1983, p. 140

2   Weizsäcker, C. F., Wohin führt uns die Wissenschaft? (Whereto Does Science Lead Us?), address on the occasion of the first official assembly of the Max-Planck Society 1950 in Cologne, in: Weizsäcker, C. F., Zum Weltbild der Physik, 13. Auflage, Hirzel Stuttgart 1990, pp. 184–199, here pp. 184, 185, not included in the English edition: The World View of Physics, Routledge and Kegan Paul London 1952

3   Nietzsche, F., Unzeitgemäße Betrachtungen, Erstes Stück: David Strauß, der Bekenner und Schriftsteller, Abschnitt 8, 3. Absatz, 1873, translated by R. J. Hollingdale: Untimely Meditations, 1, David Strauss, the Confessor and the Writer, Section 8, Paragraph 3, p. 35, Cambridge University Press 1997, available online: http://cnqzu.com/library/Philosophy/neoreaction/Friedrich%20Nietzsche/Friedrich_Nietzsche%20-%20Untimely_Meditations_(Cambridge_Texts_in_the_History_of_Philosophy__1997).pdf, retrieved 28 March 2018

1.4.2.

1   Singer, P., Practical Ethics, see Suggested Further Reading, in particular Chapter 8, Rich and Poor, pp. 218–246

2   Ebner-Eschenbach, M. v., Aphorismen, 143.–152. Tausend, Insel Frankfurt a. M. 1964, p. 13, translated by D. Scrase and W. Mieder: Aphorisms, Ariadne Press Riverside 1994, p. 29

3   Montaigne, as 1.1.[4], but Book 3, Chapter 10, Of husbanding your will, p. 769

4   Camus, A., La Peste, cinquantième édition, Gallimard Paris 1947, Part IV, p. 280, translated by S. Gilbert: The Plague, 1948, available online: http://www.24grammata.com/wp-content/uploads/2013/06/The_Plague__Albert_Camus-24grammata.com_.pdf, p. 125, retrieved 18 April 2018

5   Appiah, K. A., Experiments in Ethics, Harvard University Press Cambridge/London 2009, p. 180

6   Rorty, R., Keine Zukunft ohne Träume, Wider die Arroganz der Intellektuellen (No Future without Dreams. Against the Arrogance of the Intellectuals), translated into German by J. Schulte, Süddeutsche Zeitung, SZ am Wochenende, 30/31 January 1999, p. I (I was not able to find out if this text by Rorty was published in English.)

7   Kersting, W., Plädoyer für einen nüchternen Universalismus (Plea for a sober universalism), Information Philosophie 1/2001, pp. 8–22, in particular p. 15

1.4.3.

1 La Mettrie, J. O. de la, Ouvrage de Pénélope ou Machiavel en Médecine. Par Ale-thius Demetrius, 3 Volumes, Berlin 1748–1750, Volume I, p. 125, the original French text can also be found in: Vartanian, A., LaMettrie's L'Homme Machine. A Study in the Origins of an Idea, Princeton University Press 1960, p. 10

2 Montaigne, as 1.1.[4], but Book 3, Chapter 9, Of vanity, p. 748

3 Lichtenberg, G. Chr., The Waste Books (Sudelbücher), translated by R. J. Hollingdale, first published as Aphorisms, 1990, New York Review Book 2000, see Suggestions for Further Reading, Notebook J, p. 159; all aphorisms not found there are translated by me and, if not stated otherwise, quoted according to Lichtenberg, Aphorismen, ed. M. Rychner, Manesse Zürich 1958, in this case this applies to the second and third aphorism, Sudelbuch L, p. 472, Sudelbuch A, p. 64

4 Gontscharov, I., Oblomov, 1859, translated by D. Magarshack, Penguin Classics London 2005, Part Four, p. 458

5 Russell, B., The Conquest of Happiness, 1930, Allen & Unwin London 1975, p. 124

6 Flake, O., Schloß Ortenau (Ortenau Castle), 1955, Fischer Taschenbuch Verlag Frankfurt a. M. 1984, p. 291

1.4.4.

1 Schopenhauer, A., Aphorismen zur Lebensweisheit, Kapitel V., Paränesen und Maximen, A. Allgemeine, 1851, 3. Aufl., Goldmann München 1980, S. 114, translated by T. B. Saunders: Counsels and Maxims, being the second part of Arthur Schopenhauer's Aphorismen zur Lebensweisheit, Allen and Unwin London 1924, Chapter I, Section 3, available online: https://en.wikisource.org/wiki/Counsels_and_Maxims/Chapter_I, retrieved 21 June 2018

2 Bachmann, I., Die Wahrheit ist dem Menschen zumutbar (Humans can be expec-ted to confront the truth), Piper München 1981, p. 76

3 Russell, B., Autobiography, Prologue, see Suggested Further Reading, p. 3

4 Goethe, J. W. v., Brief an Hetzler d. J. (Letter to Hetzler the Younger), 24 August 1770, available online: http://www.zeno.org/Literatur/M/Goethe,+Johann+Wolfgang/Briefe/1770, retrieved 7 February 2023

5 Schopenhauer, A., Vorlesung Metaphysik der Sitten (Lecture on the Metaphysics of Mores), in: Philosophische Vorlesungen, Piper München 1985, p. 103, cited from: Safranski, R., Schopenhauer und Die wilden Jahre der Philosophie, p. 64, translation by E. Osers: Schopenhauer and the Wild Years of Philosophy, Harvard University Press 1991 (see Suggested Further Reading), p. 38

6 Seneca, Epistulae morales ad Lucilium, Liber II, Epistula 16, 1., see 1.3.[7], available

online: https://en.wikisource.org/wiki/Moral_letters_to_Lucilius/Letter_16, retrieved 9 October 2018

7   Goethe, J. W. v., Italian Journey 1786–1788, entry of 17 February 1787, translated by W. H. Auden and E. Mayer, 1962, North Point Press San Francisco 1982, p. 161, available online: https://archive.org/details/italianjourney1700goet/page/160/mode/2up, retrieved 7 February 2023

8   Frankl, V. E., Ärztliche Seelsorge, 1946, 8. Aufl., Kindler München 1975, p. 114, translated by R. and C. Winston: The Doctor and the Soul, II, 2, On the Meaning of Suffering, 1955, Reprint Alfred A. Knopf New York 1972, p. 107, available online: https://archive.org/details/doctorsoulfromps0000fran/page/106/mode/2up, retrieved 7 February 2023

9   Shakespeare, Macbeth, Act I., Scene III., 147

10 Schopenhauer, A., Collected Essays of Arthur Schopenhauer, On the Wisdom of Life. Aphorisms, Simon and Schuster New York 2012, p. 318. This edition follows T. B. Saunders' 1896 translation (leaving out footnotes) which handles Schopenhauer's texts quite liberally and is based on the German edition by Grisebach, now considered questionable in many respects. Up to know I could not find the original German source for this frequently passed on quotation.

11 Mann, Th., Tischrede bei der Feier des fünfzigsten Geburtstags (Table Speech at the Fiftieth Birthday Celebration), 1925, in: Über mich selbst (On myself), Fischer Frankfurt a. M. 1994, p. 362

12 Jaspers, K., Einführung in die Philosophie, p. 49, translated by R. Manheim: Way to Wisdom: An Introduction to Philosophy, pp. 121, 122, see Suggested Further Reading

13 Montaigne, as 1.1.[4], but p. 851

14 Russell, as 1.4.3.[5], but p. 25

15 Epicurus, Vatican Sayings, No. 35; available online: https://www.epicurus.net/en/vatican.html, retrieved 8 February 2023

16 Bonhoeffer, D., Nach zehn Jahren: Rechenschaft an der Wende zum Jahr 1943, Gegenwart und Zukunft, available online: https://sumsinagro.de/nach_zehn_jahren/4, retrieved 8 February 2023. English translation (various translators): An Account at the Turn of the year 1942–1943, in.: Letters and Papers from Prison, Fortress Press Minneapolis 2015, available online: https://g.christianbook.com/ns/pdf/sample/402741.pdf, retrieved 8 February 2023

17 Bonhoeffer, K., Abschiedsbrief aus der Todeszelle an seine Kinder (Farewell Letter from Death Row to his Children, Easter 1945), quoted from: Grabner, S., K. Röder, Emmi Bonhoeffer: Essay, Gespräch, Erinnerung, Lukas Berlin 2004, p. 36

18 Rushdie, S., The Satanic Verses, I. The Angel Gibreel, p. 66, 1988, Viking Penguin New York, London etc. 1989, available online: https://archive.org/

details/SalmanRushdieTheSatanicVerses, retrieved 9 February 2023, p. 46 of the pdf

19 Tugendhat, E., Das Alter. Die Herausforderung der Frustrationen (Old Age. The Challenge of Frustrations), Gespräch mit Jochen Rack, Aufklärung und Kritik, Schwerpunkt: Selbstbestimmtes Sterben (Main topic: Self-determined dying), Sonderheft 11/2006, pp. 68–77, here pp. 71, 75

20 Flanagan, O., Varieties of Moral Personality. Ethics and Psychological Realism, Harvard University Press Cambridge/London 1991, p. 336

21 Mann, Th., Joseph der Ernährer, 1944, in: Joseph und seine Brüder, Sonderausgabe, S. Fischer Frankfurt a. M. 1981, p. 1280, translated by H. T. Lowe-Porter: Joseph the Provider, Knopf New York 1944, Chapter Seven, The Lost is Found, p. 339

1.4.5.

1 Schlechta, K., Das offene Gespräch als Ausdruck der Freiheit (Open discussion as an expression of freedom), in: Club Voltaire, Jahrbuch für kritische Aufklärung I, Szczesny Verlag München 1963, unveränderter Nachdruck, IBDK Verlag Berlin 1989, pp. 222–236, here p. 222

2 Lichtenberg, as 1.4.3.[3], Hollingdale's translation, p. 185

3 Goethe, J. W. v., Faust, Part II, Act II, Scene III, Monologue of Erichto, Line 7015 to 7018, translated by A. S. Kline, available online: https://www.poetryintranslation.com/PITBR/German/FaustIIActIIScenesItoIV.php, retrieved 9 February 2023

4 Appiah, K. A., Cosmopolitanism. Ethics in a World of Strangers, Norton New York/London 2006, p. 144

5 Feyerabend, P., Killing Time, 1994, University of Chicago Press, New Edition 1996, p. 152

1.4.6.

1 Ebner-Eschenbach, as 1.4.2.[2], but p. 30

2 Pascal, see 1.2.[6], Section VI: The Philosophers, 380, p. 74

3 Robinson, R., An Atheist's Values, see Suggestions for Further Reading, p. 158

4 Singer, as 1.4.2.[1]

5 Kelsen, H., What is Justice? University of California Press, Berkeley, Los Angeles, London 1957, Reprint The Lawbook Exchange Union New Jersey 2000, 2013, available as kindle edition too, the quotation can be found shortly before the end of I., Kindle edition pos. 108; "ultimately" is supplemented by me, according to the German text ("in letzter Linie": Was ist Gerechtigkeit? 1953, 2. Aufl., Franz Deuticke Wien 1975, I., 5., p. 6) because without it the statement loses its balance

6   Patzig, G., Der wissenschaftliche Tierversuch unter ethischen Aspekten (Ethical Aspects of Scientific Animal Testing), in: id., Gesammelte Schriften I, Angewandte Ethik (erroneously called "Grundlagen der Ethik" due to an oversight by the publisher), Wallstein Göttingen 1993, pp. 144–161, here p. 148

2.

1   Stevenson, Ch. L., Ethics and Language, Yale University Press New Haven and London 1944, Fourteenth Printing, 1972, p. 215

1   Bok, S., Lying. Moral Choice in Public and Private Life, 1978, second edition, Vintage Books New York 1999, pp. 21, 22

2.1.

1   Stegmüller, W., Metaphysik, Wissenschaft, Skepsis (Metaphysics, Science, Scepticism), 1954, 2. Auflage, Springer Berlin/Heidelberg/New York 1969, p. 453

2   Hook, S., Conflicts in Ways of Belief, 2. Choice and Belief, in: Sydney Hook on Pragmatism, Democracy and Freedom. The Essential Essays, Prometheus Amherst 2002, p. 270

3   Lange, F. A., Geschichte des Materialismus und Kritik seiner Bedeutung in der Gegenwart , J. Baedeker Iserlohn 1866, p. 541, translated by E. Ch. Thomas: History of Materialism and Criticism of its Present Importance, Trubner & Co London 188, Chapter II., Christianity and Enlightenment, p. 283, available online: https://archive.org/details/historyofmateria03languoft/page/n301/mode/2up, retrieved 20 April 2023, p. 302 of the pdf

4   Popper, K. R., The Open Society and Its Enemies, 1962, fourth edition (revised), Princeton University Press 1963, Volume II, chapter 24, Oracular Philosophy and The Revolt Against Reason, II. p. 231, available online: https://archive.org/details/opensocietyitsen0001popp_c2j9/page/230/mode/2up, retrieved 15 February 2023, p. 231 of the pdf

5   Feil, E., Glaube in wissenschaftstheoretischer und theologischer Perspektive (Faith from the perspective of epistemology and theology), Ethik und Sozialwissenschaften 1 (1990) pp. 592–594, here p. 593

6   Albert, H., Traktat über kritische Vernunft, 1968, 5. verbesserte und erweiterte Auflage, Mohr Tübingen 1991, p. 74, translated by M. V. Rorty: Treatise on Critical Reason, Princeton University Press 1985, pp. 79, 80 (Mary Rorty decided to use "foundation" instead of "justification" at this point, but, as far as I can see, it remains unclear throughout the whole book according to which concept the two English words are chosen alternatively to translate the German word

"Begründung".) See also Suggestions for Further Reading

7 Albert, H., as 6, but pp. 18–21 (German edition pp. 15–18) and also https://en.wikipedia.org/wiki/M%C3%BCnchhausen_trilemma, retrieved 4 March 2025

8 Albert, as 7, but p. 101 (German Edition p. 95)

9 Albert, as 7, but p. 101 (German Edition pp. 94, 95)

10 Albert, as 7, but pp. 39–48 (German Edition pp. 35–44)

11 Topitsch, E., Das Problem der Moralbegründung (The problem of justification of morality), unkorrigiertes Manuskript der Vortragsreihe »Moral in dieser Zeit«, Bayerischer Rundfunk 1977, p. 15

12 Merkel, R., Willensfreiheit und rechtliche Schuld (Freedom of the will and legal culpability). Eine strafrechtsphilosophische Untersuchung, Nomos Baden-Baden 2008, p. 95

13 Walter, H., Neurophilosophie der Willensfreiheit, 1997, 2. Auflage, Mentis Paderborn 1999, p. 361, translated by C. Klohr: Neurophilosophy of Free Will, The MIT Press Cambridge/London 2009, p. 298, translation slightly transposed by me to match the quotation from the German text and retain comprehensibility

14 Bieri, P., Das Handwerk der Freiheit (The craft of freedom. On discovering one's own will), Hanser München 2001, in particular pp. 382–384

15 Patzig, G., Relativismus und Objektivität moralischer Normen (Relativism and objectivity of moral norms), in: in: id., Gesammelte Schriften I, Grundlagen der Ethik, Wallstein Göttingen 1994, pp. 9–43, here p. 12

16 Nida-Rümelin, J., Demokratie und Wahrheit, Drittes Kapitel, Ethische Begründung (Democracy and truth, third chapter, ethical justification), Beck München 2006, p. 84

2.2.

1 Huxley, Th. H., Agnosticism and Christianity, in: id., Science and Christian Tradition (Collected Essays Volume V), Macmillan and Co. London 1895, pp. 309–365, here p. 316

2 Hare, R. M., The Language of Morals, 1952, Oxford University Press London/Oxford/New York 1964, p. 1

3 Améry, J., An den Grenzen des Geistes, in: Jenseits von Schuld und Sühne. Bewältigungsversuche eines Überwältigten, 2. Auflage, Klett-Cotta Stuttgart 1980, pp. 33, 34, 37, translated by S. and S. P. Rosenfeld: At the Mind's Limits, Indiana University Press Bloomington and Indianapolis 1998, pp. 12, 15

4 Seneca, De Tranquillitate Animis, 1. (3) ("Tam malorum quam bonorum longa conversatio amorem induit"), Latin text available online: http://www.perseus.tufts .edu/hopper/text?doc=Perseus:text:2007.01.0021, retrieved 7 September 2020

5   Marcus Aurelius, The Thoughts of the Emperor Marcus Aurelius Antoninus, translated by G. Long, Little, Brown and Company Boston 1889, Book V, 16. (first quote), Book VII, 2. (second quote), Book VII, 59. (third quote), available online: https://en.wikisource.org/wiki/The_Thoughts_of_the_Emperor_Marcus_Aurelius_Antoninus, retrieved 22 February 2019

6   Ratzinger, J., Der Streit um die Moral. Fragen der Grundlegung ethischer Werte (The argument over morality. Issues concerning the foundation of ethical values), Festvortrag 72. Fortbildungstagung für Ärzte, Regensburg 1984, pp. 8, 9

7   Hegselmann, R., Worin könnte moralische Bildung bestehen? Ein Minimalideal (What could moral education consist of? A minimal ideal), in: Holzapfel, G., Ethik und Erwachsenenbildung, Universität Bremen, Fachbereich 12, Bremen 1990, pp. 16–40, here pp. 19, 20

2.3.

1   Camus, as 1.3.[2], p. 73, p. 49 of the translation

2   Brecht, B., Der Radwechsel, Buckower Elegien, for example in: Gesammelte Gedichte, Band 3, Suhrkamp Frankfurt a. M. 1976, p. 1009, translated and edited by J. Willett and R. Manheim, quoted from: The Cambridge Companion to Brecht, edited by P. Thomson and G. Sacks, Cambridge University Press 1994, p. 216, originally in: Poems 1913–1956, Methuen London and New York 1976, 1979, revised paperback edition 1987, p. 439

3   Although it is now also a quotation from Neil Gaiman's young adult novel "The Graveyard Book", published in Britain and the US 2008, this wise saying has been around in various versions for a long time.

4   Frankl, V. E., Psychotherapie für den Laien (Psychotherapy for the Layman), 3. Auflage, Herder Freiburg 1972, p. 28.

5   Nietzsche, F., quoted from Frankl, V. E., Man's Search for Meaning, II, Logotherapy in a Nutshell, first published in the 1962 edition, my edition Beacon Press Boston 2006, p. 104, possibly only attributed to Nietzsche

6   Gabor, D., Inventing the Future, 1963, Penguin Books 1964, p. 145

7   Kanitscheider, B., Welt-Modelle (World Models): Invarianzen und Symmetrien des Kosmos, in: Buschlinger, W., Chr. Lütge (Hrsg.), Kaltblütig. Philosophie von einem rationalen Standpunkt, Festschrift für Gerhard Vollmer zum 60. Geburtstag, Hirzel Stuttgart 2003, pp. 197–219, here p. 219

8   Blumenberg, H., Die Genesis der kopernikanischen Welt, 1975, Suhrkamp Taschenbuch Wissenschaft Frankfurt a. M. 1981, p. 793, translated by R. M. Wallace: The Genesis of the Copernican World, The MIT Press Cambridge Massachusetts/London England 1987, p. 684, translation slightly modified

9   Huxley, as Alpha[3], but p. 103

10 Kahl, J., Weltlicher Humanismus. Eine Philosophie für unsere Zeit (Secular Humanism. A Philosophy for our Time), see Suggested Further Reading, pp. 123, 124

11 Monod, J., Chance and Necessity. An Essay on the Natural Philosophy of Modern Biology, 1971, Vintage Books New York 1972, pp. 172, 173, available online: https://monoskop.org/images/9/99/Monod_Jacques_Chance_and_Necessity.pdf, retrieved 7 March 2019

12 Marquard, O., Zur Diätetik der Sinnerwartung (On the Dietetics of Expectations for Meaning), in: Achenbach, G. B., Philosophische Praxis, Dinter Köln 1984, pp. 145–160, here p. 159

13 Mynarek, H., Der kritische Mensch und die Sinnfrage (The critical human being and the question of meaning) Manuskriptdruck Berlin 1976, p. 161

14 Deschner, K. (in collaboration with F. Heer und J. Kahl), Warum ich Christ/ Atheist/Agnostiker bin (Why I am a Christian/Atheist/Agnostic), Kiepenheuer & Witsch Köln 1977, p. 188

15 Reichenbach, H., The Rise of Scientific Philosophy, University of California Press Berkeley and Los Angeles 1951, p. 302

16 Albert, H., Der Sinn des Lebens ohne Gott (The Meaning of Life without God), 1984, in: Hoerster, N. (Hrsg.), Religionskritik, Arbeitstexte für den Unterricht, Reclam Stuttgart 1984, p. 119–128, here p. 127

17 Kanitscheider, as 1.3.[7], but pp. 25, 26

18 Kanitscheider, B., Die Materie und ihre Schatten. Naturalistische Wissenschafts-philosophie (Matter and its Shadows. A Naturalistic Philosophy of Science), Alibri Aschaffenburg 2007, p. 200

19 Kurzke, H., Wirion, J., Unglaubensgespräch (Talk of Disbelief), 2005, Beck'sche Reihe Beck München 2007, pp. 112, 113

20 Moonstruck, USA 1987, directed by N. Jewison, written by J.P. Shanley, Cosmo Castorini (Vincent Gardenia) talking to his daughter Loretta Castorini (Cher)

3.

1 Jaspers, K., Karl Jaspers to Hannah Arendt 18 September 1946, in: Hannah Arendt, Karl Jaspers, Briefwechsel 1926–1969, Piper München 1985, p. 143, translated by R. and R. Kimber: Correspondence 1926–1969, Harcourt Brace & Company San Diego/New York/London 1992, p. 58

3.1.

1 Weizsäcker, C. F. v., Der Naturwissenschaftler, Mittler zwischen Kultur und Natur (The Scientist, Mediator between Civilization and Nature), Speech 1976, in:

id., Der Garten des Menschlichen, 1977, Fischer Taschenbuch Verlag 1980, pp. 66–77, here p. 69, English version: The Ambivalence of Progress. Essays on Historical Anthropology, Paragon House Publishers New York 1988, p. 76, available online: https://archive.org/details/ambivalenceofpro0000weiz/page/76/mode/2up, retrieved 5 August 2024

2   Bacon, F., Novum Organum, 1620, Aphorism 41, 42, written in Latin, quoted from the English edition by J. Devey, P. F. Collier & Son New York 1902, available online: https://oll.libertyfund.org/titles/bacon-novum-organum, p. 8, retrieved 9 March 2023. The Latin text can be found, for example, in the following edition in Latin and German: Neues Organon/Novum Organum, Teilband 1, Meiner Hamburg 1990, 41, pp. 100, 101, 42, p. 103

3.1.1.

1   Vollmer, as 1.2.[3], pp. 73, 74

3.1.2.

1   Nietzsche, F., Menschliches, Allzumenschliches, Zweiter Band, Erste Abteilung, 225, 1878, translated by R. J. Hollingdale: Human, All Too Human, A Book for Free Spirits, Volume Two, Assorted Opinions and Maxims, Cambridge University Press 1986, 1996, p. 270, available online: https://www.holybooks.com/wp-content/uploads/Nietzsche-Human-All-Too-Human-by-Nietzsche.pdf, retrieved 7 February 2020

2   Albert, as 2.1.[7], but p. 38 (German edition p. 34)

3   Dawkins, R., The Blind Watchmaker, Chapter 11, Doomed Rivals, 1986, Penguin London 2006, p. 293, available online: https://terebess.hu/keletkultinfo/The_Blind_Watchmaker.pdf, retrieved 27 June 2019

3.1.3.

1   Vollmer, G., Evolutionäre Erkenntnistheorie (Evolutionary Epistemology), see Suggested Further Reading), here quoted from 6. Auflage, Hirzel Stuttgart 1994, p. 34

2   Lamont, C., The Philosophy of Humanism, see Suggested Further Reading, pp. 126, 127

3   Weizsäcker, C. F. v., Kopernikus, Kepler, Galilei, in: as 1.2.[8], pp. 96–117, here pp. 98–103

4   Kanitscheider, B., Im Innern der Natur. Philosophie und moderne Physik (Inside nature. Philosophy and modern physics), Wissenschaftliche Buchgesellschaft 1996, p. 125

5   Einstein, A., probably a nice, concise paraphrase of similar statements by

Einstein, the origin of which cannot be traced exactly

3.1.4.

1   Lichtenberg, as 1.4.3.[3], but Notebook L, p. 226, German text, p. 457

2   Hofstadter, D. R., Gödel, Escher, Bach: An Eternal Golden Braid, Basic Books New York 1979, Six-Part Ricercar, p. 720, available online: https://readyforai.com/download/godel-escher-bach-an-eternal-golden-braid-pdf/, retrieved 31 July 2019, p. 733 of the pdf

3   Glasersfeld, E. v., Konstruktion der Wirklichkeit und des Begriffs der Objektivität (Construction of reality and of the concept of objectivity), in: Einführung in den Konstruktivismus, Piper München 1992, pp. 7–39, here p. 38. A text in English presenting the same ideas is: An Introduction to Radical Constructivism, in: Watzlawick. P. (ed.) The Invented Reality, Norton New York and London 1984, pp. 17–40, available online: https://www.vonglasersfeld.com/070.1, retrieved 12 March 2023

4   Popper, K. R., Objective Knowledge, 1972, reprinted (with corrections), University Press Oxford 1975, pp. 38–44

5   Vollmer, as 3.1.3.[1], pp. 35–40

6   Vollmer, as 1.2.[3]

7   Descartes, R., Discours de la méthode, shortly before the end of the quatrième partie, 1637, Le Livre de Poche Paris 1973, p. 61, quoted here according to: René Descartes, A Discourse on the Method of Correctly Conducting One's Reason and Seeking Truth in the Sciences, translated by I. Maclean, Oxford University Press 2006, pp. 32, 33, available online: http://www.rlwclarke.net/Theory/ SourcesPrimary/DescartesDiscourseonMethod.pdf, retrieved 14 October 2019, p. 110 of the pdf

8   Vollmer, as 5 and 6

9   Russell, see 1.2.[2] , Chapter II, The Existence of Matter, eleventh and twelfth paragraph

10 Glasersfeld, as 3, but p. 39

11 Vollmer, G., Ordnung ins Chaos? Zur Weltbildfunktion wissenschaftlicher Erkenntnis (Order to chaos? On the shaping of our worldview by scientific knowledge), in: id., Auf der Suche nach der Ordnung, Hirzel Stuttgart 1995, pp. 1–20, here pp. 18, 19

12 Dick, P. K, I hope I shall arrive soon, Introduction, Doubleday New York 1985, Paperback St. Martin's Press New York 1987, p. 4

3.1.5.

1   Freud, S., New Introductory Lectures on Psychoanalysis, Lecture XXXV, The

Question of *Weltanschauung*, translated/edited by J. Strachey, The Standard Edition, Norton New York 1995, pp. 210, 211, English text also available online: http://www.valas.fr/IMG/pdf/Freud_Complete_Works.pdf, p. 4768 (p. 4789 of the pdf), retrieved 22 October 2019

2   Sagan, C., The Demon-Haunted World: Science as a Candle in the Dark, 1996, Ballantine Books New York 1997, p. 27

3   Kuhn, Th. S., The Structure of Scientific Revolutions, 1962, 50th Anniversary Edition, University of Chicago Press 2012, XII. The Resolution of Revolutions, pp. 145, 146

4   Gordin, M. D., The problem with pseudoscience. Pseudoscience is not the antithesis of professional science but thrives in science´s shadow, published online, https://www.ncbi.nlm.nih.gov/pmc/articles/PMC5579391/, retrieved 13 March 2023)

5   Collins, F. S., The Language of God, Free Press New York 2006, p. 142

6   Mayr, E., quoted from: The Grand Old Man of Evolution: An Interview with Evolutionary Biologist Ernst Mayr, Skeptic July 5, 2004, shortly before the end of the interview, available online: https://www.skeptic.com/eskeptic/04-07-05/, retrieved 13 March 2023

7   Huxley, Th. H., An Episcopal Trilogy, in: as 2.2.[1], pp. 126–159, here p. 140

8   Vollmer, G., Kann es von einmaligen Ereignissen eine Wissenschaft geben? (Can there be a science of onetime events?) in: id., Was können wir wissen? Band 2, Die Erkenntnis der Natur, 2. Aufl., Hirzel Stuttgart 1988, pp. 53– 65

9   Popper, K. R., The Poverty of Historicism, Chapter 29, The Unity of Method, Routledge & Kegan Paul, London 1957, 2002, pp. 120–132

10 Kurtz, P., The New Skepticism, Prometheus Buffalo 1992, p. 11

3.1.7.

1   Kant, I., Träume eines Geistersehers, 1766, Ein Vorbericht, der sehr wenig vor die Ausführung verspricht, German text for example in the edition Reclam Stuttgart 1987, p. 5, translated by E. F. Goerwitz: Dreams of a Spirit-Seer, Cambridge Massachusetts 1899, A Preface which promises very little for the discussion, available online: https://en.wikisource.org/wiki/Dreams_of_a_Spirit-Seer/Preface, retrieved 12 December 2019

2   Neurath, O., Empirische Soziologie, 1931, German text in: id., Wissenschaftliche Weltauffassung, Sozialismus und logischer Empirismus, Suhrkamp Taschenbuch Frankfurt a. M. 1979, p. 183, translated by P. Foulkes and M. Neurath: Empirical Sociology, 8. Coherence, in: Empiricism and Sociology, D. Reidel Publishing Company Dordrecht/Boston 1973, p. 381, available online: https://cominsitu. files.wordpress.com/2020/11/vienna-circle-collection-1-otto-neurath-auth.-

marie-neurath-robert-s.-cohen-eds.-empiricism-and-sociology-springer-nether-lands-1973.pdf, retrieved 14 March 2023, translation modified by me

3   Schopenhauer, as 1.4.4.[1], German text: Kapitel V, Paränesen und Maximen, C., p. 154, translation Chapter III, Section 26

4   Das Streiflicht (The Sidelight), Süddeutsche Zeitung, 24–27 December 1987, p. 1

5   Lem, S., Über außersinnliche Wahrnehmung (On extrasensory perception), in id., Essays, Band 2, Suhrkamp Frankfurt a. M. 1987, pp. 7–34, here p. 9 (translated from Polish to German by F. Griese)

6   Achenbach, G. B., Äußerung in einem Interview über die Philosophische Praxis (Statement in an interview on philosophical practice), Kaffeehausblätter, 2. Ausgabe, Januar 1988, p. 25

7   Hofstadter, D. R., Metamagical Themas, 1985, p. 110, available online: https://archive.org/stream/MetamagicalThemas/Metamaical%20Themas,%20Hofstadter_djvu.txt, retrieved 22 January 2020

3.1.8.

1   Voltaire, Éloge Historique De Madame La Marquise Du Chatelet, 1752, Œuvres complètes de Voltaire, Garnier Paris 1883, tome 23, p. 520, available online: https://fr.wikisource.org/wiki/%C3%89loge_histrique_de_Mme_du_Ch%C3%A2telet/%C3%89dition_Garnier, retrieved 26 January 2020

2   Weizsäcker, C. F. v., in: Krishna, Gopi, The Biological Basis of Religion and Genius, Harper and Row New York 1971, Introduction, 5. Genius and Insanity, translated by R. Ulrich, kindle edition The Institute for Consciousness Research & The Kundalini Research Foundation 2014, pos. 589–598

3.1.9.

1   Heidegger, M., Was ist das – die Philosophie? Neske Pfullingen 1956, translated by J. T. Wilde and W. Kluback: What is Philosophy? Rowman and Littlefield Lanham 1956

2   Schnitzler, A., Entry in the friendship book of »Tutti« Fischer, 8 August 1924, later Motto of Schnitzler's collection of aphorisms »Buch der Sprüche und Bedenken« (Book of thoughts and sayings), Phaidon Wien 1927, here quoted according to the facsimile of the original entry, in: Fischer, B. B., Sie schrieben mir oder was aus meinem Poesiealbum wurde, 1981, 15. Aufl., dtv München 1995, pp. 83, 84. A small collection of excerpts from Schnitzler book was published in English in 2007 in the British Journal of General Practice (Schnitzler having been a doctor too), regrettably not containing this quotation. Available online: https://www.ncbi.nlm.nih.gov/pmc/articles/PMC2084127/pdf/bjpg57-1010.pdf, retrieved 23 March 2023

3 Nietzsche, F., as 3.1.2.[1], Volume One, 9, Man Alone with Himself, Aphorism 621, p. 196, available online: https://www.holybooks.com/wp-content/uploads/Nietzsche-Human-All-Too-Human-by-Nietzsche.pdf, retrieved 7 February 2020

4 Anders, G., Über philosophische Diktion und das Problem der Popularisierung (On philosophic style and the problem of popularisation); from Philosophische Tagebücher (philosophical diaries), New York 1949, Wallstein Göttingen 1992 (Göttinger Sudelblätter), p. 6, seemingly unpublished before this edition

5 Comte-Sponville, A., Petit traité des grandes vertus, 1996, translated by C. Temerson: A Small Treatise on the Great Virtues, Metropolitan Books 2001, Holt Paperbacks New York 2002, Humor, p. 217

3.2.

1 Hofstadter, as 3.1.4.[2], but p. 706, p. 719 of the pdf

2 Schulz, W., Vernunft und Freiheit (Reason and freedom), Reclam Stuttgart 1981, p. 122

3 Huxley, J., A Redefinition of Progress, in: see Alpha[3], but pp. 18–40, here p. 28

4 Schopenhauer, A., in this wording ("Der Mensch kann zwar tun, was er will, aber nicht wollen, was er will.") possibly only attributed to Schopenhauer. Very close is a passage in: Die beiden Grundprobleme der Ethik, zweite, verbesserte und vermehrte Auflage, Brockhaus Leipzig 1860, I. Preisschrift über die Freiheit des menschlichen Willens, III. Der Wille vor dem Bewußtseyn anderer Dinge, S. 43, available online: https://archive.org/details/diebeidengrundp04schogoog/page/n7/mode/2up, retrieved 25 January 2025, translated by D. E. Cartwright and E. E. Edwards: The Two Fundamental Problems of Ethics, Oxford University Press 2010, Prize Essay on the Freedom of the Will, III. The Will Before Consciousness of Other Things, p. 69

5 Merkel, as 2.1.[12], p. 79

6 Weischedel, as 1.3.[5], pp. 182, 183

7 Walter, H., as 2.1.[13], pp. 224, 225, further references there

8 Huxley, J., as Alpha[3], but p. 108

9 Edelman, G. M., Bright Air, Brilliant Fire. On the Matter of the Mind, Basic Books New York 1992, Part III, 12. Language and Higher-Order Consciousness, p. 136, available online: https://archive.org/details/brightairbrillia00gera/page/194/mode/2up, retrieved 28 March 2023

10 Mises. L. v., Theory and History, Part 2, Chapter 6, 2. The Secretion Analogy, 1957, Liberty Fund 2005, p. 66

11 Dennett, D. C., Elbow Room. The Varieties of Free Will Worth Wanting, The MIT Press Cambridge, Massachusetts, London 1984, pp. 169, 170. See also his later book: Freedom Evolves, 2003, Penguin London 2004

3.3.

1   Mackie, J. L., The Miracle of Theism, Chapter 14, c), The Moral Consequences of Atheism, Clarendon Press Oxford 1982, pp. 254, 255

2   Zippelius, R., Das Wesen des Rechts (The nature of law), see Suggested Further Reading, p. 101

3   Maupassant, G. de, Préface to Paul Ginisty's L'Amour à Trois (The love triangle), Paris Baillière 1884, available online:
    http://maupassant.free.fr/chroniques/amourtrois.html, retrieved 28 March 2020

4   Zippelius, as 2, p. 109

5   Kant. I., Grundlegung zur Metaphysik der Sitten, 1786, (original edition pp. 59–61), translated by A. W. Wood: Groundwork for the Metaphysics of Morals, Yale University Press 2002, pp. 42–44, accessible online: http://www.inp.uw.edu.pl/ mdsie/Political_Thought/Kant%20-%20groundwork%20for%20the%20 metaphysics%20of%20morals%20with%20essays.pdf, retrieved 6 March 2020

6   Vollmer, G., Wissenschaft mit Steinzeitgehirnen? (Science with stone age brains?), in: mannheimer forum 86/87, Boehringer Mannheim 1986, pp. 9–62, here p. 12

7   Ayer, A. J., this concrete wording may only be attributed to Ayer, but it gives the gist of what he expressed again and again, see for example: Language, Truth and Logic, Chapter VI, Critique of Ethics and Theology, 1936, second edition 1946, republication Dover New York 1952, pp. 102, 103, available online: https://archive.org/details/languagetruthlog00alfr/page/102/mode/2up, retrieved 29 March 2023

8   Vogel, Chr., Vom Töten zum Mord. Das wirkliche Böse in der Evolutionsgeschichte (From killing to murder. On the true evil in evolutionary history), Hanser München 1989, p. 60

9   Vogel, Chr., Gibt es eine natürliche Moral? Oder: wie widernatürlich ist unsere Ethik? (Is there a natural morality? Or: How unnatural is our ethics?) in: Meier, H. (ed.), Die Herausforderung der Evolutionsbiologie (The challenge of evolutionary biology) Piper München 1988, pp. 193– 219, here pp. 215, 216

10 Shaftesbury, A., An Essay on the Freedom of Wit and Humour, Part II, Section III, in: Characteristics of Men, Manners, Opinions, Times, 1711, Bobbs-Merrill Indianapolis/New York 1964, pp. 41–99, here p. 77

11 Confucius, Analects (Lun Yu) XV, 23, the text here follows the translation by Legge, accessible online (in direct comparison with other translations): http://wengu.tartarie.com/wg/wengu.php?l=Lunyu&c=24&s=15&m=NOzh, retrieved 25 March 2020

12 Kant, as 5, (original edition p. 51), p. 38 (Wood translates "universal law of nature", a term Kant has used, but not here)

13 Robinson, as 1.4.6.[3], but pp. 49–52

14 Kolakowski, L., Religion – If there is no God, Oxford University Press 1982, p. 191

15 Kant, I., Über ein vermeintes Recht aus Menschenliebe zu lügen, 1797, On a Supposed Right to Lie from Altruistic Motives, 1797, see: Immanuel Kant, Critique of Practical Reason and Other Writings in Moral Philosophy, edited and translated by L. W. Beck, University of Chicago Press, 1949, pp. 346–350, available online: https://drive.google.com/file/d/1gXotC0wKVYdZgdS0z0KpcDWRD-qiH4qk/view, retrieved 5 January 2022

16 Topitsch, as 2.1.[11], but p. 5

17 Shaw, G. B., Maxims for Revolutionists, in: Man and Superman, 1903, quoted here according to: Mackie, J. L., Ethics. Inventing Right and Wrong, Penguin Harmondsworth 1977, p. 89

18 Kelsen, as 1.4.6.[5], but V., Kindle edition pos. 326

19 Apel, K.-O., Diskurs und Verantwortung. Das Problem des Übergangs zu einer postkonventionellen Moral (Discourse and responsibility. The problem of the transition to a postconventional morality), 1988, 2. Aufl., Suhrkamp Frankfurt a. M. 1992, for our context see for example pp. 12, 13, pp. 426–431

20 Habermas, J., Faktizität und Geltung, 1992, Suhrkamp Taschenbuch Wissenschaft Frankfurt a. M. 1998, III., II., p. 140, translated by W. Rehg: Between Facts and Norms: Contributions to a Discourse Theory of Law and Democracy, MIT Press Cambridge Massachusetts 1996, p. 109

21 Hoerster, N., Ethik und Interesse (Ethics and interest), Reclam Stuttgart 2003

22 Singer, see 1.4.2.[1], on this in particular pp. 38–54, pp. 94, 95

23 Williams, B., Morality, Chapter 2, Subjectivism: First Thoughts, Cambridge University Press 1972, Canto Edition 1993, pp. 16, 17

24 Singer, P., Nicht alles Leben ist heilig (Not all life is sacred), Interview, Der Spiegel, 26 November 2001, p. 237

3.4.

1 Schopenhauer, A., Über die vierfache Wurzel des Satzes vom zureichenden Grunde, 1847, § 34, zum Beispiel in: Kleinere Schriften, Sämtliche Werke Band III, Suhrkamp Frankfurt a. M. 1986, p. 155, translated and edited by D. E. Cartwright, E. E. Erdmann, C. Janaway: On the Fourfold Root of the Principle of Sufficient Reason, Cambridge University Press 2015, p. 121

2 Kurtz, as 3.1.5.[10], but p. 237

3 Vaihinger, H., Die Philosophie des Als Ob. System der theoretischen, praktischen und religiösen Fiktionen der Menschheit auf Grund eines idealistischen Positivismus, Reuther & Reichard Berlin 1911, translated by C. K. Ogden: The

Philosophy of 'As if': A System of the Theoretical, Practical and Religious Fictions of Mankind, Barnes and Noble New York 1968, first published by Kegan Paul, trench, Trubner London 1924, this edition is available online: https://archive.org/details/in.ernet.dli.2015.101717/page/n25/mode/2up, retrieved 26 January 2025

4   Wilson, E. O., On Human Nature, Chapter 8, Religion, Harvard University Press Cambridge Massachusetts/London England 1978, pp. 169–193, for the topic of indoctinability, the readiness to be indoctrinated, see especially p. 184

5   Dennett, D. C. Breaking the Spell. Religion as a Natural Phenomenon, Viking New York 2006, p. 141

6   Hamer, D., The God Gene. How Faith is Hardwired into our Genes, Doubleday New York 2004

7   Vaas, R., Blume, M., Gott, Gene und Gehirn. Warum Glaube nützt. Die Evolution der Religiosität (God, genes, and the brain. Why faith is useful. The evolution of religiosity), Hirzel Stuttgart 2009

8   Sommer, V., Die Gene der Göttin. Einer Urreligion auf der Spur (The genes of the goddess. On the track of a primeval religion), in: id., Von Menschen und anderen Tieren. Essays zur Evolutionsbiologie, Hirzel Stuttgart/Leipzig 2000, pp. 165–182, References pp. 191, 192

9   Rossano, M, The African Interregnum: The "Where", "When", and "Why" of the Evolution of Religion, in: Voland, E., W. Schiefenhövel, The Biological Evolution of Religious Mind and Behaviour, The Frontiers Collection, Springer Verlag Berlin Heidelberg 2009, pp. 127–141

10 Wilson, D. S., Darwin's Cathedral. Evolution, Religion, and the Nature of Society, The University of Chicago Press Chicago and London 2002

11 Allport, G. W., The Individual and His Religion, Macmillan New York 1950, see especially pp. 52–74 (for "mature" and "immature" religious sentiment); and: Allport, G. W., Ross, J. M., Personal Religious Orientation and Prejudice, Journal of Personality and Social Psychology, 1967, 5, pp. 432–443, on "extrinsic" and "intrinsic" religiosity in particular p. 434

12 James, W., The Varieties of Religious Experience, 1902, Penguin Putnam New York n. y.

13 Xenophanes, Fragments 15, 16, translated by John Burnet: Early Greek Philosophy, Adam & Charles Black London 1892, third edition 1920, p. 119, available online: https://en.wikisource.org/wiki/Fragments_of_Xenophanes, retrieved 14 April 2020

14 Lichtenberg, as 1.4.3.[3], German text: Promies edition, Volume I, D, 274, p. 275, Hollingdale`s translation: Notebook D, 48, p. 51

15 Schiller, F., Was heißt und zu welchem Ende studiert man Universalgeschichte?

Eine akademische Antrittsrede, in: Sämtliche Werke in zwölf Bänden, Cotta Stuttgart 1867, Zehnter Band, pp. 260–276, here p. 265, translated by C. Stephan and R. Trout: What Is, and to What End Do We Study, Universal History? available online: https://archive.schillerinstitute.com/transl/Schiller_essays/universal_history.pdf, p. 259, retrieved 23 August 2024

16 Montesquieu, Lettres persanes, Lettre LIX, 1721, Garnier-Flammarion Paris 1964, p. 105, translated by John Davidson, 1899: Persian Letters, Letter 59, accessible online: https://en.wikisource.org/wiki/Persian_Letters/Letter_59, retrieved 13 April 2020; very similar already Spinoza, Letter to Hugo Boxel, Autumn 1674, Letter 60, translated by R. H. M. Elwes: The Chief Works of Benedict de Spinoza, George Bell London 1902, available online: https://oll.libertyfund.org/titles/spinoza-the-chief-works-of-benedict-de-spinoza-vol-2, retrieved 15 April 2020

17 Feuerbach, L., Das Wesen des Christentums, 28. Kapitel, Schlußanwendung, 3. Aufl. 1849, Reclam Stuttgart 1971, p. 401, translated by M. Evans aka George Eliot: The Essence of Christianity, John Chapman London 1854, Chapter XXVII., Concluding Application, p. 268, available online: https://archive.org/details/a581696600feneuoft/page/268/mode/2up, retrieved 15 April 2024, words partly italicised by me according to original German text

18 Lichtenberg, see 1.4.3.³, first quotation: German text: Promies edition, Volume I, J, 944, p. 785, Hollingdales's translation, 195, p. 169, second quotation: German text: Promies edition, Volume I, L, 444, p. 915, not included in Hollingdales's translation

19 Lewis-Williams, D., The Mind in the Cave, Thames & Hudson London 2002, see in particular p. 291

20 Newberg, A., Waldman, M. R., Born to Believe (originally: Why We Believe What We Believe. Uncovering Our Biological Need for Meaning, Spirituality, and Truth, 2006), Free Press New York 2007

21 Hume, D. The Natural History of Religion, XV, General Corollary, 1757, see: Principal Writings on Religion including Dialogues Concerning Natural Religion and The Natural History of Religion, Oxford University Press Oxford New York 1993, 1998, p. 184

22 Freud, S., Die Zukunft einer Illusion, 1927, for a concise summary see especially Chapters V (End), Chapter VI, German text for example in: id., Massenpsychologie und Ich-Analyse. Die Zukunft einer Illusion, Fischer Taschenbuch Verlag 1967, pp. 109–113, translated by J. Strachey: The Future of an Illusion, Norton New York 1961, pp. 29–33, available online: https://archive.org/details/sigmund-freud-the-future-of-an-illusion/page/n31/mode/2up, retrieved 23 August 2024

23 Metzinger, T., Der Ego-Tunnel. Eine neue Philosophie des Selbst: Von der Hirnforschung zur Bewußtseinsethik, 2009, Piper München 2014, Nachwort:

Spiritualität und intellektuelle Redlichkeit, p. 398, not included in the English edition of the book but an English version is available online: Spirituality and Intellectual Honesty. An Essay, https://www.blogs.uni-mainz.de/fb05philosophie/files/2014/04/TheorPhil_Metzinger_SIR_2013_English.pdf, retrieved 20 April 2020, p. 19

24 see 22, but Chapter V, p. 108, p. 28 of the translation by Strachey

25 Marx, K., Zur Kritik der Hegelschen Rechtsphilosophie, Einleitung, 1843/44, first printing in: Deutsch-Französische Jahrbücher, Paris 1844, available online: https://de.wikisource.org/wiki/Zur_Kritik_der_Hegel%E2%80%99schen_Rechtsphilosophie, translated by Annette Jolin and Joseph O'Malley: A Contribution to the Critique of Hegel's Philosophy of Right, Introduction, Cambridge University Press 1970, accessible online: https://www.marxists.org/archive/marx/works/1843/critique-hpr/index.htm, both retrieved 21 April 2020

26 Durkheim, E., Les formes élémentaires de la vie religieuse, 1912, translated by Joseph Ward Swain: The Elementary Forms of the Religious Life, Conclusion, III., pp. 437, 438, George Allen & Unwin London 1915, available online: https://ia902708.us.archive.org/11/items/elementaryformso00durk/elementaryformso00durk.pdf, retrieved 21 April 2020, pp. 453, 454 of the pdf

27 Topitsch, E., Vom Ursprung und Ende der Metaphysik (On the origin and end of metaphysics), 1958, second edition, Springer Wien 1972

28 Mackie, as 3.3.[1], Chapter 10, p. 197

29 as 28

30 Vaas, Blume, as 7, here p. 218

31 Küng, H., Existiert Gott? Piper München 1978, especially F IV, 3. p. 625, translated by E. Quinn: Does God Exist? 1980, Reprint Vintage Books New York 1981, p. 569, available online: https://archive.org/details/doesgodexistansw0000kung_p0g9, retrieved 13 April 2023

32 Schopenhauer, as [1], § 20, p. 53, English text, p. 41

33 Anders, as Alpha[2], pp. 36, 37

34 Smoker, B., Why I am an Atheist, International Humanist, April 1989, pp. 2–4, here p. 4

35 Stendhal, this bon mot, quoted again and again, is possibly only attributed to Stendhal. I could not trace its origin further back than to Nietzsche's enviously appreciative comment in: Ecce Homo. Wie man wird, was man ist. Warum ich so klug bin, 3., German text for example in: Nietzsche Studienausgabe Fischer Bücherei Frankfurt a. M. 1968, Band 4, p. 162, translated by Anthony M. Ludovici: Ecce Homo. How One Becomes What One Is, Why I am so clever, 3., Foulis Edinburgh and London 1911, available online: https://www.gutenberg.org/files/52190/52190-h/52190-h.htm, retrieved 17 April 2023

36 Busch, W., Aphorismen und Reime (Aphorisms and rhymes), Sämtliche Werke, Band II, 6. Aufl., Bertelsmann München 1992, p. 882

37 Hitchens, C., *the* Portable Atheist, Da Capo Press Philadelphia 2007, Introduction, p. XIX-XX

38 Lichtenberg, G. Chr., Philosophische Bemerkungen (Philosophical remarks), German text see Rychner's edition, 1.4.3.[3], p. 483, 484, not included in Hollingdale's translation of The Waste Books

39 Kreiner, A., Die Leiden der Welt und das Theodizee-Problem (The suffering of the world and the problem of theodicy), Aufklärung und Kritik 1/2002, pp.127–136, here pp. 135, 136

40 Collins, as 3.1.5.[5], pp. 198–201

41 Küng, as 31, especially p. 631, English translation p. 574

42 Dahl, E., Wer zur Hölle will schon in den Himmel? Ein Brevier für Ungläubige und solche, die es werden wollen (Who the hell wants to go to heaven? A breviary for unbelievers and those who aspire to be), Books on Demand Norderstedt 2010, Einleitung, S. 21

43 Weber, M., Die Wirtschaftsethik der Weltreligionen (The economic ethics of the world religions), Archiv für Sozialwissenschaft und Sozialpolitik, 41. Band 1916, pp. 1–30, quoted from: id., Soziologie. Universalgeschichtliche Analysen, Politik, Kröner Stuttgart 1973, pp. 398–440, on this pp. 423–426, translated by H. H. Gerth and C. Wright Mills under the somewhat misleading title "The Social Psychology of the World Religions", 1948, in: From Max Weber: Essays in Sociology, New Edition 1991, Reprint Routledge London 1993, pp. 267–301, in particular pp. 287–291

44 Russell, B., Letter to Mr. Major, 18 March 1958, in: Dear Bertrand Russell ... A Selection of His Correspondence with the General Public 1950–1968, Houghton Mifflin Boston 1969, p. 6, available online: https://archive.org/details/dearbertrandruss00russ_0/page/6/mode/2up4, retrieved 24 April 2024

45 Protagoras, On the Gods, translation of the beginning of his lost work, quoted here from the Internet Encyclopedia of Philosophy: https://www.iep.utm.edu/protagor/, retrieved 31 May 2020

46 Darwin, C., Autobiography, written in 1876, extract quoted here from: Life and Letters of Charles Darwin, edited by his son Francis Darwin, Murray London 1887, Volume I, p. 313, available online: http://darwin-online.org.uk/content/frameset?keywords=agnostic&pageseq=331&itemID=F1452.1&viewtype=side, retrieved 31 May 2020

47 James, as 12, p. 427

48 Küng, as 31, pp. 629, 736, English translation, pp. 572, 674

49 Mann, Th., Doktor Faustus, 1947, 37.–46. Tausend, Fischer Frankfurt a. M. 1981,

Kapitel XI, p. 121, new translation by John E. Woods, Knopf New York 1997, Vintage International New York 1999, Section 11, p. 98, available online: http://barrybeck.com/Doctor-Faustus.pdf, retrieved 30 March 2021

50 Pfahl-Traughber, A., "Bausteine" zu einer kritischen Theorie über Religion ("Building blocks" for a critical theory of religion), Aufklärung und Kritik 3/2010, Sonderheft Schwerpunkt Atheismus, p. 136–152. For the formulations I am in debt to for this résumé see especially p. 151

51 Lange, as 2.1.³, but p. 540 of the German text, p. 281 of the translation, p. 300 of the pdf

52 Simmel, G., Die Religion (Religion), 1912, 9.–11. Tausend, Rütten & Loening Frankfurt a. M. 1922, pp. 13, 14, translated by H. J. Helle: Essays on Religion, Part 5, 11, Yale University Press 1997, p. 142

53 Reemtsma, J. P., "Atheist? Allerdings!" (Atheist? Indeed!), Humanistischer Pressedienst, 23 August 2006, available online: https://hpd.de/node/85, retrieved 27 March 2021, p. 3

54 Albert, H., Richard Schröders Kritik des neuen Atheismus (On Richard Schröder's Criticism of the New Atheism). Ein kritischer Kommentar, Aufklärung und Kritik 1/2010, pp. 170–188, here p. 185

3.5.

1 Eigen, M., Perspektiven der Wissenschaft. Jenseits von Ideologien und Wunsch-denken (Perspectives of science. Beyond ideologies and wishful thinking), Deutsche Verlags-Anstalt Stuttgart 1988, p. 256

2 Behringer, W., Kulturgeschichte des Klimas, von der Eiszeit bis zur globalen Er-wärmung, 2007, 6. Aufl., Beck München 2022, p. 275, translated by P. Camiller: A Cultural History of Climate, Polity Press Cambridge/Malden 2010, p. 206

3 Meyer, Th., Fundamentalismus. Aufstand gegen die Moderne (Fundamentalism. Revolt against modernity), Rowohlt Reinbek bei Hamburg 1989, p. 185

4 Reichholf, J. H., Die falschen Propheten. Unsere Lust an Katastrophen (False prophets. Our lust for catastrophes), Wagenbach Berlin 2002, 2. Aufl. 2003, p. 135

3.6.

1 Hassemer, W.; Warum Strafe sein muß (Why punishment is necessary), Ullstein Berlin 2009, S. 31

3.6.1.

1 Popper-Lynkeus, J., Die Todesstunde (The hour of death), in: Phantasien eines Realisten (Fantasies of a realist), 1909, Neuausgabe, Erb Düsseldorf 1980, p. 103

2   Deschner, as 2.3.[14], but p. 129

3   Eckermann, J. P., Gespräche mit Goethe, Goethe zu Eckermann am 25. Februar 1824, translated by S. M. Fuller (translation slightly modified): Conversations with Goethe in the Last Years of his Life, James Munroe and Company Boston and Cambridge 1852, p. 87, available online: https://archive.org/details/conversation-swi01fullgoog/page/n6/mode/2up?view=theater, retrieved 27 July 2023

4   Hume, D., Essays on Suicide and the Immortality of the Soul, The complete unauthorized 1783 edition, Essay II., III, 4., available online: https://www.qcc.cuny.edu/socialsciences/ppecorino/phil_of_religion_text/chapter_7_souls/Hume-OnImmortality-Soul.htm, retrieved 8 May 2023

5   Jaedicke, H., Von der Kunst das Leben zu verlängern. Sterben ist doof. Alles andere ist Lüge (On the art of extending Life. Dying is stupid. Everything else is a lie), Edition BoD, Hrsg. Vito von Eichborn, Books on Demand Norderstedt 2007, p. 27

6   Russell, B., Why I am not a Christian, Watts & Co., for the Rationalist Press Association Limited, 1927, first published as a pamphlet and reissued many times since, for example in: Why I Am Not A Christian and other essays on related subjects, 1957, Simon and Schuster New York 1965, Section "The Argument for the Remedying of Injustice", p. 13, available online: https://archive.org/details/why-i-am-not-a-christian/page/13/mode/2up, retrieved 23 April 2024

7   Montaigne, as 1.1.[4] , but Book II, Chapter 6, Of practice, p. 267

8   Lessing, G. E., quoted from: Jens, W., Samariter in der letzten Stunde (Samaritan in the last hour), Süddeutsche Zeitung, October 29, 2003, p. 2 (arguably a paraphrase of Lessing by Jens)

9   Hölderlin, F., Hyperion, 1797, 1799, Hyperion to Bellarmin, fourth last letter of the first book, translated by B. Ross, Archipelago Brooklyn 2008, kindle edition, p. 53

10 Birnbacher, D., Funktionale Argumente in der ökologischen Ethik (Functional arguments in ecological ethics), Aufklärung und Kritik 2/1997, pp. 84–98, here p. 85

11 Hume, D., Dialogues Concerning Natural Religion, 1779, Part XII, for instance in: Dialogues Concerning Natural Religion and The Natural History of Religion, Oxford University Press 1993, p. 122

12 Albert, H., Das Elend der Theologie. Kritische Auseinandersetzung mit Hans Küng (The misery of theology. A critical examination of Hans Küng), Hoffmann und Campe Hamburg 1979, p. 198

13 Knight, M., Morals without Religion, International Humanist, December 1988, pp. 4–5

14 Feuerbach, L., Die Unsterblichkeitsfrage vom Standpunkt der Anthropologie (The question of immortality from the standpoint of anthropology), 1846, Kröner Stuttgart 1938, p. 28

15 Panofsky, E., Meaning in the Visual Arts, University of Chicago Press 1955, Phoenix edition 1982, p. 1, originally from Wasianski, E. A. C., Immanuel Kant in seinen letzten Lebensjahren (Ueber Immanuel Kant, 1804, Vol. III), reprinted in Immanuel Kant, Sein Leben in Darstellungen von Zeitgenossen, Deutsche Bibliothek Berlin 1912, p. 298

16 Buhl, as Introduction[3], but p. 162

17 Brecht, B., Als ich in weißem Krankenzimmer der Charité (When in my white room of the Charité), as 2.3.[2], p. 1031, translated and edited by J. Willett and R. Manheim: Poems 1913–1956, Methuen London and New York 1976, 1979, revised paperback edition 1987, Last Poems 1953–1956, p. 451

18 Edelman, as 3.2.[9], Part IV, 15. A Graveyard of Isms: Philosophy and its Claims, p. 162

19 Bovenschen, S., Älter werden (Growing Older), 2006, Fischer Taschenbuch Verlag Frankfurt a. M. 2008, pp. 106, 107

3.6.2.

1 Unger, F., Das Coma egressum – der irreversible Hirnausfall (Coma egressum – the irreversible brain failure), Münch. med. Wschr. 137 (1995) Nr. 32/33, pp. 28, 29, 510, 511

2 Hoff, J., In Der Schmitten, J., Rixen, S., Das eigene Sterben ist unverletzlich (One's own dying is inviolable), Süddeutsche Zeitung, SZ am Wochenende, 12./13.11.1994, p. V

3.6.3.

1 Birnbacher, D., Forschung an embryonalen Stammzellen – ethische Fragen (Embryonic stem cell research – ethical questions), Abschnitt 4: Embryonenforschung – kategorisch unzulässig? Aufklärung und Kritik 1/2002, pp. 5–17, on this in particular pp. 16, 17; there is also an article in English by Birnbacher expressing these views though without explicitly using the term "piety principle": The Role of Complicity in the Ethics of Embryonic Stem Cell Research, from the book "Embryonic Stem Cells", edited by C. Atwood, IntechOpen London 2011, pp. 3–19, hereto especially pp. 18, 19, available online: https://www.intechopen.com/chapters/15437, retrieved 19 June 2023

3.6.4.

1 Singer, as 1.4.2.[1], Chapter 7, Taking Life: Humans, pp. 189–190

2 Singer, as 1.4.2.[1], Chapter 6, Taking Life: The Embryo and the Fetus, pp. 153–154

3 Engelhardt Jr., T. H., The Foundations of Bioethics, second edition, Oxford University Press New York/Oxford 1996, see for example pp. 140, 141

4 Hoerster, N., Ein Lebensrecht für die menschliche Leibesfrucht? (A right to life for unborn humans? Juristische Schulung 1989, Heft 3, pp. 172–178, and (5), pp. 9, 26–28

5 Hoerster, N., Neugeborene und das Recht auf Leben (Newborn infants and the right to life) , Suhrkamp Frankfurt a. M. 1995, on this in particular p. 57

6 Chen, C., Bailey, C., Baikie, G., Dalziel, K., Hua, X., Parents of children with disability: Mental health outcomes and utilization of mental health services, Disability and Health Journal 16 (2023) 101505 (with references to other studies on related problems), available online: https://www.sciencedirect.com/science/article/pii/S193665742300078X, retrieved 8 October2024

7 Baier, K., Threats of Futility: Is Life Worth Living? Lecture at the Free Inquiry's Conference, Washington D. C., 1987, published in: Free Inquiry 8(1988), p. 47–52, in particular p. 49

8 Strzyzynska, W., "All pregnant women are in danger": protests in Poland after expectant mother dies in hospital, The Guardian 15 June 2023, available online: https://www.theguardian.com/global-development/2023/jun/14/all-pregnant-women-are-in-danger-protests-in-poland-after-expectant-mother-dies-in-hospital, retrieved 4 July 2021

9 Kuhse, H., P. Singer, Should the Baby Live? The Problem of Handicapped Infants, Oxford University Press Oxford/New York/Melbourne 1985, in particular p. 8

10 Kuhse, Singer, as 8, on this in particular pp. 78–107

11 Giubilini, A., Minerva, F., After-birth abortion: why should the baby live? J Med Ethics 2013;39:261_263, available online: https://jme.bmj.com/content/medethics/39/5/261.full.pdf, retrieved 9 October 2024)

12 Kind, C., Kritische Fragen an das Entscheidungsmodell. Das Zürcher Modell aus der Sicht eines außenstehenden Neonatologen (Critical questions concerning the decision model. The Zurich model from the view of an external neonatologist), in: An der Schwelle zum eigenen Leben. Lebensentscheide bei zu früh geborenen, kranken und behinderten Kindern in der Neonatologie, Medizin-ethischer Arbeitskreis des Universitätsspitals Zürich, Lang Bern u. a. O. 2002, pp. 145–154, in particular pp. 150, 151

3.6.5.

1 Hilgendorf, E., Sterbehilfe und individuelle Autonomie. Erkundungen und

Klärungsversuche auf vermintem Gelände (Euthanasia and autonomy of the individual. Explorations and attempts at clarification on mined terrain), Aufklärung und Kritik, Schwerpunkt: Selbstbestimmtes Sterben, Sonderheft 11/2006, pp. 31–39, here p. 35

2   BVerfG, Urteil des Zweiten Senats vom 26. Februar 2020 - 2 BvR 2347/15 -, Rn. 1-343, https://www.bundesverfassungsgericht.de/SharedDocs/Entscheidungen/DE/2020/02/rs20200226_2bvr234715.html, retrieved 4 August 2023

3   van der Waal, G., R. J. M. Dillmann, Sterbehilfe in den Niederlanden, Zeitschrift für Allgemeinmedizin 71 (1995) pp. 1621–1627

4   Gordijin, B., Freiwillige aktive Sterbehilfe in den Niederlanden. Von der Duldung zur gesetzlichen Regelung (Voluntary active euthanasia in the Netherlands. From toleration to legal regulation), Dtsch. Med. Wochenschr. 126 (2001) pp. 1307–1309

5   https://www.euthanasiecommissie.nl/binaries/euthanasiecommissie/documenten/jaarverslagen/2023/april/4/jaarverslag-2023/Annual+report+2023.pdf

6   Rietiens, J. A. C., P. J. van der Maas et al., Two decades of research on euthanasia from the Netherlands. What have we learnt and what questions remain? J Bioeth Inq. 2009 September, 6 (3): 271–283

7   Buijsen, M., Euthanasia in the Netherlands. History, Developments and Challenges, Derecho Y Religión, Vol. XVII. 2022, pp. 77–100, available online: https://pure.eur.nl/ws/portalfiles/portal/80998804/EUTHANASIA_IN_THE_NETHERLANDS._HISTORY_.pdf, retrieved 23 October 2024

8   https://www.exit.ch/en/englisch/faq/ (What Is the Procedure for Physician-Assisted Suicides), retrieved 7 August 2023

9   https://www.dghs.de/service/vermittlung-von-freitodbegleitungen.html, retrieved 7 August 2023

10 Bridgeman, P. W., quoted from Engelhardt, as 3.6.4.[3] , but p. 349

11 Dworkin, R., Do We Have a Right to Die?, Addendum 1994, in: id., Freedom's Law. The Moral Reading of the American Constitution, third printing, Harvard University Press Cambridge 1999, p. 146

3.6.6.

1   Klinkhammer, G., Baby einer Toten: Sieg des Narzismus (A dead women`s baby: triumph of narcissism), Deutsches Ärzteblatt 92 (1995), 27. Januar 1995 (1), S. A 163, available online: https://www.aerzteblatt.de/archiv/81500/Baby-einer-Toten-Sieg-des-Narzissmus, retrieved 25 August 2023

2   Jackson, J., Can Older Women Cope with Motherhood?, in: Kuhse, H., Singer, P. (Ed.), Bioethics. An Anthology, Blackwell Oxford 1999, p.118

3   Lebensrecht versus Menschenwürde? "Erlangen" und seine Konsequenzen

(Right to life versus human dignity? "Erlangen" and its consequences), Universitas 48 (1993) März 1993, pp. 205–224 (contributions by various authors) Another case report from the Czech Republic describing the birth of a healthy child after such a procedure can be found here: https://www.ncbi.nlm.nih.gov/pmc/articles/PMC8141338/ (published 2021, retrieved 28 August 2023)

4 BGH (Federal Court of Justice), Urteil vom 6. Juli 2010, – 5 StR 386/09 LG Berlin –

3.6.9.

1 Bentham, J., An Introduction to the Principles of Morals and Legislation, T. Payne London 1780, Reprint Gale Eighteenth Century Collection Online, Introduction Chapter XVII, IV^a, p. CCCIX

2 Singer, P. Animal Liberation Now, The Bodley Head London 2023, first edition in 1975 under the title "Animal Liberation", revised several times and published in its sixth version in 2023. About equal consideration of interests see pp. 4–6 and passim

3 Korsgaard, Chr. M., Fellow Creatures. Our Obligations to the Other Animals, Oxford University Press 2018, Paperback 2020, on ends in themselves and Kant`s all but outdated views on the behaviour towards animals see especially pp. 77–79 and 97–100

4 Nussbaum, M. C., Justice for Animals. Our Collective Responsibility, Simon & Schuster New York 2022, for the central ideas of the approach see especially pp. 80, 81, 95–99

5 as 4, p. 169

6 Darwin. Ch., Letter to Ray Lancaster, 22 March 1871, in: Life and Letters of Charles Darwin, 1887, reprinted by Century Bound 2022, Volume II, p. 567, available online: https://www.fulltextarchive.com/book/The-Life-and-Letters-of-Charles-Darwinx2940/7/#p248, retrieved 17 January 2024

3.7.1.

1 Kaufmann, A., Strafrechtspraxis und sittliche Normen (Criminal law and moral norms), Juristische Schulung 18 (1978) pp. 361–367, here p. 363, paragraph 3

2 as 1, but p. 363, paragraph 1

3 Singer, as 1.4.2.^{1}, but p. 305

4 Zippelius, as 3.3.^{2}, but pp. 80, 81

5 Kelsen, as 1.4.6.^{5}, but X., Kindle edition pos. 419–428

6 Hoerster, N., Rechtsethik ohne Metaphysik (Ethics of law without metaphysics) Juristenzeitung 37 (1982) 65–272, and id., Moralbegründung ohne Metaphysik (Justification of morals without metaphysics), Erkenntnis 19 (1983) 225–238

7 Zippelius, as 3.3.2 , but p. 10

8 Seneca, Ad Lucilium Epistulae morales, Letter 95, 30., translated by R. M. Gummere, Volume 3, William Heinemann London 1925, available online: https://en.wikisource.org/wiki/Moral_letters_to_Lucilius/Letter_95, retrieved 25 January 2024

9 Russell, B., source not locatable anymore

10 Zippelius, as 3.3.[2], but p. 120

3.7.2.

1 Zippelius, as 3.3.[2] , but pp. 48, 50

3.7.4.

1 Kermani, N., Das Erfolgsgeheimnis der westlichen Leitkultur (The secret of success of Western "Leitkultur"), Süddeutsche Zeitung, 2.2.2004, p. 16

2 Ferencz, B., Parting Words. 9 Lessons for a remarkable life (written by N. Khomami), Sphere London 2020, p. 76

3.7.5.

1 Kaufmann, as 3.7.1.[1], but p. 365

2 Kaufmann, as 3.7.1.[1], but p. 24

3 Aristotle, The Nicomachean Ethics, Book V, 1138a, quoted here from the translation by D. P. Chase, J. M. Dent and Sons London 1911, p. 127, available online: https://archive.org/details/nicomacheanethic0000aris/page/n5/mode/2up, retrieved 5 February 2024

3.7.6.

1 Schreiber, H.-L., Rechtliche Grundlagen der psychiatrischen Begutachtung (Legal foundations of psychiatric assessment), in: Venzlaff, U., K. Foerster (Hrsg.), Psychiatrische Begutachtung (Psychiatric assessment), third edition, Urban & Fischer München/Jena 2000, S. 1–54, here p. 6

2 Hassemer, as 3.6.[1], but p. 226

3 Merkel, as 2.1.[12], but p. 136

4 Walter, 2.1.[13], but p. 38

5 Merkel, as 3, but p. 129

6 Lüderssen, K., Abschaffen des Strafens? (Abolishing punishment?) Suhrkamp Frankfurt a. M. 1995, on this especially p. 318

7 Reemtsma, J. P., Das Recht des Opfers auf die Bestrafung des Täters – als Problem (The victim`s right to punishment of the perpetrator – as a problem),

Beck München 1999, S. 21

8   as 7, but p. 27

9   Merkel, as 3, but p. 135

3.8.1.

1   Lindemann, H., Gustav Heinemann. Ein Leben für die Demokratie (A life for democracy), Kösel München 1978, p. 26

2   Robinson, as 1.4.6.[3], but p. 161

3   Popper, K. R., Bemerkungen zu Theorie und Praxis des demokratischen Staates, Vortrag 9.6.1988, Bank Hofmann Zürich 1988, p 17 (original German text), translated by P. Camiller: Reflections on the Theory and Practice of the Democratic State, in: id.: The Lesson of this Century, Routledge Oxon 1997, p. 73

4   Eschenburg, Th., Die lupenreine Demokratie bringt sich um (A perfect democracy is killing itself), Interview, Die Zeit, 21 October 1994, p. 64

5   Montaigne, as 1.1.[4], Book III, Chapter 10, Of husbanding your will, p. 774

6   Friedman, M. and R., Free to Choose. A Personal Statement, 1980, Harcourt New York 1990, p. 295

7   Robinson, as 1.4.6.[3] , but p. 200

3.8.2.

1   Smith, A., An Inquiry into the Nature and Causes of the Wealth of Nations, Book I, Chapter II, Of the Principle which gives Occasion to the Division of Labour, 1776, The University of Chicago Press 1976, p. 18

2   Müller-Armack, A., Wirtschaftslenkung und Marktwirtschaft (Economic steering and market economy), 1946, Kastell München 1990, pp. 68–70

3   Eucken, W., Grundsätze der Wirtschaftspolitik (Principles of economic policy), 1952, 7. Aufl., Mohr Siebeck Tübingen 2004, pp. 363, 360

4   Robinson, as 1.4.6.[3], but p. 178

5   Friedman, M. and R., as 3.8.1.[6], but p. 32

6   Müller-Armack, as 2, but p. 94

7   Müller-Armack, as 2, but p. 114

3.8.3.

1   Jaspers, K., Die Atombombe und die Zukunft des Menschen, 1958, Neuausgabe, Piper München 1982, S. 247, translated by E. B. Ashton: The Future of Mankind, The University of Chicago Press 1963, p. 182, available online: https://archive.org/details/futureofmankind0000jasp/page/182/mode/2up, retrieved 25 February 2024

2   Weizsäcker, C. F. v., Wege in der Gefahr, 1976, dtv München 1979, S. 243, translated by M. Shaw: The Politics of Peril, The Seabury Press New York 1978, p. 243, available online: https://archive.org/details/politicsofperile00weiz/page/n7/mode/2up, retrieved 25 February 2024 (translation modified as to "world domestic policy" instead of "world-internal politics")

3   Bredow, W. v., Renaissance militärischen Denkens? Militärische Gewalt in den internationalen Beziehungen (Renaissance of military thinking? Military force in international relations), Universitas 49 (1994), No. 6, pp. 569–578, here p. 578

4   Höffe, O., Demokratie im Zeitalter der Globalisierung, 1999, überarbeitete und aktualisierte Neuausgabe, Beck München 2002, S. 430, translated by D. Haubrich with M. Ludwig: Democracy in an Age of Globalisation, Springer 2007, p. 311, available online: https://archive.org/details/democracyinageof0000hoff, retrieved 25 February 2024

5   Weizsäcker, C. F. v., Bedingungen des Friedens (Conditions of Peace), Göttingen Vandenhoeck und Ruprecht 1963, especially pp. 9, 13, 17, translated by A. Hentschel in: id., Major Texts on Politics and Peace Research, Chapter 4, World Domestic Policy, SpringerBriefs on Pioneers in Science and Practice, Volume 25, 2015, pp. 31–40

6   Höffe, as 4, but p. 236 and passim

7   Rawls, J., The Law of Peoples, 1999, fourth printing, Harvard University Press, Cambridge/London 2002, on this especially pp. 105–111

8   Purdy, J., Das Amerika der reinen Herzen (The pure heart), Die Zeit, 28 February 2002, p. 11 (my retranslation, article listed in Purdy's list of publications but original English text seems not to be published)

9   Lambsdorff, O., Frieden und Globalisierung (Peace and Globalisation), 2003, in: Der Freiheit verpflichtet. Reden und Aufsätze 1995–2006, Lucius & Lucius Stuttgart 2006, pp. 402–408, here p. 408

10 Rawls, as 7, but p. 11

3.9.

1   Schönwandt, W., Denkfallen beim Planen (Thinking traps in planning), Vieweg & Sohn Braunschweig 1986, p. 84

2   Pape, J., Der Spiegel der Vergangenheit. Geschichtswissenschaft zwischen Relativismus und Realismus (The mirror of the past. History between relativism and realism), Peter Lang Frankfurt a. M. 2006, pp. 207, 129

3   Schieder, Th., Ohne Geschichte sein? Geschichtsinteresse, Geschichtsbewußtsein heute (Being without history? Interest in history and awareness of history today), Walter-Raymond-Stiftung Köln 1973, S. 20

4   Popper, as 3.1.5.[9], but Chapter 33, p. 149

5   Lessing, Th., as 1.4.1.[1], here I. Buch, Erkenntniskritik der Geschichte. Schuld- und Verschuldungsursache, pp. 59, 60

6   Lübbe, H., Geschichtsbegriff und Geschichtsinteresse (The concept of and the interest in history), Schwabe Basel/Stuttgart 1977, p. 213

7   Pape, as 2, p. 14

8   Koselleck, R., "Erfahrungsraum" und "Erwartungshorizont" – zwei historische Kategorien, 1976, hier zitiert nach dem Abdruck in: id., Vergangene Zukunft. Zur Semantik geschichtlicher Zeiten, 4.Aufl., Suhrkamp Frankfurt a. M. 2000, S. 374, translated by K. Tribe: *Space of Experience* and *Horizon of Expectation*: Two Historical Categories, in: Futures Past. On the Semantics of Historical Time, Chapter 15, Columbia University Press New York 2004, p. 274, available online: https://voidnetwork.gr/wp-content/uploads/2016/09/Futures-Past.-On-the-Semantics-of-historical-time-by-Reinhart-Koselleck.pdf, retrieved 9 March 2024 (translation modified by me)

9   Eigen, M., Gesetz und Zufall bei der Entstehung des Lebens (Law and chance in the origin of life), Festvortrag (Festive lecture), 70. Fortbildungstage für Ärzte, Regensburg 1983, p. 14

10 Koselleck, R., Vom Sinn und Unsinn der Geschichte, Merkur 51 (1997) 319 – 314, in: Aufsätze und Vorträge aus vier Jahrzehnten, Suhrkamp Berlin 2010, p. 25, translated by S. Franzel and S.-L. Hoffmann: On the Meaning and Absurdity in History, III., in: id., Sediments of Time. On Possible Histories, Stanford University Press 2018. pp. 177–196, here p. 191, Kindle edition pos. 3750

11 Gabor, as 2.3.[6], but pp. 73, 123, 124

12 Hobsbawn, E., On History, The New Press New York 1997, p. 9 and more comprehensively pp. 272–277

13 Lübbe, as 6, but p. 276

14 Dürrenmatt, F., Theater-Schriften und Reden, Hingeschriebenes (Writings on theatre and speeches, Jottings), Die Arche Zürich 1966, p. 89, not included in the English selection Writings on Theatre and Drama of 1976

3.10.

1   Dewey, J., Art as Experience, 1934, Perigee Paperback New York 2005, p. 322

2   Hume, D., Of the Standard of Taste, in: Four Dissertations, A. Millar London 1757, p. 230, available online: https://archive.org/details/bim_eighteenth-century_four-dissertations-i-t_hume-david_1757/page/n1/mode/2up, retrieved 12 March 2024

3   Nietzsche, F., Götzendämmerung oder Wie man mit dem Hammer philosophirt, 1888, Streifzüge eines Unzeitgemäßen, 19., translated by R. J. Hollingdale: Twilight of the Idols or How to Philosophize with a Hammer, Expeditions of an

Untimely Man, in: Twilight of the Idols and The Antichrist. Penguin Classics London 1990, p. 89

4   Eckermann, J. P., Gespräche mit Goethe, 17. Januar 1827, translated by J. Oxenford: Conversations of Goethe with Eckermann, Wednesday, January 17, 1827, in: Conversations of Goethe with Eckermann and Soret, Volume I, Smith, Elder & Co. London 1850, p. 326, available online: https://archive.org/details/conversationsofg01goetuoft/page/326/mode/2up, retrieved 18 March 2024

5   Rosenkranz, K., Die Ästhetik des Häßlichen, 1853, translated by A. Pop and M. Widrich: Aesthetics of Ugliness. A Critical Edition, 2015, Paperback edition Bloomsbury New York/London 2017

6   Alt, P.A., Ästhetik des Bösen (Aesthetics of evil), 2. Aufl., Beck München 2011, pp. 513, 514

7   Burke, E., A Philosophical Enquiry into the Origin of our Ideas of the Sublime and Beautiful, 1757/1759, Penguin Books London 1998, see especially the beginning of Part II, p. 101

8   Kant, I., Kritik der Urteilskraft, 1790/1793/1799, siehe insbesondere § 5, Vergleichung der drei spezifisch verschiedenen Arten des Wohlgefallens (Comparison of three specifically different kinds of satisfaction) and § 28, Vom Dynamisch-Erhabenen der Natur (On the Dynamically Sublime in Nature), Originalausgabe 1793, pp. 102–109, translated by P. Guyer: Critique of the Power of Judgment, Cambridge University Press 2000, pp. 95, 143–148

9   Welsch, W., Zur hermeneutischen Verfassung der Kunst, 1994, in: id., Grenzgänge der Ästhetik, Reclam Stuttgart 1996, pp. 210–227, here pp. 227, 223, 224, translated by A. Inkpin: On the Hermeneutic Constitution of Art, in: Undoing Aesthetics, Sage Publications Thousand Oaks 1997, pp. 131, 132, 129, 130

10 Menninghaus, W., Das Versprechen der Schönheit (The promise of beauty), 2003, Suhrkamp Taschenbuch Wissenschaft Frankfurt a. M. 2007; VIII. Trauerarbeit am Schönen (Mourning at the beautiful), pp. 281–287

11 Welsch, W., Konstellationen der Wahrnehmung (Constellations of perception), 1990, in: as 9, pp. 181–196, here p. 194 (not included in the English edition)

12 Adorno, Th. W., Ästhetische Theorie, 1970, 13. Aufl., Suhrkamp Taschenbuch Frankfurt a. M. 1993, p. 184, translated by R. Hullot-Kentor: Aesthetic Theory, 1997, Continuum London/New York 2002, p. 121

13 Welsch, W., Gegenwartskunst im öffentlichen Raum: Augenweide oder Ärgernis? 1992, in: as 9, pp. 202–209, here p. 209, the whole essay can be found as Chapter 6 in the translation mentioned above: Contemporary Art in Public Space: A Feast for the Eyes or an Annoyance?, for the context of the quotation see p. 121, but this specific figurative expression was omitted by the translator and is quoted here in my translation

4.

1 Szczesny, G., Die Zukunft des Unglaubens/The Future of Unbelief (see Suggested Further Reading), p. 60 of the German text, p. 81 of the translation (modified by me)

2 Feuerbach, as 3.4.[17], but p. 12 of the quoted German edition (Vorwort zur ersten Auflage/Preface to the first edition), omitted in the Evans/Eliot translation and thus in all English editions known to me

3 Nietzsche, as 3.1.2.[1], but Aphorism 153, p. 82 of the translation

4 Knight, M., Morals without Religion 2, Talk on BBC Home Service January 1955, Dobson London 1955, available online: https://humanists.uk/humanism/humanism-today/humanists-thinking/margaret-knight-morals-without-religion/, retrieved 16 April 2024

5 Kanitscheider, as 1.3.[8], but pp. 73, 74 (Translation of the quotation from Unamuno: "In church I take off my hat, but not my head.")

6 Kahl, J., Es gibt keinen Gott (There is no god), Aufklärung und Kritik 2 (1995), Heft 2, pp. 113–118, here p. 117

7 Keller, G., Brief an Wilhelm Baumgartner (Letter to Wilhelm Baumgartner), 27. März 1851, in: Kellers Briefe in einem Band, Aufbau Verlag Berlin und Weimar 1967, p. 84

4.1.

1 Popper-Lynkeus, J., A Table Talk with Martin Luther, in: as 3.6.1.[1], but p. 57

2 Albert, H., Die Idee der kritischen Vernunft (The idea of critical reason), in: as 4.[4], but pp. 17–30 and 401–403, here p. 402

3 Montaigne, as 1.1.[4], Book III, Chapter 1, On the useful and the honorable, p. 601

4 Dawkins, R., Remark in a talk given at a conference in Monterey, California, April 2002, video available online: https://www.google.com/search?client=firefox-b-e&q=dawkins+ted+talk+militant+atheism#fpstate=ive&vld=cid:8d328b8a,vid:VxGMqKCcN6A,st:0 (13:37–13:47), retrieved 18 April 2024

5 Pew Research Center, 8 facts about atheists, February7, 2024, available online: https://www.pewresearch.org/short-reads/2024/02/07/8-facts-about-atheists/, retrieved 18 April 2024

6 Berg, K., Even in Hell You Find Norwegian Humanists!, International Humanist, December 1989, pp. 8, 9 and https://www.human.no/om-oss/norwegian-humanist-association, retrieved 19 April 2024

7 Meyer, Th., Die Ironie Gottes. Religiotainment, Resakralisierung und die liberale Demokratie (God's irony. Religiotainment, resacralisation and liberal

democracy), VS Verlag Wiesbaden 2005, p. 78

8   Meyer, as 7, but p. 77

9   Montesquieu, De l'Esprit Des Lois, 1748, translated by Th. Nugent: The Spirit Of Laws, London J. Nourse and P. Vaillant 1752, Volume II, Book XXIV, Chapter II, p. 172, available online: https://archive.org/details/bim_eighteenth-century_ the-spirit-of-laws-tran_montesquieu-charles-de-_1752_2, retrieved 23 April 2024

10 Russell, as 3.6.1.[6] , but Preface, p. VI

4.2.

1   Popper-Lynkeus, in: Idylle (Idyll) as 3.6.1.[1], but p. 371

2   Emrich, E., Feste feiern … Verlegenheit oder Chance in der Familie (Celebrating festivals – embarrassment or chance in the family), unkorrigiertes Manuskript, Bayerischer Rundfunk München 1975, p. 8

3   Kahl, J., Das Elend des Christentums, Rowohlt Reinbek bei Hamburg 1968, überarbeitete und erweiterte Neuausgabe 1993, Nachwort 1993, p. 174, quoted here from the English edition: The Misery of Christianity: A Plea for a Humanity without God, 1971, enlarged Kindle edition Royal Wave Media 2024, Afterword from 1993, pp. 204, 205

4   Russell, B., Letter to Miss Baker, 29 December 1964, as 3.4.[44], but p. 142

5   Emerson, R. W., Self-Reliance, Essays, 1841, in: id., Self-Reliance and Other Essays, Dover Publications New York 1993, p. 24

6   Marquard, as 1.[1], but p. 8 of the German text, p. 5 of the translation

7   Schlechta, as 1.4.5.[1], but pp. 231, 232

8   Kahl, J., Weihnachten. Das heitere Friedensfest im Winter (Christmas. The cheerful winter festival of peace) , in: Kahl, J., Schütt, P., Das andere Weihnachtsbuch (A different Christmas book), 3. Aufl., Weltkreis Dortmund 1986, pp. 209–234, here p. 225

9   Democritus, Fragment 230, quoted in 8, also p. 225, Greek text in: Diels, H., Die Fragmente der Vorsokratiker, griechisch und deutsch, Zweiter Band, 4. Aufl., Weidmannsche Buchhandlung Berlin 1922, p. 107, available online: https://archive.org/details/diefragmentederv02diel_0/page/n5/mode/2up, English translation here from: Freeman, K., The Pre-Socratic Philosophers. A Companion to Diels, Fragmente der Vorsokratiker, second edition, Basil Blackwell Oxford 1949, p. 317, also available online: https://archive.org/details/presocrat-icphilo0000free_s5x5/page/n5/mode/2up, both retrieved 14 May 2024

4.3.

1   Busch, as 3.4.[36]

2   Busch, as 3.4.[36], but Volume I, p. 844

3   Frederick II, King of Prussia to Voltaire, 24 October 1766, original French text available online: https://fr.wikisource.org/wiki/Correspondance_de_Voltaire/1766/Lettre_6544, retrieved 17 May 2024, not included in Holcroft's 1798 translation of the Letters of Voltaire and Frederick the Great nor in Aldington's 1927 translation

4   Albert, as 2.1.[6], but pp. 120, 121 (German edition pp. 113, 114)

5   Hume, D., Essays, Moral and Political, Volume II, Kincaid, Fleming and Alison Edinburgh 1742, IX. The Sceptic, pp. 157, 158, available online: https://archive.org/details/bim_eighteenth-century_essays-moral-and-politi_hume-david_1742_2/page/156/mode/2up, retrieved 17 May 2024

6   Feuerbach, as 3.6.1.[14], but p. 91

7   Lennox, J. C., God's Undertaker: Has Science Buried God? 2007, new updated edition, Lion Books Oxford 2009, pp. 17, 18 (Survey by Larsen and Witham, Nature 386 (1997), pp. 435–436)

8   Hoerster, N., Introduction to: id. (ed.), Religionskritik. Arbeitstexte für den Unterricht (Criticism of Religion. Working texts for tuition), Reclam Stuttgart 1984, pp. 5–16, here p. 9

9   Hoche, A. E., Die letzten Fragen (Ultimate questions), in: id., Jahresringe (Annual rings), 76.–77. Tausend, Lehmann München 1969, pp. 233, 234

10   Dawkins, R., The God Delusion, see Recommended Further Reading, The Argument from Beauty, pp. 86, 87

11   Marcuse, L., Kultur-Pessimismus (Cultural pessimism), in: as 4.[4], pp. 242–256, here p. 256

Omega

1   Huxley, Th. H., Possibilities and Impossibilities, in: as 2.2.[1], pp. 192–208, here p. 206

2   Busch, as 3.4.[36], but p. 874

3   Mach, E., Die Geschichte und die Wurzel des Satzes von der Erhaltung der Arbeit, Vortrag 15.11.1871, J. G. Calve'sche K. & K. Universitätsbuchhandlung Prag 1872, Reprint Legare Street Press 2022, p. 3, translated by P. E. B. Jourdain: The History and the Root of the Principle of the Conservation of Energy, The Open Court Publishing Co. Chicago 1911, I. Introduction, p. 17, available online: https://archive.org/details/historyandrootp00machgoog/page/n20/mode/2up, retrieved 30 June 2024, p. 21 of the pdf

4   Améry, J., Unmeisterliche Wanderjahre (Unmasterly wandering years), 1971, dtv München 1989, p. 40

Index

Hare Richard M. 80, 240, 478, 486, 503
Harris John 503, 508
Harris Sam 441
Hart-Dworkin debate 515
Hassemer 199, 326, 517
Hauser 480, 485
Hayek 524
health care system 353, 355, 525
  decisions limiting costs 357
Healy 518
heaven 179
Hegel 132, 137
hegemonic power 368
Hegselmann 85
Heidegger 132, 134, 472, 506, 537
  and National Socialism 471
Heinemann 340
Heisenberg 104, 466
heliocentrism 108
help obligation to 162
Henning 488
hereafter experiences 201
heretic 157
hermeneutics 135
heroes 151
heroism 319
highest good 148
Hilgendorf 245
Hinduism 182
Hirsi Ali 442
historicism 383, 528
historiography
  critical commitment 388
  relation to reality 383
history 32, 71, 89, 152, 370, 435, 512
  and democracy 342
  and human rights 386
  and law 316
  and objectivity 384
  and values 386
  crimes 304
  instrumentalisation 384
  meaning 385, 386

of law 310
of philosophy 310
unpredictablity 385
Hitchcock 409
Hitchens 178, 442
Hitler 177, 203, 303, 514, 528
Hobsbawn 388
Hoche 261, 429, 505, 506, 536
Hoerster 161, 225, 303, 429, 441, 486, 489, 490, 498, 513, 515
Höffe 367, 370, 438, 522, 526
Hofstadter 110, 129, 138
Hölderlin 205
Holzgrefe 527
Holzhaider 520
Homann 522
home 458
  glorification of 459
homeland 459
homelandliness 134
homelessness transcendental 188
homeopathy 117
homosexuality 163, 285
  and evolution 286, 510
  and law 289
  and religion 174
  and society 288
  discrimination 289
honesty 456
honour 163
Hook 69
hope 73, 91, 187, 200, 203, 462
  and history 386
horoscopes 127, 129
hospices 264
hostility toward disabled people 244
hour of death 204
Hrdy 455
human beings severely disabled 235
human dignity 207, 216, **217**
human experimentation 46, 447
human history 197, 205
human limitations 190
human rights 51, 317, 368, 378, 516

oxygen lack of 201

symbolism 393
Szczesny 413, 416, 439, 460

T

Tag 493
Tallack 492
Tàpies 410
taste 158, 396, 532
  standard of 390
tax evasion 155
tax revenue 359
tax system 363
Taylor 515
technical jargon 132
technology 36, 189, 192, 196
telekinesis 127
telepathy 127
termination of life on request 255
terminology 132, 133, 136
  philosophical 453
terrorism 379
testability 103
Thaler 522
thalidomide 241
theatre 398
theft prohibition of 156
theism 72, 89, 174
theodicy 178, 180, 468, 490
  problem of 103
theologians 178
theology 123, 180, 186, 461, 490
  and public universities 116, 469
  and science 115
  modern 187, 536
theories 70, 103, 109, 114, 116, 474
  speculative 123
theory 119
  and observation 466
  and practice 45, 55
theory of evolution 119
theory of relativity 119
Thieme 522
thinking
  and feeling 444

restrictions on 192
thoughts transmission 144
three worlds concept 466
tolerance 19, 37, 44, 48, 59, 60, 81,
  432
  and democracy 342
  and determinism 140
  and law 302, 323
  and society 415
  and state 344
  of religions 433
Tolmein 537
Topitsch 77, 157, 173
torture 312, 515
totalitarianism 441
tradition 84
  and knowledge 100
  and morality 80
traditionalism
  uncritical 424
traditions
  and Christianity 423
  and law 316
  cultural 484
  mystical 495
transcendence experiences 170
transience 200, 201, 204, 406, 454
  and art 410
  and happiness 94
transplantation medicine 210, 499
transsexuality 285
treatment
  "extraordinary methods" 253
  "ordinary methods" 253
  limitation of 249
tribal society 163
trickle-down economics 524
trolley problems 483
Truffaut 409
Truog 499
trust in god 185
truth 17, 36, 46, 77, 78, 123, 154,
  198, 205
  and death 496

Z